"This book is a landmark step in addressing the role of visuality in global politics. Rich, diverse, and innovative, it represents a vital contribution to understanding some of the most pressing analytic and political questions of our time."

Michael C Williams, *University of Ottawa, Canada*

"This sparkling collection of essays brings the visual aspects of global politics to the fore, challenging the traditional scholarly focus on texts. It illuminates the power of images in shaping the way we interpret and respond to global phenomena. The book will quickly become an indispensable resource for all scholars of international politics and law."

Hilary Charlesworth, *Melbourne Law School, Australia*

"This is a wonderful anthology. Typically these alphabetical collections are best for reference, but I was surprised to find myself reading through from one to the next. Many of the entries speak to each another, and together they paint the best available picture of images as 'political forces.' Visual culture studies has often made the promise of being political in a way that art history hasn't, but this is the only book that puts the politics first. It will be a useful reference for the current political moment, in which each of us has the responsibility to witness, interpret, and also produce political images."

James Elkins, *School of the Art Institute of Chicago, USA*

"We live in an age of the visual turn in politics, one in which images work upon several registers of life. But the professoriate still mostly responds to politics through the hegemony of the textual. *Visual Global Politics* takes several huge steps to redress this imbalance. Consisting of multiple image-rich essays, it engages bodies, borders, torture, climate, democracy, security and several other domains by addressing their image/word intertexts. A timely and indispensable volume."

William E. Connolly, *Johns Hopkins University, USA*

Visual Global Politics

We live in a visual age. Images and visual artefacts shape international events and our understanding of them. Photographs, film and television influence how we view and approach phenomena as diverse as war, diplomacy, financial crises and election campaigns. Other visual fields, from art and cartoons to maps, monuments and videogames, frame how politics is perceived and enacted. Drones, satellites and surveillance cameras watch us around the clock and deliver images that are then put to political use. Add to this that new technologies now allow for a rapid distribution of still and moving images around the world. Digital media platforms, such as Twitter, YouTube, Facebook and Instagram, play an important role across the political spectrum, from terrorist recruitment drives to social justice campaigns.

This book offers the first comprehensive engagement with visual global politics. Written by leading experts in numerous scholarly disciplines and presented in accessible and engaging language, *Visual Global Politics* is a one-stop source for students, scholars and practitioners interested in understanding the crucial and persistent role of images in today's world.

Roland Bleiker is Professor of International Relations at the University of Queensland, where he directs an interdisciplinary research program on Visual Politics. His work has introduced aesthetics, visuality and emotions to the study of world politics.

Interventions

Edited by: Jenny Edkins, Aberystwyth University, UK and Nick Vaughan-Williams, University of Warwick, UK

The series provides a forum for innovative and interdisciplinary work that engages with alternative critical, post-structural, feminist, postcolonial, psychoanalytic and cultural approaches to international relations and global politics. In our first 5 years we have published 60 volumes.

We aim to advance understanding of the key areas in which scholars working within broad critical post-structural traditions have chosen to make their interventions, and to present innovative analyses of important topics. Titles in the series engage with critical thinkers in philosophy, sociology, politics and other disciplines and provide situated historical, empirical and textual studies in international politics.

We are very happy to discuss your ideas at any stage of the project: just contact us for advice or proposal guidelines. Proposals should be submitted directly to the Series Editors:

- Jenny Edkins (jennyedkins@hotmail.com) and
- Nick Vaughan-Williams (N.Vaughan-Williams@Warwick.ac.uk).

    'As Michel Foucault has famously stated, "knowledge is not made for understanding; it is made for cutting". In this spirit The Edkins–Vaughan-Williams Interventions series solicits cutting edge, critical works that challenge mainstream understandings in international relations. It is the best place to contribute post disciplinary works that think rather than merely recognize and affirm the world recycled in IR's traditional geopolitical imaginary.'
    Michael J. Shapiro, University of Hawai'i at Manoa, USA

For a full list of available titles please visit www.routledge.com/series/INT

Reforming 21st Century Peacekeeping Operations
Governmentalities of Security, Protection, and Police
Marc G. Doucet

Politics of Visibility and Belonging
From Russia's "Homosexual Propaganda" Laws to the Ukraine War
Emil Edenborg

Military Intervention in the Middle East and North Africa
The Case of NATO in Libya
Susannah O'Sullivan

The Emancipatory Project of Posthumanism
Erika Cudworth and Stephen Hobden

Visual Global Politics
Edited by Roland Bleiker

Visual Global Politics

Edited by Roland Bleiker

LONDON AND NEW YORK

First published 2018
by Routledge
2 Park Square, Milton Park, Abingdon, Oxon OX14 4RN

and by Routledge
711 Third Avenue, New York, NY 10017

Routledge is an imprint of the Taylor & Francis Group, an informa business

© 2018 selection and editorial matter, Roland Bleiker; individual chapters, the contributors

The right of Roland Bleiker to be identified as the author of the editorial material, and of the authors for their individual chapters, has been asserted in accordance with sections 77 and 78 of the Copyright, Designs and Patents Act 1988.

British Library Cataloguing in Publication Data
A catalogue record for this book is available from the British Library

Library of Congress Cataloging in Publication Data
Names: Bleiker, Roland, editor.
Title: Visual global politics / edited by Roland Bleiker.
Description: Abingdon, Oxon ; New York, NY : Routledge, 2018. |
Series: Interventions | Includes bibliographical references and index.
Identifiers: LCCN 2017042159| ISBN 9780415726061 (hbk) |
ISBN 9780415726078 (pbk) | ISBN 9781315856506 (ebk)
Subjects: LCSH: Mass media and international relations. | Visual
communication—Political aspects. | Digital media—Political aspects.
| Social media—Political aspects.
Classification: LCC P96.I53 V57 2018 | DDC 320.01/4—dc222
LC record available at https://lccn.loc.gov/2017042159

ISBN: 978-0-415-72606-1 (hbk)
ISBN: 978-0-415-72607-8 (pbk)
ISBN: 978-1-315-85650-6 (ebk)

Typeset in Times New Roman
by Florence Production Ltd, Stoodleigh, Devon, UK

In memory of Alex Danchev

Contents

x *Contents*

Mapping visual global politics

Roland Bleiker

We live in a visual age. Images shape international events and our understanding of them. Photographs, cinema and television influence how we view and approach phenomena as diverse as war, humanitarian disasters, protest movements, financial crises and election campaigns. Politicians have been acutely aware of this at least since shocking images of the Vietnam War influenced domestic and international support for US foreign policy (Kennedy 2008). The UN Secretary General regularly urges photojournalists to produce more images, particularly of atrocities that seem to exist in silence and demand urgent action (Pronk 2005; Devereux 2010: 124–34).

The dynamics of visual politics reach in all directions and go well beyond traditional media outlets. The examples are numerous. Digital media, such as Twitter, YouTube, Facebook and Instagram, play an increasingly important role across the political spectrum, from terrorist recruitment drives to social justice campaigns. High-profile visual artists, such as Anselm Kiefer and Ai Weiwei, have become influential voices of political dissent. Fashion and videogames are frequently derived from and enact the militarised world we live in. Drones, satellites and surveillance cameras profile terrorist suspects and identify military targets.

We live in a visual age indeed. Images surround everything we do. This omnipresence of images is political and has changed fundamentally how we live and interact in today's world. Scholarly fields such as art history and media, cultural and communication studies have for long examined visual representations. But we still know far too little about the precise role visuality plays in the realm of politics and international relations. And we know even less about the concrete practical implications. Addressing this gap is particularly pertinent since new technologies now allow for the speedy and easy distribution of still and moving images across national boundaries.

Visual Global Politics offers a comprehensive overview of and engagement with the role of visuality in politics and international relations. It is designed as an accessible, one-stop source for anyone interested in understanding the central role that images play in today's world. At the same time, the book pushes our understanding of politics. Although we live in a visual age, knowledge conventions – both in academia and in the wider realm – are still very much focused on texts and textual analysis (see Williams 2003). What would a true political appreciation of the visual look like? What would it mean to communicate and think and act in visual ways? How would the media, books, classrooms and other realms be transformed if we were to treat images not just as illustrations or as representations but as political forces themselves?

To appreciate the wide range and far-reaching consequences of visual politics it is important to look not only at two-dimensional images, as illustrated in the examples above, but also at three-dimensional visual artefacts and performances (see Callahan, Chapter 9). The latter include influential phenomena, such as border installations, churches, national monuments and parades. Visual images and visual artefacts differ in their nature and function. For one, images have the potential to circulate rapidly while some artefacts are limited by their physical nature and location. But they are also linked in numerous ways and have at least three common dimensions, which will be explored through the book.

First: at a time of globalisation and global communication the boundaries between images and visual artefacts become more and more blurred. Consider the Vietnam Veterans Memorial in Washington DC, designed by Maya Lin. It is one of the most influential visual artefacts, a monument visited by millions of people who often leave with deeply emotional impressions. But most people around the world have "seen" the monument not as a result of a personal visit, but through images that circulate online, in newspapers, on TV and in movies. The same is the case with almost any influential visual artefact or performance, from flags to military parades and televised presidential election debates: they are always more than localised three-dimensional objects or phenomena. They are artefact–performance constellations that circulate politically through still and moving images.

Second: images and visual artefacts tell us something about the world and, perhaps more importantly, about how we see the world. They are witnesses of our time and

Figure 0.1 US veterans point out a familiar name at the Vietnam Veterans Memorial following a
Veterans Day ceremony, 11 November 2006

of times past. A satellite image provides information about the world's surface. Photographs document wars or diplomatic summits or protest movements. Monuments remind us of past events and their significance for today's political communities. Sometimes images and artefacts entrench political practices. For instance: a variety of seemingly mundane visual performances, from hairstyles to body movements, signal and normalise gendered systems of exclusion. But sometimes images can also uproot political practices. Indigenous photographs – such as the one on the cover of this book by Michael Cook – can challenge stereotypes and the colonial understanding of history associated with them.

Some credit this artistic creativity with the potential to fundamentally reorient our political world. A work of art can lead us to see the world in a new light and help us rethink assumptions we have taken for granted, including those about politics. Or so believes Alex Danchev (2016: 91), who was convinced that "contrary to popular belief, it is given to artists, not politicians, to create a new world order." Look, as an example, at Pablo Picasso's famous painting *Guernica*, which has become one of the most iconic and influential anti-war statements. It seeks to capture not the factual aspects of wars but their traumatic human and emotional dimensions. In so doing *Guernica* has become a constant public and political reminder of the moral dangers of war. Consider how, in February 2003, the US Secretary of State, Colin Powell, made a case for war with Iraq to the United Nations in New York. He had to do so outside the Security Council chamber, which features a large tapestry reproduction Guernica. For the occasion of Powell's speech *Guernica* was (in)famously hidden behind a blue cover: its visual-emotional-ethical message was too powerful and subversive to be seen. As Maureen Dowd (2003) put it: "Mr Powell can't very well seduce the world into bombing Iraq surrounded on camera by shrieking and mutilated women, men, children, bulls and horses."

Third, and already illustrated by *Guernica*: images and visual artefacts do things. They are political forces in themselves. They often shape politics as much as they depict it. Early modern cartographic techniques played a key role in legitimising the emergence of territorial states. Hollywood films provide us with well-rehearsed and deeply entrenched models of heroes and villains to the point that they shape societal values. A terrorist suicide bombing is designed to kill people with a maximum visual impact: images of the event are meant to go around the world and spread fear. James Der Derian (Chapter 50) speaks of a "war of images," a situation where visuality is a key strategic part of war, used at all levels and by all actors. In this way images become weapons themselves in a myriad of ways: not just to project fear but to recruit combatants, to sway public opinion, to guide drones and missiles – in short, to wage visual war.

I now map out the broad conceptual contours of visual global politics in an effort to understand the key issues at stake. I neither summarise the chapters – they are designed to defy easy summary – nor do I survey specialised and often narrow academic debates. Instead, I highlight, in accessible language, the key issues that are central to understanding visual global politics. I bring together insights from different disciplines in an attempt to provide a framework though which the political significance of images can be understood and further investigated. I do so in relative detail because there has not yet been a comprehensive attempt to assess the broad field of visual global politics. This is not to say that scholars have not tackled the issues at stake. They have done so in numerous and highly sophisticated manners. But most existing books focus on a particular aspect of visual politics. There are, just to mention a few examples, books that deal with the conceptual issue of aesthetic theory (Bleiker 2009; Pusca 2009; Rancière 2004), with the role of photography (Azoulay 2008; Hariman and Lucaites 2007; Levi Strauss 2003; Linfield 2010; Perlmutter 1998; Sliwinski 2011), film (Shapiro 1999, 2008; Weber 2005, 2006b, 2011), popular culture (Griffin 2015; Nexon and Neumann 2006; Shepherd 2013; Weldes 2003) and art (Danchev 2009; Danchev and Lisle 2009; Luke 1992, 2002; Martin 2014). There are books that address the more general role of the media (Moeller 1999; Der Derian 2009; Zelizer 2010) and the politics of representation (Campbell 1992; Debrix and Weber 2003; Rabinowitz 1994; Tagg 1988). There are also volumes that take on visual politics in a broad way, but they either deal with specific empirical issues, such as geopolitics (MacDonald, Hughes and Dodds 2010), peace (Möller 2013), democracy (Azoulay 2001), the role of the face (Edkins 2015) or regional conflict (Shim 2014). Finally, there are already several broad surveys, but they focus on visual culture not on visual politics (see Dikovitskaya 2005; Elkins 2003; Jay 2005; Mirzoeff 1998, 1999, 2011; Mitchell 1986, 1994, 2005b; and, for a rare take on the political, Shim 2014: 9–46).

The idea of *Visual Global Politics*, in short, is to open up debates as widely as possible. In this sense, the book is not an academic treatise but more a provocation designed to evoke reflection and discussion: a political engagement with the visual and a visual engagement with the political. While these visual–political links take place in numerous realms, I particularly flag, with Jacques Rancière (2004), how images are political in the most fundamental sense: they delineate what we, as collectives, see and what we don't and thus, by extension, how politics is perceived, sensed, framed, articulated, carried out and legitimised.

The visual turn

When characterising the nature of our world today, W.J.T. Mitchell (Chapter 34; 1986, 1994) speaks of a "visual" or "pictorial" turn, stressing that people often perceive and remember key events more through images than through verbal accounts. He writes of a "new heightened awareness" of the role of visuality, even of how the problem of our time is the "problem of the image."

In the world of politics, the ensuing implications are particularly pronounced. Our understanding of terrorism, for instance, is inevitably intertwined with how images dramatically depict the events in question, how these images circulate worldwide, and how politicians and the public respond to these visual impressions. Take the terrorist attacks of 11 September 2001. There is no way to understand the origin, nature and impact of the event without understanding the role of images. The attack was designed for visual impact. Images circulated immediately worldwide, giving audiences a sense of how traumatic and how terrible the event was. Many of these emotional images not only shaped subsequent public debates and policy responses, including the War on Terror, but also remain engrained in our collective consciousness.

Images are, of course, not new, nor have they necessarily replaced words as the main means of communication. Images and visual artefacts have been around from the beginning of time. The visual has always been part of life. Images were produced not only to capture key aspects of human existence, but also to communicate these aspects to others. Examples range from prehistoric cave paintings that document hunting practices to Renaissance works of art. Some of these images and cultural artefacts we still see today and they continue to influence our perception and under-standing of the world.

But there are two ways in which the politics of images has changed fundamentally. First is the speed at which images circulate and the reach they have. Not that long ago, during the time of the Vietnam War, it would have taken days if not weeks for a photograph taken in the war zone to reach the front page of, say, the *New York Times*. In today's digital world, a photograph or a video can reach audiences worldwide immediately after it has been taken. Media networks can now make a local event almost instantaneously global, whether it is a terrorist attack, a protest march, an election campaign rally or any other political phenomenon. But it is not just that global media networks now cover news events 24 hours a day. The issue goes well beyond the influential CNN effect (Robinson, Chapter 6; 2002). The circulation of news has changed fundamentally. Even traditional newspapers – from *Le Monde* and *Der Spiegel* to the *Guardian* – are meanwhile multimedia organisations with a substantial internet presence. They cater to an audience that consumes news increasingly through smart-phones, tablets and other mobile devices.

Second is what one could call the democratisation of visual politics. It used to be that very few actors – states or global media networks – had access to images and the power to distribute them to a global audience. Today, everyone can take a photograph with a smartphone, upload it on social media and circulate it immediately with a potential worldwide reach. Every two minutes, people upload more photographs than there were in total 150 years ago (Eveleth 2015 in Kaempf, Chapter 12).

Figure 0.2 Film and photojournalists covering an election campaign rally by Kim Dae-Jung, Seoul, South Korea, 1987

Source: Roland Bleiker.

Figure 0.3 People with smartphones documenting an election campaign event by Hillary Clinton
         in Orlando, Florida, on 21 September 2016. Barbara Kinney

Source: Barbara Kinney, www.flickr.com/photos/hillaryclinton/29845603875

Two photographs that illustrate the changes in visual media coverage are Figures 0.2
and 0.3. The first one is from a 1987 South Korean presidential election campaign rally
by Kim Dae-Jung. It is covered by conventional film and photojournalists whose images
then circulated via local and global media. The second is from the 2016 US presidential
election campaign by Hillary Clinton. It features a crowd with mobile phones more
concerned with visualising their own presence than with documenting the event.

The result is an unprecedented visualisation of both our private lives and our political
landscape: a global communication dynamic that is fundamentally new and rooted in
various networks and webs of relations (Kaempf, Chapter 12; Favero 2014: 66). Look
at the Arab Spring uprising that started in Egypt in 2011. One of the most remarkable
episodes occurred when a young woman blogger, Aliaa Elmahdy, posted a nude
photograph of herself on her blog. She did so to protest gender discrimination in Egypt
and called for more personal freedom, including sexual autonomy. Her private-cum-
public photographs circulated immediately and widely around the world. They generated
extensive public protests in Egypt and a wave of feminist solidarity abroad. Or consider
how the terrorist organisation Islamic State is using beheading videos as part of a
carefully orchestrated and well organised social media strategy, aiming at numerous
audiences simultaneously (Friis 2017).

Any group or individual, no matter what their location or political intent is, can
potentially produce and circulate images that, in today's new media language, go viral.
Historians would remind us, though, that images have gone viral before the internet era. Engravings of the traumatic earthquake in Lisbon in 1755 rapidly spread across
Europe, providing publics eager for news with visual evidence about the disaster
(Sliwinski 2011: 37–8). Likewise, a few months after Eugène Delacroix witnessed and
painted *Les Massacres de Chios* in Greece in 1823, it was exhibited in Paris and people

flocked to view the artwork. It did, in this sense, go viral and might have played a role in persuading French elites and policy-makers to change their position and support the Greek War of Independence against the Ottoman Empire (Rodogno 2012: 72–3; see also Los Angeles County Museum of Art 2015; Bellamy 2012). The difference between then and today is nevertheless dramatic: more and more people now have the ability to produce and distribute images, and the speed at which they can go viral today is unprecedented and has unprecedented consequences.

What we have here is nothing less than a visual communication revolution that has shaken the foundations and hierarchies of established media networks. We see a dismantling of the division between broadcaster and viewer, producer and consumer. While this emancipatory technology has created an unprecedented proliferation and diversification of images, voices and views, some commentators believe this process is not as democratic as it first appears (see Kaempf, Chapter 12). Various factors – from algorithms to the legacy of old media and the interference of states – structure and mediate the flow of images. Here is one example of many: political events, such as protest marches or terrorist attacks, gain immediate worldwide media attention when they take place in the heart of the Western world, say in Paris or New York or Berlin.

Figure 0.4 Women in the revolution graffiti. Note, this is not the actual photograph that Aliaa Elmahdy posted on her blog. It is a graffiti representation of the photograph and a portrayal of Samira Ibrahim, who launched a lawsuit against the Egyptian army for conducting "virginity checks" on protesters.

Source: Wikimedia Commons, https://commons.wikimedia.org/wiki/File:Women_in_the_revolution.jpg

When similar events take place in the global South – say in Beirut or Baghdad or Bogotá – they often barely make the news (for terrorism see Hanusch 2015; for protest Bleiker 2002).

The actors themselves, of course, are not necessarily democratic either. Susie Linfield (Chapter 33) says that we live in an age of the democratic image but also in an age of the fascist image. Yes, suppressed minorities now have the chance to "speak up." They have a voice they did not have before, or, at least the potential to circulate this voice and perhaps have it heard. They can now enter diplomatic debates in ways that were not possible before (see Constantinou, Chapter 13). But, at the same time, the new potential of social media also paves the way for violent encounters. Perpetrators of atrocities have for long documented and celebrated their atrocities with photographs (Reinhardt, Chapter 49). The Nazis did so, and so did the Khmer Rouge (see Hughes 2003: 23–44). But today, with the help of social media, perpetrators of all kinds can circulate their videos fast and widely, from suicide bombing of Al-Qaeda to beheadings by the Islamic State. In this instance, then, photographs or films of violence are no longer "forms of witnessing but, rather, forms of war itself." And with that, they reach "unprecedented important and political influence" (Linfield, Chapter 33).

The power of images I: icons

There are few realms where the power of images is more obvious than with icons. Robert Hariman and John Lucaites (Chapter 25; 2007) defined icons as widely known and distributed images that represent "historically significant events, activate strong emotional identification or response, and are reproduced across a range of media, genres, or topics." Some scholars go as far as stressing that iconic images are so effective in recalling political events that they often become "primary markers" themselves (Zelizer 2002: 699). This is to say that over time, an event is recognised publicly not primarily by its political content but by its photographic representation. The representation then becomes content itself.

Consider two well-known examples of iconic photographs that have come to stand for the crises they depict. First is Nick Ut's Pulitzer Prize-winning Vietnam War image of 1972. It depicts nine-year-old Kim Phúc, naked, badly burned and fleeing from her South Vietnam village after it was napalmed. At the time this photograph directed public gaze to the atrocities committed against innocent civilians. It transformed public and political perceptions of the war, so much so that it contributed to further eroding the war's legitimacy (see Hariman and Lucaites, Chapter 25; 2003: 35–66; 2007; Lee-Koo, Chapter 4). In fact, half a century later the image still stands as a metaphorical representation of the Vietnam War and the suffering it brought. The second well known example is another Pulitzer Prize-winning photograph, taken in 1993 in famine-stricken Sudan, by Kevin Carter. Carter's photograph depicts a starving child in an unfathomable manner: kneeling helplessly on the ground, her head in her heads, while a vulture watches over. It was an image that "made the world weep" and stood – as it continues to do – as a powerful marker of the problem of poverty in the developing world.

At a time when we are saturated with information stemming from multiple media sources, iconic photographs remain influential for their ability to capture social and political issues in succinct and mesmerising ways. They serve as "visual quotations" (Sontag 2003: 22). Icons, in this sense, shape public opinion because they are part of the collective fabric through which people and communities make sense of themselves.

Here is an example: a poster that has become an iconic image of US President Barack Obama. Designed by the street artist Shepard Fairey and based on a photograph by Manny Garcia, the poster came in several variations, including "Hope" and "Progress" and "Change." It played a key role during Obama's 2008 presidential election campaign for it became a symbol of support for Obama and the ideas he stood for. The image soon turned into a veritable pop culture phenomena, very quickly spreading virally and being reproduced not only on countless posters but also on T-shirts, buttons, stickers and more (Arnon 2011). On several levels the image has already achieved iconic status, most notably in its widespread appropriation. The Obama poster was followed by countless imitations, from parodies to political re-uses, including Fairey's own adaptation for the Occupy movement. But it might be too early to tell if the image will become a true icon, for it is generally assumed that at least a decade is necessary for this to occur (Hansen 2015: 271, 277; Hariman and Lucaites 2007). Today, when images are produced and circulated with ever greater speed and reach, icons can emerge in a short period. But this very proliferation of images can also lead to a situation where icons are short-lived and soon become superseded by other ones. Only time will tell which images retain their iconic status and which ones disappear from our collective memory.

Icons are powerful and there is an inevitable politics about them. The most prominent critique is that they become detached from their original setting. Once stripped of context, icons can easily be appropriated and, thus, run the risk of feeding into preconceived stereotypical narratives. Individuals depicted in icons become symbols. The ensuing dynamic erases their suffering and "the political causes of what is actually happening to them" (Dauphinee, Chapter 1). This has been particularly the case with visual depictions of "Africa," which are often embedded in undifferentiated and stereotypical media portrayals (Campbell, Chapter 17; Lee-Koo, Chapter 4; Müller, Chapter 3).

The power of images II: emotions

There is clearly something unique about images. They have a special status. They generate excitement and anxieties. "Why is it," Mitchell (2005b: 7) asks, "that people have such strange attitudes towards images?" Why is it that audiences are given a stern warning before they see shocking images of, say, war or terror or bodily mutilation or, as above, impending death? Why, Lene Hansen (2014) asks, do we not get the same warning with verbal depictions? Consider how news outlets that published images of the bombing of the Boston marathon in 2013 felt compelled to add notes that read "Warning: This image may contain graphic or objectionable content" (Haughney 2013). No such warning was given with language-based articles of the same event, even though they described the horror of the attack in equally great detail. What makes images seemingly more dangerous and powerful than words?

Part of what makes images unique is that they often evoke, appeal to and generate emotions. Pictures of traumatic events, such as terrorist attacks, natural catastrophes or airplane crashes, seem able to capture the unimaginable. This is why news coverage of such traumas is frequently accompanied by images, as if they could provide audiences with a type of emotional insight that words cannot convey. Images seem to express the pain and distress of victims better than words do. They are thus central to how audiences worldwide perceive and thus also understand and respond to crises (Dauphinee, Chapter 1; Hutchison, Chapter 47; 2016).

Film and television are visual media that appeal to feelings and emotions in a particularly powerful way. Cinematic depictions of political issues offer the viewer a very visceral experience, in part because they combine narratives, visual images and sound. But such depictions are also powerful because they are based on individual characters and the moral choices they make, offering the viewer not just an abstract depiction of politics but a form of cinematic storytelling that allows them to identify with particular individuals and their situations. As a result, distant and complex political topics become accessible through personal stories (see Plantinga and Smith 1999; Shapiro, Chapter 46). The political effects of these visual-emotional character developments can be diverse. They can give viewers historical or contemporary experiences that they otherwise would never be able to have. Consider how the recent American miniseries *Roots* – a remake of a highly successful 1977 miniseries – retraces the history of slavery through the experience of a family, thus giving viewers a sense of what it might have been like to experience the respective trauma first-hand and personally. But cinematic depictions – as for instance in the form of prevailing spy and adventure movies – can also feed "geopolitical anxieties" and designate some people – such as those of a different skin colour or religious orientation – as more suspicious and dangerous than others (Dodds, Chapter 22; Philpott, Chapter 20; Der Derian 2009: 166).

Images – in moving and still form – can clearly have very powerful emotional and political effects. They can convey the meaning of political events across time or to audiences far away. They shockingly remind us, as John Berger (1991: 42) puts it, "of the reality, the lived reality, behind the abstractions of political theory, casualty statistics or news bulletins." They serve as "an eye we cannot shut."

Allow me to briefly illustrate some of the political issues at stake by focusing on the role of emotions in visual representation of humanitarian and other political crises. An image of a child under attack, for instance, can generate not just emotional reactions by viewers but also political responses (Lee-Koo, Chapter 4). Bob Geldof, in the context of the humanitarian campaign for victims of the 1983–5 famine in Ethiopia, knew exactly that images of destitute victims, particularly close-ups of children, would solicit widespread compassion and generate donations (Müller, Chapter 3).

Key to this dynamic is the visual appearance of the face, for it is through the face that "we are thought to signal our inner feelings and our emotions." This is what marks our individuality and this is how we are being identified (Edkins, Chapter 16; 2015). But the links between images and emotions are complex. There are at least two somewhat opposing scholarly takes on the issue.

First: there is an extensive literature in social psychology that discusses the so-called "identifiable victim effect." Surveys have discovered that close-up portraits of victims are the type of images most likely to evoke compassion in viewers, whereas images of groups create emotional distance between viewers and the subjects being depicted (Jenni and Loewenstein 1997; Kogut and Ritov 2005). The question then is: what happens to those people who are not visualised through the face, such as those "hidden" behind a veil (Callahan, Chapter 9) or those, like many refugees, who are portrayed as arriving in large numbers on boats (Bleiker, Campbell and Hutchison 2014).

Second: there is the literature on compassion fatigue, presented in this volume by the influential work of Susan Moeller. The contention here is that an overexposure to images of suffering eventually renders viewers numb and indifferent. It is not that they do not care, but that the emotional situation becomes too much for them to bear:

they feel that they cannot possibly make a meaningful difference and therefore start turning away emotionally (Moeller, Chapter 8; 1999; see also Sontag 1977, 2003). Other scholars stress that while individuals and societies often block out or even deny images of human suffering, there is ample evidence that the public reacts generously when charity organisations appeal for help (see Cohen 2001; Campbell 2004: 62; 2014b; Johnson 2011: 621–43; Berger 1991: 41–4). From this perspective, the issue may not be one of compassion fatigue so much as one of media fatigue – of global news media moving rapidly from crisis to crisis (see Campbell 2014b).

How to understand the political significance of images and visual artefacts

So far I have provided two brief examples – on icons and on emotions – to illustrate the power of images and the complexity of the political dynamics associated with them. I now would like to step back in order to trace more carefully the nature and implications of visual politics.

Images work at numerous overlapping levels: across national boundaries and between the physical and the mental world. They come in complex and wide varieties: as photographs or films, as comics or videogames. Things get even more complex when we think of three-dimensional visual artefacts, such as architecture, military uniforms or monuments.

No matter how diverse and complex visual images and artefacts are, they all have one thing in common: they work differently from words. That is their very nature. They are of a non-verbal nature but we, as scholars, need words to assess their political significance. Something inevitably gets lost in this process. This is why there is always a certain excess to images, a kind of "surplus value" that escapes our attempts to explain them definitively (Mitchell 2005b: 65–110). Add to this that images often work through emotions and that emotions are notoriously difficult to recognise and understand. They have stereotypically been classified as private and purely individual phenomena. One can never truly understand how another person feels. One can only convey this feeling to others and, here too, something inevitably gets lost in the process. While a large body of literature, meanwhile, highlights the social and political nature of emotions, understanding how they actually work is far from easy (see Hutchison and Bleiker 2014b).

The challenge, then, is to explore the nature of visual politics in a way that does as much justice as possible to its unique emotional and non-verbal status (see Scarry 1994). Doing so inevitably entails scrutinising the crucial links between the visual and verbal. The issues at stake are not clear-cut. Some authors, relying on Horst Bredekamp's influential analysis, argue that images have an "auto-active" nature and thus "a voice of [their] own" (Schlag and Heck 2012: 8, 16). There is, indeed, something universal and non-linguistic about images. All cultures in the world use images – from artworks to flags and from media photos to television. As opposed to language, which requires a particular set of skills to be understood, everyone can see and "read" images, even though we might end up with different interpretations (see Shim 2014: 27). But this does not mean that images work independently of language. Mitchell (Chapter 34; 2005b: 5), for instance, argues that "all media are mixed media," that there is nothing either purely verbal or purely visual. Both elements make sense in conjunction with each other. Mitchell does, indeed, explicitly warn not to fall into the stereotypical position that "images have replaced words as the dominant mode of expression in our time." This is why – following Roland Barthes – he speaks of "imagetext" (when the two are seamlessly merged), image-text (when they are separate but connected) and image/text (when they stand in conflict or tension). These connections between text and image are particularly pronounced in some realms, such as comics, which revolve around merging visual and textual components (see Choi, Chapter 2; Hansen 2017). But they exist in all aspects of visual politics.

The dilemma then is: images are different than words (even if they are intrinsically linked to them) but we still need words to make sense of them. And we need to understand them in all of their complexity. We need to put images central and, as James Elkins (2013: 59) put it, recognise that "they need to never be fully controlled."

The key is to engage images in a way that defers authority back to them; to grant images their unique and untameable status and provide a set of commentaries that, ultimately, leave the last word with images. Doing so requires a multitude of approaches and perspectives, even if they are, at times, not compatible (see Bleiker 2015). This is precisely why this book revolves around a large number of short chapters, each tackling the world of visual politics from different perspectives. None of these perspectives can claim to offer an authentic and uncontested view. They are inevitably always partial. But taken together, this myriad of perspectives offers us an appreciation of the complexity entailed in visual politics.

In order to frame the pluralist exploration of the chapters that follow I now identify – in a more systematic way – several links between visuality and global politics. For the sake of clarity I return to images – and to photographs in particular. I do so both because photographs lend themselves more easily to analysis. Arguably they also play a particularly important political role because of the ease in which they circulate and enter "our" collective memory. I will later branch out again to the larger dynamics of visual politics, including artefacts and performances.

The politics of images I: the illusion of authenticity

Photographs are useful to illustrate how visual politics work. They deceive. They seem to give us a glimpse of the real. They provide us with the seductive belief that what we see in a photograph is an authentic representation of the world: a slice of life that reveals exactly what was happening at a particular moment (see Tagg 1988; Shim 2014: 26). This is the case because a photograph is, as Roland Barthes (1977: 17) stresses, "a message without a code." As opposed to a linguistic representation, for instance, a photograph is "a perfect analogon." Barbie Zelizer (2005: 29) speaks of a kind of "eyewitness authority."

In the realm of documentary photography, for instance, it was for long commonly assumed that a photographer, observing the world from a distance, is an "objective witness" to political phenomena, providing authentic representations of, say, war or poverty or famine (see Levi Strauss 2003: 45; Perlmutter 1998: 28; Campbell, Chapter 17). Such positions hinge on the belief that a photograph can represent its object in a neutral and value-free way, transferring meaning from one site to another without affecting the object's nature and signification in the process. Debrix (Debrix and Weber 2003: xxiv, xxvii–xxx) stresses that this belief is part of a long Western search for transcendental knowledge, be it of a spiritual or secular nature.

Few, if any, scholars today still believe that photographs objectively represent the world. Representation is meanwhile recognised as an inevitable aspect of politics. Photographs depict the world from a certain angle and are inevitably part of a range of political processes.

But it is precisely the illusion of authenticity that makes photographs such powerful tools to convey the meaning of political events to distant audiences. Jonathan Friday (2000: 365) writes of photographs as generating a near-compulsive draw to view the horror and spectacle of political and humanitarian crisis: a kind of "demonic curiosity." Spectators view and re-view crises through various media sources until the enormity of the event seems graspable. In doing so, photographs shape not only an individual's perception but also larger, collective forms of consciousness.

The illusion of authenticity also masks the political values that such photographic representations embody. The assumption that photographs are neutral, value-free and evidential, is reinforced because photography captures faces and events in memorable ways. For instance, if one looks at a close-up of a victim of a humanitarian crisis one could easily believe that one actually sees that person as he or she was at that moment. Michael Shapiro (1988: 124, 134) writes of a "grammar of face-to-face encounters." And he stresses that the seemingly naturalistic nature of this encounter makes photographic representations particularly vulnerable to being appropriated by discourses professing authentic knowledge and truth. We may succumb to such a "seductiveness of the real" to the point that we forget, as David Perlmutter (1998: 28) warns us, that "the lens is focused by a hand directed by a human eye." Add to this that the public

Figure 0.5 Lightness illusion

Source: As discussed in Anderson and Winawer (2005). With permission from the authors.

rarely sees the news media as purveyors of commercially profitable stories and images. Instead, the news is perceived as a reflection of the actual, as a neutral mediator between a subject and, in the case of most international news, an object usually located in another part of the world.

The illusion of authenticity applies across a range of visual fields explored in the chapters that follow. Rune Saugmann (Chapter 44) found that the use of surveillance images, which is ubiquitous around the world, rests on an assumption of factual evidence – all while the images in question are highly partial in a range of ways.

Before I engage the ensuing politics in detail, allow me to flag with one simple example how images can deceive or, at least, how we ought to be wary of trusting them with giving us authentic insight into what they depict.

This image above (Figure 0.5) highlights what Barton Anderson and Jonathan Winawer (2005: 79–83) called "lightness illusion." The two halves of the image illustrate the effect that layered image representations can have on lightness perception. An object's lightness as we perceive it is not as obvious as it might seem because it depends on the background against which it is depicted. Have a close look at Figure 0.5. The chess pieces in the top half seem very different than the ones at the bottom. In the top they appear white and in the bottom they appear black. But the image is deceiving us. Or, rather, our vision does. In reality, all of the chess pieces are exactly the same. The chess pieces only appear differently because they are set against a very different background, which provides the lightness illusion.

The politics of images II: aesthetic choices

Images deceive and not only because they might trick our eyes, or can be manipulated and faked. All images – still and moving ones – always express a particular perspective.

Images reflect certain aesthetic choices. They represent the world from a particular angle. They inevitably exclude as much as they include. A photograph cannot be neutral because it always is an image chosen and composed by a particular person. It is taken from a particular angle, and then produced and reproduced in a certain manner, thereby excluding a range of alternative ways of capturing the object in question (see, for instance, Sontag 2003: 46; Barthes 1977: 19).

Consider the two versions of the historical photograph reproduced below (Figure 0.6). Taken in 1944, the photograph depicts the president of the Croatian Parliament, Marko Došen, and several Catholic Church leaders, including the Archbishop Alojzije Stepinac. Both the original and the cropped version of the photograph produce a simulacrum, showing exactly what the lens and sensor capture. But the two versions show completely different political realities. The cropped version (Figure 0.7) depicts three clergy engaging in what seems a normal and uncontroversial activity. The original version (Figure 0.6) places them next to soldiers and civilians giving Nazi salutes, thus visually documenting their complicity.

The important aspect of this process, for David Levi Strauss (2003: 45), is that there are always relations of power at stake in a photograph, that there is always an attempt to tell a story, and that this story is always told from a particular, politically charged angle. Numerous chapters in this book explore this aspect of visual politics, showing, for instance, how images from satellites and drones offer always a particular and highly political view of the world (Wilcox, Chapter 14; Shim, Chapter 40; see also Tagg 1988).

Figure 0.6 Alojzije Stepinac (far right) with two Catholic priests at the funeral of President of the
Croatian Parliament Marko Došen in September 1944

Source: Wikimedia Commons, https://commons.wikimedia.org/wiki/File:NDH_-_salute.jpg (in the public domain).

Figure 0.7
Cropped version of Figure 0.6

The politics of images III: the need for interpretation

Images make no sense by themselves. They need to be seen and interpreted. They gain meaning in relation to other images and the personal and societal assumptions and norms that surround us. This is why Barthes (1977: 17–19) stresses that there are always two aspects to a photograph. There is the "denoted message," which is the above-mentioned perfect representation of a visual image. But there is also a "connoted message," which includes how a photograph is read and interpreted, how it fits into existing practices of knowledge and communication. This interpretation contains values that inevitably have as much to do with the position of the interpreter as with the content of the image itself. Some refer to this process more specifically as "secondary image construction," which takes place when photographs are "selected out from their original ordering and narrative context, to be placed alongside textual information and reports in a publication" (Hall 1997: 86). John Berger (1991: 55), for instance, points out that photographs "only preserve instant appearances." When we look at a photograph we never just look at a photograph alone. We actually look at a complex relationship between a photograph and ourselves (Berger 1972: 9).

Our viewing experience is thus intertwined not only with previous experiences, such as our memory of other photographs we have seen in the past, but also with the values and visual traditions that are accepted as common sense by established societal norms. There are inevitably power relationships involved in this nexus between visuality, society and politics. Numerous commentators in this volume highlight the issues at stake. Images, Sally Butler (Chapter 27) says, "are potentially like open-ended sentences that require an imaginative response." The meaning of climate cartoons, Kate Manzo (Chapter 5) reminds us, is like the meaning of climate itself: "it varies across time and space." This is why Lene Hansen (Chapter 41) stresses that interpreting images is not just about outlining the facts they depict. There is far more at stake.

Look at the above image of priests being implicated with fascists in Croatia. To make sense of the image we need to know something about the history of fascism in Europe. We need to know what a Nazi salute is and what it means and stands for. We need to know what kind of ideology and what atrocities are associated with Nazi rule. We also need to know a range of things about religion, from how priests dress to Christianity's presumed embrace of humane values. Without knowing all these issues the image would make no sense or would, at least, have a very different meaning.

Look at how satellite images are often seen as authentic depictions of the earth. David Shim (Chapter 40) points out how they seem to offer a "perfect resemblance of an external reality." But, in fact, they are highly constructed images. In order to make sense they need to be processed and tweaked to correct distortion in the raw data. Cloud formations and snowfall, for instance, obstruct views. The final image is thus compiled from a range of different shots, taken at different times. Such forms of collated images would, in photography, be dismissed as "photoshopped" and fake and, yet, in satellite imagery they are the very essence of how the image is constructed.

Look, in this very context, how the US Secretary of State, Colin Powell, argued for the invasion of Iraq at the United Nations' Security Council by displaying satellite and other images that allegedly proved the existence of weapons of mass destruction. Powell (2003) fully recognised that these images are "hard for the average person to interpret" and that doing so requires "experts with years and years of experience, poring for hours and hours over light tables." But once these highly technical and inevitably subjective

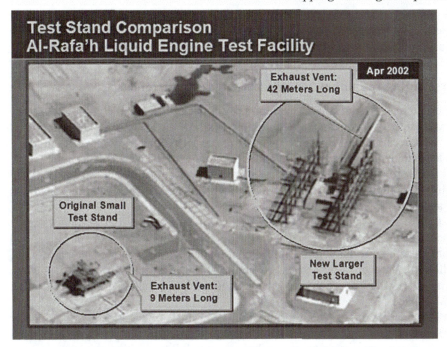

Figure 0.8 "Test stand comparison Al-Rafa'h liquid engine test facility," from Secretary Powell's Remarks to the UN Security Council

Source: Powell 2003.

interpretations are imbued with the legitimacy of political authority they become a form of hard evidence. They form an empirical base for policy choices. And yet, as the world found out later, this allegedly irrefutable visual evidence was mistaken: there were, after all, no weapons of mass destruction in Iraq (see also Shim, Chapter 40).

Look at what happened when bombs from a US drone killed twenty civilians in Afghanistan in 2015. A drone's vision system – interpreted with confidence by military sources – identified the target as military. This mistake could happen, Wilcox (Chapter 14) argues, because an interpretation of an image is always dependent on the values of the interpreters. In an environment permeated with fear, as was the case here, "the lack of evidence of weapons becomes evidence of weapons based upon what is felt must be true." This is how, as she puts it, the fear of Afghan insurgents "can stick to any body visible through the camera of the drone."

Look at the torture photos at Abu Ghraib. They do not speak for themselves. Viewers around the world saw and interpreted them differently depending on the views they had of the War on Terror. Some might have seen the photographs as part of a "shock and awe" military strategy. Others saw them as an expression of an increasingly violent American society. Others again saw them as a manifestation of American imperialism (see Dauphinee, Chapter 1; Linfield, Chapter 33).

Look at one of the most iconic images of the past few decades, the "Tiananmen Man" image, depicting a lone protester in front of a series of tanks. This image immediately makes sense for many people around the world, as long as they know about the historic event, the occurrence of the protest movement and its suppression by the police. But many people inside China, for whom depictions and reportage of the Tiananmen massacre remain censored, do not have the background knowledge necessary to interpret this photograph, let alone recognise it as an icon.

Understanding the impact of images and visual artefacts

So far one thing is clear: images matter. They matter politically. We know that they do or, at least, have a corresponding intuition. But how do we actually know that what we know is accurate? For instance, what is the exact political impact of an image – say a photograph of a tsunami victim on the front page of the *New York Times*? People around the world are inevitably influenced by seeing a humanitarian tragedy depicted through the photograph of a suffering individual. But what is the exact impact of this image and how do we know?

The task of understanding the precise impact of images is not easy. Images work in complex ways, crisscrossing a range of geographical and temporal boundaries – all the more since new technologies, from global media networks to new media sources, now allow for an ever faster and easier circulation of images.

Let me start with two examples where images clearly mattered and had a direct political impact.

First is the debate on the use of torture in the War on Terror. As early as the summer of 2003, it was publicly known – in part through reports from Amnesty International – that US troops were using torture techniques when interrogating prisoners in Iraq.

Figure 0.9 An unidentified Abu Ghraib detainee, seen in a 2003 photo

Source: Public domain; ineligible for copyright. Pictures taken by US military personnel as part of that person's official duties are ineligible for copyright in the United States.

There was, however, little public interest or discussion about the issue. Nobody seemed to care. Domestic and international outrage only emerged in the spring of 2004, in direct response to graphic photographs of US torture at the Abu Ghraib prison facilities. All of a sudden there was a massive public outcry and discussion about whether or not torture is a legitimate way of waging the War on Terror. This shift was not linked to the knowledge of torture, which was always there, but to audiences worldwide witnessing the demeaning nature of torture though graphic and emotional images. While these visual shifts may not have fundamentally altered US foreign policy, they stand for years to come as symbols of America's abuse of power and loss of legitimacy and prestige (Hansen, Chapter 41; 2015: 264–5).

Second is the European refugee crisis of 2015. Key here is a photograph of a three-year-old Syrian refugee, Alan Kurdi, found dead on a beach in Turkey on 2 September 2015. That image circulated immediately around the world, reaching 20 million screens in 12 hours (Vis and Goriunova 2015). People reacted with a level of empathy that was unusual. All of a sudden, public attitudes toward refugees changed across Europe but particularly in Germany, where one witnessed the emergence of what was called a *Willkommenskultur*, a culture of welcoming refugees. There were images of refugees arriving in Munich and being welcomed to cheers by German people. Everywhere, Germans were helping out. This shift directly correlated with the image of Alan Kurdi going viral. An empirical study shows that there was not only a massive spike in social media discussion of the crisis but also, and more importantly, that the positive word "refugee" increased far more than the more pejorative term "migrant" (Vis and Goriunova 2015) This one image of a dead boy clearly played a key role in this shift. Of course, we all empathise with a three-year-old boy. Children are innocent, and to see an innocent victim is something that rallies people. As Katrina Lee-Koo (Chapter 4) puts it, images of children feed into "pre-existing narratives" so much so that they often generate political action. In the case of Alan Kurdi, the image changed both public attitudes and policies: the German Chancellor, Angela Merkel, adopted a much more progressive policy toward refugees. She famously declared "wir schaffen das" – "we'll manage that." But the public mood changed after the terrorist attacks in Paris in November 2015, which killed 130 people, and after a large group of mostly immigrant men assaulted over a thousand women during New Year's Eve celebrations in Cologne. By then, the *Willkommenskultur* had been replaced by an "Abschiebekultur," a culture that favours sending refugees back. But despite this backlash, the image of Alan Kurdi did, at least in the short run, have an impact on public attitudes and policies.

Alan Kurdi and the debate on torture illustrate the power of images to shape political debates and phenomena directly. But in most cases it is much more difficult to ascertain if images have a direct impact.

Only in rare instances do images directly cause political events. In most cases the impact of images is more diffuse. There are, for instance, clear links between the dramatic images of the terrorist attacks on 11 September 2001, the highly emotional rhetoric of good versus evil that emerged in response, and the ensuing War on Terror. But these links would be very difficult – if not impossible – to assess with cause–effect models. As Jacques Rancière (2004: 63) put it: "Politics has its aesthetics, and aesthetics has its politics. But there is no formula for an appropriate correlation."

Causality is not the right concept to understand the impact of images, at least not if approached in a conventional social scientific manner. But one could perhaps speak of "discursive causality" or "discursive agency" (Hansen 2006: 26, see also 2015: 274–5;

Bleiker 2000: 208). This would retain a notion of impact but acknowledge that images work gradually and across time and space. They transgress numerous borders – spatial, linguistic, psychological and other ones. They work inaudibly but powerfully: by slowly entrenching – or challenging – how we view, think of and thus also how we conduct politics. Images, in this sense, are political because they frame what William Connolly (1991) called "conditions of possibility" within which politics takes place. This is why the thorny issue of how to approach impact is crucial and thus needs further elaboration.

The politics of visibility and invisibility

The most prominent advocate of such an approach to images is Rancière. He speaks of the "distribution of the sensible," that is, of how in any given society and at any given time, there are boundaries between what can be seen and not, felt and not, thought and not, and, as a result, between what is politically possible and not. These boundaries are arbitrary but often accepted self-evidently as common sense (Rancière 2004: 13; see also Rockhill 2009: 199–200).

Images influence the distribution of the sensible. They frame or reframe the political, either by entrenching existing configurations of seeing, sensing and thinking, or by challenging them. The boundaries between what is sensible and not sometimes shift rapidly, as in the case of torture debates, but mostly they evolve gradually as the visual world around us shifts and evolves. Images reveal and conceal. They show and hide, and, as Costas Constantinou (Chapter 13) points out, we often are not aware of what is excluded and what political consequences follow. Take the issue of sexual violence during conflict and war. Much of this violence takes place without being directly documented, visually or otherwise (Azoulay, Chapter 36). Add to this that sexual violence is so pervasive that, as Marysia Zalewski (Chapter 42) argues, "it is increasingly difficult to know what it is that we are seeing and what it is that we keep missing." This is why Elspeth Van Veeren (Chapter 28) believes that "visibility and invisibility are mutually constitutive." Any claim about visual politics contains, in some way or another, a concept of invisibility.

An immediate and normal reaction to a concept of politics as a struggle over visibility is: what happens to people, issues and phenomena that we do not see? What happens when we do not see violence, human rights violations, mass rape during war? Numerous authors explore such issues (for instance Reinhardt, Chapter 49; Azoulay, Chapter 36; Zalewski, Chapter 42). Some stress that the absence of images is "the most significant form of distancing and forgetting" (Robinson, Chapter 6). The genocide in Rwanda, for instance, killed up to a million people in a few months in 1994. Because there were very few images circulating in global media at that time it was possible to dismiss the tragedy as a mere local conflict (Robinson, Chapter 6). Even today, many of the world's most deadly conflicts, particularly in Africa, are not covered by global media because there are no Western geopolitical interests at stake (Kirkpatrick 2016: 91, 97).

Likewise, look how the evolution of warfare has very much been intertwined with what we see and what we don't – from emerging camouflage practices in the nineteenth century to attempt at controlling the spread of images during the Vietnam War (Van Veeren, Chapter 28). But recent conflicts, most notably in Afghanistan and Iraq, have shown that control over the flow of images is almost impossible to retain in the face of social media, which allows any individual or group to take images of the war zone and circulate them immediately (see Dauphinee, Chapter 1).

Figure 0.10 Man in a bear market – losing money in the markets, Jack Moreth

Source: Jack Moreth, www.stockvault.net/photo/193457/man-in-a-bear-market---losing-money-in-the-markets/
Freely available at Stockvault.

A related problem is about what happens to political phenomena that are hard to visualise? How can we "see" finance, Brassett (Chapter 19) asks? We can't. It is always represented by something; a banknote, a cheque, a bank statement. And yet, finance is surrounded by visual metaphors – from bankers in suits to bulls and bears to storms and tsunamis and rising and falling stock indexes – that often give us a misleading sense of what is going on. Religion, likewise, cannot be seen as such. It is visually represented through symbols, such as churches, mosques, clothing, hairstyles, shrines or praying individuals. These visual representations are imbued with preconceived, arbitrary and very political notions of what religion is (Wilson, Chapter 38). Or look at democracy: do we have more transparency today as greater aspects of democracy are made visible through television, film and the internet? Not necessarily so (Chou, Chapter 10). And what about peace? We have numerous visual icons that signify war but is there is not even a concept like peace photography? If peace is seen as the absence of violence, then there is literally an unlimited and meaningless number of images that can depict this (Möller, Chapter 32).

While the relationship between visibility and politics is complex, one can depict a range of historical evolutions as struggles over what is seen and not. Nicholas Mirzoeff (2011: 2) reminds us that the very term "visuality" goes back to the nineteenth century and signifies "the visualisation of history." He goes on to stress that visualised techniques, developed during plantation slavery, paved the way for the type of centralised leadership that lies at the core of contemporary political orders (Mirzoeff 2011: 10, 22–3). One could go back and observe these links between visuality and politics in almost all

Figure 0.11 How to visualise peace? United Nations Buffer Zone in Nicosia, Cyprus, July 2014

Source: Roland Bleiker.

realms. Look at how maps have always portrayed the world in political ways. In the early modern period in Europe, when new cartographic techniques emerged, they also paved the way for a new form of politics. As opposed to showing overlapping forms of governance, as had been previously the case, new maps designed territories in a way that carved out linear divisions of mutually exclusive territories. This technique facilitated the emergence of the nation-state, holding exclusive political authority over a well-defined territory (Branch, Chapter 45). Or consider how human rights and humanitarianism have emerged in tandem with photographic technologies. Sharon Sliwinski (Chapter 24) argues the history of human rights can be told and understood by looking at the circulation of images, how people emotionally reacted to them and what political consequences followed (see also Lee-Koo, Chapter 4; Fehrenbach and Rodogno 2015). One could find similar patterns when looking at images in relation to war, or colonialism, or gender relations, or any kind of political subject.

The division between what is seen or not inevitably has far-reaching political consequences. But the respective boundaries are not clear-cut. Making something visible is not necessarily positive. Visibility can also entrench existing political patterns. The above example of visual metaphors for finance and financial crises might be widespread and recognisable, but they do not necessarily provide us with adequate insight into finance. Indeed, these visual metaphors present finance as a technical affair related to stock prices and market movements. They gloss over complexities and mask the politics that underlie them. For instance, they normalise and legitimise neoliberal values and hide from view the human cost associated with economic crises or simply with regular market economics.

Likewise, invisibility is not inevitably always a negative. Indeed, Rune Saugmann Andersen and Frank Möller (2013: 206) stress that the invisible can be just as important if not more than what we actually see. Look at how suppressing photographic evidence of the killing of Osama bin Laden only spurred the public's imagination and generated suspicion and conspiracy theories (see also Mitchell 2011). Saugmann Andersen and Möller (2013: 207) go as far as arguing that invisibility can actually "activate the imagination" because the process of alluding, rather than showing in full, shatters the illusion that images somehow are authentic representations of reality.

Art plays such a powerful role precisely because it neither tries to visually represent the world as it is nor rely on familiar visual patterns. The very power of art lies in stimulating our imagination by creating a distance between itself and the world. The political significance of art is located in its self-conscious engagement with representation – an issue that is ignored by most approaches to politics. Many social scientists, for instance, tend to assume that we can have authentic knowledge of the world as long as we employ the correct methods of inquiry. By contrast, aesthetic approaches speak of the brokenness of political reality, of the fact that there will always be a gap between a particular representation and what it represents (see Ankersmit 1996; Bleiker 2009; Gadamer 1986; 1999: 88). Invisibility here is not a lack, but a way of allowing a reader to understand the complex emotional and political dimensions of reality and its visual appearances. The most extreme form of legitimising invisibility is abstract art, which defies all forms of representability.

Consider the Australian artist David Rankin. Much of his work is both abstract and, at the same time, directly concerned with political issues. His engagement with the Holocaust legacy, for instance, consists of a series of abstract paintings that appeal to the viewer's senses and invite her or him to imagine, reflect and contemplate the deeper meaning of pain, trauma and loss. Because familiar depictions of Nazi atrocities are

Figure 0.12 Prophecy of Dry Bones – Red Night, David Rankin, 1997

Source: David Rankin, 1997. With permission from the artist.

absent and yet known to everyone at the same time, abstraction is a way of using invisibility to depict the impossible and its political consequences.

What images and visual artefacts do

Reading and interpreting images and visual artefacts is one thing, and an important one. But just as crucial – if not more – is trying to understand what they do. Mark Reinhardt (Chapter 49) stresses that the politics of photography relates, mostly, to how they "are used, and by whom." Nayanika Mookherjee (Chapter 29) speaks of the need to "explore the social life" of images and how they "perform or co-construct a global politics."

Images are not just used and abused for political purposes. They do political things themselves. One of the most striking recent examples here is controversies over cartoons depicting the Prophet Muhammad. The issue here is not just a matter of how these cartoons are differently interpreted – inconsequential and harmless to some, a form of freedom of expression for others, extremely offensive to yet others. Just as important, if not more, is what these cartoons did, for they themselves became triggers for massive controversies and even violent attacks that killed cartoonists and bystanders in Paris and Copenhagen (Hansen, Chapter 41).

Images and visual artefacts obviously do a lot of things. So let me just focus on one realm as an illustration. It is an important realm: how images and artefacts visually depict and perform and thus politically frame a sense of identity and community. This

Figure 0.13 Mausoleum of Mao Zedong, Beijing, 1987
Source: Roland Bleiker

is why iconic images are important: they shape public opinion and the type of ideas and ideologies that underlie political communities (Hariman and Lucaites, Chapter 25). But it is not just icons that do so.

There are a multitude of images and visual artefacts that together mark identity and community. Flags, parades, religious symbols, monuments and mausoleums are just the most obvious examples. Look at the Mao Mausoleum, located at Tiananmen Square in Beijing. It is a national monument designed to celebrate China's revolutionary spirit and foster a sense of identity, unity and purpose. Even today, when the Chinese government has moved on from the radical and violent revolutionary spirit of Mao, thousands of people still line up and wait for hours to pay their respect to the preserved body of the Chairman.

Iver B. Neumann (Chapter 26) reminds us that identity needs to be represented so that people can identify with it and gain a sense of common purpose, a sense of community. He goes on to stress that these constructions of identity often focus on "others," which is why "it is always worth pondering where they lurk." And they lurk everywhere. Prominent movies, such as James Bond, depict the world as one in which threats lurk permanently and have to be addressed quickly and violently to pre-empt disasters. All this matters not just on the screen, for if these types of images and depictions appear and reappear in films, on television and elsewhere, then they start to be part of societal values and assumptions, constituting some ideas and people as legitimate and others as dangerous or at least deviant (Dodds, Chapter 22).

The notion of communities being constituted in a stark inside/out manner and in relations to a threating other is well accepted (see Walker 1993). But the visual aspects of this dynamic has not yet been sufficiently explored. This is why Klaus Dodds (Chapter 22) wants us to pay attention to how the "reel and the real" interact and co-constitute each other. Take an example from Simon Philpott (Chapter 20). He points out how television coverage of the terrorist attack of 11 September 2011 was very much based on and presented according to the techniques refined in Hollywood disaster movies. This is how the coverage not only made sense to the public but also already framed the parameters of the political response. The prevailing script had already delineated what it meant to stand up in times of crisis; how to rally around the nation and its ideals; and, not least, how to act and retaliate with purpose and determination (see also Der Derian 2001; Hutchison, Chapter 47). The result was the War on Terror which, not surprisingly, entrenched hostile perceptions of others and eventually led to more violence and terrorism. In short, it is impossible, as Cynthia Weber (2006b: 8) put it, to separate "theatres of culture from theatres of war."

Images and visual artefacts perform and frame identity not just in the realm of foreign policy but in all aspects of life. Few domains are more imbued with visual politics than gender norms. Almost all aspects of sex and gender are in one way or another prescribed through visual norms, including how men and women are meant to dress, walk, talk and interact. Linda Åhäll (Chapter 21) examines how gender is performed visually in relation to societal rules and conventions. She stresses that the ensuing practices are "as much about invisibility as about visibility" because there are always bodies left out of and silenced by prevailing forms of gender visualisation. There are countless examples of such practices. Here is just one: veiling. For Callahan (Chapter 9) this visual performance is linked to very black-and-white understandings of gender, race, ethnicity and religion. Significant implications follow because veiling is not just a private issue but a highly political one. Some states enforce a mandatory practice while others have banned it – using female bodies and their visual appearance as political markers of culture or of secularism respectively.

Visual power: domination and resistance

Images and visual artefacts are neither progressive nor regressive. They can entrench existing power relations or they can uproot them. But they are inevitably linked to power and this power is, as Mitchell (Chapter 34) puts it, "for good and evil." Before I hand over to the contributors of this volume, I want to flag how some of the chapters explore these links between visuality, politics and power.

There are plenty of examples of how visuality entrenched existing political structures, even authoritarian ones. The paradigmatic case here is Leni Riefenstahl. Her stunning films of Nazi rallies, such as *Triumph of the Will* or *Olympia*, helped the Nazi regime turn mere propaganda into a broader mythology that was instrumental in gaining popular support for a racist and militaristic state apparatus: "fascinating fascism," as Susan Sontag called it (Sontag 1975; see also Steele, Chapter 43; Philpott, Chapter 20; Bach 2007). Socialist realist art, likewise, played a key role in glorifying and legitimising authoritarian Communist practices in the Soviet Union and elsewhere. Some also see new fascist trends emerging in current rise of right-wing populism across Europe and the US. They stress how particular visual and rhetorical strategies – electoral theatre – disregard evidence and reasoned argument in an attempt to exploit people rendered vulnerable, anxious and resentful by widespread economic insecurity (Connolly 2016; see also Chou, Bleiker and Premaratna 2016).

A recurring theme is how the global North, influenced by liberal Western values, visually depicts the rest of the world. Television and photographic portrayals of celebrity engagement with famine, for instance, tend to revolve around a patronising view of Africa, depicted as a place of destitution, where innocent and powerless victims are in need of Western help. Tanja Müller (Chapter 3) shows how such visual representations rely on simplistic, black-and-white narratives that distort the everyday lived realities on the ground. Katrina Lee-Koo (Chapter 4), likewise, writes of how, in the context of children involved in violence, images tend to promote simple narratives, based on binary constructions of us versus them. Even when development institutions try to break through these visual patterns, they fall back on other stereotypes. Kalpana Wilson (Chapter 11) examines how ad campaigns recently challenged the problematic tendency of depicting women in the global South as passive victims. But in doing so, they harked back to another stereotype infused with power: the notion of an adolescent girl, working harder and more diligently than her male counterparts, becomes an agent of development and an ideal neoliberal vehicle for investment.

Or consider the seemingly non-political world of fashion. Laura Shepherd (Chapter 30) shows how fashion trends that rely on military attires – from cargo pants to camouflage garments – inadvertently legitimise practices of militarisation in today's Western societies. They generate a "positive public disposition towards militaristic ideas and ideals" and become part of a certain set of societal values – in this case, values linked to the belief that military solutions are both desirable and necessary to tackle some of the world's problems.

But just as images and visual artefacts entrench power relations they can also uproot them. Here too, there are plenty of examples from the global South. Photography was, of course, an integral part of the colonial project, documenting and reinforcing a range of cultural assumptions that reflected European prejudices of colonial "subjects" (see Lisle, Chapter 48). But photography also turned against colonial rule. Stephen Chan (Chapter 7) points out that during the early struggle against colonialism photography was about documenting who was there. The photographs were very static as a result. With the advent of lighter cameras and the ability to circulate photographs things changed. This is how the struggle against colonialism became news, and the news spread around the world. "Suddenly black faces and their hopes and fears were part of the same monochrome industry."

Or look at images of trauma. They often entrench existing forms of community and power – mostly a nation-state and discourses that juxtapose a safe inside from a threatening outside. But they can also transform, as Hutchison (Chapter 47; 2016) shows, creating new emotions, resonances and solidarity among people, as for instance in the wake of the 2004 Asian tsunami, where the worldwide circulation of trauma images created an unprecedented level of support and donations.

Or look at how visual media, particularly video clips, have been used to counter what Weber (Chapter 18) calls fear-based patriotism in the United States – a kind of orientalist patriotism that marked dark-skinned people wearing certain "Arabic/Muslim" body coverings as suspicious. A new diversity patriotism campaign visually celebrated the integration of people from different backgrounds into the American community – though, as Weber writes, not without subconsciously harking back to the problematic practices they sought to distance themselves from. Visuality works both ways.

Or look, as the final example, at a photograph that came to symbolise the so-called Black Lives Matter movement: an online and street protest movement by African

Figure 0.14 Taking a Stand in Baton Rouge, Jonathan Bachman

Source: https://widerimage.reuters.com/story/taking-a-stand-in-baton-rouge/ Printed with permission from Reuters.

American communities designed to draw attention to the systematic racism towards black people. The photograph in question was taken by Jonathan Bachman in August 2016 during a protest in Baton Rouge. It shows a woman, named Ieshia Evans, confronting two police officers – and many more behind them – clothed in full riot gear. The photograph symbolises a politics of resistance. It shows one unarmed civilian woman confronting a large group of uniformed, armed soldiers, presumably men. The photograph not only captures the tension between civilian and police, dissident and authority, but also harks back to a long history of non-violent protest during the civil rights movement, from Rosa Parks to Martin Luther King. The photograph was picked up by countless news organisations around the world and went viral, so much so that it not only came to symbolise the protest but also took on a political role itself.

Jacques Rancière believes that photography and other art forms play a particularly important role in challenging political narratives and pushing the boundaries of what can be seen, thought and done. He portrays art as the meeting ground between existing configurations of the sensible and attempts to reconfigure our sensory experience of the world (Rancière 2004: 9; Rockhill 2009: 200). Sally Butler (Chapter 27) does, indeed, show how art has for long played an important role in the struggle of Indigenous Australians for rights and self-determination. Michael Cook, whose photograph is featured on the cover of this book, visually reverses how colonial Australia has rendered the Indigenous population invisible. But Indigenous art has not just revealed aspects of Australia's past that were hidden from colonial view, but also served as protest forms that eventually contribute to political and social change (see also Bleiker and Butler 2016).

This is, of course, the very power of art: to make us see the world anew, to make us see a different reality from the one we are used to and the one that is commonly accepted (Whitebrook 1992: 5, 7). Art is thus political in the more basic sense of offering insight into the processes through which we represent – all too often in narrow and highly problematic ways – political facts and challenges. Comic books work by means of exaggeration and distortion and, in doing so, "stretch the boundaries of our imagination" (Choi, Chapter 2). Photographers challenge deeply entrenched stereotypes about Roma people and provide us with views and insights that we would otherwise not be able to get (Pusca, Chapter 39). Artists serve as moral witnesses, Alex Danchev (Chapter 51) stresses. They embark on visual adventures that makes us see the world anew, that "rubs it red raw." They help us re-view, re-feel, and re-think politics in the most fundamental manner. Images, in this sense, make, unmake and remake politics. This is why, as flagged at the beginning of this introduction, Danchev (2016: 91) believed that "contrary to popular belief, it is given to artists, not politicians, to create a new world order."

Style and format of the book

Before we start a few words are in order about the rather unusual format and style of *Visual Global Politics*. It is structured around short chapters written by experts from numerous different disciplines, ranging from international relations, geography and art history to media studies, anthropology and literature. The authors draw on their specialised research but then present the results in an accessible language designed to reach not just specialised academics but a broad range of readers.

A large number of short chapters – a structure inspired by *Theorizing Visual Studies* (James Elkins, Kristi McGuire *et al.* 2013) – is best suited to cover the wide range of issues at stake. Each chapter engages a particular political topic and does so in the context of a particular visual realm. The chapters intersect and intersperse, overlap and criss-cross each other in a way that Gilles Deleuze and Félix Guattari (1980) wrote of rhizomes: constellations that have no beginning or end but, instead, multiple entryways and exits; a middle from where they expand and overspill. Rather than offer a comprehensive survey of a topic, the idea of short chapters is to provoke and to illuminate, to offer a range of views that depict the world from different angles. We follow Nietzsche (1982: 278) here, who wrote in aphorisms and believed that thinking deep thoughts is like taking a cold bath: "quickly in and quickly out again."

Even though all chapters engage with a particular visual realm, they are arranged by political themes. I could have organised the book by visual themes too, and I started off this way. Distinctions could then have been made between, say, old and new media, moving and still images, high art and popular culture. But these divisions are highly arbitrary. Where are the boundaries between these realms? Take photography. Is it an art form or part of popular culture? A documentation practice or a form of journalism? Do photographs take on a different political role when they are printed or digitalised, when they appear in a gallery, a newspaper or on a social media platform? To make these divisions is not only arbitrary but also runs the risk, as John Berger (1991: 45) puts it, of forgetting "the meaning and enigma of visibility itself." Add to this that key political phenomena, from war to diplomacy and from colonialism to sexual violence, cut across these diverse visual fields. Any concept and structure is, of course, always an imposition of a preconceived idea upon a far more complex and messy reality. Nietzsche (1969: 80) already knew that all concepts in some way elude a clear definition, for "only that which has no history can be defined." But define we must. And so I ran with political themes that show how visuality plays a key role in global politics and this across a wide range of different realms. For the same reason, I opted against a linear narrative and against grouping the chapters into thematic and ultimately arbitrary sections. The chapters now float freely or, at least, alphabetically. Readers can engage them in any order they wish.

Finally I would like readers to know that I had originally planned to write a conclusion. In the end I refrained from doing so to leave the last word to the late Alex Danchev, who died a few months before this manuscript was completed and to whom the book is dedicated. His insightful chapter on "Witnessing" offers as fitting a conclusion as is possible: it shows us how the visual both traces our political past and opens up important opportunities for the future. This is the case because the visual – in its various forms – is intrinsically linked to politics and ethics. Art can help us imagine the unimaginable. In doing so it becomes a form of moral consciousness and an expression of political hope because it ruptures and transcends the language of habit that surrounds us and circumvents what is and is not politically visible, thinkable and possible.

Note

I build here on the following sources, which also offer further elaborations on the topics in question: Bleiker (2001, 2009, 2014, 2015); Bleiker, Campbell and Hutchison (2014); Hutchison, Bleiker and Campbell (2014); Bleiker, Campbell, Hutchison and Nicholson (2013); Bleiker and Kay (2007); Hutchison and Bleiker (2014b, 2016); Bleiker and Butler (2016).

1   Body

Elizabeth Dauphinee

Our culture is suffused with images of death and injury in war. Our ability to engage critically with these images depends on our capacity to recognise and challenge the politics of pain – the politics that is often obliterated by the image itself. The photograph – and even the video – no matter how horrific or painful, does not speak for itself. It is mediated by the photographer's framing of the scene, by the viewer's gaze, and by the explanatory (political) narratives that circulate around the image. And while the photograph might purport to express some "truth," this truth is not self-evident in the image, nor is it politically neutral. For example, the American soldiers who photographed the torture of prisoners at Abu Ghraib likely did not anticipate that their snapshots would become evidence in what has become one of the most infamous torture scandals in US history. Rather, they were more likely performing the act that we would normally associate with the tourist souvenir (Winn 2004; see also Lisle 2000). Steven Winn (2004), writing for the *San Francisco Chronicle,* described the photographs from Abu Ghraib as tourist-like – the "hurried, candid action shots of a camera hungry to catch it all." But as with any text, the author's intention is not an indicator of how something will be received.

We know, of course, that the "souvenir" photos from Abu Ghraib unleashed a storm of criticism and outrage at the conduct of the US invasion of Iraq. There was no shortage of attempts to explain both the photographs and the torture. Feldman (2005: 204) argued that the photographs from Abu Ghraib can be understood as part of the whole "shock and awe" program that framed the invasion of Iraq. Others viewed the photographs of the torture as evidence of the increasing brutality in American life (Sontag 2004b), or as proof that the US intervention in Iraq, presented in part by the Administration as a salvific enterprise, was, in fact, a hypocrisy (*The Nation* 2004). And, seeking to downplay the photographs and the torture they depicted, conservative American commentators, such as Rush Limbaugh (2004), argued that the torture was no more than a "hazing ritual" equivalent to "emotional release" for combat-weary US soldiers. Donald Rumsfeld, the US Secretary of Defence, refused to discuss the word "torture," instead using the word "abuse" to describe the violence against Iraqi prisoners (Rumsfeld, cited in Sontag 2004a).

Body

Historically, studies focusing on what we today call "global politics" generally ignored the obvious point that *bodies* are the targets of war and war-related violence. In her path-breaking book, *The Body in Pain*, Elaine Scarry (1985: 63) made a simple and extremely powerful observation: that the purpose of war is to injure. It is an obvious truth that war produces torn, bleeding, burnt, and obliterated bodies. These bodies are the currency with which wars are "won" and "lost." To train the weapons of war on landscapes, cities, and infrastructures is to target the human bodies that built these spaces and that dwell within them. Of course, one claims (and must claim) that there are other "goals" in war – goals more noble and important than the destroyed bodies and lives that are required to achieve them. But regardless of the "political" causes of war, the tactic of war is universal: to out-injure one's opponent to the point of submission.

The simplicity of Scarry's observation feels almost tautological. It seems obvious that the logic of war is bodily injury and death. But images of dead, torn, and bleeding bodies do not just circulate in unregulated or apolitical contexts. Governments work hard to hide the volume of injury and death that war-making entails. At its most instrumental level, this involves the outright attempted control of the images associated with dead and injured bodies. For example, Richard Nixon successfully opposed the use of the Freedom of Information Act to suppress the images associated with the massacre at My Lai in Vietnam in 1968 (see Liptak 2009). Both George W. Bush and Barack Obama have attempted to block the release under the same Act of images depicting US soldiers torturing Iraqi detainees. The US Office of War Information suppressed many images of the Second World War, including those that showed the effects of the atomic bomb on the residents of Hiroshima and Nagasaki (slavick 2009).

We see here that the drive to catalogue and circulate the bodily injuries of war is juxtaposed with the simultaneous desire to hide these injuries from the public eye. In some cases, the scale of injury and death is so profound that the volume of information required to keep track of it is mind-bogglingly enormous. The massive volume of people who died in Nazi concentration camps, for example, required an entire bureaucracy to document the deportations and manage the killing operation. While the methodical execution of millions of people can be documented over time in well-organised bureaucratic contexts, this is no longer the case with the advent of the nuclear age. The physicist Leo Sartori, writing in 1983, notes that "In the case of all-out nuclear war, the scale of destruction is so great that the specific numbers almost don't matter." In a world where total obliteration is technically (and maybe also morally) possible, it is hard to conceive of the destruction as perpetrated against *individuals* – instead, we see whole societies of people destroyed or reduced to the constant threat of destruction. In a world that has seen the mechanised death camp obliterate generations, it is easy to forget the assault to the individual's body in the larger political context of "genocide." That the murder of the body is the goal of war is almost ancillary to the optimal train timetable that ferries people to their deaths, to the air burst of an atomic weapon over a city, to the remote performance of a massacre via drone strike, or to the torture of prisoners at Abu Ghraib, Guantánamo Bay, and elsewhere. And in this modern world, the click of the camera arises to document all of it.

Managing images

With the advent of photography and its vehicles of mass dissemination – the television broadcast and later the internet – the effective management of the body-in-war became more difficult. Governments could enforce the ban on publication of grotesque photographs during the Second World War; but by the time of the Vietnam War, a television in virtually every American household made this control much more difficult.

Nixon's attempts to suppress the images emerging from Vietnam were ultimately fruitless. Despite attempts to tightly control the press in Afghanistan and Iraq by embedding them directly with US forces, it has proven to be impossible to control the images that circulate electronically, including those of the torture of prisoners at Abu Ghraib.

But if dead and injured bodies are the currency of war, why is there such a drive to hide this from the public eye? What do we actually encounter when we see the images of this kind of bodily degradation and pain that threaten the acts associated with war?

The answers are more varied and complex than the images themselves might at first suggest. We might be able to identify the use of war photography for a number of seemingly apolitical "purposes." For example, photography is a key part of the scientific information-gathering process on the damage that various weapons can inflict on human bodies. In Hiroshima, US scientists meticulously documented the injuries that the atomic bombing caused to bodies – including flesh burns, keloid scarring, tumours, cancers, and organ failure. Importantly, the bodies were examined, but not treated (slavick 2009). This scientific documentation helped to build a corpus of knowledge about the bomb that would in turn contribute to a more complete understanding of the medical and biological impacts of radiation. The goal was not to treat the victims, but to gather information about the injuries. To put it bluntly, American scientists continued to "test" the bomb long after it was detonated by gathering intelligence on its biological effects. In 2008, the Walter Reed Army Medical Centre published a book of photographs of combat trauma alongside the surgical procedures of acute battlefield "injury care." While this textbook shows some of the most horrific bodily wounds of war, its goal is not to shock nor is it to simply document injury, but instead to show how such massive wounds are triaged and treated. The value of the lives in the photographs does constitute an important politics – namely, that injured US soldiers can and should be treated and saved. But as a "medical" text, it also depoliticises the war conditions within which the injuries were sustained and prevents us from asking the deeper questions about why these people were sent to participate in an activity *whose very goal* was always the destruction of their (and others') bodies.

When we see photographs of destroyed and tortured bodies, we are predictably fascinated and horrified. Organisations like Human Rights Watch, the International Committee of the Red Cross, and Amnesty International rely on this anticipated feeling of horror and utilise photographs of violence in order to generate support for political campaigns that seek the elimination of torture and other human rights violations. They rely on the ability of the photograph to communicate the reality of bodily pain to people who are not experiencing that pain – to people who can only imagine that pain (Scarry 1985: 9).

Here, we begin to witness the development of 'iconic' photographs, such as the girl Kim Phúc running from her napalmed village in Vietnam, or the hooded, crucified prisoner at Abu Ghraib. However, these photographs come to be "iconic" in ways that erase the suffering of individuals and the political causes of what is actually happening to them – that is, their war-mediated trauma. The photograph becomes an "empty signifier" – a pornographic image of others' pain and suffering that becomes little more than a repellent curiosity. Sliwinski (2004: 154) argues that "the helplessness and horror of bearing witness to suffering brings with it the demand for a response, and yet one's response to photographs can do nothing to alleviate the suffering depicted."

The still photo also tends to petrify the artefacts of violence. This petrification lends itself to all kinds of different narratives, with different ethical and political implications. Bodily pain and death are easily pressed into the service of various political projects. But Sliwinski (2004: 151) argues that "despite the drive to narrate, at some point in the encounter with images, the viewer falls silent, too, suggesting the technology demands narrative, but also resists that demand." There is no necessary politics associated with the images and, in fact, the images themselves flatten the physical pain and sensationalise the terror associated with the torture such that it becomes almost impossible for a viewer to respond.

What is instructive here is that, in delivering the testimony of their torture, the prisoners at Abu Ghraib stated over and over again that they were stripped, injured, raped, and terrorised, and that all of this was then photographed or filmed, suggesting that the filmic aspect of recording the prisoners' ordeals was understood by them to be part of the torture (see Dauphinee 2008).

Images of pain

Why are we horrified by images of people in pain? Is it because "they" are "others" to us, as Sontag claims? Perhaps. But there is also something about the bodily pain experience itself that isolates the sufferer. The drive to make visible the body-in-pain alienates the viewer of the image. This is because the body-in-pain cannot narrate its calamity. Joanna Bourke (Bourke 2014: 41; see also Wilcox 2015a) observes that pain "[evicts us] from the land of the human." For Scarry (1985: 5), pain is unsharable because it resists objectification in language. Unlike other interior bodily states, pain takes no object. If we love, we love someone or something. If we are hungry, it is hunger *for* something or someone; if we have fear, it is fear *of* something or someone. But pain resists this objectification. Because of this, Scarry understands pain to be uniquely world- and language-destroying. This does not mean that we can't "see" the pain-filled body, but that our ability to connect with that pain is automatically reduced, whether we are witnesses to or perpetrators of the pain. Bourke (2014: 45) understands this when she says that "The voyeuristic jolt of seeing a stranger weeping at a road accident should not be compared to the sadist's delight in inflicting injuries. Both, however, point to an element of cruelty in human culture."

These elements form or are formed within the crucible of our socio-political and philosophical orientation toward our relationships with other people. The torturer isolates the victim from himself and from his world, which includes the language that cannot express the interiority of the pain. Pain is therefore mainly narrated as an experience that isolates the sufferer. Scarry (1985: 13) argues that to have pain is to have certainty; to hear about another's pain is to have doubt. Because of this, the image of the body-in-pain inevitably flattens the experience of pain – it reduces people to representations of their plight, to images of starvation, of dismemberment, terror, torture, and agony, where images become stand-ins for human suffering, where people become bodily canvases for the torturer's inscription of pain and the political interpretations that follow. For Hannah Arendt, the suffering of the concentration camps was so indescribable that the survivor could hardly narrate his experience. Had he returned from the camp to report on his experiences, he would not have been believed, she wrote (Arendt 2000: 125). Similarly, she (2000: 120) notes that "anyone speaking or writing about the concentration camps is . . . regarded as suspect; and if the speaker has resolutely returned to the land of the living, he himself is often assailed by doubts with regard to his own truthfulness, as though he had mistaken a nightmare for reality."

Because the experience of the body-in-pain cannot be easily accessed, its imagery is also an obscenity. However, for all our voyeuristic fascination with pain, pain is also associated with an elemental unpleasantness – even impoliteness. Bourke (2014: 42), for example, observes that "Mind–body dichotomies are so engrained in Western culture that chronic pain is routinely viewed as something blameworthy and disruptive." At some level, then, it is simply *impolite* to be a victim of torture – to have one's ruined body ruin another's breakfast. Paul Kirby (2016: 156) writes about his encounter with the image of a Congolese fighter clutching the severed genitals of some unnamed enemy: "I come across this in a glossy Saturday supplement magazine which asks its readers to consider this photo alongside others culled from war zones, and to judge which is 'the best.' This is during breakfast. I cannot purge that shot or the manner of its discovery, and reproduce it in my thesis." As Kirby's experience also suggests, however traumatic our encounter with the war-image might be, the range of our possible responses is governed by a deep sense of isolation. In the helplessness of his revulsion, all he can do is reproduce the image. This tells us something about the political and ethical hopelessness associated with our in-ability to respond meaningfully to the suffering of others (Sontag 2003).

Constrained already by the inability to corroborate the experience of pain in the body of another, the introduction of photographic imagery further inscribes this distance. As we have seen, Sliwinski (2004: 151) argues that "the technology demands narrative, but also resists that demand." In simpler terms, the photograph never speaks for itself, but any attempt we make to speak for the photograph is also deeply limited, and says more about us than it does about the victim of torture in the photograph. In this sense, pain is cultural and ideological as much as it is physical. For Sliwinski (2004: 158), "there is something to be seen and therefore known in images of suffering, but it is not the traumatic experiences of others. Rather we are asked to look and imagine their terror, but in this looking [we encounter our] own failure to see." Bal (2005: 159) expresses it this way: "Compassion without an identification that is both specific and heteropathic leads us to an emotional realm where the fear of violence can be made objectless." Put plainly, this means that our visceral reaction to images of violence are about *us* – about our ruined breakfasts and the anxieties associated with the experience of vicarious trauma.

The visual politics of the body

In the silence that Sliwinski identifies, there *are* possibilities for making a different response. The body is an ideological entity before it is anything else. It is our socio-political culture that enframes our engagement with the body and with the body-in-pain. While Scarry notes that pain itself takes no object, bodily pain can be and is routinely mobilised into narratives of war and conflict. We suffer "for" something, or "because" of something – because American soldiers need "emotional release," or because American cultural life is increasingly brutal. Whether as martyrs, tortured prisoners, or battlefield casualties, pain and suffering are ascribed meaning – both socio-political and ideological. The task for those of us who have only the photographs is to ask how else we might understand the things we do to one another.

2 Borders

Shine Choi

As Nevzat Soguk (2007: 283) poetically put it, "Borders have lives of their own. They move, shift, metamorphose, edge, retract, emerge tall and powerful or retreat into the shadows exhausted, or even grow irrelevant." I explore the life of the inter-Korean border and how it is brought to life in the South Korean comics *Oh! Hangang* by Hur Youngman.

I examine image–text relations in comics and how *drawing* the world by hand creates an aesthetic of exaggeration and distortion that helps us understand what borders are and do. Borders are inherently spaces of contradictions. They are spaces of encounters and divisions that separate and unite. They are visible yet invisible, fixed yet mobile, rigid yet porous, and remote yet so central to politics. Comics are a form that exploits contradictions between, among others, image and text, interiority and exteriority, visibility and invisibility, and movement and action stopped in motion. Studying borders through comics provides an animated way of making sense of the contradictions and politics of borders.

Comics as a form

A basic definition of comics is that they are drawn images that are put in sequential order to tell stories (Eisner 2008; McCloud 1994; Chute 2010). Comics work by exaggerating the world, ourselves, and our ideas. Caricatures are visual exaggerations *par excellence*, and the comic form stretches out how caricatures work by exploiting the relationship between image and text. As a literary form more than a pure visual object, images in comics are drawn to interact with texts to tell a story on a page.

I explore, to borrow Miodrag's (2013: 92) words, the "aesthetic impact" of drawings and what melding image and text creates that is greater than its parts. The cartoonist Daniel Clowes (2005: 4) makes this point in the episode "Harry Naybors, the Comic Book Critic" by drawing the figure of the critic into a view that shifts the argument made about comics as a genre. In this episode, Harry Naybors, the comic book critic, explains in a series of word bubbles that comics, unlike cinema, work through exteriority as he goes about his personal business (e.g. scratching his bottom, peeing, having breakfast undressed) in the privacy of his home. Drawing the body behind the voice doing particularly intimate things in an intimate place cuts through the authoritative voice of the text. By undercutting the text through his drawing, Clowes *shows*, not tells, how the image and text combination produces something that exceeds the sum of its parts. This excess is created by *exaggerating* the tension between the image (painfully intimate) and text (painfully authoritative). Not all image–text relations in comics work through tension but by exaggerating this point, Clowes shows us what comics do best. They exaggerate, caricature and animate how we imagine and tell stories, and in so doing, stretch the boundaries of our imagination.

Border experiences at the 38th parallel

As it was in 1988 when *Oh! Hangang* was first published, the Korean peninsula remains divided today along the 38th parallel. Two separate rival states, the Democratic People's Republic of Korea in the north and the Republic of Korea in the south, maintain a fragile truce afforded by a composite "buffer zone" along the 38th parallel that "ended" the Korean War. Installed in 1953 in place of a peace treaty, a complex system of military installations maintains several limit lines designed to keep the buffer zone empty – the Military Demarcation Line, the Southern and Northern Border Lines, and the Civilian Control Line (Gelézeau 2011: 328–30; 2013: 13–23). These lines today create a crowded border, filled not only with military activities that maintain the division, but also with a range of hostile posturing, from annual US–South Korean joint military exercises to equally regular North Korean missile testings and satellite launches. Also crowding the inter-Korean border are peace festivals, environmentalists and bird watchers, reconciliation media events big and small, women-for-peace marches and summits, balloon-launching North Korean defector activists, K-pop-blasting loudspeakers, Korean artists, Irish artists, good tourists, amateur photographers, Nordic documentary filmmakers, American university study tours, good-will gesture herded cows heading to the North, returning revolutionaries and heroes, and solitary looks to the sky wondering what all this is about.

Hur Youngman's *Oh! Hangang* shows us how political borders, even a heavily militarised border like the inter-Korean one, have always been spaces crowded with competing meanings, activities and contradictions. Borders that seek to empty out the space for pure demarcation and separation by brute force are never empty. They are always porous and complex social spaces that are part of larger ideological apparatuses that order and manage human lives (Newman 2003; Paasi 2011; Rajaram and Grundy-Warr 2007).

Oh! Hangang maps this social world historically from Korean liberation in 1945 through the Korean War (1950–3) and to the era of the divided peninsula. The era of Korean division is also an era of Cold War ideological contestations between US-led capitalist liberal democracy that builds faith in strong private property rights and the free market in the name of liberty, and Soviet-led socialism and communism that promise freedom from the shackles of capitalism through top-down centralised communal ownership and containment of market forces. In examining this Cold War comic today, and in light of how Hur has risen as the godfather figure of the Korean comic scene, my suggestion is that sensation and poetics in *Oh! Hangang* continue to compose and maintain the inter-Korean border.

Borders and their contradictions are central to *Oh! Hangang*. The narration tells us of borders that divide and keep out. We read of maintaining borders, of crossing and surviving them. And we see how comics use an aesthetic of contradictions and exaggeration to bring to life these harrowing Cold War border experiences.

The central narrative of *Oh! Hangang* follows Lee Gangto, a farm hand in a southern village who goes to the big city through the good graces of his landowner's progressive daughter, criss-crosses the Korean border, and wrestles with the new two-state system to emerge as a celebrated hyperrealist painter and a proud middle-class head of family. The 38th parallel importantly shapes Gangto's life. The border first appears in the story when Gangto decides to cross it and go to the North to help build a new revolutionary society. This is before the war and before the military institutionalisation of the space, so crossing the border is swift, quiet and uncontested. Yet, the border even in this instance is riddled with contradictions. Gangto, deep in thought, brings into this space contradictory feelings of dismissing the leftist intellectual "weaklings with shallow principles" that he is leaving behind, yet revelling in being finally accepted in his departure as an equal by the people he rejects (Hur 1995, Book 1: 257).

The final panel in this sequence resolves this contradiction by shifting to a retrospective narrative voice that laments his youthful decision to cross the 38th parallel owing to his own heroism. This textual resolution offered through a retrospective perspective is visually supported by turning the landscape into a black vacuum for the white text to shine through. Previously straightforward (desolate) border landscape becomes pitch

Figure 2.1 Hur Youngman (허영만), "Gangto crosses the border," in *Oh! Hangang* (오!한강)

Source: *Oh! Hangang* (오!한강) (Seoul: Seju Munhwa Publishing Team Mania, 1995), Vols 1–4. With permission from the author/artist, Hur Youngman.

Figure 2.2 Hur Youngman (허영만), "Violence at the border during the Korean War," in *Oh!
Hangang* (오!한강)

Source: *Oh! Hangang* (오!한강) (Seoul: Seju Munhwa Publishing Team Mania, 1995), Vols 1–4. With permission
from the author/artist, Hur Youngman.

blackness that holds words. Here words become an image in the sense that the panel
turns text into a visual experience achieved through blanking the exterior world. This
resolution works by exaggerating text–image relations – that is, by blanking out an
image to turn text into an image. Exaggeration, then, is a marker of tension and
contradictory feelings at the border as much as it is a way to create meaning.

When the war breaks out, this inter-Korean border is sealed, tensions escalate,
caricatures take over. The story that Gangto's wife tells about crossing this wartime
border is illustrative of the shift. In contrast to Figure 2.1, there is no interior world
of text at this border. The border is all surface images of the brute force that maintains
it as an uninhabitable empty space.

Silhouette figures in the dark dodge barbed wire and bullets. The figures come to
life, abruptly, in action panels, as seen in the last panel in Figure 2.2 where the "cartoony"

body of soldiers accompanying Gangto's family are stiff from the full impact of the bullets. The caricature of struck bodies stopped in motion makes visible the force of violence in ways that caricatures singularly can: swiftly, dramatically, in full velocity. As in cinematic action scenes, we almost immediately "get" the emotion of the picture, and in its swiftness of impact, the figure punctures and animates the grey darkness preceding the scene.

The two styles of drawing in this episode – silhouettes and action caricatures – not only blend together to tell a story but also work in similar ways, that is, by making visible only the outermost lines and evacuating details. They direct our vision to how borders turn space into a grey vacuum, a non-space where the human can only be a vanishing dot as seen in the final panel of the episode. Both styles of caricature work by drawing stark contrasts and simplifying features to create an experience of exaggerated aesthetics. To draw is to manipulate lines. Manipulation of lines that distort our perception is what makes caricatures compelling. By making the real false, it is able to direct our eyes and make the exteriority of who we are and our world – things on the surfaces – matter. In short, caricatures interrupt the privileged location that interiority, things that we ultimately cannot see, has in our understanding of what is true, authentic, real. Caricaturing how the inter-Korean border was sealed through force makes the violence of the featureless, impenetrable non-space visible, palpable and arresting. What these caricatures offer is a poetic visual experience of how a border is sealed. They connect us to bodies that try to break through and in doing so stretch out our political imagination.

Maintaining the 38th parallel

The contradiction, then, is that the border zone is never an empty space. For borders to perform their function as firm, solid lines that demarcate space, they need to be established and maintained by humans and human-created and -operated machineries, social or otherwise. Following Gangto and later his son in their role as soldiers gives us the perspectives of those who create and maintain borders. The border area for the two men is a line that pins them down against their will with little option but to defend the division. Their analogous experiences provide a contrasting view of border politics during and after the war.

The absurdity and desperation of maintaining the frontline bubbles to the surface early on when Gangto and his arch-rival are chained together to the trenches to prevent defection. Two full pages of panels foreground, visually, how Gangto is literally pinned to the ground and frozen to stillness. Textually, we follow Gangto deep in thought turning to the recesses of his memory, his life in Pyongyang, his mistakes, how foolishly he got swept into other people's ideas, how he had failed as an artist, his need to live yet how everything is over (Hur, Book 2: 83). Turn the page, we abruptly arrive at an animated scene where Gangto bolts up to his feet to protest this unacceptable fate to his superior. As quickly as we happen upon this scene, we realise that this too was just the stuff of his mind.

Just as border crossings produce contradictory feelings and desires, so does being pinned at the border to maintain it. Riddled with feelings and experiences that are more animated than the exterior world, these feelings spill out and metamorphose into full image-text panels that interrupt the boundary of real and imagined. Contradictory feelings also emerge in the reader–comic relation. There is humour in the cartoonish

Figure 2.3 Hur Youngman (허영만), "Gangto pinned to the trenches during the Korean War," in
      Oh! Hangang (오!한강)

Source: *Oh! Hangang* (오!한강) (Seoul: Seju Munhwa Publishing Team Mania, 1995), Vols 1–4. With permission
from the author/artist, Hur Youngman.

way Gangto jumps up from the trenches or in the downturned mouth of the onlooking
soldier in the background. In short, Gangto's desperation and the absurdity of occupying
the frontline are both funny and depraved at the same time. Hur Youngman (in SBS
2015, my translation) is a firm proponent that "*Manhwa* [comics] has to be fun. If it
is not fun, it is not a good *manhwa*." That the *drawings* produce this effect gives
readers permission to experience this contradictory feeling and own it because it is
decidedly drawn in and unambiguously intentional. Again, war seals the border but
the space is crowded with contradictions and tensions that extend to and draw in the
readers from our detached positions.

    If Gangto fought to stay alive while pinned down at the frontline, then Gangto's
son, Seokju, fights the boredom of keeping the border in a time of ceasefire. The
border in Seokju's time is a site where the politics from out there in the civilian world
(where real action is taking place) seep in and animate the boring monotonous uneventful

life at the 38th parallel. For instance, politics arrive at the border in chocolate wrappers that keeps him abreast of the student protests and political developments back there in the outside world. We also follow Seokju on his leave that returns him to the heart of leftist student activities, home demolition and displacement of residents in the name of urban development. In these episodes, we get glimpses of the growing divide between the winners and losers of the South Korean society in the era of Korean division. Only when reinserted into the larger social world that Seokju brings with him does the watch at the "hottest" border of the Cold War become a time and place for politics. Thus, the border is crucial in maintaining the inter-Korean division but to perform this function, the border becomes a space where politics is kept out. War in Seokju's time is not only occurring uneventfully at the frontline but also on the homefront, in the larger society. War, then, is not something that occurs in a specified time or place but *is* wherever and whenever contradictions, tensions and exaggerations erupt and/or are contained.

Image–text entanglements

Oh! Hangang was first published in 1988 and owes its birth to the now defunct South Korean Ministry of Culture and Information, which approached Hur to author an anti-communist series in the popular comic magazine *Manhwa Gwangjang*. In all his accounts, Hur (1997; in SBS 2015) takes much care to point out how he agreed to the proposition on the condition that the ministry did not interfere with the process. The publication platform for *Oh! Hangang* is curious. The magazine editorial notes and insertions at that time make clear that it is an anti-establishment underground public space. The aim of the magazine aligns with its name, which means "comic public square" in Korean. It aims to provide "mental rest and sense of leisure" for the tired modern individual and use "the acute and poignant communicative power" of comics to offer political content that surpasses critical essays, investigatory reports or hours of political speech (*Manhwa Gwangjang* 1987a: 389, 1987b: 16). That the Korean government used this space for anti-communist control and that *Oh! Hangang* is a production from this effort certainly makes it a weapon of the South Korean state-driven ideological war. At the same time, it can also be seen as an example of how ideological warfare might be as entangling as it is divisive, as boundary-crossing as it is boundary-making. Comics *animate* our imagination by distortion, exaggeration, simplification and deception without apology.

Stories come to life when texts gain visual dimensions, when action is stopped and exaggerated, when ideas gain a façade, an exterior. Perhaps part of how comics animate is through entanglement with the establishments that they reject, ideas that they oppose and seductions of acceptance they heroically denounce.

3   Celebrity

Tanja R. Müller

Visual representations of celebrity campaigns have changed in recent years. They have moved away from depicting starving children towards featuring agitated celebrities. But this has not altered the underlying gaze and patterns of engagement. These are based on patronising, quasi-imperial definitions of compassion, not on a form of solidarity that respects its counterpart as equal. Even where celebrity campaigns have moved from humanitarian crisis to political engagement, like in the Sudan campaigns made prominent by George Clooney, representations of conflicts follow a "Western" logic that relies on the "white" saviour but lacks real understanding of local contexts. This representation unites the celebrity and general audiences in a constituency of compassion, and ultimately plays a role in demands made from "Western" political leaders.

I examine media representations of "Africa" and the surge in celebrity engagement in the global South. I trace these phenomena back to the 1980s famine in Ethiopia, whose iconic TV coverage resulted in the creation of Band Aid and subsequent celebrity activism. I argue that this engagement centres on a one-dimensional representation of "Africa" as a place of destitution where "innocent" women and children need "Western" compassion – a compassion often denied by ruthless and predominately male leaders.

Famine reporting and celebrity humanitarianism

While engagement of celebrities with "humanitarian" causes has a long history, a defining event was the 1983–5 famine in Ethiopia (Littler 2008; Müller 2013a). Made possible by new patterns of real-time visual media coverage, it laid the ground for the subsequent high-profile engagement of a brand of celebrities in humanitarian and political issues in the global South. For TV audiences of a certain generation, the emblematic pictures of starving people in white robes, hunched together on the plains of Korem, became an engrained imaginary of what life in "Africa" looks like. Those pictures were a watershed in crisis reporting. Filmed compellingly by the late cameraman Mohamed Amin, the key visual message was re-enforced by voice reporting from Michael Buerk that described a "biblical famine, now, in the twentieth century" (Franks 2013).

First aired on the BBC on 23 October 1984, the Amin/Buerk report was shown by 425 broadcasting organisations around the world to an estimated audience of 470 million people. It has subsequently been called "the most famous and influential humanitarian recording in history," a claim justified when one considers its relation to the surge in celebrity humanitarianism combined with the meteoric rise of global NGOs (Vaux 2001: 52).

But why had this specific piece of media reporting such a lasting effect? After all, devastating famines have a long history in Ethiopia and other reports of imminent starvation accompanied by visual footage had been sent from Ethiopia many months earlier (Müller 2013a).

A closer look at the reality manufactured by this BBC report reveals its lasting impact: Amin/Buerk sent their report from Korem, in normal times a hamlet of some 7000 people on the main road from Addis Ababa to Asmara in the north. But at that time, it was one of the biggest relief camps, housing an estimated 40,000 to 60,000 people. The report invoked biblical tropes and suggested that camps like Korem have been part of the scenery of Ethiopia since times immemorial. In reality the emergence of a camp signifies a state where all means of survival have collapsed. It is also interesting to note what the report does not show in order to sustain the analogy with the forces of God and nature: Ethiopia was at the time engaged in two counter-insurgency wars just north of Korem, in Tigray and Eritrea. It has in fact been argued that the famine was to a large extent caused by those wars (De Waal 1997). The television viewers remained largely oblivious to those dynamics. They did not see the multiple rocket launchers that occupied the plains of Korem, nor hear the frequently encountered sound of Ethiopian fighter jets on their way north to bomb rebel positions (Vaux 2001: 52).

In contrast, the anti-political explanation of famine propagated by the Amin/Buerk report was vital in making musicians like Bob Geldof and Western audiences sit up and respond. This was famine represented in aesthetically beautiful fashion as a result of (biblical) forces outside human control, not caused by power struggles that would demand a political response. In showing starving women and children up-close, this representation played a decisive role in transforming the abstract reality of multiple deaths into a dramatic story of individual suffering (Benthall 1993).

Bob Geldof immediately understood the power of this direct gaze at destitute victims to elicit widespread compassion. In no time, he enlisted fellow musicians, and little more than one month after the BBC broadcast from Korem the Band Aid charity record "Do they know it's Christmas?" was released and went straight to number one in the charts.

Geldof's role in the foundation of Band Aid (and subsequently other high-profile activities) made him the archetype of a particular form of celebrity engagement with the suffering of others, the "celebrity of common-sense humanitarianism." Tester (2010: 34) defines "common-sense humanitarianism" as "the humanitarianism of media audiences who rely on unquestioned myths to make sense of the suffering of others." It serves the purpose of soliciting an affective response in a way that does not question "our" potential responsibility for such suffering but, rather, legitimises the unequal global order. The celebrity humanitarian plays an important role here in sustaining imaginings about "us" and "them" and at the same time helps create what Edkins (2000: 122) calls "the new humanitarian international community" – that is, people who feel a personal responsibility to react towards far-away suffering without a threat to their own lifestyles.

This double role of the celebrity, upholding distance while at the same time acting as mediator between the far-away suffering and "us," is captured in the photographs from Geldof's visits to Ethiopia in the course of the Band Aid relief effort. Explicitly avoiding being photographed with starving children, he nevertheless used the possibilities of the media in full to give expression to a youthful idealism as he walked as a (white) Jesus-like figure with (black) children holding each of his hands. Such visual representations are oblivious to – or are ignoring – the fact that his visits were stage-managed by the Ethiopian authorities in order to convey a message supportive of the regime's objectives. The late David Blundy reported from one visit with Geldof to Korem in 1985 that after Geldof's departure people were herded onto trucks by government militias and driven to resettlement centres. This was a highly controversial counter-insurgency policy by the Ethiopian government at the time, partly facilitated by the famine relief donations and resulting in many casualties (Clay and Holcomb 1985).

We, the audiences, have contributed to this seemingly "innocent" but in fact highly political relief effort through committing an act of everyday consumption, having bought Band Aid products. The activism asked for by the celebrity humanitarian, primarily to buy, at the same time exposes its character: it is based on the myth of "just capitalism" that legitimises a global order based on capitalist exploitation. Resulting contradictions between global wealth and destitution are addressed through "compassionate consumption" (Richey and Ponte 2011).

The majority of aid agencies (though there were some notable exceptions, see Müller 2013b for details) supported this representation and made a conscious decision against speaking about the complex realities on the ground for fear donations would cease. They remained "caught up in the fabulous fundraising of . . . the Band Aid movement" that had fundamentally changed perceptions about charity (Franks 2010: 81).

Figure 3.1 Bob Geldof in Ethiopia during the famine of the 1980s

Source: reproduced in the *Daily Record*, 4 September 2014, www.dailyrecord.co.uk/entertainment/celebrity/bob-geldofs-top-sweary-quotes-4163415#vygRdtVSbRdZXri7.97

This representation raises important questions about modes of solidarity and compassion, and the possibility of progressive politics. It also invites us to interrogate whether a more political way of celebrity humanitarianism can be imagined. I now do so by looking at celebrity engagements in a more recent famine in Somalia in 2011.

Beyond "Band Aid" representations?

The UN officially declared a famine for two regions of Southern Somalia on 20 July 2011 and predicted around 3.7 million people would be affected. The major relief agencies put out calls for immediate action that, together with media headlines, provoked a two-strand celebrity-mediated response.

The first was an urgent appeal by the likes of Save the Children, who enlisted the widow of Bob Marley. Under the slogan of the Marley song lyric "imgonnabeyourfriend" this campaign evoked a representation of "Africa" reminiscent of the 1980's media coverage (Müller 2013b). More interesting was a second type of celebrity response. It was advanced by ONE, an advocacy organisation co-founded by Bono from U2. It included a number of celebrities who, since Band Aid, have engaged in such causes. Under the slogan "Hungry No More" and with the subtitle "Drought is an act of nature. Famine is man-made" it calls "famine the real obscenity." It also proclaims not only to "fxxx famine" but to know "how to stop it," citing a catalogue of early warning systems, food reserves, better seeds, irrigation, peace and security.

The ONE campaign showed no famine footage and focused exclusively on the trope of the angry celebrity. In doing so the image of the innocent sufferer is upheld. The only "people" mentioned are "30,000 children [who] have died in three months" and "12 million women and children [who] are on the brink." ONE is "not asking for your money" but "asking for your voice." Instead of clicking to provide a donation (as is the case in the Save the Children campaign) viewers are invited to click in order to lobby their politicians to put an end to famine or address other issues ONE advocates, such as dealing with poverty and preventable diseases. The anger voiced in the ONE campaign remains stuck in a particular interpretation of the world that is in essence anti-political, even if and when the language of social justice is being used.

Looked at in more detail, the ONE-sponsored campaign reduced the complex realities of famine in Somalia to the suffering of women and children in an area controlled by a vicious Islamic militia, Al-Shabaab. This is combined with remarks about the need for security that imply a "bad" (African) 'other' is standing in the way of such security. It thus perpetuates an understanding of famine that concurs with the Western hegemonic narrative of security and the War on Terror.

This is important because celebrity humanitarianism is playing an increasingly important role in the wider conceptualisation of relations between the global North and South. Celebrity endorsement influences philanthropic, NGO and government spending and thus social and political priorities. Some observers point out that phenomena like Band Aid coupled with new communication technologies have resulted in a "global meritocracy of suffering" where all deserving causes eventually attract international support (Clifford 2002). Others give credit to celebrity activism in shaping "social meaning and inspiring civic engagement" and describe its "'non-confrontational' reordering of economic forces in the service of higher goals" as a new model of visionary leadership (Huddart 2005). But as the following section will show, celebrity humanitarians occupy an important function within a system of personalised Western politics that interprets the world through a one-dimensional lens (Dieter and Kumar 2008; Donini 2010).

Enduring features of celebrity humanitarianism

A celebrity cause in "Africa" that seems to take into account political complexities is the intervention into the political and humanitarian crises in Darfur and South Sudan. Most prominently advanced by George Clooney and Dan Cheadle, this campaign proclaims that African-Christian South Sudan had fought a battle for independence from the Arab-Muslim "chauvinist" North. Hollywood celebrities depict this fight in almost biblical terms, not unlike the BBC broadcast of famine in Ethiopia. We see here the heroic struggle of David, the Christian-African underdog, against Goliath, the more powerful and resource-rich Muslim-Arab adversary who is at the same time supported by the likes of undemocratic China. In that version of events, the complex realities of the various conflicts in Sudan, and the fact that they do not run along faith-based or racial lines, were nowhere to be found. Like in the cases of Ethiopia and Somalia, causes that are worthy of celebrity engagement are those that can be represented in clear binary terms of right and wrong.

Figure 3.2 President Barack Obama discusses the situation in Sudan with actor George Clooney
during a meeting outside the Oval Office, 12 October 2010

Source: Wikimedia Commons, https://commons.wikimedia.org/wiki/File:George_Clooney_-_White_House_-_October_2010_(cropped).jpg (in the public domain).

What the Sudan engagement has shown, however, is a shift in the role of celebrity humanitarians. They moved from Geldof's call for direct engagement (buying) and now aspire to assume the role of mediator between those moved by empathy on behalf of the innocently suffering "other" ("us", the audience) and "our" respective governments. In Tester's words (2010: 34), the celebrity of "common-sense humanitarianism" has mutated into a "professional humanitarian" whose engagement is founded upon explaining to general audiences what types of action to demand from their respective political leaders.

While there is a danger of overstating the actual role of celebrity humanitarians in global politics, they do play an important part in transnational advocacy networks. Such networks are at their most successful when focusing on simple narratives that can easily be reported by the media and have a clear moral message. One of the archetypes of such a story was the BBC broadcast on famine in Ethiopia in 1984. Since then, the agendas promoted by celebrity humanitarians have relied on moral values and discourses shared by the larger public. Once it was about feeding the starving children of Ethiopia, now it is about speaking out against "evil" or highlighting threats to "our" way of life by "barbaric" others.

Ultimately, the focus on the innocent sufferer and the evil perpetrator, combined with partisan interpretations of local realities, prolongs a global order based on 'Western' superiority that at the same time undermines local responses.

Visualising celebrity humanitarianism

I have examined the surge in celebrity humanitarianism on the African continent and its intertwinement with media representations that can be traced back to the visual representation of the 1980s famine in Ethiopia.

This "Band Aid" representation of famine has emerged more generally as a potent symbol of African collapse, the crisis of the post-independence project and the recurring need to alleviate "innocent" suffering. "Humanitarian" interventions are thus often determined by a combination of media representations, aligned aid agency advocacy, and high-profile celebrity engagement. Celebrity protagonists cast themselves ultimately in the role of altruistic saviours of a suffering "other," a figure of the present with little individual history or identity and thus easily spoken for by the benevolent celebrity (Watts 1991).

In this way celebrity humanitarians are instrumental in dividing the world into the "humanity that suffers" and the "humanity that saves" (Douzinas 2007: 12). The original Amin/Buerk broadcast was instrumental in producing the archetype of the category of "victim" worthy of celebrity engagement and wider moral compassion. This "victim" is the innocently suffering, not for example the freedom fighter with a Kalashnikov ready to battle a system that denies people their basic rights and dignity. As Suzanne Franks (2014) pointed out in a recent commentary for the *Guardian,* fundraising for the contemporary humanitarian disaster in Syria has been difficult, as here we find "a complex story without clear goodies and baddies," a story not easy "to convey, either for journalists or NGOs." Nor for celebrity humanitarians, one could add. It is a crisis that is being left to fester, like so many others. And celebrity humanitarian engagement that speaks truth to power has yet to be found.

4   Children

Katrina Lee-Koo

There is a line that the liberal global citizen does not like to cross. That line concerns the use of direct political violence against children. After all, children are innocent in the face of political violence. In an ordered world, they should not need to confront it. Those who commit it are barbaric and those who witness it have an innate duty to "do something." This straightforward narrative can undercut the most complex political machinations. Far from the hard-headed strategies of global conflict, a single image of a child experiencing political violence can galvanise an unwavering emotional-political response and produce a clear underlying narrative: "This war is wrong"; "These people are poison"; "This continent is a basketcase."

This is why images of children under attack are powerful. Without us realising it, they creep into our consciousness, feeding into pre-existing narratives of global politics, to compel action and shape political landscapes.

Children and narratives of global politics

The images shown in this chapter have had this galvanising effect upon the liberal mindset. These images are powerful because they pull an emotional trigger that reinforces familiar narratives about liberal order and illiberal disorder. In 1972 the picture of Kim Phúc escaping a napalm attack in her South Vietnamese village appeared on the front page of the *New York Times*, winning photographer Nick Ut a Pulitzer Prize. According to Denise Chong (1999: xiii) "this picture stopped the Vietnam War." Its publication immediately scripted nine-year-old Kim into the role of an innocent victim of a problematic conflict, while compelling the US public to confront its role in the violence. Visuality, particularly in the form of moving images, had already played a central role in graphically presenting the human side of conflict to US audiences. However, this remains one of the most iconic photographs of the twentieth century that speaks of the human costs of war. Particularly once the anti-war movement appropriated it, the image came to embody the troubled internal moral turmoil that characterised US involvement in Vietnam.

Four decades later, US Secretary of State John Kerry described the image of a seven-year-old Australian boy Abdullah Sharrouf holding the severed head of a Syrian official as "really one of the most disturbing, stomach-turning, grotesque photographs ever displayed" (Kerry 2014) It has been reported that the boy's father, Khaled Sharrouf, an Australian jihadist who had recently relocated his family to Syria from Australia, forced his son to pose with the head and then celebrated the image via Twitter with the comment: "That's my boy!" Its reproduction in the Western media – which censored the child's eyes and the deceased's face – reinforces an existing narrative that describes Islamic State (IS) as "so far beyond the pale with respect to any standard by which we judge even terrorist groups" (Kerry 2014). In doing so, it foregrounds public awareness of the barbarity of IS and warns of its capacity to infiltrate liberal societies. This provides a platform from which liberal states like Australia might morally justify military engagement against IS abroad and infringements upon civil liberties at home in the name of countering violent extremism. According to *The Australian* newspaper (2015), which first published the image on 14 August 2014, it "is sure to remain one of the defining images of this conflict, like the photograph of naked Vietnamese girl Kim Phúc fleeing a napalm attack during the Vietnam war."

The iconically stylised image of an African boy holding an AK-47 has similarly become symbolic of global power relations between a developed liberal order and an underdeveloped illiberal disorder. The dividing line here, presented in the child's race, is not between an imagined "East" and "West," but rather "North" and "South." The image of the lone African child soldier has come to symbolise not just childhood innocence lost, but also the loss of an entire continent. Kate Manzo (2008) argues that the narratives generated by such images morally empower a western humanitarianism that re-establishes a colonial set of power relations. In each case, these images of a violated child provoke an emotional response that creates or reinforces imaginings of global political power, providing liberal actors with moral justification for action.

Consequently, the power of these images derives from their capacity to prompt simple narratives of global politics built upon binary constructions of "us" and "them," "right" and "wrong" and "good" and "bad." It is a narrative code that is easy to decipher. Confronted with these images on the front page of a newspaper, or in a charity advertisement on the side of a bus, the viewer knows that the person responsible for

Figure 4.1 Kim Phúc, centre, with her clothes torn off, flees with other South Vietnamese children after a misdirected American aerial napalm attack on 8 June 1972 (Nick Ut)

Source: Nick Ut, *Daily News*, www.nydailynews.com/news/world/iconic-napalm-girl-photo-vietnam-war-turns-40-article-1.1088201

Figure 4.2 African boy holding an AK-47
Source: UNICEF

this violence is immoral and poses a threat not just to the child, but also to "our" way of life. This is because there is – in theory – nothing more fundamental to "our" way of life than preserving the innocence of children. In the words of US President Barack Obama (2012) in the aftermath of the Sandy Hook Elementary School shooting in 2012, "This is our first task – caring for our children. It's our first job. If we don't get that right, we don't get anything right. That's how, as a society, we will be judged."

Confronted with violence against children, the liberal viewer is immediately given a role. As the desperate child's eyes look directly out, that role is clearly marked as one of responsibility. Any responsible adult must act against the abuse of a child, must do whatever is necessary to stop the abuse and defend against its proliferation. Acknowledging this, former First Lady Laura Bush (2001) said in her radio address on the eve of the US-led war against Afghanistan in 2001, "All of us have an obligation to speak out. . . . Fighting brutality against women and children is not the expression of a specific culture; it is the acceptance of our common humanity." In short, those who commit political violence against children must be stopped.

The violence can only be stopped, however, through direct confrontation with the child's abusers. The images impose a liberal narrative of conflict where the liberal order is scripted as hero and the illiberal order as the villain. Consequently, Abdullah Sharrouf can only be saved once his father is dead and IS are obliterated; Kim Phúc cannot be saved without ending the war in Vietnam; and child soldiers cannot be demilitarised until Africa accepts a path towards liberal development. The scripting of characters into good and evil, or light and dark, offer stark characterisations. This is reinforced by the fact that the villain is unseen – the child appears in the image alone and isolated. Karen Wells (2009) argues that global charities often use images of a child alone to imply that their community has abandoned them. Portraits of lone child soldiers allow the imagination to assume he is orphaned or otherwise rejected by local adults. Similarly, in the background to the image of Kim Phúc are South Vietnamese soldiers. Yet they are not looking at her or rendering any assistance, protection or apparent concern. Audiences are told directly that it is Abdullah Sharrouf's father who has given him a severed head and ordered him to pose with it, demonstrating complete parental negligence. Within this context, the message these images transmit is that liberal society must assume responsibility for addressing the threat posed to these children by absent or abusive carers.

Rescue is an important theme of the narrative. In 1994, Gayatri Spivak argued that post/colonial relations are often justified through a narrative of white men saving brown women from brown men. To some extent, we can put children in the same role as women: victims who need saving. In the case of children we can argue that responsible adults (read the liberal order) must save children from those who would commit political violence against them (read the illiberal order). This provocation can then be woven into the familiar narrative of global politics that Spivak identifies. In this sense, the image of the child resonates with pre-existing identity politics and power relations to complete this narrative of global politics. The image of an African child soldier becomes a metaphor for the continent itself in a continuing colonial narrative of savagery, under-development and the white man's burden. The child soldier is Africa – lost, futureless, infantile, uncivilised and barbaric. The guiding hand of the liberal order can step into the absent parent role to provide structure, education and direction towards liberal order (Manzo 2008). Similarly, the brutality of radical Islam is the backdrop to the image of Abdullah Sharrouf – vicious and primal – a movement moving backwards rather than forwards. Again, Kim Phúc is Vietnam – an anguished girl child whose skin is burnt off her body by a destructive war. Marita Sturken (1997: 92) writes, "As a young, female, naked figure, Kim Phúc represents the victimised, feminised country of Vietnam." Much of the political power of these images therefore resides with those and that which are unseen in the image.

The children themselves are merely subjects who do not wield political power. In fact, the power of the images is fuelled by the subject's lack of power. In the face of the politics that engulf them, they are apolitical, passive and bound by the private sphere. Within a liberal idea of childhood, children are thought to be generally unable to comprehend the adult world of politics surrounding them. Lacking political capacity, children in liberal societies do not vote, and cannot enlist to fight in state-based militaries. These are seen as acts of protection – protecting children from the harsh, outside world of politics. An image of a child holding the decapitated head is therefore particularly confronting and vulgar – a breakdown in social order and a failure of adult responsibility to remove children from politics.

The liberal idea of childhood as a passive state is reinforced by a legal framework that defines rights and responsibilities according to age. For instance, many liberal states designate 18 years of age as the point at which children become politically responsible adults. The important point here is that at this point "adult" decisions become *their* choice and *their* right. Therefore an image of an 18-year-old soldier does not provoke the same moral outrage in liberal societies as an image of a 15-year-old soldier. Liberal audiences assume the latter has made a fully informed choice to join an armed force, but the former was forcibly recruited. Guy Westwell (2011: 4) notes that in the editing of the image of Kim Phúc, a shadow over the child's groin was removed so as not to give the impression it was pubic hair. This in turn would ensure that she was identified as a young girl. Westwell (2011: 4) suggests that the mistaken shadow would act "as signifier of adult sexuality and adult consciousness [which] would have lent greater agency to the Vietnamese victim and demanded a different, more complex, response from an adult viewer in the U.S."

Finally, the revulsion these images inspire is informed by a liberal understanding that the world can be demarcated into spaces that are politics-bound (the public sphere) and politics-free (the private sphere). Children belong in the private sphere – of the home – where the state and its politics should not tread. Jennifer Tilton (2010: 51) writes that "our normative definition of childhood locates children in the family, safe and secure in private homes and off the streets." In this space children should not need to encounter, or be invested in, political contest. Nine-year-old Kim Phúc, running naked down a public street, offers a stark demonstration of public sphere politics exploding into her private world in a violent and graphic violation of the laws of armed conflict.

Furthermore, the visuality of the photographic image – as opposed to moving images – reinforces this conceptualisation of childhood. These children are mute and paralysed; seen but not heard. They are incapable of responding to the politics around them and it is left to the viewer to use their own preconceptions to imagine the child's fear as politics descends upon them. These images portray them as dwarfed by their contexts. Kim Phúc runs from an ever increasing and rapidly approaching explosion behind her. She cannot escape it as it burns her skin and has forced her to remove her clothes. The African boy is dwarfed by an AK-47 – routinely referred to as a small arm and light weapon – it seems as long as he is tall. Abdullah Sharrouf needs both hands to hold up a severed adult head the size of his own torso, bowed slightly at the weight of it. Juxtaposed to the politics around them, these children are tiny, trapped and alone.

The undeniable victimisation of these children makes "doing nothing" morally indefensible. Yet we need to be careful about what kinds of politics we allow these images to enact, particularly when a broader liberal imagining purchases them. Politics enacted in the name of saving children do not always have that net effect. After a decade of conflict in Afghanistan, the well-being of children in that country is arguably worse than prior to 2001. There is little evidence that US-led forces sought to mainstream the well-being of children into their operational goals, despite Laura Bush's appeals that these children needed saving (Lee-Koo 2013). It can therefore be argued that they were used for propaganda effect – a way of clearly distinguishing between the civilised "us" who spoke of protecting children and the barbaric "other" who were not only abusive carers but taught their children to decapitate the enemy.

Current speculation in Australia about whether radicalised children *can* be saved has crystallised around the case of Abdullah Sharrouf. His Australian grandmother has pleaded for the return of her grandchildren from Syria to Australia in the wake of reports of both parents' deaths. However, Australian politicians are concerned that these children will pose a threat to society. It is recognised that these children are victims of their father's terrorist activities, but in their victimhood they are nonetheless super-empowered by an unnatural exposure to violence. Leader of the Opposition Bill Shorten (in Wigham 2015) summed up this widely held view that children were "victims of child abuse" but he "wouldn't feel comfortable with these children being reinserted into a playground with my children." In evocative descriptions of wayward boys, journalist Robert Kaplan (1994) similarly described the threat to the liberal order posed by militarised children in the conflict-ridden states of west Africa. Ill-bred, deprived and anarchic, he described scenes with children "as numerous as ants" who "defecate in streets filled with garbage and pigs." Kaplan's message is that these savage yet super-empowered youths, in their hoards, present an imminent threat to the liberal order. While Kaplan's claims have been much critiqued, it has resonated throughout aspects of the liberal community (Lee-Koo 2011: 732) and provided an extreme view of the suspicion with which children who are victims of political violence can be treated.

The global East/West discourse reverberates in these debates. Ultimately, this debate is warped. As Nordstrom (1999: 26) points out:

> It is both dangerous and unrealistic to look at the abuse of children, in war, in another country, in another context as if that were somehow different and more barbaric than the patterns of abuse that characterize our own everyday cultures, in peace and war.

These debates allow too many viewer-driven assumptions about these children to inform understanding and, more troublingly, drive political action. Michael Wessells (1998: 641) argues that images of conflict-affected children used to explain global and local politics "oversimplify a complex reality and invite a host of damaging errors." The conversation that the images prompt – sometimes in the form of military violence – is between the viewer and the perpetrator of violence. Inevitably, this negatively affects more children.

Stepping outside of the image

There is an alternative to this, however. Let children speak. Why not transition children, some of whom are captured in these graphic images, from passive and static subjects into agents of political change?

In the decades since a napalm attack drove Kim Phúc from her village, she has become a voice for forgiveness and peace. She (quoted in Newton and Patterson 2015) noted, "I realized that if I couldn't escape that picture, I wanted to go back to work with that picture for peace. And that is my choice." Throughout her life Kim Phúc has not just been a static symbol for peace, but an advocate for it. Her life-story became an important corrective to propagandised clichés of a single image (see Chong 1999) and spoke to the complexity of her identities as a girl, a woman, Vietnamese, Canadian, victim and survivor. Children can and do narrate their own political lives. They do have agency to effect political change. In order to use this to its fullest advantage, the liberal order needs to give children a voice with which to speak, and an opportunity to be heard.

This begins with challenging liberal understandings of childhood. Yes, children (like many adults) are innocent victims of political violence. Kim Phúc is undeniably an innocent victim of war. But that is a fragment of her identity. As a child she was also a survivor. In itself this was an act of agency that allowed her to challenge the politics around her. More recently, Pakistani schoolgirl Malala Yousafzai, a 2014 recipient of the Nobel Peace Prize, has similarly demonstrated the interplay between victim and advocate. These examples are not isolated to celebrated cases. Memoirs and research of former child soldiers expose diverse accounts of their political lives, all of which trouble the simplified narrative of child-victim. Children can demonstrate comprehension of the politics that has embroiled their homelands, and justify a personal investment in it (Huynh 2015). This investment might be advocacy for peace, or it might be participation in armed conflict.

This is not an argument to afford children adult responsibilities. Children should not have to experience violence, and adults should be responsible for their protection. Posing a child with a severed head or an AK-47 – with all the attendant politics – is an appalling act of violence. Mistakenly bombing a village with napalm is a horrendous war crime. However, before decisions are made as to how to "save" these children, the children should be allowed to speak for themselves. Let them consider the circumstances in which they might put down their weapons or stop running. The result may be politics that not only allow children to participate in their own protection, but the protection of whole communities as well.

5   Climate

Kate Manzo

Climate, which comes from the Greek *klima* meaning "area," usually refers to a region's long-term weather patterns. This is measured in terms of average precipitation (i.e. the amount of annual rainfall, snow, etc.), maximum and minimum temperatures throughout the seasons, sunshine hours, humidity, the frequency of extreme weather, and so on (Met Office [UK] 2013).

The term "climate" has two significant meanings, one literal and the other metaphorical. Climate literally "refers to what the weather in a certain place is *usually like* . . . so you should think of climate as *average weather*" (Klein and Bauman 2014: 12). Time and place are both central to literal understandings of climate. Average weather is derived by meteorologists from weather patterns measured over a period of time, with thirty years being the standard set by the World Meteorological Organization (WMO n.d.). Climate is thus a shorthand term for the generally prevailing weather conditions of a particular place – possibly a particular planet, such as Earth. In a metaphorical sense, climate is also shorthand for "the prevailing attitudes, standards, or environmental conditions of a group, period or place: *a climate of political unrest*" (Dictionary.com n.d.).

I show how climate iconography, that is, images and symbols used to portray weather, has worked to visualise global political dangers and threats. The chosen aesthetic realm is political cartoons, for two reasons. First, previous work shows that cartoons can represent complex issues in simplified and accessible form (Manzo 2012). This doesn't mean that cartoon messages are comprehensible to all; cartoons' visual languages can be ambiguous or culturally opaque. Subject-specific historical knowledge is also required to decode all but the most current cartoons. Nonetheless, cartoons which conventionally appear in popular newspapers – as accompaniments to news stories and editorials – are politically useful. In educational terms, cartoons can work like the illustrations in textbooks; drawing attention to the news of the day and facilitating general understanding thereof.

In political terms, cartoons that embed political commentary, analysis and critique go beyond objective journalistic reportage to raise awareness of relations of power. The standard use of caricature, lampooning and satire in political cartooning is demonstrably not without political risk. The killing of cartoonists (among others) at the headquarters of the satirical magazine *Charlie Hebdo* in Paris in January 2015 was a cogent reminder of the potency of political cartoons.

Cartoon sources and collection

The British Cartoon Archive (BCA) at the University of Kent is a repository for all cartoons published in British newspapers since 1904. In addition to the images and their artists, the Archive usefully catalogues the source and date of publication, the caption, embedded text, and the subject matter addressed in the cartoon. A wide range of subjects can be covered in even the simplest cartoons. This demonstrates both the dual character of climate iconography (i.e. its literal and metaphorical aspects) and its political versatility. Recognisable symbols of weather are a form of visual language used to illustrate a variety of political issues.

To explore the use of climate iconography to visualise global politics, I began by searching the BCA archive using the "simple" and "advanced" search options. The latter gives a further choice to search by either "any text" or "subjects." A click on the subject tab "climate" suggests using the word "weather" as a synonym. The total number of records returned for a search by the words "climate" and "weather" came to 2,648, of which only 438 were classified as "climate." Further searches were for "climate change" (121 entries), "global warming" (142) and "Cold War" (527). Taken together, the search terms designed to capture the literal and metaphorical meanings of the word "climate" returned a total of 3,438 records.

In addition to a small cartoon image, the result of each search I conducted listed the artist or creator, the title of the cartoon, the name of the publisher, and the date of publication. Analysis revealed that the top four publishers are all so-called tabloids. Within the broadsheet category, the *Daily Telegraph* is well ahead of the *Guardian* (with 251 published climate cartoons), followed by the *Independent* (222), and the *Observer* (60). This finding echoes the argument that "more pictures/less text" is a defining feature of tabloid journalism (McLachlan and Golding 2000: 78). However, the idea that tabloids generally publish "fewer political/parliament news stories" than broadsheets (McLachlan and Golding 2000: 78) is less clearly supported. The cartoons in the next section suggest more of a reliance on visual modes of storytelling (like cartoons) in tabloid news.

In terms of weather or climate type, there is "a well-worn cliché that Britons are obsessed with the wind and rain" (O'Mahony 2012: 1). Many cartoons published in British newspapers were therefore expected to reference those conditions. At the same time, climate is a multi-scalar concept, and climate cartoons are not necessarily parochial. Given UK newspaper coverage of international debates about climate change and global warming (see Manzo 2010a) many "hot" and "extreme" climate cartoons were also expected.

An array of *cold* weather cartoons were also featured in the Archive. The first theme is national. A 2013 survey found that Britons "complain most about unpredictable weather and it being too cold" (Bains 2013: 1). *Coldness* is therefore a negative signifier of British weather. The second factor concerns language. Metaphors are a part of everyday English, helping to "structure how we perceive, how we think, and what we do" (Lakoff and Johnson 2003: 4). The blog "Metaphors in American Politics" shows how American media employ the terms *frozen* and *cold* to describe abstract political concepts (Burgert 2013). Cold weather metaphors more generally can attach to a broad array of abstract concepts and experiences, for example, fear (getting cold feet, a cold chill down the spine), austerity (hiring freeze, wage freeze) and lack of emotion (a cold fish, cold-hearted, etc.).

The other two factors are planetary or global. A theory of global cooling that "picked up support from some pretty reputable scientists" was circulated by American media in the mid-1970s along with apocalyptic visions of a coming Little Ice Age (Struck 2014: 4). A key signifier of climate threat at that time would therefore have been ice rather than sun. The current equation of climate change with rising average global temperatures is historically contingent, only becoming newsworthy since the 1990s. Last but not least, the so-called Cold War between the United States and the Soviet Union ran from the end of the Second World War until the collapse of the Soviet Union in December 1991 (Cold War Museum n.d.). *Coldness* has thus long been a powerful signifier of global conflict – even pre-dating the Cold War, as the next section shows with reference to a select number of illustrative cartoons from the data set.

Cold weather iconography: visualising global conflict

Polar bears stranded on ice floes are conventional symbols of global warming; dominant signifiers of the Earth's vulnerability to climate change (Manzo 2010b). Drawn in July 1941 at the height of the Second World War and published in the *Evening Standard*, a cartoon by David Low entitled "Unexpected winter in Indo-China" tells a different story. The mixed weather metaphors applied to the central figure, called Jap War God, suggest political indecision or inaction. He is sitting on an ice floe and not standing – a sign of inactivity further insinuated in the accompanying text box: "If he no move smartly now then Hon feet soon grow cold, yes?" At the same time, he is letting off steam – an indicator of emotional heat or arousal in both the English language and Japanese Manga comics (Wikipedia n.d.). Such mixed metaphors suggest a moment of political hesitation on the part of Japan – a country further symbolised in the cartoon by the rising sun in the background. Japan is also known as Nippon – the Land of the Rising Sun.

The embedded text "US Freeze" refers to the freezing of all Japanese assets in the United States by President Roosevelt on 26 July 1941 (two days before the cartoon's publication) in retaliation for Japanese occupation of French Indo-China. Britain and the Dutch East Indies soon followed American suit and froze Japanese assets. This event was captured at the time in American cartoons – one of which attributed political cold feet to the US and Britain (see Rice 1941). Five months later, following the Japanese attack on Pearl Harbour, the US officially entered the Second World War by declaring war on Japan and then Germany.

The complex geopolitics of a subsequent war – the Cold War – is portrayed quite simply in the Figure 5.1. Drawn by Victor Weisz (pen name Vicky) and published in the *Daily Mirror* in early January 1957, it depicts events that temporarily united the post-war superpowers on the same side of a conflict. Palm trees in sand are a picture postcard depiction of the western desert in Egypt. The cartoon appeared on the day that Anthony Eden resigned as British Prime Minister, following a short-lived invasion of the Suez Canal by Israel, Britain and France. The nationalisation of the Canal by Egypt's Gamal Abdel Nasser (an ally of the USSR) had prompted the attack in late October 1956 amid concerns about continued access to Middle East oil, which is portrayed in the cartoon by the rigs. The downturned mouth of the out-of-place snowman symbolises mutual American and Soviet distaste for the conflict; both demanded a cease-fire at the United Nations in early November. The invaders then agreed to withdraw and were replaced by UN troops, but this did not prevent the very thing that had prompted the invasion in the first place. At the end of that month, the Eden government re-introduced petrol rationing amid growing fuel shortages at home.

There were also a lot of cartoons that illustrate the domestic and foreign policy connections. Consider an untitled cartoon by Michael Cummings, published by the

" WELL, SOMEBODY **HAD** TO FILL THE VACUUM ... "

Figure 5.1 "Well, somebody had to fill the vacuum," Victor Weisz, *Daily Mirror,* 9 January 1957

Source: Victor Weisz, *Daily Mirror*, 9 January 1957. Mirrorpix, British Cartoon Archive, University of Kent. Printed with permission.

Daily Express in June 1961 with the caption: "Excuse you Mr Macwonder, could you spare a moment for the Hot War at home?" It juxtaposes cold weather iconography with references to heat. The hot/cold dichotomy can be read here as a commentary on political priorities. A figure with a large telescope is Eden's successor Harold Macmillan – a Conservative Prime Minister known by the nicknames Supermac (first in a parody of Superman by Vicky) Macwonder and later Macblunder (by political opponents). The Soviet leader Nikita Khrushchev is drawn as a cartoon snowman. A tiny figure in his hand, waving a Berlin banner, is a reference to the Berlin crisis of 1961 that culminated in the building of the wall between East and West Berlin.

In looking east, Macmillan is apparently pre-occupied with Cold War politics and inattentive to "the Hot War at home." Behind Macmillan's back are symbolic representations of two divisive political issues. One portrayed by a heavily-armed masked man is crime: calls "for the reintroduction of corporal and capital punishment continued into Macmillan's second term of office [1959–1963]" (Jarvis 2005: 53). Another, small figure with a Union Jack is an iconic image of a banker. He stands for debates about economic recession, notably rising inflation and the wage increases that "were outstripping productivity growth" at the time (Evans and Taylor 1996: 122). Chancellor Selwyn Lloyd responded in July 1961 with austerity measures and an increase in the bank rate. Another metaphorical freeze – a seven-month wage freeze imposed later by the Prime Minister – was to prove "deeply unpopular" (Evans 2010: 1).

Hot weather iconography: visualising global warming

The other key theme of climate iconography is global warming. I start with a classic parable about complacency and conceit. Icarus was a character in Greek mythology who flew too close to the sun. The wayward youth plunged to his death after ignoring repeated warnings from his father, Daedalus, to steer a middle course. Represented as Earth in Figure 5.2, Icarus cuts a small-scale figure in relation to the neighbouring Sun. The mythological reference, giant Sun and overwritten capitalised text all suggest reading the cartoon itself as a latter-day Daedalus, warning of planetary death as a consequence of ignoring the dangers of global warming.

Another possible Daedalus emerges from the BCA's accompanying notes to the cartoon. These differentiate between "people depicted" (Icarus) and "people referred to" (John Selwyn Gummer). Also known as Lord Deben, Gummer is the current chair of the UK's independent Committee on Climate Change. In 1995, as Environment Secretary, he introduced the Environment Act. A year later, Gummer argued for an international effort to try to cut greenhouse gases during the second annual Conference of the Parties to the United Nations Framework Convention on Climate Change. The Icarus cartoon appeared on the last day of a conference that recognised the need for a binding protocol on the reduction of greenhouse gases. The Kyoto Protocol, committing Parties to set internationally binding emissions reduction targets, followed in 1997.

The Conference was held in Doha, Qatar, in 2012 and marked the first time that climate change negotiations took place in the Middle East. Like Figure 5.1, an untitled cartoon by Peter Schrank that the *Independent on Sunday* published in December 2012 places a cold climate figure in the midst of a desert. Although stranded on the side of a road instead of an ice floe, the solitary polar bear remains a potent symbol of the consequences of global warming. The distressed animal asks a question to a group of camels: "Where are the wise men?" We see here another example of Christian iconography at work in climate change visualisation (Manzo 2012), recalling as it does the biblical story of the three wise visitors to baby Jesus at Christmas. As the watching camels on the other side of the road are immobile, the fate of the polar bear seems to rest with unidentified humans. Since none of the animals look at the sign to the Conference in the background, the sought-after "wise men" appear to be absent from the proceedings. The cartoon was published two days after the end of a conference remembered for the Doha Amendment, which established a second commitment period (2013–20) for the Kyoto Protocol.

Visual climate metaphors

In *Metaphors We Live By,* Lakoff and Johnson (2003: 4) argue that "most of our ordinary conceptual system is metaphorical in nature." Climate metaphors and icons are among the tools used by visual storytellers, political cartoonists included. I explored some of the literal and metaphorical ways in which "climate" is used to make sense of, and represent, different aspects of global politics over time.

Figure 5.2 Untitled, *Daily Telegraph,* 19 July 1996

Source: Nicholas Garland, *Daily Telegraph,* 19 July 1996. Telegraph Media Group Ltd, British Cartoon Archive. Printed with permission.

The aim was not to suggest that climate cartoons necessarily facilitate understanding of complex and/or contested phenomena. Meaning is like climate itself; it varies across time and space. Political cartoons are designed to be commentaries on the events of the day; their meaning may be lost for irregular consumers of news. This is why there is a need for historical knowledge to make sense of cartoons. The same can be said, of course, of news stories of any variety. It is not a problem unique to the visual realm.

The historical perspective adopted here demonstrates the significance of cultural literacy in political storytelling as well as the role played by climate iconography in portraying political issues. Ice floes and polar bears, palm trees and oil rigs have stood the test of time along with mythological and biblical figures. As politicians come and go these are the things that live on.

Note

The author would like to thank Elena Campbell for research assistance.

6   CNN effect

Piers Robinson

The so-called CNN effect emerged during the 1990s and was linked to the potential for a global political consciousness predicted in Marshall McLuhan's (1962) famous "global village" vision. The term quickly came to be associated with the emerging humanitarian-intervention debate of the 1990s and the idea that media representations of human suffering, communicated via the new 24-hour global media, were playing a pivotal role in mobilising (Western) responses. The role of CNN – the Cable News Network – epitomised the political role and impact of this new global media phenomena.

I discuss the CNN effect and focus, in particular, on the powerful role of images in relation to humanitarian crises. I proceed in three sections: first, the CNN effect debate is defined and then related to current debates surrounding the "visual turn" in world politics. The following section outlines the historical backdrop to the debate and the broader topic of the role of the image in shaping responses to humanitarian concerns. Here the importance of the visual dimension of mediating suffering is discussed with particular reference to the persuasive power of images. In the third section, the argument will be developed that images need to be understood as part of strategic attempts to exercise power through so-called organised persuasive communication. For the viewers of images, this realisation demands that we always look beyond the image to understand the political context from which it emerges, whose interests might be being served, and the strategic intent of the source of the image.

The CNN effect and the visual turn

The CNN effect became closely associated with the debate over intervention during humanitarian crisis. Consider the interventions in northern Iraq (1991), involving the creation of "safe havens" for Iraqi Kurds, and Operation Restore Hope in Somalia (1992–3), involving the deployment of US forces to aid food delivery. In both cases media representations of suffering people were seen as pressuring policy makers to intervene for humanitarian purposes. The key issue of the debates that emerged was whether or not traditional elite dominance of foreign policy making had been usurped by non-state actors and media representations.

The underlying premise of the CNN effect was that advocacy journalism was transforming the conduct of states and underpinning a fledgling norm of "humanitarian" intervention. The ensuing challenge was to explore how a post-Cold War global media environment was shaping global power regulations. Particularly important was how new communication technologies helped non-state actors to increase the visibility and transparency of "distant" crises.

The CNN effect debate was not only about one particular US-based global news provider, the Cable News Network. The issue was much broader, capturing a range of phenomena associated with the impact of news media on foreign policy formulation and global politics. As new global media organisations established themselves and the internet became ubiquitous, new hypotheses have emerged, such as the "Al Jazeera effect" and the "YouTube effect." Although the technologies associated with each are different, they all speak to similar concerns regarding the power of media to shape political processes.

For scholars of the visual turn, the CNN effect is part of a broader dynamic in which the immediacy, ubiquity and perceived veracity of film and photographic images have transformed global politics, "reconfiguring the political terrain itself" (Hansen 2011: 52). Although suspicious of "cause and effect" assumptions entailed in the CNN effect debate, scholars of the visual turn have been interested in broadly the same set of concerns. As Bleiker (2015: 889) puts it, the aim is to "understand how images frame the conditions of possibility; how they influence what can and cannot be seen, thought and discussed; in short, how they delineate and shape the political."

It is impossible to understand the importance of visuals without also understanding how they interact with the linguistic (verbal and written) dimensions of communication, the context in which a news report is broadcast, and the pre-existing knowledge and cultural backdrop of the audience. Visuals rarely work in isolation and should be understood as one component of communication, which includes verbal and textual (language) forms, as well as physical acts, including posture, gesture and violence. For example, the opening salvos of "Shock and Awe" in Iraq 2003, which included highly visible attacks on buildings in Baghdad, were aimed at communicating a message to the Iraqi people. It is also very difficult to separate visuals from other aspects of a communicative event. For instance, written captions and spoken language often anchor the meaning of visuals, guiding how they should be interpreted by an audience. At the same time, verbal and written communication can serve to conjure up images in the mind of the reader. Expressed in other words, visuals are not the only form of communication that possess the attributes of immediacy and longevity. Sound-bites too can have this effect. Think how Nike's trademark tick and its logo "Just do it" are both powerful and enduring symbols, one visual and the other verbal.

Visualising human suffering: from empathy to emotional distance

The role of the image in reporting humanitarian crisis has a long history. For example, during the 1960s, civilian suffering in the Nigerian–Biafran War (1967–70) was brought home to Western audiences in a highly visual way. The 12 July 1968 cover of *Life* magazine, showing two sorrowful-looking children and headlined with "Starving Children of Biafra War," was an early example of what was to become a stereotypical visual representation of humanitarian crisis involving a focus on suffering women and children. A second significant example of the power of images to elicit global responses to suffering came with the 1984 Ethiopian famine. On 23 October 1984, a BBC evening news broadcast was presented by journalist Michael Buerk narrating a powerful news report, filmed by Mohamed Amin. Buerk (Harrison and Palmer 1986) described the famine as being of "biblical proportions" and, for almost ten minutes, UK audiences were presented with desperate images of death and starvation. The power of such

Figure 6.1 Starving children of the Biafra War, cover of *Life Magazine*,
         12 July 1968

Source: *Life Magazine*, 12 July 1968. *Flickr*, www.flickr.com/photos/falmouthpubliclibrary/
6264316141

images to move audiences became clear with the ensuing international civil society response to that crisis, which culminated in the famous Live Aid concerts.

There are a number of reasons why such images are understood as essential to humanitarian reporting and the CNN effect thesis, all of which pertain to the power of such media reporting to *persuade* audiences that something must be done to help. As Hutchison, Bleiker and Campbell (2014) explain, images of the suffering and the dying are "essential for audiences to feel," and it is precisely this emotional impact which drives people to feel both empathy for the suffering that they are seeing and, in many cases, to demand that action be taken to alleviate that suffering (see also Robinson 2002: 27–30).

Images perform this role more effectively than written or spoken words because of both their immediacy and their ability to capture the "visceral and strangely visual nature of catastrophe" (Hutchison, Bleiker and Campbell 2014). In particular, images that focus on individuals, rather than anonymous masses, help to connect an audience directly with an individual with whom they can start to emphasise (Bleiker *et al.* 2013). Images of women and children reinforce this persuasive power for they are people often understood to be in particular need of protection and, in the case of children, being undeniably innocent victims (van der Gaag and Nash 1987). Of course, images are also powerful because they "seem to authentically reflect what they depict" (Hutchison, Bleiker and Campbell 2014). Seeing is believing and, whatever the potential for image manipulation through digital technology, people tend to believe photographs and films to be truthful representations. Beyond the persuasive power of the image itself, visuals are also important in terms of the overall visibility of a humanitarian crisis as defined by how much media attention it receives. News values based upon the ugly mantra of "if it bleeds, it leads" capture the importance of drama, immediacy and shock value. Also, the circulation of images in today's internet-based and highly visual media environment is said to have increased the "humanitarian space" by widening and deepening awareness of humanitarian suffering (Hutchison, Bleiker and Campbell 2014; Hansen 2011: 57).

However, frequently humanitarian crises are obscured by a style of reporting that works to create distance between the audience and those who are suffering. For example, in their analysis of media coverage of the 1994 Rwandan genocide, Myers *et al.* highlight this particular dynamic in which the conflict, and the genocide itself, was framed as a "regular round of tribal bloodletting" emanating from Africa's "heart of darkness" (Myers *et al.* 1996; see also Robinson 2002: 110–16). A key part of this distance framing was the lack of images of the killing and suffering. Recently, Bleiker *et al.* (2013) documented the dehumanising visual representation of refugees arriving in Australia. Here, emotional disengagement is enabled by rarely showing images of individual refugees and, instead, frequently representing them with images of a faceless mass of people arriving on boats. Perhaps most frequently, media coverage of humanitarian crisis is characterised by the absence of reporting and the lack of images. As Hawkins (2011) argues, news media repeatedly fail to spotlight the world's most serious crises and, here, invisibility is undoubtedly the most distancing form of (non)representation.

The variability of visual representations, oscillating between visuals that encourage us to care and visual representations that persuade us to distance ourselves and not to care, are a clue to the importance of the political dimension of humanitarian reporting. As Hutchison, Bleiker and Campbell (2014) state, "there is always power, interest and politics in all visualisations of humanitarian crisis," and, if that is the case, the question arises as to why we are sometimes asked to care while, at other times, we are encouraged to forget about the suffering of others.

Persuasion and power: beware the image

Understanding that the images we see might reflect power, interests and politics brings us directly to the phenomenon of so-called organised persuasive communication (Robinson 2014: 474–7). This refers to all organised activities aimed at influencing beliefs, attitudes and behaviour. Euphemisms such as public relations (in short PR), strategic communication and public diplomacy are often used. The scale of these activities is impressive: today PR workers outnumber journalists three to one while, between 2002 and 2012, the US federal governments spent 16 billion dollars on outside PR ads. Importantly, such activities often involve significant levels of manipulative communication and deception. Indeed, Corner (2007: 57) argues that patterns of deception and manipulation have become integral to contemporary society such that "almost all types of promotional behaviour slide – perhaps sometimes plunge – into forms of deceit." A clear recent example of deceptive communication is the distortions of intelligence estimates regarding Iraqi weapons of mass destruction capabilities in the run-up to the 2003 Iraq invasion (Herring and Robinson 2014).

What does this all mean for the imaging of humanitarian crises and the question of how we are persuaded to think, feel and act? Sometimes, when we see the image of a starving child, it is because humanitarian actors seek support to alleviate suffering. Most of us would not see such attempts to persuade as problematic or deceptive. At other times, images of suffering are brought to our attention because political actors attempt to persuade us of the legitimacy of a particular policy. In fact, one of the key findings of research into the CNN effect and the humanitarian interventions of the 1990s was that seemingly apolitical and altruistic interventions were often underpinned by selfish national interest. In this light, images of suffering people became part of the public justification of particular foreign policies. For example, NATO's 1999 air war against Serbia was initially designed as an act of coercive diplomacy (Robinson 2002: 94–110) and actually preceded the major humanitarian crisis caused by Milošević's expulsion of Kosovar Albanians. Indeed, US policy makers were specifically advised that bombing would worsen the humanitarian situation in Kosovo (Robinson 2002: 96). Perversely, the humanitarian crisis that followed the start of the air war then became a justification for it as NATO spokespersons directed public attention to the TV images of refugees fleeing Kosovo. As a result, the complex and ambiguous politics behind the intervention became submerged in a simplistic and indeed deceptive NATO-promoted "narrative" that the intervention was a straightforward response to a humanitarian crisis.

In recent years we have often witnessed such appropriations of humanitarian narratives in order to justify Western military action (Robinson *et al.* 2010: 170–2). Images of troops delivering food aid in Iraq, or of liberated Afghans flying kites over Kabul following the fall of the Taliban in 2002, have become part of strategic attempts to persuade audiences of the moral legitimacy of wars that are often disingenuously presented in humanitarian terms. Here too images are a part of deceptive communication that leads us to believe that our government's actions are righteous, when, in reality they may well be profoundly harmful. Reports such as the one published recently by the group Physicians for Social Responsibility (2015), which estimates deaths associated with the "War on Terror" to be in the region of 1.3 million, should give pause for thought whenever we see images of suffering and relief from wars prosecuted by "our" governments.

The absence of images of human suffering is, as noted above, perhaps the most significant form of distancing and forgetting. What then of the conflicts that we do not get to see and where suffering remains invisible? Approaching this issue through the lens of organised persuasive communication, which encourages us to think about the political interests and objectives behind reporting, raises the question of why some conflicts remain invisible. The genocide in Rwanda 1994 was, at the time, obscured through its representation as a "regular round of tribal bloodletting," as noted above. The ensuing war in the Democratic Republic of Congo (DRC), involving the loss of millions of lives, however, has remained almost entirely absent from Western media reporting (Hawkins 2011). Only very recently have academics started to examine British and American activities in the region and their role regarding the bloodshed and suffering (Cameron 2013; Herman and Peterson 2014). Is it perhaps the case that we have not seen the suffering precisely because that suffering might raise awkward questions for our governments? Images of suffering children, of which there have been countless in the region, are not something that the US and UK governments have sought to promote.

The visual politics of the CNN effect

The process by which images arrive on our TV screens, tablets, laptops and newspapers is rarely random. The kind of sustained media campaigns associated with any given humanitarian crisis are usually the result of actors working hard to bring those images to our attention with the intent to persuade us to feel one way or another about the suffering that is being witnessed. For us, as the viewing public, an important first step is recognising the organised and persuasive intent behind such images. Once we do that, we are in a position to critically evaluate whether or not we want to allow ourselves to be persuaded. Sometimes, we are being asked to care because political actors are genuinely seeking to alleviate suffering. At other times, attempts to engage our sympathy are to do with political actors securing our support for policies that may, in fact, be a source of great harm. When we see nothing of the suffering in a conflict, even when perhaps we know full well that there must exist suffering of almost unimaginable proportions, we must ask why that is the case and whose interests might be being served by that invisibility.

Our key challenge, then, is to become critical viewers of images and the absence of images. The challenge is as gargantuan as it is crucial for it is an essential first step in our defence against manipulation and deception.

Note

Thanks to Roland Bleiker and Stefanie Haueis for comments on earlier drafts.

7 Colonialism

Stephen Chan

The film *Tsotsi*, by director Gavin Hood, is set in Johannesburg and contrasts the modern central city with the slums of Alex and Kliptown. There was no need to build special sets for the film. The locations were as grimy as the director needed. Kliptown is the poorest part of Soweto, and was the site of the 1955 Freedom Charter. Thousands of people, in a remarkable piece of underground organisation, made their way across South Africa to the Congress of the People and signed a document that established the goals of liberation. It was an immensely social democratic document, and the delegates assembled for photographs before the police waded in.

No photographs survive of the Kliptown the delegates saw. The spot where they declared the charter is now Walter Sisulu Square, and the modern Soweto Hotel has balconies that overlook the site, and look out towards a giant funnel that houses an engraved version of the charter, funnelling sunlight upon its various sections. But all around the square and hotel, Kliptown is the same as it was in 1955 – with the curious addition of chemical toilets in street after street. It is the African National Congress (ANC) government's only substantial "improvement" to the suburb. One still meets aged veterans of 1955 in the streets, or at Bolo Blom's community centre, where they tell their stories and Bolo shows off his photographs of Kliptown as it is now, curating the identikit images of what it was like then (Rebergen and Rebergen 2015), before finally the ANC bulldozers come and "renew" the slum with "modern" housing units with toilets inside them. If the bulldozers come. Should they come, the residents will oppose them. It's their slum. They want sanitation, but they don't want destruction of the neighbourhood that houses their memories.

Liberation's monochrome

Bolo, his nickname taken from the Bruce Lee film *Enter the Dragon*, leads a mini-industry of liberation tourism. He takes visitors through the rubbish heaps and shanty houses where Mandela, Sisulu and others stayed or hid; where such and such a figure made a speech – he shows the exact stone upon which she stood – even the rusty barbed wire is the same wire from 1955.

It is clear Bolo is creative, but he is also rightly evocative. The photos of 1955 are static and are a record only of those who came, not to where they came. In them, Trevor Huddleston towers over almost everyone, the tall white priest who came to give solidarity, and it is remarkable how many women were dressed in their Sunday best. There are no photographs of the local Jewish butcher and Chinese greengrocer who fed the visiting masses – no photographs of the police wading in, and no photographs of the crowd

Figure 7.1 Kliptown house from where security forces controlled the movement of ANC dissidents, David "Bolo" Meyers

Source: David "Bolo" Meyers. Printed with permission.

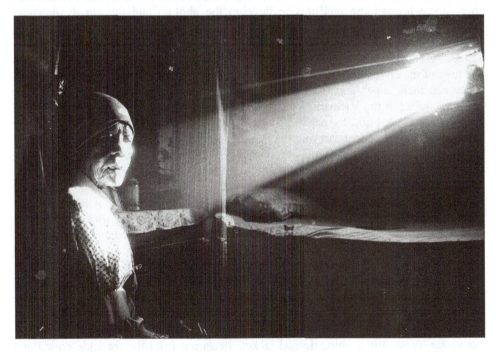

Figure 7.2 One of the Kliptown houses where ANC dissidents were hiding, David "Bolo" Meyers

Source: David "Bolo" Meyers. Printed with permission.

shielding figures like Mandela as they slipped away. If Mandela was there at all. But the legend would not be complete if he had not been there. The Soweto Hotel has wall-sized photographs of him, and of the South African and American jazz greats. The liberation struggle had music, but like the lack of photos, there are no surviving recordings of whether the delegates sang or what they sang. Bolo's photographs are destined for the wall of a museum, the pages of a glossy book to be sold in art shops.

That is one of the problems of photographs. They become static portrayals of a moment that is lost in terms of its energy and passion. They become icons that cannot give blessings to a new generation, and not one inured to moving images that can be manipulated, replayed, recolored, given music at the touch of a finger. The earlier the photographs, particularly of the struggle against colonialism, the more static they are. Underground and guerrilla fighters didn't take photographers with them into the field. They are photographed in rows at their camps where the photographer is away from danger. They always look gallant and determined. There are very few moments captured in a brilliant monochrome, perfectly framed, of terror or savagery. There is no Don McCullin (2003) of the colonial struggle, no embedded photojournalists of the struggle. The early shots of Ethiopian warriors in lion head-dresses and armour, mustering to fight the fully equipped Italian colonial army, do not show whether they hesitated before charging against machine guns. Wilfred Thesiger (1980), as a young student, took some of them. The Ethiopians won, incidentally, but there are no photos of the battlefields and the battle fatigue that comes from having lived while realising one is standing amid the bodies of those who did not.

Photography came into its own, that is, beyond the static moment of a record of who was there, with the advent both of lighter cameras (and those who could afford them and who had the facilities to develop the photos) and the slowly dawning international interest in colonialism and the need to decolonise. The vicious police intervention in Sharpeville in 1960 was captured brilliantly and in all its savagery by Ian Berry and featured in a double-page spread in *Life* magazine. But this was also the time of the civil rights movement gathering steam in the USA, and suddenly black faces and their hopes and fears were part of the same monochrome industry. The industry spread to the Vietnam War, so that the terror of a naked girl, later identified as Pam Thi Phúc, burnt by napalm in 1972 (taken by Huynh Cong "Nik" Ut) is the same anguish of a student carrying the fatally wounded Hector Pieterson in the Soweto uprising of 1976 (taken by Sam Nzima). Suddenly, oppression and the oppressed were news, and the news was spread, if not with sensationalism, then with the editorial need to have people say, "how horrible." Monochrome became a middle-class consciousness-raising device, and it was quickly supplanted by the moving image of telecasts from frontlines, until anything visual became a font of fatigue in the daily diet of news from everywhere, and news from nowhere as people became inured, tired and then resistant. Susan Sontag (2003) wrote of Jeff Wall deliberately contriving to pose photos that were brutal beyond reality in order still to infuse some horror in his viewing audience.

Where monochrome still had effect was when it dealt not in violence at all. Robert Lebeck's 29 June 1960 photos of the Congolese independence celebrations are a case in point. King Baudouin of Belgium is the guest of honour and stands in an open-topped car in a slow-moving motorcade. He is in a white uniform with a sword. A youngster, dressed in a shirt, tie and jacket, steels out from the roadside crowd and deftly takes the sword out of the king's scabbard. The king seems not to notice. For a few brief moments he is dancing in the street, the king's car having obliviously

Figure 7.3 Women looking through the Kliptown house from where security surveyed ANC dissidents, David "Bolo" Meyers

Source: David 'Bolo' Meyers. Printed with permission.

passed on, waving the king's sword. We don't know what happened to him. The final shots are of Congolese soldiers capturing him. But the photos are of a moment when the people, or at least one of the people, captured independence from the politicians who then plunged the country into war and subsequent generations of kleptomania – captured the symbol of rule from the decolonising king. Given how atrociously his predecessor King Leopold treated the Congo, and how much was looted, and how many people were enslaved, it is almost a tame moment, but an evocative one.

Visualising the struggle against colonialism

In 2015, an exhibition called 'Human Rights, Human Wrongs' was held in London, at the Photographers' Gallery, just off Oxford Street. It was ambitious and attracted a double-page spread in the *Guardian* newspaper – but was, in terms of the crowds walking down Oxford Street every hour, poorly attended. It worked off two texts: the first was Article 6 of the Universal Declaration of Human Rights on recognition before the law, and Frantz Fanon's (1986) work on how colonisation dehumanises the subject. The exhibition, over two floors, depicted dehumanisation and the fightback against it. It was a glorious recapitulation of moments of history – but was also totally decontextualised. Che Guevara is there alongside Martin Luther King. An anti-Vietnam War protest in the US is there alongside battlefield casualties in lands some viewers would never have heard of. Mexico was there alongside the uprisings in 1968 in Paris.

If Fanon wrote that cruelty is an omnipresent in colonialism and works precisely because it is casual, that is, it can be continued without remorse, then viewing its artefacts casually is its counterpoint. The exhibition was meant to give pause for reflection and sober acknowledgement that the West had much to answer for – but that struggle took place within the West as well. It showed bodies of dead Vietnamese guerrillas but also exhausted American soldiers, flopped on the ground, their arms outstretched like Christ-figures. Those who killed and those who died are undifferentiated. The complex dynamic of political calculation is not represented, and the air-conditioned and besuited direction of wars from the White House to the Kremlin – casual pointing of fingers towards a map and glancing up at flowcharts of casualties and expenditures – is matched by the casual turning away from one photograph to another, and a perhaps nervous exit to the coffee-bar below.

Even so, this exhibition from the archives of the Black Star Collection was an achievement. This is probably the best photo-reportage collection to do with international struggle. The exhibition was meant to be didactic, but what it did was to educate people that there had been struggles. Yet, individual monochromatic photographs do very little now. The specificity only makes sense by an immediate click-through to Wikipedia – and then the instant of "knowledge" passes. The assault of two floors of photographs from many struggles leads to a generalised *ennui*, without even the possibility of a plausible bank of knowledge that makes combined sense, and not a sense that can be divided into separated wars and causes and the inspirations to undertake risk and suffering in order to resist. There is neither critique nor invitation to latter-day action. All the action displayed has gone. It took place in other lands, at a different time. It is a different world. No doctrine and no solidarity and no remorse emerge into the surrounding daylight of Oxford Street and its shops.

Having said that, let me dwell on two photographs that were not in the exhibition. They are from the trial of Waruhiu Itote. George Rodger took the 1954 photo sequence where the guerrilla known as General China was flanked by four African guards. In the first photo, they are all are facing the camera except Itote, who is looking away, his face caught in a three-quarter angle although his shoulders are square on. He is wearing a short-sleeved white shirt and his hair is in the beginnings of dreads – the hallmark of Mau Mau fighters. He is gaunt with pronounced cheekbones, very dark, and he knows he is about to be condemned. There is another photo in Rodger's sequence, and that has Itote talking to his Asian lawyer, A.P. Kapila. Itote is in the same three-quarter profile, but listening carefully. Kapila, in full profile, is whispering into his ear. Whether this was the beginning of what became a post-sentence plea-bargain, or whether it was just another moment in the trial, we do not know. In the end, after being sentenced to hang, he was reprieved as a result of a peace-deal. He was kept in prison, and was incarcerated with Jomo Kenyatta – whom Itote had opposed as being too moderate. Kenyatta however looked after him in prison and taught him English. But this means that Kapila was talking to him in Kikuyu.

This cross-cultural resonance is lost in the photos, as is the fact that the white-shirted prisoner had been a member of the King's African Rifles, and had fought in Burma for the British, albeit in a segregated unit. In the photos, he looks like a bewildered clerk.

He was freed at independence and in 1982, I met him. I didn't know who he was. He was then 60 and the commander of the Kenya National Youth Service and, somehow, I was inspecting the young recruits. We had tea together. He poured my cup like an

English gentleman. Afterwards, my escorts from the host government ministry whispered to me in hushed and awed tones: "Do you know who that was? That was General China."

In a way, they were waxing ironic: they had taken a Chinese person to meet General China. In another very clear way, they were genuinely in awe that they had met the liberation legend. At the time, I was simply meeting another fat commander of another para-military, a uniformed apparatchik who had seen better military days if he had seen any military days at all. One of the officials even took a photo of me with General China, although I never saw it. If it had been on display at the 2015 London exhibition, it would simply have depicted a military square somewhere in Africa. A Chinese man in a light green suit, white shirt and tie – a Chinese man with longish hair – is shaking hands with a taller, portly, uniformed African officer in khaki. Perhaps they are smiling. Perhaps they are sharing a joke – in English. But the photograph would have told nobody anything about the African officer. There were ranks of young uniformed recruits in the background, standing to attention in straight lines.

Itote had not been a gentleman guerrilla. Part of his job was to execute "traitors." He committed atrocities. He struggled for freedom. He was regarded by the British colonial authorities as a terrorist. After independence, the whole Mau Mau insurrection was hushed up, as Kenyatta wanted to portray a national image of a modernising and "civilised" Kenya. Writers like Ngugi wa Thiongo railed against this suppression of a national history where the fighters were marginalised and those who had not fought grew rich and powerful. Only in very recent years has the British colonial effort to suppress Mau Mau become evident in court cases brought against the British government of torture of suspects. Photos emerged of the suffering then. They had a momentary shock value. We were terrible then. We must compensate them now. Then we must move on. And now we have. We have more wars and more photos and, above all, more moving images to be getting on with and, really, nothing shocks us any more – or not for very long.

Photographs as oxygen of publicity? Monochromes as mono-realities

This is the problem Susan Sontag (2003) grappled with as she began her book, *Regarding the Pain of Others*, with a quote from Virginia Woolf that we should be horrified and disgusted by photos of war, carnage, death and mutilation. Woolf certainly was when she saw photographs from the Spanish Civil War and wrote about it in her *Three Guineas*. She wanted war abolished (Sontag 2003: 3–4) – something that seems to us today both desirable but also totally naïve. But, with the advent of non-state actors taking on state actors, the canvas of war has moved on. Such momentary horrors we might have are reserved for the moving images on the internet of executions, beheadings of kneeling men in orange by masked men in black. The colours are calibrated and the desert backdrops form neutral settings for the clash of colour taking the fatal stroke to colour. These are often spread on Facebook sites so that the surrounding messages and pictures are sufficiently trivial to sensationalise the executions – and the comments reflect the sense of sudden horrified sensation. Then Facebook takes down the videos on the grounds of their extremity and the publicity they give the militant causes. But the removal of the pictures does not stop the violence.

So we enter a modern realm where the image is an incidental phenomenon to wars that continue whether we see anything of them or not. The fact that often those executed are journalists whose editors wanted us to see wars, because they assumed we also wanted to see them, or thought we should see them, becomes the debate – not the stopping of wars but, at very best, whether the oxygen of publicity for them might slow wars or perhaps change the tactics of horror used in wars, and that we would want wars to slow down, but are too worldly in the twenty-first century to believe they can be stopped.

There is no more need for Jeff Wall's elaborate exaggeration of war's effects, so well described by Sontag. Despite the limits of gruesomeness imposed by editors, images leak. There is nothing that can any more be exaggerated beyond their awful reality. What this means when we look back on the still photos of colonialism and the struggle towards decolonialism is that we view a series of often disconnected and static images in a monochrome that also allows us to constitute a mono-morality: we express disgust and move on, not to any anodyne safety from such images, but to the real-time, vibrantly coloured, moving, almost interactive images of our contemporary horrors. Of the history of nations being violently born long ago, we see nothing any more but their places in archives or galleries.

Or we move on to vacuous modern pursuits of triviality. As Don McCullin put it of photojournalism, "it's had it. Nobody wants to look at spreads of dying children," when there are cleavages of fake-tanned starlets to look at (cited in Cadwalladr 2012).

The dead Hector Pieterson is remembered in a memorial museum in Orlando, Soweto. Pam Thi Phúc (now Kim Phúc) lives in Canada. As for General China, his appointment to the Kenya National Youth Service was a sanitised rehabilitation of those who fought the British as insurgents – those loosely called the Mau Mau. He was not given a proper rank in the army: just in a para-military with community development, as opposed to full military functions. He was not celebrated in public. He had a good salary and pension. He died in 1993 at the age of 71, of a stroke. He was a farm manager at that time. Somewhere in the countryside far from the cameras of the city. I suppose I should say he is very static and monochrome now. But I could find no photographs of his funeral.

Note

As this volume went to press, Bolo Blom, a.k.a David 'Bolo' Meyer, passed away.

8   Compassion fatigue

Susan D. Moeller

A thought experiment

Look at the screengrab in Figure 8.1. This woman's picture appeared in an October 2014 photo essay in the online site of the British newspaper the *Guardian* (Chaim 2014). Do you want to look at the woman – or do you want to look away? Do you find yourself examining her chest or scanning her eyes? If you learn that she is a Syrian refugee who was attacked with acid in her hometown, do you want to know more, or is it enough to know that?

Figure 8.1 Syrian woman burned with acid. *Guardian,* 16 October 2014

Source: 'The sons of war: Syria's refugees – in pictures,' *Guardian*, 16 October 2014, www.theguardian.com/media/gallery/2014/oct/16/the-sons-of-war-syrias-refugees-in-pictures/.

The image of the woman is arresting, even in this black-and-white version. But in the original published colour photograph her flowered dress and shawl add to the power of the image – the femininity of what she is wearing highlights the angry puckering of her scars. The photo silently documents this woman's past, yet does so incompletely. The woman is looking just a shade beyond the camera lens: is she sad, or resigned, or depressed? Does the scarf covering half her face hide greater scarring, or does it signal something else?

It's not easy to look at refugee faces such as hers, even in the privacy of one's own environment. But it's also hard to turn the page. The woman's gaze demands attention, it asks that viewers respond to her plight – her look asks that viewers react to her as an individual, that viewers take at least some responsibility for her welfare.

But if those who look at the faces of the refugees don't know how to help relieve the refugees' distress, how quickly do the viewers click off the page? And if the viewers do move on with their lives, are they left feeling guilty? How long does the guilt last? A minute? Hours? Days? As a consequence of the guilt that is felt, how eager are those viewers to look at more photos of Syrian refugees, to listen to, watch, read articles on the conflict? Are they perhaps a little wary, thinking that if they see other images of refugees or read more about the conflict those accounts will trigger more guilt, will make them feel a bit more helpless, a bit more powerless?

If this thought experiment connected with any of *your* actual reactions to this photo, then you now have a sense of why people might contract what has been called "compassion fatigue."

Compassion fatigue: emotions on overload, but no outlet for relief

At its most basic, "compassion fatigue" is a response to seeing or reading about too much horror or tragedy for too long.

What is too much? How long is too long?

Compassion fatigue is not prompted, per se, by what many would consider a surfeit of coverage – say wall-to-wall 24/7 coverage – of a breaking news event. Compassion fatigue can occur after a brief period of reporting or after an extended period. Compassion fatigue is typically triggered by audiences' belief that they themselves are helpless in the face of the trauma described – trauma often graphically depicted via photographs and videos.

In that respect, compassion fatigue, as I explained in my eponymous book, is not always what it is taken to be (Moeller 1999). Compassion fatigue does not describe what is happening when audiences turn away from explicit images out of revulsion for the horror shown. Nor does it describe the scenario when political reactions keep audiences away from a story – when liberal or conservative sensibilities are offended by the way a story is told. Nor does it explain the situation when simple boredom with a news account alienates readers and viewers.

I recently read one junior scholar argue that "compassion fatigue" couldn't possibly explain the media's coverage of a specific event because the journalists at issue did express compassion for the victims of the tragedy. But the "theory" of compassion fatigue is not reliant on whether journalists show sympathy for those they write about, nor does the theory suggest that audiences who succumb to compassion fatigue are or will become psychopaths, with no feelings for victims of trauma.

Compassion fatigue occurs when a reader's or viewer's emotions are deeply engaged by a tragedy, but there appears to be no easy or meaningful contribution that the individual can make in response to the news of tragedy – no five dollar contribution, no vote, no online petition will fix the problem.

Compassion fatigue is essentially a response to emotions on "overload." People respond to that overload by shutting down all that troublesome input, by turning away from the news. Compassion fatigue may be especially prevalent when audiences are physically distant from the crisis being covered; audience members feeling as if they can't do anything to ameliorate a crisis can trigger a reluctance or even an aversion to being confronted with more news and more coverage of the same set of events.

And compassion fatigue can be triggered when similar situations repeat in a droning monotone like the Talking Heads' refrain: "Same as it ever was, same as it ever was, same as it ever was." If the previous famine / civil war / massacre / refugee crisis was never resolved, what hope is there for this one? In this sense, compassion fatigue emerges out of people's belief that they – or perhaps anyone or even any group or institution – are inadequately equipped to do something meaningful to *make the tragedy stop* . . . so they try to stop the inflow of images and stories of the tragedy. They avoid the news of the situation, turn the page on a story of it when it appears, click past teaser photos, or simply, fail to click through at all to any sites they assume might be triggers for distress.

Then there's the compassion fatigue that is a response to what people perceive as their own moral failure. Those at especial risk are those who keep up with what's happening in the world, but for whom items in the news are interchangeable data points in a never-ending scroll. In other words, it's not the activists among us who typically fall into this kind of compassion fatigue funk; it's not those who staff the Red Cross volunteer shelters, or work on the Habitat for Humanity teams, or those who tithe their earnings to send to charity. It's the rest who are at risk: those who are casual and oft-times frivolous visitors into others' lives. Those who are comfortable in their own status quo. Those who don't want to change their lives even if doing so might be a small contribution towards resolving others' tragedies. Those who don't want to confront the fact that they do not invest much time or many resources into tragedies beyond their own personal borders. Those who would prefer not to be reminded of their own shortcomings. Those who avoid the news stories that remind them.

Those are the people who fall into the stupor of compassion fatigue.

Images of a crisis

Media share responsibility for the disheartening phenomenon of compassion fatigue but they also have the power to provoke the public into feeling compassion and empathy for distant others, even well into an ongoing event.

That latter takes strategic planning across news cycles as well as innovative thinking about why and how audiences can come to care about the news. Media flex that power rarely.

Some digital outlets try to direct viewers' short attention spans by using the tools of clickbait. Consider the headlines of three of the top BuzzFeed News stories on Syria in mid-2015: "ISIS propaganda magazine briefly listed for sale on Amazon" (Dalrymple II 2015), "ISIS justifies taking of Yazidi 'slave-girls' as concubines" (Hernandez 2015), and "A suicide bomb instructor in Iraq accidentally killed his students" (Clayton 2014). It's easy to imagine surfers deciding to read those stories, but hard to imagine that such stories would prompt readers to care more about what was happening in Syria and its surrounding neighbours.

Then there are other ways media try to break through and capture the public's attention. In early 2015, actor, director and activist Angelina Jolie (2015) wrote an op-ed in the *New York Times* about the desperate circumstances of the Iraqi and Syrian refugees she had visited in her role as special envoy of the United Nations High Commissioner for Refugees.

"What do you say," she wrote, "to the 13-year-old girl who describes the warehouses where she and the others lived and would be pulled out, three at a time, to be raped by the men?"

The *New York Times* online illustrated Jolie's shattering op-ed with two images. At the top of the page was a photograph of Jolie in a refugee camp, smiling in response to a multitude of hands reaching to touch her own outstretched ones. Dressed in a black down jacket, with hair dishevelled, Jolie was not glamorous. But she was, still, recognisably the celebrity Angelina Jolie.

Then, midway down the article, was a line drawing, effectively a cartoon, of sad children, and at their feet a small city of UNHCR tents.

The editorial decision to run those two images illustrates a continuing concern in the news media's coverage of international stories: how should editors and producers tell the news fairly, accurately and immediately, especially of long-running and tragic events, when the audiences appear to be dazed by the flurry of daily facts and the unremittingly grim images of what's happening?

Angelina Jolie's op-ed made the case that Americans should "help Syria's neighbours bear the unsustainable burden of millions of refugees." While a casual consumer of her opinion piece might not have stopped to assess why those two images accompanied her article, media-literate readers could have asked: why did the opening photo picture the author of the opinion piece rather than the Syrian and Iraqi victims of ISIS who are the focus of the op-ed? Shouldn't the audience be shown what Jolie was describing? Shouldn't the public have been given some "real" glimpse of the horrors about which Jolie wrote, rather than a cartoon version of traumatised children? (Disclosure: I used to draw op-ed cartoons for the *Washington Post*.)

Jolie's article was compelling, passionate, informed. The choice of that photo of Jolie alongside her words was jarring, however. Did the *New York Times* shy away from depicting visually what Jolie put into words? Did the editors think a photo of the "mother with tears streaming down her face" that Jolie described would be less interesting than the one they published of Jolie? Who was the news here? Jolie, or the Syrians whose stories Jolie told?

Perhaps the *New York Times* believed that its readers were so surfeited with news from Syria that they would turn the page on this article – or ignore the story altogether – if they didn't see a picture of Jolie or if she was not the headliner. The *New York Times* did literally put Jolie prominently in the photo accompanying the piece, as well as in the page's (sub)headline: "A New Level of Refugee Suffering: Angelina Jolie on the Syrians and Iraqis Who Can't Go Home." The editors' assumption must have been that Jolie's small-font byline alone would not be noticed by their readers. The editors made the decision to arrest the wandering eyes of the *New York Times'* readers by making Jolie's face and name prominent – and by actively promoting the story on its home page and via its daily listservs and app. Jolie's full name appeared three times on the first screen of the online story – and the opening word of the first two paragraphs was the word "I."

The threat of compassion fatigue suggests one reason at least why the *New York Times* page editors made the choices they did about the Jolie op-ed. The *Times* editors must have believed – and perhaps had the data to prove – that their online visitors (and print subscribers) were not reading about Syria and Iraq. So how to change their audience's "been-there, seen-that" attitude? Reel the public in with a celebrity name at the top.

It's clear that the United Nations and Jolie herself understand how the game works. After all, celebrity UN ambassadors have been around for a long time: not just Angelina Jolie, Shakira and Emma Watson in our world, but Audrey Hepburn and Danny Kaye in past decades. Celebrities are news, and media follow the "biggest" celebrities wherever they go, even if it's to the ends of the earth. Audiences are curious to see how celebrity ambassadors manage in the world's crisis areas, and the audiences' curiosity about the famous names brings attention to the zones of disaster and catastrophes they visit. The lesson learned by UNHCR, UNICEF and other UN agencies is that signing up attractive celebrities known for being light and entertaining (as well as smart and passionate) is good business. Not only do they attract media attention, but putting celebrities centrally into stories of global challenges offsets the otherwise leaden and depressing news from the crises themselves.

Angelina Jolie's op-ed in the *New York Times* can then be understood as just one more example in a long history of examples of how celebrities have been used to attract audiences to remote tragedies. (The Jolie op-ed trended as a top story in the paper and attracted 514 comments.) The celebrification of so much news may not, then, be entirely caused by the public's low tastes for gossip and rumour; it may be encouraged at times by mainstream news outlets themselves and abetted by some of the most "serious" media institutions in the world. Jolie's op-ed, a powerful story in arguably the globe's top news outlet, is one continuing indication of the impact of what I have called "compassion fatigue" on media coverage of international affairs.

The impact of compassion fatigue on media

The possibility of an audience reacting to coverage of a newsworthy, but traumatic event by "turning the page" helps explain how media choose – upfront – to cover such events.

Faced with telling the story of pain and trauma – especially one at a geographic and psychological remove from their home base – media outlets worry that members of their audience will turn away from their publication and go to some other news outlet because the viewers and readers feel too emotionally exhausted, too helpless, too weary of unending disaster, too morally bereft. Even the *threat* of some of their audience coming down with "compassion fatigue" can cause editors and producers on all platforms to tinker with their coverage. And the data available from digital platforms means that today editors and producers know if and when their audiences *are* avoiding coverage of an event – and they know what has kept audiences tuned in to (or turned off from) similar events in the past.

The consequence of certain audiences turning away from difficult news stories is that the media have had to figure out how to forestall audiences avoiding those stories. Newsworthy, but tragic events can be covered in many ways, from formulaic, to gee-whiz, to sensational. Traumatic events can be treated as just another who-what-where-when-why-how story, with bland, neutral-voiced summaries of the news, and with numbers accounting for what happened, including such "facts" as how many died. Coverage can also be tipped to prioritise the diplomatic consequences of an event, the consequent security status of the location, the regional implications of the situation, the economic fallout, and the often favourite approach of media outlets: what does this event mean for us (the audience)? Why should "we" care? It's that latter approach, for example, that gives rise to headlines such as the *Toronto Star*'s front-page breaking story on 18 July 2014, about the Malaysian Airlines plane shot down over Ukraine: "Canadian among 298 dead in crash."

Media coverage can also be "in your face," especially when dramatic images exist of an event. Images can be played as so much visual effluvia, deployed for their quick hit, attention-getting, noxious shock value. The problem however is that while publishing them often works – there can be significant short-term benefits, with a quick uptick in readership and viewership – there can be a significant long-term downside for the event itself and for journalism writ large. It's hard to hold an audience at fever pitch. Horrible images may grab attention, but audiences rarely stay around after they've seen the climax. The result is that desperate faces bleed into other desperate faces, and little is learned beyond the lesson that, yes, something awful has again happened to a population of people far away. And by reporting the news in such a way, journalism itself has ratcheted up the temperature of sensationalist coverage, only to have to ratchet it up again the next time.

Yet it's not a mistake for media to put trauma front and centre – large photos, slide shows, videos, multimedia, narrative accounts of suffering can all personalise what has happened for an audience geographically and psychologically distant. If care is taken not to horrify viewers and readers with too-graphic accounts, but to use imagery and stories to prompt empathy as a compelling lead-in to nuanced accounts of what has happened, then highlighting the trauma can be a "best" approach to coverage. Audiences tend to remain with news stories when they find the coverage absorbing and personally meaningful. Media outlets that know how to nurture their audiences through all the ramifications of an event, and do so over time, can be rewarded with audiences staying with the coverage.

So what's the takeaway? That this kind of multi-variant approach occurs more rarely than it should. Even given the exigencies of the audience, deadlines and the budget-pressed business, there is less coordination and less mindfulness about the range of coverage of events than there should be.

News outlets need to show the faces of those who have been caught in the maelstrom of conflict and disaster. Some in the audience will look away, others will struggle with compassion fatigue. But ultimately the bottom line in news is fair and accurate, nuanced and compelling coverage. Media outlets need to push back their fear of compassion fatigue. They need to deploy all means possible to bring attention to news that matters, including working with celebrities on occasion. Ultimately the test of coverage should be: "Is the news outlet prioritising its news values differently than the 'news' itself would suggest, because of the fear that some in the audience will turn aside?" If the answer is "No," then the means taken to bring the story to the public eye are appropriate.

9 Culture

William A. Callahan

The attack on the satirical magazine *Charlie Hebdo* in 2015 demonstrated how visual artefacts play an increasingly important role in shaping international political events and our understanding of them. This event also showed the uneasy relation of culture and politics, especially when cultural activities in civil society become engulfed in global politics.

'Culture' is a complex idea, which has shifted in meaning and significance since the end of the Cold War. In the 1990s, the process of globalisation eroded many national cultures as it challenged state sovereignty. But in the post-ideological climate of the 2000s, there has been a reassertion of state sovereignty, both in international fora and in everyday life. Consider, as an example, how asserting and safeguarding "cultural sovereignty" is a key issue for China's new National Security Commission. Increasingly this is the global norm, rather than the exception. Culture is (re)nationalised in the service of the state for domestic politics. At the same time, culture gets "civilisational-ised" for global politics, as shown by the debate over Huntington's "clash of civilisations" thesis.

I examine the visual politics of the veil as an illustration of how visual images, artefacts and performances are a key site for this uneasy mix of culture and global politics. Rather than trying to nail down "culture" as a distinct and coherent analytical term, I will show how cultural sovereignty invokes cultural governance by the state, and also provokes cultural resistance in various spaces.

Veiling/unveiling

It is not an exaggeration to say that veiling constitutes one of the most provocative political and cultural statements in the world today. Reactions are strong, both in defence of veiling and attacking it; and these reactions are expressed in personal space, community space, national space and global space. Veiling here is not only a religious but also a social practice, done by specific women at specific times and places. It reflects political notions of concealing and revealing, dark iron curtains and bright transparency, veiling and unveiling.

While most analyses of visual culture look to photographs and film, I explore how the veil provokes visual global politics as a material artefact. Analyses of the veil characteristically turn this material object into a symbolic discourse, and then use hermeneutic methods – for example, interpreting the Qur'an and/or French law – to reveal its true meaning. Alongside this hermeneutic analysis, I will also explore what happens when you take the materiality of veils seriously, and appreciate them as

82   *William A. Callahan*

artefacts where visual politics is represented, performed and experienced through more embodied, affective and everyday encounters on the local, national and world stage.

The guiding image of the veil is of a woman wearing a burqa, a black garment that covers the face and the body, somewhere in the Middle East. Such visual cultural performances produce essentialised self–other relations, which in turn evoke other sites of identity/difference: race, ethnicity, religion. A woman recently described how, when she wears a headscarf on the streets of London, people assume that she is "Arab," while she describes herself as a "white British Muslim convert:" "People outside the Muslim community have a hard time believing I'm white. It's like I can't be white and Muslim. If I didn't wear the hijab they wouldn't have a problem accepting I'm white" (Amer 2015).

Veiling here is a visual cultural performance that marks communities of race and religion in the popular culture of everyday adornment; it is a choice, an assertion of a woman's "cultural sovereignty" at the personal level. It is much more than an image – it is an embodied interactive participatory performance.

Yet such sartorial politics is not merely a personal choice. States are involved as well, both in prescribing dress codes in some Middle Eastern countries, and proscribing them in some European countries. Saudi Arabia and Iran do not agree about much, but both have official dress codes for women, and morality police to enforce them. According to Iran's Islamic establishment, the "hijab is protection from sin" for both women and men, and the morality police see themselves as a "kind of hijab for the society of the Islamic Republic" (*Guardian*, 19 December 2013; 27 May 2015; also see Eltahawy 2015: 49).

Figure 9.1 "A white British Muslim"

Source: With permission from Amena Amer.

Rather than being an obstacle to public life, here the veil provides women with "security" to enable them to enter the public sphere, especially when society is seen as a space haunted by dangerous moral temptations (see Heath 2008). Indeed, for many, to unveil is to reveal oneself as "naked" (Eltahawy 2015: 46). The cultural logic also appeals to global self–other relations: "pious Iran" versus "the Great Satan." Sometimes it is directly invoked in international politics: in 2015 Iran's reformist President Hassan Rouhani was criticised for the loosening of morality rules as a way to attack his government's nuclear agreement with the Group of Six world powers (*Guardian*, 27 May 2015). Yet even within Iran, such fundamentalism lends itself to ridicule: one young woman (in the *Guardian*, 27 May 2015) recently criticised the morality police: "what right do you have to say whether my hijab is proper or improper? Can you show me the hijab-o-meter they issued you when you took this job?"

In *Headscarves and Hymens* (2015), Eltahawy recounts her personal experience of veiling and unveiling in the wider context of daily life in Egypt, London and Saudi Arabia. Many women celebrate the veil in terms of emancipation and security, and criticise white Western feminists for exacerbating Islamaphobia through their misunderstandings of the practice (Scott 2007; Heath 2008). Thus when Eltahawy asks "Why do you hate us?" one expects a similar East versus West argument. Eltahawy, however, reframes the issue to Arab men hating Arab women. For her (2015: 10), the veil is seen as an expression of patriarchal power relations, in which women are seen as the "walking embodiment of sin" and where "clerics [are] obsessed with female orifices." Morality police here are not promoting piety, but cynically using their power to commit sexual harassment at Islam's holiest site in Saudi Arabia: the veil didn't protect Eltahawy, rather it actually enabled the police officer's anonymous grope (2015: 50–1).

Likewise, the Islamic Republic's "cultural revolution," described in Satrapi's graphic novel *Persepolis*, shows how sartorial politics can be very personal and very threatening: among Iranian women debate was not between East and West, but between "the veil" and "freedom" (Satrapi in Heath 2008: 248–9).

Veiling is also politically charged in France. Curiously, much like in Iran and Saudi Arabia, the French state appeals to legally defined dress codes to control veiling: in 2004, it banned girls from wearing headscarves in public schools, and then banned public burqa-wearing in 2011. Visual global politics invaded French beaches in Summer 2016 with the burkini ban. Supporters of the bans argued that the veil is problematic not just as a practice, but conceptually as well: it poses a challenge both to the liberal ideological order of French secularism (*laïcité*, laicity) and to the liberal world order in the global War on Terror. This concern was expressed in terms of "women's rights," and figured veils as a sign of female submission in the patriarchal culture of Islam. While many girls and women in France argued that they had freely chosen veiling, the counter-argument was that one cannot have free choice in such a male-dominated culture and society. French girls, according to this logic, needed to be saved from their family and their community.

At the local and global level, the veil ban invoked a "clash of civilisations" logic that sees Islamic values and Western values as incompatible. While it is popular to criticise Huntington's monolithic view of culture, a leading Muslim cleric actually confirmed the incommensurability of Islam and laicity (Joppke 2009: 31, 112–13). French president Jacques Chirac thus saw the headscarf as a "kind of aggression" and a state commission concluded that veils were part of Islam's "permanent guerrilla war against laicity" (in Joppke 2009: 4, 47). This concern was not just domestic, but is part of a global visual economy of veiling: some feared that "the experience of Iran was about to be imported into France" (Scott 2007: 176). Veil bans thus were criticised by many for exemplifying a deeper Islamophobic racism (Scott 2007; Heath 2008).

Globally, many Muslims saw France's veil bans as an attack on Islam as a whole. Indeed, the crusade against the veil has Orientalist overtones: Conquering the East by de-veiling Muslim women is a recurring Western male fantasy from the colonial period, which continues in the present. While the Muslim clerics may see unveiled women as "naked," this unveiling/naked dynamic is also found in paintings by Manet, Renoir, Matisse, and Picasso (Heath 2008: 14). In the realm of popular culture, colonial Algeria produced a whole genre of postcards for French soldiers that showed unveiled women as naked (Alloula 1986). More recently, the veil – and unveiling – is a popular topic for cartoons in *Playboy* magazine (Shirazi 2001: 39–61).

Like in Iran and Saudi Arabia where morality police saw the absence of veils as a threat to moral order and social order, in France veiling became a matter of cultural sovereignty, cultural governance, and resistance to it. Iranians resist by challenging the veil, and in France one resists by veiling. Indeed, some feminists turn the question around to ask why white men (and women) continually feel the need to save brown women from brown men (Zuhur in Heath 2008).

But like with *Charlie Hebdo*'s controversial Muhammad cartoons, the veil also became a site of art, fashion, satirical activism in France. "Princess Hijab" uses graffiti art "to spark debates about fundamentalism and feminism" by drawing veils with a black marker pen on fashion posters in the Paris Metro (Christafis 2010).

Two young women, who call themselves "NiqaBitch," protested the veil bans through a video of themselves walking around Paris dressed in niqab that covered their faces and upper bodies, along with hot pants and high heels that displayed their bare legs.

Figure 9.2 Visual cultural resistance by Princess Hijab

Source: Anonymous artist, *Guardian*.

Figure 9.3 Screenshot of "NiqaBitch shakes Paris"

Source: Anonymous artist, http://vimeo.com/15747849

The video shows how they get "thumbs up" support from many on the street, and even a request for a fun photo from the policewoman guarding France's Ministry of Immigration and National Identity. Here timing was crucial – when the law went into effect a few months later, the same policewoman would be obliged to fine them for the same veiling activity (NiqaBitch 2010). Princess Hijab's guerrilla art and Niqabitch's performance art both are fascinating sites of resistance, mixing the sacred and the profane to question how culture, visuality and tolerance work in Republican France. They show how veils work as material artefacts to performatively provoke visual global politics.

Veiling/unveiling beyond East/West in China

To recount, the debate over veiling/unveiling in Europe and the Middle East can be summarised as debates between women and men, and between East and West. Many supporters of veiling see it as a practice that distinguishes Eastern/Islamic/Arabic communities from Western ones. Many critics of veiling call for the liberation of women from patriarchy. This figuration makes sense when the debate is located in Europe and the Middle East. But what happens when we relocate it to China, a non-Western country with an ethnic minority group – Uyghur – that is Muslim? How does it complicate the notions of Islamic modernity as an alternative to the West, and struggles within liberalism?

In many ways, the situation in western China displays the cultural governance/cultural resistance dynamic seen in France. Veils were not really an issue until the 2000s, when Uyghur women started re-veiling as part of the global Islamic revival that includes this global Islamic fashion trend. Beijing became concerned about this cultural practice in 2009, after riots erupted in Xinjiang between Uyghurs and Han Chinese. "Islam" in Xinjiang thus was increasingly understood as a foreign threat to China's national security and cultural sovereignty, and the veil was seen as a visual provocation of what Beijing calls the "Three Evils" of separatism, extremism and terrorism.

Like in Iran and France, such cultural performances were seen as a legitimate site for state intervention. Sartorial engineering is not new in China. During the Cultural Revolution (1966–76), people were required to wear the military-inspired Mao suit. In 2001, the "Han clothing movement" emerged as a grassroots movement to resist what is seen as the Manchu "bastardisation" of Chinese civilisation. While sartorial engineering in Xinjiang is a local issue, it is also located in the global visual politics of national security. The concern is foreign terrorism, and the goal is social stability along China's Central Asian frontier. Since 2012, the veiling practices of Uyghur women has been a topic of intense study by Han men and women in the party-state (see Jin 2015). The concern is that vulnerable women are being "brainwashed" into wearing the veil by foreign fundamentalists. De-veiling thus is presented as an issue of women's liberation, which has the added benefit of fighting the "Three Evils" of separatism, extremism and terrorism (Leibold and Grose 2016).

China is interesting because it combines the Iranian proscription with the French prescription of female fashion: the visual culture of the veil is presented as the problem, and the visual culture of an alternative authentic sartorial form is presented as the solution. Rather than relying on just legal measures to ban veils as in France, Beijing looks to its own kind of morality police. Tens of thousands of party cadres were sent around Xinjiang to urge women to discard the "regressive fad" of veiling. This campaign was positive in the sense that women who de-veiled were rewarded with cash prizes. It was negative in the sense that these red arm-banded party cadres created intelligence files to monitor uncooperative women. Likewise, citizens who report veiled women to the authorities are rewarded, and stores that sell cloth suitable for veiling are penalised (Jin 2015; Leibold and Grose 2016).

In addition to proscribing veils, in 2011 the Xinjiang government launched an $8 million five-year "Beauty Engineering" project to prescribe the proper dress for the veil-free "new-style woman": atlas dress, doppa hat and braided hair. As an official newspaper (cited in Leibold and Grose 2016) explains:

> Women represent the love and beauty of the world and they should personify beauty and serve as emissaries of love. Wrapping oneself up is not only not beautifying, it can also destroy one's body and mind. One's heart and soul can wither due to long periods in the dark.

While fashion is a site of cultural resistance in France, it is a site of cultural governance in Xinjiang, where officially organised fashion shows encourage women to "expose their pretty face and allow their beautiful hair to flow free" (see Jin 2015; Leibold and Grose 2016). The Beauty Engineering project yielded benefits at the national level in 2013, when a non-veiled Uyghur woman won the Miss China beauty pageant. The new official version of authentic garb for Uyghur women gained international exposure in a fashion show at the China-Eurasia Expo held in Urumqi (2012, 2014, 2016).

Certainly, in China there is a wide range of resistance to both veiling and de-veiling. Some Uyghur agree that veils are an improper import from the Arab world, and some women complain that they have been pressured by their husbands to veil. However, rather than see it as foreign and backward, many Uyghur women celebrate veiling as an important activity in global Islam's modern cosmopolitan fashion.

The Chinese case also shows the problems of cultural sovereignty in both domestic and international politics. Beijing responds to threats to cultural sovereignty not just by controlling national identity – by prescribing what (not) to wear to be Chinese – but also controlling ethnic/religious identity – by positively defining the proper ethnic dress for Uyghur women. Here visual culture (i.e. the veil) is not simply a problem; as the Beauty Engineering project shows, visual culture is also the solution. Like in other countries, the Chinese party-state seeks to nail down the meaning of the veil through official definition and moral policing; and like in other countries, the more it seeks to enforce a stable meaning, the more veiling/unveiling resistance it creates. Once again, culture, visuality and global politics bleed into each other in complex ways; but the Chinese experience complicates the East/West framing of the debate in unexpected ways, making us think again about the proper role of culture in state–society relations.

The visual politics of the veil

I have consciously avoided the problem of explaining "culture" as a distinct and coherent analytical term. Instead, I explored the controversial dynamics of the veil in visual global politics. Like "culture," the veil means different things to different people. Many analysts thus conclude that we should not concentrate on veiling because it distracts us from the real issues of the day: the physical violence and poverty suffered by women (Heath 2008), racism in the West (Scott 2007), and the political contradictions that define the liberal polity (Joppke 2009).

For me, this replays many of the ideological arguments of the twentieth century, where "culture" was largely seen as a distraction from the true nature of class, race and humanity in the ideologies of communism, fascism and liberal democracy. Rather than help us to clarify the essence of these grand ideological narratives, the provocation of veiling shows how culture can move us in emotional and bodily ways. As any engaging cinematic experience shows, it is difficult to reduce analysis of visual culture to accurate representations. The performance – in public veiling, as in public diplomacy – invokes an excess of meaning beyond what can be expressed in words and encapsulated in ideology. Here we go beyond hermeneutics to appreciate veils as material artefacts that "do" politics through more embodied, affective and everyday encounters on the local, national and world stage. Hence rather than reveal the truth-value of veiling, we can appreciate the "cringe-value," the uneasy excitement, of the heterogeneous encounters it provokes (Callahan 2015).

Even so, veils are a challenge not only to the liberal polity, but also to larger ethical debates. Consider how, on the one hand, Derrida encourages us to provide unconditional hospitality that welcomes the "Other" into our home, without either judging them or seeking to convert them to the self (Derrida and Dufourmantelle 2000). On the other hand, Levinas (1969) stresses how we must not simply tolerate difference, but actively engage it through person-to-person, face-to-face, eye-to-eye encounters. Bleiker, Campbell and Hutchison (2014) likewise conclude that to have an ethical relation with refugees as people (rather than as invading hordes), we need to see their faces, up close and in person.

But what of the veil: does it deny this ethical encounter? Are veiled women actually judging non-veiled women as impious (Eltahawy 2015; Heath 2008)? Or does it mean that we need to think about the limits that the visual poses on global politics?

10 Democracy

Mark Chou

Alexis de Tocqueville was said to have detested America at first sight. The frenetic pace of New York City, where his boat had docked in May of 1831, overawed his senses. Never having set foot outside Europe, the bustling city streets appeared to him as garish and chaotic. There was none of the usual order or mannerisms which he, a French aristocrat, was accustomed to at home in Versailles. America was part of the New World. It was also a democracy.

Everything that Tocqueville saw in those early days only worked to validate the views he had held about democracy (and America) up till that point. It was a government run by fools for fools. While the people he encountered seemed congenial enough, it worried him that no one possessed any real sense of direction or purpose in life. Not even America's chief political leaders – those whom Tocqueville met included Andrew Jackson, John Quincy Adams and Charles Carroll – showed much foresight or discipline. The country's politics, in this sense, was as chaotic as its city streets. Not long after he landed, Tocqueville arrived at an important insight: if what he had seen thus far was anything to go by, then democracy was surely doomed to fail.

But in his account of Tocqueville's travels, the renowned British scholar David Runciman tells us that the young aristocrat did eventually see things differently. Though it took some time, Tocqueville discovered that democracy had unseen virtues. Hidden away from everyday view was a political system that worked, and worked well (which is not to say that democracy was free of problems). "This was the most important thing Tocqueville discovered on his travels," writes Runciman (2013: 2): "democracy is not as bad as it looks." Sure, outward appearances did not fill Tocqueville with much confidence. On this matter, he believed that the aristocracies of Europe were much better at putting on a show. Yet looks at face value can be deceiving in a democracy. Political philosophers since Plato have known this fact. Now, Tocqueville knew it too. But whereas Plato had thought that what was obscured in a democracy was potentially dangerous, Tocqueville took the opposing view. Writing in the first volume of his *Democracy in America*, published in 1835, Tocqueville (2000: 221) surmised that democracy's "faults strike one at first approach, but its qualities are only discovered at length."

Tocqueville implicitly shows us that there is a visual dimension to the politics of democracy. There are things about democracy that can be seen instantly and things that can only been seen with time. One of the defining features of a democracy is its transparency – an assumption as commonly held in Tocqueville's day as in ours. What you see is what you get; that is what sets democracy apart from other systems of government. As Thomas Paine (2000: 181–2) once wrote: "Whatever are its excellencies and defects, they are visible to all." That is democracy's genius: thanks to transparency, everything is visible. Yet Tocqueville's observation contradicted what many at the time celebrated as democracy's greatest strength. What he observed was that democracy is not transparent at all. From one moment to the next, one never really sees what is truly going on. In other words, there are things which a democracy reveals, and things it conceals. Transparency is merely an illusion.

This insight into democracy's lack of transparency did not come to Tocqueville immediately. In fact, as we learn, it was only revealed after a period of observation. As Tocqueville and his companion, Gustave de Beaumont, travelled through America – heading from New York to New Orleans and then back again – he had ample time to observe and to reflect during the many train, steamboat and horseback journeys they took. The pace of their travels gave Tocqueville a unique perspective on American society.

In a recent essay on slow theory and democratic representation, the prominent democratic theorist Michael Saward makes reference to an exhibit in the "Moderna Exhibition" at Stockholm's Modern Museum called *My Country (Somewhere in Sweden)*. The exhibit, as Saward (2011: 2) recounts, used "images, stills, and sound on a number of adjacent screens" to capture "a slow ride on horseback over several weeks, heading south through Sweden." At first glance, the work appears unremarkable, offering spectators an almost slow-motion visual representation of the minutiae of the Swedish landscape as viewed by the artist Ann-Sofi Siden on horseback. But for Saward, the work's purposefully curated pace made spectators painfully aware of the small things we miss when travelling at speed. Speed things up and Siden's landscape becomes a blur. She might have saved time travelling by car or aeroplane. But she would have lost sight of her surrounds. More importantly, as Saward points out, Siden's art work "shows us that moving slowly through town and country may prompt an unusual, perhaps unsettling, sense of unfamiliarity with otherwise familiar features of life and landscape." The point, returning to Tocqueville, is this: had he travelled any other way, had he not given himself the time to see and absorb all that was around him, perhaps the crucial insights into the hidden nature of democracy in America might have been missed.

Both transparency and time are central to how we see and perceive things. It takes time, as Tocqueville learned, to see things as they really are. Even when something appears transparent, like democracy for instance, slow observation is needed to see both what is seen and unseen.

I now reflect on the visual politics of democracy through its troubled relationship with transparency and time in our own age. While contemporary democracies have become no more transparent than the fledgling democracy Tocqueville observed almost two centuries ago, there is today a popular sentiment that, even at its worst, democracies are more transparent than they have ever been. Particularly in an age where vast amounts of information and images can be instantly accessed and transmitted with the touch of a screen, it has become easy to think that things are more apparent than they actually are.

Taking cues from Tocqueville, I want to critically explore what impact the instantaneous transmission of information and images – said to ensure ever greater political transparency – has on our capacity to sense what may be unsettling and unfamiliar about democracy today. To address this question, I will also draw on a visual medium, the popular Netflix series *House of Cards*, to illustrate what can be at stake when democrats fail to take the time to see past the illusion of transparency.

The trouble with transparency and time

Democracies are meant to be transparent. At least that is what we are told. Today, when we think about what makes democracy distinctive, it is characteristics such as openness, accountability, and representativeness that we think of. Transparency is essential to all these attributes. Citizens must be able to *see* who their representatives are, and what they are doing, if they are to keep them accountable. So much is this the case that there is now a widely held belief that "transparency has become synonymous with democracy" (Hollyer, Rosendorff and Vreeland 2011: 1191).

But even in the age of democracy as transparency Tocqueville's insights have not completely lost their currency. Against the popular discourse of open and accountable governments, there continues to be a "veil of ambiguity" that shrouds the inner workings of democracy from public view (Flinders 2012: 26). It may seem odd given what we know about democracy. Yet as scholars like Joseph Stiglitz (2002) caution, democracies have never been completely transparent beasts. Unlike authoritarian regimes, democratic governments that expose things as they truly are risk potential popular backlash. Given this, the supposed free flow of information in democracy can sometimes be less free than we might imagine. Truth has to be doctored now and then to hide what is displeasing to public sentiment.

This is particularly the case in today's multimedia-saturated democracies. We may believe that there is greater political transparency when televisions, laptops and mobile phones allow us to see and be seen from a great distance. And certainly Twitter feeds and images captured with mobile phones possess the capacity to instantly expose otherwise hidden government secrets to millions of people. Yet media-savvy governments are not oblivious to these capabilities. Governments everywhere have, by necessity, also become more adept at manipulating reality, making it "multiple and mutable" (Keane 2013: 108). The Australian democracy scholar John Keane has a term for this. For him (2013: 108), most established democracies today are also "mediacracies," that is to say, a system of "organized political fabrication" that has "all popularly elected governments . . . engaged in clever, cunning struggles to kidnap voters mentally through the manipulation of appearances."

Now more than ever, the public needs new ways to "keep an eye on power and its supposed representatives" (Keane 2013: 103). Luckily, or so Keane (2013: 78) believes, there is an increasing "multitude of monitory or 'watchdog' mechanisms operating within a new galaxy defined by the ethos of communicative abundance." WikiLeaks, the best known among these monitory mechanisms, has become renowned for ensuring "a climate of transparency and accountability necessary for an authentically liberal democracy." These monitory mechanisms and institutions, many of which are controlled by everyday private citizens, are said to promote transparency because they provide "publics with extra viewpoints and better information about the operation and performance of various governmental and non-governmental bodies" (Keane 2009).

If Keane can be charged with an oversight, though, it is perhaps his eagerness for what the rise of monitory democracy represents. Keane might have us believe that the growth of monitory mechanisms and tools coincides with a growing global democratic transparency. However, this is not the case. Monitory democracy may well be part of the solution posed by the "new galaxy of communicative abundance." But it is also part of the problem. The prominence of organisations like WikiLeaks and whistle-blowers like Edward Snowden is directly related to the increasingly sophisticated ways in which governments have become accustomed to operating in the dark. The same technology that empowers publics to capture and disseminate images of government brutality in real time likewise enables governments to make their dirty laundry instantly disappear. In this way, the age of monitory democracy may just be the latest iteration of democracy's troubled relationship with transparency (or the lack thereof).

Regrettably, there is now little hope of even seeing the so-called veil of ambiguity, let alone past it, without the aid of these networked monitory mechanisms and tools. Politics has become so fast-paced, so complex and so globalised that the only way for everyday citizens to catch up is to speed up. This is what the monitory mechanisms and tools which scholars like Keane write of enable us to do. There is no disputing that the recent pictures and videos tweeted and texted out of places like Syria and Egypt confirm that the speed of monitory tools can save lives and expose the underhanded tactics of governments. The scrutiny the international community was able to bring to bear on these wayward governments was due in large part to the role played by everyday monitory democrats wielding monitory tools. Without these monitory and networked technologies, publics would simply be swallowed up by the vast amounts of information, the sophisticated surveillance technologies wielded by governments and corporations, not to mention the 24/7 news cycles constantly being hurled at them (Navarria 2014).

Yet the very speed of these tools, which helps us respond to the pace of contemporary politics, to see the otherwise hidden secrets and violations of governments, is not politically neutral. As Siden's installation shows, some things will simply be lost – or be less visible – when they are sped up. This is as true of democracy as it is of the Swedish landscape. It may now seem counterintuitive, but democracies function best in slow motion. Unlike tyrannies, democracies are not conducive to speed (Barber 2000). Just because vast amounts of information, pictures and videos are instantly available to us does not mean we require any less time to observe and deliberate with each other. To truly see what is going on, we need to be prepared to take our time. The more complex the situation, the more we need time to deliberate.

John Stuart Mill (1991: 109) once wrote that "the mere time necessarily occupied in getting through bills, renders Parliament more and more incapable of passing any, except on detached and narrow points." The good democrat takes their time, is Mill's point, even in the face of the "sheer impossibility of finding time to dispose of." To this end, the monitory mechanisms and tools which scholars like Keane have been defending may be helping citizens to see more – more quickly. But without slowing down, what is seen will soon become a blur, which is its own kind of veil. And transparency will continue to remain nothing more than an illusion.

Peering behind the veil of ambiguity: *House of Cards*

Jumping to a television series may seem a puzzling move, especially one said to encourage audiences to binge-watch entire seasons at a time. But the current Netflix series *House of Cards*, I think, reveals precisely what can become invisible to democrats if they fail to slow down when all that surrounds them is speeding up.

In this hugely popular television show about American democracy and political deception, series creator Beau Willimon plays on the idea that democracies are meant to be transparent. In a third season episode of the series, House majority Whip turned Vice President turned the President of the United States Francis Underwood tells the

American people in a televised speech that "for too long, we in Washington have been lying to you." He is there to come clean he says; to admit to the public that politicians like himself have become accustomed to deceiving their electorates in order "to stay in power." "That ends tonight," Underwood tells his citizens: "Tonight I give you the truth."

But the transparency Underwood offers is merely the illusion of transparency so often produced within a democracy. Politicians like Underwood may talk regularly about truth and accountability. Sometimes, they will even admit to their own untruths and deceptions. Yet all that only adds to the veil of ambiguity, of which there is much in this series. But *House of Cards* does make an effort, imperfect as it is, to pierce through that veil on the occasions it has Underwood flaunt to us – the unseen viewing audience – what he cannot so frankly say to his fictional constituents.

During such moments, the action pauses; it almost stops in fact. Underwood turns to the screen and speaks candidly to disclose what he really thinks and desires. In one such moment, during the series' second season, Underwood peers through his car window and confides to the unseen audience: "Do you think I'm a hypocrite? Well, you should. I wouldn't disagree with you. The road to power is paved with hypocrisy. And casualties. Never regret." These rare intervals of actual transparency make for fascinating viewing because they brazenly, sometimes comically, expose the open secret that democracy is not transparent. This deceit, or so the series has us believe, is shameless and structural. What is more, it is just barely concealed.

In making this point, *House of Cards* also makes an important point about time. And it is this: there is a game of deception going on; it is not actually hard to see if we take the time to look. That many contemporary citizens cannot see, choosing instead to live with a sort of democratic myopia, may be due to the pace of politics that leaves them with little time to pause, to slowly contemplate and to see what is actually right before their eyes. In the series' opening credits, viewers are offered an unusually profound glimpse at our pace of life and what can become visibly obscured at that velocity. Viewers of the series will be familiar with the time-lapse images of DC in which all but the infrastructures of America's democracy are sped up. There is a rushed blur of individuals in cars and on walkways who, it seems, have no time to slow down and see things clearly.

We cannot see them through the blur. Just as importantly, they cannot see their political representatives, nor what actually goes on just behind the emblematic monuments of American democracy – despite it being right there before their eyes.

The visual politics of democracy

Not all that long ago, Paul Virilio (1986) made the observation that speed has the power to alienate and dissociate us from each other, as well as from the world that surrounds us. The faster we move through time and space, the less of any particular thing we are able to see. Finally, when all is blur, we lose touch with what is real. There is now a genuine danger that as the pace of life – and politics – speeds up, we are losing sight of what democracy really is. We may think what we are seeing – periodic elections, accountable representatives and monitory mechanisms and tools that ensure greater transparency – is real. We may think that just because we are seeing more, more often, we have seen everything. But that, as Tocqueville discovered almost two centuries ago, is merely part of the illusion that blinds people to the inner workings of democracy. The visual politics of democracy should begin with the realisation that transparency only makes some things visible. Citizens should not think that simply because something is transparent that there is nothing hidden from view. Precisely when all appears clear and instantly visible is when citizens should slow down, pause, to see if what is there is there at all.

11 Development

Kalpana Wilson

I examine here how development institutions visually represent women in the global South. I explore, in particular, how the figure of the adolescent girl is presented as a vehicle for "investment" in future growth and an ideal neoliberal subject of development. From the 1990s onwards policies promoting the use of "positive," active images of "poor women in developing countries" were adopted by international NGOs, donor governments, the World Bank and other development actors. This was the result of several closely interrelated factors: first, widespread critiques of existing – and still prevalent – representations of "Third World women" as a homogeneous category of "passive victims;" second, the transformation of concepts of participation, empowerment and agency; and third, a growing emphasis on extending women's labour as a strategy of global capital accumulation.

I examine these processes through a discussion of a series of videos circulated by the ongoing Girl Effect campaign. I show that these new visualisations of "agentic girls" in the global South contribute to and extend racialised and gendered regimes of representation and rely upon and reinforce, rather than challenge, multiple relations of inequality.

"Smart Economics," gender and neoliberalism

The neoliberal approach to gender equality in development is epitomised by the World Bank's slogan "Gender Equality as Smart Economics" (World Bank 2006; World Bank 2011). Smart Economics is premised on the assumption that women will always work harder, and be more productive, than their male counterparts; further, they will use additional income more productively than men would. Therefore, greater gender "equality," understood as an increase in women's participation in labour markets, will have a significant impact on economic growth.

Neoliberal approaches to gender and development are deeply racialised in their production of hyper-industrious, altruistic entrepreneurial female subjects. They are now represented alongside, while by no means fully displacing, earlier constructions of "Third World women" as passive recipients of development (Mohanty 1986; Spivak 1988). Mohanty (1986: 338) argued that Third World women are constructed within gender and development discourses as "a homogeneous 'powerless' group often located as implicit *victims* of particular socio-economic systems." In this depiction, women are waiting to be liberated by Western feminists, in a reiteration of missionary women's narratives of rescue and salvation (Abu-Lughod 2002).

Critiques of these representations have contributed to a much greater emphasis on identifying women's agency and the active role that women play in the context of development. But this shift, which goes back to the late 1980s, has been incorporated into a liberal discourse that sees women as individuals who exercise "free will" and maximise self-interest. The emphasis on women's "choices" and rational decisions to conform to gendered expectations or collude in the oppression of other women neglects both the power of gendered ideologies as well as the persistence of structural inequalities and violence. The global tendency of women to work harder than their male counterparts and to expend more of their resources on their children is celebrated as "efficiency," without acknowledging the oppressive social and economic pressures which compel women to do so (Wilson 2008).

The increasingly ubiquitous citation of women's agency and empowerment was consistent with a shift in neoliberal development policy in the 1990s. The World Bank and other institutions sought to address deepening poverty, but in a way that retained the neoliberal model. Empowerment and participation became closely related to ideas of individual responsibility and self-help. The burden of responsibility for mitigating poverty was thus shifted on poor households, and specifically poor women, who were simultaneously directly subordinated to the disciplines of the market in new ways (Molyneux 2008).

As a result, the last two decades have seen a growing emphasis on the extension and intensification of women's labour as central to sustaining neoliberal capital accumulation. On the one hand, the global contraction of workers' share in profits is achieved through an increasing use of waged and unwaged labour of women who are increasingly often responsible for the survival of poor households (Perrons 2012). On the other hand, the further incorporation of women into global labour markets is seen as an important on-going source for expanded reproduction of capital (Wright 2006). These two processes taken together form the core of a gendered understanding of "accumulation by dispossession" (Harvey 2004; Hartsock 2006). Rather than lifting gendered constraints on women's time and mobility or challenging the unequal division of household labour, these processes actually depend on and further deepen existing gendered inequality.

In this context, the hyper-industrious entrepreneurial "girl" from a low-income household in the global South has emerged as a central visual trope of twenty-first-century neoliberalism. Just as representations of contented and productive women workers in colonial enterprises "symbolically affirmed the need for empire" (Ramamurthy 2003), so these contemporary representations implicitly confirm the "empowering" potential of neoliberal globalisation and erase questions of structural injustice (Wilson 2011).

"She will do the rest": Representing adolescent girls in development

The rise of the "girl" in development discourse and policy has been markedly corporate-led (Chant 2016). Although the idea that girls' education could be an "investment" in future reductions in the birth rate can be traced back to a 1992 speech by Lawrence Summers, then Chief Economist at the World Bank (Murphy 2012), it was the Nike Foundation, set up by Nike in 2004, which arguably led the way in focusing on adolescent girls in the global South as the "solution" to the "problem" of development more generally. The Nike Foundation was set up in partnership with the Population

Council and subsequently established partnerships with the World Bank and the UK government. Nike's notion of the "Girl Effect" has since been adopted and promoted much more widely (the Girl Effect itself became an independent organisation in 2015). In 2007, several UN organisations established an Interagency Task Force on adolescent girls. In 2008, the World Bank founded its Adolescent Girl Initiative (Koffman and Gill 2013: 86). This has been followed by campaigns such as the UN's Girl Up, and Plan International's "Because I am a Girl," as well as multiple corporate social responsibility projects by transnational corporations (Murphy 2012).

I now look at a series of short online videos produced by the Nike Foundation. "I dare you" (Nike Foundation 2006) directly addresses perceptions of girl children and young women in the global South as victims and objects of pity. The video deploys the notion of the "gaze" with a voiceover that states: "I dare you to look at me without pity, fatigue, dismissal. . . . I dare you to rethink what it means to look at a girl." This is accompanied by a series of shots of girl children (some clearly much younger than the target group of the campaign) silently and expectantly returning the viewer's gaze. The message here is clearly not that women are already acting to change the conditions of their lives, but that they have the potential to be the individual instruments of change if only the viewer recognises it and gives it shape and direction.

The disembodied adult woman's voice – clearly marked by its inflections as African – then explains that a girl is "not a burden, not an object, but the answer." A series of statistics relating to the impact of girls' education on population increase, levels of HIV, malnutrition and economic growth are now superimposed on shots of girl children and women working alone (carrying water, digging soil) in various rural landscapes. The use of these scenes of gendered labour is ambiguous: the focus is on the desirability of girls' education (implying an alternative to the child labour we see), but simultaneously they underline "developing world" women and girls' gendered propensity for hard work and altruism as the reason why girls' education is an effective means of development.

The latter is made most explicit in the final "statistic" we are presented with: "when an educated girl earns income she reinvests 90% of it in her family, compared to 35% for a boy." Thus in the course of two and a half minutes the video moves swiftly from appropriating critiques of the racialised notion of the passive and victimised "Third World woman" to promoting a new racialised figure of the Third World woman as an instrument of neoliberal development who continues to be self-sacrificing, while now regarding gendered familial obligations as an "investment" (Wilson 2011).

"The Girl Effect" (Girleffect 2008) marked the project's launch of the Girl Effect "brand" and the removal of all reference to the Nike Foundation. This video was groundbreaking, particularly in the context of development publicity. It was based exclusively on an extremely pared down and simplified textual narrative in which individual capitalised words flash on an empty screen. This, along with a complete absence of any markers of place or culture, would appear to avoid some of the more obvious forms of objectification. Yet paradoxically, as a result of its generality, it is also free to deploy racialised tropes familiar to the viewer from more explicit photographic images and texts used by NGOs and the media. In the central sequence in the video, the word GIRL appears in the middle of a white screen and soon several tiny versions of the word FLIES are "buzzing" around her. The word BABY appears. A second later the word HUSBAND in very large letters falls on top of her, followed in quick succession by the appearance of HUNGER and HIV.

This memorable chain of effects also serves to locate the causes of suffering (HUNGER and HIV) firmly and exclusively at the level of the local, the cultural (i.e. early marriage) and the individual, and in particular in the person of the oppressive HUSBAND.

The format allows the viewer to become a powerful initiator of change, responsible for releasing and directing the entrepreneurial agency of the "600 million girls in the developing world." The viewer is invited to "pretend that you can fix this" and, as if at the click of a mouse, the FLIES, HUSBAND and BABY fall away and the GIRL becomes a microfinance entrepreneur who miraculously banishes poverty from her community, generating global STABILITY.

The speed with which these processes occur in the video is clearly intended to make links with popular cyber-culture. It suggests that the potential viewer has very little time to "waste" and wants quick and visible "results." We see here an implicit contrast between the Nike Foundation's market-led "business" ethos and earlier development initiatives. The "developing world" GIRL is now an "investment" whose gendered propensity for labour can be instrumentalised to the point where her very life is speeded up: no sooner do we "put her in a school uniform" than we see her "get a loan to buy a cow" and "use the profits to help her family." This is made explicit in the penultimate slogan: "Invest in a girl and she will do the rest."

Not only is the education of girls instrumentalised as "Smart Economics" (Chant and Sweetman 2012), but the "Girl Effect" model continues, rather than challenges, pressures on women to be hardworking and altruistic. Representations of girls and women as having an infinite capacity for labour, now recast as entrepreneurship and free choice, are both racialised and gendered (Wilson 2011). As Murphy (2012) argues, this figure, "typically represented as South Asian or African, often Muslim – has become the iconic vessel of human capital."

The Girl Effect consistently portrays girls as at risk from "cultural" practices such as early marriage, or from highly racialised figures of predatory men in their own communities. What we do not see, however, are the structural causes of poverty. Nor are existing gender divisions of labour questioned. In "Smart Economics" (Girleffect 2014), a hypothetical girl in rural Ethiopia is portrayed as having to do "five times as many chores" as her brother, at the expense of her studies. This situation is then shown to be mitigated simply by the provision of a fuel-efficient stove, with no redistribution of "chores." We next see her simultaneously cooking and studying, symbolically embodying the racialised hyper-industrious and entrepreneurial female subject.

Meanwhile adolescent girls' own bodies, sexuality and fertility are repeatedly represented as the most significant threat to their potential productivity, invoking the population discourses which are central to "Smart Economics" (Wilson 2015). Women in the global South are portrayed as "excessively reproductive" and requiring inter-vention (Wilson 2012). This is particularly explicit in "The clock is ticking" (Girleffect 2010), in which a black stick figure, marked as a girl child by her "two bunches" hairstyle and triangular "dress," abruptly grows breasts when she "turns twelve," faces early marriage and childbirth, and, most strikingly, is then menaced by sinisterly elastic black hands, which extend predatorily towards her body from all directions. Having escaped these through the simple "solution" of school attendance, the figure rapidly transforms into a mother "when she's ready," raising a "healthy" daughter of her own. Again, the "girl" is represented as conforming to historically gendered patterns of social reproduction, but now on terms dictated by global capital.

Gendered and racialised visions of development

The Girl Effect is significant in that it establishes the adolescent girl as a key agent of development. It marks the transition from liberal to neoliberal feminism in development. After an initial investment in her human capital, the responsibility shifts entirely to the individual figure of the girl: "she will do the rest," says the video (Girleffect 2008). Any critique of structures is rendered irrelevant. Even liberal feminist critiques, which highlighted gendered discriminations that ostensibly prevented markets from functioning effectively, are now silenced. The focus on adolescence, which is rapidly replacing any consideration of adult women's lives, is thoroughly neoliberal: intervention via education is constructed as necessary only to produce the idealised neoliberal subject, who will be able to negotiate unfettered and unregulated markets with ease, while simultaneously assuming full responsibility for social reproduction.

In this sense, the Girl Effect and other similar visual campaigns also address their largely young and female target viewers in the global North in new ways: they are no longer asked to help or save, but to *create* new agents of development. The "girl" in these discourses is always understood in relation and in contrast to her already empowered Northern counterpart. "Girls" in the North are invited to endorse feminism but only in relation to the South. They themselves are represented as "more educated, socially connected and empowered than ever before" (Koffman and Gill 2013: 92). This difference is also marked in the representation of sexuality, where the "global girl" as sexual subject and self-commodifier (McRobbie 2008) stands in marked contrast to the "localised" girl in the global South, whose sexuality is presented solely in terms of the threat posed by her "dangerous" and "excessive" fertility, which potentially undermines her productivity for the global economy (Switzer 2013).

12 Digital media

Sebastian Kaempf

Digital media technology started to emerge in the early 2000s in the form of smartphones, interactive websites, and social media applications such as Facebook, Twitter, Flickr, Instagram and WhatsApp. The ensuing technological sea change has fundamentally transformed the global media landscape, multiplying and diversifying the type of actors, voices and images that participate in, and influence, global politics. Alongside traditional media platforms, such as newspapers, radio and television, digital media has brought about an unprecedented multitude of information and visual perspectives on global politics. We now live in a visual age like never before.

This recent development – which I examine here in the context of the visuality of conflict and war – has led many commentators to highlight the democratising potential of digital media. They stress that the multiplication and diversification of voices and visual perspectives allow for more accurate insights into the politics of conflict. Digital media has certainly fragmented the global media landscape by allowing for more diverse visual perspectives. But the processes through which the visuality of war arrives at the screens of our smartphones, tablets and computers are far less diverse and random than most commentators want to make us believe.

I examine the arguments for and against these alleged democratising effects of digital media, highlighting four particular aspects that limit what we actually see about today's wars.

The hyper-visual dimension of digital media

The emergence of digital media technology in the early 2000s has fundamentally transformed the global media landscape – and with it the visualisation of politics and war. Up to the early twenty-first century the nature of traditional "old" media technology, such as newspapers, radio and television, required vast specialised infrastructures, massive financial investments and high levels of human expertise in the form of professionally trained journalists, editors, typesetters and producers. As a result, these forms of media could only be afforded by a small number of actors, such as empires, states and more recently media conglomerates (Kaempf 2013). Add to this a clear structural separation between sender and receiver (Rid and Hecker 2009), and you end up with media monologues through which information is diffused by a small number of powerful producers to a mass of passive consumers. This technological configuration meant that the visualisation of war remained relatively narrow because states were largely able to control the flow of images that reached the media-consuming public (Kaempf 2013).

The digital media revolution has shaken the structural foundations and hierarchies of the old media landscape. Its interactive nature has dissolved the old separation between sender and receiver. Its cheap and user-friendly nature has enabled the average citizen to become a media consumer *and* producer at the same time.

Digital media technology has not only multiplied but also diversified the number of media actors and possibilities. There are now numerous ways of tweeting, texting, posting, messaging, uploading, commenting and linking media content. By the end of 2014, it was estimated that – for the first time – there were more mobile phones on the planet than people. In 2016, Facebook announced that it had 1.7 billion subscribers. If that were a country, it would make it the largest on the planet, ahead of China and India. Within the space of a few short years a completely new and all-encompassing media environment emerged: a new digital ecosystem.

The visual dimension of digital media technology is particularly important. To realise why, it is worth putting recent changes in a broader historical context. The photo camera was invented in 1826 by Joseph Niépce. The oldest surviving photograph depicting a human being dates back to 1838, taken by Louis Daguerre, showing the Boulevard du Temple in Paris.

Because of the long exposure that was required, it took Daguerre over 10 minutes to take this one photograph. A lot has changed since 1838. Not only has camera technology become faster, cheaper and easier to use, but also cameras and images have

Figure 12.1 The Boulevard du Temple, Louis Daguerre, 1838

become ubiquitous thanks to smartphones, social media platforms and digital devices. There has been an astronomical increase in the number of photographs taken and uploaded. In 2014, Snapchat users shared 8,796 photos online every second. In 2013, users uploaded 350 million images to Facebook every day. On Flickr, 670 million public pictures were uploaded in total in 2014. This is 1.83 million pictures per day on average (Michel 2015). In just a single minute on the web, three days' worth of video is uploaded onto YouTube (Woollaston 2013). Overall, in 2014, we were uploading an average of 1.8 billion pictures to Facebook, Flickr, Snapchat and WhatsApp every single day (Woollaston 2013). To put it differently: every two minutes, people are uploading more photos than ever existed in total 150 years ago (Eveleth 2015).

Within a few years, digital media has generated a historically unprecedented visualisation of our daily lives. And while the majority of images uploaded today are either selfies or images of pets (Eveleth 2015), this new visual dimension extends also into the realms of conflict. Never before has war entailed such a visual dimension – a dimension that will continue to increase since a big part of the human population is still to gain access to the internet.

This emancipatory dimension of digital media technology has generated a multiplicity of new perspectives on and visualisations of war. Citizen journalists, individual soldiers, activists, NGOs, street protestors, non-state armed groups and freelance journalists all have contributed to a more diversified image of conflict. They have lent their voices to a conversation about war that had previously been confined to a handful of powerful media outlets.

But there is a paradox: despite the abundance of images we know relatively little about the visual dimension of politics and war. Although more and more research on images is now emerging, David Campbell (2007: 358) remains correct in saying that we have yet to grasp what the visual dimension of politics means.

The democratising effect of digital media's visuality and its counter-tendencies

For many commentators, the rise of digital media constitutes a process of democratisation. Everyone with a smartphone and internet connection can disseminate news. The ensuing dynamics hold the potential to offer more balanced views of world politics. We can now disseminate and engage in a multitude of perspectives, allowing us to get clearer, better and more objective insights into world politics. For instance, the Syrian civil war exposed us to a multitude of media actors, ranging from the embattled Assad regime to opposition forces, ISIS fighters, average citizens, religious leaders, humanitarian aid workers, international human rights groups and global news networks.

While each of these multiple insights comes with its own political agenda and spin, the sum of all seemingly allow for a more nuanced and arguably more accurate depiction of the conflict.

Digital media has certainly diversified the global mediascape. But the processes through which images arrive on our screens, and through which they enter into our minds, are far less diverse than some commentators suggest. At first sight, this might seem counterintuitive. But looking behind the screens of our computers, phones and tablets reveals technological processes and political dynamics that limit which visual representations can appear on our screens.

I highlight four factors that compromise our ability to experience the promise of digital media in its full diversity.

First, while digital media has shaken the foundations of the global mediascape, there still remains a vast discrepancy between established news outlets and digital ones. Traditional outlets, such as television and newspapers, still attract significantly higher numbers of readers, listeners and viewers. While younger generations have been the biggest driving force behind the growth of digital media, very few of these outlets can rival established ones in terms of mass consumption and followership (Mitchell and Holcomb 2015). Established news outlets are perceived to be more objective, professional and ethical (Louw 2010; Gillmor 2010). They remain trusted media actors and thus hold significant political power.

Second, digital media technology, and the internet in particular, has become increasingly controlled by states. Two decades ago most governments barely thought about the internet. Very few even had internet policies. Fast-forward to today, and cybersecurity has become a key priority for most governments. This development has generated a new market, where the interests of states and the internet economy converge around the need to collect, monitor and analyse as much data as possible. Consider how companies that market facial recognition technologies service both Facebook and governments, from the CIA to authoritarian regimes (Deibert 2013). Internet firms, which were once associated with wiring the world, are now offering off-the-shelf software for social media infiltration, computer network attacks and mobile-phone tracking that have the potential to turn into weapons of repression and warfare (Deibert 2013).

These developments heavily influence the ability of digital media to serve as tools for social mobilisation and dissent. A few years ago, many saw the so-called Arab Spring as a symbol for how digital media can contribute to ending authoritarian rule.

The reality is more complex, as seen in the case of Syria (Morozov 2011; McChesney 2013; Shirky 2008). The same online dynamics that challenged governments can also be used by governments. Groups sympathetic to the Assad regime employed off-the-shelf malware crime-kits that infiltrate social networks in order to gather data that then led to the identification, arrest and murder of dissidents (Deibert 2013). This was not an isolated incident. In many parts of the world dissidents and human rights activists have been targeted by advance spyware, manufactured by Western companies (Deibert 2013). Content filtering, social network mining, mobile-phone tracking and even computer network attack capabilities are being developed by Western firms and put into the hands of policy makers. These digital tools are often used to limit democratic participation, identify dissidents and infiltrate the networks of adversaries.

The growing role of the state in cyberspace means that digital media platforms are increasingly governed and policed. In turn, dissident voices are finding it harder to reach their target audiences.

Third is the role of algorithms, which limit the availability of otherwise very diverse information in digital media (Podolny 2015). Asked by a journalist about the algorithmic logic of the Facebook newsfeed, Mark Zuckerberg (in Kirkpatrick 2011: 296), the company's director, answered that "a squirrel dying in front of your house may be more relevant to your interests right now than people dying in Africa."

Facebook and most other digital media platforms organise information according to this logic because algorithms largely determine how information flows online (Luckerson 2015). Take Google: if two people, at the same time and location, use the same search engine to search for the very same word, such as "Syria," they tend to get different search results. The reason for this is that Google uses 57 different signals to generate personally tailored information, ranging from the user's location, the type of device and browser used, to the user's digital footprint and browsing history. The *Huffington Post*, the *New York Times*, and *Yahoo! News* now all use personalised newsfeeds (Podolny 2015; Jolly 2014).

This means that we have moved into a world where digital media shows us things that it thinks we want to see. This might, of course, not be what we want or need to see. As Eric Schmidt (cited in Jenkins 2010), CEO of Google, said: "It will be very hard for people to watch or consume something that has not in some sense been tailored for them." In other words, the algorithmic nature of digital media platforms generates filters that decide, for the media consumer, what enters a screen and what is edited out (Jolly 2014; Luckerson 2015). The user no longer decides what is relevant, important, uncomfortable or challenging to his or her worldview. Instead, with algorithms increasingly deciding what we get to see and what not, digital technology has moved us further away, rather than closer, to the idea of generating a diversity of views about world politics.

The fourth factor that limits the democratising promise of digital media is the behaviour of the media consumer her-/himself. While consumers have more news sources available than ever before, they tend to feel overwhelmed by the sheer number of them (Mitchell and Holcomb 2015). Average consumers tend to rely on news sources that confirm their existing political, religious or ideological worldviews (Gillmor 2010). They have become increasingly disinclined to consume news that challenges their assumptions or that contradicts their worldviews, thus inevitably leading to more one-sided and narrow political positions (Mitchell and Holcomb 2015).

The visual politics of digital media

Digital media has fragmented the global mediascape and allowed for a multitude of voices and visualities to emerge. But the processes through which images and texts arrive at our screens are far less conducive to promoting true diversity. Although images abound on the internet and in social media, they do not necessarily help media consumers to gain a more critical understanding of politics and conflict. Disconcerting as this might sound, it also highlights that citizens and societies need to become more media-literate and take an active interest in the politics of media technology. We need to be far more aware that looking behind the screens of our computers and phones reveals technological processes and political dynamics that – knowingly and unknowingly – determine which images we see and which we don't and how this shapes our understanding of politics and conflict.

13 Diplomacy

Costas M. Constantinou

Diplomacy is commonly associated with the artful use of language, continuous negotiation, and dialogues between states and/or other actors (Nicolson 1963; Watson 1982). As a verbal means of communication, it entails a specialised lingo, carefully employing words, coded terms, euphemisms and loaded silences to make representations and induce specific actions or inactions with regard to international relations. By practising diplomacy, one can speak for or against a specific side, policy or cause, develop and spin narratives, draft written agreements or gloss over disagreements through constructive ambiguities.

The visual plays a crucial role in diplomacy, even though diplomacy is usually seen as predominantly a language affair, emanating from the long historical association of diplomacy with oration and advocacy. Traditionally, the visual has figured as part of the dignified milieu or the ceremonial trappings of power that support the linguistic environment of diplomacy, an honorific assisting substantive verbal and written work. But the importance of the visual goes beyond ceremony, with scholars highlighting numerous historical and contemporary cases that illustrate the impact of visual culture and non-verbal communication on diplomatic practice (e.g. Cohen 1987; Jönsson and Hall 2003).

The theme of this short chapter is visual diplomacy, focusing on the ethical implications of "enframing" and the "distribution of the sensible." That is to say, it examines visual engagements that hide or remain oblivious of what they exclude, or how their disclosures support but also limit our understanding of the world (Heidegger 1977; Rancière 2004; Bleiker 2009). I examine these conceptual issues and illustrate them through practical examples. I first look at how a classic painting can be used to reflect on what diplomacy is or should entail. I then investigate how diplomatic practices have changed at a time when digital communication provides states and non-state actors with a range of new opportunities to create and disseminate images. I call this new period the "post-protocol era."

The diplomatic frame and its exclusions

The painting in Figure 13.1 is often depicted as a classic "picture" of diplomacy. Scholars show it for pedagogical purposes or as embellishment, illustrating the broad range of diplomatic activity (e.g. Berger 1972; Barber 1979; Der Derian 1987; Carroll 1993). But we can learn a lot more from this painting. How does diplomacy emerge, what kind of diplomacy is framed into being, and what alternative possibilities are erased? This painting is an exemplar of how the representation of diplomacy is not given and fixed but dependent on how states – and other actors and spectators – recognise and interpret it.

In a detailed analysis of the painting I stressed that by elevating the ambassadorial identity of the portrayed men, a diplomatic framing takes place through which particular diplomatic readings are rendered plausible and legitimate (Constantinou 1994, 1996). *The Ambassadors* – crucially, not titled as such by Holbein – was painted more or less at the same time as the publication of Machiavelli's *The Prince* (1533). Both works have been invariably read to reflect Renaissance power shifts, the rise of secular humanism, the advent of the territorial state, the challenges of the Reformation and the progressive decay of medieval political authority. Holbein's painting is said to encapsulate the changing political landscape but also the brave new world that characterised life and politics in early sixteenth-century Europe, a world that begat and supported a new, vibrant diplomatic culture, kindled by the consciousness of the "discovery" of the "new world" (Carroll 1993).

With a diplomatic frame in mind, one can indeed "enter" the picture and engage in numerous intellectual puzzles that have fascinated art historians for centuries, rationally linking the various artefacts in the painting, directly or indirectly, to events, developments or anxieties of diplomatic practice. Note, for example, the lute with the broken string depicting perhaps the religious disharmony in Europe. Or look at the curtain that covers the crucifix symbolising the end of an era, the demise of religious universalism and

Figure 13.1 The Ambassadors, Hans Holbein, 1533

Source: Hans Holbein, 1533. National Gallery, London. With permission from the National Gallery Picture Library.

the advent of a new scene of secular diplomacy and particularism. Then there are the mathematical, astronomical, religious and cultural items at the centre. They can symbolise a humanist and knowledge-savvy attitude in diplomacy keen to critically engage questions of political authority and humanity. Finally, regard the anamorphic skull at the bottom of the painting. It can serve as a *memento mori*, a reminder of diplomacy's failure and its deadly implications but also of its continued necessity and avoidance of hubris (Carroll 1993; Constantinou 1994; Foister, Roy and Wyld 1997; North 2004; Devetak 2005).

Overall and so far, what we tend to "get" in this painting is the dominant vision of diplomacy, one that is historically specific, Eurocentric, state-centric, and courtly. Other images and perspectives are rendered invisible, for through this painting we remain captive admirers of an aristocratic portrait of diplomacy and the elitist cosmopolitanism that it portrays. We miss, for example, all the pre-modern cultures of diplomacy that included a multiplicity of actors and agents, diverse cultures that were defeated by progressively restricting the *ius legationis* – the right to send and receive embassies – only to sovereign territorial units (Constantinou and Der Derian 2010). That is to say, we miss practices of diplomacy before the monopolisation of the *ius legationis* by sovereignty. We fail to see all the instances when *ambassadors* were people commonly sent by local rulers, cities, monasteries or universities (Queller 1967) or the sub-national diplomats of our times (Cornago 2013). We furthermore miss the indigenous cultures of diplomacy that were treated as uncivilised and inferior, and consequently pushed aside by the expansion of the European society of states; diplomatic cultures that even today strive to be recognised yet remain unacknowledged or end up being belittled as exotic practices (Beier 2009; McConnell, Moreau and Dittmer 2012).

Re-imagining the ambassadors

Let us now conduct a visual thought experiment. Let us see how a different frame or picture can help us understand diplomacy in broader and more complex ways. I have altered Holbein's painting in Figure 13.2. In doing so I want to highlight two forms of alternative possibility. First, replacing the two "ambassadors" in the picture with two other "ambassadors" who bear the title but whose work is not commonly associated with official diplomacy: namely St Paul and Angelina Jolie. Second, replacing the anamorphic skull that dominates at the forefront of the painting with an aboriginal Australian, so that what serves as a *memento mori* in Holbein's painting would now serve as a *memento colonialis* in our revised version. By altering the classic "picture of diplomacy" I seek to broaden our understanding of ambassadorship and capture political issues and phenomena that would otherwise go unnoticed.

St Paul, as the "Apostle to the Nations," signifies a key moment in the history of diplomatic thought (Constantinou 2006). He is a pioneer of the missionary culture, the proliferation of religious as well as secular missions to save humanity. Paul is a self-designated not Jesus-appointed ambassador, insisting that he received his credentials from the cause he served and those he helped rather than from a secular power. He stressed that he was an apostle living off his own means; an "ambassador of Christ in chains" (Ephesians 6:20) distinguishing himself from the esteemed status, comfortable lifestyle and immunity enjoyed by the Roman *legatus* at the time.

Angelina Jolie, as a celebrity Goodwill Ambassador of the United Nations, signifies another key moment in the history of diplomatic thought (see Cooper 2008). Jolie's diplomacy is valuable and effective when viewed through what Debord (1994) called the "society of the spectacle." For Debord (1994) the confluence of mass media and capitalism means that social life has been supplanted by its representation. As a result, the interaction of nations, peoples and individuals could be said to take place less through physical encounters of actual diplomats but primarily through the images and appearances of mediatised representatives.

Finally, replacing the *memento mori* at the forefront of *The Ambassadors* in my revised picture of diplomacy, the aboriginal representative can serve as a *memento colonialis* – a reminder of the perished or unaccredited embassy that strives for recognition. Consider, in this regard, the Aboriginal Tent Embassy outside the old Parliament House in Canberra, which started with the planting of a beach umbrella in 1971, developed into a makeshift office and was viewed as symbolic of the struggle for indigenous rights in Australia (Foley, Schaap and Howell 2013). The *memento colonialis* in the picture of diplomacy is thus symbolic of contemporary struggles for a more inclusive diplomatic system.

In short, whereas Holbein's original painting can provide an insight into a historically specific, exclusive understanding of diplomacy, it can also be reframed to provide a more open, dynamic and inclusive understanding of diplomacy, which seeks to redress exclusion and accredit unrecognised embassies and everyday diplomacies (see further, Constantinou 2013 and 2016).

Figure 13.2 The Ambassadors Revisited, conceived by Costas M. Constantinou, drawn by Vasilis Argyrou, 2016

Source: Costas M. Constantinou – Vasilis Argyrou. With permission from the artists.

Visual representation in a post-protocol era

Visuality in diplomatic practice has been commonly associated with the arts of power and the splendours of the state. Architecture, sculpture, paintings, icons, mosaics, processions, musical and theatrical performances in European courts were an instrumental means through which domestic and foreign audiences entered "a world of fantastic allegory," and which "enabled a manipulation of visual and aural experience perfectly attuned to the ideological demands of the courts of baroque Europe" (Strong 1984: 4–5). Some of the archaic ceremonies of state diplomacy continue today and constitute an inheritance that symbolically sets apart "official" and "professional" diplomacy from its non-governmental, plebeian versions.

Besides courtly visuals, the World Wide Web has considerably extended diplomatic space and multiplied opportunities for visual diplomatic representation. In state diplomacy representations tend to be closely regulated by diplomatic protocol, which codifies and routinises the social behaviour of diplomats, aiming to "frame . . . the picture" and minimise the unintended impact of the visual (Foreign Service Institute 2013: 2). The electronic proliferation of "unauthorised" images that are being disseminated at the same time, however, challenge official diplomatic protocols. The diplomatic plot is no longer controlled and stage-managed from a single sovereign source, participation no longer restricted and hierarchical. Today, any person with the ability to use social media can disseminate transgressive counter-images that challenge the official narrative (see Table 13.1 summarising this shift).

To that extent, diplomatic interaction becomes less predictable in today's so-called post-protocol era. Non-state actors have more and more abilities to produce and circulate powerful images that support their ideas and activities. Diplomatic signalling – the use of non-verbal signals through which diplomatic agents tacitly communicate with each other and more broadly with the public – is no longer limited to professional diplomatic corps (Sharp and Wiseman 2007; Cohen 1987). Major technological advances mean that all kinds of activists and representatives can choose their own stage and medium for action (Copeland 2009). They travel around the globe and make their advocacy and representations felt "on the ground." They interlace the virtual and the physical, filtering their "mission" in and through social media. The classic media landscape is increasingly overtaken by new interactive media that empower individuals to produce, manipulate and respond to visual and textual information. One can become an everyday ambassador on different stages and through different mediums – making representations, capturing attention and demanding action (Otto 2015).

A recent striking example of everyday visual diplomacy concerns the abduction of hundreds of schoolgirls by Boko Haram from Chibok in northern Nigeria. The mothers of the abducted voiced their demand for national and international action via placards displaying the emotive motto "Bring Back Our Girls!" – a message globally disseminated through the mass media and social networks. This mission was embraced by a range

Table 13.1 Protocol and post-protocol eras

Diplomatic protocol	Conventional protocol	Digital post-protocol
Participation	restricted/hierarchical	broadly open/democratic
Plot	official/state-centric	unofficial/transgressive
Interaction	predictable	unpredictable

of other actors, by symbolically holding placards with the same message: human rights and women's NGOs, ordinary people and celebrities, ranging from the Pakistani Nobel laureate Malala, who survived an assassination attempt by the Taliban for pursuing her right to education, to Michelle Obama, who held the same placard inside the White House (see Figure 13.3).

Through this visual engagement and its electronic reproduction anyone could join "the mission" to save the Nigerian girls. Parallel to the official deliberations between the Nigerian government, the US and the African Union, countless concerned citizens around the globe have become "Chibokgirls ambassadors," advocating and campaigning for their release. But, at the same time, people started to appropriate this now symbolic image of holding placards in support of the Nigerian girls. For example, there were images showing Michelle Obama holding the same placard but with an altered message: "My Husband Kills Kids with Drones." That is, given its iconic status, this image was employed to draw attention to a different issue, an equally dramatic and emotive one: that of drone strikes and their violations of international humanitarian law. In short, the image was used to visualise other pressing issues and to challenge the narrow and elective ethics of diplomatic actors.

Visual diplomacy and the politics of spectacle

In *The Society of the Spectacle*, Guy Debord suggests that the spectacle hypnotises modern society, stupefies the masses and serves as a paradigm of power. Its "specialized

Figure 13.3 Michelle Obama campaigning from the White House

Source: Wikimedia Commons, https://commons.wikimedia.org/wiki/File:Michelle-obama-bringbackourgirls.jpg (in the public domain).

role," he argues, "is that of spokesman for all other activities, *a sort of diplomatic representative of hierarchical society at its own court*, and the source of the only discourse which that society allows itself to hear" (Debord 1994: section 32, my emphasis). In other words, spectacle has become the dominant form of representation, a kind of diplomatic plenipotentiary that is exclusively accredited and monopolises representation in contemporary society, dominating over and above the physical experience of events. Images speak louder than words and activities; or, differently put, all words and daily activities seem to be spoken for in advance or framed by images and imagers.

Debord's position is too absolutist but it has polemical value because it helps us appreciate the power of images. Diplomats increasingly recognise the importance of the production and circulation of images that has led to the "mediatization of diplomacy" (Pamment 2014). Digital diplomacy has amplified the opportunities of many actors – state and non-state ones – to publicise their concerns on a global scale (Bjola and Holmes 2015). These engagements are particularly effective when they are accompanied by striking images. The tactical use of images in support of diplomatic narratives can have a tremendous impact. This is why diplomacy today is no longer limited to the imperial, aristocratic and hierarchical picture of Holbein's "ambassadors." The "new ambassadors" can also be found beyond the official diplomatic corps, and can increasingly display multimedia and digital literacy as well as being more aware of the visual framing and decoding of their diplomacies. But note that images can be used just as effectively by those who challenge prevailing state-based policies. The result is a *post-protocol world of diplomacy* in which imagery is used by multiple actors, operating at multiple levels, and pursuing multiple objectives.

14 Drones

Lauren Wilcox

> Drones have not only eyes but also ears and many other organs.
>
> (Chamayou 2015: 41)

Drones represent a qualitative shift in technologies of visualisation in war. They are often seen as a disembodied form of warfare in which operators use drones to wage war on people and populations from thousands of miles away. But this is not the case. Grégoire Chamayou's description of drones as having far more embodied capacities than sight is a welcome reminder that vision is always embodied and tied to other ways of knowing and creating the world.

The visual in drone warfare is about far more than just obtaining more precise images of buildings, vehicles or people. The visualisation that occurs through drones is a highly political process that represents and constitutes targets and the world around them in very particular ways. Of key importance here is how bodies are viewed and interpreted. Expressed in more academic terms: visuality in drone warfare is both embodied and embodying. That is to say, it is a visual practice embodied in drone pilots and their equipment and it is also embodying in the sense that drone warfare works through the emotions of fear and hatred that shape the bodies that are subjected to the violence of drones. Donna Haraway's critique of the violent, masculine and militaristic politics implicit within certain visual ways of knowing takes on renewed salience in considering the visual politics of drone warfare. Haraway criticises the notion that we can have knowledge that is somehow separated from our bodies and from how these bodies are part of power relations. She highlights the so-called situatedness of knowledge and stresses (Haraway 1988: 585) that "vision is *always* a question of the power to see – and perhaps of the violence implicit in our visualising practices. With whose blood were my eyes crafted?"

Drones and voyeuristic violence

One of the most striking features of the use of drones in warfare and targeting assassinations is what Matthew Power (2013) called "voyeuristic intimacy": a situation in which surveillance of targets may last for days or weeks. In the words of one drone operator (quoted in Chamayou 2015: 117), "you see them wake up in the morning, do their work, go to sleep at night." Or, as former drone operator, turned outspoken critic, Brandon Bryant (quoted in Woods 2015: 176) put it: "We're the ultimate peeping toms. No one's gonna catch us. No one's going to hear or see a Predator drone flying at the distance and height that we flew at." This form of voyeurism creates an intimacy with the objects of surveillance and violence, even from a great physical distance (Wilcox 2015a: 140–2).

In drone warfare, the people operating the drones often have what seems like a clear vision of the bodies they surveil – thus fostering a sense of closeness that is at odds with the ease with which drones are used to kill. This unsettles the assumption that a soldier's resistance to killing is diminished the further she or he is located from the targets. In this view, long-range targeting, such as from snipers or aerial bombardment, is considered to foster a higher resistance to killing than hand-to-hand combat (Grossman 1995: 98; Chamayou 2015: 116; Daggett 2015).

How does this play out in practice? Look at what happened when, in February 2010, bombs from a US-operated drone and armed helicopter killed twenty people in the Uruzgan province of Afghanistan. The convoy was "positively identified" as carrying combatants that posed a threat to nearby American ground troops. The evidence was furnished by a "drone's eye view" and a series of conversations between the Predator drone crew, troops on the ground, "screeners" at headquarters in Florida and an armed helicopter crew (Cloud 2011). But the ensuing confidence in the ability to distinguish between combatants and civilians was wrong. There were civilians in the convoy, revealing the inadequacies of drone images to positively identify a threat and a legitimate target.

Even if total visual transparency were possible, the nature of contemporary counter-insurgency means that it is difficult to distinguish between combatants and civilians because they and their equipment are often visually indistinguishable (Gregory 2011: 200). Distinctions between civilians and combatants are also not permanent, as people might shift from one category to another. Add to this that images from drones are often blurry, and that video feeds contain frequent gaps in satellite and communications links.

Embodying violence

Transcripts of the messages from the drone crew that was tracking the convoy over-whelmingly suggest their desire to identify the people as dangerous and thus as targets (Cloud 2011). Spotting of individuals "holding cylindrical objects" is taken to indicate the presence of weapons. The lack of clear evidence of weapons is taken as evidence of weapons, even though the presence of weapons is not itself indicative of being a militant: "It's what they've been doing here lately, they wrap their [expletive][*sic*] up in their man dresses so you can't PID [positively identify] it" (Cloud 2011; US Air Force 2011:12). The Predator pilot and sensor operator discuss seeing two "military-age men" struggling with something in the back of a truck and decide it is a "human shield." Other such examples include the designation of prayer as a signal of intent to do something nefarious, the movements of vehicles away from the location of US ground forces as a "flanking maneuver" (US Air Force 2011: 38). The presence of only men and supposedly only adolescents or older suggests that greater accuracy of vision offered by the drones does not necessarily suffice as a mechanism to ensure greater distinction between civilian and combatants when the bodies perceived are already considered dangerous.

The attack on this convoy was stopped when members of the Predator drone crew noticed that some of the people fleeing from the wreckage ("squirters," in the military slang) were wearing brightly coloured clothing usually associated with women.

Safety observer:	are they wearing burqas?
Sensor:	that's what it looks like.
Pilot:	they were all PIDed ["positively identified"] as males. No females in the group.
Sensor:	that guy looks like he's wearing jewellery and stuff like a girl, but he ain't . . . if he's a girl, he's a big one.

(US Air Force 2011: 62)

The appearance of bodies seen to be female disrupts this scene for it is taken to indicate the presences of civilians (Becker and Shane 2012). The eventual decision to "call out" or officially register the presence of women and children suggests the inadequacy of the visual field to signify gender and, relatedly, combatant/civilian status. It also sheds light on how race and gender are visually and affectively incorporated into decision-making. In a war justified by colonial narratives of saving Afghan women from despotic men (Shepherd 2006; Wilcox 2009; Abu-Lughod 2013), the killing of women and children undermines both the mission and its underlying ideological justification. Yet, at the same time the idea that all "military-aged men" are legitimate targets is reinforced by the attack's classification as a mistake hinging upon the presence of women and children.

Scholars have long described how political links between bodies, race and gender come into being through visual practices. Judith Butler, for instance, notes that white paranoia makes it difficult or impossible to use visual images to establish the "truth" of racial brutality. Writing in the early 1990s, Butler describes the video evidence of the Rodney King beating by police officers in Los Angeles. She stressed that most of the predominantly white jury viewed the victim, a black man, as the true cause of violence – and this regardless of the brutality of the attack (Butler 1993). Race and gender structure not only our interpretations of images, but also our sense of which lives matter: who is worth protecting, saving or grieving or, conversely, which bodies are considered threatening and thus must be separated from us or eliminated through violence (see Butler 2009).

The visual politics of drone warfare has elements of what Frantz Fanon's first-person account of the black body already pointed out: that such a body is defined as dangerous prior to any move or gesture. He illustrates this by showing how a little white boy fearfully reacted to Fanon's visual presence: "Mama, see the Negro! I'm frightened" (Fanon 1986: 111–12). Sara Ahmed (2014: 63) argues likewise that it is through the movement of emotions like fear and hate that bodies are socially shaped and formed. Embodiment in this sense works through contagion, through the fear and hatred of certain bodies spreading and "sticking" to other bodies.

In such a racialised and fear-laden environment, the *lack* of evidence of weapons becomes evidence of weapons based upon what is felt *must* be true. Generic attributes, such as dangerousness, become associated with certain types of bodies, leading to what can be termed a shift from "looks like" to "seems like" (Puar 2007: 187). Surface appearances are then taken as internal "truths" (Puar 2007: 186).

It is in this way that the fear and hatred of Afghan "insurgents" or "militants" can stick to any body visible through the camera of the drone. Because the predator drone crew, based in Nevada, has a pre-determined desire to attack the convoy they fail to recognise signs that identify the convoy as posing no danger. The fear that the people in the convoy could be militants is linked to the fear of not being certain. The body of the enemy is depicted though these techno-political processes of drone warfare in ways that simultaneously produce a body and destroy it. At the same time, the legitimacy of this violence is established through gendered and racialised assumptions about which bodies intrinsically constitute a threat to other bodies. The construction of certain bodies as threatening is thus less a matter of how they visually appear and more linked to a deep-seated desire to make bodies into what we already know they must be (Wilcox 2015b).

The visual politics of drone warfare

This massacre in Afghanistan ended up being more visible than most, leading to a high-profile military investigation. Apologies and payments were made to the victims and their families. Transcripts and other records related to the events were made public. This specific massacre is thus "exceptional" as it is well documented, frequently discussed by journalists and academics, and serves as an example in which the US military has admitted to faults within the chain of command. General Stanley A. McCrystal, the top US commander in Afghanistan, apologised to Afghan President Hamid Karzai. Several letters of reprimand were issued to officers and other forms of disciplinary action taken in relation to the incident (Cloud 2011).

Meanwhile thousands of people have been killed in drone warfare. These deaths are accepted as legitimate because of the alleged visual precision of drones. The focus on "exceptional" and particularly abhorrent killings, such as this particular convoy in Afghanistan, renders invisible the bodies of those whose deaths were not investigated in the same way. Add to this that bombs fired by drones strike with such force that the bodies killed are often rendered unrecognisable. Any sign of identity is being destroyed (Gregory 2015).

Drone warfare as a visualisation practice thus contributes to constituting certain bodies as legitimate targets and as lives that do not matter, even though the inaccuracy of this vision is not able to ascertain for certain the distinction between insurgents and civilians (Wilcox 2015a: 160–2). Such problematic forms of warfare cannot be justified by the often-made distinction between "intended" deaths and "unintended but acceptable" ones. The visual component of drone warfare, and the political context within which it operates, simply cannot deliver the accuracy needed to distinguish between legitimate and illegitimate targets. There can thus also be no accidentally but acceptably dead.

The visual technologies of drone warfare can never guarantee that violence will be limited to appropriate targets, if such a categorisation can even be made. Rather, appreciating how the interpretation of drone images always already constitutes certain bodies as likely enemies reveals how visuality is implicated in the production violence. Drone warfare is thus less a mode of disembodied warfare than one that strives to conceal the violent practices of embodiment that are enabled by its visual practices.

Note

This chapter draws on Wilcox (2017: 11–28).

15 Empathy

Nick Robinson

In our increasingly visual age, the public overwhelmingly experiences war through television news coverage, popular culture and entertainment. All of these centre on visual spectacles, on what Roger Stahl (2010) calls "militainment." Central to this dynamic are military videogames, played by tens of millions of people around the world. Spurred by this success, videogame-based campaigns have increasingly been used to recruit soldiers. Even terrorist organisations, like Islamic State, base their visual campaigns on videogames.

I examine military videogames from a counterintuitive perspective: by focusing on how they project and enable empathy. Videogames seem, at first sight, an unlikely vehicle for such a discussion. Military war games even less so. They have frequently been criticised both for promoting violence and for offering inappropriate racist depictions of stereotypical "enemies." I counter this form of caricature and show how videogames – even war videogames – can play an important role in generating empathy. I define empathy as allowing a person to feel what someone else feels from their perspective.

Videogames are a highly visual medium. They offer depictions of often fantastical worlds with ever increasing levels of sophistication and realism. I focus on how visuals interact with what is called the "possibility space" of "gameplay": the constraints related to what the player can and cannot do (Bogost 2007). Here I argue that empathy is experienced by players based on what they are allowed to do, and how and what they are allowed to see.

I trace the move towards empathy in war-based videogames along the following lines: from games in which players are meant to empathise with the US as a victim following 9/11; to games that give players the chance to feel what it is like to be a soldier; to games that allow players to take on the role of victims of war. The variety of these empathetic connections points to the political significance of videogames but also offers challenges for understanding the relationship between player and games.

Feeling for the USA?

Archetypal military shooter videogames are typically set in a contemporary conflict in which the player represents a member of the US military or its allies. The player is engaged in war against uniformed soldiers from an enemy clearly identified with a particular state, most frequently Russia, China, North Korea or a country in the Middle East. The only method of success is through shooting and destroying the enemy.

Empathy seems at first sight absent from such a simulated militarised world. And yet, mainstream military games frequently encourage the player to make an empathetic connection with both the soldier and his homeland: the USA is portrayed as an innocent victim of violence.

Typical of the genre is *Call of Duty 4: Modern Warfare* (2007), which begins with US marines drawn into conflict in the Middle East following a *coup d'état* in an unspecified Middle Eastern country. Thirty thousand American troops are subsequently killed by a nuclear bomb which is detonated by the coup leader. As a first-person shooter, the player is literally thrust into the role of one of the soldiers who witnesses the mushroom cloud which graphically signifies the bomb's detonation. The soldier then crawls through the post-nuclear wreckage before dying of radiation poisoning. The USA is thus depicted as moral and righteous; it is the victim of "barbaric" forces who are beyond negotiation.

Mainstream military shooters thus present the USA and its soldiers as co-constitutive: the empathetic connection between player and character is assumed and uncomplicated. Frequently played in first person so that the player literally comes to "embody the soldier," the player sees through the eyes of a soldier with the dominant view being along the barrel of a gun. Visually the screen also presents strategic information such as a direction indicator to their next objective, and levels of health and ammo. Action is near continuous, such that, by the game's end, the player has killed literally hundreds (perhaps thousands) of enemies to return the US to a state of stability.

The emotional response sought in the player is one of heroic complicity in fighting the War on Terror. The hyper-stylised visuals of these games, which contain frequent explosions and intense, rapid battlefield action are matched by their narrative, music and sound, all working together as the soldier/player utilises hi-tech, cutting-edge weaponry to perpetrate "clean" and "virtuous war" (see Der Derian 2009). Such war resists any empathy with the enemy, scripting out the impact of the player's actions through the absence of both civilians (there are no civilian casualties in these wars) and any portrayals of post-conflict instability. The player thus both identifies and suffers with the US as a victim and an agent who seeks just retribution and vengeance for unjustified wrongs inflicted upon it.

Feeling for soldiers?

It would be a mistake, however, to suggest that mainstream military videogames lack any critical capacity. There are ambiguities at the heart of a number of mainstream games that suggest a more complex potential set of empathetic responses. For example, *Call of Duty: Modern Warfare 2* (2009) exposes rogue military forces at the heart of government that are complicit in driving the onset of global war. Similarly, *Splinter Cell Conviction* (2010), *Call of Duty: Advanced Warfare* (2014) and *Army of Two* (2008) all reveal private military corporations working alongside malevolent government forces to mobilise the state for war (Robinson 2015: 468). The US government is thus exposed as co-complicit in the very war that is being fought by the player. Yet any sense that the US as a whole is implicated in causing contemporary war is immediately closed off as the player's actions are crucial in exposing and destroying these malevolent forces. Justice is wrought on rogue government agents not through the judicial system but through the barrel of a gun. Thus the empathetic connection between the player and the soldier character remains clear: the games *never* challenge the motives or actions of the soldier. Any moral complexity here is caused by the actions of political and military elites, not the soldiers who fight in their name, caught up in a political game over which they have no control.

Soldiers as blameless; families as victims

The message that soldiers are blameless victims is captured in a number of games in which one of the main playable characters is killed (e.g. *Call of Duty: Modern Warfare* series, *Battlefield 3*), underlining the ultimate cost of war on combatants and pulling powerfully on the empathetic connection between player and soldier. When the player's character is killed, a striking visual contrast is drawn between their death – often depicted in close-up, with death a slow and intimate affair in which the action comes to a halt – and that of the enemy, in which death is routine and normalised, distant and near instantaneous.

The game *Medal of Honor Warfighter* (2012) is highly unusual within the military shooter genre in that it explicitly seeks to demonstrate the cost of war for soldiers' families: cut-scenes woven through the game (based on the conventions of naturalistic TV drama) portray conversations between the soldier/player and his wife centred on the sacrifices they are making as a family for the "greater good." Towards the end of the game, one of the lead characters (Mother) is captured and graphically and needlessly tortured to death by the terrorist antagonists. The game ends with a two and a half minute long cut-scene centred on Mother's military funeral in which the player's family and comrades are at the graveside as Mother's heroism is commemorated. Thus, the game takes the theme of sacrifice into a very personal place, demonstrating the consequences for those left in the homeland of fighting the War on Terror.

Critical empathy: the reflective soldier

Spec Ops: The Line (2012) is perhaps the first game explicitly designed to force the player to reflect on the efficacies of war and on the consequences of war for the player/soldier. Taking inspiration from Joseph Conrad's *Heart of Darkness*, the game places the player in the role of Captain Walker, the leader of a three-man squad of US Special Forces, charged with undertaking a rescue mission designed both to reconnect with US military soldiers trapped following a sandstorm in Dubai – whose leader, "Konrad," is slowly revealed as a parallel figure to Kurtz in Conrad's book – and to rescue civilians.

Essential to *Spec Ops: The Line*'s empathetic capacity is its synergy between visuals and gameplay. The setting of the game is crucial, providing an allegorical representation which juxtaposes Dubai's prior opulence and wealth with the devastation which has been wrought upon it by the sandstorm, shown in the depictions of skyscrapers and luxury hotels which have now fallen into ruin.

Marking a further crucial difference between this game and the "first-person" games discussed above, *Spec Ops: The Line* is a "third-person" game in which the player's character is fully visible at all times. At the beginning of the game, the player's character (Captain Walker) is presented as a virtuous military archetype: clean-cut, courteous to his colleagues and respectful of the rules of military engagement. Yet as the game unfolds, it forces the player into an increasingly morally ambiguous series of actions including killing US soldiers and local civilians – the devastating impact being made visually manifest in the battering and scarring of Walker's body.

Central to the empathetic power of the game is the critical position which it takes on the role of military technology. While in the "virtuous war" of most military shooters, military technology is universally "clean," allowing the player to kill overwhelming numbers of enemies with minimal collateral damage and no risk to civilians, in *Spec Ops: The Line* technology has a devastating effect. Perhaps the most infamous example occurs about half-way through the game in the mission "The Gate" in which Walker utilises a hi-tech mortar containing white phosphorous in order to overcome a heavily fortified enemy encampment. While this is ostensibly a choice (in a cut-scene Walker and his colleagues argue over whether to deploy the weapon) the game's structure requires the use of the mortar to advance the story.

But where other games script out consequences, *Spec-Ops: The Line* makes them all too clear for both character and player. In a highly graphic and visually unsettling scene, Walker and his colleagues are forced to walk through the carnage they have created. Initially, they encounter the burning bodies of soldiers, screaming in agony – legitimate targets, the characters rationalise. But as they continue, the characters and player are confronted with a horrifying truth: the soldiers were protecting civilians and both groups burnt to death in the white phosphorous attack.

The power of the game thus comes from the synergy of visual representations and the deliberate limits that it places on the scope of what the player can do: the player is *forced* into the unfamiliar role of perpetrating acts of violence against both US soldiers and innocent civilians which the player is then forced to experience. The consequences of this are seen by the player as their character is increasingly battered and physically scarred – an allegory for the violence they have unleashed on others. Yet, Walker also descends into madness as a result of these conflicting pressures. As the game ends, Walker's loss of reason is complete. He is confronted with a series of hallucinations of people he has killed, with Konrad's voice, inescapably taunting, locked inside his head: Why did you do what you did? Why have you perpetrated acts of indiscriminate violence?

All of us who play military shooters have killed thousands of people. Walker's character forces us to ask the question – who is evil? The enemy, Walker or the player? *Spec Ops: The Line* thus represents the possibility of deploying the empathetic connection between player and character in a different, critical way.

Victims/civilians

I have considered the potentials and challenges of the empathetic connections between players and their soldier characters in mainstream military videogames, where civilian victims are usually absent or graphically, passively dead. Two recent games – *Sunset* (2015) and *This War of Mine* (2014) – work differently: they place the player in the position of the civilian victim, using the empathetic connection between player and character to enable a different understanding of the effects of war.

Consider *This War of Mine*, which is loosely based on the siege of Sarajevo during the conflicts in the former Yugoslavia. Paweł Miechowski (cited in Reynolds 2014), one of the game's senior writers, explicitly argues for the power of the game environment to create empathetic understanding of war: "if you think about it, in movies such as *The Pianist* or *Saving Private Ryan* or many other war movies, you're always the spectator. In games, you're in the middle of the experience or the story, so it can be the perfect way to cover a serious topic."

Played from a sideways-on point of view, the game tasks the player with trying to keep multiple civilian protagonists alive, initially taking control of three civilians caught up in the conflict who have been forced to take refuge in a war-damaged house.

Visually, the game uses a predominantly monochrome colour scheme offering representations of war-damaged urban buildings such as houses, churches and supermarkets – its deliberate darkness seeking to invoke a sense of depression in the player given the hopelessness of the plight confronting the civilians represented in the game. The game is separated into a day–night cycle, with the day taken up by cooking, sleeping and building objects such as a bed or radio to improve the civilians' physical and mental well-being, while the night is taken up by scavenging for ever scarcer resources.

The in-game rules make the game extremely difficult. First, the game provides no instructions of the most effective strategies for survival. Players have to figure things out for themselves as they work through the game, and frequent missteps make death inevitable. Second, the game deliberately limits the player's resources: he or she is thus forced to take risks and leave the shelter of their house to scavenge for resources at night. Yet scavenging confronts the player with a series of ethical and moral dilemmas: valuable objects such as medicine and food, which are essential to your survival, will frequently be "owned" by other civilians. Stealing them may result in violent confrontation and death to you or the other civilians. Even when conflict is avoided, stealing results in your characters becoming depressed as they reflect on the costs of their actions on their victims. Even those items which are not owned, such as wood or scrap metal, have to be carefully chosen as characters have limited capacity to carry items each night.

The difficulty of the game is further enhanced by the fact that scavengers may also steal your resources at night while you are away. While you can leave house members

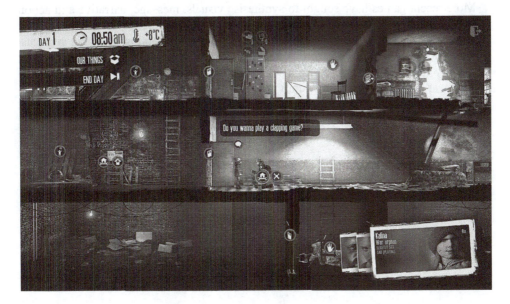

Figure 15.1 This War of Mine: civilians confront the hopelessness and horrors of survival in a war zone

Source: *This War of Mine*, www.thiswarofmine.com/Printed with permission.

to defend your property, allocating them to guard duty carries costs in terms of their lack of sleep and the fact that they may become injured by other scavengers. Valuable resources can be used to board up your property to make it more secure but this also comes at a cost – these resources cannot be used for heating or cooking, for example.

In a third-person game in which players care for civilians, the power of the game comes from its ability to make the player understand both the very real consequences of living through war, the horrible moral choices to be made, and the impact they have on the lives and mental well-being of civilians.

The visual politics of videogames

Videogames – played by millions of players around the world – are important sites of visual global politics and offer valuable insights into the role of empathy in understanding and experiencing such politics. Players (and their characters) are challenged by games to think, feel and experience multiple perspectives on war and its consequences. Whereas much past criticism perhaps understandably suggested that the focus within mainstream war games was exclusively on the heroic celebration of the soldier (clearly demarcated from an enemy "other"), military videogames have always been more complex than that. Even the mainstream invokes spaces that allow a more complex set of potential emotional connections. Like films, games have exposed the military–entertainment complex and questioned bureaucratic incompetence to ask why states and their soldiers are involved in conflict. Games such as *Medal of Honor Warfighter* reveal the consequences for soldiers killed in action and their families. Yet arguably all of these games subsume the critical intent of their narratives and stories by the action-centric pattern of play which places a premium on relentless action that serves to celebrate conflict and restricts space for reflective empathy.

More recent games have sought to synthesise visuals, message, narrative and action to create empathetic connections between player and character. *Spec Ops: The Line* explicitly engages the consequences of military violence for both soldier and civilians. Games such as *This War of Mine* connect players with the harrowing consequences of war by forcing them to care for civilian victims. The growth of this new genre of critical war game marks a significant moment not only for the games industry but also for a form of politics that forges more critical and empathetic pathways towards understanding of war.

16 Face

Jenny Edkins

The way we think about global politics is largely conditioned by the idea that one of the most important questions – maybe the most important question – is: "How can we best live together?" If the world is made up of people of different backgrounds and divergent interests living alongside each other, how can we find a way of living together harmoniously and without conflict? How can we overcome what divides us? However, this question rests on an unspoken assumption: that we are separate individuals that come into the world as distinct beings, each independent from the other, who only learn to live together later. It is through this learning process that we overcome our inherent selfishness and egoism and become civilised, able to live and work together. Our learned ability to do this distinguishes us from the criminal, the primitive and the savage, who remain in a so-called state of nature, where life is "solitary, poor, nasty, brutish, and short" (Hobbes 2008: 84).

I would like to suggest that a more appropriate political question might be one that turns this assumption on its head. Instead of starting from a premise that we are separate beings who have to learn to live together, what if we were, in contrast, to assume that we are inherently interconnected? That, rather than being distinct individuals, we are who we are only through our connection, our relation to other beings – both animate and inanimate? The political question we have to ask then changes. It becomes: "How is it that we think of ourselves as separate in the first place?" Is it the way we are brought up to think that makes us see ourselves as individuals, and not some fact of nature? If so, how does that come about? And, more importantly, how might it be challenged?

Our individuality is often seen as symbolised by the face. We recognise people by their facial features: most of us can immediately identify someone we know by their face, and the documents that we carry bear our picture so that officials we encounter can compare the person in front of them with the image to validate our identity. The face is a signal of a discrete, identifiable individual, each separate from the other. The face is also seen as a window on the soul. Through the face we are thought to signal our inner feelings and our emotions, and we see the face of another as a way of reading their reactions to us, their intentions, and even their past experiences. There are people who do not interact in this way: who cannot recognise faces, even of their nearest and dearest, or who cannot move their facial muscles to express emotion – and perhaps cannot even feel emotion as a result (Edkins 2015). But a face is still seen as reflecting the person behind the face: someone who is separated from us by the face but whose internal life is understandable through the signals transmitted by their facial expressions. The face is a signal of our existence as separate, distinct beings, and marks the line between inside and outside.

There are many practical examples that challenge this common-sense view, and the chapter explores one in particular. I will call this facelessness. There are people whose faces are not what we expect: those who have facial injuries or disfigurements. Exploring our response to unusual faces can show how strong our desire for a face that reconfirms our individuality and separation is. In this chapter, I suggest that the desire to repair the face is motivated by a need to conceal the vulnerability and interconnectedness that the intact face hides. It is our wish to retain the notion that we are separate individuals that compels us to restore the integrity of the face.

I begin by discussing a novel and a video performance that pose the problem of facelessness, and see the face literally and metaphorically as a mask that can or cannot be removed. There is an argument that, by concealing the face, the burka produces the horror of facelessness. In the second section, I explore face transplants, and in particular the first face transplant, where the recipient was a Frenchwoman named Isabelle Dinoire. The portrayal of Dinoire reinforced the idea that, to be a whole, separate individual, a person has to have a face that is intact. Face transplants are based on that logic. However, Dinoire's own thoughts about what she experienced, which I discuss in the third section of the chapter, appear to challenge this reasoning. They reveal how her transplant led her to see herself, not as once more a whole, singular individual, but, rather, as a person now intimately and literally connected to and responsible for someone else: her dead donor.

Mask, face and facelessness

One of the most powerful explorations of imaginaries of face, facelessness and the face as mask is Kobo Abe's (2003) novel *The Face of Another*. The narrator of the novel, a scientist whose face was destroyed in a laboratory accident, builds himself a new face, to replace the mask of bandages he has been forced to wear. His face has been eaten away by chemicals, leaving only a horrific mass of wheals and scar tissue. Feeling unable to appear in public in that state, he conceals the horror behind bandages. That does not work either, and he decides to construct a new face/mask. Behind the mask, modelled on the face of another, he can see while remaining invisible. He sets out in this new face/mask to seduce his own wife, who later tells him she was aware of his deception while still playing along with it. This story is more than a story of a new face, as indeed is Isabelle Dinoire's face transplant. Abe's novel – first published in 1964, long before the possibility of face transplants was mooted – is an account that questions the fundamental meaning we assign to face and personhood, truth and deception. In the end the protagonist of the novel is unable to distinguish between the mask and his real face: the mask becomes just another face, and the real face nothing but a mask – but a mask with nothing behind it, a mask that cannot be removed.

While reading Abe's novel or watching the film version (Teshigahara 1966) can be disturbing, the video performance, *Omnipresence*, by French artist ORLAN (1993) is perhaps even more challenging. It takes place in an operating theatre. ORLAN remains conscious as her face is marked up for surgery, and as the surgeons make their incisions. The whole is streamed by live video to audiences worldwide. Parveen Adams (1996) describes watching as the performance reaches what for her is its climax, when the knife severs the face "to the point where we see that the face is *detachable*." The

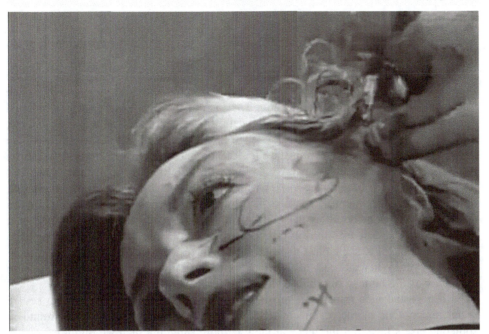

Figure 16.1 After making an incision around her ear, the surgeon begins to lift and separate ORLAN's face, screenshot from *Omnipresence*

Source: Screenshot from *Omnipresence*. Myriapodus Films and ORLAN. https://vimeo.com/66967753 at 14 min.

surgeon makes an incision around the ear, and begins, with her fingers, to separate the skin from flesh. The power of ORLAN's work is "in the space which is opened up . . . between the bloodied place which we see all around her ear and the face as it lifts from its customary base. . . . There is, suddenly, no inside and no outside" (Adams 1996: 153–4).

A similar gap arises when the face is masked. Slavoj Žižek (2010) asks why a woman wearing a burka triggers anxiety. He argues that it is not because the usual face-to-face encounter cannot take place, so that we cannot read expression and intention in the face, or interact in the usual way, but rather that the burka hides the protective mask that the face provides. The face conceals the awful way in which we are all ultimately unfathomable to each other; the face makes us appear understandable, "normal," acceptable. On the other hand, Žižek argues, the covered face forces us to confront the uncanny horror of the incomprehensible other person directly, without a face as a reassuring "protective shield," a pretence of knowability. He asks us to consider "the opposite of a woman taking off her burka and revealing her natural face." What happens if, instead, we "imagine a woman 'taking off' the skin of her face itself, so that what we see beneath her face is precisely an anonymous dark smooth burka-like surface with a narrow slit for the gaze?" (Žižek 2010). How would it then be possible to relate to this person without a face? A woman in a burka appears faceless, like someone whose face has been torn away, and thus exposes our fear of our own precarious personhood.

The first face transplant

In normal cosmetic surgery, of course, patients do not witness the operation; they do not see the face peeled away. They do not see the face lifting, the relation between inside and outside is obliterated. The skin is replaced, sutured back into place, and the face – the screen that conceals the horror – reinstated. For the recipient of a face transplant, things are more problematic. The face of the donor must have been lifted quite away from the flesh, still living, beneath: that much they (and we) must realise, though we might choose not to acknowledge it. And the recipient has to deal with the knowledge that they are wearing the face of another – not like a mask that can be removed, but as a face that they have to live with indefinitely. Before the transplant, they will have been brought face-to-face with their own lack of face, their own mortality, or animality. As recipient of the first face transplant, Frenchwoman Isabelle Dinoire (in Châtelet 2007), says, it is the stuff of nightmares: "My face was the face of a monster. The hardest was the nose, because you could see the bone. . . . That bone made me think of a skeleton. Of death." They have seen themselves with the face-mask torn off. Whereas most of us can look in the mirror each morning to reassure ourselves of the fantasy of wholeness and individuality, they cannot.

Full or partial face transplants are becoming more frequent in response to severe facial injury. One of the major concerns had been the impact of walking around in someone else's face, but the medical view is more sanguine than we might expect. A review (Infante-Cossio 2013: e264) notes that, although longer-term psychosocial outcomes remain unknown, as yet "there have been no problems regarding the transfer of identity and the body image changes." The longer-term effects of the indefinite use of immunosuppressive drugs to ensure the foreign tissue is not rejected remains a strong concern; the side effects of "converting a healthy person with a disfigured face into an unhealthy person who looks more normal" can be severe and life-threatening (Iain Hutchison quoted in Donnelly 2011). There is a sense that surgical teams are searching for a patient who will be suitable for surgery, rather than responding to patients' needs (Taylor-Alexander 2013). Surgeons involved in transplants gain significant prestige and there is also a strong element of nationalism involved as countries compete to be first in this new field.

Another, rarely remarked-on aspect of face transplantation is the impact of the procedure on the donor family. There is considerable work on how best to recover a face from a brain-dead heart-beating donor – a time-intensive process. While the removal of solid organs from a donor is invisible, facial composite tissue allotransplantation removal, to give it its full nomenclature, "involves a very distorting defect in the donor's face." In order to "restore [a] donor's body to make it look as normal as possible before returning [it] to the family," a mould is taken of the donor's face before tissue is removed, and a resin or silicone mask made to take its place (Infante-Cossio 2013: e268). Even the dead need faces it seems.

Isabelle Dinoire's experience as the first recipient of a partial face transplant – nose, lips and part of the chin – is widely documented, most notably in the book *Le baiser d'Isabelle*, by Noëlle Châtelet (2007), and a BBC Horizon programme (Austin 2006). The first pages of the book show that the surgeons at Amiens recognised as soon as they saw her that she was the "ideal patient" they had been waiting for. She had been bitten by her dog while unconscious, following an overdose. Unusually, her lips and nose had been detached with almost surgical precision (Châtelet 2007: 25). They did not tell her straight away what they were thinking. As soon as she knew what was planned, she began to think about the donor and their family. One thing that concerned her was the fact that it would mean returning a body without a face to the family: "For me, that was a terrible picture. Their daughter, faceless!" (Châtelet 2007: 59). The staff reassured her that the face would be replaced – they would show her photographs and she wouldn't be able to see the difference. There was a long wait for a suitable donor, but the operation was successful and Dinoire returned home to begin a period of adaptation – both to life with a "new" face and to media attention as the world's first face transplant. She appeared before a press conference just over a year afterwards (Lichfield 2006).

Living with another

Dinoire describes how it felt immediately after the operation. It wasn't so much her appearance that was difficult to accept, but the feeling of being inside someone else's mouth. When she looked in the mirror, though, she saw only "the other." She couldn't forget the donor, without whom she wouldn't be there herself. She talked to her (Châtelet 2007: 239, 244). At the start of course there was no feeling in the transplant; when sensation returned as the nerves started to reconnect, things were not so bad. But she still felt that she couldn't forget, and didn't want to forget, the donor, who was, she said, like a twin sister. Dinoire had taken an overdose; the donor had committed suicide. The face became her face insofar as she was the one who had reanimated the dead woman's face and now kept it alive and gave it movement – but it was still the donor's face: the donor lived on, as part of her (Châtelet 2007: 262). Châtelet's book ends with Dinoire's realisation that she no longer has the right to think of suicide. She has a responsibility to the medical team, and to her donor, to live (Châtelet 2007: 318). As Marc Lafrance (2010: 158) puts it, "Dinoire chose to welcome the other into herself; an other whom she would protect, defend and, most importantly, remember." Lafrance contrasts this view with the "spare parts" view adopted by the surgeons, who wanted Dinoire to appropriate the face and regard it as hers. He (2010: 159) suggests that we need "to dispense with the idea that the mind is the seat of the self and the body a set of exchangeable and replaceable parts."

In the case of the face in particular, maybe we need also to dispense with the idea that the face is a mirror to the soul, a window on emotion, and a signifier of a unique, inviolable and recognisable identity. Dinoire was never, Lafrance points out, presented with the possibility of living with a disfigured face. Disfigurement "exposed her body – and, by extension, all bodies – as open and vulnerable to the other [and] called into question the sovereignty of the subject." This was an unacceptable disruption to "the notions of separation and distinction that underlie Western understandings of the autonomous self" (Lafrance 2010: 151–2). It is perhaps the fight to maintain this distinction that motivates medical advances, as much as national pride, personal prestige or even patient care. Ironically, these advances may do the reverse, revealing the inevitable intermixing and vulnerability of flesh and personhood.

The intermingling that Dinoire feels, but that her medical team does not seem prepared to countenance, is expressed in part by her reference to the donor as her twin. Unusual embodiments, like conjoined twins, represent an ambiguity that many people find difficult to cope with (Shildrick 2002). There is a medical and cultural imperative to separate conjoined twins. We cannot accept the idea of two people in one body.

Separation is conducted wherever possible and is narrated as giving each of the twins the possibility of a "normal," autonomous, fully human existence. The alternative seems to be monstrosity. Although medical advice about the chances of success is important, it tends to be assumed that if separation is possible, then that should be the choice parents make. Separating conjoined twins and transplant surgery share the same narratives of bodily integrity, and similar results for those involved: "the implications of attempting – as with conjoined twins – to split a singular morphology into self and other are paralleled by the incorporation of the organs of another into an existent self" (Shildrick 2008: 38). Dinoire cannot forget her twin sister. She is now responsible for keeping her donor alive, for making her donor's face live on, as both hers and not hers at the same time.

The faceless – or rather, those with faces that appear unacceptable, dismantled, effaced – challenge the way we expect to visualise the world. We require the face to sustain what we call social reality (Žižek 1989). It is there to enable us all to operate within a fantasy of the world as made up of separate, independent individuals, each with a core self behind the face that they present to the world. Transplanting a face from one to another does not change prevalent fantasies of self and other, but, rather, conforms to and confirms those fantasies. Or, rather, it does *almost*, but not quite. If we listen to those like Dinoire, we find that face transplants, like other transplants but perhaps even more so, reveal an existence of multiple persons in one body that disturbs our comfortable and comforting fantasy of individuality and separation.

Note

A longer version of this chapter appears in Edkins (2015: 158–64); material used with permission.

17 Famine

David Campbell

In the twentieth century, more than 70 million people worldwide died from famine, making it the most famine-stricken period in history. In the twenty-first century, this extreme mortality continues. Given that the capacity to abolish famine globally was achieved in the twentieth century, preventable mass death on this scale constitutes an atrocity, one increasingly connected to conflict (see Devereux 2000: 29; Graham-Harrison 2016). Framing the issue in this way radically revises conventional understandings of famine and poses a fundamental challenge to the way famines are photographed.

There have been two shifts in how famine has been understood in recent times. While famine is by definition a food crisis, the nature of such crises is many and varied, such that simple interpretations of famine as a natural disaster have been superseded by more complex understandings that highlight political responsibility (Devereux 2000: 3; for an overview of these shifts, see Devereux 2006: 1–14). With over 80 per cent of famine deaths in the twentieth century located in China and the Soviet Union, and all those deaths occurring before 1965, the importance of political context is clearly paramount (Devereux 2000: 9). Indeed, we can extend the focus on political responsibility and conclude that "nothing 'causes' famine: people commit the crime of mass starvation" (Edkins 2006: 51).

The fact that famines are inescapably political is underpinned by the second important development in the twentieth and twenty-first centuries, whereby food crises are now located almost entirely in sub-Saharan Africa, where the intersection of political conflict and natural factors has been most acute (Devereux 2000: 3; this persists in Nigeria: see for example, Sieff 2016). This means that states previously free of food crises have become prone to conflict-induced famines. The first and most notable of these crises was Biafra in the late 1960s, yet this region of Nigeria was devoid of famine before the civil war and has remained free from famine since (Devereux 2000: 15).

While our understanding of the causes and context of famine has undergone major revision, the photographic portrayal of food crises has remained largely static through the use of stereotypes. A stereotype is something preconceived or oversimplified that is constantly repeated without change. Stereotypes involve icons, which are figures that represent events or issues. Icons have a sacred history but the attention they attract as objects of our gaze can produce a range of effects depending on time and place. The photographic deployment of particular icons via an established aesthetic to represent famine is a clear example of stereotypes at work. It is well illustrated by the 13 July 2003 cover of the *New York Times Magazine* designed to feature a story on "Why famine persists" (Bearak 2003). With a montage of 36 black-and-white photographs depicting famines in various African countries between 1968 and 2003, the unchanging reliance on portraits of either lone children or women in distress was there for all to see. The cover included images from well-known photographers – including Abbas, Eve Arnold, Stuart Franklin and Chris Steele-Perkins of Magnum – but the article did not address the persistence of this photographic style across time and place.

I examine the iconography of famine, asking how and why stereotypical portraits of famine victims continue to be produced and how they shape our understanding of the political complexities of food crises. I illustrate the issues at stake by going back to the case of Malawi in 2002. I do so because of the way this food crisis demonstrates clearly the political nature of contemporary famine, and because of the way one of the iconic photographs from this context travelled across the media to be used in a number of different ways.

The Malawi famine of 2002

"Africa's dying again" was the *Daily Mirror*'s page-one story on 21 May 2002 (see Imaging Famine 2002a). This "shock report" was illustrated on the cover by staff photographer Mike Moore's picture of Luke Piri (Figure 17.1), taken during a trip to Malawi with journalist Anton Antonowicz to uncover what the paper (Antonowicz 2002) described as the "world's worst tragedy since Ethiopia."

The colour photograph of Piri was one of at least three of the boy Moore took while in Ludzi near the Malawi–Zambian border. Two of the images show Piri posed against a bare wall, dressed only in pants, and looking directly if plaintively into the camera. One of the photos (not published in the paper) has Piri holding up an empty white bowl, chipped on the rim and containing no more than a single spoon, as though imploring the viewer for food. Another (that appears inside the paper alongside an equally emaciated girl) looks down on Piri as a staff member at the feeding centre holds him. Piri's dark eyes offer the only expression on an otherwise blank face. The caption – "HOPE: Luke Piri, three, clings to life" – anchors the message.

Moore's photograph of Piri was constructed as a portrait of atrocity. The three images of Luke Piri demonstrate the photographer organised the pictures, getting the boy to stand in front of a blank backdrop, and directing him to either hold a bowl or stand with his hands by his sides. As such, it follows in the footsteps of similar pictures, such as Don McCullin's (1992: 124) photograph of the Biafran girl Patience, which McCullin took after getting a mission orderly to arrange her with hands obscuring genitalia for the sake of dignity. It is another of the icons that make up the stereotypical representation of famine.

Moore's Malawi photographs were framed by both the purpose and presentation of the newspaper's story. In the second paragraph of the article (Antonowicz 2002), the function of the image is laid bare: "the emaciated body of the three-year-old in our front-page picture is covered in scabies. His belly is distended. His ribs racked. His suffering a symbol of famine stalking this tiny, landlocked nation." In conjunction with the headline about the scale of the imminent disaster, and opposite a half-page image of an outstretched hand displaying the dry grass that is said to substitute for food, the story is designed to jolt readers into action. With another banner headline, declaring "crops have failed, food prices have rocketed . . .," the paper is asking people to make charitable donations, and details of how to contribute to a Save the Children fund appeal are prominently displayed at the bottom of the page.

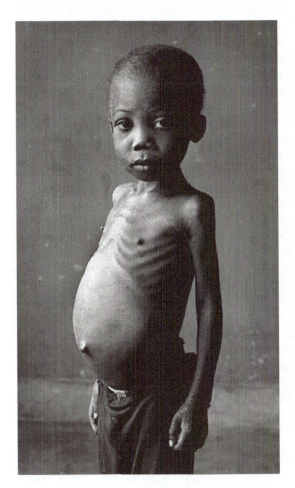

Figure 17.1 Luke Piri, aged three, suffering severe malnutrition, with his ribs exposed and distended belly he waits for his first meal since arriving at an orphans' feeding centre in Ludzi, eastern Malawi. Mike Moore, May 2002

Source: Mike Moore, "Africa's dying again," *The Daily Mirror*, 21 May 2002. Printed with permission from Mirrorpix.

The text of the article claims that both "excessive rains and prolonged drought depleted the maize harvest" and led to food shortages, giving credence to the idea that this is another natural disaster. However, the article also includes a range of political factors responsible for the crisis, including the liberalisation of agricultural policy foisted on a corrupt Malawian government by the International Monetary Fund (IMF), which resulted in the selling off of grain stocks that could have provided cover for food shortages. The situation in Malawi in 2002 embodied, therefore, the new understanding of famine as political.

Malawi is a country "in a perpetual state of food emergency" (Devereux 2002: 16). A litany of development statistics underscore the population's ongoing vulnerability to food shortages: two-thirds of the population live below the national poverty line, more than a quarter live in extreme poverty, and a third of the population have consistently poor levels of nutrition (Menon 2007). This vulnerability was made more acute by the combined effects of international and national governance strategies. More than a decade of structural adjustment policies promoted by the IMF, the World Bank and major donor countries removed subsidies for small farmers, dismantled price controls and privatised social agencies that had previously eased food insecurity (Owusu and Ng'ambi 2002: 10–11).

These changes in Malawi's political economy were evident in the sell-off of the Strategic Grain Reserve in 2002, only a few months after the Minister of Agriculture had warned the country's donors that a food deficit was forthcoming. In April 2002, shortly after international donors removed Malawi from the Highly Indebted Poor Country Interim Debt Relief Program over concerns about government corruption, the IMF recommended Malawi sell two-thirds of its grain reserves to repay a commercial South African bank loan. Going beyond the IMF position, the Malawian government sold all its grain stocks, resulting in private traders hoarding supplies in order to maximise profit. In the absence of price controls, the cost of maize had risen by 400 per cent in the six months to March 2002, so the confluence of these forces greatly hindered access to food (Owusu and Ng'ambi 2002: 10–11, 14; Devereux 2002: iii). As Devereux (2002: 15) makes clear, "famines are always a problem of disrupted access to food as much as restricted availability," and the political economy of access is more important than the restricted availability flowing from natural triggers.

The *Daily Mirror* story stated the natural triggers for the 2002 food crisis in Malawi were "only part of the picture" and they are surely correct in that assessment. We have to question, therefore, whether the photographs of Luke Piri are consistent with a story that encompasses both natural and political dimensions, and in which access to food is more significant than simple availability. Do the stereotypes allow for an understanding of the inherently political nature of famine? If not, what is their specific function and how do we explain their persistence?

The meaning of famine icons

Portraits individualise the social, and the photograph of Luke Piri, as a portrait of atrocity, conforms to the "ideologically Western mode" whereby "famine becomes the experience of the lone individual" (Kleinman and Kleinman 1996: 7). Regardless of the content of any supporting text, photographs of this kind suggest the individual is a victim without a context. Indigenous social structures are absent and local actors are erased. There is a void of agency and history with the victim arrayed passively before the lens so their suffering can be appropriated (Kleinman and Kleinman 1996: 7; Bleiker and Kay 2007: 149).

As appropriations of suffering, photographs are affective rather than simply illustrative. They are designed to appeal emotionally to viewers and connect them with subjects in a particular way. The message is that someone is suffering, we should be sympathetic to his or her plight and moved to do something. However, the lack of contextual support means that viewers regard action to alleviate suffering as coming from outside (Kleinman and Kleinman 1996: 1, 7). This structuring of the isolated victim awaiting external assistance is what invests such imagery with colonial relations of power.

As a historical and political formation, colonialism involves the governance of an indigenous population by a distant power. The practices of governmentality through which indigenous lives are managed are asymmetrical and unequal relations that structure the relationship of self and other, us and them, as superior/inferior, civilised/barbaric, developed/underdeveloped and so on. The colonial relationship between self and other can be conducted in a number of different modes, from violent suppression to a humanitarian concern with the well-being of colonial subjects, and it is the latter that the photographic stereotypes of famine invoke.

This is especially evident when the famine icons are portraits of children. The efficacy of the child as symbol flows from a number of associated cultural assumptions: children are abstracted from culture and society, granted an innate innocence, seen to be dependent, requiring protection and having developmental potential (Burman 1994: 238–53; 2008). By removing context while indicating the future, such imagery turns a particular individual into "a universal icon of human suffering," thereby depoliticising the circumstances through which the life of the photographed individual has been produced (Manzo 2008: 637). At the same time, because these tropes have a long colonial history, stereotypical photographs embody colonial relations of power that contrast an adult and superior global North with the infantilised and inferior global South. This is evident from the *Daily Mirror*'s use of the Luke Piri photograph on its cover alongside the headline "Africa's dying again." The continent is constructed in relation to the photograph, thereby infantilising and homogenising a space home to a billion people in 61 diverse political territories, most of who are not subject to famine.

The photographs of Luke Piri had a long life and travelled to other locations. For example, only weeks after appearing in the newspaper the same picture (albeit reversed) was used by a UK charity for an appeal advertisement (Imaging Famine 2002b). While similar pictures continue to dominate charitable appeals regardless of the time, place or issue, aid organisations working to provide assistance in the global South have signed up to codes of conduct designed to limit both the proliferation and negative effects of stereotypical images. However, there is no escaping the fact that because photographs are polyvalent, they can sustain paradoxical readings. In this sense, the malnourished child can be both a sign of humanitarian values and the symbol of an infantile, inferior and helpless zone of despair (Manzo 2008: 652; for a discussion of how this also operates in other issues, see Kozol 2004).

The possible need for famine icons

Famine iconography should be roundly condemned as simplistic, reductionist, colonial and even racist. But before we are satisfied with this comprehensive rebuke, we have to ask a couple of difficult questions. First, would we be better off without these photographs altogether? Of course, that depends on who the "we" is. It might be easy to say that it would be better for us in the global North to be free from portraits of atrocity, but does the same apply to citizens of the global South? What would it mean to have no images of atrocities like famine? Notwithstanding their critique of the appropriation of suffering in famine iconography, Kleinman and Kleinman (1996: 17) argue that the absent image is equally a form of political appropriation and that – thinking about the visual lacunae of the Chinese famine of 1959–61 – "public silence is perhaps more terrifying than being overwhelmed by public images of atrocity."

Second, if we want to dispense with the negative, what might be the positive that should take its place? In their *Images of Africa* report, Nikki van der Gaag and Cathy

Nash (1987) noted research showing photographs of smiling, satisfied individuals conveyed the idea that "we must have helped them" so that viewers believed "all Africans had become 'aided Africans.' " This means the scopic regime that produces "Africa" as a place of lack is so strong that many positive images only reinforce the colonial relations of power embodied in the negative images (van der Gaag and Nash 1987: 17; see also Campbell and Power 2010). Indeed, one of the few studies on the effect of atrocity images from "Africa," "The Live Aid legacy" (Voluntary Service Overseas 2002), demonstrated that "80% of the British public strongly associate the developing world with doom-laden images of famine, disaster and Western aid," thereby establishing a relationship where we are superior because of our humanitarian aid and charitable giving, and they are inferior, passive and dependent on us.

The coeval relationship of the negative and positive suggests that we need to move beyond these terms in framing our options. The South African photographer Guy Tillim (2009) put it well in an interview:

> One has to be careful with the positive/negative thing. Just because one takes images of dance halls in Lagos, and people being happy, it might end up being as much of a cliché as the suffering image. Positives images are one[s] that are self-aware or are interesting, penetrat[ing] and original no matter what they look at. Negatives images are ones that perpetuate the issue.

Tillim helps recast our sense of what is positive and negative by moving us towards an appreciation of the need for visual strategies that, by being reflexive and penetrating, understand what the stereotypes are and how they can be contested. This involves much more than rejecting one aesthetic and replacing it with another, not least because of the importance of continuing to see photographic records of atrocity. While their persistence and problems need to be analysed, this means we need to be less concerned about the *presence* of famine icons and more concerned about the *absence* of alternative, critical visualisations that can assist in capturing the political context of crises, thereby potentially shifting the scopic regime from the colonial to the postcolonial.

In moving beyond negative versus positive as the limit of our critical understanding, we also need to appreciate that there are moments when famine icons might be necessary in order to address the political context. Indeed, there are moments where we might understand famine iconography as being produced by the complex political circumstances they generally fail to capture. This can be demonstrated by a return to the case of the Malawi famine of 2002.

There was advance warning of food shortages in Malawi, but because of their strained relations with the government international donors "were not well disposed to reports of food shortages" (Devereux 2002: 14). The Malawian government was also resistant to stories of food crises from local NGOs. It was, in part, the production and circulation of famine iconography that broke this indifference. As Devereux's (2002: 15) postmortem of the crisis observed, "only after the media started reporting starvation deaths in Malawi did the donors reverse their hard-line stance and offer food aid unconditionally." The same dynamic has been repeated in other crises, such as the 2005 Niger famine, where the World Food Program (WFP) began reporting a looming crisis in October 2004 and called for donor assistance, but international assistance was minimal until the media got involved in July 2005. Anthea Webb (in Gutierrez 2006), WFP's senior public affairs officer noted:

All information is available. The problem is to turn information into providing food to people in need. In Niger we had practically nothing until we got footage on video of people dying of malnutrition to the BBC. But it is much better to help people before it is too late. In Niger we had made a very clear plea. The problem is getting the message across.

Although a free press has been regarded by many as part of a famine early-warning system, this record indicates the media is caught in a tragic conundrum. Governments and international institutions are not moved by information alone, and without official activity the media lacks a hook for a story. A story becomes possible when there is visual evidence of disaster, but in the case of famine that evidence cannot be easily visualised (at least in terms familiar to the media) until people start showing an embodied trace of the food crisis (as in Luke Piri's distended stomach and prominent ribs) or start dying. By that time, however, because of the indifference of governments, the final stages of a food crisis have begun, the possibility for preventative action has long passed, and the only course of action is humanitarian and remedial.

In Malawi, the *Daily Mirror*'s claim of two million facing death turned out to be a gross exaggeration, with the best estimate being that 1,000–3,000 people perished (Owusu and Ng'ambi 2002: 14; Devereux 2002: 18). That does not diminish the seriousness of the event, because at the height of the crisis of 2002, nearly 70 per cent of farming families faced food shortages. However, it wasn't until evidence of "excess mortality" could be pictured that the media had a way of telling the story, and because that is the end of the disaster, coverage emphasises the shock value, thereby "idealizing the photograph's power to repair the wrong" (Sliwinski 2006: 356).

Accordingly, "the media is a *late* indicator of distress, not an early warning. Journalists ... [are] like observers at a car crash, to report on the tragedy, not to prevent it" (Devereux 2002: 8). While we can criticise the *Daily Mirror*'s story and pictures for their reproduction of famine iconography, we have to appreciate how the recourse to stereotypes is often a function of the political context they seek to address but cannot represent. Importantly, this means "compassion fatigue" is not the issue with respect to the relationship between pictures and policy. People continue to respond to the humanitarian structure of feeling induced by photographs like that of Luke Piri. The problem is official indifference and the media's entrapment in that indifference until it is too late.

The ultimate challenge for photography as a technology of visualisation is to find compelling ways of narrating the story so that the political context of famine can be portrayed in a timely manner. Sometimes there are visual stories that achieve this, as in the *New York Times* photo report detailing how the new Malawian government rejected neoliberal policies, reinstated fertiliser subsidies and oversaw increased food production and reduced famine (*New York Times* 2007). Of course, journalists don't bear the primary responsibility for preventing famine but they need a better understanding of global malnourishment – of which famine is just an acute and more visible part – in order to represent the issue before it is too late.

Note

This chapter draws on my essay "The iconography of famine" (Campbell 2011).

18 Fear

Cynthia Weber

> The oldest and strongest emotion of mankind is fear, and the oldest and strongest
> kind of fear is the fear of the unknown.
>
> (H.P. Lovecraft 1927/1945: 1)

Fear of the unknown plays a significant role in global politics. In the field of security
studies, what most insecure populations, nation-states and global organisations fear is
not just what they know, but what they do not or cannot know. Very often, global
insecurities about knowing and not knowing are related to global insecurities about
seeing, not seeing or imagining what we see. As in the horror genre H.P. Lovecraft
describes, global political practices produce, circulate and mobilise fear through their
tactical use of visibilities, invisibilities and their related imaginaries.

This comes as no surprise to those familiar with the US-led War on Terror. One of
the enduring lessons of this war is that sovereign nation-states can craft their security
policy in opposition to not just the sometimes visible acts of terrorism by sometimes
visible (yet often imaginary) terrorists; they can also craft their security policy in
opposition to the more often invisible emotion of "terror" (Bleiker and Hutchison
2008). Among the ways the US linked visibilities, invisibilities, terror and security
during the War on Terror, I suggest here, is through its crafting of a particular kind
of US patriotism, what I call "fear-based patriotism."

Fear is not the first thing we typically think about when we think about patriotism.
This is because patriotism is traditionally understood as national loyalty that takes the
form of love, devotion, support and the defence of one's country. Yet patriotism also
takes the form of hate, loathing, rejection and the attack of those people, places and
organisations that are deemed to be a threat to the nation. During the War on Terror,
patriotic US citizens and their coalition partners learned to convey their patriotism by
denying (Weber 2003, 2006a), embracing (2006b) or (re)mediating (Debrix and Weber
2003; Weber 2003, 2008a) their fear of terrorists and terrorism. Yet no matter how it
was expressed during the War on Terror, patriotism inevitably manifested itself as or
in relation to fear-based patriotism.

This fear-based patriotism drew upon long-standing Western orientalist visual
traditions that primarily marked racially darkened people wearing "Arab," Muslim,
and Sikh bodily coverings (beards, hijabs, turbans) as evil individuals who represented
evil civilisations (Ford 2001; Huntington 1996; for critique, see Said 2001). Primed
by cinematic encounters that circulated these visual tropes as causes of terror and
terrorism that justified domestic and global wars (McAlister 2005; Weber 2006b,
2008b), Western audiences were taught to associate "*reel* bad Arabs" with real bad

terrorists (Jack G. Shaheen 2015). They were also taught that real bad terrorists could take innumerable forms, some of which had not yet explicitly been associated with "the terrorist." This allowed a Western fear of reel/real bad "Arab" terrorists to progressively expand the category of "the terrorist" to include any person or group who opposed "national values." It was this expanded fear-based patriotism that came to ground and epitomised what it meant in official Western coalition discourses to be a patriot during the War on Terror.

At the same time, another form of patriotism sat alongside this fear-based patriotism – what Evelyn Alsultany (2007, 2012) calls "diversity patriotism," a patriotism that makes the celebration of diversity its foundation for feelings of national unity. Diversity patriotism is produced in many ways, including through visual strategies found in public service announcements – public interest messages designed to raise awareness of social issues with the aim of changing public attitudes and behaviours.

In this chapter, I examine one of the most iconic forms of visual media through which diversity patriotism was circulated immediately after 11 September 2001: the American Advertising Council's "I am an American" public service announcement (hereafter, "the ad"). By discussing the visual strategies employed in the ad, I explore how diversity patriotism – which would appear to be antithetical to fear-based patriotism – is premised upon fear-based patriotism (for an extended reading of the ad's aural and textual strategies as well, see Weber 2013).

Diversity patriotism in the American Ad Council's "I am an American" public service announcement

On 21 September 2001 – 10 days after 9/11 – the American Ad Council launched its "I am an American" advertising campaign (Ad Council 2004a). The campaign featured 30- and 60-second public service announcements broadcast on US television in which a montage of US citizens of various ages, races, religions and ethnicities look directly into the camera and declare, "I am an American" while emotive American music plays in the background. The US motto appears on the screen, first in Latin, then in English – "E Pluribus Unum," Out of Many, One. The final shot is of a young girl – possibly Arab, possibly South Asian, possibly Hispanic. She rides her bike in Brooklyn Bridge Park across the river from where the Twin Towers used to be. Smiling broadly, the little girl waves a US flag. According to the Ad Council (which is the leading producer of public service announcements in the US), the "I am an American" campaign "helped the country to unite in the wake of the terrorist attack" by "celebrat[ing] the nation's extraordinary diversity" (Ad Council 2004a).

The "I am an American" ad illustrates "diversity-patriotism, whereby racialised groups are temporarily incorporated into the imagined community of 'Americans'" to the point that "[d]ifference is identified as defining the nation" (Alsultany 2007: 598). The cinematic strategies the ad employs to achieve this diversity patriotism are masterful. It saturates the visual space with a diversity of sharply focused unnamed US Americans and softly focused familiar Americana backdrops, like a fire station in lower Manhattan or the Golden Gate Bridge in San Francisco. It saturates the aural space with the repetitive yet performatively varied mantra "I am an American" uttered with an array of accents, inflections and intensities. It sets these visual and aural representations to the emotive American music "Short Trip Home" by Edgar Meyer that has a Coplandesque quality to it. And it literally spells out what its message is –

"E Pluribus Unum," Out of Many, One – a phrase that, according to the makers of the ad, communicates "out of many faces, religions, geographical backgrounds, and ethnicities, we are one nation" (Ad Council 2004b).

By employing these cinematic strategies, the "I am an American" ad constructs not only difference but also the ideal of the visible *tolerance of difference* as the foundation of the modern US nation (Brown 2006; Weber 2007, 2008b). It is as if the US identity announced in the original US motto "E Pluribus Unum" (which in 1776 referred to the uniting of different US colonies into one federal system) always referred to the visible "melting" of individual racial and ethnic differences of US Americans into the visually united citizenry of the United States, and as if this melting and the acceptance of all those melted into this pot by all US citizens were a long-ago accomplished fact (Berlant 1997; Fortier 2008; Marciniak 2006). The ad achieves this feat by attempting to solve what R.B.J. Walker (1990) refers to as the three problems facing the author-isation of the sovereign nation-state – the need to resolve the relationships between (1) the universal and the particular; (2) the self and the other; and (3) space and time.

The ad resolves the universal/particular problem by attaching to the sign "America" a plurality of apparently visible individual bodily differences (skin colour, age, sex) of US American citizens while at the same time denying these individual citizens any invisible, private signs of difference (their names, their lived histories, their easy or complicated relationships with the US state). The ad resolves the self/other problem by appearing to dissolve all visible differences within the sameness of the US melting pot, while it nonetheless excludes or leaves ambiguous differences that might disturb the national melting pot ideal. For example, apart from two visually ambiguous indivi-duals who might be either "Arab" or Muslim but cannot be definitively identified as such, the ad includes "no visible markers of anything Arab, Muslim, or Sikh [which is misread as Muslim by some US Americans], no veil, no mosque, no turban, no beard; no distinctive Arab, Muslim or Sikh clothing" (Alsultany 2007: 598). In this way, Alsultany (2007: 598) concludes, "the Ad Council affirms the binary between 'the citizen' and 'the terrorist'" both inside and outside the US nation-state. Finally, the ad resolves the space/time problem by domesticating a particular identification – the claim to be "American" – within the United States rather than within the larger continent that goes by this name and by excluding histories past and present that might make this claim contingent. It does this not only by taking famous US landmarks as backgrounds in some shots. It also does this by excluding any unambiguous visual signs of Indigenous Americans in the ad, a population that even today is not containable in the national imagery of either a territorial state like the United States or within the modernist history of progress narrated through the melting pot myth (Sollors 1996; Shaw 2009).

It is on the basis of this specific yet universalisable construction of a visibly collective US national identity in which body is nation, diversity is identity, and tolerance is patriotic citizenship that the ad hails every US citizen to actively tolerate those differences that compose this "America." But because of the necessary visual exclusions and ambiguities the ad employs to assemble this ideal "America," what the ad also does is remind US Americans of how distinct they are from those whose differences – foreign and domestic – cannot be melted into this "America." It is these unseen differences that the ad implicitly instructs US Americans not to tolerate, for these are the differences embodied by those who presumably hate "us." It is these US Americans who are to be feared because they embody the fear of known terrorists or the fear of unknowable terror itself.

In this respect, then, the ad draws a line between the normative white or normatively melted US citizen and the threatening Muslim, "Arab" or Sikh terrorist, as Alsultany argues (2007: 598). By representing some "culturalised" differences as acceptable and failing to visually represent other "culturalised" differences at all, the ad encourages a more amorphous, unanchored fear of any unseen, unknown or imagined difference – not only racial and religious but also indigenous, sexual and political – that is not clearly represented in the ad.

For example, the US singer Pat Boone tapped into this fear of amorphous, unanchored difference when he connected LGBTQI rights activists with terrorists. He did this by labelling gay rights activists working in 2008 to overturn California's ban on gay marriage as "sexual jihadists." Writing about these activists in the context of the November 2008 Mumbai terrorist attacks, Boone (2008) made the following comment:

> What troubles me so deeply, and should trouble all thinking Americans, is that there is a real, unbroken line between the jihadist savagery in Mumbai and the hedonistic, irresponsible, blindly selfish goals and tactics of our home-grown sexual jihadists. Hate is hate, no matter where it erupts. And by its very nature, if it's not held in check, it will escalate into acts vile, violent and destructive.
>
> (Boone 2008; see also Weber 2016)

By failing to visually represent indigenous, sexual and political differences as melted into the US ideal of itself, the ad leaves open the possibility that these differences, too, might be threatening to US citizens and the US nation-state now or in the future. In this way, the ad even more narrowly draws a line around what Alsultany (2007: 596) calls "the limits of cultural citizenship." And it is only within the limits of this narrowly drawn, acceptable cultural citizenship that US citizens are hailed by the ad to transform the aesthetic illusion propagated by the ad of a united (albeit exclusive) US national identity into a practical fact.

Visualising diversity and difference

Contrary to its intended purpose of preventing "a possible backlash against Arab Americans and other ethnic groups after the [9/11] attacks" (Ad Council 2004a), the Ad Council's "I am an American" ad helps to organise a specific visual US national imaginary in which some but not all bodies are equated with the US nation, some but not all differences are equated with US identity, and some but not all forms of tolerance are equated with patriotic citizenship. In so doing, the ad simultaneously anchors itself in a celebration of diversity on the one hand and a fear of difference on the other (for a critical reading of the ad as an illustration of "filming the fear of difference," see Weber 2007, 2008b, 2010, 2013). For even though individuals, societies, nations and states regularly conflate the two, the celebration of diversity does not necessarily equate to the celebration of difference. Rather, the celebration of diversity often explicitly refuses difference and thereby refutes the politics of difference (Fortier 2008).

It is through this simultaneous conflation of diversity with difference and strategic visual separation of these two terms that the ad effectively constructs a complex, mobile system of differentiation in which some differences mark citizens as "safe citizens" and others mark them as "unsafe citizens." "Safe citizens" are those citizens whose differences can be made to normatively conform to national ideals during the

War on Terror historical moment so that they not only pose no threat to their state but, rather, they defend their state from threats by confirming these national ideals. In contrast, "unsafe citizens" are those citizens who either will not or cannot make their differences normatively conform to the national ideals of this particular historical moment, making them real or potential threats to "unifying" national ideals and to the US state's vision of itself.

It is these unsafe citizens – US citizens who are beyond the limits of US cultural citizenship – who are cautioned by the ad to keep their "culture" (a euphemism for "disturbing differences") private so that their differences do not endanger the US nation-state or frighten the US citizenry (Brown 2006). For if these unsafe citizens do not melt into/mesh with the US image of itself after 9/11, they are likely to find themselves on the wrong side of the us/them divide, whether they are "American" or not. This has proved to be another unfortunate legacy of the US-led War on Terror, which continues to play itself out in contemporary forms of Western fear-based patriotisms.

The "I am an American" ad, then, is not only a visual celebration of US diversity patriotism; it is a visual form of fear-based patriotism that warns "different" US Americans to align with the national side by keeping what could be their disturbing cultural differences private or face the consequences. As such, the ad reinforces the message President George W. Bush made before a Joint Session of the US Congress the day before the "I am an American" ad was broadcasted – "Either you are with us or you are with the terrorists" (Bush 2001). For even though President Bush's words were directed to foreign nations that harbour terrorists, his words, like the "I am an American" ad, attempted to persuade US citizens and Western coalition citizens more broadly to underwrite the sovereign power of their state in the War on Terror or face the possibility of having their own state's sovereign power unleashed against them.

19 Finance

James Brassett

Recent years have seen an unprecedented level of popular and critical interest in finance. Finance is a subject of daily news coverage, intense political debate, as well as everyday struggles and resistances like Occupy, Strike Debt, and the Indignados movement. Ideas of crisis, austerity and "banker bonuses" have become a commonplace of financial journalism.

Interestingly, over a similar time period, the academic study of finance has broadened beyond a specialist circle of economists and financial historians to include a burgeoning critical literature on the everyday and cultural political economy of finance that draws from international relations (IR), geography, social studies of finance, English literature and art (Langley 2008; Marsh 2011; North 2014). This new-found pluralism is not just a reflection of responsive academic business models, but points to a growing recognition of the complex and nuanced politics of finance. Gone are the days when the study of finance could be limited to the technical study of "efficient market hypothesis" and the various algorithms of investment, risk and volatility that build from it. Now there is a widespread understanding that finance entails ambiguity, limitation, instability, power, hierarchy, winners and losers. In short, finance carries a host of political dilemmas that are increasingly known, represented and discussed across popular, policy and academic circles.

This growing recognition of the political dimension of global finance presents a dilemma for critical thought: why has nothing changed? If there is a growing appreciation that finance is problematic, unstable, hierarchical, contestable and changeable, then surely this would hasten the reform objectives of critical policy makers and civil society as well as fostering practices of resistance by alternative financial organisations and individual financial subjects? But quite the reverse is so. The past decade has seen an intensification of private and public debt, securitisation and speculative practices, all hastened by the rise of 24-hour seamless global markets and "curiosities," like high-frequency trading and the accommodation of central banks via low interest rates and "quantitative easing." In the words of one liberal scholar (Helleiner 2014), this has been "the status quo crisis." The financial element of everyday global life continues to expand in quantity and quality at a relentless pace and even as we become more widely aware of the uncertainties entailed.

In this chapter I want to argue that part of the reason for the relative lack of change relates to the visual politics of finance. By this I mean to suggest that finance, per se, does not "exist." One cannot point at finance. Finance is always-already a product of representation. It is in the process of representation that much of the politics of finance is shaped, I will argue, so as to govern the expansion of financial life. What do I mean by this? Take something as commonplace as money. While we can point at, even touch money, only a very small proportion of money takes on a physical form. There is electronic code, of course, and money can be – in principle – printed to match the theoretical quantities that exist. But what you see when you look at a bank note is better understood as a representation of money, the value of which is both unstable and uncertain. Think about the intermediation function of banks, for instance. Banks take deposits and make profits by lending out those deposits over longer periods at higher interest rates. This means that on any given day, the value of actual money which banks hold is drastically smaller than the amount their depositors are theoretically able to draw (Rethel and Sinclair 2012). On this view, a bank run is actually more rational than might be supposed; and money is a collective agreement not to talk about it.

What are we not talking about? In a word, *value*. Money, like gold or shiny cars, is a representation of value, and value is a social relation of subjective judgement(s). People value what they believe other people will value, and this process is itself potentially reflexive over time. On this view investment markets have less to do with instrumentalities of demand and supply: instead they work through participants' judgements of what other participants will value. Thus, the value of any value can go up or down depending on all sorts of inter-subjective factors. Some basic implications of this strange way of valuing value include the question of how a covered garage in the centre of London can be worth a million pounds, how high-frequency trading vehicles can work so well that they short circuit the New York Stock Exchange, and how the value of foreign exchange markets can exceed the *annual* value of global gross national product in less than five trading days. The issue for anyone interested in the politics of finance is that all of this uncertainty is itself priced into the market via risk and so, in a sense, uncertainty becomes an element in stability. So let's not talk about it.

The visual politics of finance is not simply a story about "big" "bad" financiers duping us all once again, but is intimately intertwined with the critical repertoires of engagement and reform. The first section considers visual representations of normal and abnormal finance. The second section unpicks those "critical" visual representations of finance that do exist and asks how they also work to distract from genuine reflection on the contingency and mutability of finance.

Visualising (ab)normal finance

Finance lends itself to visual images and metaphors. For all the preponderance of financial products, practices and issues in everyday life, it still carries a certain esoteric or opaque quality. While some might understand the nature of their credit card or mortgage debt (all too intimately), it is quite another thing to speak about foreign exchange reserves, debt swaps, derivatives or sovereign credit ratings. Often ignored as too complicated for the general public to understand, when financial news stories break, the media tends to draw on pictures and metaphor. The stock market is depicted through large groups of men in a room, shouting across each other; in moments of turmoil they touch their faces. A bank run is depicted in movies and news as people queuing round the side of a bank. Even the apparently more "sober" or "solid" elements of finance carry a stock set of visual tropes: the City is gleaming skyscrapers, the banker is a man in a suit, the insurer has a bowler hat. But in recent decades the idea of *finance gone wrong* has become a central idea.

An important visual trope of the 2008 sub-prime crisis was the idea of a financial tsunami. This metaphor – often depicted in cartoon form – was a popular image used and deployed across a range of media depicting the 2008 sub-prime mortgage crisis as a financial tsunami that was "spreading across the world." The idea was that this financial tsunami had a foundation in the US mortgage market, but that the shockwave would spread across the globe. As a visual discourse of finance, such images suggest that financial crisis can be understood as an acute natural disturbance with profound and destabilising implications. A simple emergency therefore has clear implications: financial crisis is bad and we need to stop it. While global finance has often relied upon metaphors of size and heroism – "global finance" as a "phoenix risen" and populated by "rocket scientists" – the history of finance demonstrates how metaphorical tropes have worked to produce such "positives" against the negative of finance in crisis. Marieke de Goede (2000: 72) argues that a stable rising market is associated with cold reason, a rational mastery of the fundamentals, whereas a plummeting market is produced as hysterical or mad:

> The argument that situates financial crises in the realm of delusion and madness sustains a discourse of transcendental reality. By locating financial crisis in the aberrant domain of mad behaviour, the normal, regular and sane workings of financial markets are reaffirmed. Irrationality, excess and greed are located externally to the financial system; they may disturb the system from time to time, but have no proper place in it. Thus, the financial system is imagined as a coherent and rational whole.

When financial markets go out of control there is often a sense that some higher power – be it fortune or nature, is making itself felt. Here, we can begin to see a line from the notion of finance as rational (and financial crisis as irrational) through to logic of nature as a disturbance (to the scientific, masculine dominion of finance). For instance, we are quite used to thinking about "market turbulence," where traders are forced to "weather the storm." Indeed, the Asian financial crisis in the early nineties was commonly referred to as a "hurricane" in significant policy papers (see for example, Goldstein in Peterson, Goldstein and Hills 1999: 6). Such metaphorical images work to produce finance as normal, and crisis as abnormal. And such binary performances of (ab)normal finance work to obscure hierarchies, ambiguities and contests in favour of maintaining order.

Complex financial arrangements are rendered as immutable, something we live with, rather than something we make. Interestingly, the discourse of the sub-prime crisis drew upon and developed such natural metaphors by focusing most directly on their traumatic qualities. Rather than nature, divorced from context, a "financial tsunami" whose foundations were the sub-prime mortgage market, threatened to engulf the world. As Ngaire Woods (2009) argued, "Just when many of the world's poor countries have fought their way back – and started building democracies that work, businesses that grow, exports that sell – a tsunami is swelling up out of the banks of the rich world."

The idea of presenting the financial crisis as a "tsunami" is an interesting one because it promotes a discourse of natural disaster with potential humanitarian effects. This idea of a financial tsunami was common across a range of media commentators and policy actors, including Gordon Brown who called for an early-warning system akin to the early-warning system he endorsed around the time of the actual tsunami.

Indeed, the use of imagery like "tsunami" draws upon (now) common understandings of mass death associated with the 2005 tsunami that hit Thailand, Sri Lanka and India. The implicit suggestion is that the sub-prime crisis was not only an example of the awesome power of natural finance, but also an "event" literally capable of threatening the lives of hundreds of thousands of people. Savers were depicted in fear for their money, homeowners were quizzed about what they would do if the bank foreclosed or their house prices went down. Understandably, when told about the onset of a "financial tsunami," popular emotions were indeed marked by shock and fear, but interestingly there was also a mobilisation of other traumatic emotions, including shame – both individual and collective – as well as anger for the alleged perpetrators.

Visualising excessive finance: men and sex

The "blame game" that emerged sought to identify numerous candidates and make them feel guilt for their role. Clearly the excesses of bankers, predatory lending and high remuneration were major issues, but equally, perhaps, there was a more general reflection upon the way that we were *all personally* responsible: we had borrowed too much, and had not learnt from the mistakes of our predecessors in the Great Depression (Brassett and Clarke 2012). This move to visualise finance through ideas of natural disaster, trauma and fear allows the politics of finance to be simplified. There has been a traumatic event and we need to respond quickly and urgently by bailing out the banks and monitoring for future events. Even the apparently critical turn to blame bankers can be understood as a move to avoid "talking about" finance. It establishes a further dividing practice between normal and excessive finance.

If the dramatic images of a financial tsunami were part of a (limited) repertoire of humanitarian governance that seeks to re-frame sovereign power for new circumstances, surely there are possibilities for resistance? Indeed, the period of the global financial crisis has been a powerful spur for critical and popular movements "against" finance. However, one of the key visual images of excessive finance – the male banker – has become a limit for critical thought. Here we might think about popular media debates about the role of men in the financial crisis, which ask questions like: "If Lehman Brothers had been Lehman Sisters, run by women instead of men, would the credit crunch have happened?" Or as Robert Peston (2009) put it: is the financial crisis just a story about "men behaving badly"?

Most explicitly, the critical documentary *Inside Job* (2011) presents an aesthetic of banking reminiscent of Oliver Stone's *Wall Street* (1987): gleaming skyscrapers adorn high-powered individuals. Bankers are portrayed as living a high life of exciting experiences and vast amounts of money. Investment bankers receive special treatment as exotic others: six-figure bonuses, sports cars and so on. *Inside Job* portrays one Icelandic banker who buys a pin-striped private jet, for instance. In this way, the personal mores of bankers are brought into question. They are all (apparently) men, who regularly take cocaine and visit strip clubs and prostitutes. Indeed, the film interviews a high-class prostitute about her business relations with Wall Street bankers said to run into the thousands. The objective appears to be to portray a particular form of immoral financier, a footloose, non-embedded metaphor for capitalism: "In an industry in which drug use, prostitution, and fraudulent billing of prostitutes as a business expense occur on an industrial scale, it wouldn't be hard to make people talk if you really wanted to" (narrator, *Inside Job*).

In the fallout of the crisis, pundits blamed the testosterone-driven culture of investment banking and asked whether finance needed to be more feminine, understood as: more risk averse, nurturing and sharing. Such representations worked to essentialise gender roles, drawing on assumptions about how women are (allegedly) more patient and caring, more nurturing – mindful of the long-term well-being of their families – and thus, more akin to the type of finance to which we want to return. In contrast to the naturalised images of financial catastrophe in the tsunami image, suddenly the idea of nature was mobilised through the image of the woman – and the mothering potential of figures such as Angela Merkel and Christine Lagarde – to promote a "return" to stable finance (Brassett and Rethel 2015). This use of gender as a register for critical engagement worked to naturalise finance and render its politics in simple terms. As Robert Peston (2009) remarked:

> I think there may be a sense (and here I'm on very dangerous territory) in which masculine vices played a dominant role in fomenting the crunch. . . . if we're looking to prevent a repetition of the kind of financial calamity we've just endured, it mightn't be a bad start to appoint a woman as chief executive of Citigroup (or HSBC), or as chancellor of the exchequer or even (heaven forfend) as governor of the Bank of England.

The visual politics of finance

The visual politics of finance promotes the idea that finance "is something" that "does something." This is an alluring idea since it suggests that finance might be "good," even if it is sometimes "bad," and thus (understandable) modes of political engagement can be entertained, for example, "stop the crisis," "recover."

However, such simplification – with its naturalising metaphors of "hurricanes," "tsunamis," "naughty boys," and "good mothers" – is a distraction that both re-produces the problematic of financial expansion (if only we get it right this time) and therefore doubly disarms agency. We are blind both to the role of agency in the constitution of finance – finance-as-social-practice – and thus to the possibility of thinking of alternatives. For instance, everyday practices of local currencies can set parameters on community exposure to risk and circuit capital in reciprocal terms. Equally, local banking practices have long suggested a move away from credit scoring and, sometimes even, the very idea of interest. In these ways the visual economy of finance may need to be thought beyond images of shock, devastation or blame, and towards "small," practices of everyday finance: the coins we carry, the wider financial arrangements we engage or refuse.

20 Foreign policy

Simon Philpott

Visual culture is rich with references to foreign policy. Imagery of the making and consequences of foreign policy are ubiquitous, whether in fine art, television news reporting of international conferences, photos of world leaders clad in "awkward Apec fashion" (Anonymous 2015), images of human beings in flight from conflict, or the backstories to videogames.

It is perhaps film – in either its factual or fictional version – that has provided the most sustained engagement with foreign policy over decades. Documentary film has generally taken a clear-eyed and unsentimental view of foreign policy by focusing on its often disastrous consequences. By contrast, popular cinematic accounts of events like the Cuban missile crisis, such as *Thirteen Days* (2000), are political thrillers that put suspense and tension, and so perhaps a certain glamour, at the heart of foreign policy decision making. That is not to say that all lavishly produced fictional accounts of foreign policy are necessarily without historical merit or that each made-to-a-budget documentary film is burdened with impenetrable fact at the expense of its visual appeal. Rather, along the fact–fiction continuum different genres of film, whether popular and fictional or truth-seeking documentary, engage with the visual in distinctive ways.

The threat or advent of conflict has often spurred Hollywood to make popular films that address the foreign policy challenges of the United States and other Western democracies. This was in no small part because the governments of the Soviet Union and National Socialist Germany quickly recognised that film was not only a powerful means of communication but also an ideal way to realise their political projects. With her *Triumph of the Will* (1935), Leni Riefenstahl set new standards in political communication and provided a breath-taking visual account of Germany's new regime, one designed not so much to convince as to impress (Rotha 1967: 588). Similarly, cinema was the vehicle used by the Soviet Union to communicate the supposed superiority of its system and by the early 1930s was its principal means of expression (Rotha 1967: 219). Frank Capra's legendary *Why We Fight* (1942–5) documentaries are one of the earliest direct responses to the perceived threat of National Socialist Germany. It is also an early example of collaboration between the United States government and the creative industries to persuade ordinary people of the need to take difficult foreign policy decisions. As Capra (1971) observed, Riefenstahl's film "fired no gun, dropped no bombs. But as a psychological weapon aimed at destroying the will to resist, it was just as lethal."

Hollywood and the visualisation of conflict

It is not just the content of films that is influential in shaping the understanding of complex foreign policy issues. Consider how in the first hours after the attacks on New York and Washington in 2001 television networks had to make do with fragmentary shots of the crashing planes. But as they found and assembled footage during the subsequent days, so-called "continuity editing" became possible: "By the second or third day, viewers brought up on the technique of Hollywood disaster movies were able to watch a sequence of images that made dramatic sense" (Bolter 2005: 10–11). Shocking and traumatic in their own right, it is nonetheless Hollywood genre conventions that provided substantive meaning to the attacks. Given the expectations created by Hollywood – expectations that the red, white and blue of the American flag are colours that don't run – it is highly likely that a policy of military aggression may have appeared as the only acceptable course of action to George Bush and his policy advisers. Yes, the administration longed to topple Saddam Hussein in Iraq, but not to have responded militarily to the attacks on New York and Washington may have confounded Americans to the point of loss of confidence in the government of the day. In other words, it is not merely the plotlines of popular films that matter but that the very medium of visual entertainment itself creates, over time, entrenched expectations of what the conduct of foreign policy should look like. It is here that documentary film, less glamorous, generally produced on far smaller budgets, often with little visual candy, struggles to be seen and heard in reminding audiences of the hard lessons of foreign policy misadventure learned in past conflicts.

In the decades since the Second World War, there have been perhaps thousands of films that have in one way or another engaged with foreign policy and its making. They have explored many themes, including the threat of nuclear war, espionage, terror, natural disaster and environmental crises. Most often cinema has delved into foreign policy through the genres of drama and thriller, but comedic accounts, such as *Dr Strangelove*, have also revealed the paradoxes and at times absurdities of foreign policy and its performance (see for example, Erickson 2012). But while war, crisis and espionage are common themes in popular cinema about foreign policy, it is no accident that economic relations between states are largely neglected. The most skilled directors struggle to make interesting days, weeks and months of drawn-out negotiations about economic policy primarily carried out by middle-aged and older men (Gregg 1998: 9). Indeed, films about foreign policy are often obliged, even when seeking to faithfully reproduce an event or crisis, to indulge in a certain poetic crafting of events. As Robert Gregg notes, literal accounts of history are often dull and weighed down by ambiguities and are unlikely to satisfy cinema audiences (Gregg 1998: 7). Directors must attend to quenching the desire of audiences for both plot and visual satisfaction.

Loners and mavericks: heroic and masculine depictions of foreign policy crises

The use of artistic licence to fulfil established popular expectations leads cinema to offer a view of foreign policy that bears little resemblance to how politics is routinely conducted. Often we encounter an exaggerated depiction of an individual who intervenes in crisis situations, turns disaster into success and saves his country or the world from a catastrophe.

Rebels, mavericks, loners and, indeed, sociopaths of many kinds make up the world of foreign policy on film. Frequently, these well-meaning loners act against direct instructions because they believe they have a better grasp not only of the situation at hand but also of their country's best interests. Indeed, such mavericks often act against the interests and instructions of mainstream politicians, who they believe have corrupted the values of their country. As the journalist John Allemang (2001) wrote on the day following the attacks on New York and Washington in 2001: "Hollywood has schooled us to see the response to terrorism and disaster as a heroic human story." The phenomenal popularity of Sylvester Stallone's John Rambo rests in part on the idea of a man of integrity wronged and abandoned by a system corrupted by politicians who no longer act in the interests of the United States. Likewise, whatever else one may want to say about the private war he is waging, Marlon Brando's Colonel Kurtz (*Apocalypse Now*) frames his activities as an explicit critique of American foreign policy. Jake Gyllenhaal's Douglas Freeman (*Rendition*) acts in defiance of orders and against a key aspect of US foreign policy when he releases a supposed terrorist because he recognised that torture has prompted a false confession (Klein 2005). British spy James Bond has made a career out of skirting authority and maintaining a deeply narcissistic attitude. Most of these heroes are white men, presented to audiences not just as righteous but also as sexually desirable.

It is not just the fictional characters of popular film that are framed as loners and mavericks. Mike Shapiro highlights how George Bush's advisers went to great lengths to script his actions in the mode of a Hollywood western, as a frontier hero who charges ahead with the moral certitude necessary to seek retribution for the attacks of September 2001. Recognising the power of popular film, Bush's advisers were keen to frame the War on Terror as a black-and-white story that opposes "us" versus "them," "good" versus "evil." In this civilisation versus barbarianism narrative the capture of Osama bin Laden, dead or alive, raised no significant moral questions (Shapiro 2004: 174). American vigilantism found expression or was read into films such as *Memento* (2000), *In the Bedroom* (2001) and *Collateral Damage* (2002). Each of them is about revenge and retribution. The key protagonists take matters into their own hands, outside the bounds of law.

How fiction film depicts war in simplistic ways

The motivations for foreign policy action (and inaction) are often complex and driven not just by one's own perceived interests but by those of others. However, viewers of popular fictional films are often only given one perspective on a foreign policy issue. Given the dominance of Hollywood in producing films for Anglophone audiences it comes as no surprise that the perspective that viewers most frequently encounter is that of the United States. Yet Hollywood's examination and exploration of American foreign policy is rather mixed. For example, Hollywood had little to say about the war in Vietnam while it was ongoing. And yet, numerous subsequent films were made, often to critical acclaim, and with great success at the box office. Hollywood's aversion to tackling the war in Vietnam during the period of American involvement is widely regarded as arising from a blend of Hollywood's caution after the traumas of McCarthyism and the moral ambiguities of the war itself (Augé 2002). Unlike the Second World War, which Hollywood portrayed as a just and necessary war against fascism in Europe and militarism in Asia, the war in Vietnam was depicted in much more ambiguous terms (Weber 2006b). Films released after the conflict portrayed it as an American tragedy, often focusing on how the war degraded the physical and mental health of US combatants and eroded their capacity for sound moral judgement. But, at the same time, there is hardly a credible Vietnamese character to be seen and almost no perspective offered on what the war meant to those trying to repel the world's most significant military power.

Hollywood and the UK film industry have engaged more directly and immediately with recent US foreign policy in a number of films made about the wars in Iraq and Afghanistan. Unlike the Vietnam films, these entail at least some character development of "enemy combatants" who share with audiences their grievances about US foreign policy. For example, Nick Broomfield's *Battle for Haditha* (2007) depicts the lives of ordinary Iraqis, including those implicated in the detonation of a roadside bomb that provoked a retaliatory massacre carried out by US troops. One of the bombers (Ahmad) is a middle-aged former Iraqi military officer, incensed about the economic insecurity arising from his demobilisation by US occupying authorities. We see him in the loving embrace of his family and yet sufficiently enraged by the invasion and subsequent insurgency that he takes action against US forces for reasons of revenge and personal reward. The simple visual device of locating Ahmad with his children serves to humanise him and provides a space of reflection on the consequences of US foreign policy. However, few of these films, which are often critical of US foreign policy, fared well at the box office. Most were savaged by right-wing commentators and film critics. It was not until the release of the genre-transcending (and Academy Award-winning) *The Hurt Locker* (2008) that a War on Terror-themed film achieved both critical and commercial success.

How documentary films challenge foreign policy conventions

Documentary film, very much the poor relation to fiction film, has a rather more impressive history of analysing the making and consequences of foreign policy. Indeed, the genre is replete with films and directors who have challenged foreign policy conventions and the harm done by particular choices in foreign policy making. Numerous contemporary documentary filmmakers continue the genre's tradition of exposing the effects of great power foreign policy decision making. Among them are Errol Morris, John Pilger, Michael Moore, Alex Gibney, Werner Herzog, Robert Greenwald, Laura Poitras and Deborah Scranton. Indeed, the list of films nominated for Academy Awards that are examinations of US and Western foreign policy making is extensive. While not all are direct explorations of foreign policy decision making, films like Joshua Oppenheimer's *The Act of Killing* (2012) and *The Look of Silence* (2014) delve into human tragedies that in part arise from the structures of Cold War politics and, particularly, from the confrontation of communism in East and Southeast Asia by the United States and its allies. Since 2010 there have arguably been seven Academy Award contenders that deal with aspects of (primarily) US foreign policy, including 2015's winner *Citizen Four* (2014). A review of earlier decades reveals a similarly steady stream of Academy Award-nominated films that have probed the consequences of foreign policy making.

Documentary films are usually made on much smaller budgets and make little use of special effects. They are rarely afforded the kind of marketing efforts that Hollywood's fictional films enjoy. Nor do they feature the star-power draw of blockbuster movies. One possible exception is *Fahrenheit 9/11* (2004), which grossed nearly US$24m on its first weekend and broke a range of records for documentary film, largely because of the notoriety of its writer, director and star, Michael Moore. Unlike fictional accounts of foreign policy, which tend to revolve around melodramatic narratives and sweeping conclusions, documentary as a genre tends to be more complex (Brown and Rafter 2013, 1019). They often wrestle with issues of ethical representation, strive for ambivalence, resist premature closure and seek to disorient their audiences such that the potential for transition from spectatorship to witness may be realised (Brown and Rafter 2013: 1019–20). Bearing witness to the ethics and consequences of foreign policy is a key area of departure between fictional and documentary accounts.

Why films of foreign policy matter

Why does all this matter? It matters because cinema, in particular, is where people go to learn something about the world and its events, issues and conflicts. It matters because of the long history of Hollywood demonising peoples, cultures and ethnicities. For example, many people have noted how Hollywood entrenches highly negative views of the US's various others. Muslims and Arabs have long been at the receiving end of unsparing portrayals of their supposed character, cultural and moral shortcomings. Jack Shaheen (2001) points out that in a survey of some 900 films made between 1980 and the early 2000s, representations of Muslims and Arabs are almost without exception unfavourable. Things only worsened after the attacks of September 2001 (Shaheen 2008). Arabs, argues John Eisele (2002: 69–70), have been "cinematically streamlined" and steadily reduced to "raving, maniacal terrorists, devoid of human decency and morality." Such popular visualisation of supposed enemies strips them of their humanity and makes their killing not just possible but desirable. Conversely, those that are charged with implementing such foreign policy on the ground are routinely portrayed as heroic, even if their work is particularly distasteful.

In film as in life, the world of foreign policy is dominated by white men, whether they be government officials or the mavericks who set out to correct the failings of politicians and the systems they inhabit. Such an approach to foreign policy implies that "the truth is out there" and that it can be quantified, accessed, understood and made tangible by those operating with the correct motivations.

The complexities and compromises of foreign policy are of little interest to those "putting right" the sins of policy makers. Indeed, there are few films that honestly attempt to portray the duplicity of Western powers and how entrenched problems in global politics arise from such decision making. Western audiences are unlikely to see films that explore the "toxic residue of resentment and conflict" that currently have UK Foreign Office officials "brainstorming anxiously" about how to commemorate the centenary of the Sykes–Picot Agreement (1916) and the Balfour Declaration (1917) (Black 2015). Nor are there likely to be any popular films that will expose what Arabs call the tripartite aggression of the Anglo-French-Israeli collusion in the invasion of Egypt in 1956. These examples of "western duplicity and high handedness" (Black 2015) have had a lasting impact on the geopolitics of the Middle East and are little known let alone understood by cinematic audiences. What we see instead are the problems of the Middle East framed in terms of ethnic and religious tensions. Non-

Western peoples are depicted as unable to manage their own affairs – a deeply entrenched stereotype that has informed Western foreign policies for decades if not centuries (Black 2015). On this understanding, the absence of democracy in the Middle East is not a failure of Western foreign policy but of the character of Arab peoples. Few fictional films challenge this view. But this is precisely what a critical cinematic approach to foreign policy should and must do.

21 Gender

Linda Åhäll

I engage with gender and visuality in two ways: as representation and as performance. Building on Judith Butler's influential work on gender as performative and inspired by Raewyn Connell's work on masculinities, I focus on gender as a social practice that constantly refers to bodies, to what bodies do (or don't do) and to how bodies matter, visually. Drawing on Jenny Nordberg's book *The Underground Girls of Kabul* (2014), I use the cultural phenomenon of *bacha posh* in Afghanistan, a practice in which girls are brought up as boys, to demonstrate the visual politics of gender and sex. I aim to show how visuality is not only essential to how gender is understood and communicated but also offers opportunities to challenge associated cultural practices. I conclude by highlighting that we miss out on understanding key aspects of how global politics works unless we pay attention to visual logics of gender.

Officially they don't exist, but when Nordberg stumbles upon the phenomenon, she finds out that there is a specific term for a child who is neither a son nor a daughter: it is *bacha posh*. *Bacha* means "boy" and *bacha posh* translates as "dressed like a boy" in Dari. Female-to-male cross-dressing is of course nothing new: there is a long history of women who, in order to achieve something they would not otherwise be able to do, choose to "pass" as male. In this case though, it is important to note that the gender change is the decision of the parents (and/or other adults), rather than the wish of the child. Add to this that this gender change is temporally limited: *bacha posh* are expected to change back into "real" girls when they reach puberty. They are meant to marry and have children of their own, although not everyone does. Interestingly, Nordberg learns that the practice has long historical roots, although most international "experts" on Afghanistan have never heard about it.

The reason for having a daughter become a son varies. For poor families it might simply be the case that one of the daughters must generate an income, something a girl is not otherwise allowed to do. For upper- or middle-class families, it can be a question of cultural resistance: "I wanted to show my youngest what life is like on the other side," as one mother (in Nordberg 2014: 15) puts it. Most often though, being a *bacha posh*, or having a daughter become a *bacha posh* is a cultural advantage: in a social context where having a baby boy is seen as a success, whereas giving birth to a baby girl can be seen as a humiliating failure, "everybody knows that a made-up son is better than none at all" (Nordberg 2014: 48). As an aspiring politician, Azita decided to let one of her daughters become a son to make the *image* of the family complete; to make herself a legitimate representative of her local constituency:

After five or ten minutes, they used to ask about my son, and the entire discussion was about why I don't have a son. "We are sorry for you. Why don't you try next time to have a son," they would say. And I don't want to stop this talking [politics] inside my home. They think you are weaker without a son. So now I give them this image.

(in Nordberg 2014: 60)

Although there are several ways to analyse "gender" in the *bacha posh* practice, I use it as an illustration of how "sex" is a gendered category and, importantly, how "sex" is sustained, performed and normalised through three interlinked processes of visual signification: "dressing," "looking" and "walking."

What is gender?

During recent decades feminist scholars and activists have successfully put gender on international policy agendas and influenced, at least to an extent, academic debates on what counts as security and global politics more broadly. On the one hand, "gender" has become a buzzword: the passing of UN Security Council resolution 1325 in 2000 has led to gender "mainstreaming" in international organisations and development programmes. At universities, many modules include "a week on gender," and scholarly textbooks usually feature a chapter on either gender or feminism. But feminists have pointed out that although gender has become more visible, these formal inclusions might actually also be detrimental to long-term feminist goals of political transformation. A focus on "gender," whether as policy or in academic research, is not necessarily feminist (see Carver 2003). Also, because women have historically been left out of "high-politics" and because the on-the-ground role of women in conflict situations is often ignored, a great deal of feminist interventions have remained focused on "woman." While there is nothing wrong with this – women are still marginalised as legitimate actors in global politics – there is a risk that gender research gets dismissed as something that only concerns women.

The conflation of "gender" and "women" is problematic for several reasons. Because both men and women "have genders, experience gender, and live in a gendered world" (Sjoberg 2015: 7). Because gender as identity is not fixed, something one is assigned "naturally" at birth, but rather subject to social and historical variation. Because the gendering of identity is always intersected with other factors, such as class, race, age and disability. Because "the work masculinity is doing" (Zalewski 2015) remains invisible. Because it excludes people who identify as *both* or *neither* men and women. And, finally, because it fails to problematise what the binary categories of "man" and "woman" mean in the first place: how they are formed, performed and reinforced.

Among feminist scholars there is no agreed-upon definition of what gender is or how gender should be studied. There are by necessity many feminisms: different feminist perspectives, guided by different political conundrums, treat gender as an analytical category differently. I approach the political conundrum of gender and visuality with an analytical focus on bodies; how bodies are informed by a visual, gendered logic. We all have bodies, which is why thinking about gender as a social practice needs to look at what bodies do and mean. It enables us to see how bodies are valued differently; how bodies are "sexed" visually and how this means that certain bodies matter visually while others do not. In this way, a focus on bodies puts the visual logic of gender at the centre of politics.

The sexing of bodies

Judith Butler famously criticised the naturalness of sex in her books *Gender Trouble* and *Bodies that Matter*, both originally published in the early 1990s. By discussing drag performances, Butler drew attention to the political practice of gender and construction and reiteration of sex as an ideal construct. What Butler suggests is that sex is not a simple fact or static condition of a body, but a *process* whereby regulatory norms materialise sex and achieve this materialisation through a forcible reiteration of those norms (Butler 2011: xii). This means that sex is as culturally constructed as gender, and that sex is itself a "gendered category" produced through repetition (Butler 2006: 5). For example, when a child is born it is "called," or "interpellated" to use Butler's term, as either a girl or a boy; the baby has moved from being an "it" to a she or a he. In this naming a girl is "girled," but the key point Butler makes is that this initial medical interpellation is then continually repeated and reinforced by various authorities and practices so that it becomes seen as "natural": "The naming is at once the setting of a boundary, and also the repeated inculcation of a norm" (Butler 2011: xvii).

I am using the *bacha posh* practice as a site where a certain "drama of sexual difference" (Butler 2011: 22) plays out. Here gender is a social practice that attaches meaning not only to the "shape of our bodies," but also to the *assumed* shape of our bodies (Shepherd 2015: 26). Expressed in other words: it is about how *bacha posh* bodies matter visually as a fantasy of the male sex and how these bodies then metamorphose into their adopted gender.

In Afghanistan's gender-segregated society what sets boys and girls apart is all exterior: it is about visual signs to do with dress, hairstyle, and body language. While some *bacha posh* are "called as boys" immediately after birth, others are much older and self-aware of their gender change. For an older child, the first step of a successful gender change is a change in dress and hairstyle. Mahnoush was six years old when her parents asked her if she wanted to "look like a boy and dress like a boy, and do more fun things like boys do, like bicycling, soccer, and cricket." Mahnoush said yes and with a new haircut, a pair of pants from the bazaar and a denim shirt with "superstar" printed on the back, she became, in a single afternoon, Mehran – the spiky-haired boy (Nordberg 2014: 14). While the statement "it's a boy" might be sufficient for the change of an infant's gender, if the child is older the gender change also needs the support of others in the child's immediate surroundings, particularly from those who know that the child is in fact a girl biologically. According to Nordberg (2014: 75), neighbours, colleagues, doctors, teachers are usually accommodating, precisely because they understand that having a made-up son is simply better than none. In the case of Mehran, when a male Koran teacher demanded her to cover her head, a baseball cap solved the problem.

To some *bacha posh* posing as a boy is a part-time "duty." To others the sexing process is the only way of living they know. Fifteen-year-old Zahra has lived as a boy as long as she can remember. She lacks most traditional feminine traits and speaks for herself right away as if she were a boy: her adopted gender is "natural." Even

Figure 21.1 Zahra/Naveed (Adam Ferguson)

Source: Adam Ferguson. With the permission of the photographer.

though she knows that she is a girl biologically, Zahra has no intention of changing back to a girl/woman.

> My mother always tells me that I am a girl. But my neighbours call me a boy. I feel like both. People see me as both. I feel happy I am both. If my mother had not told anybody, nobody would know. I say I am Naveed to those who don't know.
>
> (in Nordberg 2014: 104)

While assessing the effects of this practice on individuals is beyond the scope of this chapter, the story of Zahra illustrates that these cross-dressers are involved in complex narratives of identity, belonging and exclusion relating to the social boundaries that they transgress. A year later, Zahra no longer feels like "both" a man and a woman. "People use bad words for girls," she says. "When I am a boy they don't speak to me like that." Instead, she fantasises about changing her biological sex to fit her male gender (Nordberg 2014: 97, 147).

The visual code of "dressing" might be relatively easy to achieve, but the *bacha posh* must also practise their gender according to appropriate cultural norms: they must perform their new gender without raising too much suspicion. I now focus on two additional bodily attributes and capacities that function as visual signs or codes of gesture involved in how bacha posh perform and practise the fantasy of the male gender: "looking" and "walking."

Figure 21.2 Mahnoush/Mehran (Adam Ferguson)
Source: Adam Ferguson. With the permission of the photographer.

The performance of gender

Some *bacha posh* adapt well to their new life. Mehran's father even talks about her as a him: "He looks like a boy, and he behaves like a boy. He is a good son for us. . . . To be honest, I think of him as a boy. When I see him, I see my only son" (in Nordberg 2014: 89). Thinking about practices of "looking" offers one glimpse into how Mehran passes as a boy:

> When I take pictures of the girls [Mehran's twin sisters], or when they take pictures of one another with my camera, Benafsha and Beheshta strike well-rehearsed poses, pouting their lips and batting big flirty eyelashes, sometimes pointing fingers at each other and swirling their arms as they perform a little Bollywood-style dance routine. . . . Mehran goes in the exact opposite direction – looking angry, staring into the camera, hands on her hips.
>
> (in Nordberg 2014: 83)

Mehran has learnt how to practise a boy's gender rather than a girl's. She actively controls the gaze and seemingly models her behaviour on her father and other boys. At school, she refuses such activities as sewing and doll play in favour of cycling, football and running. In a similar way, Zahra has learnt that her look or "male gaze" is key to how she performs her adopted gender:

> She does not greet us with a smile. Nor does she lower her gaze, an impulse ingrained in most Afghan girls. She is unafraid, looking me straight in the eyes,

resting one hand on her hip. And why would she not? Her exterior is of the ruling gender; mine is not.

(in Nordberg 2014: 96)

In Afghanistan, and arguably to varying degrees in most cultures, female bodies are supposed to take up a minimum of space and "walking" is therefore equally important for how Zahra practises the fantasy of a male gender:

> She has an exaggerated and clunky way of walking, as if there were something between her legs. With high, tense shoulders, and hands hanging by the thumbs in her pockets, she strides forward in broad, duck-footed steps, in her preferred outfit of an oversize hooded plaid short, jeans and flip-flops. She keeps her head low, face close to her chest, and looks up only if someone directly calls her name. She knows her power is in the exterior, and her walk successfully signals that she is a typical teenage boy with some attitude.
>
> (in Nordberg 2014: 98)

Zahra in this way claims space normally only available to boys. "Walking" as a visual code in how *bacha posh* learn and unlearn the practice of appropriate gender behaviour is also obvious in the story of Shukria, a *bacha posh* who after changing back to a woman as an adult is struggling to perform her "real" gender appropriately:

> She would tiptoe around in her burka with what she had worked out was a suitably ladylike gait that replaced the way she swung her arms by her sides or put her hands in her pockets while taking long strides and moving along quickly. When a burka was no longer required, she continued walking in her new, feminine way. Often, she forgot the most important part – to keep her head submissively bent – but she was constantly reminded to do so by those around her. No woman should walk with a straight back and a raised neck, she learned. Instead, she trained herself to hunch over as soon as she stood up, and she is careful to inhabit a far smaller physical space than she used to, by keeping all her extremities close.
>
> (in Nordberg 2014: 175)

Bacha posh Shukria learnt how to be a boy by imitating her older brother. But when she changed back, she had to re-learn how to be a woman by observing and imitating women's behaviour. Still, as Nordberg (2014: 176) puts it:

> For Shukria to retain herself to be a woman remains a work in progress and a language in which she may never be entirely fluent. The male side of her "stuck" in a way that she describes as "natural." It was her first spoken language and her first body language, and boys were her first friends. Everything else – everything female – she has to constantly correct and remind herself of.

In this way, the performance of gender is intimately linked to processes of learning and unlearning through both images and language. This is how thinking about gender as a social practice is useful for studies of visual global politics.

The visual politics of gender

Thinking about gender as a social practice means that it concerns us all. We all live gender, because we live in gendered societies and because we all have gendered bodies. For some this is a choice, for others it is not something one pays much attention to, for others still, as the case of *bacha posh* in Afghanistan, it is a rational choice made by the parents in view of obtaining financial and/or cultural advantages.

I have used the *bacha posh* practice as an illustration not only of how bodies matter visually but also of how a focus on visuality facilitates an analysis of how gender politics is resisted and challenged everyday. Although I have focused on only three of many visual codes – "dressing," "looking" and "walking" – I show how common-sense knowledge of gender is by no means fixed. Children are not born gendered but learn social codes of behaviour and how to reproduce themselves in culturally appropriate ways, sometimes successfully, sometimes less so.

The wider significance of thinking about gender as a visual language of meaning-making, formed through processes of learning and unlearning, is that we need to remain open to the visual global politics of gender. The key issue is about those bodies that are left out, made invisible, missing, silenced; it is about invisibility as much as visibility. It is about how silences, gaps and invisibility are produced through what is either "seen" or "not seen." It is about how gendered bodies intersect with other visual identity markers, such as class, race, age and disability.

In short: without paying attention to the visual logics of gender and sex we miss out on a whole lot of what is going on in global politics.

22 Geopolitics

Klaus Dodds

The formal academic history of geopolitics from the early twentieth century onwards is one characterised by a number of trends; a belief in the material significance of geographical and even geophysical factors in shaping world politics; a conviction that state power was intimately linked to demography; a social Darwinist belief that states were in perpetual competition with one another for resources and territory; and, finally, a predilection for visual objects, such as the map and globe, which would function as accomplices to state-sanctioned imperial imaginaries. To think and practise geopolitics was for many scholars and practitioners a shorthand term for statecraft and power politics (Ó Tuathail 1996).

Over the last two decades, geopolitics has undergone a substantive transformation, and a new academic field called "critical geopolitics" has consolidated itself (see Dodds, Kuus and Sharp 2013). This body of literature was eager to distance itself from the legacies of "classical geopolitics" and its colonial-imperial footprint. As with other strands of academic geography, the 1980s and 1990s witnessed a flourishing of work reflecting on the power–knowledge regimes and practices underwriting cartography, geography and geopolitics. Critical geopolitics, furthermore, identified geopolitical ideas and practices as multi-faceted, using the designation "formal, practical and popular geopolitics" to convey how the worlds of the universities, governments, policy making and popular culture co-existed. In other words, geopolitics was not just the preserve of the academic expert but something that manifested itself in numerous other realms, ranging from, say, "State of the Union" presidential speeches to Hollywood films about the role of the United States in the world.

This move towards visuality and popular culture was significant because conventionally geopolitics was associated only with the sombre world of international politics – a realm that, at the time, seemed far removed from the visual world of film, television, photographs, radio and advertising (Hughes 2013). The introduction of popular geopolitics owes a great deal to the pioneering work of Joanne Sharp (2000) and her study of how *Reader's Digest* textually and visually constructed the Cold War Soviet Union as "Other" for its American and international readership. By focusing on the textual and visual elements of this monthly magazine, she considered how the Soviet Union was conceptualised as a particular kind of place governed by a series of Communist Party-led regimes, intent on spatial expansion, the domination of place and ideological struggle across the globe. Much of the subsequent work, especially in the 1990s, tackled the neglect in traditional geopolitical research of the popular and the everyday. A distinction was drawn between formal geopolitical reasoning, the practical geopolitics of governments and the popular geopolitics to be found in media outlets, such as films and television. Research was dominated by an interest in speeches and textual sources, with an abiding concern for how popular geopolitical sources ended up naturalising and legitimising the practical geopolitical narratives and identities of governments such as the United States.

Some of this literature bears similarities with international relations scholarship, which advanced post-positivist and post-realist agendas. Pertinent is the intersection between aesthetics, popular culture and world politics because it connects with popular geopolitics (for example Bleiker 2001; Weber 2006b; Shepherd 2013). These strands have been brought into a more explicit conversation with one another in numerous journals and blogs. The recent edited collection entitled *World Politics and Popular Culture* (Caso and Hamilton 2015) illustrates this dialogue between critical geopolitics and international relations. Both share an interest in how the geopolitical world is represented within and beyond popular culture, and in particular how threats, allies, identities, danger and (in)security are portrayed and embodied.

More recent iterations of this "popular cultural" have placed emphasis on the everyday, the local, the household, the embodied and the politics of emotions such as fear, dread and hope (Moore and Shepherd 2010). This has encouraged a new generation of scholars to re-direct popular geopolitics away from textual analysis per se towards a concern with how individuals and communities are embedded and affected by geopolitics (Dodds, Kuus and Sharp 2013). Some of this might appear mundane at first sight but, as feminist scholars note, the declaration of a War on Terror had profoundly different consequences for people depending on class, gender, race, sexuality and other factors (Puar 2007). A popular geopolitics of the War on Terror would take account of the embodied experiences and the manner in which emotions, such as fear, play a vital role in designating some people as more suspicious, more dangerous and more worrisome than others. Popular sources, such as film and television, play an important role in feeding those geopolitical anxieties.

In this chapter, I examine the role of visual culture and associated representations. Focusing on film depictions of the British super-spy James Bond, I show how representational practices portray the British agent and his American allies as operating in a dangerous political world characterised by permeable borders, mobile threats and a perpetual danger that needs to be addressed quickly and violently lest it affect the capital cities such as London.

Popular geopolitics and representational logics

The representational logics of film and television matter, especially if there is a recurrent pattern of depicting some places, ideas and communities as deviant and dangerous, and some others as righteous and legitimate. Some film types proved very popular with North American and global audiences. After 9/11, the superhero film rose in popularity, as figures such as Batman, Superman, Iron Man and Captain America enjoyed impressive box office returns. By contrast, war movies about Afghanistan and Iraq were less profitable (Dittmer 2005; Holloway 2008). Despite their popularity, superhero films, such as *Man of Steel* (2013), were accused of trading in "disaster porn," capitalising on the visual images associated with urban destruction, such as the attacks in New York.

The idea that one might capitalise on visual images both for aesthetic and commercial gain is noteworthy but so is the recognition that images not only command authority but also are commanded by authority (Hughes 2013). While disaster and superhero movies were caught up in debates about aesthetic exploitation of the 9/11 tragedy, there is sufficient evidence that the War on Terror was staged in particular visual ways. Consider how the US Secretary of State Colin Powell used a graphic PowerPoint presentation at the United Nations Security Council to persuade sceptics that Saddam Hussein posed a clear and present danger. Or look at how the US presidential adviser Karl Rove held a meeting in November 2001 in Beverley Hills with representatives of the entertainment industry. The idea of this meeting was to help support the War on Terror through, for instance, the production of "patriotic" movies and television programmes.

The key links between the visual and geopolitics were clearly understood by the US government. Movies, photographs and television bulletins were meant to depict US personnel and technology being put to work in the fight against Al-Qaeda and others who threatened the territorial integrity and security interests of the country. How those threats and dangers facing the United States and its allies are articulated and visually depicted deserve critical scrutiny. The seeing and scripting of the world in popular films might help us think further about how geopolitical imaginaries work and how friends and allies are distinguished from enemies and suspicious others.

Film images often appeal to feelings and emotions (Hughes 2013). In *The Kingdom* (2007), for instance, a group of FBI officers are flown to Saudi Arabia in order to investigate the ruthless slaying of American citizens by terrorists. After confronting US and Saudi official intransigence, the team eventually track down the terrorist mastermind but in so doing they rely on a supportive Saudi police officer. Using a variety of filming techniques (the close-up, the long shot and montage) the narrative arc of the film draws the viewer into an experience of Saudi Arabia saturated with anger, delay, frustration and revenge. Early on in the film, the terrorist mastermind is shown making a young child watch the bloody attack itself and later the same terrorists kidnap an FBI officer and threaten him with beheading. When the leading FBI officer whispers to a colleague "kill them all," the audience has been prepared for such a summary judgement. The terrorists have *shown* themselves to be murderously incapable of restraint and undeserving of any mercy. The film concludes with their extra-judicial killing.

James Bond: saving Britain and the world

The international political world is of abiding interest for the popular British spy James Bond. Created by Ian Fleming in the 1950s, the first Bond film was released in 1962. Based in Jamaica, it used the storyline of an evil genius called Dr No, eager to precipitate a conflict between the Cold War superpowers by interfering with respective space programs. As earlier films demonstrated, but the Bond films were to exemplify, the figure of the spy was central to Cold War geopolitics. Aided and abetted by American allies, Bond/007 proved himself to be adept not only in cultivating local allies in Jamaica but also in understanding and appreciating that Cold War antagonisms were being used opportunistically by a criminal-terrorist network called SPECTRE. Bond's ingenuity, physical strength, technological prowess and sexual confidence were placed in sharp relief to the physically impaired and apparently asexual Dr No. Bond's body, gender, ethnicity, sexuality and patriotism made him an attractive and popular cinematic figure (Funell and Dodds 2017).

Enjoying success at the box office ensured that Bond continued in his missions and established a pattern for both the narrative arc and representational qualities of the film itself. In narrative terms, Bond's trajectory quickly became formulaic: called into MI6 in London to learn of his new mission he then enters the "field" and confronts the adversary and the threat posed either to Britain and its special ally the United States or even the world itself. Having successfully neutralised the source of danger, Bond was then shown to enjoy the fruits of mission success, usually courtesy of a female accomplice. Representationally, the MI6 headquarters in London are shown to be calm and orderly in contrast to the threatening world Bond inhabits, which encompasses the secret lairs of villains, chaotic cities in the Middle East and the global South (e.g. Bangkok, Cairo, Istanbul and Rio de Janeiro) and villains who are represented as corrupt, demonic, disfigured, greedy and insane (e.g. Drax, Goldfinger and Stromberg).

Attentive to the rhyme and rhythm of Cold War geopolitics, the long-running series also shifted the geographies of the missions and degree of interaction with the Soviet Union and its allies. In *The Spy who Loved Me* (1977), for example, Bond joins forces with a Soviet counterpart in order to defeat the evil genius Stromberg and his plans to cause nuclear Armageddon. As Cold War tensions worsened in the late 1970s and early 1980s, Bond films such as *For Your Eyes Only* (1982) and *Octopussy* (1984) depict a world where rogue elements of the Soviet intelligence and military are prepared to team up with criminals and terrorists for personal gain. While the Bond films rarely

Figure 22.1 From Russia with Love
Source: James Bond film poster, 1963.

depict the Soviet leadership as hell-bent on global domination, the Soviet Union is invariably shown to be politically unpredictable, with the possible exception of the Soviet intelligence chief who is shown to be capable of restraint. Bond and his superiors at MI6 are shown to have a grudging respect for their fellow espionage professionals and recognise that in a dangerous and unstable world such work, however unpleasant, is a geopolitical necessity.

What makes the more recent iterations of Bond noteworthy is how the geographies of threat and danger became more localised and immediate. Until *The World is Not Enough* (1999), MI6 in the Vauxhall area of London had never been shown to be under threat. If there were dangers they were usually represented as being either located elsewhere or simply global because of the scale of the criminal mastermind's planning. That sense of physical, even epistemic, security is shattered when MI6 is blown up by a bomb and Bond is forced to chase a master terrorist-criminal Renard across the former Soviet Union and finally Turkey. With the Cold War seemingly diminished in intensity, the 1990s witnessed a persistent representation of the former Soviet Union as unstable, open and capable of hosting a series of adversaries posing a threat to the UK and its allies.

Arguably the most dramatic example of an overturning of the geopolitics of James Bond occurs in *Skyfall* (2012), when a disgruntled former agent again attacks MI6, and M (played by Judi Dench) is the subject of further attacks. Never before in the history of the franchise has such a significant portion of the film been based in London and shown MI6 as a vulnerable and exposed "centre of calculation." Bond's desperate attempts to track the former British agent witness him running through the streets of London, stalking the London underground, and finally driving M to his former childhood home in Scotland. The narrative arc is radically different from the earlier Bond films: London is not safe, leading allies and colleagues perish, political superiors scrutinise the *modus operandi* of the British intelligence community, and even Bond's physical prowess appears to be in doubt as he struggles to recover from serious injury.

What started as a film series in which Bond saves the world in places far away from London is now one where the geographies of threat and safety are overturned. Bond and his superiors are no longer to act with limited political scrutiny. The more recent Daniel Craig-era films (*Casino Royale, Quantum of Solace* and *Skyfall*) depict an intelligence agent ridden with existential angst. He is haunted by the loss of his lover Vesper and exposed to a world where his physical and intellectual abilities are questioned routinely. Set against the backdrop of the 7 July 2005 terrorist attacks on London, *Skyfall* (2012) suggests that the source of Britain's insecurity can also lie in past encounters, as the disgruntled agent responsible for London's mayhem was embittered by his imprisonment and torture by Chinese agents in the run-up to the handover of Hong Kong in 1997.

The cinematic figure of the spy is just one example of how particular roles and occupations, such as the soldier, the housewife, the vigilante, the refugee, the border guard and the police officer, can play important roles in popular geopolitics. One way to further scrutinise James Bond would be to think about how audiences might react if the figure of Bond was female rather than male, uneducated and blue-collar rather than well educated and white-collar, black or Asian rather than white, gay rather than heterosexual, Chinese rather than British. We might then consider how both the narrative arc and accompanying representational logics contribute to an *intersectional* popular geopolitics. In other words, a popular super-spy working for a popular cause (the safety of Britain and the wider world) precisely because he is white, able-bodied, heterosexual and British (Dodds 2014). We might also note that while Bond can and does confront female adversaries (they are invariably attractive and sexually alluring), and the villains are usually depicted as physically disfigured, asexual (and occasionally homosexual) and often non-white.

Visuality and popular geopolitics

The visual dimensions of popular geopolitics contribute to how the "reel and the real" co-constitute one another. After all, most people will never knowingly meet a spy but they will have been introduced to them courtesy of spy films and spies such as James Bond. Our ideas of signals and field-based intelligence-gathering are far more likely to come from visual popular entertainment, such as *Enemy of the State* (1988); from film serials, such as Jason Bourne; and from children's movies, such as *Spy Kids*. Many Western viewers at least have the privilege of being often far removed from the conflicts depicted in films, such as the plight of the illegal migrant to the battle spaces of the Middle East and Central Asia. When conflict is closer to home, as in the terrorist attacks of 9/11, then terror, horror and disaster movies have played an integral part of shaping how viewers see and interpret these events as well as the political responses to them.

23 Humanitarianism

Lilie Chouliaraki

Humanitarian organisations have always struggled to settle the question of how to visualise suffering and how to inspire our feelings and actions on it. One of their challenges is to safeguard the legitimacy of their activities in an increasingly competitive market (DeChaine 2005). It is this struggle over legitimacy that is reflected in the visual practices of humanitarian campaigning, for, as critics claim, no style of campaigning seems to do justice to the moral claim of solidarity. Early "negative" imagery of emaciated children was denounced for dehumanising the sufferer (Benthall 1993). "Positive" imagery campaigns of smiling faces were accused of glossing over the misery of suffering (Lidchi 1997; Smillie 1995). Most recently campaigns were accused of what has been called a "commodification of solidarity" (Nash 2008).

Why is this so? Why are visual appeals to the morality of solidarity set up for a perpetual failure of legitimacy? Addressing this question sheds light onto broader ethico-political tensions of humanitarianism as a practice of power suspended between empowering and subjecting, humanizing and othering those it cares for. So let me briefly comment on these, by way of exploring the two most prominent historical forms of humanitarian visuality: negative and positive humanitarian appeals.

"Negative" humanitarian appeals

Early examples of humanitarian appeals rely on a documentary aesthetics that authenticates suffering by representing it in its "plain reality." Emerging in the context of de-colonisation and new aid and development projects, these appeals rely on what Jenny Edkins (2000: 39) calls the "medicalization of famine." Ignoring systemic inequality as the cause of food scarcity, this medical conception of famine focused on relief, that is the need for immediate nutritional and medical support for those who suffer. "Relief", as Edkins (2000: 39) puts it, "is aimed at preserving the life of the biological organism rather than restoring the means of livelihood in the community". Early appeals consequently rested on visualising the effects of starvation on the human body.

We see here a form of "raw realism" that depicts human bodies in an extreme state of starvation. These so-called "ideal victims" (Höijer 2004) are often children and they are visually depicted in generic form: they are devoid of individualising features and taken out of their living context. They are naked or half-naked. Their self-abandoned nudity exposes emaciated ribcages, arms and legs. Captured on camera, these body parts, sitting in a row as they are, become "fetishized" (Hall 1997: 223–80). They do not reflect real human bodies with a life history. They are, rather, curiosities of the flesh that mobilise a pornographic spectatorial imagination between disgust and desire (Lissner 1979).

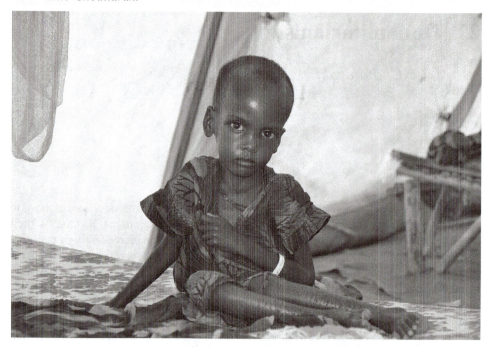

Figure 23.1 Malnourished child in an MSF treatment tent in Dolo Ado, 2001

These visual appeals are "victim-oriented," where the sufferer is the passive object of our contemplation (Cohen 2001: 218). Such appeals thus establish a social relationship anchored on the colonial relationships of suffering and premised on a maximal distance between "them" and "us" (Hall 2001 [1992]; Lidchi 1997). It is precisely this social relationship that Silverstone (2006: 283) refers to as the "immorality of distance": a relationship of power whereby the figure of the spectator is fully sovereign in her/his agency over the sufferer. The spectator is in charge of recording the suffering, appealing for help and providing charitable giving (Pinney 1997). The sufferer remains unaware, quasi-human.

The immorality of distance that these "negative" appeals enact is consequently associated with the "grand" emotions of shame and indignation (adapted from Cohen 2001: 214). Resting on the historical asymmetry between the "bare life" of these sufferers and the comfortable life of Western spectators (see Agamben 1998) these negative emotions throw into relief the logic of "complicity" that informs this asymmetry, in the first place (Singer 1972/2008: 388–96). On the one hand, the logic of complicity evokes the legacy of the colonial West and, with it, of the European responsibility for systematically disempowering distant others through imperial rule. This is a sense of historical complicity that figures in Western consciousness as a sentiment of collective guilt (Cohen 2001). On the other hand, the logic of complicity renders the individual spectator a witness of the horrors of distant suffering and so makes our inaction towards suffering a personal failure to take responsibility for such horrors – thereby motivating a personal sense of distant suffering that taps into feelings of shame (Ahmed 2004: 105).

Complicity is, in this sense, a primary source not only of negative emotion but also of the moral agency of these appeals: failure to act, it implies, is failure to acknowledge our historical and personal participation in perpetuating human suffering. Guilt and shame, however, pivotal emotions as they may be in this type of imagery, do not exhaust the communicative repertoire of "negative" appeals. In its most powerful manifestation, the logic of complicity transforms these emotions, often regarded as introverted modes of feeling towards suffering, into the more extrovert and assertive emotion of indignation. Here, the social relations of complicity can become political: they are externalised from the individual to society, as in the solidarity of revolution (Boltanksi 1999: 61–3). Consequently, the figure of the persecutor is objectified in the form of unequal structures of power. Moral agency is linked to the imperative of social justice: *outrage into action* was Amnesty International's campaign slogan during the early 1990s.

The distinction between guilt and indignation is, no doubt, crucial in differentiating non-political from politicised forms of activism, with guilt encouraging more privatised, charity-oriented acts while indignation privileges public protest against injustice. The distinction granted, however, there is an inherent tension in all visual strategies of moralisation that rely on the logic of complicity. By evoking guilt, shame or even indignation, critics argue, "negative" appeals seek to turn grand emotions into action, by, at least partly, identifying the figure of the persecutor in the very audiences they address as potential benefactors – aren't we, as the critique of empire would put it, part of this Western legacy, unwillingly but surely participating in the systemic inertia that reproduces the power relations between global North and South? Guilt and indignation, in this sense, inform an ambivalent form of moral agency that both presupposes the Western spectator's complicity in world poverty, collectively and individually, and at the same time enacts this complicity in the power relations that it seeks to expose and redress (Hattori 2003b: 164–5). The immorality of distance, which the "negative" imagery establishes between those who watch and those who suffer, captures precisely this ambivalent moral agency that makes the West the benefactor of a world that it itself manages to symbolically annihilate.

A popular response to such "negative" imagery is the compassion fatigue syndrome (Moeller 1999: 2; Chapter 8, this volume), which entailed two risks: the "bystander" effect and the "boomerang" effect. The former risk refers to people's indifference or reluctance to act on suffering as a reaction towards these flows of negative emotion that ultimately leave people feeling that there is nothing they can do. Cohen (2001: 194) puts it this way: "a sense of the situation so utterly hopeless and incomprehensible that we cannot bear to think about it." The latter risk refers to people's indignation not towards the imagined evil-doer but towards the guilt-tripping message of the "negative" campaigns themselves: "for bombarding you with material that only makes you feel miserable and guilty" (Cohen 2001:214). Rather than encouraging a moral agency of solidarity, these risks ultimately undermine it.

"Negative" appeals, in summary, rely on a realistic imagery of victimhood as "bare life" that reproduces the colonial relationships between the safe West and its suffering others and moralises Western publics through the logic of complicity, thereby risking compassion fatigue and apathy.

"Positive" humanitarian appeals

As a direct response to the affective and ethical impasses of "negative" appeals, "positive" ones also rely on photorealistic strategies that try to represent the reality of suffering "as-it-is." The difference is that these appeals reject the imagery of the sufferer as a victim and centre on the sufferer's agency and dignity.

The two key characteristics of this style of appealing are on the one hand, the personalisation of sufferers, by focusing on distinct individuals and by portraying these individuals as actors (for example, as participating in development projects); and, on the other, the singularisation of donors, by addressing each one as a person who can make a concrete contribution to improve a sufferer's life (for example, through child sponsorship). It is now the presence of the benefactor, rather than the persecutor, that is instrumental in summoning up a new affective performativity of "empathy, tender-heartedness and gratitude" (adapted from Cohen 2001: 216–18).

Rather than complicity, the moralising function of this affective performativity relies on "sympathetic equilibrium," a communicative logic that orients the appeal towards a responsive balance of emotions between the sufferer and the spectator as potential benefactor (Boltanski 1999: 39). Specifically, sympathetic equilibrium is established through the ways in which the imagery of suffering provides subtle evidence of the sufferer's gratitude for the (imagined) alleviation of her/his suffering by a benefactor and the benefactor's respective empathy towards the grateful sufferer.

This new link between the donor and the receiver is visually articulated in photos of smiling children, in the sentimental texts of child sponsorship, or in the eye-witness accounts of aid workers. The use of emotion here not only empowers the sufferer,

Figure 23.2 A child waits outside a medical clinic as part of Western Accord 2012 in Thies, Senegal

Source: Wikimedia Commons, https://commons.wikimedia.org/wiki/File:A_child_waits_outside_a_medical_clinic_as_part_of_Western_Accord_2012_in_Thies,_Senegal,_June_10,_2012_120610-Z-KE462-197.jpg (in the public domain).

giving her a voice, but, in so doing, also further animates the donor's "moral imagination" – an invitation to acknowledge the suffering of others in the context of a shared humanity that is absent in "negative" appeals. But there is also a singularisation of the donor, presented as an individual who can make a difference in a practical way. Donors now are empowered by images that suggest how their actions may lead to concrete and real change.

The moralisation strategies of "positive" appeals seek therefore to produce a new form of agency that avoids the evils of "negative" appeals. We no longer have a sense of powerlessness towards distant suffering (the bystander effect) and people's resistance to the negativity of campaigns themselves (the boomerang effect). Importantly, however, these visual practices – and the images associated with them – remain closely linked to a notion of humanitarianism as intervention: one that goes beyond relief and incorporates demands for progress and improved livelihood for vulnerable others.

Even if these positive image campaigns manage to provide us with a more authentic understanding of the complexity of global divisions, however, they conceal crucial aspects of this complexity. Promoting sustainable social change might be the aim of this intervention, but it is, at the same time, linked to very specific neoliberal and market-oriented understandings of humanitarianism (Hattori 2003a, 2003b; Cottle and Nolan 2007).

There are always power relationships involved in questions of humanitarianism and development. They emerge out of this very visual spectacle of hope and self-determination, for they gloss over the fundamental asymmetry between the two parties. They assimilate difference under "our" norm, leading to a classic instance of what Bourdieu (1977: 183–97) calls "misrecognition": the euphemistic concealment of systemic power relations by the image of smiling children.

Central to the operation of misrecognition in "positive" appeals is the visual and moralising depiction of gratitude and fellow-feeling. Gratitude relies on the social logic of the gift between unequal parties – whereby the reception of a gift without the possibility of reciprocation, as is the case of development, binds the grateful receiver into a nexus of obligations and duties towards the generous donor. At the same time, the generosity and tender-heartedness of the West unite donors in a community of virtue that discovers in its own fellow-feeling for distant others a narcissistic self-contentment (Hattori 2003b). Criticism against the "positive" performativity of appeals centres precisely on this ambivalent moral agency that their imagery makes possible. While it appears to empower distant sufferers through discourses of dignity and self-determination, "positive" imagery simultaneously disempowers these sufferers by appropriating their otherness in Western discourses of identity and agency.

Benevolent emotions operate as instruments of power, insofar as they render others the perpetual objects of "our" generosity. Simultaneously, risks of misrecognition feed into an increasing compassion fatigue for "positive" styles of appealing too. First, there is the risk of positive examples of "aid in action" suggesting that the problems of the developing world have been fully addressed. The result is inaction on the grounds that "everything is already taken care of" (Small 1997: 581–93). Second, there is the risk that the plethora of smiling child faces may be misrecognised as children like "ours." The result here is inaction on the grounds that "these are not really children in need" (Cohen 2001:183–4). Rather than enabling action on vulnerable others, "positive" appeals can thus deepen the crisis of pity in that they introduce an element of suspicion in the spectacle of suffering.

"Positive" imagery, in summary, is defined by a performativity of benevolent emotion, which claims authenticity by reference to a realist aesthetics of the empowered child and moralises the West through the logic of sympathetic equilibrium and its emotions of empathy and tender-heartedness. Unable to resolve the problem of suspicion, however, "positive" imagery runs risks of compassion fatigue similar to those of "negative" imagery.

The visual politics of humanitarianism

The historical controversy around appeals highlights the paradoxes of humanitarianism. Despite showing human vulnerability "as-it-is," the photorealistic authenticity of suffering can neither depict the "truth" of suffering nor sustain legitimate claims to solidarity.

By seeking to confront us with the reality of distant suffering in two of its most authentic forms – shocking destitution and hopeful self-determination – the visualisation of human vulnerability is suspended between two impossible public (im)moralities: the immorality of distance and the immorality of identity. The former animates guilt and indignation to lead us into action but such negative emotions tie action to our own complicity in global injustice and run the risk of ultimate fatigue and apathy. The latter animates gratitude and tender-heartedness to persuade us to act, but such positive emotions tie action to a suspicious view of development as unreciprocated gift, which glosses over deep asymmetries of power and runs the risk of denying the very need for action on the grounds that it may be unnecessary or, even, unreal.

There are alternatives. I have recently examined a digital, playful style of appeals that co-exists with previous ones but departs from them. This emergent style can be characterised as "self-reflexive" or "ironic" (Chouliaraki 2013b). Unlike the previous two, this approach does not seek to legitimise claims to solidarity by resolving the paradoxes of appeals but, in contrast, renders these paradoxes the very object of our contemplation and reflection. Such reflexive or "ironic" appeals entail an ambivalent logic; one that seduces us into a "cool" activism, while keeping us in a comfort zone that offers neither justifications as to why we should act on the suffering of others nor the opportunity to confront the humanity of those others.

My initial question then remains: how can human suffering be communicated as a legitimate cause of humanitarian engagement? We still have no definitive answers. What my overview of humanitarian spectacles hopefully enables, however, is an informed awareness of the difficulties of representing suffering as an object of solidarity and a practice of sustained reflexivity that keeps the promise of new spectacles alive – spectacles that avoid the traps of "grand" emotion and self-centred activism in favour of empathetic and justice-driven commitment to acting on vulnerable others without asking back.

Note

This text draws on Chouliaraki 2010.

24 Human rights

Sharon Sliwinski

It is one of the most recognisable passages in the United Nations' Universal Declaration of Human Rights (UDHR) – that slightly oblique and yet grave reference to the Nazi death camps: "Whereas disregard and contempt for human rights have resulted in barbarous acts which have outraged the conscience of mankind." These barbarous acts were front-page news in most of the Allied countries in the spring of 1945, at the very moment when the United Nations was founded at a conference in San Francisco. The newsstands were filled with photographs from the newly liberated Dachau and Buchenwald camps. Illustrated magazines such as *Life* and *Picture Post* brought the public face-to-face with the Nazis' mass manufacture of corpses. These dramatic images provided the backdrop as members of the new intergovernmental organisation began to call for an international bill of rights. This demand ultimately manifested in the UDHR, which was adopted by the UN General Assembly in 1948. All to say, this particular iteration of universal human rights was born amid one of the twentieth-century's most dramatic visual scenes.

Reading the UDHR from this perspective – as an anxious response to the encounter with the visual representation of the Nazi atrocities – can produce a novel interpretation of this foundational document. This is a bit like catching a "tell" in a game of poker: recognising the unconscious sign that gives away the other player's hand. In contrast to the UDHR's outwardly triumphal pronouncement that all human beings possess an inalienable dignity and rights, the newsstands and newsreels had just provided potent evidence that the world was utterly bereft of any such creature. Read with this visual context in mind, the particular vision set forth in the UDHR – a world where human beings are "born free and equal in dignity and rights" and "endowed with reason and conscience" – begins to seem like a profound fantasy invented to cover up the Final Solution's dramatic rent in the very idea of humanity.

Approaching the UDHR from the vantage of its visual context might lead us to critique this document's particular definition of universal human rights. Such an analysis would, of course, have to find its place within a long tradition that has critiqued these ideals (Burke 1790; Marx 1844; Arendt 1951; Lefort 1986; Agamben 1998; Douzinas 2000; Asad 2003; Brown 2002; Žižek 2005; Rancière 2010; Moyn 2010; Nguyen 2012).

Approaching human rights from this vantage leads to questions about how politics intersects with aesthetics – to an investigation of how our most cherished political concepts are so often born out of rich visual scenes. In other words, while the struggle for universal human rights can be told as a story of political machination and juridical reform, it can also be told as a story about the circulation of visual images and spectators' complex, emotional experience of viewing them. The history of human rights – and the history of their abuse – is a richly illustrated one. Thinking through the way this venerable political concept intersects with the visual realm can, perhaps, yield fresh insights – both about the concept, but also about all the human passions that bind us together and tear us apart.

Everything old is new again

The visual history of human rights does not have to begin with the signing of the UDHR in 1948, or for that matter, with the photographs from the liberation of the Nazi lagers. One could begin this history in April of 1792, when William Wilberforce stood up in front of the British Parliament to introduce his second bill on the abolition of the slave trade. Wilberforce had learned from his initial political failure. The first time around, he had relied upon a closely reasoned presentation of facts to persuade the Members of Parliament. The second time, he played directly to sentiment. He lingered over the grisly details that the Society for the Abolition of the Slave Trade had gathered over the years: the brutality of the men who made it their business to traffic in human beings, the way the slaves were packed like sardines into the hulls of ships, and the cruel, short life that awaited them on the sugar plantations of the West Indies.

In his 1792 speech to Parliament, Wilberforce lingered over the story of a single girl who was beaten to death by the captain of a slave ship for allegedly refusing to "dance" (the common means of forced exercise for the slaves during the long voyage). As he began the story, Wilberforce feigned a dramatic apology: he wished he could forever drop all such recitals, narratives that could only prove the cruelty of those involved in the slave trade, but this one instance could not be ignored. The case involved a fifteen-year-old girl, a young slave who found herself in an "indecent situation" while on board the ship (she had been raped and likely infected with a venereal disease) and subsequently refused to "dance." The captain of the vessel took this as an opportunity to mete out punishment. He tied the girl up by her wrists and placed her in a position so as to make her a spectacle to the whole crew whereupon he began to beat her. Not thinking this exhibition sufficient, the captain then tied her up by her legs to continue the beating. But even this did not bring an end to it. The captain strung her up by a single leg and continued the assault, whereupon the girl lost all sensation, and died of her wounds three days later.

Wilberforce's account of this incident nearly aroused a riot. Members began to shout from all corners of the House, demanding the captain's name. He eventually supplied the information to quell the uproar: John Kimber, captain of the slave ship *Recovery* owned by Bristol merchants. Debate about the slave trade raged throughout the night. The young Prime Minister, William Pitt, delivered a defence of Wilberforce's bill that itself ran for over an hour. A compromise solution of "gradual abolition" was eventually passed, though this initial victory only ended up serving those who sought to delay the end of the trade. Abolition was eventually passed into law in 1807, but full emancipation would have to wait until the Slavery Abolition Act of 1833.

The British abolitionist movement is often cited as the first grassroots human rights campaign. Less often discussed is the fact that this early campaign was a thoroughly visual affair. One week after Wilberforce's momentous speech, Londoners were able to gaze upon the fifteen-year-old girl's murder for themselves. A hand-coloured print (Figure 24.1) began appearing in coffee houses and pubs all over London, produced

*Figure 24.1 The Abolition of the Slave Trade; or, The inhumanity of dealers in human flesh
exemplified in Capt'n Kimber's treatment of a young Negro girl of 15 for her virgin
modesty*, Isaac Cruikshank, hand-coloured etching, April 1792. © Trustees of the
British Museum

by the Scottish caricaturist, Isaac Cruikshank (father to the well-known political
cartoonist, George Cruikshank).

The print belongs to the emerging genre of editorial cartoons; it was part of a large
body of such ephemeral images that circulated during the period. This particular print
depicts the murder at its apex: the mostly naked girl is strung up by one leg on the
deck of Kimber's ship, with the captain himself leering over the scene, whip in hand.
The picture seized the public's attention – galvanising concern about this particular
murder and providing a platform for the larger debate about abolition.

Like the backdrop in which the United Nations' Universal Declaration was drafted,
this early human rights campaign was steeped in a complex and profoundly problematic
visual scene (Wood 2000). The British public had become familiar with the "Brookes"
slave ship diagram, which circulated throughout the country in newspapers, pamphlets
and even via posters pasted at pubs and coffeehouses (Figure 24.2).

Wilberforce had used a wooden model of the ship in his speech to the House of
Commons to demonstrate the abominable conditions of the Middle Passage.

The public would also have widely recognised the emblem that Josiah Wedgwood
created for the abolition movement (Figure 24.3). The medallion pictured a kneeling
male slave gesturing in a supplicating manner, accompanied by the inscription: "Am
I not a man and a brother?" Wedgewood's emblem grew so popular it began to be

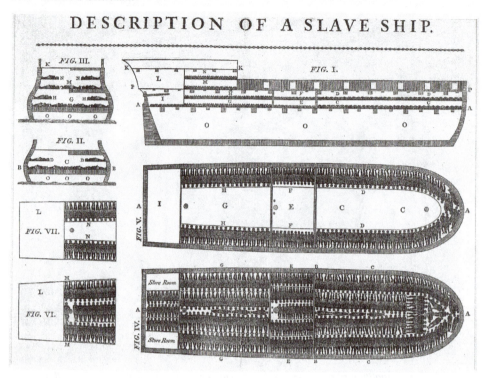

Figure 24.2 Description of a slave ship, © Trustees of the British Museum

Source: Trustees of the British Museum. Printed with permission from the British Library.

Figure 24.3
Oval cameo, inscription: "Am I not a man and a brother?" designed by Josiah Wedgwood for the Committee for the Abolition of the Slave Trade, 1787. © Trustees of the British Museum

Source: designed by Josiah Wedgwood for the Committee for the Abolition of the Slave Trade, 1787. Printed with permission from the National Maritime Museum.

reproduced in all manner of forms: it was printed on plates, enamel boxes and tea caddies. Ladies wore the medallion in the form of pendants, bracelet charms and ornamental hairpins. As Thomas Clarkson (1808: 192) remarks in his history of the abolitionist movement: "At length the taste for wearing them became general, and thus fashion, which usually confines itself to worthless things, was seen for once in the honourable office of promoting the cause of justice, humanity and freedom." The now familiar and uneasy alliance between social justice campaigns and souvenirs has deep roots.

The world spectator

Defining human rights as an aesthetic scene involves more than treating images and objects as illustrations of political action proper. Indeed, apart from studying these images and objects, there is also the question of the spectator to consider. Aesthetics can mean many things, but in a philosophical context, it refers to that specific mode of thought that is called upon in our engagements with representational objects. The German philosopher Immanuel Kant defined it as a particular operation of human judgement. In fact, around the same time as Wilberforce was fighting for abolition of the slave trade in the British House of Commons, Kant was pursuing his argument that aesthetic judgement was a unique mode of thought in so far as it is "merely subjective," by which the philosopher meant that spectators must rely upon their own feelings as the only authority. The principles that guide this special mode of thought cannot be borrowed from a higher power. Aesthetic judgement uses particular instances to aim toward universal principles. Or as Kant (2001 [1798]: 13) put it, such judgement has "a principle particular to itself upon which laws are sought."

This version of aesthetics – as a mode of judgement – is generally associated with the history of art, but Kant himself provided an avenue to consider the spectator's judgement as a properly *political* matter. When the French Revolution exploded in 1789, the philosopher seized upon the distant event as a spectacle that demonstrated a truth about the human condition. More specifically, he argued that the Revolution exhibited evidence that humanity was progressing perpetually toward the better. One might be tempted to test his thesis in relation to the revolutionary wave of demonstrations and protests of the recent Arab Spring. Kant (2001 [1798]: 143–4) singled out the figure of the spectator (*der Zuschauer*):

> This event [the French Revolution] consists neither in momentous deeds nor crimes committed by men whereby what was great among men is made small or what was small is made great, nor in ancient splendid political structures which vanish as if by magic while others come forth in their place as if from the depths of the earth. No, nothing of the sort. It is simply the mode of thinking [*Denkungsart*] of the spectators [*Zuschauer*] which reveals itself publicly in this game of great revolutions, and manifests such a universal yet disinterested sympathy for the players on one side against those on the other, even at the risk that this partiality could become very disadvantageous for them if discovered.

For Kant, the Revolution's significance did not lie in the political events themselves – the storming of the Bastille, or the toppling of the *ancien régime*. Rather, the significance of these events lay in the way in which they elicited a special "mode of thinking" from distant spectators. For the philosopher, this particular mode of thought was important because it displayed a disinterested enthusiasm. Our passionate response to distant events does not imply that we are tempted to participate; the spectator should not be confused for a political actor. Rather the goal of this figure's public regard is a *purposiveless interest in the other*: a passionate sympathy or a vicarious delight that is fashioned from watching events unfold at a distance. For Kant, spectators' passionate response to such events constitutes a subjective form of judgement that nevertheless aims at universality, what he termed *sensus communis*. This passionate mode of thought holds humanity together.

These nascent speculations about the spectator's role in political life remained largely confined to philosophy until Hannah Arendt delivered a set of lectures in 1970 on what she described as "Kant's political philosophy." Through careful reading of the philosopher's late work, Arendt began to revise her own definition of the political arena (which she had previously set out in *The Human Condition*). She argued, after Kant, that political events become transformed into world events – something of larger significance to human history – through the judgement of distant spectators. In the course of her analysis, she transformed Kant's *Zuschauer* into a *Weltbetrachter* – the "spectator" became a "world spectator" whose judgement of distant events provided the ground zero of politics itself. In her thirteenth, and final, lecture, Arendt (1992: 75–6) proposed:

> You judge always as a member of a community, guided by your community sense, your *sensus communis*. But in the last analysis, you are a member of a world community by the sheer fact of being human; this is your "cosmopolitan existence." When you judge and when you act in political matters you are supposed to take your bearings from the idea, not the actuality, of being a world-citizen and therefore also a *Weltbetrachter*, a world-spectator.

Arendt's analysis helps us understand how human rights are called into existence through the collective exercise of human judgement, and more specifically, the collective judgement of *particular* world events. Such judgements rely on the world spectator's feelings about the idea, not the actuality of being a world citizen. "Cosmopolitan existence" thus belongs to the life of the mind, even though the spectator's judgement is not simply a matter of private sentiment or personal feelings. Our complex aesthetic response to world events – what Kant described as our "enthusiasm" – contains something that is universally communicable, possesses an exemplary validity, and collectively presupposes a shared, sensuous realm of public life.

One can catch a glimpse of how this version of visual politics plays out in relation to the founding of the Universal Declaration of Human Rights – or for that matter, in the abolition of the slave trade. Both of these important political moments were grounded in an aesthetic scene, and the demand for rights was voiced by world spectators, that is, by individuals situated at a remove from the events themselves who based their demand for human rights in an exercise of exemplary, universal judgement: "Whereas disregard and contempt for human rights have resulted in barbarous acts which have outraged the conscience of mankind." Our recognition of human rights is inextricably bound to aesthetic experience in this respect. To speak of human rights is, first of all, to speak of *the spectator* of human rights.

The visual perplexities of human rights

Formulating human rights through the idea of the world spectator does not resolve the profound antinomies that surround this political concept. Indeed, thinking through these visual dimensions only adds another layer of critique.

Hannah Arendt (1949: 37) was one of the earliest and most vociferous detractors of the UN's new declaration. She dryly noted that the document's "lack of reality" was "rather conspicuous." More gravely, she argued that the plight of stateless people exposed the inadequacies of the new declaration as a means for securing rights. These protections, she proposed, were only granted by having access to a political community. Building on Arendt's seminal critique, recent scholars have added a new layer. Those in the Marxist tradition have diagnosed universal human rights as an ideological revision of nineteenth-century bourgeois rights which only re-entrench class exploitation and oppression (Brown 2002). Postcolonial theorists have argued that the UN's version of human rights relies on a false universalism that has served as a tool of Western cultural imperialism – a means to subsequently implement neocolonialist economic policies and justify military interventions (Nguyen 2012). Critical legal scholars have also analysed the limitations of appeals to both human rights and constitutional rights as a means of gaining power for minority groups in liberal constitutional states (Mutua 2008). Feminist theorists have noted the limitations human rights impose by naturalising a masculinist notion of an unencumbered and self-sufficient subject as the model rights-bearing individual (Engle 1992).

To this list, we can now add the myriad critiques emerging from visual culture, from Susan Sontag's (1977) early, caustic criticism of photography as an "act of non-intervention" to the increasingly intricate debates about the ethics of spectatorship and media witnessing (Boltanski 1999; Sontag 2003; Reinhardt, Edwards and Dugane 2007; Frosh and Pinchevski 2009; Butler 2009; Hesford 2011; Rentschler 2011; Apel 2012; Chouliaraki 2013a; Kozol 2014).

Critiques aside, the visual presentation of world events continues to be the means through which the international community communes. Circulating more quickly and in more venues than ever before, these images function like the stage material of a grand, tragic play – providing the medium through which world spectators exercise their capacity to imagine humanity as one entity. For better or worse, the ideals of human rights are tethered to this fraught arena of representation.

25 Icons

Robert Hariman and John Louis Lucaites

A Buddhist monk self-immolates on a crowded street in Saigon. A solitary Chinese man calmly stands before the muzzle of a tank near Tiananmen Square. A father and son crouch behind a rusting barrel in Gaza seconds before they both are killed. A hooded individual stands precariously on a cardboard box inside Abu Ghraib prison, his arms extended with wires attached to his hands.

These and many other photographic images are icons of a global public culture. They stand out among the thousands of photographs that are disseminated by media institutions every day. Their circulation persists long after the initial coverage of the specific event. Although the designation "iconic" appears frequently in media commentary on images ranging from smiley buttons to the latest celebrity gesture, the iconic news image has specific features that shape a distinctively public mentality. We define iconic photographs as those photographic images appearing in print, electronic or digital media that are widely recognised and remembered, are understood to be representations of historically significant events, activate strong emotional identification or response, and are reproduced across a range of media, genres or topics (Hariman and Lucaites 2007: 27).

Despite the religious connotation of "icon," these images do not have universal or transcendental meanings. They are open to a wide range of interpretative responses and their use will change over time until they, too, disappear. In fact, they have much in common with many other outstanding photographs of significant moments in the ongoing cascade of media production. Nonetheless, the iconic photographs acquire distinctive capacities for shaping public identity, thought and action.

Image analysis

Iconic photographs provide important resources for constituting people as citizens, forming public opinion and motivating participation in specific forms of collective life. They relay social knowledge and dominant ideologies, shape understanding of specific events and time periods, model relationships between civic actors, and provide figural resources for subsequent communicative action. They accomplish these ends either through the embodiment of symbolic resources that are available throughout the print media, or by presenting what cannot be said well or at all in print. In any case, the visual medium is particularly good at activating aesthetic patterns that can shape audience response. In order to understand how an iconic photograph might function, several hermeneutical principles can be applied. These include shifting the dominant modality from representation to performance; entering into an emotional scenario;

identifying an array of semiotic transcriptions; and discerning how the image manages a basic contradiction or recurrent crisis.

Performances are aesthetically marked, situated, reflexive examples of restored behaviour presented to an audience (Bauman 1989). Photography is grounded in phenomenological devices crucial to creating the performative experience. Framing, for example, marks the image – that 1/500th of a second – as a special selection of reality that acquires greater intensity than the flow of experience before and after it. As they are framed, photographs become marked as special acts of display. This aesthetic status heightens awareness of the stylistic features of any subject, and prompts a second-order, reflexive consciousness that comes from foregrounding signifying practices and the communicative role of the photograph itself.

Such performative engagements are inevitably emotional. Performances traffic in bodies. They evoke emotional responses precisely because they place the expressive body in a public space. The image displays emotions as they operate within repertoires of social behaviour, activates available structures of feeling within the audience, sets a mood for understanding the event, and bonds participants and spectators affectively. These emotional signs and responses operate reliably and powerfully because they are already presented within the broad conventions of public comportment (even as their particular meanings can vary across cultures). Thus photography operates not just as a record of things seen, but as a way of seeing that creates emotional resonances that can be relayed across cultures, media, genres and topics.

The social repertoires activating emotional response are but one of the many patterns of identification coded into an iconic image. The icon coordinates a set of semiotic transcriptions, each of which could suffice to direct audience response but which together provide a dynamic mediation of complex events. Because the camera records the *décor* of everyday life, the photographic image is capable of directing the attention across a field of gestures, interaction rituals, social types, social structures, political discourses, political styles, artistic motifs, cultural norms and other codes as they intersect in any event. Thus, the icon provides strong economies of transcription to organise a range of interpretations for a public audience. This intensive coordination of semiotic codes through performative embodiment is the reason that the iconic photograph is not limited to the conventional journalistic function of reporting information.

The final and most important feature of the iconic photograph is its capacity to manage or negotiate a basic contradiction or recurrent crisis within the political community. Any polity has foundational contradictions that lead to repeated conflicts. Politics in particular involves the negotiation of incommensurable goods, such as liberty and security, or individual rights and majority rule (Berlin 1982), while class conflict, racism, factionalism and other biases, exclusions and denials remain widespread problems. In any case, and whether to defer or address the problem at hand, symbolic mediation is essential, even as the media of representation are themselves incapable of providing comprehensive representation of the social totality (Ankersmit 1996). Although other media are entangled in these problems as well, iconic photographs are distinctively capable of staging these constitutive tensions for public deliberation.

An interpretive method focused on these elements of visual articulation provides a basis for understanding how the iconic photograph inflects conceptions of citizenship. What it means to be a "citizen" sits at the fulcrum of many modern political contradictions and crises. If citizenship is to be an actual mode of participation in the community, rather than a merely legal construct or regulative ideal for decision-making, then it has to be articulated in a manner that encourages emotional identification with other civic actors (Azoulay 2008). Indeed, in the modern era, which is defined in part by large, heterogeneous states maintained through technologies of mass communication, citizenship may depend on visual modalities that can enact the relationship of the abstract individual to the impersonal state. Likewise, the modern nation-state requires transference of passionate identification with local, embodied, organic institutions to a superordinate, procedural governmentality. This shift in identification is accomplished in part through images of virtual embodiment that reframe locality within a national context while grounding national symbols in the social experience of everyday life. As the world becomes increasingly interconnected these processes expand from national to global scale.

Put differently, the iconic photograph becomes the command performance of what it means to see and to be seen as a citizen, and as such it opens itself to a wide array of usages, not least in the ways in which it is appropriated beyond its initial production and dissemination to engage, challenge and celebrate the norms of civic life. The repetition of an image in the same place, whether a history book or a billboard, doesn't necessarily signal an icon. If you see the same image in history books, roadside memorials, political campaign posters, editorial cartoons, commercial advertisements, T-shirts, tattoos, graffiti and so on, across topics and over time, then you have an icon. By following the copies, imitations and parodies that produce iconicity in the international media environment, one can get a glimpse of public culture in a global context. A primary example of how an image can become a global icon is the photograph of the lone protester in Tiananmen Square.

Tiananmen Square

It all began in mid-April 1989 as students and urban workers congregated in Beijing's Tiananmen Square, demanding liberalisation and democratic reforms from an authoritarian Chinese government. By the middle of May, martial law was declared and nearly 300,000 troops were mobilised to manage the more than one million people occupying the square. The turning point came on the evening of 3 June when the military deployed troops and tanks to clear the Square. A massacre ensued. On the morning of 5 June a lone individual blocked the path of a column of tanks on Chang'an Avenue, just outside the Square.

This is one of several nearly identical photographs that are used interchangeably. It became the focus of an international media blitz (Perlmutter 1998) and is generally recognised as the iconic photograph of "Tiananmen Square."

The lone individual is standing up to authority – literally, courageously, remarkably so. It is an inspiring performance of democratic dissent, but it is not a photograph with a single message. The tension between state authority and the individual citizen is palpable, but the image is also a dramatic vehicle for managing other tensions between relatively liberal and democratic conceptions of citizenship, between realist and idealist conceptions of political power, and between national and global definitions of civil society. Each of these cannot be traced here (see Hariman and Lucaites 2007: 208–42), but we can suggest how the aesthetic coding of the image inflects response toward a relatively abstract, liberal and global conception of citizenship, rather than toward solidarity with democratic revolution in China or elsewhere.

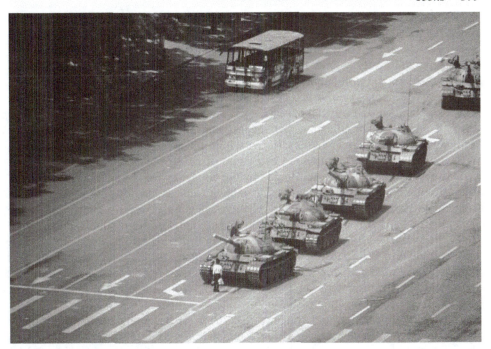

Figure 25.1 Tiananmen Square, Stuart Franklin, 1989
Source: Stuart Franklin, 1989.

The political drama of popular opposition to a repressive regime provides the obvious context for the photograph. The man confronting the column of tanks is a picture of contrasts: the lone civilian versus the army, the vulnerable human body versus mechanised armour, the human spirit of courage and hope versus the unrelenting apparatus of state power. But the critique of authoritarian regimes and the celebration of liberal-democratic virtues is only one order of perception activated by the composition. More important is to see that the dramatic standoff is positioned within a modernist perspective toward pictorial space.

The dominant aesthetic frame of the image unfolds from the vantage of the photographer who is above and at some distance from the unfolding drama. The tanks are still impersonal, but so is the scene as a whole. The viewer is thus disconnected from the event, positioned as a distant spectator who can neither be harmed by nor affect the action unfolding below. The viewer of the picture thus acquires the neutral, "objective" stance of the camera. As James C. Scott (1998: 79) has demonstrated, whenever we view unfolding events with an objective detachment afforded by a purportedly neutral point of view, we are "seeing like a state." The authoritarian state positioned within the picture is subordinated to the individual standing freely before it, but both alternatives are subordinated to a modernist scheme of representation. The event unfolds on almost completely deserted public space, a model of the abstraction characterising modernist design. There is no place to sit, congregate or talk, and its dimensions are not to "human scale" but proportioned instead to accommodate the flow of vehicular traffic – a point underscored by the rectilinear grid of parallel lines and directional vectors.

Of course, modernist abstraction is complicated by other codes of modern political order, not least the disciplined exercise of power: the constitution of the subject through controlled use of the body within a zone of surveillance (Foucault 1979). Notice how the photograph neatly sutures these two transcriptions: a silent body in public view generates the authority of public opinion in opposition to the state's use of force, while disciplinary technologies of urban design and visual representation frame the scene as if it were being viewed from an observational tower. The photograph is a paradigmatic case of modernist simplification that reduces and intensifies the political conflict in terms that are most legible and reassuring within the assumptions of a universalising, Western narrative of the continuing expansion of modern technologies.

This abstract orientation is reinforced by the anonymity of the man before the tank. Almost nothing in the image marks a distinctive Chinese identity (the sole exception being a red star on each tank). Rather, what we see is a transparent, seemingly legible depiction of a modern individual standing in an empty, uniform public space before a generic symbol of routinised state power. From this perspective, the photo has in a stroke transformed Chinese political identity into a globalised version of that "revolutionary political simplification of the modern era: the concept of a uniform, homogeneous citizenship" (Scott 1998: 32). If you did not know that this scene was in Beijing you could imagine it was in any city in the world.

The interpretive range and trajectory of the icon become evident in its many appropriations. It circulates regularly as a template for editorial cartooning – both in the USA and elsewhere – and it has been adopted by political activists, spoofed by parodists and used to advertise everything from anti-drug campaigns to rock concerts; it has even been featured in a Super Bowl ad for Chik-fil-A restaurants. Some of these adaptations suggest a general drift from the image's specific historical reference, but they underscore the fact that multiple patterns of definition – and most notably, democratic revolution on the one hand and liberal autonomy on the other – are present and recognisable within the image. Their presence, and a shift from one political concept to the other, can be seen in several appropriations of the photograph by *Time* magazine over a period of nearly twenty years.

Time originally featured the iconic photograph on its 19 June 1989 cover above a headline that read "Revolt against communism." The photograph was then reproduced on a two-page spread that introduced the standard Cold War narrative promoting democratic revolution against a communist state. As the story unfolds, the man stands for the Chinese people, who are citizens acting collectively, and the state is silent while he is given the power of speech. Nine years later the magazine shifted its focus in commemorating the event, noting that "it's unclear how much the agitators for democracy actually achieved," while dubbing the lone protestor as "an Unknown Soldier in a struggle for human rights" (Iyer 1998). Human rights are very important, of course, but they are not the same thing as a successful democracy. *Time*'s commemoration thus acquiesces to the regime's refusal to accept democratic reform, while emphasising instead the icon's embodiment of liberal ideals.

But the story does not end here. As in 2006, *Time* appropriated the image in support of a story titled "Google under the gun," concerning Google's decision to impose Chinese government censorship on its web searches in China (Grossman and Beech 2006).

The illustration that accompanied the story includes both democratic and liberal inflections of the image. Some elements of the artistic rendition emphasise the original

Figure 25.2 Red Tank, David Wheeler

Source: David Wheeler. With permission from the artist.

story's Cold War framing of resistance to Chinese oppression, locating the image directly in Beijing, moving the star to the front of the tank that now is red like the flags and imperial city in the background, elongating the barrel and putting it directly in the man's personal space, and changing the point of view to bring the viewer closer to the man's experience of the tank's authoritarian power. But instead of standing in a public square the man now is sitting in a private space. He is not standing up to the tank but staring into a virtual environment of icons and other images that happen to be encased in the tank's mechanical apparatus. The liberal individual who should be free to move unhindered through a global communications medium is being intruded upon by an overbearing state. Free access of information becomes the key factor in this vision of a global civil society, which will develop by aggregating individual preferences. A prior democratic moment becomes the background for a liberal future of individual consumption and abstract connectivity in global cyberspace.

The visual politics of icons

Iconic photographs rarely have much news value – and certainly not for long – but they serve as moments of visual eloquence that provide symbolic resources for mediating fundamental tensions within a polity. Within an increasingly global (and globalised) visual environment, iconic images may be suited both for adaptation for communicative action within many different locales and for articulation of a global public culture. But therein lies the rub, for as we have argued about iconic photographs more generally, from the beginning of the twentieth century to the present the interpretive inflection increasingly evident in patterns of circulation and appropriation has shifted from an emphasis on democratic solidarity to liberal autonomy. And so the question must be, what is the future of the iconic photograph as a marker of global citizenship?

26 Identity

Iver B. Neumann

On the level of groups, identity spells similarity between some, and difference from the rest. The We, the Self, has to be continuously limned off from the Other. One obvious way of representing the Other is as conquered by and at the mercy of the Self. I want to chart how this has been done historically in visual stone media – palettes, narrative reliefs, monuments. The point made is a basic one: predicating the identity of the Self on suborning Others may seemingly prop up self identity, but it also produces anxiety.

Identity

Groups are an essential part of human life. The larger a group, the more imperative it is to its cohesion that there exists some kind of glue, some marker of commonality, some integration. It is impossible to act collectively without a preconceived scheme of who is acting. A collective that knows itself to be a "we" is simply more productive, with a larger capacity for action than one with a weaker sense of group identity.

Since humans are without a group mind that can orchestrate the behaviour of each and every individual, identity has to be represented, so that individuals may be inter-related to join it. Tales about the past play a constitutive role here, for history is identity's chronological dimension. As Halbwachs ([1925] 1992: 38) put it almost a century ago, "the past is not preserved but reconstructed on the basis of the present." Bartelson (2006: 37) alerts us to how

> [t]he relationship between collective memory and identity is always a two-way street: there is no community without a corresponding memory that records its trajectory in time, and no such trajectory without the active construction of a past order to support or debunk a given identity in the present.

Groups are relational. The "we" exists because it is different from other groups. In the decades following the Second World War, this theme was elaborated upon in ways which made it into the very cornerstone of social analysis of collective identity by philosophers like Emmanuel Levinas, Simone de Beauvoir and Jacques Derrida. In terms of method, the breakthrough came within the social science that has specialised in identity since its inception, namely social anthropology. In Bergen, in 1969, Fredrik Barth and associates published the book *Ethnic Groups and Boundaries*, which argued that ethnic groups could be studied by examining their borders and could be characterised in terms of which differences the groups themselves held to constitute them. Social anthropology never looked back, and over the last thirty years, the other social sciences have followed suit.

Identity is a key precondition for foreign policy. Maintaining boundaries (territorial as well as social) is a question of identity maintenance, as well as a question of security. The delineation of a "We" is inherent to any identity formation, and since this question goes to the core of who We are, it may at any time become a political or even security question. Identity – understood as the question of who We are, who our Others are, and what kind of relations exist between Us and Them – is a key precondition for foreign policy (Connolly 1991; Campbell 1992; Walker 1993).

It is a transhistorical phenomenon that the Other is produced in multiple sites, some of which are visual. In order to stress this basic fact, I have chosen to begin my inquiry by looking at one of the world's oldest surviving artefacts, the more than five-thousand-year-old so-called Narmer Palette. I then look at a 3,200-year-old narrative relief and trace the theme through a genre that has been particularly historically stable, namely monuments (Carrier 2005: 16). The way of thinking about how to secure the Self by limning it off from Others that gives the impetus to the building of a monument is bound to fade and fail. By the same token, Selves change radically through history. And yet, the visual genre of the monument lends a certain stability to the exercise.

Egypt

The motif of the triumphant king crops up in the thirty-first century BCE (Baines 1989). The so-called Narmer Palette, a stone artifact presumably used for ritual purposes, centres on Narmer, pharaoh of the First Dynasty, holding a captured enemy by the hair. The obverse side has the pharaoh and soldiers parading in front of the corpses of beheaded enemies that are subsequently shown being eaten by wild animals. Narmer is huge, other humans are small. This is what art historians call hierarchic scale. We are witnessing an entire cosmic order here, with the Self embodied by the king, and the Others suborned. The Narmer Palette may or may not depict an event, which may or may not be the unification of upper and lower Egypt. What is quite obvious, though, is that this is a representation where the Self takes sustenance from lording it over the Other.

During the early Bronze Age, Egypt's major Others were other great powers, like Hatti, the polity of the Hittites. During the late Bronze Age, however, it became nomads. The manual on kingship by Merikare (Dollinger 2003), written somewhere between 2000–1700 BCE, is fairly typical:

> Speak thus concerning the barbarian: As for the wretched Asiatic . . . He does not dwell in one place, being driven hither and yon through want, going about [the desert] on foot. He has been fighting since the time of Horus; he never conquers, yet he is not conquered, and he does not announce a day of fighting, like a thief whom a community has driven out. . . . Do not worry about him, for the Asiatic is a crocodile on his riverbank; he snatches a lonely serf, but he will never rob in the vicinity of a populous town.

In the twelfth century BCE, the theme of the suborned Other made a transition to a new medium, namely Egyptian temples. Consider the reliefs on the temple at Medinet Habu, Thebes, which is Ramses III's (d. 1155 or 1156 BCE) final resting place. The

Figure 26.1 Narmer Palette

Source: Wikimedia Commons, https://commons.wikimedia.org/wiki/File:Narmer_Palette.jpg (in the public domain).

drawings on the temple depict a triumphant Ramses lording it over captured "Sea Peoples": raiders and traders from elsewhere in and around the Great Green, that is, what we know as the Mediterranean. Why would the Other make such a dramatic entrance on historic monuments?

The answer seems to lie in a need to reestablish superiority. As argued most fully by Allan Megill (1998), memory takes on a particularly urgent importance when identity is experienced as being under threat. The Self seems to be challenged by some Other and one way of shoring up the Self is to invoke narratives of how things used to be. In 1550 BCE, Egyptians finally managed to dethrone the Hyksos. This was a major event, so much so that the reestablished series of dynasties is known as the New Kingdom. The Hyksos seem mostly to have been Semitic-speakers who migrated into Egyptian lands (Booth 2005). With the help of Indo-European war technology (composite bows, chariots, stratagems) from the Eurasian steppe, probably brought to them by Hurrians (who also made up part of their number) and definitely new to the region, they were able to establish themselves as pharaohs. The intermezzo left a memory of what migrants could do that was not lost on later pharaohs, however, and when the so-called Sea Peoples emerged, by sea and over land, to raid and migrate into the kingdom, memories of what in-migration could do were still fresh.

The Sea Peoples is a catch-all for waves of migrants that had been on the move from around 1600 BCE (Manning 2014). What is important here is, I think, a basic functional point. With the increased strain on what we are definitely warranted in calling the body politic, inasmuch as the body of the pharaoh was the *pars pro toto* of the polity, the maintenance of political authority called for a wider broadcast of depictions of how the cosmic order was being upheld. Since it was impossible to further enhance the divinity of the pharaoh by representational means – he was already a god – this was done quantitatively, not only in the sense that depictions increased in size, but first and foremost by making these images widely available by having them engraved on public monuments. The hierarchic scale of the depicting itself – the pharaoh looms over his enemies – is reinforced by a blowing-up of that scale. The campaigns against the Sea Peoples took its toll, and it seems to have been in this context that the Sea Peoples become the first Other in history to appear in represented form on temple gates, where all who passed could watch the larger-than-life representations of Ramses II (1279–1213 BCE) defeating foreign soldiers and lording it over captured enemies. The ploy did not work. Around 1140 BCE, only some fifteen years after the death of Ramses III, his dynasty went down in the general cataclysm known as the Bronze Age Collapse.

Uptake

Egyptians reacted to the social strain by placing the suborned Other on public display on temple gates. Greeks evolved a tradition of hanging pieces of captured armour from tree branches, and there was at least one monument raised that depicted such armour (Garlan 1975: 60), but it was left to the Romans to echo the Egyptian depicting of the suborned Other. Roman triumphal arcs emerge from the early second century BCE (Claridge 2010: 55) and are full of reliefs of conquered enemies. One example would be the Arch of Titus, built around 82 CE by the Roman emperor Domitian to commemorate his brother Titus and his victories, which included the sack of Jerusalem. Captured Jews being led away in chains and booty, including a menorah (a Jewish seven-pronged candelabra), feature prominently. The arch was built where this very procession had passed into Rome, so the reliefs were presented as a representation of an *in situ* event. The Arch of Titus became something of a touchstone for later monuments depicting similar themes. One practice of the Renaissance, that is, the European mnemonic ethno-politics which commemorated past greatness, was (from the sixteenth century onwards) to build arches of triumph, and the Arch of Titus was a favoured exemplar.

Now, why would Greeks refrain from depicting suborned Others directly on monuments, while Romans would feature them prominently? The standard work on the Arch of Titus tells us no more than that arches grounded the building of colonies and the arch was a Roman power symbol (Pfanner 1983: 95). Once again, it seems to me that the question is social strain. Greeks were famously fighting a number of comers, but Greek *poleis* were not that cosmopolitan. With the exception of Corinth, which owed its stature to trade, and which owed its trade to its strategic position and the canal that made it possible to cross the isthmus on which it was placed, and which due to its trade, harboured a number of foreign traders at any one time, Greek *poleis* were fairly homogeneous affairs. In imperial Rome, on the other hand, the known world rubbed shoulders. Order, the famous Pax Romana, was predicated on showing these people, and also people in the colonies, their respective places, with Roman citizens on top, other free men in the middle, and everybody else at the bottom. This was made perfectly clear on monuments, as everywhere else.

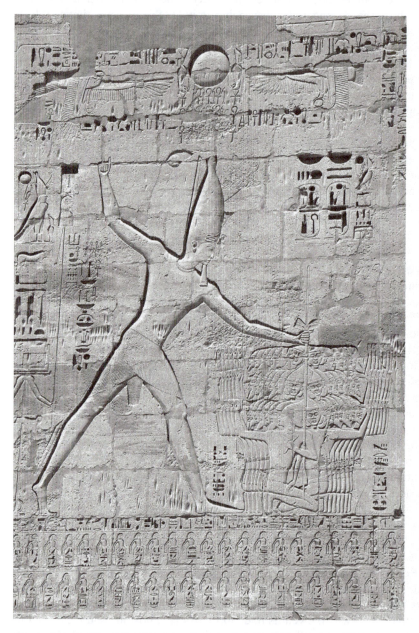

Figure 26.2 Ramses III smiting his enemies, Temple of Ramses III, Medinet
Habu, Nick Dawson

Source: Nick Dawson. Flickr Creative Commons, www.flickr.com/photos/nwb_dawson/
7152400029/in/album-72157629585864018/With permission from Nick Dawson.

Note however, that, as time wore on, monuments specified how the Other could become less radically different. For example, on the Arch of Severius from 203 CE, captured Parthians are not only in chains, but also out of them, and only handled by Roman civilians, as opposed to soldiers. This monument begins to depict incorporation into the Self (there is some evidence that this was also done by Egyptians, but it is inconclusive).

With the Renaissance or rebirthed Europe, the arch reappeared, with the suborned Other still in place, but usually as a fighting force, not as a captured one. The arch was a particularly blatant example of early modernity's penchant for "spatial marks of identity that could be deciphered in terms of those virtues that had been appropriated from the ancients" (Bartelson 2006: 48). The most famous of them all, the Arc de Triomphe de L'Étoile, was built by Napoleon following his triumph at Austerlitz in 1806 and stands in the heart of Paris. Formatted on the Arch of Titus, it has battle scenes prominently displayed, so the Other is back in view, but this is not the vanquished and integrated Other highlighted by Romans. There is no social contact or hybridisation on display here, only the Other depicted as a fighting force. The Other is reduced to some other detachment of humanity, distinct from the Self. Nationalism thinks of humanity in terms of a series of distinct, backward-looking, rebirthing detachments of sameness, be that when the Self is celebrated with the Other absent or, as in arches, when the Other is present as a force about to be suborned. Quite fittingly, the Arc de Triomphe was also to become the first grave to the Unknown Soldier (Kattago 2009: 154) – the homogenised Other was joined by the homogenised Self.

We also have a parallel genre that depicts the suborned. Perhaps we may think of the Roman triumphal arch having split in two, with the arches themselves keeping the topic of fighting the Other, and some equestrian statues taking up the discarded topic of the resulting suborned Other. One example may be found in Saint Petersburg, in Catherine the Great's statue to her predecessor and founder of the city, Peter the Great, who is depicted on horseback while putting down a snake, a metaphor for Sweden. Such depictions of the Other as animal (fantastic or otherwise; there are dragons galore) abound in the period. Later on, there are also examples of the Other being depicted in human form. One example would be the equestrian statue of Eugene of Savoy. It hails from the year 1900, stands in Buda Castle and depicts how Eugene liberated Budapest from the Ottoman Empire at the Battle of Zenta (1697). Reliefs with fighting scenes and statues of defeated Turks crowd the plinth, so this particular monument actually takes up both aspects of the Roman arch – the fighting of the Other as well as the resulting suborned Other. The relational presentation of the Other in monuments that began in Egypt and thrived in Rome is still with us, it still crops up where heavy social strain is in evidence, and it still represents the Other as suborned or about to be suborned.

A caveat is in order. An overarching discussion like this one cannot go into depth about different ways of representing the suborned Other. I simply note that the overwhelming majority concern the Other suborned in battle or taken prisoner after battle. There are variants, however, such as the 1888 Columbus Monument in Barcelona, where grateful child-like natives may be seen kneeling down to sundry Christian cultic specialists.

Figure 26.3 Prince Eugene of Savoy's monument at the Castle of Buda, Budapest, Hungary

Source: Wikimedia Commons, https://commons.wikimedia.org/wiki/File:Budapest_princ_Eugen_1.jpg (in the public domain).

The visual politics of monuments

At present, seemingly universal monumental buildings seem to be all the rage. Monumental representations of the Other as suborned are still all around us, but new monuments tend to find other ways of celebrating the Self. If the Other makes the Self by being the marker of where the Self ends, however, the Other will not disappear just because it is not depicted. Others are constitutive of our own identity, and so it is always worth pondering where they lurk. It may be progress that we no longer celebrate our own identities by depicting vanquished enemies – or it may mean that we have simply found new and more indirect ways of doing exactly that.

Note

The chapter is part of a project on Images and International Security based at Copenhagen University and funded by the Danish Research Council for Independent Research, grant no. DFF-132-00056B.

27 Indigeneity

Sally Butler

The term indigeneity attained new political significance with the 2007 United Nations (UN) Declaration on the Rights of Indigenous Peoples. It aims to support the rights of indigenous peoples around the world and sets international standards for domestic political institutions. The UN, however, resists any definition of what constitutes indigenous people, deferring instead to principles of self-determination. This is demonstrated in the UN's Permanent Forum on Indigenous Issues that states "an official definition of 'indigenous' has not been adopted by the UN-system body" (United Nations Permanent Forum on Indigenous Issues: 2015). Preference is given to a process of self-identification framed by various conditions: historical continuity with pre-colonial/settler societies; strong links to natural resources of homelands; and distinct social, economic, or political minorities with distinct language, culture and beliefs. In short: the Declaration is wedded to an ethos of self-determination that is deeply ambiguous about what the concept of indigeneity means and how it should be approached politically.

Visual art arguably has greater efficacy in conveying an image of international indigeneity. Images are more ambiguous than words and thus seem more suited to convey ambiguous concepts, such as international indigeneity. The cultural theorist W.J.T. Mitchell (2005b) claims that the visual image is essentially propositional in nature: it poses questions and prompts us for words and ideas. Roland Barthes (2003 (1964): 117) similarly regards images as implying a "floating chain" of "signifieds" that keep meaning in flux. Images are potentially like open-ended sentences that require an imaginative response, and it is in this imaginative space that a coherent image of global politics can take shape while remaining speculative, experimental and, as Mitchell argues, propositional.

I examine images of international indigeneity created by the Australian artist Michael Cook (born 1968). Art plays a significant role in the history of Australian indigenous people and their struggle for political recognition and rights (Foley 2006; Leslie 2008; McLean 1998). Cook's art represents local Australian indigenous struggles, but it also expresses them in terms of a more global fight for minority rights. In his 2014 series of photographic artworks titled *Majority Rule,* Cook conveys a sense of the strategic ambiguity inherent in the concept of international indigeneity. Cook's aesthetic asserts simultaneous local and global perspectives and a profound uncertainty regarding indigenous identity. This strategic ambiguity makes visible the struggle of indigenous people for political recognition *on their own terms,* and advances understanding of what is at stake in upholding a principle of self-determination for political minorities.

Majority Rule

Minority politics sits at the heart of Michael Cook's art. He is an artist of Australian indigenous heritage whose work discloses the historical, social and political marginalisation of his people. An ongoing strategy of role reversal in his art encourages viewers to see history otherwise – how it could have been.

Techniques of reversing the invisibility of indigenous Australians subvert conventional attitudes that continue to perpetuate racial stereotypes. Cook uses the medium of (tinted) black-and-white photography to imply a sense of the historical archive, but then populates this archive with an indigenous presence using digital imaging techniques. The aesthetic alludes to parallel histories superimposed over each other and events that disturb and dislocate familiar narratives about the past (Cook 2010a and 2010c). Indigenous figures and faces that colonialism rendered invisible emerge to populate familiar images of Australian discovery, settlement and sovereignty. Portraits of Australia's founding fathers recede under a double exposure with indigenous faces (Cook 2010b). In the *Civilised* (Cook 2012) series, indigenous figures wearing fashionable colonial attire await their fate on the shores where invading boats first landed. These ironic overlays question what constitutes "civilisation" and a heroic "settlement" of the land and create ambiguous perspectives of Australian history and society that are complicated by a more visible indigenous presence.

Cook's strategy of role reversal politicises the minority status of Indigenous Australians but in *Majority Rule,* the imagery becomes more global in scope through allusion to what Nicholas Mirzoeff (2006: 54) calls "minoritarian collectivity." Mirzoeff uses this term in reference to nineteenth-century aesthetic practices that sought to subvert the serial pathology of orientalism. Following Homi Bhabha's writing about the "solidarity of a partial collectivity," Mirzoeff (2006: 53–4) argues that a nineteenth-century culture of improvisations by certain performing artists constituted "disoriental affiliations" that subverted racial stereotypes of the time. Racial minorities assumed a partial collectivity through these essentially visual practices by conveying a strategic ambivalence and incoherence that resisted racial definition and categorisation. In his twenty-first-century visual art practice, Cook employs similar strategies of ambivalence, incoherence and ambiguity, correlating Australian indigenous politics with a global minoritarian collectivity.

Majority Rule consists of seven digitally engineered photographic artworks where Australian indigenous politics is internationalised through the uncertain symbolism of an urbane dark-skinned businessman whose repetitious presence dominates city spaces of commercial and political power. The same man appears multiple times within each image, and throughout the series. His multiplication makes him a dark-skinned everyman and representative of a new form of "majority" on the global scene.

Indigenous Australians are stereotypically invisible in these sites of power but this role is reversed in *Majority Rule*. Locations include the (former) Australian Parliament building and House of the Senate; the High Court of Australia; a War Memorial rotunda; and various scenes of city commuting. While some of the scenes feature iconic Australian sites, others could be any city in the world where businessmen commute on their daily routine. *Majority Rule* shifts between the local and the global as it configures an image of an ambiguous non-white majority in control of society.

Different kinds of suits and hats worn by the businessmen serve to diversify and globalise the historical contexts of these spaces. In *Majority Rule (Memorial)* the figures

Figure 27.1 Majority Rule (Senate), Michael Cook, 2014

Source: Michael Cook, 2014. Image reproduction with permission from the artist and Andrew Baker Art Dealer.

Figure 27.2 Majority Rule (Tunnel), Michael Cook, 2014

Source: Michael Cook, 2014. Image reproduction with permission from the artist and Andrew Baker Art Dealer.

Figure 27.3 Majority Rule (Bus), Michael Cook, 2014

Source: Michael Cook, 2014. Image reproduction with permission from the artist and Andrew Baker Art Dealer.

wear white three-piece suits with black bowler hats that suggest late nineteenth- or early twentieth-century Western society. City commuters in *Majority Rule (Bridge)* and *Majority Rule (Tunnel)* are clothed in suits and hats alluding more to mid-twentieth-century commercial life. In *Majority Rule (Bus)*, the figures again wear waist jackets reminiscent of earlier times while the man at the front of the bus reads a copy of *Walkabout* magazine that was published in Australia between 1934 and 1974 (Bolton 1964). *Walkabout* was responsible for significant racial stereotyping of Australian indigenous people as nomadic, and habitually depicted romanticised anachronistic images of indigenous people as hunter-gatherers rather than modern citizens. The bus in this image also recalls the vehicle used for protests against indigenous segregation in Australia in 1965 (Curthoys 2002). This Australian successor of the United States freedom rides creates awareness of the global context of minority groups fighting for civil rights.

Pictures such as those in *Majority Rule* present ambiguous perspectives of time and place in order to disorientate conventional perceptions of historical and geopolitical order and to redirect the political imagination toward new associations. In particular, the dynamics of visual perception also incorporate a unique mode of viewer involvement that can invoke a sense of political accountability.

Cook employs a method of direct address to the viewer that is similar to what Mitchell describes as a "demand" on the viewer in his book titled *What do Pictures Want?*. He (2005b: 36–40) refers to the direct address employed in the infamous "Uncle Sam wants you" poster used for Second World War USA recruitment and argues that it takes us deep into the political unconscious of the nation at the time. The demand from Uncle Sam embodies what the nation lacks (or needs) and the gaze looking out directly at the viewer personalises the demand. In *Majority Rule,* each image in the series includes a figure located at the centre of the image who looks directly at the viewer (except for one where the figure's head is bowed in respect). This central figure is alone in looking directly at the viewer and elicits a galvanising "demand" similar to that described by Mitchell. The direct address is an assertive but ambiguous demand that implicates the viewer in the proposition of the indigenous majority. It questions why this majority should be so unlikely. Why are minorities so alien to these sites of power? As Mitchell suggests, the picture foregrounds a lack that potentially translates as a political appeal, or demand, for action. The visual power is a kind of front-line assault where the imperative is acute even though the course of action remains ambiguous. Cook's aesthetics in *Majority Rule* thus incites awareness of the strategic ambiguity that lies at the heart of what constitutes international indigeneity.

Minority collectivity

Majority Rule offers insight about the nature of minority collectivity that extends to considerations of how international indigeneity relates to global politics. The strategic ambiguity involved in international indigeneity arguably involves the same mind-set required for global politics to negotiate a co-existence of difference. In *Majority Rule,* Cook's "everyman" alludes to those populations who are marginalised from seats of power in any city in the Western world. It seems that while determinations about indigenous identity in a local context are various and self-determined, indigeneity in a global context relates more to a particular form of political minority collectivity. The UN itself resists defining indigenous peoples except to assert that they "form non-dominant groups of society" (UN Permanent Forum on Indigenous Issues 2015). Francesca Merlan (2009: 303) describes international indigeneity as an ambiguous term that "has come to presuppose a sphere of commonality among those who form a world collectivity of 'indigenous peoples' in contrast to their various others." As mentioned previously, the cultural theorist Homi Bhabha describes a transaction of minorities in the context of orientalism as a "process of affiliation . . . based on the solidarity of *the partial collectivity*" (in Mirzoeff 2006: 53).

Robert Niezen (2003: 15) reminds us that despite its representation of so-called ancient cultures, international indigeneity is a "quintessentially modern phenomenon" representing an estimated 300 million people and over 4,000 different cultures. So international indigeneity is inevitably ambiguous and resistant to definition. Visual practices sustain this strategic ambiguity. Mirzoeff describes the political potential of visuality's "imaginative analogies and symbols" as a mode of flash cards or triggers rather than legible signs. He refers to visuality's inherent ambiguity as a weapon similarly to how Walter Benjamin (in Mirzoeff 2006: 54) conceives our apprehension of the past "as an image which flashes up at the instance it can be recognised and is never seen again." We comprehend the solidarity of international indigeneity in the moment of looking at the image, but it resists attempts to define its essence. Mirzoeff (2006: 54) continues: "to recognize the image is not, however, to name it. It remains incoherent, deterritorialized, and collective."

Mirzoeff's point here is to separate practices of recognition and identification. This is precisely what an international collective of ambiguous indigeneity requires. Global indigeneity seeks political recognition while local indigenous communities seek *"self"*-identification. Recognition politics and identity politics are thus at odds across the spectrum of global and local perspectives. Similarly to the aforementioned UN Declaration, visuality's demand for political recognition resists defining the subject.

Majority Rule's strategy of role reversal is a method of dealing with this complicated relationship between recognition and identification. The replicated "everyman" asserts the anonymity of the individual but the imagery nonetheless demands recognition of an indigenous minority collectivity. If Cook (2013) simply wanted to make a point about indigenous people posed as a majority he could have populated the scenes with a diversity of indigenous people. But the strategy in replicating just one indigenous person ostensibly demands recognition while resisting attempts at identification. Cook is quoted on this topic in an interview where he claims, " 'Indigenous' is many things and physical characteristics have little to do with this identification. So while looking Indigenous has nothing to do with Indigeneity, in my aesthetic I seek out a strong character in a model's physicality" (cited in Louise 2014). Cook's "strong character" is the element in his imagery that seeks indigenous political recognition but the anonymity achieved through replicating the same figure resists identification. An image that seeks recognition for an ambiguously identified concept involves complex processes of perception, and *Majority Rule* achieves this through visual strategies that suggest, imply and propose, rather than simply representing a subject. Cook's aesthetic brings the awkwardly coupled principles of political recognition and self-determination into a coherent image of international indigeneity.

A further dimension of role reversal in *Majority Rule* alludes to links between minority collectivities and a model of global politics that the sociologist Ulrich Beck (2006) termed cosmopolitanism. Although this concept is criticised widely as an unrealistic ideology of global humanism, Beck advanced the principle of cosmo-politanism as *an image* of a global society that upholds diversity and multiplicity and resists homogeny. The word *image* is significant here because it infers a "big picture" perception of the world, and a reconfiguration of time and space, in the spirit of what Andrew R. Russ (2013) describes as a radical political imagination. The time-space reconfigurations of Beck's (2006) model of cosmopolitanism are fundamentally ambig-uous because the concept internalises otherness, the co-existence of rival lifestyles, and the acceptance of culturally diverse viewpoints and behaviours. Cosmopolitanism fundamentally rejects the image of the global melting pot and aims to maintain the local in the global.

The politics of art

Michael Cook's *Majority Rule* artworks explore how strategic ambiguity about indigenous identity is inherent in the concept of international indigeneity. Cook's aesthetic asserts simultaneous local and global perspectives and a profound uncertainty regarding indigenous identity. This strategic ambiguity makes visible the struggle of indigenous people for political recognition *on their own terms*, and advances under-standing of what is at stake in upholding a principle of self-determination for political minorities.

Majority Rule brings together the simultaneity of a co-existence of difference, but the pronounced sense of sterility in the staged affect of the photographs implicitly critiques practices of assimilation and homogeneity. All of the characters in the series assume the pose of a global society's model citizens but they are all the same. The bland mechanical nature of their poses seems to reject the concept of a majority at all – indigenous or any other. *Majority Rule*'s stilted ritual of life suggests that majority politics is not the image for a global society of the future, so much as a shifting and ambiguous field of minority collectivities that battle for simultaneous political recognition and self-identification.

28 Invisibility

Elspeth Van Veeren

Invisibility, like visibility, is a set of practices and ideas that order the world and its politics. While the workings of visual politics are increasingly documented and understood, the same cannot be said about explorations of the relationships between invisibility and politics. Part of the answer lies in being more attentive to how visibility and invisibility are mutually constitutive. The answer also lies, however, in understanding that, like visibilities, invisibilities operate in multiple modes that depend on different, and often competing, understandings of how knowledge and common sense are constituted. To fully grasp the breadth of what visual politics offers is to understand the different ways in which the visible *and the invisible* are produced, ordered and normalised.

This chapter therefore offers an initial typology of four modes or conceptions of invisibility, the assumptions made about the nature of knowledge and the politics that results: invisibility as barrier, as inexpertise, as culture and as absolute. Making claims about visual politics requires, implicitly if not explicitly, at least one, if not multiple, conceptions of the invisible in order to make sense of the power associated with seeing.

Invisibility as barrier

The metaphor of window or screen often characterises and shapes our thinking about visibility (Friedberg 2009). Likewise, invisibility is often imagined through metaphor: most often as a barrier or veil that occludes and confuses sight. Over the years these barriers have variably been imagined as magic caps, cloaks, rings, spells, powers and potions, used by gods, spirits and their guardians, as well as in connection with developments, or misadventures, in science and technology. Governments, militaries, security agencies, investigative journalists, civil rights campaigners, activists, religious leaders, occultists, novelists, artists, designers, inventors and engineers often conceive of invisibility as a barrier, developing practices that look to control what cannot and should not be seen alongside what can and should be seen.

Invisibility as barrier is therefore intertwined with cultures of secrecy and security discourses: that something cannot be seen is either articulated as safer, meaning it needs to be kept secret and concealed, or more threatening and it has to be revealed. Within this conception of invisibility as a barrier, this tension between invisibility as safer or as more threatening is productive in a number of ways, including the (re)production of social, political and religious hierarchies as they are used to differentiate between those who can see and those who cannot. Barriers, or invisibility practices, also gain in significance as they help create, for example, economies of secrecy around the trade and development of invisibility barriers and the practices and technologies that work to reveal invisible things.

For example, within this last century, invisibility as barrier is identifiable in the innovations associated with the Cold War document classification system and redaction schemes (among a set of associated secrecy practices (Anaïs and Walby 2016)) used by the US to shield nuclear secrets from the Soviet Union or in new strategies for misinformation or misdirection (Van Veeren 2011; Bakir 2013; Van Veeren 2013; Van Veeren 2014; Nath 2014). It can also be seen in the sizeable investment and development associated with defence technologies such as the ongoing expansion of practices associated with modern camouflage, in the range of stealth and signal jamming technology, in stun grenades ("flash bangs" that overwhelm the senses), and in the expansion of cyberespionage and online surveillance (Shell 2012; Brunton and Nissenbaum 2015; Thornton 2015). At the same time, technologies and practices to see through these barriers are also continuously under development. New forms of radar, sonar, infrared and long-range telescopes and telephotography continue to emerge to see through the barriers of air, water, distance and visual "noise." In other words, infrared and night-vision goggles, satellite imagery and remote sensing, or smartphones and social media enable new visibilities. But they are also interdependent with new invisibilities as they form part of (spiralling) patterns of hide and seek.

Finally, within these conceptions, invisibility is also productive as it treats invisibility as a tool which hides the ordinarily visible, where the invisible is associated with the intentionally hidden, and where what is hidden is, at least in principle, knowable (see Solnit 2010: 12; Dean 2002). This conception of invisibility therefore reproduces a simpler model of communication and knowledge where knowledge exists independently and is distinguishable from these barriers, masking over, in the process, its own productive and contingent power.

Invisibility as inexpertise

While the barrier approach conceives of invisibility as that which is hidden, invisibilities are also understood as that which cannot be sensed (is insensible) except by those with specialised knowledge. This conception, more common in scientific and technological discourses (Knorr Cetina 2009; Daston 2015), though overlapping significantly with discourses of security and secrecy, understands invisibility as that which is impossible to see "in plain sight" even in the absence of a physical barrier. This conception of invisibility, like invisibility as barrier, therefore requires the equivalent of a visual prosthetic (such as a telescope or microscope) in order to render the invisible visible. For example, the origins of everyday photographic technologies and practices have as central to their history the desire to push into new "frontiers of vision" by making visible the invisible. Early experiments in photography, in particular, were driven by the desire to see the traces of the spirit world (Smith 2013: 5).

Invisibility as inexpertise also means that a simple amplification is not enough. Specialist knowledge and even oblique approaches to the things under investigation are required in order to make visible. Conceptions of invisibility as insensibility and inexpertise therefore move towards a more complex understanding of communication and knowledge, with corresponding implications for political communication and democratic politics.

First, within this conception of invisibility, rather than things becoming visible or revealed, investigations into the invisible often rely on identifying the traces of things: the Large Hadron Collider does not amplify impossible-to-see particles, but instead measures their momentum or changes in the magnetic field in order to see them; the Hubble Space Telescope cannot help viewers see far away galaxies directly, but instead detects variations in light on the visible and invisible spectrum.

Second, when invisibility is conceived as insensibility and inexpertise and when visual prosthetics are needed to amplify sight and to detect the traces of the invisible, expertise and mastery become essential for seeing. Expertise is needed to see and to decode what is revealed. Teams of specialists are needed to capture and interpret the images produced for medical purposes through X-rays and computerised tomography (CT) scans or through magnetic resonance imaging used to see into (or screen) our bodies (Cartwright 1995; Carusi *et al.* 2014). Experts in digital data abound in order to produce and decode the cryptographic codes and algorithms that increasingly affect our everyday lives (Amoore 2013; Kurgan 2013). Without this expertise, the technological tools to see into the invisible will not work. And without this expertise, the traces will remain encoded even as they are revealed. Within the conception of invisibility as inexpertise seeing these particles, galaxies, cellular structures, codes and algorithms relies on technologies, elaborate practices and specialist knowledge in order to make visible what is invisible.

But, in the process, invisibility as inexpertise nevertheless produces its own invisibilities. While dependent on a promise to push the "frontiers of vision," to decode the natural mysteries of the world, or pre-empt future and invisible threats, these practices and technologies are as enmeshed in producing new visualities and new ways of ordering the world with corresponding invisibilities: Photography captures moments, allowing viewers to look more slowly and to see greater detail, but loses out movement and context (Lisle 2009; Van Veeren 2011). Big data offers new perspectives on shifting patterns within groups but pushes out outliers and uncertainties (Amoore 2013). And like barrier conceptions of invisibilities, certain groups over others also gain power through claims and associations with these expert ways of seeing. Finally, through the drive to extend the "frontiers of vision," rendering the invisible visible may change and even produce the very things that are observed (Eisenstein 1980; Barad 2007).

Invisibility as culture

Beyond the technological or expertise-driven understandings of invisibility, seeing, and therefore not seeing, is also understood as a product of the cultural codes and practices that order our world. Within the "invisibility as culture" conception, things, and more usually people, are rendered invisible as a form of violence, often through racial, classed, gendered, sexed and ablest discourses. This violence can be direct and visible, but is often also structural and cultural, reproducing its own cultures of secrecy and insecurity.

Within this understanding, invisibility is most frequently associated with powerlessness. As Ralph Ellison (1952) explained: to be invisible is to cease to exist. Politics is therefore replete with calls to render visibility to the invisible, from refugees and prisoners, to the victims of sexual and racial violence, in order to obtain rights and protections (see for example hooks 1992; Simon 2007; Casper and Moore 2009; Azoulay 2012).

Invisibility however is also a sign of power. As Carol Anderson (2016) argues, for example, the Black Lives Matter movement is a highly visible and public campaign directed at securing the right to exist, and to thrive, for African Americans. For Anderson what remains invisible is powerful and historically dominant "white rage": the forms of white resistance and violence that continue to perpetuate racial injustice. This power derives its force from its invisibility.

Invisibility as culture is therefore connected not only to the disempowerment of certain identities, but also to the cultural forces that reproduce these identities and associated inequalities and insecurities, rendering them "commonsensical" and therefore harder to overcome. They are dispersed, pervasive and interconnected (Cohn 1987; Enloe 1996; Doty 1996; Weber 2016), popularised (Weldes *et al.* 1999), intensified (Amoore 2007), and even hardwired into the invisible infrastructure of our daily lives (Burrington 2016), for example, in the algorithmic coding of facial recognition software that fails to recognise non-white facial features (Introna and Nissenbaum 2000). To date, as the discourse of "invisibility as culture" suggests, only a select few have the power to move in and out of these cultures (Sanchez and Schlossberg 2001; see also Johnson 2002).

So, while some call for greater visibility of the invisible powerful and the powerless within the conception of "invisibility as culture" there is an argument to be made that invisibility offers (temporary and limited) security: that there should be a right not to look or to be looked at until the structural forms of power shift in a more egalitarian way.

Invisibility as absolute

Finally, invisibility may be conceptualised as an absolute. In this understanding, invisibility is not the product of barriers, inexpertise or exclusively culture, but may be, first, the result of phenomena and ideas exceeding any capacity to render visible. In short, invisibility is understood as a failure of visual representation and understanding. This conception is often used when trying to communicate the complexities and sensations associated with pain, love, death, awe, the effects of time or the uncertainty of the future, or the scale and horror of violence, such as war and poverty. Absolute invisibility means accepting the idea that the world cannot be transparently represented or understood.

Second, conceptions of "invisibility as absolute" are also connected with a more relational understanding of knowledge. Here, invisibility and visibility are always intertwined; working together rather than against one another. Frames, filters, orders and barriers help make sense of the world and its visibilities through their selective inclusions, but this requires exclusions. It also requires the selection of viewpoints, or "situated knowledges" (Haraway 1988), as within cultural conceptions, but with the recognition that there will always be multiple views and viewers that render others invisible. This interplay between inclusion and exclusion, between the visible and the invisible, and the positioning of viewers, is what makes things understandable. And this interplay, a mutual dependence that is always subject to change, is where power resides and politics takes place.

Within the conception of "invisibility as absolute" there will therefore never be tools or practices that result in total visibility and there is no moving or thinking past visuality and the cultural production of invisibility. Visibility and invisibility, or in/visibility, are always limited, tied to the viewer and history, and in need of reproduction. Others, and the experiences of others, will always be both invisible and opaque. Edouard Glissant (in Britton 1999), for example, calls for the ability to resist being looked at because of the impossibility of ever being seen, and therefore understood. Invisibility is inescapable.

The politics of visibility and invisibility

In its different conceptions, invisibility is part of a set of practices that order the world and our knowledge of it. This includes how we understand invisibility itself as constructed, mobilised, contested and enforced through and for political aims – whether calling for the end of invisibility and total transparency or celebrating its ambiguities. In other words, invisibility has been and is itself constituted in several different ways with very different political effects and consequences: as barrier, as inexpertise, as culture, and as absolute. As we must investigate the visual for its interconnections with politics, we must also be alert and curious about invisibilities. There is politics beyond the edge of sight.

29 Memory

Nayanika Mookherjee

I am often asked by others about what I work on: I respond that I work on the public memories of wartime sexual violence. This response to my answer – "Memory! How would you know it is true?" – not only hints at the perceived unreliability of memory: this comment also reminds us that the evidence, sources and processes of historical memory – primarily through human recall in the past or present – are often suspected of being incorrect, imagined or constructed and, hence, questionable sources of evidence. In this context, where the validity of memory as evidence of a past is often interrogated, how are memories of violent events remembered, forgotten or remembered to be forgotten (Mookherjee 2006)? This is more so the case as the recall of violent events is always deemed to be difficult and fragmented. More specifically, what are the artefacts through which violent memories are recalled? How do they become part of history? What is the relationship between history and memory?

In trying to explore the role of objects of memory and their relationship with global visual politics, I examine how public memories of wartime sexual violence perpetrated during the Bangladesh war of 1971 are remembered through photography.

I show how visualising wartime sexual violence contributes to the politics of a public memory of wartime rape, enabling the "internationalising" of the issue and shaping in various ways the public debate about the figure of the raped woman. Through this discussion, the limits of global visual politics are also identified. The key insight of this chapter is its attempt to show that rather than romanticising either history or memory as distinctive, authentic tools, my work on the public memories of wartime sexual violence is a contribution to the scholarship that focuses on the interrelationship between memory and history. I show how dominant historical accounts on sexual violence draw from the individual memories that are in circulation. And it is the circulation of private memories that provides the very terms of recall for the visualised dominant history of sexual violence. The legitimacy generated from these individual memories also highlights the limits of the visual nature of global politics.

Memory, history and global visual politics

Memory is often situated in a hierarchy of credibility distinctive from history (for different positions on this distinctiveness, see Halbwachs 1980; Nora 1989). Memories are deemed to be contradictory ways of dealing with the past. History is considered to be objective, based on evidence, and the official version of experiences, while memory is seen to be subjective and provided by fallible human subjects. History is thereby deemed to start when social memory is fading away. Also, history is meant to be a scholarship for the few while collective memory is shared by the whole community. Others have, however, distinguished true memory from artificial history. To Pierre Nora (1989: 8), memory is the authentic vehicle of recalling the past, whereas history is a reconstruction and incomplete. History as a usable past is based on a constant struggle between different power blocs which want to impose their idea of the past as the hegemonic and national one. Memory is seen to be the mode through which this hegemonic history can be resisted, and alternative versions of history can be brought to the surface: the practices of remembering and writing are the means through which resistance is seen to be encoded.

In instances of violent events in global politics, it is often assumed that memories of atrocities are shrouded in silence. Memory-making thereby becomes the resistive process through which these untold stories can be brought to the surface and a suppressed, even subaltern account can be made part of history. Memory-making can occur through interviews and oral history projects. The accounts arising from these methods are then made part of objects which are seen to represent these memories. So, for example, intergenerational family memories, Holocaust, and Second World War memories can be transmitted orally through stories and interviews. They can also be located in language, bodily practices and rituals. These accounts can also be represented through various material, external memories, whether as objects of memory like the poppy. Photographs, films, literature – as well as structure and organisations, such as memorials, museums and archives – can come to represent and/or exhibit different aspects of these memories. The processes of preserving memories, whether through that of remembering, silences, forgettings, contestations, reconciliation and redress, also highlight the objective of this memory-making. Finally, processes of memory-making seek to establish the relationship between meaning and identity as expressed, claimed and contested through representation of the past in voice and text.

What is the role of visuality in this memory-making process? Does a visually rich object like a photograph enable stronger memorialisations, particularly when the memories of violent pasts are in question? I explore these aspects of a visual global politics by examining the role of photographs in representing the memory of sexual violence perpetrated during the Bangladesh war of 1971.

Visualising wartime sexual violence

In late 1971, Bangladeshi photographer Naibuddin Ahmed took a photograph of a woman (Figure 29.1) who had been raped by the Pakistani army during the Bangladesh war of 1971. This photograph depicted the woman with her dishevelled hair and her crossed, bangle-clad fists covering her face. Smuggled out of Bangladesh, the photograph drew international attention to the Bangladesh war, through which East Pakistan became the independent nation of Bangladesh, a war in which rape was common. Faced with a huge community of rape survivors, in December 1971, the new Bangladeshi government publicly designated any woman raped in the war a *birangona*, meaning brave or courageous woman. The Bangladeshi state uses the term to mean "war heroine" (see Mookherjee 2015). Even today, the Bangladeshi government's bold, public effort to refer to the women raped during 1971 as *birangonas* is internationally unprecedented, yet it remains unknown to many outside of Bangladesh.

Among many other images, Ahmed's photograph is iconic, symbolising the horrors of 1971, connoting the supposed shame and anonymity of the raped woman. It is also

Figure 29.1 The *birangona* "hair" photograph, Naibuddin Ahmed
Source: Naibuddin Ahmed. With permission from the artist.

Figure 29.2 Autograph ABP exhibition: Ahmed's photograph in *Bangladesh 1971*, a major
documentary photography exhibition at Rivington Place Gallery, London, April–June
2008

Source: Rivington Place Gallery, London, April–June 2008. With permission from Autograph ABP.

one of the most often-cited and widely circulated visual representations of the *birangona*. This image has been used on the cover of an English translation of a Bengali book on women's oral history of 1971 (Akhtar *et al.* 2001). In the spring of 2008, a photographic exhibition titled *Bangladesh 1971* displayed this picture at the Rivington Place Gallery in Shoreditch, East London, as the visual "trace" of the raped woman of 1971 (Figure 29.2).

In 2013–14, a London-based theatre company Komola Collective announced its intention to stage a play in the United Kingdom and in Bangladesh on the *Birangona: Women of War,* based on the testimonies collected from a group of poor *birangonas* in Sirajganj. It included Ahmed's photograph on its poster to announce the play (Figure 29.3). Unlike Ahmed's photograph, where the raped woman uses her hair (as well as her fists) to cover her identity, the theatre group altered this photograph to portray the *birangona* as looking out through her dishevelled hair. In this version, she holds up her fists in protest above her mouth while revolutionary women emerge out of the folds of her sari. The connotations of shame and anonymity in Ahmed's image have been replaced by the *birangona*'s demands for justice for the killings and rapes of 1971.

Along with these and other photographs representing the raped woman, portrait photographs of *birangonas* also exist in large numbers. In the 1990s, portraitures of *birangonas* in newspapers accompanying their stories of wartime rape become the prevalent modes through which they are visualised. These photographs not only brought

Figure 29.3 Ahmed's photograph as part of the poster for the play *Birangona: Women of War*, staged in the United Kingdom and Bangladesh in 2013–14

Source: With permission from Caitlin Abbott.

the *birangona* out of the shadows of "statistical anonymity," but also provided the public with a face for and an idea of a *birangona* (Sekula 1982). After this moment of truth, those seeking to document the testimonies of rape in 1971 had to visualise the war heroines through portraits. This is because the snapshot of the war heroine elevated "vision as the noblest sense" (Fabian 1983: 106) and rendered "a higher semiotic order to the photograph than the vagaries of the pen or the brush or the dishonesty of local testimony" (Pinney 1997: 108).

The Ahmed photograph of the *birangona* of the 1970s brought the horrific events of 1971 to the attention of an international public. The portraiture photographs of the *birangonas* in the 1990s brought to light the post-conflict life trajectory of the *birangona* and the still unresolved wounded history of Bangladesh. The visuality of these photographs not only represented the *birangonas* but also helped to constitute the image and idea of who the *birangona* is. If here, the "memory museum is mostly a visual one" (Sontag 2004a), what kind of recognition and meanings do these images legitimise? And what implications does such a role of visuality have on public debates on the *birangona*? Unravelling these questions would also lead us to the limitations of such a visually inflected global politics.

Visualising rape

In attempting to ascertain the impact of memorialising by visualising a political event like wartime rape, I am reminded how various Bangladeshis from different classes told me that they viewed the woman's dishevelled hair in Ahmed's photograph as signalling her "abnormal" state after the rape. By "abnormal" they refer to her being psychologically affected as a result of being raped. References to the photograph also directed me to the presence of a huge corpus of visual and literary representations of the *birangona* and the need to explore how they are interwoven with and contribute to the public memory of the history of rape in 1971. The circulation of this photograph and of other visual portrayals of the raped women of the Bangladesh war of 1971 underlines the presence of a public memory of wartime rape. It also suggests the importance in Bangladesh of visually identifying the raped woman. In fact, on a number of occasions during my fieldwork, people narrating encounters with the "raped women" would refer to the photograph: "Have you seen 'the famous hair photograph?' The raped woman covering her face with her fist and hair? The women we saw looked very much like that. They had become 'abnormal' (mentally unstable) as a result of the rape."

In the public memory of rape there exist visual ways of identifying the raped woman as "abnormal." Here, these real-life encounters with the "abnormal" *birangona* inter-twine with similar portrayals of the raped woman in the existing literary and visual representations to arrive at a sedimented image of who a *birangona* is. The image alone cannot create that sedimented image and a visual global politics cannot alone sustain performing and co-constructing the history of wartime rape. It is the cross-reference of this image with one's experiential encounters that makes the "abnormal" visuality of the *birangona* real.

Similarly, turning to the portraitures of *birangonas* prevalent in the 1990s, their photographs would always be accompanied by the caption "*birangona*" and a testimonial account of the event of rape. Hence, here the photograph alone would have been inadequate, as a woman could not be identified as war heroine without her caption and testimonial account. The photograph thereby needed a supplementary text, a "verbal register" (Sekula 1986: 30). In the 1990s, journalists gave individuality to these images through testimonies, in order to overcome the inadequacies of visual empiricism. These long testimonies accompanying the *birangona* portraits were found in the press with headings: "*Birangona* Bokul in the mental hospital" (*Bhorer Kagoj* 13 May 1998) or "*Birangona* Rizia is leading a life of poverty" (*Doinik Songbad* 16 March 1997).

The camera swept like a fishing-net throughout the country, capturing these faces of *birangonas* looking straight into the camera, erect, cautious and cut off from their family members, everyday surroundings and activities. The 1990s testimonies typically begin with the commencement of the war in 1971, then describe the day of a rape, the names and number of Pakistani army personnel involved, the names of local collaborators, the response of family members, the psychological or physical ramifications of the attack, and a perfunctory mention of the kinship structure within which the woman would be located (or from which she would be dislocated) now. The conjunction of these portraitures with the testimony of rape and the absence of family members, common in newspaper accounts during the national days of commemoration, made them all part of the archival grid of the collective memory of rape and the war heroine in the 1990s. In turn, the women themselves counted as *birangonas* when they linked or were linked to the aforementioned characteristic codes and "marks" that make her a "case."

In thinking through the visual global politics of wartime rape, it is thereby important to note that Ahmed's photograph of the *birangona* is enabled not just by being able to visualise her. The success of this visuality is also dependent on the circulation of this image in different contexts: in the *Washington Post*, for instance, and in Bangladeshi newspapers commemorating the war and in international exhibitions. It is its cross-referencing – in different texts, contexts and times – with witness accounts that has significantly contributed to the efficacy of this representation of the raped woman. Similarly, the portraiture images of the *birangonas* are only visually co-constructive with the event of wartime rape when they are placed alongside the captions of the images and the text of their testimonies.

That this repetitive memorialisation of the visuality of the "abnormal" *birangona* has contributed to a skewed idea as to who is a *birangona* and what state she is in today, is revealed by the following questions I would be asked about my research by the left-liberal community. I spent eight months of my year-long multi-sited fieldwork in Enayetpur and surrounding villages in a western district in Bangladesh, working among the four *birangonas*, their families and communities. To protect their anonymity I gave them fictional names: Mosammad Rohima Nesa, Kajoli Khatoon, Moyna Karim and Rashida Khatoon. Like many other women, they were raped by West Pakistani soldiers in their homes during the Bangladesh Liberation War of 1971. Four poor, landless women, they have since lived with their husbands and children in villages in this part of Bangladesh. During my fieldwork, when I would return to Dhaka from Enayetpur, people – NGO activists, human rights lawyers, intellectuals, writers, journalists, academics, feminists who knew about my research – would invariably ask the following questions about the war heroines: Are they married? Do they have a family, children, *kutumb* (in-laws)? Did their husband know of the incident of rape? My answer to these questions would amaze them: the poor, rural and illiterate women continue to be married to their landless husbands with whom they were married even before 1971, *in spite of* the rape. These frequently occurring, repetitive questions point to a sedimented imaginary of the war heroine among the activist community. Just as the image in the hair photograph gives an idea of the *birangona* as "abnormal," various literary and visual representations have contributed to the perception that the war heroine's kin networks have abandoned her and her family have not accepted her as a result of the rape.

The potentials and limits of visual memories

The significance of visuality in being a supplement to existing oral histories and memory-making is undoubted. That visuality in global politics has provided a trigger to seek justice for past violence is a significant fact. In fact oral and visual histories created the conditions which enabled various women to narrate their violent histories of 1971 and post-1971 life trajectory in Bangladesh. While drawing on oral and visual history, researchers also need to identify the limitations of depending solely on image. I am particularly cautious of how oral history, visual representations, testimony and memory are often invoked uncritically in retrieving "untold stories" of a "real past" and that speaking/having a voice/being imaged is alone deemed to be healing and contributing to an archive of memory.

Instead, a visual global politics needs to explore the social life of these images to examine how images need to be intertwined with other contexts, texts, to perform or co-construct a global politics. Through this alone the political functions and the social ramifications of witnessing through images within national and international processes would be highlighted.

At the same time, it is important to ask: what kind of victim is necessary for a visual global politics? In Bangladesh, the authentic victim is marked by "trauma" which is determined by a physical condition resulting as a consequence of rape. It also identifies the real war heroine as one who has no familial and community support. The politics of remembrance here is based on an assumed impact of that of sexual violence, the consequential trauma and a necessary traumatised post-event trajectory of life story. Here the reinscription of personal stories into national and international domains obscures the richness and complexities within which memories of visualities of global politics are located.

30 Militarisation

Laura J. Shepherd

This chapter explores the visuality of militarisation through the medium of fashion. I first explain the phenomenon of militarisation, before moving on to explore how fashion trends that draw on the aesthetics of military attire contribute to the dynamics of militarisation in contemporary Western societies. I conclude with an argument that links everyday representations of militarism, such as those found in fashion, with a changing contemporary security environment that relies on such representations for the normalisation – and therefore acceptance – of war.

Explaining militarisation

The relationship between war and the state has long fascinated scholars of politics and sociology. Classical political theories about state behaviour all comment on how states and governments engage in war and mobilise support for war. Governments can decide to embark on armed conflicts, they can distribute state resources to military projects, and they can train soldiers. But states cannot wholly control public support for war, nor can they control how the public conceives of the military as an institution. It is the process of militarisation that creates a positive public disposition towards the military and towards militaristic ideas.

Militarisation is a complex and interwoven set of practices that contribute to the production of a militarised society and an ethos of militarism. A militarised society is one in which people have come to believe that a military solution to a problem is the best solution; it is the production of a set of ideas and beliefs about how the world works. Militarism is an ideology, a way of thinking about political issues that structures a society's understanding of violence through a prism of acceptance of the use of force and the valorisation of military institutions. In short, militarism as an ideology works – as most ideologies do – to shape the parameters of what is considered to be "common sense" in a society.

Militarism becomes depoliticised once it is accepted as a dominant ideology and, as such, shapes how people think about war and the use of force in ways that they are not even conscious of. "Common sense" is never the subject of political debate but "just the way it is." This is why Stuart Hall (1985: 105) declared the acceptance of common sense "the moment of extreme ideological closure." Accepting militarism as an ideology creates a militarised society: one in which military institutions, approaches and even aesthetics are depoliticised, detached from their original imbrication in violence and war.

Militarism comes to be accepted as an ideology through the process of militarisation, which has been described as "the contradictory and tense social process in which civil society organises itself for the production of violence" (Geyer in Davies and Philpott 2012: 43). This account presupposes that the impact of militarisation is limited to "the production of violence." I contest this assumption and propose that militarisation is linked not only to direct violence, as exercised by the police and military, but also to beliefs about other forms of political activity: the exercise of authority, the concept of legitimacy, and the experience of civilians. Militarism informs how we think of ourselves as citizens of a particular state, how we relate ourselves to formal politics, and how we engage with others both inside and outside our own territorial boundaries.

Militarism sustains particular assumptions about power and authority. Many feminist scholars have interrogated the concept of militarisation, linking gender, power relations and fetishisation of the military. Cynthia Enloe (2007: 4) explains:

> To become militarized is to adopt militaristic values (e.g. a belief in hierarchy, obedience, and the use of force) and priorities as one's own, to see military solutions as particularly effective, to see the world as a dangerous place best approached with militaristic attitudes. . . . Most of the people in the world who are militarized are not themselves in uniform. Most militarized people are civilians.

Enloe goes on to explain how assumptions about an association between masculinity and authority in turn create an association between masculinity and military power. In the context of militarisation, this means that a militarised society or institution assumes that the natural power-holders in society should be masculine.

A militarised society – one in which most people have consciously or unconsciously adopted an ethos of militarism – also generates assumptions about how to engage with those people who are not part of that society. This is evident in how militarised societies both protect their borders and deploy troops overseas. The concept of border protection leads to further militarisation: the state is responsible for "protecting" the domestic population from an unspecified threat and this unspecified threat is associated with everyone who is not part of the population. A militarised response to the threat is justified by and also perpetuates the ethos of militarism. In the US, the UK and many other parts of the world borders are guarded by heavily armed representatives of the state. Bodies moving through these spaces are meant to behave in particular ways in the face of this exercise of state power. The expectation that civilians will know what to do – that they will acquiesce to demands, that they will be docile, obedient, unquestioning – is intimately related to the values of a militarised society.

The decision when or whether to deploy troops overseas can also be interrogated as evidence of a militarised society. There are two elements here.

First is the creation of an ethos of militarism that suggests it is a good thing to join the armed forces and participate in the military as an institution. There are many ways this happens, such as by telling war stories to motivate new generations of fighters. As far back as imperial Rome, stories of the glory of war have been told to civilians, with the intended or unintended outcome of creating communities willing to perpetrate violence on behalf of the state. Horace's *Odes*, published in 23 BCE, include the now famous line "dulce et decorum est pro patria mori," which loosely translates as "it is a sweet and glorious thing to die for one's country." This phrase is inscribed on the wall of the chapel of the Royal Military Academy at Sandhurst in the UK.

The second element of militarisation relates to the conduct of soldiers overseas. This is a much more direct and visible form of militarisation. There is always a purpose to employing troops in foreign countries. The armed forces are meant to have a specific mission that should have a positive effect. Whether or not troops achieve their objectives, the underlying assumption is that the presence of the military is a good thing because it will help resolve a crisis situation. In a militarised society these assumptions are rarely questioned, even though they often mistakenly imply that a foreign military presence works better than local forces and that a militarised response is the most effective response (White 2002; Duffield 2007).

The militarisation of fashion

Having outlined how militarisation is linked to an ethos that has clear socio-political effects, I now explore how visual practices are part of the militarisation process. Militarisation does not just reside in the "high politics" of border protection, humanitarian intervention and strategic military deployment. Aesthetic sources, including fashion, also reveal and conceal a lot about militarism in society. Fashion has not received a great deal of attention so far, even by scholars who work on militarisation and popular culture (Lutz 2002; Giroux 2004, 2008; Davies and Philpott 2012; for notable exceptions see Collins 2003; Salzinger 2003; Elias 2004).

The idea of "military chic" has a long fashion history, dating back to the early twentieth century. Military materials came to be used in the post-war period because alternative fabrics were scarce. Military styling was employed in the tailoring of jackets, skirts and trousers, in homage to the uniforms of soldiers (Steele 2006 [1997]: 5).

The emulation of military styling is not simply practical or stylistic. There is a politics to it too. Jane Tynan (2013: 78) notes that "fashion discourses continually draw on military discourses to exploit the spectacle of war." The "exploitation" of war by fashion relates directly to the concept of militarisation. Indeed, the creation of military-inspired outfits, garments and fabrics is both a result of militarisation and a way of reproducing these very militarised values.

Many items of clothing that are military in origin are now "civilised" to the extent that their military connection is no longer recognised. Examples include the trench coat, the pea coat, Dr Marten boots and cargo pants (see Gunn and Calhoun 2012).

Such cargo pants are popular with people of all ages and genders. Their military origins are obscured by their normalisation in mainstream fashion. Cargo pants are widely and cheaply available. By the 1990s they were selling to "suburban teens . . . punks and rappers alike" (Gallagher 2013). The aesthetic of cargo pants was derived from their military utility. Multiple pockets resulted from reworking a British Army model by US American Army designers, who create pants that paratroopers could wear to keep all necessary items close to hand when parachuting (Gallagher 2013). In keeping with their military origin, the pants are usually available in muted or dark colours, or even camouflage print. They tend to have several large pockets, each fastened with a single large button or heavy-duty Velcro, harking back to the need for soldiers to be able to open the pockets quickly and easily. Even if those who wear these pants today do not know their origins, the widespread availability and visibility of a garment with such a strong military aesthetic contributes to the militarisation of societies.

A more obvious example of the militarisation of fashion can be seen in the use of camouflage print material to create garments for civilians. When my son was born,

Figure 30.1 Cargo pants, worn by a woman, seen in Florence, Italy

Source: Photo by Mattes. Wikipedia Commons, https://commons.wikimedia.org/wiki/File:Cargo_pant,_female.JPG (in the public domain).

I was sent a set of baby clothes, accessorised with tiny bootees and a tiny beanie hat, all in forest camo colours of brown and dark green. From baby clothes to wedding dresses, all manner of clothing is available in camo print. The gendered and sexualised dynamics of militarisation are evident in the framing of many of these images, where the juxtaposition of femininity with the masculinity of the military is evident.

The use of camouflage print materials in the construction of civilian clothing has widespread appeal. "Camo is the trick birthday candle of patterns," said Jonathan Evans, fashion director of menswear e-commerce site East Dane. "Every time you think it's gone out, it starts back up again" (in Gallagher 2015). Part of this appeal is related to the enduring quality of militarism in society. As Tynan (2013: 84) states, "army clothing militarises bodies." Where army clothing is so widely accepted, so popular over so long a period of time, the bodies it covers must be thoroughly militarised. Aesthetic choices are never apolitical, which is why the producing and consuming of military chic amounts to a perpetuation of militarism: it is the very practice of militarisation (see Bleiker 2001, 2009).

Militarisation and war politics in the everyday

We can find militarisation in any number of places throughout society. Militarisation – the process of creating a positive public disposition towards the military, and towards

Figure 30.2 Finnish fashion model Anniina Mäkelä in jacket and bra

Source: Photo by Flickr user /-\nniina Loves U, CC BY 2.0. Wikimedia Commons, https://commons.wikimedia.org/wiki/File:Finnish_fashion_model_Anniina_Mäkelä_in_jacket_and_bra.jpg (in the public domain).

militaristic ideas and ideals – is evident in news media reportage, television shows, films and poetry. These are all modes of representation. How we, as a society, represent war constitutes the meaning we make of it as well as its institutions, including the military. "People go to war because of how they see, perceive, picture, imagine, and speak of others; that is, how they construct the difference of others as well as the sameness of themselves through representation" (Der Derian 2009: 238).

Fashion is a subtle but important aesthetic practice that is implicated in militarisation, for it is implicated in how people see themselves, others and war. Studying popular culture – of which fashion is a part – is important because it recognises that politics is not just the preserve of formal institutions of governance and elected representatives. Politics happens also in the street, in the kitchen; it can be laid bare in internet memes, coffee cups and architecture. Politics surrounds us, constituting our everyday lives.

I study fashion as the medium for investigating militarisation because how we choose to cover our bodies is not often overtly politicised. One of the very few exceptions here is the so-called "*affaire du foulard*," or the debate over religious veiling. But the politics of military fashion has often been ignored. And yet, clothing is both militarised and militarises. The popularity of a military aesthetic in mass-produced clothing – from baby clothing to wedding dresses, by way of high-street chain-store jackets and pants – suggests a widespread acceptance, what might be termed a normalisation of militarism in the everyday. Cynthia Enloe (2007: 143) recounts an anecdote that captures this dynamic beautifully:

> On the last day [of my visit], Kaori Hirouchi was seeing off a mainland-Japanese colleague, Amane Funabashi, and me at Okinawa's main airport. Kaori brought her little seven-month-old baby with her to the airport. When she saw me, she exclaimed, "Look what a friend just gave me!" . . . She pulled out a pair of cute little baby socks . . . the miniature cotton socks were khaki and were decorated with images of little bomber airplanes. . . . Can one militarize "cuteness?"

I suggest that it is not only "cuteness" that is militarised here, but also the infant and childhood itself. Enloe wondered, as I did with the package of baby clothes I was sent when my son was born, would these socks have been sent for a baby girl? The gendered politics of militarised fashion deserve further interrogation and so does the overall process of militarisation.

31 Nation

Shirin M. Rai

Murals, statues and inscriptions adorn the Indian parliament, a colonial building that houses India's democracy. They tell a story of "India that is Bharat": its past glories, the struggles for independence, the leaders who led these and their aspirations – in artistic styles that represent different regions of the country. Bharat is a term used in the Indian constitution to bring together the British and ancient Indian names of the nation.

Why were these murals, portraits and statues commissioned? And what do they tell us about contemporary struggles over aesthetics and political meaning that continue to mobilise as well as agitate political actors?

While sympathetic to Bourdieu's understanding of distinction and open to Rancière's promise of/for aesthetics, my approach focuses on the production of art by and through the state. I examine how this art affects the reproduction of privilege as well as its contestation (Taylor 2000). I turn to insights developed by postcolonial theorists, who try to understand not only the role that art played in movements of independence, but also how the form that art takes is framed by the histories of colonial inequality, nationalist aspirations, and collective imaginaries of freedom and modernity (Brown 2009a; Mitter 1995, 2007; Guha-Thakurta 1992; Sachs 1983).

I argue that these imaginaries are framed by privilege and affirm the legitimacy of the modern postcolonial state. They do so even as they continue to struggle with the palimpsest of colonial histories that refuse to entirely fade away. However, they are also contested, reshaped and even ignored as new civilisational debates evolve.

Before I start I would like to flag that all of the murals I discuss in this chapter can be viewed at the website of the Parliament of India: http://rajyasabha.nic.in/rsnew/picture_gallery/mural.asp/.

Imagining the nation, inventing its traditions, representing identities

Bhabha (1990: 1) notes that "nations, like narratives, lose their origins in the myths of time and only fully realise their horizons in the mind's eye." Focusing the eye, however, involves casting the spotlight on and leaving in darkness different images, materials and memories. The imaginings and representations of the Indian nation before and after independence tell an interesting, if predictably elitist, story of the nation.

India came into being in a moment of openness that allowed new possibilities to take shape. But there was closure too, for the partition of India into two countries gave shape to different citizen(ship)s and national subjectivities. To be Indian, rather than a subject of empire or member of a religion, had to be redefined in the wake of the partition's bloodbath. This encompassed the establishment both of new hegemonic discourses through constitutional and legal arrangements and of new economic and military infrastructures that allowed knitting together disparate populations into one stable political entity: the independent nation-state. Postcolonial India also tried to resolve a paradox that haunted the nationalist struggle: how to be modern and Indian; how to reach forward and back to build a new political imaginary for a new nation (Brown 2009a: 1)?

Marking the nation in public spaces was an important mode of translating freedom into the everyday materiality of citizenship. The nation was performed, given authoritative sanction and legitimised through various symbolic markers, such as changes to the names of streets or the removal of imperial public art installations in favour of new ones. As Walzer (1967: 194) has pointed out, "politics is an art of unification; from many, it makes one. And symbolic activity is perhaps our most important means of bringing things together, both intellectually and emotionally."

Nation-building

I now focus in particular on the installation of new parliamentary murals, statues and commemorations in the Indian parliament.

Two aspects of this aesthetic project need to be emphasised. First, the process of commissioning the murals was highly centralised. In an attempt to tell the "right" story about India, a committee was established. It was chaired by the Speaker of the parliament and included luminaries from the worlds of politics, history and art. Second, the form that the murals took was revivalist rather than modernist. The Indian "orientalist" style of the Bengal School was preferred over the modernist/realist traditions that had developed during the late colonial period. Thus, these murals do not reflect the struggles between revivalism and modernism that were characteristic of other aesthetic forms, such as architecture (Brown 2009b). Rather, the murals' Indian revivalist aesthetics was one of nationalism and modernity.

Although the Speaker, G.V. Mavalankar, was inspired by a Western parliamentary aesthetic, he believed India had its own history of decorating public buildings, which the loss of patronage to the arts under British rule had obscured. It was thus, he felt, the responsibility of the government of independent India to patronise traditional and modern Indian artists. Western architectural styles were rejected in favour of "bold attempts for the revival of traditional art" (Parliament Secretariat 1953: 2–3).

The sub-committee charged with planning the murals considered three different methods of producing them: fresco, marouflage and tempera. The latter was chosen, which means that the murals were painted directly on a prepared wall. The other two styles were rejected for different reasons: fresco because of lack of expertise available in India, and marouflage because of the adverse effect of the climate on the canvas upon which marouflage murals were painted. The announcement of the project and this list of proposed subjects for the murals inevitably provoked a public response, questioning the inclusions and exclusions of history to be visualised (Mohite 1955: 6; Choudhary 1955: 6).

In the end, 59 panels were completed and displayed in the outer corridor on the ground floor of the Parliament House. Out of 43 artists employed to paint the murals there were only two women and one Zoroastrian male. Most were Hindu upper castes.

Many painters and their supervisors selected for this project (Ukil, Mukherji and Bendre) were influenced by modernist abstract tradition, but the panels do not reflect this. Rather, they represent traditional modes of Indian painting: Mughal painting style to depict Akbar's court, for example, or the revivalist aesthetic of the Bengal School in Panel 4, showing establishment of Ramrajya. Similarly, while nationalist artists, such as the sculptor Karmarkar, were inspired by subaltern subjects, the murals do not reflect this concern for and inspiration from "the local poor" (Mitter 2007: 156).

The themes of the murals were carefully selected to inspire citizens by "depicting the outstanding episodes in the nation's history" (Parliament Secretariat 1953: 4). The state wanted to build an aesthetic bridge between India's ancient culture and its emerging identity as a modern nation-state. The artists were, in short, given very clear instructions and were not allowed to give free rein to their imagination. This provoked criticism from some (Adib 1957: 6):

> What do you want the murals to do? Romanticise the past? Flatter the present? ... Why do you have to impose ... on the artist? ... Why don't you leave him free to do as he pleases?

For many painters involved in this project, the recognition of the new state and its patronage were also at stake. Many of the artists and supervisors led colleges of art in metropolitan cities, where postcolonial visuality and aesthetics took form.

The narrative structure of the murals

So, what is the story that these murals tell? I suggest that they depict the idea of "India that is Bharat" through two narratives. The first one is about forging the nation invoking myth and/as history. This involves remembering and forgetting historical moments; reshaping the diverse political landscape, and reconfiguring gender relations as well as recovering India's "democratic past" to secure its place as a modern democracy. The second narrative is about cementing the legitimacy and accountability of the new nation through multicultural secularism and India's international profile (Brown 2009a). I now comment briefly on each of these.

Forging the nation

Myth is central to constructing the origins of any nation; it ties the past with the present, the mythic with the real, the religious with the secular. Panel 1 depicts a scene from the third millennium BCE: "The seal of Shiva as Yogi showing the Indian ideal of meditation. Also bull and unicorn from Mohenjodaro." Here mythology meets history to show the start of cosmic and historical time. Despite the fact that the name Bharatavarsha only found its way into the popular vocabulary in the 1860s (Jha 2006: 6), the development of the ancient Hindu imaginary of Bharat suggests a narrative of a seamlessly elided "Indian civilisation." This elision shows in Panels 3, 4 and 5, where scenes from the Ramayana and the Mahabharata are reproduced as part of the historical narration of the nation. The fact that both of these are Hindu texts is troubling in a constitutionally secular country.

The recovery of the idea of India goes together with the representation of the excellence of Indian philosophy and statecraft. Visualised as well in several murals is a tolerance of difference. Panel 45, for example, depicts the court of Akbar, with his "seven jewels": musicians, advisers, philosophers from both Hindu and Muslim communities. They constitute a medieval "government of all the talents." Similarly, Panel 20 depicts Kanishka's Buddhist council (first century CE), described as an age where different cultures mingled, such as Zoroastrians, Buddhists and Brahmanicals.

Representations of Indian statecraft are accompanied by the absence of representations of Indian colonial humiliations. Not a single mural depicts the oppression of the Indian people. There are, for instance, no scenes of the massacre of Jalianwala Bagh on 13 April 1919. When murals do depict resistance, it is through images of heroic leaders of the nationalist struggle. In these murals, Indian leaders are agents of their destiny, rather than victims of colonial rulers. Mural 59 depicts the leaders of the Great Revolt of 1857, Rani Laxamibai and Tantia Tope. Panel 115 shows Gandhi's Dandi March in 1930 against introduction of tax on salt. Panel 117 depicts India's independence day through the hoisting of the national flag at the Red Fort on 15 August 1947.

Mostly absent, however, are average Indian people. Subaltern faces, bodies and acts are folded into the iconography of the heroism of elites. They are the ones who challenge colonialism, recover from depredations with honour and with history intact, and face the nation forward towards the future.

Gender has been a recurring foundational motif in nationalist discourse. While social reform was considered a priority by all post-colonial elites, it was also emphasised that the "essential distinction between the social roles of men and women in terms of material and spiritual virtues must at all times be maintained" (Chatterjee 1989: 243). This produced tensions that are visible in the murals in parliament. The figures chosen to represent Indian women sit well and comfortably in the nationalist discourse of postcolonial modernity. They challenge the constructed traditions, which were so effectively used to legitimise colonial subjection. Far from being oppressed and awaiting rescue, Indian elite women, such as Rani Jhansi, are shown in these murals to be defenders of family and kingdom (Panel 59), educated, creative and leading a life outside the traditional family norm (Panels 6 and 63). The women in these murals, such as the philosophers Gargi and Maitrayee, stand in for how the Indian elite sees gender equality: as a kind of project that does not disturb gendered social relations.

Legitimacy and accountability in state-building

The legitimacy of independent India rested on its post-partition secularism, democratic institutions and rule of law. But wrapping these concepts around the idea of the nation created tensions, which were largely papered over in these murals. In Panel 5, we have Manu the Hindu law giver described as "the first law giver" and also as the one who legitimised the caste system and the subordination of women to male family members. But these problematic aspects are not highlighted, for the emphasis rests on Manu's laws signifying that Indian society was a civilised, law-abiding society for centuries before the rise of Western power.

Indeed, despite Gandhi's struggles against caste oppression and of Ambedkar's rejection of Hinduism, there are no murals that depict the violence of caste-based exclusions that marked Hindu society or the struggles against it. Instead, we have formal encounters of benign sovereigns and supine subjects (Panel 3). In these murals, reclaiming the right to rule thus builds on deep historical foundations of the civilised Indian state. This theme is reinforced by several panels that portray a democratic and enlightened past through marginal/tribal groups (Panel 3), philosophical gatherings (Panel 6) and kings in conversation with religious monks.

Statehood needs recognition not just of the citizens but also of the international community. The murals depict flourishing trade and state relations between India and the wider world. Examples include Asoka sending emissaries abroad to spread the word of Buddha (Panels 14 and 15); foreign ambassadors arriving at courts of Indian princes (Panel 18); a map of India's trade relations with various Asian countries (Panel 27); and trade delegations from China (Panel 28). There are other panels depicting Indian courts as cosmopolitan spaces, where intellectuals, philosophers, travellers and traders mingled and paid homage (Panels 31, 33, 36 and 37).

Reviewing the murals, no one can be in doubt that they attempt to retrieve Indian historical achievements as well as post-colonial national ambitions for the future. These murals invoke the particularity of Indian democracy, secularism and legitimate statecraft. And yet they are silent about colonial and caste oppression and everyday democratic struggles.

Aesthetic reception: the influence of architecture and art

We have not yet focused on one question: who was the intended audience of this public art? Was it the people who visit parliament every year? Or the people who work in the parliamentary precincts? Paying attention to these murals could be seen as the "emotionally and symbolically charged signs of club membership" (Hobsbawm and Ranger 1999: 11).

The narratives produced through the murals, while forming a backdrop to politics, impinge less and less on the struggles of the present. As India opens its doors to the world as a neoliberal success story, the production of the state's autobiography suggesting an unbroken line between Asoka's Buddhist peace emissaries and of post-independent India's role in the non-aligned peace movement. This is a palimpsest at best. Today's leaders and spectators rush past the earlier careful enunciation of India's aspirations towards new horizons of neoliberal success. In part, this neglect or normalisation is the success of the vision of the state-commissioned work displayed in parliament. On another level, however, it is also a challenge to that early vision.

In sum: I have attempted to show that aesthetic approaches to studying politics can allow us to read politics in different ways (Bleiker 2009). While many scholars have sought to understand how we consume political art, my attempt has been to show how this art is produced – by state and non-state actors – through commissioning, interpreting and challenging art and its installations. In this, my approach is different from those scholars who have focused on the transformative potential of art (Marcuse 1978; Rancière 2003), as well as from those who have argued that aesthetics represent as well as reproduce power (Bourdieu 1984). Through this reading of political aesthetics in the Indian parliament, I suggest the politics of art and the art of politics are conjoined in the production and consumption, as well as in the message and the form that that message takes.

Note

This chapter is based on a longer piece, Rai 2014.

32 Peace

Frank Möller

Peace photography – in contrast to war photography – does not exist as a concept in the professional discourse on images. Only a few authors ask what a photograph of peace might look like (Allan 2011; Ritchin 2013: 122). This omission tells us much about visual global politics focusing on violent conflicts, wars, famines and other disasters rather than on peaceful change and reconciliation. It also reveals something about global politics because "how we now – today – understand what photography is and how it works tells us something about how we understand *anything*" (Thompson 2013: 4). Does the absence of peace photography as a concept imply that visual images of peace – visions of peace – do not exist either?

Visions of negative peace

If peace is understood negatively as "absence of violence of all kinds" (Galtung 1996: 31) then both peace and images of peace are impossible. Accordingly, peace is referenced in much visual work negatively by depicting its absence (Wilkes Tucker, Michels and Zelt 2012). Peace can be referenced by focusing on the horrors of war as in much documentary work aiming to acknowledge suffering, to raise awareness or to create solidarity. There are many dangers inherent in this approach. For example, the people depicted may be reduced to, or even visually constructed as, victims without agency, in need of help from others. Peace can be referenced by capitalising on the power of the invisible. It can also be referenced, as Robert Capa did during the Spanish Civil War, by depicting "the temporality of the everyday" (Dell 2010: 46). This temporality, however, was shaped by war, not peace – islands of seeming non-violence in an environment otherwise dominated by war and destruction.

Even aftermath photography, commencing when physical violence has stopped, is inseparably connected with the preceding violence as the condition of possibility for its existence. Such photography can show that for many people and in many cases suffering is not over once the use of physical force has stopped, but the move from aftermath to peace is difficult to visualise. Even such a formidable conflict photographer as Philip Jones Griffith is said (Kennedy 2014: 53; emphasis added) to have shown in his book *Vietnam at Peace*, that Vietnam "is *not* yet 'at peace' with itself." Aftermath photography offers important visualisations of human affliction but it does not unconditionally qualify as peace photography. Expanding the conception of the aftermath seemingly endlessly and thus establishing temporal distance between a photograph and the violence it references (Baker and Mavlian 2014) is not a convincing approach to peace photography either, because its main reference point remains violence. Indeed, photojournalism assigns priority to representations of violence rather than peace.

If peace is understood as absence of direct, physical violence, then peace photographs are redundant, threatened by irrelevance. This is the case because the vast majority of images, including the most trivial ones, do not depict violence and would thus qualify as peace photographs. The concept of peace photography would be devalued by endlessly expanding it. Furthermore, seemingly peaceful photographs might hide forms of violation and exploitation as well as traumatic memories that cannot easily be visualised, giving the impression that peace exists in situations where it does not exist.

The concepts of visions of peace or peace photography are derivative of underlying concepts of peace. It is for this reason that there cannot be such a thing as a body of photographic work that is *universally* regarded as peace photography: peace is a contested concept; so is peace photography. Any understanding of peace photography depends on and reflects the political and cultural configurations from which it emerges and beyond which it cannot be generalised. Only with regard to these configurations can a given peace photography concept claim validity. The search for a single and universally recognised peace photograph will be in vain because of this interpretative openness: a viewer's experience will always be dependent on the context within which it takes place. Furthermore, it will be very difficult to establish causality between an image and peace. Even seemingly obvious cases, such as selected Vietnam War photographs and their influence on US culture, become more complex when analysed carefully (Perlmutter 1999: 203–6). However, photography and peace may be connected with one another *episodically*, which means that "their placement either in space or time asks us to think them together" (Taylor 2003: 274).

Peace photography depends not only on underlying political and cultural con-figurations but also on verbal or written designations of meaning in connection with a given body of photographic work. War photography is a social construction, contingent, and changeable over time, and so is peace photography. Concepts are not fixed but evolve by people "doing" them, creating, affirming, modifying or abandoning them (McSweeney 1999: 165). Thus, no photograph is *by itself* a peace photograph. Rather than asking what a photography of peace might look like, it is therefore more appropriate to reflect upon the question of what body of photographic work might meaningfully be referred to, and thus be constructed, as peace photography. *Meaningfully* means that any such designation, in order for it not to be arbitrary by merely reflecting the speaker's first-person assumptions, has to be aware of conceptual understandings of peace, war and conflict developed in the social sciences and humanities.

At least three elements have to be taken into consideration when thinking of peace in the context of visual global politics. First, the relationship between images and peace is episodic, not causal. Second, visions of peace reflect specific cultural configur-ations; they cannot claim universal validity. And, third, just as conflict transformation requires adequate approaches to both the past and the future (Galtung 1996: 109–11), visions of peace, without ignoring the history of violent encounters, have to go beyond constantly referring back to what was and, instead, point forward to what will be or to what might be, to peace or to peace as a potentiality. Such photography would at the same time be linked with *and* decoupled from preceding violence, the existence of which it nevertheless acknowledges. I suspect that the combination of these three elements results in a fourth one, namely, that visions of peace will have to add a focus on process to the traditional photojournalistic interest in "icons."

From the aftermath of conflict to peace

What role can peace photography play in the aftermath of conflict? Visions of peace may show gradual reductions in levels of violence. They may highlight the practical possibility of non-violence in situations that would earlier have been dealt with violently. Photography can also visualise post-conflict cooperation between former perpetrators and victims, preferably emerging from the community rather than being imposed by policy-makers. Such documentation can contribute to the normalisation of cooperation and perhaps to reconciliation. None of these approaches, however, will create peace photography without assistance to be provided by linguistic designations of meaning shared by a significant number of people.

Peace photography may also reference a point in time when the preceding violence has stopped being the single most important reference point for individuals and groups of people formerly exposed to violence. Using security community terminology, it may be said that such photography visualises the replacement of experiences of violent change with expectations of peaceful change while simultaneously acknowledging that this is not a linear process but one characterised by ups and downs, progression and regression. Such replacement is arguably the subject of Rineke Dijkstra's acclaimed photographic series *Almerisa*. At the age of six, Almerisa and her family came to Amsterdam from then war-torn Bosnia. Dijkstra photographed her in an asylum centre in Leiden for a project on children of refugees. Subsequently, Dijkstra took pictures of Almerisa over a period of 14 years at one- or two-year intervals, always in similar settings, always in front of a neutral background, always sitting on a chair – first a plastic one, then a wooden one (Marcoci 2010). This change is important, as Almerisa (in Chauhan 2012) explains: "When I came to the Netherlands it was all unstable like the plastic chair, and now I am sitting on a wooden chair with more stability, with my feet on the ground, and holding my first-born child." Does such a simple material object as a wooden chair, then, symbolise the transition from aftermath of war to peace? Does a photograph of Almerisa sitting on such a chair show a vision of peace when regarded in comparison with earlier photographs showing her on a plastic chair? At what point in time did the violence experienced in Bosnia stop being the single most important reference point as to the construction of Almerisa's identity and the (re)construction of her life (if it ever stopped)? At what point in time did expectations of peace begin to replace experiences of war? Only Almerisa knows the answers to these questions; viewers can only speculate; they cannot know. The photographs do not give them assurance but may invite them all the same to think of photography in terms of peace and not only war.

Peace photography and participation

The process character of visions of peace has another dimension. It is one of the important ingredients of participatory and collaborative work in photography and the visual arts to help transform people who had been subjects of representations of others into agents of their own image. This can be done either by distributing picture-producing devices among people who do not themselves possess such devices or by increasing the degree of cooperation between "artist" and "subjects" to such an extent that the subjects are being transformed into co-artists who produce images together with the artist. Such transformation requires time; it is a process, and this process can be photographed. The process of an image coming into being is as important for the people involved in it as is the resulting image (Möller 2013: 99–123). This importance, however, is often disregarded in discourses on images with their interest in the resulting pictures (and the search for "icons") and their celebration of selected professional photographers. Being an agent of their own image gives people the chance to present *their* points of view, to break with visual stigmatisation and standard patterns of representation, and to confront viewers with unexpected images, thus potentially altering how others see and understand the subjects depicted and their living conditions. Being an agent of their own image is also important because it challenges some of the criticisms regularly articulated in connection with photographic representations of human beings, especially criticisms of exploitation and subjugation relating to images of human suffering and people living in what seem to be unfavourable conditions.

Being an agent of their own image is important, too, because – regardless of what happens with the resulting images and regardless of how audiences respond – the experience of having participated in the production of works of art *not* as (voluntary or involuntary) subjects of an artist's visual project but as co-artists is something that nobody can take away from the people involved in these projects. This "something" can be grasped with reference to recognition, self-esteem, pride, perhaps even peace of mind. Peace is not always about the big stories of peace among nations; it also has an everyday dimension referencing processes in the course of which individual people – often referred to as "ordinary" people – gain something that helps them cope with the conditions within and with which they have to live. This is also an important ingredient of those participatory photography projects where people who have formerly been represented by others take their own pictures by means of cameras given to them by those in charge of the projects. This is so regardless of the limitations of such collaborative projects – and the occasional hyperbole linking such projects with emancipation, democratisation and empowerment.

From war to peace photography

If, as Susan Sontag (1977: 12) claimed, "the act of photographing ... is a way of at least tacitly, often explicitly, encouraging whatever is going to keep on happening," then there would seem to be many possibilities for image-producers to engage in a "proactive photography" (Ritchin 2013: 123). Pro-active, that is, with regard to peace. Peace photography or visions of peace do not exist as concepts in the professional, academic discourse on image making. Exhibitions and books celebrate war photographers. However, one of the most famous among them, Robert Capa (in Whelan 2007: 131), wrote as early as 1938 that the "war photographer's most fervent wish is for unemployment." Concepts such as peace photography or visions of peace are social constructions, and no one prevents us from defining *peace* as the main event visual culture should reference. The possibilities of visual culture are endless; so are the possibilities of peace photography. In the digital age, there are many more image producers than ever before and some of them might produce a body of work that can meaningfully be referred to as peace photography or visions of peace. If, as Jerry Thompson (2013: 4) suggests, everything we try to understand is in some way related to photographs, then a pro-active peace photography has relevance far beyond the narrow confines of image production and scholarly work on photography.

Note

Many thanks to Alex Danchev for directing my attention to Rineke Dijkstra's work.

33 Perpetrators

Susie Linfield

We live in the age of the democratic image. Cell-phone cameras – along with YouTube, Facebook, Instagram, and all the other wonders of social media – have allowed citizens, and would-be citizens, from around the globe to reveal countless forms of oppression and the struggles against them. Think, for instance, of the photographs that poured out of Iran during the exhilarating Green Movement demonstrations of 2009. Although Iranian photographers were under attack and most of the foreign press had been expelled, the whole world was watching.

We live in the age of the fascist image. Cell-phone cameras and lightweight video equipment – along with YouTube, Facebook, Instagram, and all the other wonders of social media – have allowed perpetrators of atrocities to document, and celebrate, virtually every kind of violence, no matter how grotesque. (The main exception is sexual violence, which is such a key part of modern warfare and remains largely hidden.) Think of the photographs pouring out of Syria from the Bashar al-Assad regime, from the Nusra Front and ISIS, from Hezbollah: they show starvation, torture, suicide bombings, burnings, beheadings. Syria is considered the world's worst political *and* humanitarian crisis, and once again, the whole world is watching. But the whole world does not agree on the meaning of what it sees.

Photography and film have always been double-edged swords, so to speak. They have always been used both to fight injustice and to perpetrate it. This has never been truer than it is today, when virtually everyone has the ability to make and distribute images. Never before has the dual nature of photographic images been so starkly apparent, so confusing and, at times, so terrifying. We live in the age of the grassroots image; but that has turned out, alas, to be the age of the perpetrator image.

Confused about the image

Perplexity about photographic images is nothing new. Such confusions were especially acute during Germany's Weimar period, a time that, like ours, experienced dazzling technological advances and that ended, of course, in the catastrophe of Nazism. In the midst of political crisis and economic turbulence, Weimar citizens witnessed an explosion of overwhelming, bewildering, widely available forms of new media: photographs, movies, newsreels, advertisements, and hundreds of illustrated journals, tabloids, magazines and newspapers. The philosophers and critics of the Frankfurt School, who perceived that they were living atop a political volcano, were genuinely, deeply puzzled by these new mediums; this was particularly true of Walter Benjamin and Siegfried Kracauer, who worked as a film and cultural critic for the widely read *Frankfurter Zeitung*.

Kracauer and Benjamin saw, and desperately hoped, that photography and film might be revolutionary forces. Mechanically produced images opened up the possibility of a mass, democratic audience viewing the world, *experiencing* the world, in new and expansive ways. New forms of vision, including those that disoriented the viewer and fragmented conventional meanings, could break through ossified ways of thinking and feeling and function as a kind of truth serum. But these critics also perceived that photography and film were highly emotional and dangerously seductive. Kracauer, in particular, argued that photographs offered a misleadingly superficial view of the world and could not explain the complexity of political events. Like an Old Testament prophet, he thundered (1995: 58): "The 'image-idea' drives away the idea. The blizzard of photographs betrays an indifference to what the things mean." For similar reasons, revolutionary playwright Bertolt Brecht claimed, albeit with characteristic overstatement, "Photojournalism has contributed practically nothing to the revelation of the truth about the conditions of this world. On the contrary, photography, in the hands of the bourgeoisie, has become a terrible weapon against the truth" (Brecht cited in Kahn 1985: 64). Here was a paradox: it was precisely the democratic nature, the *demotic* nature, of photography and film that made them so dangerous.

This is glaringly, painfully true today, in the age of the perpetrator image.

Perpetrator images, then. . .

Perpetrator photographs are taken by those who commit crimes and atrocities to record and extol their own power and to humiliate their victims. They are the most unnerving genre of photography possible, and this is not only because what they show is often (though not always) disgustingly brutal. Equally dismaying is what these images say about those who took them. The questions tumble forth: Why did they take these pictures? Why are they not ashamed of what they've done? Do the makers of these images think that viewers will share their contempt for their pitiful, powerless victims? Are they right?

The most notorious groups of such photographs, and certainly the most extensive, were those taken by the Nazis in the ghettos, in the camps and on the Eastern Front. Indeed, visually speaking, most of what we know about the Nazi state and the Jewish genocide comes from this source. The Nazis – official photographers and soldiers on their own – were diligent recorders of their activities: thus we see the starving, emaciated, crushed prisoners of the ghettos; the slave labourers; the ingenious persecution of Jews in cities and towns across Europe; the mass executions and mass graves on the Eastern Front; even Auschwitz, which boasted two SS photographers and a crew of photographer-inmates. Today, in gleaming, reconstructed Berlin, visitors flock to the Topography of Terror, a museum built on the site of the former Gestapo headquarters. There, one can study, in detail, the story of Nazi terror within Germany from 1933 to 1945, courtesy of official German photographs. The photographs are fierce and blunt; they left me feeling stunned and breathless. The museum is aptly named. But even the Nazis refrained from photographing the gas chambers and the "pure" extermination camps like Sobibor. They suppressed most of their perpetrator images and denied news of the genocide as it seeped out to the world; in fact, as the Soviet and American troops advanced, the Nazis made desperate though unsuccessful attempts to hide the evidence of their crimes.

Perpetrator photographs are not always bloody, nor do they always show overt acts of violence – though fear and pain are always their subject. Although quite different from the Nazi images, the photographs taken in Stalin's notorious Lubyunka prison, mainly in the 1930s, are another version of this genre. These are true portraits, taken with slow film and natural light; their subjects were executed quickly after being convicted in phony trials for phony crimes. Unlike the anonymous victims of the Nazis, these victims were well-documented: we know their names, addresses, ages, occupations, party affiliations, nationalities. (The Soviet Union did in fact attract the workers of the world.) They are a diverse lot: writers, housewives, workers. What madness led the Communist state, for which so many of them had struggled, to murder them? Their torment, and the sheer injustice of their deaths, live on in these photographs.

A more overtly brutal set of perpetrator photographs from prison – taken, like those at Lubyanka, for unfathomable reasons and hidden until the fall of the regime – are those from the Khmer Rouge's notorious S-21. Approximately 14,000 people were tortured and killed there; seven are known to have survived. We see thin, black-garbed peasants, sometimes wounded, sometimes chained, caught with alarm in the glare of a flash. Mothers with babies, and very young children, confront us (genocide spares no one); even they would be executed as enemies of the state. They meet the camera, and what they knew would be their imminent deaths, with anguish, with fear, and sometimes with inexplicable calm.

The category of perpetrator photographs is too capacious. Saddam Hussein's Baathists, Somalia's Hizbul Islam, Sierra Leone's Revolutionary United Front are all known to have recorded some of their atrocities. Among the most infamous images of this kind were those taken on cell-phones by American soldiers in the Abu Ghraib prison; once revealed, these images instantly ricocheted around the world to billions of people. It was not only the vicious treatment of the prisoners that repelled so many; worst of all were the smiles on the soldiers' faces. Here, as so often in perpetrator photographs, is the incontrovertible evidence that the torturers have stripped themselves, and not only their victims, of all that we like to call "humanity." These smiles – this *joy* in the suffering of others – constitute the most disorienting and sinister aspect of perpetrator photographs. They shred the connective tissue between people, and peoples, that documentary photographers have sought to create.

... And now

Though the lineage of perpetrator photographs is long, the situation today differs from the past: perpetrator photographs have assumed an extraordinary, and unprecedented, importance and political influence. New forms of politics and new forms of technology have combined to create the perfect storm. Groups like Al-Qaeda and Hezbollah videotape their assaults, suicide bombings and executions and then use the footage, sometimes accompanied by rousing musical soundtracks, to propagandise; the Taliban, which outlawed photographic images when it was in power, now has its own video production unit to film and distribute its operations. Amedy Coulibaly, the jihadist who killed shoppers in a Parisian kosher supermarket in the *Charlie Hebdo*-related attack, came armed not just with a Kalashnikov and a submachine gun but with a video camera and laptop, the better to quickly upload images of his carnage onto the web. Here we find the most morally astonishing, the most despair-inducing, change between "then" and "now": atrocities that, in the past, were denied and concealed – by the Nazis, the Stalinists, the Khmer Rouge – are now brandished in front of the world. Murder in the making is no longer hidden; now it is loudly proclaimed, joyously affirmed, and used to create a new sort of Internationale. Welcome to the era of the terrorist selfie.

Ground Zero in this war of images is Syria, the site of what Amnesty International has called "unthinkable atrocities" committed by all sides (Kareem Shaheen 2015). If the Spanish Civil War was, photographically speaking, the first "modern" war – documented by Robert Capa with unprecedented intimacy, both in the midst of battle and behind the lines – the Syrian Civil War is the first postmodern one. For the first time, many of the images that we see are not only made but also disseminated by those within the conflict. Some of these images are taken by ordinary civilians, or by citizen journalists, and show their immense suffering; consider, for instance, the graphic videos documenting the 2013 chemical attacks. But many of these images are made by the combatants themselves – made, that is, by those fighting for and against the Assad regime.

There are several reasons for this. The Syrian government has barred many foreign journalists and photographers, and has imprisoned and killed domestic ones; for obvious reasons, it views the press as an enemy. Similarly, many of the groups fighting Assad have declared virtual war on photographers and journalists: kidnapping, torture and execution can be their likely fate. Combatants on all sides have vigorously rejected the traditional idea, the *civilisational* idea, of *any* neutrality: journalists and photographers – in addition to doctors, humanitarian workers and, of course, civilians – are all fair game.

People across the globe have been transfixed by the ISIS images, which revel in pure sadism. Shock-and-awe is their mission: thus the burning-alive, in a cage, of the Jordanian pilot, and the video of an ISIS-trained child beheading a Syrian soldier. It is these very images, this very barbarism, which has helped draw many recruits to the group. The whole world may be watching, but the whole world is not horrified. ISIS and others have taught us, if we needed to be taught yet again, that there are untold numbers of people who will cheer images of cruelty and pain. So while we may not have a clash of civilisations, I believe that we have a clash of images: between those who use images to expose violence and those who glory in it.

The Assad government, too, creates death and images of it. Pro-Assad forces distribute images of torture and carnage; in 2014, newspapers across the world reported the discovery of the so-called Caesar photographs. This was a cache of 55,000 images smuggled out of the country by a police photographer who had made some of them. They show thousands of grotesquely skeletal corpses – some bruised and beaten, some with eyes gouged out – who were executed in Assad's jails. The pictures were not intended for distribution; indeed, Caesar risked his life by downloading and distributing them. It is nevertheless extraordinary that they were produced. Like the Nazis and the Khmer Rouge, the Syrian government *wanted* to record at least some of its crimes. This reveals an ominous confidence on Assad's part: clearly he thinks that neither he nor these photographs will ever end up in the Hague. He has gambled on winning, and he may well be right.

Many documentary photographers in the twentieth century, and especially the early war photographers, believed that the revelation of violence and oppression would lead to saving action. Some even dreamed of a world without war and exploitation. The photographs taken by Assad, ISIS and others of their ilk turn this hope on its head. The camera has become a tool with which to bolster, rather than fight against, the most hideous aspects of war and the most fearsomely dictatorial regimes. Photographs of violence are no longer forms of witnessing but, rather, forms of war itself. The dream of photojournalism has become a nightmare.

Fighting back: the humanist image

One of the wonderful things that photographs offer – despite the claims of Kracauer and Brecht – is a freedom of interpretation to the viewer: she does not necessarily see what the photographer assumed she would. I'm pretty sure that I, and millions of others, view the Nazi, Khmer Rouge and Abu Ghraib photographs quite differently than the people who made them intended. Perpetrator photographs can be turned against themselves: they indict the photographer for his cruelty rather than the victims for their presumed weakness, shame and defeat. And perpetrator photographs have always been met with counter-images, counter-narratives, and what I would call a counter-humanity. Think, for instance, of Mendel Grossman, a prisoner of the Łódź Ghetto, who left us with a trove of quietly harrowing photographs, taken in secret, which document the ghetto's savage conditions and demonstrate how the machine of death actually worked.

Though its aesthetic and political conditions are quite different from Grossman's, I think he would have cheered the work of a contemporary underground Syrian film collective called Abounaddara. Every Friday, the day of protest in the Arab world, its anonymous "snipers" release what they call a "bullet" film. (In Arabic, *abounaddara* means "the man with glasses.") These are short videos – some last less than a minute, most no more than four – that provide unique perspectives on life (and death) in Syria today. Eschewing narrative voiceovers and historic context, they plunge us into unsettling, previously unseen realities. But "bullet" and "snipers" may be misleading: Abounadarra opposes images of gore and violence; it also mocks the grandiosity of "resistance" and "victory," the empty bravado of militarised patriotism and the glorification of "martyrdom." In ironically titled films such as "With our souls, with our blood," "The mother of the hero" and "Vanguards" – which shows earnest Syrian schoolchildren learning the fascist salute – it reveals the callousness of these weary concepts.

Abounaddara understands that clichés foster sentimentality and negate clear thought, and so it aims to surprise on both aesthetic and moral levels. (It dedicated a film about a murdered colleague to his assassin.) And though the collective adamantly opposes Assad's criminal regime, it does not hesitate to criticise the opposition – see, for instance, "The Islamic State for dummies." Abounaddara's filmmakers embody the spirit of freedom itself. Rather than dictate responses or positions, they want viewers of their images to doubt, to question, to investigate, to imagine, to think critically – even, perhaps, to laugh. Their films are profoundly anti-dogmatic and anti-authoritarian, which is to say, anti-fascist and anti-fundamentalist.

Instead of concentrating on bombed cities or torn bodies, Abounaddara's films show the *ethical* wreckage of ordinary Syrians, whether fighters or civilians, perpetrators or victims – and show, too, how painfully conscious they are of their ruin. In "What justice?," a victim of torture quietly but forcefully ponders what kind of punishment would befit his tormentor, then kicks us in the stomach with his parting thought: "You've uncovered the monster inside me – happy now?" In "The unknown soldier (Part 3)," an anguished, bewildered member of the Free Syrian Army admits to a beheading: "My body cut his throat, and my soul wept." Many of Abounaddara's films focus on women (the collective reportedly has many female members), who are particularly outspoken, even spiky. In "Marcell," a self-described "girl of the revolution" explains why she stopped wearing the veil precisely when Islamist militiamen began "meddling . . . in my hair business." The young woman of "How the regime didn't fall in Aleppo (Part 1)" tenderly recalls her first demonstration – "My God, it was so lovely!" – and why she relinquished this treasure when the black flag of jihad began to darken the protests. In "The woman in pants," a middle-aged teacher wearing a headscarf wonders why a woman wearing trousers is considered blasphemous but a jihadist hiding behind a mask is not, and she ridicules ISIS: "Talk about a state! It's more like a small gang that takes advantage of people's fear."

Consciously drawing on Benjamin's ideas of the dialectical image as a political intervention and of history as a series of catastrophic ruptures, Abounaddara creates a cinema of unpredictability and subversion – and of humanism too. Yet its images, unlike those of Capa's from the Spanish Civil War, exist within a context of widespread political confusion. We, and I mean those of us in the West who consider ourselves democrats and who thrilled to the Arab Spring's initial uprisings – we simply have no answers when it comes to Syria. We can respond to Abounaddara's films as human beings, but we don't know how, as citizens, to *use* the images that its members risk their lives to present. As a *New York Times* headline about the Caesar photographs read, "Syrian's photos spur outrage, but not action" (Gordon 2014).

"Stop watching!," an Abounaddara film urgently commands as a train speeds towards us. "We are dying!" Though the collective's spokesman disavows any particular program or plan (especially for Westerners), there is a challenge here, one we should not avoid. And so after we look, and after we think, and after we mourn, we are left with the question – the very title, in fact, of Abounaddara's 2011 manifesto: What is to be done?

34 Pictorial turn

W.J.T. Mitchell

We live in a global culture of images, a society of the spectacle, a world of semblances and simulacra. We are surrounded by pictures; we have an abundance of theories about them, but it doesn't seem to do us any good. Knowing what pictures are doing, understanding them, doesn't seem necessarily to give us power over them. I am far from sanguine that my work, or any scholarly contribution, can change the situation. Perhaps our main task is one of disillusionment, of opening a negative critical space that would reveal how little we understand about pictures and how little difference mere "understanding" alone is likely to make. Images, like histories and technologies, are our creations, yet are also commonly thought to be "out of control" – or at least out of "someone's" control.

We may, as a result, find that the problem of the twenty-first century is the problem of the image. Scholars in numerous fields, from philosophy to art history and politics, have started to engage these challenges, so much so that we can perhaps speak of a pictorial turn: a new and heightened awareness of the role that the visual plays in the world today.

I am, of course, not the first to suggest that we live in a culture dominated by pictures, visual simulations, stereotypes, illusions, copies, reproductions, imitations and fantasies. Anxieties about the power of visual culture are common. Everyone knows that television is bad for you, and that its badness has something to do with the passivity and the fixation of the spectator. But then people have always known, at least since Moses denounced the Golden Calf, that images were dangerous, that they can captivate the onlooker and steal the soul. We can go even further back in time and find examples of how images have offended. God creates a human creature in his own "image and likeness," and that creature then sets about disobeying its Creator's orders. If the first crime against God's law is the acquisition of forbidden knowledge, the second, and equally grievous transgression, is the creation of "graven images" or idols, explicitly prohibited by the second commandment.

Why is it that people have such strange attitudes towards images, objects and media? Why do they behave as if pictures were alive, as if works of art had minds of their own, as if images had a power to influence human beings, demanding things from us, persuading, seducing and leading us astray?

We want to know what pictures mean and what they do: how they communicate as signs and symbols, what sort of power they have to affect human emotions and behaviour. What we need, then, is a critique of visual culture that is alert to the power

of images for good and evil and that is capable of discriminating the variety and historical specificity of their uses.

I will provide a brief sketch of such a critique here, drawing on my previous work
(Mitchell 1986, 1994, 2005b) and making one central point: when identifying a pictorial
turn and highlighting the crucial role that images play in politics, it is important not
to fall into the commonly held view that images have replaced words as the dominant
mode of expression in our time. The key, rather, is to understand how images and text
mutually constitute each other, interacting in a dialectical constellation that I have
called the "imagetext" (if word and image are seamlessly united), image-text (if they
are distinct but connected) and image/text (if they are in conflict or tension).

A crucial terminological clarification is in order. In common parlance, "picture" and
"image" are often used interchangeably to designate visual representations on two-
dimensional surfaces; it is very difficult to avoid some version of this usage. In general,
however, I think it is useful to play upon distinctions between the two terms: for
example 1) the difference between a specific material object (the picture that one
frames and hangs on a wall) and the image that appears *in* the picture, as an illusion
or simulacrum that can be copied and reproduced in another medium; or 2) the difference
between a unique, individual specimen (the picture) and the species to which it belongs
(the image).

Imagetext: pictures and words as mixed media

In *Iconology* (1986), I asked three basic questions about pictures: What are they? What
is their relation to language? And why do the answers to these first two questions
matter? Why does it matter what pictures are, how they relate to language?

The answers to these questions are complex and cannot possibly be explored in a
short chapter. But I would like to flag one particularly important issue: the need to
appreciate the mutually constitutive interaction of pictures and texts. All media are
mixed media, and all representations are heterogeneous. There are no "purely" visual
or verbal fields, though the impulse to purify media (for example, in abstract painting
as described by Clement Greenberg) has been a key strategy of modernism in the
visual arts.

All we have, ultimately, are imagetext constellations, what Foucault described as
the "seeable and sayable," the "visible and articulable," or the realms of representation
and discourse. A promising way forward is to go beyond merely describing image–text
interactions and to actually trace these imagetext constellations to issues of power,
value and human interest. Foucault's (1973: 9) claim that "the relation of language to
painting is an infinite relation" seems to me true, not just because the "signs" or "media"
of visual and verbal expressions are formally incommensurable, but because this fault-
line in representation is deeply linked with fundamental ideological divisions. The
"differences" between images and language are not merely matters of form: they are,
in practice, linked to things like the difference between the (speaking) self and the
(seen) other; between telling and showing; between "hearsay" and "eyewitness"
testimony; between words (heard, quoted, inscribed) or objects or actions (seen, depicted,
described); between sensory channels, traditions of representation and modes of
experience. We might adopt Michel de Certeau's (1986) terminology and call the
attempt to describe these differences a "heterology of representation."

The politics of visual-verbal representations

Tensions between visual and verbal representations are inseparable from struggles in cultural politics and political culture. Issues like "gender, race and class," the production of "political horrors," and the production of "truth, beauty and excellence" all converge on questions of representation. The basic contradiction of cultural politics and the links between word and image are mutually symptomatic of deeply felt shifts in culture and representation: anxieties, on the one hand, about the centrality and homogeneity of such notions as "Western civilisation" and, on the other, about the sense that changing modes of representation and communication are altering the very structure of human existence. Culture, whether the advanced research carried on in university seminars, the diverse ideologies propagated in "liberal arts" curricula, or the dissemination of images, texts and sounds to a mass public, is inseparable from questions of representation. Politics, especially in a society that aspires to democratic values, is also deeply connected with issues of representation and mediation, not only the formal linkages between "representatives" and constituencies, but also the production of political power through the use of media.

Separating word and image is a problematic but commonplace distinction between types of representation, a shorthand way of dividing, mapping and organising the field of representation. It is also the name of a kind of basic cultural trope, replete with connotations that go beyond merely formal or structural differences. The difference between a culture of reading and a culture of spectatorship, for instance, is not only a formal issue but also has implications for the very forms that sociability and subjectivity take, for the kinds of individuals and institutions formed by a culture. This is not quite so simple a matter as dividing the terrain of "Word and Image," between "television" and "the book" (see Cheney 1988). Books have incorporated images into their pages since time immemorial, and television, far from being a purely "visual" or "imagistic" medium, is more aptly described as a medium in which images, sounds and words "flow" into one another (Williams 1974: 92). This doesn't mean that there is no difference between the media, or words and images: only that the differences are much more complex than they might seem at first glance, that they crop up within as well as between media, and they can change over time as modes of representation, technologies and cultures change.

The question of what role images play in politics can thus not be settled by arriving at a set of values and then proceeding to the evaluating of images. Images are active players in the game of establishing and changing values. They are capable of introducing new values into the world and thus of threatening old ones. For better and for worse, human beings establish their collective, historical identity by creating around them a second nature composed of images that do not merely reflect the values consciously intended by their makers, but radiate new forms of value formed in the collective, political unconscious of their beholders. In short: what we need to understand is the politics of mutually constitutive and constantly changing imagetext formations, the artificial world of signs, symbols and media that we have created around ourselves. The transformation of nature called the "Anthropocene," when human beings become a casual agent in the biosphere, has been anticipated for millennia by its predecessor, the universe of semiosis and mediation. It is as if the old metaphors of the book of nature, the music of the spheres and the mythic tapestry of constellations have, in our time, been literalised and made real.

35 Protest

Nicole Doerr and Noa Milman

Social movements are loose networks of individuals and organisations with common values. They pursue political aims by relying mostly on unconventional forms of participation (della Porta and Diani 1999). Digital communication, social media and other aspects of globalisation have inspired an increasing number of social movements to use visual strategies of communication.

Addressing the visual dimension of transnational protest, students of social movements have argued for the importance of systematic empirical analysis of the actors or historical factors behind global media reporting on protest and contentious political events (Doerr, Mattoni and Teune 2013). Interested in global audiences, some scholars studied the transnational diffusion of visualisations of protest, focusing on global symbols of injustice (Olesen 2015) or migrants' rights protests as well as populist right-wing cartoons (Doerr 2010). Researchers studying protest networks and their transnational diffusion face the opportunity and also the challenge to study a great variety of images spread by activists through social media sites, such as Facebook and Twitter (Mattoni and Teune 2014).

To understand the visual dimension of transnational protest, we examine the actors behind the creation of images. Following Roland Barthes (1967), we could say that once an image is "out" in a global digitalised public space, the authors can no longer control its interpretation. However, we know much less about the actors behind the images that spread transnationally – particularly if those actors are small, non-institutionalised social movement groups who create images that become viral. Who created an image that went viral in social media, and which brokers (e.g. media actors, sympathisers, officials) have been engaged in the process of diffusion? Which audiences are addressed by each image, and how do audiences in different national and political contexts interpret and react to the image?

Picturing and framing transnational protest

Photographs are a key strategy used by protestors to frame their message and reach out to different national and transnational audiences, sometimes with ambivalent consequences given the complex and culturally diverse nature of global publics (Müller and Özcan 2007). An example from our research on social movements illustrates both challenges and advantages of including images in research. We examined the use of photographs in press coverage that dealt with single mothers in the context of protest movements against austerity and welfare reforms (Milman 2013). We revealed that ensuing visual representations were biased with regard to race, sex and class depending on their specific national political context (Doerr and Milman 2014). In the United States, for instance, photographs of single mothers focused on angry black and Latina women. The children of protestors were pictured in overcrowded social housing projects, symbolising poverty and neglect, suggesting promiscuous mothers overwhelmed by their task of bringing up five and more children with running noses and fearful faces (Milman 2014). These images tapped into familiar stereotypes of minority women and constructed a negative image of protestors as irresponsible mothers, discrediting them and undermining the claims advanced by the activists. It is not surprising, then, that racist and gendered stereotyping of ethnic minority groups and of women in particular have become increasingly politicised and contested by grassroots protesters, for example by the US Black Lives Matter movement. Most recently, sexist images of minority women have become a key issue in national public debates in the context of the US presidential election of 2016.

Alternative photographs and visuals created by protestors

To examine the actors behind the creation of alternative images of protest we now look at the political mobilisations of the original EuroMayday protests on the issue of social precarity (Mattoni 2012; Doerr and Mattoni 2014). EuroMayday protesters were one of the first transnational social movements in Europe working with an alternative type of social media or *media sociali* (Mattoni 2012).

EuroMayday is a particularly interesting case of protest because this network of activists used visual communication strategies instead of text-based discourse to spread their message to protesters in different European countries. The movement succeeded in mobilising a large number of mostly young people – despite significant linguistic and cultural barriers (Doerr and Mattoni 2014). In 2005, on the traditional occasion of Labour Day, hundreds of thousands of citizens and migrants across Europe participated in unconventional street parade performances and other direct actions within a transnational network of local protests against social precarity and the transformation of previously stable jobs into temporary and cheap labour (Mattoni 2012). There were street parades from Milan to Maribor, and from Athens to Helsinki (Doerr and Mattoni 2014). In Italy, many organisers of EuroMayday protests were in precarious job situations and belonged to a generation of students and young people that had previously been portrayed as politically disengaged (Mattoni 2012). While EuroMayday organisers clearly disagreed on whether or not "Europe" was their shared political frame, it was surprising to note that activists produced a range of visual representations that symbolised Europeans as a "precarious people" of migrants and citizens struggling in a precarious labour market (Doerr 2010).

Particularly interesting are alternative images of migration, a good example of which is a poster designed by EuroMayday Milan that shows two young figures in front of an urban skyline.

The poster was designed and put online by EuroMayday Milan in 2008. It was originally based on a photograph and features a variety of notable traits, such as the flashy and figurative style and colours. The couple standing in the centre adopt a dynamic posture. The male figure is presented in a seemingly resistant posture, with his arms crossed, while at the same time smiling. The female figure, though, is just a little bit darker in hue. Texts are combined with visual designs, with an English-language slogan addressing the European dimension of the protest (*Let's conspire and fight for*

Figure 35.1 Milan EuroMayday poster. Zoe Romano, 2008
Source: Zoe Romano, 2008. With permission from the author.

the Other Europe) as well as an Italian subheading addressing precarious workers and migrants participating in the protest parade in Milan. Listed in the subtle green hue at the left margin of the poster are all of the European protest cities involved in the EuroMayday network, while the red dot on the right side marks the place and time of the local protest in Milan. Referring to how the couple are visually portrayed, the Italian text mentions migrants first and precarious workers second, emphasising the political relevance of migrants within this protest event. Regarding the question of what is represented and what is hidden in this poster, notice – in the comparison of text and visual elements – that the visual layer does not highlight Europe as a topic, though it is mentioned three times within the text. The different colours produced in the poster symbolise different ideological groups in the local Milan coalition of protestors. For example, take the use of the colour pink. It stands for queerness as a new radical subjectivity beyond traditional left workers' mobilisations in the distinct context of Milan.

The creator of the poster, who is also one of the founders of EuroMayday in Milan, explains why she put together the poster after intense discussion within her group. Here is an extract (in Doerr 2010) from an interview we conducted with her on 6 November 2008:

> I made this poster based on a photograph we took. The female figure is a migrant; the male figure is a precarious [worker]. This poster stresses migration as a topic, and the struggles for migrants in our own network, as also written in the text. At the beginning, EuroMayday was very much a network on precarity. In 2008 for the first time, migrants participated actively in the process of constructing the EuroMayday parade so we felt *they* should be protagonists with us on the poster.

There is an interesting intersection of visual and verbal symbols here. The local Mayday group in Milan imagined itself as both (undocumented) migrants and left libertarian Italians. The groups' pluralist composition, and its discussions about restrictive immigration laws from the Italian government, inspired a new "we-group" imaginary in the words of the interviewee herself, as her group symbolises a joint struggle of labour migrants and other activists previously part of EuroMayday Milan.

Visualising protest

We have looked at the actors behind the creation of protest images. We have explored how activists as well as mainstream media actors and political institutions create and diffuse distinct images of protest. As we have tried to show through the examples we studied, images are used and spread by authorities and media actors to discredit social movements, but they are also an important resource for protest actors to express themselves. Because images mean different things in different national public spaces and for different audiences, we have proposed a critical, self-reflective approach to understand images of protest.

36 Rape

Ariella Azoulay

Over the course of several weeks in 1945 in Berlin, anywhere between a few hundred thousand and two million German women were raped. This took place even in urban spaces, where cameras were present as the destruction of buildings was carefully recorded in numerous trophy photographs. The rapes are discussed, though not in depth or at length, in quite a few historical accounts. There is no disagreement among researchers about the widespread occurrence of rape – only about the precise number of women who were violated.

Many of the publications that mention the mass rape in Berlin include a small collection of photographs. But rape is always absent from these collections. To ask where the photos of these rapes are, then, is not to search for evidence that women were systematically raped. Such evidence abounds. Instead, this is a political question which has to do with the boundaries that determine which photographic information withheld in the body of the camera can be decoded and how. These priorities and presumptions limit what can be learned from photographs.

When so many oral accounts from victims of rape describe the destroyed urban fabric and the presence of armed soldiers in the streets as the arena of their rape, we cannot refrain from asking, how come none of these photos of destruction became associated with rape? What are the expectations implied by the dismissal of these photos – that only a photograph in which a rapist or a group of rapists are captured in the same frame with an attacked woman could be recognised as a "photograph of rape?"

The co-presence of cameras and rape in zones of systemic violence

I am writing against the scarcity paradigm common to archival searches. I do not expect that, after seventy years, during which photos from this systemic violence of rape did not circulate, all of a sudden the archive will provide us with some rare, unseen images of torn bodies. Instead of inhabiting the corresponding imperial role of a discoverer of a large-scale and known catastrophe, I limit my study to available images. After all, the aim of a photographic archive should not be to endorse the known number of raped women with photos of their wounded bodies. When we speak about conditions of systemic violence, we should not look for photographs *of* or *about* systemic violence, but explore photographs *taken in* such zones of systemic violence. The places recorded in them are exactly the same places where rape took place. Maybe not on the third floor, but on the second; maybe not in the apartment on the right, but in this one on the left. Maybe only three soldiers and not four, and so on and so forth. The impossibility of stabilising this kind of information, which may be crucial for individual cases, is counterbalanced by the possibility of exploring, through photographs, the destroyed urban spaces in which hundreds of thousands of women were held hostage, raped and ruled by produced food shortages as modes of politico-physical subjugation.

Destroyed cities were quickly crowded with photographers, some of whom acted as if nothing could stop them as they journeyed through the destruction, seeking out sights that constituted prime objects for the photographic gaze. The presence of rape, including both what preceded and followed the physical violence, did not require any special haste to detect. It was ubiquitous, but still, it did not appear as a prime object for the gaze of these photographers, in the way the large-scale destruction of cities did.

In the centre of Figure 36.1, we can see a photographer holding his camera ready in his left hand; but in a broader sense, we also discern an interest in the photographer as a figure who is always already ready, as this same photographer becomes the subject of another photograph being taken by the photographer featured to the right. This attention to the presence of photographers in zones of war and violence is of course reinforced by still another photographer, the one who took the photograph that pictures these two photographers in front of a tank and the destroyed Brandenburg Gate.

In the context of the alleged absence of photographs of rape, we should better look at this photograph slightly differently, and ask, where are the photographs of rape that these photographers took or could have been taking in a city plagued with rape? Did they not witness these rapes first-hand, or did they choose not to use their cameras when women were raped in front of their eyes?

Until the moment we encounter a "photograph of rape" in post-Second World War Berlin, we can use this photograph as a placeholder in a photographic archive in

Figure 36.1 Photographers at the Brandenburg Gate, Berlin, May, 1945

Source: Author's own photograph collection.

Figure 36.2 Exhibition: The Natural History of Violence
Source: Curation and photograph by the author.

formation, and relate to it as a particular species: the *untaken photograph of rape*, the *inaccessible photograph of rape*, *the undeveloped photograph* or the as yet *unacknowledged photograph of rape*, depending on the circumstances under which the photographs were – or were not – taken, given or disseminated, and on the position of spectator that we negotiate. For now, this placeholder can be named an *untaken photograph of rape*.

Photographs should not be thought of as raw archival material, or positive facts whose intrinsic meaning as primary sources is to be spelled out through research. They should be read with and against other material, often considered "secondary," and they deserve special attention since what they encapsulate is always more than what those who produced them intended to record. If photographs are not associated with the rapes that often took place at the precise moments when they were taken, it is this dissociation that I'm attempting to foreground and overcome. "What was there" is made equal to "what made it into the frame" and photographs are conflated with photography.

In zones of systemic and omnipresent violence, the co-presence of cameras and rape in the same unit of time and space should be enough in order to reject the axiom according to which there are no images of rape. In such zones, when *there are no photos at all*, ALL photos should be explored as photos of the very same violence. I propose to ask in which kinds of images this systemic rape is located, even if it remains somewhat elusive. I want to bring rape to the surface of the photograph, side by side with other, more visible phenomena. Photos showing the massive destruction of built environments are my first sources in this effort. I propose to read these perforated houses, heaps of torn walls, empty frames, uprooted doors, piles of rubble – all those elements that used to be pieces of homes – as the necessary spatial conditions under which a huge number of women could be transformed into an unprotected population prone to violation.

Figure 36.3 Battered Berlin, 11 July 1945
Source: Author's own photograph collection.

Spectatorship and violence

Already in July 1945, the absence of rape was constructed carefully through tropes of substitution and displacement. Figure 36.3 is an urban trope of displacement. The chaotic, dilapidated environment that formed the arena of systemic rape had been remodelled and replaced by discrete destroyed objects on relatively cleansed sidewalks like the building in the photograph. The way it was described by one of the workers of the agency that distributed it deserves attention: "this is one of the scenes presented to the eyes of the allied soldiers who entered war-shattered Berlin" (as noted on the back of the photo). The description focuses on the way the "battered city" was given to the eyes of Allied soldiers. Rather than displaying interest in the way people experienced life in their battered city, the photo caption assumes the manifest permission of those who destroyed the city to continue to seize it, administer it and view it, and to act as if they are not the destroyers but those who come to explore, assist and restore order.

It is the use of violence that grants authority to take up certain positions, like that of the spectator, inhabited by the Allies without remorse, even though they are not just spectators but those who occupy and dominate the city, and bear responsibility for the spectacle the city was forced to perform. In accordance with the familiar imperial protocol, the plight one perpetrates becomes one's trophy, an object of one's gaze.

This is made possible since the plight of certain segments of body politics or entire populations doesn't etch historical time. There are no memorial dates, or even dates that are remembered by people other than the victims, dates in common that would make certain catastrophes tangible in time. "I've lost all concept of time," Anonymous (2000: 102) wrote in a city from which all concept of space was already removed. Thus, a photograph taken three months after the Allies entered the city, in which women are seen walking casually in the street, and not as if they had just seen their first daylight after being forced to live for weeks as "cave dwellers," can be distributed as a representation of the scene the Allies first saw when they stopped bombing the city from above and entered it by foot. Weeks of terror simply do not exist in the timeline of imperial powers' news desks.

Using Anonymous' diary *A Woman in Berlin* (2000) as an index for my reading of these photographs, I was able to relate to the photographic information along a different temporal axis. When photos record the presence of well-dressed girls and women in open spaces, like in this "battered Berlin" photo, we should remind ourselves that these women are in a very early moment of experiencing anew the meaning of walking in their city without the threat of being violently captured and raped, or forced to choose a cruel deal of being provided with enough food to survive in exchange for their body and work. This is through a photo of a city from which the omnipresent rape was wiped out in order to clear the way for its survivors to be shaped as consumers by the Marshall Plan devised for them.

Figure 36.4 The capital of the Third Reich after the storm, Berlin, April 1945

Source: Author's own photograph collection.

When the Allies walked into Berlin after heavily bombing it, smoke was often still hanging in the air, while the streets were carpeted with rubble, dead bodies of people and animals, and a few refugees on the run, carrying small bundles. These elements gradually disappeared from the city, and the degree of their presence in photographs can be used as a timeline of the rape that took place in this *décor*. Shortly after Allied troops entered the city, the screams of women being raped or resisting rape could be heard. This sound should be associated with images where the level of rubble and density of smoke are still high.

When the photo in Figure 36.4 was taken, probably by an anonymous Russian infantry soldier, women's screams were likely still audible. It doesn't seem like the dead corpse of the horse, still attached to the damaged carriage, attracted the photographer; nor did the scale of the destruction, as is clearly the case in the photo whose focus is a collapsed building. In this image, the photographer's gaze is closer and more intimate. The photo was not taken in order to show the house or the street. It seems more like an idiosyncratic souvenir the photographer wanted to carry with him. He would have been familiar with this particular building: he probably knew how to get in and out of each of its holes, and wanted to keep some memories of the many evenings and nights he spent there with one woman or maybe many, first having to "grab her wrists," "jerk her around the corridor" and "pull her, hand on her throat, so she can no longer scream," and later providing some vodka, herring, candles and cigarettes after he raped her. There are no existing statistics, but many women preferred to shelter themselves from multiple gang rapes in these types of relationships. These men became friends, of sorts, welcomed insofar as they could prevent foreigners from intruding and raping the women more brutally.

Consider W.G. Sebald's *On the Natural History of Destruction* (2004). He (2004: 29) is attentive to the movement of refugees, "numbering one and a quarter million, dispersed all over the Reich, as far as its outer borders," but oblivious to what happened to them on the roads, in the woods, in the refuges they found in their homes or along the way in tattered buildings. It is unlikely that Sebald didn't know about the mass rape of German women in this mesmerising *décor* of destruction, or about the controversy in Germany every time women sought to publicly raise the issue of those rapes and how they were silenced, as if the numerous children to whom they gave birth after these events living in Germany simply did not exist.

When photos of catastrophe are not studied, but merely made into tokens of destruction, details like the density of smoke, the height of rubble, the latter's position in the entrance to a building, women's grimaces, features and clothes are neglected, and appear as more of the same. When imperial violence is made into ether, these details can be helpful in making it palpable again. After all, there are innumerable photographic records taken in imperial arenas of violence. Careful attention to smell, colour, sound and other tactile aspects is necessary to endow this etheric violence with material presence in photographic archives.

Visual documents of rape

Visual documents of rape are not missing; this is just another cliché rooted in the imperial fusion of perpetrators' points of view with neutral facts. Visual documents of violence perpetrated in the open should be located within available images, falsely declared not to be images of rape, even though they were taken in the same place, and at the same time, as the rapes. With the help of the Anonymous diary, not much is required in order to hear the convulsing voices of women while being raped and resisting rape.

Seen this way photos of destruction are also photos of an arena of rape. In these perforated and porous dwellings, women, children and the elderly lived with no windows, no doors, no water, no gas, no electricity and very little food. They moved from the upper floors to the basement and up again, depending on the data they could gather on the behaviour of their rapists. Some of the rapists, they learned, were too lazy to climb to the upper floors, especially when drunk; others felt less comfortable raping women in crowded places like basements, where, after the aerial bombing, people stayed since their apartments were made inhabitable. Young girls in particular hid in closets and other less accessible parts of what was left of their or others' homes. Some of the women managed to reduce the number of men who raped them by making deals with individual soldiers, who would protect them from the others and, in exchange for access to these women's bodies, provide some food. The rubble that blocked buildings' entrances didn't stand in the way of those who came to rape women. On the contrary, the chase after women was part of the adventure, as can be read in Anonymous' diary. Even though the buildings were not secure, women still preferred to stay in them rather than going outside and walking to their predators.

37 Refugees

Heather L. Johnson

The way we imagine "the refugee" has changed. Gone from our public representations are images of the immediate post-war period, featuring proud, close-knit families, ready to begin a new life. Gone, too, are the brave, heroic and talented figures of the Cold War: dancers, athletes and politicians who, in standing up for their political convictions, were forced to flee the Soviet Union for the West. Instead, typical images of refugees today depict desperation and displacement in the global South. We see a large number of malnourished, powerless individuals in tattered clothing. We see women and children seeking protection from events outside their control.

Images are powerful. They not only illustrate the physical or material appearances – the colour and lines that capture a moment in time – but also reflect and inform our assumptions about people and politics. Embedded in this context are our own suspicions and fears, and political forces related to gender, race and class. An image tells us who refugees are and what status they occupy: are they "legitimate" or "threatening," "in need" or "suspicious?" Images thus shape how we respond to the flow of asylum seekers across international borders.

I examine images used by the United Nations High Commissioner for Refugees (UNHCR). I draw from the landmark publication *Images of Exile* (UNHCR 1991) as well as from current campaigns and online photo galleries. I trace broad trends in visual representation, reflecting upon how the changes in images correspond with changes in policy in Western countries. Images of refugees changed as politics shifted from the Cold War to economic protectionism and then to a preoccupation with security. As a result of these shifts, refugees have become less welcome. They are no longer seen as brave and defiant and masculine, standing up to oppression. They are viewed either as economic burdens or as security threats. They are feminised, disempowered and in need of charity.

1951: the international refugee regime

Images played a crucial role in the political acceptance of the refugee regime. Understood initially as a temporary measure with only a three-year mandate, the UNHCR has become a permanent feature of global politics. The mandate – then and now – was to provide a framework for international refugee protection and to seek and implement permanent solutions to the "refugee problem." The provisions for such "solutions" are laid out in the 1951 Convention Relating to the Status of Refugees (UNHCR 1951), but they rely entirely upon a state's willingness and capacity to implement them effectively. The incorporation of the Convention into domestic state law varies widely according to state interpretation of the requirements and parameters of protection, and is directly influenced by public support and the ever-changing dynamics of the balance between border security needs and the individual human right to claim asylum.

The images published by the UNHCR are crucial to these political dynamics. They both reflect and shape public expectations of who a refugee is – and what is possible for that person's protection. Humanitarian funding for the UNHCR's activities is dependent on strong public support. The UNHCR relies upon voluntary donations for the vast majority of its budget and, facing increasing demand on these limited resources and pervasive donor fatigue, there is an intense focus on fundraising. Achieving strong public support in Western states is a priority for the organisation, not only to facilitate the resettlement of refugees, but also to support global protection activities. To raise funds "refugees must be visible," argues Harrell-Bond (in Baines 2004: 36), and this visibility is achieved by images, deliberately and carefully chosen to shape a particular understanding of refugees and their needs and capacities.

At the founding of the UNHCR in the early 1950s, images of the refugees overwhelmingly focused on Europe. Pictures reflected families and individuals who are easily identifiable as being from the global North.

We see white and often male bodies, Western-style dress, suitcases. The depicted people are heroic, determined and have a personal identity and individual story. These

Figure 37.1 Germany, European refugees, UNHCR, 1953
Source: UNHCR, 1953. With permission from UNHCR.

images directly reflect the founding assumptions of the UNHCR, which were firmly European. Both the organisation itself and the Convention that guides its work were established in response to the displacement of eight million refugees in the Second World War and, subsequently, the displacements that resulted from the onset of the Cold War. The persons of concern were thus of European origin. They were fleeing states that were hostile to the West (Sobel 1979: 2–3; Hyndman 2000: 9). Pictures clearly communicated to the Western public that refugees were not to be feared, and that they were individuals and families that could integrate easily into host societies. Overlaid over the pictures are discourses of race, gender and class.

Refugees were depicted so they could be welcomed: as representing familiar values and ways of being that were non-threatening and non-disruptive. Such representations actively shaped the anticipated public response to the preferred "solution" of resettlement. The visual representation conveyed to the Western public that refugees were "like them," and could contribute to society. Resettlement in host countries was seen as not only viable, but also desirable in the long term.

It is important to recognise that these early conceptualisations valued the political nature of the refugee. This is reflected in the emphasis on individual identities and stories, conveyed with dignity and pride. The 1951 Convention defined a refugee in ways that placed emphasis on individuals who are active, valorising specific experiences of persecution. By contrast, generalised violence and mass displacements were not part of the official focus of the UNHCR. This understanding emphasised who a refugee was, situating his actions and choices as essential components to his identity as a refugee (gendered language here is deliberate). The refugee was inescapably political and had ideological value; he was said to be "voting with his feet" by fleeing to the West.

Myths of difference

As the 1960s began – barely ten years after the establishment of the UNHCR – events outside Europe began to challenge the temporal and geographical limits in the Convention. Independence struggles in the colonies of Africa and Asia, and events such as the Chinese cultural revolution, the Algerian civil war and the wars in Indochina generated massive displacements across continents (Neuman 2004: 42; Baines 2004: 5). No frameworks beyond the UNHCR existed to adequately address the challenges and needs of the "new" refugees. These pressures ultimately resulted in the signing of the 1967 Protocol. The refugee definition became global.

As the geographical focus of the regime shifted, so too did the popular imagination of the refugee. In the 1960s, the image of the refugee was no longer that of a white European individual giving voice to an affirmative and heroic political position. A competing figure had emerged: a victim, poverty-stricken and fleeing violence and war. Chimni (1998) argues that a "myth of difference" arose as refugee flows in the South were represented as radically different from those in Europe. This difference is clearly articulated by the UNHCR (2000: 6) itself:

> These refugees were different in many ways from those envisaged in the 1951 UN Refugee Convention. In most cases they were people who had fled their homes not because of a fear of persecution but because of war and violence related to the process of decolonisation. Most of them did not seek to integrate in the country

of asylum, but wanted to repatriate when their own countries became independent or when the environment became more secure. Rather than dealing with individual refugees on a case by case basis, UNHCR now found itself dealing with mass flows of refugees.

This myth of difference is played out starkly in the pictures of the era. Rather than white, middle-class and heroic, the new images were of poverty-stricken and desperate people. The reasons for flight were no longer individual political circumstances or actions, but instead conditions of war and violence, compounded by poverty. These are generalised "causes" not easily captured by the individualist political framework of the 1951 Convention.

The depiction of mass movements is immediately evident. In the UNHCR online galleries, the pictures from the 1960s onwards are dominated by images that show a massive number of refugees from Africa and Asia.

What is significant in contrasting the two categories of images – those of European refugees, and those of refugees in the South – is the removal of a sense of personal identity and experience. As the refugee becomes a figure from the global South, any sense of migration being as a result of personal, political choice disappears from the frame. Refugees are depicted as victims of forces beyond their control. Rajaram (2002: 247) argues that humanitarian agencies represent refugees in terms of helplessness and

Figure 37.2 African refugees in the 1960s, UNHCR/S. Wright, 1961

Source: UNHCR/S. Wright, 1961. With permission from UNHCR.

loss. Heroism, defiance and determination are deemphasised, while desperation and vulnerability are the key markers of experience. Individual stories no longer matter. This removal of individuality is a strategic attempt to counter the fears and suspicions. Emphasising need is meant to shore up public support.

The international refugee regime was established in the context of the Cold War and the conflict between two superpowers. Its shift to the global South, however, was conditioned by the pervasive power relations between North and South and the continuing legacies of colonialism. Framed by the context of a global economic crisis in the late 1970s and 1980s, a colonial suspicion took hold. The assumption was that refugee migration from the South to the North was motivated not by need for protection, but by the conscious desire for economic betterment. Amid reports of mass population movements, refugees came to be understood as unacceptable economic "burdens."

The multi-layered dynamics of class were central to the push-back from Western societies: perceived differences in education and skill levels underscored fears that newly arrived refugees would not – could not – "contribute to society." Such differences are visible in popular images of the time, in style of dress and the condition of the clothing. Important as well were racial and colonial differentiations between poor and rich, "civilised and uncivilised." A crisis of authenticity emerged for asylum seekers as their claims were presented as spurious and inauthentic. The suspicious figure of the economic migrant became a foil for the legitimate refugee.

As Western/Northern states became more hostile to refugee resettlement, the images produced by the UNHCR emphasise greater need. As choice became a reason to be suspicious of refugee claims – because "choice" had come to mean not a political or ideological decision, but an economic one – the "forced" nature of refugee migration was emphasised through representations of desperation. Political choice was no longer to be celebrated, but was de-emphasised.

Since the 1990s, and particularly since the terror attacks of 11 September 2001, the figure of economic migration has been joined by the figure of the terrorist. Refugee flows are seen as potentially providing effective cover for combatants and terrorists (Adamson 2006). The emphasis on security threats has only increased as the wars in Iraq and Afghanistan, and now in Syria, have generated massive refugee flows that overlap in origin, religion and identity with the popular imagination of the Islamic jihadist terrorist. Border control has become increasingly restrictive (Dauvergne 2007), and asylum policy is characterised by what Chimni (2009) refers to as "the non-entrée regime." Discourses of "preventative protection," which aim to prevent movement across borders or between regions, have overtaken provisions for the resettlement of refugees. The clear policy preference is to protect refugees in their regions of origin. As security concerns have become increasingly dominant, the victimisation of the refugee in official images has been consolidated around a rejection of the politically active (and therefore threatening) refugee in favour of a desperate individual subject to circumstances beyond her control.

Imagining the female refugee

Present-day asylum advocacy and humanitarian activities rely upon discourses of victimisation that depoliticise the refugee. The denial of a capacity for being political, for being powerful, is embedded within a disempowering victim discourse (Malkki 1995: 11–12). Refugees today are depicted as quiescent, passive and fundamentally non-political. This victimisation and depoliticisation of the refugee is explicit in UNHCR literature, which describes the refugee's life as:

> desperately simple, and empty. No home, no work, no decisions to take today. And none to take tomorrow. Or the next day. Refugees are the victims of persecution and violence. Most hope that, one day, they may be able to rebuild their lives in a sympathetic environment. To exist again in more than name.

(cited in Soguk 1999: 9)

To be effective, however, this discourse must be embodied in an imagined figure of the refugee. Contemporary refugees are depicted as poor, a condition assumed to deter (or make difficult) political action as survival becomes the overwhelming goal of daily life. However, this also creates suspicion about the economic motivations for migration, which has seriously damaged the credibility of refugee claims, and thus the openness of the system. In this way, poverty creates both vulnerability and sinister intent. It is gender that plays the crucial role in creating the vulnerable refugee. Samara argues that the UNHCR has capitalised on the images of refugee women and children (in Baines 2004, vi).

The use of women and children to depict mass mobilisations began with the recognition of the refugee crisis of the global South. By the 1980s the image of a "Third World" mother and child had become emblematic of "the refugee."

Figure 37.3
A woman covering her face exemplifies the shift to depersonalisation, victimisation and feminisation of the refugee, UNHCR/J. Mohr, 1968

Source: UNHCR/J. Mohr, 1968. With permission from UNHCR.

The emphasis on women and children in collections of refugee images is consistent with empirical numbers. However, it was not until 1990 that the UNHCR first considered a gender-specific policy (Goodwin-Gill 1996: 256; Forbes Martin 1992). Multi-faceted vulnerability defines the female refugee. Socio-economic poverty coupled with greater familial and care obligations make migration far more difficult for women than for men. Women refugees are non-threatening in this aspect, as they are seen as unlikely to migrate for "economic reasons." Similarly, they are excused from the security discourse, as the imagination of the "terrorist" is overwhelmingly male. Instead, refugee women are generalised into a category that is both dependent and in need of protection.

The construction of the vulnerable refugee woman, therefore, is used as a tool for the mobilisation of support behind humanitarian intervention and refugee work (Rajaram 2002: 252). It is part of a larger process through which refugees are visualised and politicised. Paying attention to the ensuing dynamics is as important as ever, not least since the global refugee regime is currently struggling to meet the largest refugee crisis since the Second World War. Western public support for emergency assistance of refugees is high, but political support for longer-term solutions, including resettlement, is low. Embedded in a context of heightened security and economic austerity, both are sinking. Images remain a crucial element of the ongoing politics of asylum, and in the face of hostile attitudes to refugees we are now seeing images of children, and of death, dominating the public campaigns. This is not a break from trend, but a continuation of the victimisation of the refugee and the depiction of powerless desperation and need. The implications of these visual trends are important for they shape how refugees are to be protected, integrated and given the chance of safe and dignified lives.

38 Religion

Erin K. Wilson

Visually rendering "religion" in contemporary global politics reflects similar challenges and assumptions to those encountered when attempting to make sense of the category of religion with the written word. We do not really know what "religion" is, or at least there is little consensus on how to define this intangible dimension of the human experience. We grasp at elements of what might be called "tradition," "the sacred," "the supernatural" in an attempt to depict religion. Largely, however, "religion" is a category that resists definition and concreteness, shifting in its meaning from one context to the next (Hurd 2015; Beaman and Sullivan 2013). Efforts to clearly define "religion" reflect influence from secular worldviews, which assume that the religious and the secular can be and should be clearly delineated from one another, maintaining the dominance of the secular over the religious (Wilson 2012, 2017). When specific definitions are made about what religion is and does, it is frequently an exercise of power. These exercises of power may take place internally within a specific religious tradition, to claim access to the "true" religion and authority over all other interpretations; or externally, often by political actors who seek to control religion and harness its influence in the pursuit of largely secular Euro-American Enlightenment goals and values, including specific interpretations of democracy, human rights, human dignity and development. It is important to bear in mind, however, that just as "religion" is a category that resists definition and concreteness, so too does "secular."

Let us pause for a moment and consider – close your eyes and imagine, please humour me for a little while – what are the images that appear in your mind when you think of "religion?" What are the most common representations of "religion," the "sacred," the "divine" that we encounter in global politics and the media?

Now, did you see:

- Large imposing buildings, with ornate architecture and visible symbols?
- Stained glass windows, depicting stories from the life of Jesus Christ?
- Authority figures (predominantly middle-aged men) in ornate robes and odd-looking hats standing behind or beside pulpits and lecterns?
- Leather-bound, ancient, tattered books containing words considered sacred by a community of followers?
- Candles being lit inside cold, bare, stone rooms?
- People with heads bowed, eyes closed and hands clasped together in an attitude of prayer?
- Individuals wearing religious dress, distributing aid to the poor in conflict zones and developing countries, Mother Teresa-like?

- People holding guns, wearing traditional head dress and waving flags with Arabic script on them?
- Cartoons and caricatures that ridicule or mock religious figures and religious beliefs, such as the *Jyllands-Posten* cartoons, or the pages of *Charlie Hebdo*?

These may or may not have been what you saw in your mind's eye, yet these visual tropes frequently appear in media reporting on issues where religion, politics and public life intersect. They are all implicitly imbued with dominant assumptions about what religion is and does in contemporary global politics. Such prevailing assumptions reflect the influence of the Christian tradition, and the secular Enlightenment critique of this tradition, embedded in the Euro-American worldview that has come to permeate global institutions, global media and the global public sphere (Gutkowski 2014). This is not to suggest that there is only one kind of secular Euro-American worldview. There are numerous variations, manifesting differently in and across diverse cultural, geographic, linguistic, political and historical contexts. Yet they possess certain family resemblances, including particular assumptions about the category of religion (Wilson 2017). Predominantly, these assumptions position "religion" as institutional, individual and irrational (Wilson 2012), and as either "good" or "bad" on the basis of whether it contributes to or hinders the pursuit of peace, democracy and human rights as conceived in the Euro-American political imaginary (Hurd 2015).

Let us briefly consider these images in turn.

Figure 38.1 Westminster Abbey

Source: Wikimedia Commons, 2004, https://commons.wikimedia.org/wiki/File:Westminster_Abbey_West_Door.jpg (in the public domain).

The imposing buildings, the authority figures, stained glass windows, sacred scriptures and candles all reinforce assumptions about the supposedly inherent institutional nature of religion. Religion is governed through institutions and hierarchical leadership structures that are predominantly patriarchal. Its adherents gather together on a regular basis in formally designated and sanctified locations, engaging in established, officially authorised rituals.

Yet, while an important part of numerous Christian denominations, this institutional dimension of religious experience is less relevant in other traditions and contexts. By reinforcing this association between "religion" and formal religious institutions, visual representations of religion contribute to a marginalisation of religious traditions and experiences that do not fit with the dominant definition of religion that is built on the Christian experience. They perpetuate notions of "right" and "wrong" forms of religious practice; that there are institutions and individuals who are part of those institutions, who are authorised to determine what constitutes "correct" religious practice and engagement, and others who are subversive, heretical. This occurs within and across different religious traditions, extending to the marginalisation of indigenous spiritualities and cosmologies (Conway 2013; Sullivan 2005: 104).

The political consequences of these assumptions about what constitutes "religion" and what does not become particularly acute in relation to the legal protection of the right to freedom of religion or belief. When spiritualities and cosmologies are constituted as "cultural traditions," rather than "religious beliefs," they can sometimes be denied the protection of the law (Beaman 2012; Sullivan 2013).

What about images of people themselves – in prayer, distributing aid to the poor, brandishing weapons and flags while wearing traditional dress? What do these reveal about the assumptions that we make regarding what religion is and does?

First, they perpetuate the notion that "religion" is a personal, individual and oftentimes largely private activity. Images of individuals engaged in prayer suggest the assumed intimate and private nature of much religious activity. Even the images of religious buildings and institutions contribute to this notion of religion as a private affair – religious institutions and buildings are separate and distinct from other buildings such as those that are government- or commerce-related. Each sphere – political, economic, religious – is represented as separated from the other. Religion is a matter that is and should be kept private, in order to protect religion from undue interference by the state and vice versa. This individualised, private nature of religion supports the assumption that religion and politics can and should be kept separate (Wilson 2012).

Images of religious individuals distributing aid or carrying weapons feed into the "good/bad" religion narrative, or what Elizabeth Shakman Hurd (2015) referred to as the "two faces of faith." "Good" religion supports secular development goals, provides comfort and support to those in need, does not challenge the power and authority of Westphalian state or market institutions. "Good" religion is peaceful, unobtrusive, non-subversive. "Bad" religion, on the other hand, disrupts established forms and institutions of power. It is violent, chaotic and reactionary, oppressing people, preventing the realisation of their human rights and dignity, undermining the power and authority of state and market institutions.

Permeating these visual renderings of religion is the implicit assumption that religion is pre-modern, backward and irrational, only engaged in by individuals and communities who are "unenlightened," "uneducated," "un- or under-developed," requiring salvation by modern secular Euro-American Enlightenment democracy. This assumption is

Figure 38.2 A man praying at a Japanese Shintō shrine, Kalandrakas, 2007

Source: Kalandrakas, 2007. Wikimedia Commons, https://commons.wikimedia.org/w/index.php?curid=2156163 (in the public domain).

perhaps most explicit in cartoons and caricatures and the debates they inspire, in which the right to freedom of expression appears to trump any claim to sacredness and reverence made by religious adherents. Indeed, freedom of expression is a necessary part of Enlightenment, of pointing out the irrationality and pre-modern nature of any form of religious belief, "saving" people from oppression and ignorance and bringing them into secular, rational, Euro-American modernity.

I have until now considered how these assumptions about what religion is and does permeate visual images in global politics and media in general terms. In the remainder of this contribution, I consider three recent events and how visual renderings of religion intersect with the debates and assumptions about these events. They are the refugee crisis in Europe, the rise of ISIS and the threat of extremist terrorism, and the debates around the hierarchy of the right to freedom of religion or belief versus the right to freedom of expression generated in the wake of both the Danish cartoons affair and the *Charlie Hebdo* attacks. These phenomena are not independent of one another, but are entangled in complex ways, as the visual imagery associated with them makes clear, and are also connected with broader questions about power and inequality within Europe and in the global community.

Religion and the refugee crisis

The refugee crisis in Europe dominated headlines for much of 2015 and 2016 and will continue to be a central policy concern for several years to come. Multiple news articles on the journey of refugees to Europe were accompanied by images of refugees praying as they arrived on the shores of Greece, spreading out their prayer mats beside train tracks or the roadside as they travelled through eastern Europe. In these images, the category of religion and the category of refugee are entangled, mutually reinforcing prevailing assumptions about both. "Religion" is seen as an irrational activity and is associated with people, such as Muslim refugees from Syria, who are "pre-modern." It suggests that religion is only something that people engage with when they have nothing else, when they are desperate. It is not an activity of rational, enlightened people who have full access to their human rights and are able to live in dignity.

The irrationality of religion here intersects with assumptions about the vulnerability of refugees. In these moments of intimacy with the divine, refugees are rendered vulnerable and sacred, stripped of their agency and any identity they possess beyond being Muslim refugees, completely at the mercy of global forces and power structures, reliant on the generosity of host states for the achievement of their human rights. Such images reinforce the power imbalance between refugees and host nations, while at the same time fuelling the association between "refugee" and "Muslim" that has become increasingly commonplace in contemporary global politics. It renders refugees as wholly "other," as separate, distinct, foreign, alien in the imagined Christian/secular enlightened European context.

From this association of "refugee–Muslim," it is only a short jump to "terrorist," as the post-9/11 political environment has ensured that "Muslim" and "terrorist" are entangled (Mamdani 2002). This nexus of "refugee–Muslim–terrorist" is one of the many ways in which the European refugee crisis, the rise of ISIS and debates over freedom of speech and freedom of religion are intertwined. This discursive nexus is aided and abetted by existing assumptions about the category of religion more generally – its irrationality, its primitiveness, its violent and chaotic tendencies. The irony generated by these assumptions is that the refugees fleeing ISIS in Syria and Iraq are feared to be agents of ISIS seeking to carry out terror attacks in Europe, threatening "our way of life" (Gambino, Kingsley and Nardelli 2015; For a more detailed discussion of the nexus between "refugee," "Muslim" and "terrorist," see Wilson and Mavelli 2016).

ISIS and extremist terrorism

Visual representations of ISIS in global media reinforce this association between religion, violence and irrationality. Photographs and imagery show groups of people in camouflage gear engaged in ritualistic activities – marching, displays of allegiance to the ISIS flag, mass prayer and committing mass atrocities – implying a form of group fanaticism. Again, such assumptions and representations are assisted by existing ideas about religion itself, its violent and irrational tendencies. These images also support the "good/bad religion" narrative. ISIS is "bad" religion, specifically "bad" Islam, or "false" Islam. "Good" or "true" Islam is peaceful, supportive of and compliant with Euro-American secular democracy and human rights (Radwan 2015).

Leaving aside normative judgements on ISIS itself, the question arises as to who or what has the power to designate particular forms of religion as "good," "right" and "true" and other forms as "bad," "wrong" and "false." There is inevitably an exercise of power involved in such designations. While the excessive abuses and violence of ISIS should be opposed, it is nonetheless important to recognise the power plays that are going on in such designations of "bad," "wrong" and "false" religion. After all,

Martin Luther King Jr was at one time designated a dangerous outsider and extremist, inciting his followers to hatred and violence. The problem with making normative claims about something whose meaning and application are as fleeting and shifting as the category of religion is that others will do the same. Representing religion as either good or bad, true or false, assumes a neutral universal position possessing criteria against which such designations can be made, when arguably these designations are always an exercise of power. In the case of ISIS, these claims are being made for a multiplicity of purposes by politicians, atheists, Christians, Islamic theologians, journalists and activists.

Charlie Hebdo, the Danish cartoons and freedom of expression versus freedom of religion or belief

Such power plays are also evident in the third phenomenon, cartoons and caricatures of religion and religious adherents that have generated significant debate and violent reaction in Europe and beyond, namely the Danish Cartoons Affair and the *Charlie Hebdo* attacks. In 2005, the Danish newspaper *Jyllands-Posten* invited prominent cartoonists to contribute drawings of the Prophet Muhammad and Islam. The exercise was framed as an explicit reassertion of the right to freedom of expression in the wake of what Fleming Rose, the editor of *Jyllands-Posten*, saw as increasing restrictions on that right owing to the growing presence of Muslims within Europe (Klausen 2009: 14). Cartoonists, it was argued, should be able to draw and represent Muhammad and other aspects of the Muslim faith as they wished, without fear of recrimination. Many of the resulting cartoons linked Islam with terrorism, one depicting Muhammad's head as a bomb, another showing a line of suicide bombers attempting to enter heaven only to be told that they should stop, as they have "run out of virgins." In response, the Danish Muslim community sought meetings with the prime minister to discuss the media's vilification of Islam, which were declined, so as not to compromise freedom of expression of the press (Hansen 2011: 62). Global reaction was less conciliatory, including protests burning the Danish flag and embassies set alight in numerous Middle Eastern and Asian countries (Klausen 2009: 107).

Existing assumptions about "religion" generally as violent and irrational provide a cultural backdrop against which these images convey a particular message – that Islam specifically, but religious believers in general, are irrational, unenlightened, potentially violent and dangerous. It is the responsibility of newspapers, magazines, artists and authors to point out the flaws and dangers in religious beliefs, regardless of the offence that this may cause. Freedom of expression is paramount.

The *Charlie Hebdo* cartoons that came to prominence following the attacks in Paris of January 2015 exhibit a similar hierarchy of values – that freedom of expression is absolute, and includes the right to mock and ridicule the beliefs, people, traditions and rituals that religious adherents hold dear. The subsequent debate over the right to freedom of expression had little space for nuance or critique – a group of writers who criticised the decision to present *Charlie Hebdo* authors and cartoonists with a courage award at the Pen Writers Awards were accused by Salman Rushdie of supporting the terrorists, when their goal was to raise questions regarding the extent to which freedom of expression should be regarded as the right to offend people and to ignore or devalue the things that they hold to be sacred (Flood and Yuhas 2015).

In both instances, a struggle between the hierarchy of the religious and the secular seems to be taking place, represented by the assertion of the right to criticise and ridicule religion as part of freedom of speech, over and against respecting the beliefs and values of religious people. It is arguably a thinly veiled rendering of the assumption that religion is irrational, pre-modern, violent and reactionary, while the secular Euro-American worldview is enlightened, rational, modern and peaceful.

Visualising the politics of religion

Surrounding images and representations of religion are social and political inequalities that make them all the more powerful and significant.

First, there is the ongoing contestation and struggle between the secular and the religious. While arguably the secular has held sway over the religious for some time in the public life of many secular Euro-American states, growing religious diversity in these countries is complicating this struggle. Perhaps it is not so much that the secular has dominated the religious, but that the secular has prevailed over the Christian. As different religious traditions emerge in these contexts, the secular and the Christian are to an extent realigning, to ensure the continued dominance of Christian symbols, traditions and values in the public sphere in these countries, if not as religion, then as culture and cultural heritage (Beaman 2012).

Second, and related, the inequalities experienced by Islam and Muslims across multiple contexts in contemporary global politics are made acute in each of the images I discussed. Muslims, as a clearly identifiable minority, were the target of both *Jyllands-Posten* and *Charlie Hebdo*. Multiple analyses have argued that the rise of ISIS, along with other Islamic terrorist organisations, has occurred as a result of perceived injustices and inequalities towards Muslims and Muslim-majority countries within contemporary global politics.

Finally, the images of refugees are both premised on, and reinforce assumptions about, religion as a personal, private and irrational matter. They visually represent the consequences of the inequalities and power imbalances between the secular and the religious, between moderate and extremist Muslims, between refugees and host nations.

Images show how religion is entangled with numerous and diverse aspects of contemporary global politics. They highlight that there is substantial contestation over what "religion" is and does and that the designation of specific institutions, actors, beliefs and practices as "religious," and further, as "good, right, true" or "bad, wrong, false" religion, involves a substantial exercise of power by those both within and outside various religious traditions. The consequences of these exercises of power extend far beyond what we have traditionally considered the realm of the religious. They influence state and global institutional policies on migration, conflict, human rights and development. The images suggest that the neat separation of religion and politics that has been aspired to in Euro-American societies since the Enlightenment may be unravelling, or may never have existed.

Note

My thanks to Roland Bleiker and to the members of the History and Theory in International Relations Colloquium at the University of Groningen, whose comments and feedback substantially strengthened this chapter.

39 Roma

Anca M. Pusca

A photograph captures its subjects at a unique and irreversible moment in time, which is then prioritised over others. Unlike film, which is able to reproduce to a certain extent the fluidity of time, photography purposefully segments it, allowing us the opportunity to pause and absorb. This segmentation serves not only to transform the ephemeral moment into a material trace that can be recalled at any moment, but also to purposefully separate its subjects from everything that lies outside the frame, both spatially and temporally. Many have argued that this separation and prioritisation of a particular historical moment/space through photography, a medium that is now easily reproduced ad infinitum, is in itself a political act that radically transforms how the enframed subjects are perceived as well as how history is remembered.

I focus on Roma photography, which is defined simply as the photographing of people of Romani ethnic descent. Such photography has often been controversial, from its early association with Nazi anthropologists, to more recent art and human rights photography that appropriates specific images to make political claims on behalf of Roma. I explore the work of several emblematic Roma photographers, focusing on how their photographs condition how we look at Roma today: from the photographs of Hanns Weltzel and Eva Justin in Nazi Germany; to Josef Koudelka's famous photographs of Czechslovakian Roma; and Chad Evans Wyatt and Livio Mancini's contemporary human rights Roma photography.

Photography as a political act

Before dealing with specific Roma photography, a few remarks are in order about how photography has historically been conceptualised as a political act.

The photographed world has largely become an aesthetic resource that can be sold, circulated, cited and copyrighted for economic gain. Heidegger (1977) was particularly weary about the ability of technology, such as photography, to almost completely transform how we look at the world into a limited utilitarian view. Art, and presumably art photography as well, was different in that it prioritised expression over utility, with the artist becoming a conduit through which the true nature of things can emerge. Diarmuid Costello (2012: 111–12) argues that (art) photography is thus able to "internally resist the reduction of human beings to a faceless, interchangeable, quantum of resource."

Walter Benjamin (1968) most famously talks about the relationship between technology and the work of art in his essay on the "Work of art in the age of mechanical reproduction." He argues that by virtue of becoming increasingly de-contextualised as well as widely distributed, mechanically reproduced art, such as photography, becomes particularly susceptible to political manipulation. He refers here particularly to the rise of fascism in Germany, which strategically coincided with the rise of technologies such as photography and film, and benefited significantly from the ability to use them in their strategic interest. Benjamin, however, was also aware of the ability of art, and presumably art photography, to resist political manipulation: he referred to this as "politicising art" as opposed to "rendering aesthetic."

One way in which contemporary photography is increasingly politicised is through its focus on what Susan Sontag (2003) calls "the pain of others." Although photography turns its attention frequently on "exotic" others facing the extreme violence of starvation, migration, armed conflict, poverty, disease or death, it often fails to elicit the expected empathetic response from viewers. Documentary photography, and its narrower subfield of human rights photography, actively seeks to solicit an emotional response that appeals to a wider, presumably universal, moral base. Many however question the means through which it does so, and the extent to which they might serve to reinforce stereotypes.

Photography is thus politicised in different ways: from its ability to turn images into utilitarian resources that can significantly, and often negatively, impact how we look at the world and others; to its ability to resist objectification and stereotyping by aesthetically transforming its narrow subject into something that carries a wider meaning and value.

Photographing Roma in Nazi Germany

Photography played an instrumental role during the Roma genocide in Nazi Germany: Roma photographers, whether self-employed or working for the German state, actively contributed to the genocidal project of the so-called Race Hygiene Research Unit within the German Ministry of Health. This Race Unit sought to find a genetic basis for criminality among the Roma population and use that as justification for their extermination. Photographs helped establish Roma racial profiles and trace the genealogy of Roma families, serving as "evidence" that would later be used to deport Roma to work and extermination camps. Within the Race Unit, photographs were used both as an investigative tool and as an instrument of intimidation and violence, with uncooperative Roma being photographed naked or while humiliated through practices such as forced hair cutting and physical striking (Rosenhaft 2008).

Images of photographers and Roma ethnographers, such as Hanns Weltzel (who photographed Roma Sinti families in Central Germany between 1932 and 1939) and Eva Justin (who was employed by the Race Unit as an ethnographer and Romanes speaker) show a more complicated picture of the interaction between the photographer/ ethnographer and Roma/Sinti communities in Germany. While a number of these pictures were ultimately used to trace specific Roma families, many of which were later taken to Nazi camps, they also capture a Roma community that was fascinated by the medium of photography – in some cases almost enchanted to have their photographs taken. Weltzel's and Justin's ethnographic journals hint at their emotional ties to the community and warmth towards certain Roma families. They talk about how the camera and the gifting of photographs allowed them closer access to the community.

Although aware of the evidentiary role that photography played in their genocide, Roma survivors continued to maintain an attachment to photographs taken of their community and family members. Many actively sought out lost copies of portraits and

Figure 39.1 "Roma around the table," Georg Althaus, 1962

Source: Photograph by Georg Althaus, 1962, with permission from the University of Liverpool Library, Reference GLS Add. GA 3. Georg Althaus photographic archive.

negatives of photographs taken by Race Unit-implicated photographers. Rosenhaft (2008) uses this to argue against the tendency to ascribe a violent subtext to all photographs of Roma taken in Germany during the 1930s. She argues for a more nuanced reading of some of these photographs, which acknowledges the presence of positive emotions within the encounter between Roma and non-Roma.

The politicisation of these images through the violence of the Roma genocide erases a much more complex reality in which the Roma were not just helpless subjects within this photographic encounter. They also were rather active participants who saw photography as a fascinating modern technology which allowed them to see themselves and their community through entirely new eyes. One must not forget that German Roma were not just victims of photography, but also photographers, owners/managers of movie theatres and active participants in the early discovery and use of photography and film.

Joseph Koudelka and Roma photography in communist Czechoslovakia

Josef Koudelka started photographing Roma in the context of 1960s Czechoslovakia, a time of forced settlement for the Roma, which tied many of them to rural isolation and poverty. This was also a time of great unrest in the country, particularly after the 1968 Russian invasion. Koudelka is not a Roma, and although he had a rural upbringing, his village did not have any Roma. The choice of Roma as a subject, as he explains it, was quite arbitrary at first, mainly as a result of his love for Roma music and his personal friendship with several Roma musicians and poets. He saw his photographs of Roma in Slovakia as being directly connected to his own identity as Slovakian and has always argued that his photographs of Slovakian Roma were better than those he took of Roma elsewhere, suggesting that he experienced a different kind of connection not only to the subject of his photographs, but also to the familiarity of the setting. His photographs were not meant to "inform others" or support particular causes. They were "for himself," taken with almost an instinctual approach to the subject (Farova 2002: 122).

Koudelka managed to cross over the invisible border between Roma and Gadje (majority groups), and catch a glimpse of the normality of life on the other side: for anyone familiar with rural life in communist Eastern Europe, this reality is not that much different, albeit perhaps a bit poorer. The Roma on the other side turn out to be just as human, just as religious, and often adherent to similar cultural traditions. Although physically separated from the rest of the community, they are still, in many ways, very much a part of it. Evidence of crossover permeates Koudelka's photographs: the Roma are involved in village activities, such as agricultural work, or as blacksmiths, musicians and horse dealers. In the photographs, they stare back in confidence because they trust the author and are willing to share some of the most intimate moments of their lives with him: the death of family members, baptisms, weddings, arrests. This level of trust is unique and almost unprecedented, creating representations that stand out not for their ability to depict Roma as "different," but quite the opposite, for their ability to depict them as in many ways living a life similar to other Czechoslovakian peasants.

Koudelka captured the "pain of others" subtly, in the eyes of a handcuffed child walking out on his own with his community as well as the police standing behind him at a distance; in the frozen stillness of a group of mourners around an open casket; in the coins carefully placed on the eyes of the deceased. Everywhere there is a strange sense of calm and acceptance. His subjects have accepted their pain, and their place in society. There is no sense that anything is out of the ordinary. The viewer/spectator has nothing to offer them. Instead, each photograph appears to be a silent conversation between the subject and the photographer, which we simply happen to witness. We are not a part of that conversation nor are we really meant to be. Unlike many other representations of the Gypsy community, many of which are carefully staged to achieve particular desirable results and call upon particular stereotypes and emotions, there is a certain honesty to Koudelka's photographs; not in the sense that they reveal the "true" identity of his subjects, but in the sense that they are able to somehow "disperse comfort rather than aggravate pain" (Koudelka 2007).

Although initially taken for his private collection, Koudelka's photographs of Roma have since become emblematic of his work. After his association with Magnum, his photographs were widely circulated across the globe and became some of the most visible contemporary representations of Roma. This transition from private collection to worldwide visibility has exposed Koudelka's photographs not only to increased admiration, but also to criticism that sees them as reinforcing stereotypes of poverty, criminality and backwardness. Their wide contemporary circulation, many years after the fall of communism, has had the perverse effect of creating a false iconography of contemporary Roma, which are seen through the same historical lenses despite significant changes in the way in which Roma communities exist today.

The unique politicisation of his Roma photographs through a problematic decon-textualisation serves to show how easily images can be manipulated. Photographs cannot control their distribution and for contemporary audiences it is often difficult to appreciate the specific historical context in which they were taken.

Roma human rights photography today

One of the most recent trends in Roma photography is that of finding ways to resist a constantly negative portrayal of the group, while at the same time finding ways to capture the struggles of the community with poverty, isolation, marginalisation and abuse. Sponsored by Roma rights groups such as the Open Society Foundations, Roma rights photography acts as an openly political tool aimed at creating positive spaces and frames through which Roma groups can exercise more control over how they are seen. But success has been mixed, as its audiences are not only significantly smaller, but also generally part of an intellectual elite that already accepts the legitimacy of Roma groups to claim positive spaces.

Photographer Chad Evans Wyatt recently embarked on a project to portray a different kind of Romani people: the middle- and upper-class professionals who are often thought not to exist. The result, www.romarising.com, collects black-and-white photographs of over 250 Roma professionals from across Europe and Canada, which seek to

Figure 39.2
"Victoria Petrova," Chad Wyatt

Source: Chad Wyatt, with permission from the photographer.

"engage the viewer in an unfamiliar conversation, an honest discussion between equals" (Wyatt 2014). They represent respect, calm, formality, intelligence, human ambition, as opposed to the most common "ingredients" of Gypsy photography: exoticism, otherness, "a theatre of grotesque characters, irremediably different, without redemption, often emphasising poverty, unbridled ecstasy, rootlessness, irresponsibility" (Miroslav Vojtechovsky in Wyatt 2014). The photographs identify those depicted by their full name, accompanied by a short paragraph which describes their achievements and current role. They are an eclectic group of incredibly accomplished, proud citizens.

Wyatt's documentary photography stands out through its ability to thwart Roma stereotypes. However, most Roma human rights photography struggles with finding the difficult balance between depicting the struggles of the Roma community – including poverty, migration, abuse – and fighting stereotypes of criminality and backwardness. Often, the same photograph depicting Roma poverty can be used as a record of human rights abuse as well as to incite fear within majority communities. Livio Mancini's (2012) now famous photograph of a Roma boy holding a toy gun in a rundown camp in Kosovo is a case in point. Originally taken to showcase the poverty faced by Roma Kosovars in the context of the post-war reconstruction, the picture was later used by a Swiss magazine to draw attention to the rise in robberies by Roma in Switzerland, using the caption: "The Roma are coming" (Goodman 2012). Cropped so that the gun appears real and pointed directly towards the viewer, the picture is highly confrontational. The boy's silly playfulness with a plastic gun he found in a pile of trash was easily turned into perceived aggression through a mere change of context, caption and crop.

Figure 39.3 "Roma boy with a gun," Mancini

Source: Mancini, with permission from the photographer. Chad Wyatt, *RomaRising* series (www.romarising.com/).

The misuse of photography is not new or uncommon. Ed Kashi, who has also photographed Roma communities in the context of a wider project on ethnic profiling, argues that photographers, representing agencies and the wider media, have a responsibility towards the appropriate use of photographs: making sure they are not taken out of context, that captions and descriptions are accurate, and that permissions are always sought and discussed. However, upholding such a "visual ethics" is difficult, as Kashi (in Cohen 2012) explains, particularly when photographic assignments are becoming increasingly specific, demanding that photographs take a particular line. The photographer is thus expected to "find" that line among the multitude of stories available and often ignore or keep to themselves the wider context of their encounter that is not necessarily present in the photograph (Kashi in Cohen 2012).

Even human rights and documentary photography is susceptible to the forced decontextualisation imposed by media agencies and human rights groups who have an interest in inscribing photographs with a singular reading. But as photographers are quick to point out, the reading of photographs is difficult to control: there is no way to insure that capturing the "pain" of Roma will only be seen through empathetic eyes, or that images of struggle and abuse will trigger the desire to rectify the cause. As we have increasingly seen in the case of Europe, the effect of these depictions can often be quite perverse, with Roma communities increasingly blamed for their own struggles and poverty, and perceived as irrecoverable. Despite their desire to control the political message of human rights photography, human rights groups have often failed to grasp the fact that images cannot be inscribed with a single political message, but remain open to interpretation through their unique and often unexpected encounter with the wider public.

Visualising Roma

I have sought to address some of the different ways in which Roma photography has become politicised by focusing on a series of specific case-studies: Roma photography in Nazi Germany, Roma photography in communist Czechoslovakia, and contemporary Roma human rights photography. While emblematic of certain key moments in the depiction of Roma groups, these case-studies are certainly not exhaustive or comprehensive in nature: Roma photography covers a much wider spectrum and leaves room for a number of different political interpretations.

Roma photography has become politicised either through its association with particularly violent events, such as the Roma genocide, or through its de-contextualisation as a result of wide circulation years after the initial photographic moments, or through problematic practices of cropping, which purposefully distort the original intention of the photograph.

I have deliberately left an interpretative gap between the short theoretical section at the beginning and the case-studies that followed, in order to allow readers to ponder on the different ways in which photography becomes a political act. There are multiple parallels that can be drawn between Heidegger's concern with the objectifying and utilitarian tendencies of technologies such as photography; Benjamin's discussion of the potential for political manipulation of different aesthetic forms of representation such as photography; Sontag's fear of our indifference to the "pain of others"; and Roma photography as described here. In an intentionally political move, I will leave it up to the reader to draw those individual interpretive parallels.

40 Satellites

David Shim

In November 2013, the Ukrainian government suspended an association agreement with the European Union. The suspension acted to forestall the development of closer ties with Ukraine's European neighbours and triggered a series of domestic protests, the so-called *Euromaidan*. These protests culminated in the ouster of President Viktor Yanukovych a couple of months later. In the aftermath of *Euromaidan*, civil unrest unfolded across Ukraine, in particular in the eastern and southern regions where Yanukovych had his political base. Eventually, negotiations between Ukraine and the EU were resumed, and the new head of state Petro Poroshenko signed the association agreement in June 2014. The events surrounding the Ukrainian revolution – character-ised, for instance, by the annexation of the Crimean peninsula by the Russian Federation, the downing of a Malaysia Airlines passenger plane, as well as the armed conflict in the Donbass region of Ukraine – led to a prolonged international crisis.

During the crisis, satellite imagery emerged as a pivotal factor in making, and refuting, particular knowledge claims. For instance, in April 2014, the North Atlantic Treaty Organisation (NATO) showed several pictures to media outlets, five of which were included in a press release (NATO 2014a; see also Figures 40.1 and 40.2). The military organisation argued the pictures, tagged with a March 2014 date, show Russian army units stationed close to the border with Ukraine. While the Russian military responded that these pictures contained images of an August 2013 training exercise in which Ukrainian troops also participated, a statement by NATO called these claims "cate-gorically false" (NATO 2014b). Furthermore, a high-ranking NATO official saw evidence in the images of the "destabilising effect" of the depicted units which "present serious implications for the security and stability of the region" (NATO 2014a).

A couple of months later, in August 2014, NATO distributed another series of five satellite pictures to a wider public (NATO 2014c). In its release, the alliance claimed to have evidence of Russian troops engaging in military operations inside the territory of Ukraine. The asserted movement of Russian forces into Ukrainian territory was well conveyed through the images themselves. Whereas in NATO's first release of pictures Russian military equipment was shown to be immobile, passive and stored (see Figures 40.1 and 40.2), the movement from what can be called a Russian outside to an Ukrainian inside has been presented by NATO with depictions of activity (e.g. moving vehicles) and units in action (e.g. firing positions of artillery; see Figures 40.3 and 40.4).

What can be ascertained from NATO's deliberate use of satellite images is, first, a shift in its visual narrative of the crisis: images are shown as picturesque snapshots with orderly and static units located in the outside; then, they "become" images of war and disorder with intervening units placed in the inside. Second, and more important,

Figure 40.1 Artillery battalion, 10 April 2014 release of a satellite image by NATO

Source: 10 April 2014 release of a satellite image by NATO. Image reproduced with permission from and following NATO guidelines.

Figure 40.2 Su-27/30 Flankers, 10 April 2014 release of a satellite image by NATO

Source: 10 April 2014 release of a satellite image by NATO. Image reproduced with permission from and following NATO guidelines.

Figure 40.3 Russian self-propelled artillery inside Ukraine, 28 August 2014 release of a satellite image by NATO

Source: 28 August 2014 release of a satellite image by NATO. Image reproduced with permission from and following NATO guidelines.

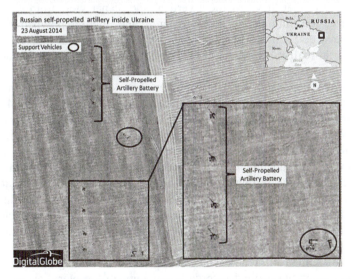

Figure 40.4 Russian self-propelled artillery inside Ukraine, 28 August 2014 release of a satellite image by NATO

Source: 28 August 2014 release of image by NATO. Image reproduced with permission from and following NATO guidelines.

NATO's crisis representation in and through these images reveals the centrality of satellite vision for contemporary geopolitical practice.

Governments, militaries and intelligence agencies around the world rely on the view from above to gather information, facilitate decision-making and convince national and international audiences of particular actions that need to be taken. Indicating the geopolitical implications of satellite imaging, these measures include diplomatic warnings, economic sanctions and military intervention. The inclusion of satellite ways of seeing into the fact-finding missions, decision-making processes and communication strategies of state actors, and increasingly of non-state groups as well, makes them a prime example of a *visual* geopolitics. It becomes clear that such images play a crucial role in creating the conditions of possibility in which current politics takes place (see also Bleiker 2015). Therefore, questions of seeing and showing, as well as of not seeing and not showing, via satellites in areas of conflict deserve closer scrutiny.

I will first examine the status of satellite images, particularly how they are often imbued with objectivity and veracity. They appear to speak nothing but the truth. However, and similar to other aesthetic modes, they always already entail a particular visual-political perspective. I then address the politics inherent in satellite ways of seeing and showing. Attention is paid to the selectivity of the satellite's gaze, which works according to a logic of inclusion and exclusion. In the end, I discuss the wider significance of the findings for critical visual inquires in international studies.

Status of satellite vision

As a technology of remote sensing, satellites gather information by means of distant observation. Similar to other vision-enhancing systems, such as drones or planes, satellites offer a particular form of tele-visuality. Almost all satellite images feature a similar visual perspective in that they provide a vertical and planar view from above onto the earth's surface. Resembling the genre of landscape photography/painting, satellite images capture wide territorial spaces within a single frame and mediate an enlarged sense of pictorial realism, overt naturalism and a colourful diversity (Dodge and Perkins 2009: 498).

Images obtained from sensors mounted on satellites draw on a techno-scientific discourse, which endows them with authority and authenticity (see Campbell 2014a). The precision of high-resolution satellite images is the result of electro-optical processes that allow them to look like mimetic reflections of geographical surface. The application of sophisticated technology, as well as its scientific uses, sustains the perception that remote sensing impartially documents places and spaces. Seemingly stripped of subjective interference, satellites promise to offer transparent insights into major processes of the world. Because these instruments of observation are capable of recording images at any time and from anywhere, they are believed to transcend natural obstacles and elemental boundaries. Analogous to the gaze of the all-seeing eye of God, satellites, arguably enhanced through their geostationary position in outer space, appear to be outside of any sphere of human influence. Therefore, pictures stemming from these orbiting machines seem to be undistorted records that document the world as it is – and not as we wish it to be. In this regard, satellite images share inherent traits with other visual media, such as film or photography, as they provide their viewers with an unmediated access to truth. In Walter Benjamin terms, satellites function as a technology of the "optical unconscious" because they expand human vision beyond its natural scope (in Edwards 2006: 4).

As satellites continuously orbit and scan the earth, they are able to reveal sites which would otherwise remain invisible to us. The ability to make visible certain places and phenomena – and not others – indicates the relations of power that operate through remote sensing. Because satellite images are a means of watching, representing and governing world affairs, they appear as a pervasive form of geopolitical knowledge. That is to say, since these images are involved in making the world knowable, they go *as* knowledge themselves and not as mere illustrations thereof. This is why satellite pictures are often used as geopolitical arguments in conflict (see Dauber 2001). In the aftermath of the *Euromaidan*, remote sensing has been invoked by many states including Russia, Ukraine and the United States in their geopolitical reasoning. For instance, in July 2014, the Russian Defence Ministry presented satellite images which it suggested show the possible involvement of Ukrainian military forces in the downing of a Malaysian Airlines jet; claims which were immediately rejected by the Ukrainian and the US government (Razumovskaya 2014). A couple of days later, the US Department of State distributed an overhead picture, declassified by the Office of the Director of National Intelligence, which it said proved the shelling of Ukrainian military units by Russian forces (DeYoung 2014). While noteworthy that these images came directly from the US administration and not, for instance, from commercial providers of satellite data, a spokesman of the Russian government pointed out that it is in fact the Ukrainian military which is shelling Russian settlements causing civilian casualties.

The point to mention here is that satellite images are not necessarily meant to support a claim – often they are the very claim. This rationality remerges time and again in international conflicts. This was – perhaps most (in)famously – the case in 2003, when then US Secretary of State Colin Powell, in an attempt to gather support in the UN Security Council for a military invasion of Iraq, presented satellite images of what was supposed to show facilities related to Baghdad's weapons of mass destruction programme. Other examples include Iran, Syria and North Korea, whose nuclear programmes constantly have been the object of distant observation. Satellite images seem to speak for themselves – they "speak security" – so that no subjective interpretation is needed.

Politics of satellite vision

Satellite photographs seem to be the perfect resemblance of an external reality. This is why they function as transparent mediators of and to the world. However, this impression obscures the complex technical processes that accompany their production – something which reveals the constructed nature of satellite vision. For before it can be presented and viewed in a meaningful way, satellite imagery has to be processed and tweaked so as to correct distortions in raw data. For instance, season-related weather constraints, including cloud formations and snowfall, impede the technology getting a comprehensive overview of the earth's surface. Only after digital processing can satellite images acquire their "proper" visual appearance (Campbell 2014a; Parks 2005). It makes satellite vision peculiar in that these pictures are simultaneously artificial *and* authoritative. This is in contrast to other visual media/genres such as news photography, which immediately loses its value and validity if its photoshopped nature is exposed. Also, due to their geostationary orbit, it takes time for satellites to be positioned over the right place. Therefore, often these images are compiled out of parcels of shots from different times to create a clear view on the ground free from cloud cover.

Post-processing is due to the vast amounts of data involved, which are transmitted through the electro-optical sensors of satellites to terrestrial stations, where they are converted into a visual form of analysis (Marmor 2008). Much of what satellites capture is rarely analysed and archived. Important to note is that satellite data only becomes real, that is a photograph, after it has been sorted, arranged and circulated (see Campbell 2014a). To put it differently, these images only say something after they have been *made* to speak.

The impact of satellite images is also enhanced due to various accompanying explanations and captions, as well as other graphical and technical means (e.g. Figures 40.3 and 40.4). That is, remote sensing is always embedded in a set of other visual-textual signs. This not only makes it accessible to a wider audience, but also ensures that photographs are read in the "right" way. In other words, accompanying signs work like visual instructions, which narrow down the range of interpretations that are available to the viewer.

Because of remote sensing's peculiar visuality – the synoptic view from above – satellite pictures, perhaps more than any other visual representation, demand (profes-sional) interpretation (Parks 2005). A common example of this is weather photographs, which have to be put in a particular context by meteorologists so that a lay audience can understand them. In fact, the analysis of satellite images is a matter of expert knowledge, as a distinct body of work and institutions suggests (e.g. Baker *et al.* 2001; Conway 1997; Lillesand, Kiefer and Chipman 2008). As such, what has to be considered a characteristic feature of satellite images is that they can be mobilised as compelling sources by various actors or signify nothing but a view from outer space.

Furthermore, even though satellites have superior capabilities of detection – "the all-seeing eye" – it should be kept in mind that they do not necessarily reveal what is meant for concealment. Clandestine activities on the ground may be part of a deceptive strategy by the observed party simply to mislead the observers and make them believe that something "suspicious" is going on. That is to say that satellite images do not tell us whether particular developments on the ground are indicative of genuine covert activities or whether they are merely a show set up for the watchful eyes in the sky.

The efforts to challenge the "promise" of the satellite image – to show the world as it is – are not meant to question its content or substance. Phenomena that have been depicted by satellite are not denied. Thus, the accuracy of seeing is not the issue here, but rather satellites' inherent politics of imaging and showing. For the question of what is to be captured by these vision machines in the first place as well as which images ought to be shown to an audience is highly selective and requires evaluation, inference and weighting. Remote sensing is, hence, not an objective instrument of sight, but a subjective point of view concerning what deserves distant observation – and what does not.

For instance, NATO's practice of designating certain sites as what it calls "areas of interest" points to the interpretive dimension of imaging and showing. While the designation of particular locations determines the alignment of satellites' sensors, it has to be asked what counts as an area of interest and who is behind such a decision. Also, NATO's choice to publish only five photographs in a press release – the original series contained at least 28 figures (see Figure 40.2) – raises the question of what NATO wants others to see and points to the need of remote sensing to select, highlight and distribute only certain depictions. Thus, the satellite gaze is not a view from nowhere, but always a view from somewhere. Remote sensing, to paraphrase one of IR's most eminent scholars, is always for someone and for some purpose (see Cox 1981).

The selective character of remote sensing gives reason to ask, for instance, why only particular places and events are pictured and presented to an audience and not others. For while satellite images have been used by Western governments to document war crimes and human rights violations in conflict areas – for example, 1995 in Bosnia (Crossette 1995) and 2009 in Sri Lanka (Pallister 2009) – none of them have been invoked, by NATO for instance, in the conflict in Ukraine, where all sides reportedly have committed atrocities according to nongovernmental organisations (Amnesty International 2014; Human Rights Watch 2014). Part of the answer lies in whether such images serve certain political purposes as they are employed to "do" something; that is, to give evidence, convince audiences and/or bestow certain actions and statements with legitimacy. What becomes clear then is, in short, that they are a means to an end and not the end itself. As Lisa Parks (2005) put it, satellite imagery assumes importance only when it has relevance to current geopolitical affairs. Satellite vision is, hence, not an innocent mode of representation, but subject to political appropriation.

The visual politics of satellites

The use of satellite imagery is widespread in global politics. To many state and non-state actors, remote sensing is promising to offer genuine insight into current world affairs. Satellite images, however, have also become part of people's everyday life with popular geospatial information services, such as Google Maps. Therefore, the view from above is now a central way of seeing *and* knowing the world.

Because satellite images affect how we make sense of the world, we need to employ them with diligence and vigilance. This entails asking a range of questions which aim at the fundamental problems of remote sensing: What does a satellite image tell us about the intentions of an actor? What can we conclude from what we (want to) see and how we (are made to) see? How can we ensure the "proper" interpretation of images when they lack any inherent meaning? And, how can we account for what satellites make visible on the ground with what the observed party wants the observer to see? Karen Litfin (2002) reminds us that even though we can reach consensus on what a satellite image depicts, it does not tell us what has to be done about it. The ambiguity of satellite imagery points to the need to take into consideration the discourses through which it is made meaningful.

I have stressed that the constitution of geopolitical agency is connected to the ability to see and to show; that is to make things visible and to grant someone else vision. Pursuing further the multifarious relationships between the visual and the (geo)political, with this volume being one of the first attempts, is thus of vital importance for future international studies.

Note

For permission to reproduce parts of my book chapter "Seeing from above: satellite imagery and North Korea" (Shim 2014), I would like to thank Routledge. I am grateful to Ansgar Fellendorf, who has provided valuable background research on the conflict in Ukraine and to Chris Lamont and Yaroslava Marusyk for helpful comments.

41 Security

Lene Hansen

As Roland Bleiker (2015) points out, images do not speak by themselves and are there-fore always in need of interpretation. At the same time, because images are produced and "read" in cultural and historical context, there are not an infinite number of inter-pretations that are realistically possible. I focus on those particular images that are part of security politics. "Security images" are used to support claims that something is a threat to our security. Images may also be seen as so offensive that they are seen as threatening to our sense of self.

As Ole Wæver (1995) has put it, to use the word "security" is to make a "speech act" that "does something": it is to claim that something or someone is threatened in such a fundamental way that "we" need to do something to stop it. To make something a matter of security is thus to move it to the top of the political agenda. Security has historically been tied to the protection of state borders from hostile states and governments ensuring that they were not dethroned by domestic "terrorist" enemies. This way of understanding security has been captured by the label "national security." Today, if we look to the way that "security" is used in world politics, it has been expanded to cover a wider array of issues, for instance pandemics like HIV/AIDS and Ebola (Elbe 2006). No longer is it just the state that can claim that its security must be protected. The concept of human security has, for example, been a way to promote the view that individual human beings, not states, should be at the centre of security policies.

As the examples of pandemics and human security show, the concept of security is not a fixed entity (Buzan and Hansen 2009). Like images, security problems are not objectively given, but a matter of interpretation. Being assigned the status of "security issue" has advantages in terms of getting political attention and economic resources. As a consequence, there are always more potential security issues being advocated than there are spots on the security agenda. What becomes a security problem is not random. There are individuals and institutions who speak from positions of power that provide them with more resources to get their understanding of security through. There are linguistic and conceptual traditions that influence how security can be imagined. Security is a matter of communication, contestation and negotiation. What gets to be defined as security is, in short, an inherently political process.

Images enter into the political process of defining security in multiple ways: as proof that *this* issue is one we should assign the status of security, as representations that are seen as so offensive that they threaten our very being, and as emotional communi-cation that makes insecurity something that real human beings concretely experience. I now will examine each of these three ways in turn.

Photographs as proofs of insecurity

As students of world politics, we can study the battles that go on over how security should be defined. Yet, for many of the political actors that are involved in these battles, security is not an open concept, but something that can be objectively decided.

Images enter into these political debates over what security is and how we should respond to security problems as "evidence." If we start with the traditional conception of security as threats to state sovereignty, frequently used images include those that feature weapons in the possession of enemy forces. Today such images are often taken from a considerable distance, by satellites, drones or cameras located far from the scene. As a consequence, it might be hard to see what an image shows. Quite literally, such images are in need of interpretation. Such interpretations might themselves be political, and thus not simply about explaining facts. A prominent case of visual-political interpretation of photographs took place in 2003 when US Secretary of State Colin Powell told the United Nations Security Council that photographs helped prove that Iraq possessed weapons of mass destruction. When forces entered Iraq, no such weapons were found. Yet, even when visual media produce pictures of weapons that are "easy to read," such images need to be connected to somebody with the intention and capacity to use them. The representation of "those with weapons" with a particular identity is thus required for weapons to become threats.

Images need not feature traditional weapons to become linked to political-military security issues. Take the videos of the planes crashing into the World Trade Center in 2001. These videos were soon located within an American discourse that interpreted the attacks as signs of an exceptional evil with little if any historical precedent (Der Derian 2001: 687). Those who are "evil" are so radically different from "us" that we cannot really understand them as agents with political agendas and motivations, only as being "other" (Campbell 1992). More recently, Islamic State's videos showing the beheading of Western journalists have been widely condemned as "visual proofs" of Islamic State's quintessential evil nature (Friis 2015). Yet, as powerful as the images of burning World Trade Center towers and kneeling hostages are, they do not speak security without politicians, media outlets and other actors granting them a particular security reading.

To say that something is a security issue is to lift the issue above normal politics and in that sense there is an element of exceptionality built into the very logic of security (Williams 2003).

The image of the World Trade Center collapsing became an instant icon that underscored that here was something exceptional at stake: exceptional threats and exceptional enemies (Hansen 2015). But spectacular events – and the images that go with them – are not the only route through which security problems can get onto the agenda. Using the example of environmental insecurities, Buzan, Wæver and de Wilde (1998: 83–4) point out that there can be creeping disasters that gradually build up to the point where conditions are sufficiently bad that they must be seen as security problems. Images can play a role in such processes by providing visual representations of how smaller events add up. The image of a polar bear stuck on an ice floe, like the one in Figure 41.1, has for example become an iconic representation of how the poles are melting, threatening not only the habitat of the bear, but human civilisation as well.

Somewhere between the spectacular and the smaller events are those images that maintain a security issue on the political agenda. Figure 41.2 shows the dead body of Lance Corporal Ryan J. Sorensen, killed by a gunman in November 2005 in Husaybah,

Figure 41.1 Polar bear on ice floe, Sven-Erik Arndt

Source: Photo: Sven-Erik Arndt, with permission.

an Iraqi town near the Syrian border. When Sorensen died, the US had lost more than two thousand service members in Iraq since the invasion in 2003, yet this was said to be the first image in US media showing the body of a casualty. As such the image is exceptional, yet also depicting something that happened on a daily basis. As a sign speaking security, the image was located within a political debate over what policy the US should pursue. One way to read the image was as proof that Iraq was a violent place in need of US troops on the ground. A contrary reading was that American lives were being lost without there being any progress in sight; as a consequence, it would be better to pull out and let the Iraqi forces take responsibility for stopping the violence. In short: this photo speaks security, but not in a way where there is an unambiguous policy message to be derived (Hansen 2011).

Images as threats to who we are

Photographs like the ones in Figures 41.1 and 41.2 document events that would happen irrespective of whether there was a camera around. They speak security by being witnesses (Mortensen 2015). Other images, like the beheading videos of Islamic State are more complicated in how they speak: the visuals document events that are taking place, yet these events are also performed for the camera. Had we known about the beheadings from eyewitness testimony, or even from images that had been captured without the knowledge of those performing decapitations, the security message would have been different. Like the iconic photographs from the Abu Ghraib prison, the beheading videos provide a mixture of documentation and performance.

Figure 41.2 Dead US Marine, Husaybah, Iraq, Johan Spanner. Printed by the *New York Times*, 7 November 2005

Source: Johan Spanner. Printed by the *New York Times*, 7 November 2005. With permission from the photographer.

A particular category of security images are those where the image itself is seen as the security act. In this case, there is nothing "real" captured by a camera, but the creation of an image by, for example, an artist. In recent years, we have seen examples of such images becoming the subject of intense confrontations with governments, political parties, religious leaders and international institutions holding that the essence of their beliefs and being have been fundamentally threatened. A prominent example is the cartoons allegedly depicting the Prophet Muhammad published by the Danish newspaper *Jyllands-Posten*, by the Swedish artist Lars Vilks, and the French satirical weekly newspaper *Charlie Hebdo*. Since the first cartoons were published in 2005, there have been attacks on embassies, the office of *Charlie Hebdo*, boycotts and demonstrations, culminating with the killings of cartoonists and bystanders in Paris and Copenhagen in early 2015.

Do these images challenge our opening claim that images cannot speak on their own? There is no shortage of voices who argue that they can say for sure what these images "say." Yet, there is no agreement among those voices on which interpretation is the right one. If we take the most well known of the Danish cartoons – one by Kurt Westergaard that shows a bearded man with a bomb in his turban – there is one reading which argues that this drawing demonises all Muslims by showing Muhammad as a terrorist. The cartoon is thus deeply offensive, particularly to Muslims. A counter-reading holds that the cartoon is a satirical comment, not on all Muslims, but on how religion is taken hostage by fundamentalist, terrorist forces, a reading Westergaard himself has offered support for. Which one of those readings is the right one? Both: the drawing does not by itself clearly say whether the individual head that is shown is Muhammad, and even if it is, if it refers to "Muslims," "terrorists," "fundamentalists" or "religious believers." There is in short an interpretive gap between the individual in the picture and the larger identities it might say something about. This interpretative gap has if anything been widened rather than closed over the years. We should understand images, particularly iconic ones that are continuously circulated and talked about, not with fixed meanings, but as open. They are being used, and used differently, across time and place and what they say changes. As students of world politics, the question is less how to decode a security image as a free-standing entity, but how to examine the political debates over visual representations.

The fact that images are discussed and their meaning often contested is an indication that visual representations are important to policy makers and others who seek to set the security agenda. There are several ways in which an image might be said to have an impact on security politics (Bleiker 2015). One is where an image is published and there is an immediate response from policy makers. Those cases are however quite rare. Even the Danish Muhammad cartoons did not receive much attention when they were first published and it was only after five months of political mobilisation that they became an international crisis. Images may have an impact in a longer time perspective and in a more indirect way that is harder to measure. What is significant about iconic visuals like "The hooded man" from Abu Ghraib is thus not their short-term impact on security policies – the Bush Administration did not drastically change how it was fighting the so-called War on Terror because of the photos from Abu Ghraib – but the way such images crystallise over time in a security message. "The hooded man" may not have changed US foreign policy in 2004, but it is now firmly established as a sign of American abuse of power and the US's loss of prestige at the global level.

Feeling insecurity

One of the most important things about visual representations is their ability to invoke emotions (Hutchison 2014). When viewed through the lens of global security, images are significant because they are capable of moving across borders in a way that words do not. Words need to be spoken or translated into a language you can understand, images by contrast can be read by all. In reality, we all read images through our social context, so the point is not that we get the same message, but that we assume we will be able to "get something." As we are looking at security images, there is also an assumption that such images make us care. They make us feel that this is important enough that it is a matter of security.

The representation of something as a security issue through words is to some extent abstract: it is about threats to "us." Visual representations, particularly those of humans, can embody such abstract representations in something concrete and specific. Security images may mobilise a range of emotions as they make the abstract more concrete. In the classical definition of security as concerned with the protection of the state against other states, fear is the main emotion that comes into view. If we expand the conception of security to include threats to non-state groups and individuals other emotions appear such as compassion, care and pity (Bleiker and Kay 2007). These emotions are particularly central when we are dealing with calls for making the insecurity of "other" individuals and populations something "we" should be concerned about, even if our own national security is not threatened. Visual representations of human beings are

Figure 41.3 House being searched, Husaybah, Iraq, Johan Spanner. Printed by *Newsweek*, 12
        December 2005

Source: Johan Spanner. Printed by *Newsweek*, 12 December 2005. With permission from the photographer.

particularly at stake here as studies have shown that the likelihood that people will
donate money increases as the number of humans depicted go down (Slovic 2006).
The human face allows for identification; or, alternatively for the feeling of fear or
repulsion. The question is whether there are humans in the picture or not, and what
those humans look like. There is an important difference, for example between depicting
migrants as young men climbing fences or as dead children washed ashore. Or contrast
the photo in Figure 41.2 with the one in Figure 41.3. Both are from the same military
operation, but in Figure 41.2, it is hard to read the facial expressions. In Figure 41.3,
we are able to clearly see the faces of the Iraqi woman and the US soldier.

On the one hand, the emotional responses of the Iraqi woman and the US soldier
are visible for us to see; on the other hand, there are multiple ways in which these
might be read. Should we see the woman, whose house is being searched, as an
accomplice to the "jihadists" who killed Lance Corporal Sorensen, or is she an innocent
civilian whose property is being violently picked through by occupational forces? Is
the young soldier looking at the woman because he is concerned that she might flee
or because he wants to console her? The photo speaks, but in more than one voice.
And if it is decoupled from the context of the US deployment in Iraq in 2005, it opens
itself up for additional readings, for example of gender and race in the context of
armed conflict.

Visual representations of humans might occupy a particular position as images that
make us feel security. But humans are not alone. Look at the polar bear in Figure 41.1.

Its ability to represent the dangers of climate change are also related to its visual appearance as a cute and cuddly animal that has been anthropomorphised by movies, toys, posters, and so on. Romanticised landscapes and cherished artefacts like monuments may also be reproduced in ways that generate an affectional response.

Visualising security

The radical transformations in communication technologies that have taken place in the last twenty years make it seem like images are everywhere. That everything can be captured and everything can be circulated. This democratises security politics in that it is much harder for governments and others to commit atrocities without someone noticing. Although we know that images can be altered, it is still the case that images count as harder evidence than words. Yet, we should also be conscious that the visualisation of security introduces new hierarchies. Not every potential security problem is easily captured. Wartime rape, for example, is largely invisible, or captured by perpetrators, not victims. There might also be an unintended "visual security dilemma" as images produced in one context are circulated to audiences that see them through a radically different lens.

Note

Research upon which this chapter is based was funded by the Danish Council for Independent Research – Social Sciences, grant number DFF-1327-00056B. Many thanks to Johan Spanner for his permission to reproduce the photos in Figures 41.2 and 41.3.

42 Sexual violence

Marysia Zalewski

Sexual violence: an everyday "domestic" occurrence and a seemingly ever present feature of international conflict. In the latter, a wide range of authoritative sources, including the United Nations, suggest the incidence of sexual violence is immense; the figure of one in three or four women will suffer this form of violence in a lifetime is regularly quoted (World Health Organization 2016). To stem what Ban Ki-moon (in UN News Centre 2014) has dubbed a "scourge," calls for action and policy are profuse and are supported by an increasing number of UN Security Council Resolutions as well as national initiatives. The incidence of sexual violence has also drawn increasing attention from high-profile celebrities. These celebrities, who once directed their (and "our") colonial gaze to poverty and HIV/AIDS, now home in on specifically conflict-related sexual violence. Most often the "poster-child" of this attention has a female face, one clearly presented as deserving of humanitarian compassion (see Kapoor 2013; Zalewski and Sisson Runyan 2015).

The involvement of Angelina Jolie, Emma Watson and similar others has invited a plethora of opportunities for visual depictions both of them and, perhaps less so, of the victims. Yet a major paradox exists; despite the increasing hyper-attention and the abundance of political rhetoric and international policy, there is a persistent failure to stem the incidence of sexual violence. Saturated in this globalised sea of images of the sexually violated and their "saviours," it is increasingly difficult to know what it is we are seeing and what it is that we keep missing.

The image I have chosen to focus on to think about this paradox and the visualisation of sexual violence on the contemporary international stage is from the film *UNWATCHABLE* (2011). This is a short documentary film, just 6.14 minutes long, which places sexual violence front and centre and champions a very strong political message. Moreover, the story is centrally located in the context of international politics, international political economy and international sexual violence more precisely. The opening credits are these:

> Save the Congo have released the film *UNWATCHABLE* as part of their campaign to lobby the EU and mobile phone manufacturers to stop the trade in blood minerals in the Congo which is fuelling violence and mass rape. It is estimated that one person a minute is raped in the Congo.

I will first describe the film, then move to analyse some of the work of the film paying special attention to one still image.

UNWATCHABLE

The film is based on an event that happened to a (real) African (black) family in "the Congo." It depicts a horrific event, but with a putatively more horrifying twist: the family in the film is white. It portrays the brutal gang rape of a teenage girl with both penises and rifle butts. The "finale" shows the husband/father being shot, his penis severed, which the wife/mother is forced to eat. The film is set in a landscape that might be described as "idyllic middle-class England," not the Congo. It begins with a young blonde-haired girl, aged about six or seven, playing in the very large grounds of the family's very large lovely house. The teenage daughter returns home from school chatting happily on her mobile phone. "Mum" is washing dishes in the kitchen. "Dad" is in the garden washing the car. A helicopter appears overhead. The young girl with freshly picked flowers in her hands looks up and innocently waves. Mum and Dad look puzzled. The helicopter lands on the impressive lawn and a phalanx of white solders in military fatigues get out and bulldoze their way into the house. They proceed to rape the teenage girl on the kitchen table while Mum looks on screaming uncontrollably, restrained by one of the soldiers, while the others take their turn to rape the teenager. Dad is pinned to the floor howling.

The little girl peers through the window. She catches the eye of one soldier, the one who is sitting on the floor just outside the kitchen crying and clutching what appears to be a teddy bear. The child turns and begins to run.

The scene moves outside. Filmed from above, the man is shot in the head and the soldiers proceed to cut off his penis; though we only really "see" a pool of blood spreading round his genital area. And we know from the "real" story (see Hall 2011) but don't "see" here, the woman is forced to eat her husband's penis. From a closing aerial shot we see the small child running across the grass towards a clump of trees. Behind the trees, we see more soldiers with rifles running right in her direction. We

Figure 42.1 The little girl in *UNWATCHABLE*, Mark Hawker, 2011

Source: *UNWATCHABLE* (2011) Dir. Mark Hawker. Darkfibre Entertainment. Available at https://vimeo.com/25341404.

"know" she will not escape. The angelic blonde-haired child in a white dress is still clutching flowers.

A documentary film like this with its overt well intentioned politics of humanitarianism and social justice, clearly seeks to use the medium of the visual to tell a story which will move, indeed surprise and shock, people to action. Though this story should not be surprising given it is well known, not the specific one perhaps, but the generic story of rampant sexual violence most especially in conflict zones (particularly those in Africa) is well publicised in Western media and is a common feature of popular culture. The film's title tells us what this violence should be: unwatchable. Though the message is more that this violence should be undoable, unimaginable, and perhaps more pertinently, we might see its violence better when sited in the "wrong" place and in the "wrong" bodies. And that we might be moved to action more swiftly, or indeed moved to action at all. One of the opening credits poses the question "could we ever imagine it happening here?" As such the surface story-line is clear; (white) people can still be shocked or more precisely, *surprised* that they/we do (or at least might) think differently about injury and damage depending on the race/colour of the bodies on whom violence is visited. What if this happened to people "like us?" is the less than subtle message of the film.

Though the white, wealthy middle-class, heteronormative family depicted in the film may not be who most of "us" are, even in the affluent West, the idea that such an event *might* happen to this "perfect" family is likely to be shocking to viewers. This is especially so given the quality of the film; it is beautifully shot and acted. And there is a crystalline aura of clarity and transparency (the whiteness, the blondeness, the water for washing of dishes and the car), all of which aid the narrative intentions of the story. Yet like any authorship (here primarily directorial) ownership of the intended ideas and meanings can never be guaranteed or controlled. The explicit use of "white" in *UNWATCHABLE*, for example, paradoxically feeds off traditional and violating racial stereotypes – perhaps alerting us to one of the fuels for the paradox I opened with, namely that hyper-visualised attention is questionably correlated to stemming its incidence.

To think further about the work of the visual in this film, I return to a quotation from René Magritte: "Everything we see hides another thing." Magritte's paintings famously evinced surface "simplicity" while simultaneously suggestive of underlying danger and violence. His classic painting *Treachery of Images* – an image of a pipe with the caption "this is not a pipe" – disturbingly depicts, as its title implies, the treachery of images (Harris and Zucker 2011). My claim is that the very clarity of visual knowledges about sexual violence hides a multitude. It surely is the case that everything we see hides a multitude of things which disappear *en masse* in the camouflage of contextual casings. And this "disappearing" is so often the case with violence as its brutality is very hard to show. In *UNWATCHABLE*, we might say that the effect of this is to *erase* violence right in the centre of its celluloid gory explicitness. But it is not a simple erasure, it is, in fact, a re-positioning of violence right back into sites and bodies in which it is more comfortably "not seen;" quite at odds with the explicit intentions of the film. Let me move to clarify this through one still image from the film.

The little white girl

The little girl peers through the window. She catches the eye of one soldier, the one who is sitting on the floor just outside the kitchen crying and clutching what appears to be a teddy bear. The child turns and begins to run.

I think this scene captures the heart of the film both directorially as well as epistemologically. As the little girl peers through the window frame, viewers are invited to think she sees the crying young soldier. Her gaze is mesmerising. Though who is the spectator here? Who is looking? The little girl? The young soldier? The eyes of the Western white world, the clear target audience for this film? The film's audience and the two characters here are all viewing through the window frame, which is interesting given one of the central roles or work of framing/frames in film is to have the audience "notice" as little as possible in order to get them to see what they are intended to see. And as viewers, we are seductively drawn into the narrative and the emotional and aesthetic imaginary of *UNWATCHABLE*. Yet the "frame" here, most especially given it is a window with glass which "naturally" we cannot "see," works beautifully in its alleged transparency to camouflage much of what is "doing work" in the film.

Let us dwell a little more on the figure of the little girl, the pre-pubescent very slender child. She is, in a Western imaginary, the essence of pre-sexual innocence. Historically, blondeness has been synonymous with white and beauty as well as the "virgin ideal," still a powerful image when housed in the pure white bodily form of the – "this" – little girl. She is the perfect picture of "unsullied femininity," that which is not "dirtied by sex" (Dyer 1997: 77). And there is little "dirt" in the film, no urine, no excrement, no malodorous leaking or smearing, apart from white flour thrown pitilessly in the teenage girl's face in the midst of rape. Directorial intention may be more explicitly at work here, installing a stark contrast with the imagined dirty, sweaty and dusty heat of "the Congo." And white is not the only colour performing this kind of aesthetic and epistemological work in the film; blue eyes, blue/white porcelain cups, Mum's blue dress, the teenager's blue school cardigan, Dad's blue car. Perhaps blue is not a colour we associate with hot, red earthy "Africa" or "the Congo;" not even the more urbane (and accurate) "Democratic Republic of Congo," evoking the popular "jungle"/Tarzan films which still hold a dear colonial place in the Western film-addicted imaginary (Dyer 1997). But more than the absence of dirt, there is no blood, no nakedness. To be sure, the film is intended to be seen by as wide an audience as possible and censorship rules apply. But again, the persistent focus on the little girl, the imagined epitome of sexual and Western innocence, reproduces a comforting colonial fantasy that dirt is/should be the fate of "others." To be white, after all, is to have "expunged all dirt, faecal and otherwise" (Dyer 1997: 76). Inevitably absent here is also the smell of rape, the seeping of squalid fluids given the rupture and leaking are inevitable, not least given the pounding of the teenage girl's vagina with rifle butts. Perhaps the screaming spectacular message of the film, as with so many similar "mega-spectacles" (Kellner 2004) in contemporary global mediatised cultures affirms something other (than intended).

Camouflaged in the film, despite its clear visual centrality, is the purity and beauty of white particularly through the "perfect" normative heterosexual form so well depicted in *UNWATCHABLE*. Crucially, the mask of whiteness imparts a clear narrative of "white" as saturated with the weight of the power of reason and persuasion. What this might imply to the white Western viewers to whom the film is addressed is that "we" *cannot* imagine it happening "here." Indeed the work of "white" re-secures the distasteful traces of racialised bestial masculinity – the "real" perpetrators behind the white actors; the explicit political narrative about race in the film obscures the liminal but solid suturing of "white" with all manner of things "good." The connections between innocence and purity, alongside the association of white with pure and wholesome knowledge and truth, are made more, rather than less, secure through the spectacular aesthetic work of this film. Pure form is exquisitely apparent in the body of the small fair-haired white girl in a white dress. But in its explicit whiteness, and specifically whiteness as attached to "perfect" bodies, whiteness begins to disappear, and as such begins to re-perform its traditional work (over) again. As Richard Dyer (1997: 45) tells us, "true whiteness resides in the non-corporeal," though we "see" bodies as white, or non-white (typically), the influence and the power and privilege of "white" works at deeper and less visible or accessible levels than "simple bodies."

In a curious deviation from the main theme, one soldier is depicted crying and clutching a teddy bear. Is this a gesture toward the potential for change in masculinity, which so many writers on this topic suggest is *the* solution to reducing sexual violence (e.g. Bourke 2007; Leatherman 2011)? Perhaps this soldier has not yet fully learned appropriate militarised masculinity, indicated by his non-participation in the raping, and his clutching an icon (at least in the West) of innocent childhood: a teddy bear. This gestures towards another thing "hiding" among what we (think we) "see." If the little girl represents the innocent hope of white humanity that must be protected, her coming "face to face" with that other normative hope in which a plethora of narratives about sexual violence pin their optimism – un-trained, reformulated masculinity – we begin to get glimpses of ways in which the intentional politics of this film have little chance of succeeding.

Visualising sexual violence

> Hegemonic forms gain currency by being unnoticed.
>
> (Ahmed 2007)

The contemporary proliferation of images of sexual violence, sometimes in putatively graphic forms as in *UNWATCHABLE*, work on the principle that vision has prime explanatory and persuasive powers. This principle has a significant lineage going right back to the foundational Cartesian idea that "sight is the noblest ... of the senses" (Descartes 1998: 116); "the eye functions as the organ of truth" (Elsaesser and Hagener 2010: 82). But the visual is languaged in intricate ways, working with multiple senses and stories in order to impart the surface story. In an overtly political film like *UNWATCHABLE*, it is important to think very carefully about the hidden range of stories and "things" that are working, which may result in what are conventionally called "unintended effects."

I began by suggesting that it is increasingly difficult to know what it is we are seeing and what it is we keep missing. I also claimed that a major paradox exists in the realm of conflict-related sexual violence: despite its hypervisibility, violence is not diminishing. This is especially problematic in the context of Western-style liberal humanitarian activities. Scrutinising well-intentioned films like *UNWATCHABLE* may appear as politically and ethically problematic. But noticing that such activities may be feeding the very violence they admonish needs to be scrutinised very closely if we are to gain accurate insight into the visual politics of sexual violence. An important question to end with is, whose pain is being assuaged by films like *UNWATCHABLE*?

43 State

Brent J. Steele

I explore the visual politics of the state. The term state is often used interchangeably with other similar terms, such as country, nation or nation-state. Conventionally,
scholars examine the "state" within both historical and functional contexts. Historically,
the state seems to have emerged around the time of the Peace of Westphalia (1648),
which was a series of treaties ending the Thirty Years War and embedding the modern
nation-state as an entity with authority within a bounded territory that borders other
states. This authority is hierarchical. It is not, in other words, overlapping with other
authorities within the same bounded space. Of course, the process of the "state"
becoming the main unit of international politics is a bit messier than the conventional
understanding would tell us (see Ashworth 2014), and including a period of consolidation
and struggle that happened both before and after the Peace of Westphalia.

Functionally, states are thought to have a variety of purposes. One scholar (Spruyt
1994: 185) suggests that "in the long run, sovereign states won because their institutional logic gave them an advantage in mobilising their societies' resources." States
actually have several institutional logics that made them more efficient at mobilising
resources than other forms of political organisation. First, modern states seem to have
been the most efficient at protecting borders. In the words of Charles Tilly (1975: 42),
"war made the state and the state made war." States also developed, eventually, large
bureaucracies to collect taxes or mobilise populations, again often for war-making.
Third, states include national identities – that is, subjects and citizens become attached
to the state as an entity that not only keeps them safe but also fulfils some sense of
meaning and purpose in their everyday lives (Hall 1999). Fourth, states also were
sovereign – that is, had both internal sovereignty (the ability to monopolise violence
within particular borders) and external sovereignty (borders recognised by their neighbours – collectively considered the "international community") (Bull 1977).

Protection, bureaucracy, identity and sovereignty – these focus attention on a state's
physical presence and presentations. That is, to focus on the physical presence of the
state, we might examine the state's functions in the form of its leaders, government
agents, police, military and border officers, as well as its infrastructure, its institutions,
government offices and the like. Yet, the importance of identity, and on recognition
via sovereignty, suggests something more than just a connection to the physical aspects
of a state. It also indicates an affective connection to a state's ideas, ideals and principles.
These connections are mediated *visually* – from military parades through film and
television – in a process that constructs what Benedict Anderson (1983) famously
called an "imagined community."

The visual politics of "the state" is about the state's *aesthetic representation*, about how it is displayed, seen, sensed or felt. One of the best ways to understand how the aesthetics of the state operates is to draw an analogy to the aesthetic practices of individuals. We engage in cosmetic practices so we not only feel good but *look good* as well. Some of us wear makeup and/or work out to have more "attractive" bodies. We may even go through cosmetic surgery (botox, implants, tummy-tucks, etc.) so that we will *look* better to others and even to ourselves. Look at how popular media stars are constantly and carefully crafting their "image" in visual ways. Paparazzi often scour beaches and nightclubs to get action shots that catch glamorous individuals off-guard – perhaps appearing dishevelled, intoxicated. Such stars otherwise carefully attend to their appearances. The strain of the visuality of individuals is that they cannot "look good" all the time – yet it is precisely the temporal condition of images that makes them so insecure. Captured in a seemingly arbitrary moment, the image can nevertheless last *for ever*. For those who are especially under the limelight of the media, one cannot look less-than-ideal. Of course, it's impossible to maintain this cosmetic perfection forever, hence the insecurity that attends to those particularly attuned to their appearances.

Now, it may seem silly to think that states pursue such aesthetic practices as well. Insecurity for states includes the same sorts of physical concerns individuals have – how to protect the integrity of their physical boundaries, how to keep their citizens or subjects safe, and how to promote the general welfare. And because they provide meaning for their citizens, states promote their image as well. They want to be recognised as legitimate. They promote this image in all visual realms, from television to the internet, and from flags to parliamentary buildings.

A state's visual politics is important for at least two audiences: their own national political communities and the broader international society. The former are audiences who connect their own identities with that of the visual representation of the state. A state can also shape its representation to be attractive to other states and other actors. Global corporations, for instance, may see a state as a potentially attractive market. The phenomenon of "state branding" is one strategy to attend to this goal. Just like corporations seek out a "brand" for their products, states seek out ways to re-brand themselves. Jeremy Youde (2009) examined the "Brand South Africa" campaign that unfolded after the collapse of the apartheid regime in 1994. He highlights how "governments want to make or re-make their image in the world to gain clout *vis-à-vis* their neighbours to achieve certain political ends" (Youde 2009: 126). Brands fix and clarify the ambiguity of state identity for others *and themselves*. In branding, a state not only seeks out an identity to project to others, but also exemplifies a "certain level of control" over an identity encapsulated by a visual brand (Youde 2009: 130).

The complexity of states' visual politics

But how do states know which images and representations will correspond to a particular audience? And how do they know what kind of impact images have? The challenges of controlling those images, and how the *same image* is subject to multiple inter-pretations, make it difficult for states to craft their aesthetic representations. Scholars focused on the visual politics of the state have taken special notice of how technology democratises the dissemination of images, videos, discourses and stories about states

(Steele 2010). But other actors have access to these distributive means too – they include terrorist organisations (like ISIS and Al-Qaeda) as well as non-state groups like WikiLeaks and Anonymous. They challenge the control states have over their visual self-representations.

Yet, even when a visual representation breaks through and captures the state in a particularly forceful (positive, negative or otherwise) light, there are no guarantees that the audience will interpret the messages of that image in the same way. We must thus keep in mind the possibility of an aesthetic state's visual representations being so-called polyvalent: having different, even opposing meanings or functions, of the same image. What may appear to be an ugly, or immoral, or problematic representation to one audience member or group, may be considered powerful, inspiring or satisfying to others.

Some of these receptions vary internationally, conditioned by particular cultural contexts. One important illustration of this comes to us from Orwell (1941), particularly from an essay he wrote early in the Second World War:

> The goose-step, for instance, is one of the most horrible sights in the world, far more terrifying than a dive-bomber. It is simply an affirmation of naked power; contained in it, quite consciously and intentionally, is the vision of a boot crashing down on a face. Its ugliness is part of its essence, for what it is saying is "Yes, I am ugly, and you daren't laugh at me," like the bully who makes faces at his victim.

What Orwell missed is that the goose-step may seem like naked power to the Englishman, but its rhythmic synchronisation may also be reassuring, and even beautiful, to Germans. In fact, while the English may have considered it ugly, we know that some of Germany's allies, including especially Italy, mimicked the goose-step in ways that would seem at odds with Orwell's interpretation. Even today, goose-steps are practised at public gatherings – as for instance in North Korea.

The practice of aesthetic representation is important to a wide variety of states. Both large states like Russia and smaller status-seeking states like Norway demonstrate an interest in their visual representations (de Carvalho and Neumann 2014). Sometimes the visual politics of the state valorises a leader, which can develop into a "cult of personality," as evidenced by Turkmenistan's Saparmurat Atayevich Niyazo or North Korea's Kim Jong-il.

A particularly compelling example of the visual politics of the state is Nazi Germany and, in particular, the propaganda films made by Leni Riefenstahl. Examples include *The Victory of Faith* and the infamous *Triumph of the Will*, which documented the Nuremberg rallies of 1933 and 1934. The latter increased the Nazi party's popularity. Riefenstahl would go on to make films about the German military (*Day of our Freedom: Our Armed Forces*), the 1936 Summer Olympics in Berlin (*Olympia*), as well as several parade or victory films after the Germans defeated Poland in 1939 and France in 1940.

Riefenstahl's films are important in several ways. First, they combine images of Nazi Germany with music and the synchronisation of troops marching. These combined elements, as well as the political speeches by German leaders, helped to stir emotions that are an integral part of the visual politics of states. Second, *Olympia* especially disclosed the importance of international sporting events to provide a world "stage" for host countries. This form of visual politics we see practised even in contemporary sporting events, including the Olympics and the Football World Cup. Third, Riefenstahl's films were distributed widely within and outside Germany in the 1930s. Riefenstahl's films demonstrate how significant visual politics is – then and now – for the legitimacy of states.

The visual politics of aesthetic states

"What" the state "is" depends upon which functions we focus on. On first sight, states seem much more objective and physical – covering territory and performing security functions – than visual or aesthetic. Indeed, the protection of states' borders remains one of the primary responsibilities and functions. Nevertheless, states go through great lengths to develop their visual politics because how they are represented to the world remains important. With our smartphones, laptops, social media sites and cable news, the visual politics of a state remains one of the primary ways through which we experience them. While the physical borders of states do change, such change is less frequent than the contestation that occurs time and again over the visual politics of states. In any day – any moment – a visual representation of a state can serve to dislodge, or reinforce the image that the viewer has of that state. We need to be aware of the political consequences that follow from these visual practices.

44 Surveillance

Rune Saugmann

Where does global visual politics meet surveillance? Surveillance relies on more than images. Images, as readers of this book will undoubtedly insist, can do much else besides assist in surveillance. So what is the connection between surveillance, politics and the image? Even if there are thousands of different visual surveillance systems in global politics, they all make one connection between politics and images: using images in surveillance relies on understanding images as facts, as transparent and objective copies of the world. This understanding of images is a particular one, and it relies on forgetting that images are also bewildering, subjective and unintelligible. Sometimes this understanding appears persuasive and sometimes not, yet visual surveillance relies on us forgetting the alternatives.

Visual surveillance and global politics

Images and image-producing devices are often deployed as part of the surveillance systems – made up of technologies, rules, bureaucracies, laws, databases, knowledges and procedures – that record and analyse phenomena of relevance to global politics. As surveillance plays a part in the management of ever-increasing spheres of social and biological life, the phenomenon under visual surveillance in the name of global politics can be almost anything: people's behaviour in subway systems is monitored for security reasons; the melting of Arctic ice caps and the growth of algae in summer months are visually monitored to gain knowledge about the causes and effects of climate change; migratory roots of humans as well as animals are monitored albeit for entirely different reasons; inner-city neighbourhoods, university campuses and the habits of a tall man in a compound in Abottabad are surveilled as part of anti-terrorism politics. A comprehensive theory – or even a list – of what is under visual surveillance in the name of global politics quickly becomes impossible. May there, then, be commonalities in the logics or rationales for such surveillance? Here, perhaps, we are on a little safer ground, as visual surveillance connected to global politics in some way connects or responds to such politics. It is deployed, we may say, to produce knowledge about the world, knowledge that can assist in making political decisions or knowledge about the phenomena politics seeks to regulate.

Yet, even this extremely broad formulation applies mainly to phenomena that are under visual surveillance by institutions with clear motives. To complicate matters, any naturalistic, representative image can become part of a surveillance system even if it was not produced with the intention of being so – especially if these images are digital. If, for example, you happened to upload a video from a political street protest that turned violent or was otherwise suspicious to capable organisations, or from the Boston Marathon a few minutes before a bomb went off there (Leonard 2013), your video would be likely to end up as part of the post-hoc surveillance of the event. Such practices are so common that NGOs concerned about privacy and the right to assembly have developed guidelines for citizens in politically charged crowd situations to practise "safe filming" that makes it difficult to use the images for surveillance purposes (Nunez 2012).

Bureaucracies are not the only ones that can do visual surveillance – surveillance studies have long focused on private companies, which have been leading in developing new visual surveillance technologies for commercial purposes (Ferenbok and Clement 2012). Also, NGOs such as Greenpeace are actively doing visual surveillance with global politics aims.

Recent conflicts have seen a meeting between these two trends, the use of private citizens' photography in surveillance and surveillance done by others than state bureaucracies. Citizens' images are increasingly being appropriated for surveillance purposes by bloggers (e.g. Higgins 2015), NGOs (e.g. Czuperski *et al.* 2015), as well as states (see Damon, Pearson and Payne 2014). As civilians live a "media life" that inevitably leaves a trail of digital images (Deuze 2011), there are millions of images freely available for anyone to use for surveillance purposes. The point, all in all, is that visual surveillance is a way of using images, rather than something that takes place by producing "surveillance images." This means that there is no such thing as a surveillance image, or a naturalistic image immune to being used in surveillance.

Knowledge by visual surveillance: hindsight and foresight, evidence and vigilance

Two quite different logics are at play in the use of images in surveillance, following from whether this surveillance is aimed at providing visual foresight or visual hindsight. Both of these forms of knowledge are widely used in global politics.

On the one hand we have surveillance systems, the rationale of which is to provide *foresight*, to anticipate what will happen in the future. This kind of surveillance is based on risk calculation and precaution, logics developed in the insurance industry (Ewald 1999). In politics, it is deployed in order to predict and prevent undesired futures, be that terrorist attacks or climate change. Amoore (2007: 221) has characterised the use of images in anticipatory surveillance as the development of a "vigilant visuality" in which "the act of seeing becomes an act of foreseeing." Image data is often coupled with other data streams to produce risk profiles or other forecasts that can be used in social sorting of a population (Lyon 1994). The use of foresight surveillance at borders has led Bigo (2006) to argue that the combination of security and surveillance produces a "ban-opticon" where surveillance-produced foresight underpins the denial of entry and rights in the name of security. Interestingly, Amoore (2007: 220) argues that the paradigm of vigilance extends to foresight or vigilance in everyday seeing, leading to a surveillant sociality in which the fellow citizen is also "the vigilant onlooker." The UK anti-terror poster in Figure 44.1 shows how the vigilant onlooker works to supplement visual surveillance in official anti-terrorism discourse.

On the other hand, we find visual surveillance practices that follow a rationale of providing *hindsight*, a forensic aim to make the past known and transparent through making it visible. Here the desire driving the implementation is one of defining the

A bomb won't go off here
because weeks before a shopper reported
someone studying the CCTV cameras.

Don't rely on others.
If you suspect it, report it.

Confidential Anti-Terrorist Hotline
Call 0800 789 321

Figure 44.1 UK anti-terrorist poster combining surveillance (CCTV) and vigilant citizen seeing

Source: With permission from the copyright-holder, the UK National Police Chiefs' Council.

past, making it known and transparent through the establishment of visible facts. The attribution of responsibility is also often a vital part of such visual surveillance, producing a forensic visuality of witnessing that "intervenes in the world through the generation of testimonial claims" (Chouliaraki 2013a: 5). This places the spectator (usually an institution with some kind of authority in relation to global politics) in a judicial position, judging on the basis of forensic images. Occasionally forensic surveillance enables ordinary citizens to become judges of global politics – for instance when war surveillance images are leaked to the public (Shapiro 1990; Laustsen 2008; Allan and Andén-Papadopoulos 2010; Saugmann Andersen 2015) or when amateur images are used as evidence of political upheavals and natural disasters (Chouliaraki 2013a). Yet, often, the authority of the ordinary spectator has been dismissed in favour of incomprehensible official interpretations. When WikiLeaks published a leaked gun-camera video showing clear war crimes, it was brushed aside by the US administration as "probably unfortunate." In these cases, fragmentation of the video evidence has often been key to claiming that citizens cannot judge for themselves what is seen (Saugmann Andersen 2015).

The everyday seeing equivalent of the forensic surveillance deployed to provide hindsight is the eye-witness recounting an event that is already history; not the vigilant onlooker reporting anything suspicious. This idea of visual surveillance can be likened to Bentham's panoptic prison where every transgressive act can be seen, and as the Foucauldian tradition of surveillance research maintains, such witnessing of transgressions has important disciplinary effects on those subjected to it.

The semiotic foundations of visual surveillance

Common to both foresight and hindsight types of visual surveillance, and irrespectively of whether the images used are produced for surveillance purposes or taken from citizens, visual surveillance relies on viewing images as transparent and objective statements of facts rather than as opaque and subjective views (Bolter and Grusin 2000). To use images as facts requires that we regard them as clear and objective imprints of the world rather than partial, subjective and possibly misleading statements that depend on our interpretation to tell anything about the world. Roland Barthes (1977: 44) long ago described this as "a new space-time category: spatial immediacy and temporal anteriority . . . an illogical conjunction between the *here-now* and the *there-then*." Even the use of images in forecasting is dependent on the view that they neutrally record the world of the past, producing facts from which predictions can be made. This view is the key political move in making images into surveillance images.

A poignant illustration of this, already mentioned, occurred when the US administration was faced with a gun-camera video leaked from a gunship deployed in the battlefield in Iraq. The video showed the killing of at least fifteen people in a series of "engagements" where there was no visual evidence of hostile activity (on the contrary, some of the images showed children in a van that came to the rescue of wounded strangers; some showed people – maybe armed – going into a house; some showed photographers with telescopic lenses among people carrying weapons). Faced with the video, then US Secretary of Defence Robert Gates told the public that they couldn't trust what they could clearly see (US Department of Defense 2010), deploying the metaphor of the "fog of war" to counter the claim to veracity of surveillance images (Saugmann Andersen 2015: 217).

The use of images in surveillance relies on a particular configuration of the image as not distorting but recording reality, configuring sight as what Amoore (2007: 223) has termed a "sovereign sense" on which state security decisions and risk calculations can be unproblematically grounded. This is a configuration that powerful actors seek to strategically deploy and withdraw to influence what is seen as true and what is not.

Undermining governance by surveillance: two strategies

Two very distinct strategies seek to resist the "sovereign sense" by working with its reliance on seeing images as transparent mediators of neutral facts, mirrors of the world-as-it-was.

These strategies have been used to resist the governance of politics and political conflicts by visual surveillance. In doing so, they not only are part of a political project (which one may agree or disagree with) but also help show how surveillance relies on images-as-facts.

The *first* strategy relies on co-opting the authority that officials attribute to surveillance images when they endorse images-as-facts in order to govern politics. This strategy turns the authority of surveillance images against the state by directing the forensic potential of images against the state rather than letting it work in the service of it.

One example of co-opted surveillance occurred in Copenhagen in the summer of 2009, after a police action to evict refuge seekers from a church where they had taken public refuge to avoid deportation. The Copenhagen Police took the unprecedented step of releasing their operational video surveillance tapes, interrupting a tradition of only using police surveillance videos in court, in training and for investigation (Copenhagen Police 2011). Statements by government ministers accompanied the publication, endorsing the police surveillance videos as proof – endorsing their "epistemic strength" as reliable knowledge about the world (Saugmann Andersen 2015) – to denounce the troublesome priest of the raided church. The Minister of Justice was shown reviewing the surveillance tapes (*BT TV* 2009: 01:30) with the headline "Minister: Priest lying;" another government minister (in Clemmensen 2009) spelling out that "it is a bold lie . . . and this video proves it."

Yet activists were soon able to co-opt the efforts of police and government officials. When the police turned to video to denounce a competing societal institution – the church priest – they empowered video in the debate in general. The new positioning of video and images as a central arbiter of truthfulness in the debate soon allowed activists to use videos to contradict and thus undermine police claims of telling the whole story, forcing the police to ultimately apologise for their handling of the case (Gjerding, Geist and Clemmensen 2009; Ritzau and information.dk 2009; Rømer 2009).

As this strategy for resisting governance by surveillance points out, surveillance is not one-directional in the sense that it is necessarily the authority that watches the citizen. Once images are seen as facts they can also be turned against the authority that authorised them as facts in the first place.

The *second* strategy is directly opposite to the first in that it works through disrupting rather than co-opting the belief that images present facts. Governing by visual surveillance can also be countered by showing that images are *not* transparent providers of facts, and that treating them as factual recordings of the world, as visual surveillance does, is highly problematic. By photographing security and surveillance installations in ways that make them extremely hard to see or to recognise, the art photographer Trevor Paglen challenges the idea that we can know the world by just pointing a camera at it. Paglen's photographs depict the distortion produced by the process of photographing something, rather than depicting the something that the camera is pointed at. By taking photographs of classified sites from extremely far away, Paglen (Paglen and Solnit 2010: 145) produces images in which we can hardly see the site depicted for all the noise produced – for instance by the "atmospheric conditions and temperature differentials between air and land." These are photographs that show how the photography distorts, how it is *not* a transparent window onto a world we can know through it.

This work points to another condition for visual surveillance – which is that surveillance depends on "reading the image as evidence of something other than itself"

(Saugmann Andersen and Möller 2013: 210). Rather than co-opting the belief in surveillance images as statements of fact, this second strategy for countering surveillance seeks to undermine that belief, showing that we cannot expect to know what it is that we see in an image.

Visual surveillance and the magic of seeing

Rather than being linked tightly to the idea of the panopticon – the disciplining effect of knowing that everything we do is visible – visual surveillance is linked to a specific understanding of images and seeing, one in which we can know the world by seeing it through surveillance images, and one in which we would all see the same in these images.

I have stressed how any naturalistic image can be used for surveillance. Visual surveillance, therefore, is not a *kind* of image (e.g. those taken by surveillance cameras), but a special *use* of images. This use can be directed at providing foresight, calculating scenarios based on visual information; or hindsight, establishing what happened in a specific situation. But both depend on understanding images as objectively capturing facts of the world, an understanding that is misleading even if it is common.

The use of visual surveillance with reference to global politics is already too vast to map, and it is sure to expand in the coming years. Among the most interesting and potentially problematic further developments is the use of automated visual surveillance to produce autonomous devices – weapons, cars, and so on – that are to navigate in societies based on (not exclusively but prominently) automated software readings of the image feeds produced by the camera sensors inbuilt in these devices. This may be feasible in closely regulated areas of sociality – highways or train tracks being one example – but what happens when visual surveillance is used as the foundation for a device to act in a much more complex and unpredictable social situation, for instance in a war zone with its multiplicity of civilian and combatant roles and lives?

45 Territory

Jordan Branch

Territorial boundaries are one of the defining features of sovereign statehood. States assert absolute authority over what goes on within those lines and are expected to make almost no claims beyond them. Why is political organisation defined in this particular way? Without the ideas and practices made possible by one visual medium – mapping – states would look very different today. Cartographic techniques and images, in short, played a key role in the origins of territorial states and continue to reinforce the dominance of this form of political organisation and interaction.

What is territory?

Although *territory* can appear to be a naturally occurring phenomenon, an area of land, it is actually more than that. Territory is, in short, a strategy of political control (Sack 1986). It involves a particular way of delimiting political authority: drawing lines between spaces to determine who controls what. As Stuart Elden (2013: 7) notes, this assertion represents a specific expression of "the relation between place and power" – *specific* because other strategies have existed. Even though drawing territorial boundaries feels today like a natural way to make political claims, it is in fact neither permanent nor inevitable as a feature of social and political organisation. It is, instead, one possible structure of rule, with historical origins in the early modern period.

This territorial form of politics emerged out of the breakdown of medieval European political structures. The Middle Ages saw politics organised with a combination of spatial and non-spatial claims. Authority was focused on centres of power, such as major cities or fortified locations, and only loosely asserted over frontiers, which were gradual zones of transition between rulers' domains rather than clear demarcations. Of course, some linear boundaries existed, particularly when waterways were used as divisions between realms. But linear borders were rare and frequently not demarcated. Non-spatial forms of organisation predominated, with feudal ties of vassalage or personal bonds between rulers and subjects providing the foundation for most political organisation. The result was a collection of political units and actors with unclear divisions between them, relationships involving hierarchical authority as well as interaction among equals, and a combination of spatial and non-spatial organisation (Ruggie 1993; Sahlins 1989).

In the modern state system, by contrast, politics is defined by territorial delimitation. In theory at least, states assert absolute authority within their boundaries and are not supposed to make claims beyond them. Even exceptions such as "failed" states or humanitarian interventions are defined by their violation of the ideal of territorial sovereignty. Statehood is historically recent, with a particular genealogy that is ignored by the common assumption that states – or something like them – must have always existed (Elden 2013).

Mapping and the modern state

The territorial structure of modern politics emerged out of a complex set of processes in early modern Europe, in which developments in the technology of mapping played an integral role. Political ideas and practices interacted with – and, in certain key ways, followed upon – cartographic depictions, a process revealed by a comparison of medieval European mapping traditions with the more familiar mapping practices that came after.

Maps can be defined as "graphical representations that facilitate a spatial understanding of things, concepts, conditions, processes, or events in the human world" (Harley and Woodward 1987: xvi). Maps are *not* limited to those images that have the recognisable features of cartography today: latitude and longitude, a key or legend, consistent scale, and so on. Any and all visual images of spatial relationships may have – and, in fact, often have had – connections with political ideas and practices. Since mapping has changed dramatically over time, it is essential to recognise and analyse those changes without focusing only on "improvements." Any type of map, no matter how simple it appears to be, may serve the purpose for which it was created. Furthermore, all maps, no matter how accurate or scientific, show certain aspects of the world and leave out or underplay others. These inclusions and exclusions and how information is presented visually both embody the ideas, interests and beliefs of mapmakers and, simultaneously, shape the ideas and knowledge held by map readers (Harley 2001; Pickles 2004; Wood 2010).

Medieval European maps were rare, widely varied, and different from the maps with which we are familiar today (Harley and Woodward 1987). In fact, written texts were used for many of the purposes that we might assume would require graphical images: property delimitation, political claims and even navigation by land or sea. Nonetheless, several visual traditions can be categorised as maps, albeit with diverse purposes, authors and audiences. *Mappaemundi* were world maps centred on Jerusalem and showing, schematically, the three known continents of Europe, Asia and Africa. These large paintings, often hung in cathedrals, depicted important places or events from biblical history. *Portolan charts* were maps of coastlines that accompanied written sailing directions for maritime navigation, highlighting coastal features and the compass directions between them. For travel by land, *itinerary maps* showed a single route, following from place to place without depicting the surrounding countryside or geographic features. All three mapping traditions emphasised particular places (such as towns) over spatial expanses, showed no boundaries between political entities, and underscored non-geographic relationships, such as religious importance.

These graphical images, as well as the written texts that served similar purposes, embodied and simultaneously reinforced a particular understanding of the spatial character of the human world. Spatial expanses were less emphasised than the unique characteristics of particular places. Distances and relationships were understood in human terms, such as travel time or spiritual importance, rather than in terms of geometric spatial measurement (Padrón 2004).

In the European Renaissance and the centuries after, mapping changed dramatically, as did the way that the world was understood. Maps went from being extremely rare manuscripts to being mass-printed objects, with an explosive growth in the number of maps in the sixteenth century – from a few thousand to millions (Woodward 2007). It was not only the quantity of maps that changed dramatically but also the way in which maps depicted the world. This transformation is conventionally traced to the fifteenth-century Latin translation of Ptolemy's *Geography* (a classical Greek text). The *Geography* contained instructions for drawing maps according the coordinate grid of latitude and longitude, and then mathematically projecting those spherical coordinates onto a flat map. Even though Ptolemy's projection methods were soon superseded and his geographical information was out of date even by fifteenth-century standards, the *idea* of depicting geographical information in this geometrically measured way was a fundamental transformation and has dominated the pursuit of mapmaking ever since. By the late sixteenth century, maps were widely produced for a commercial market, both in individual prints and in atlases. These cartographic tools were being put to a variety of uses, from navigation to education, similar to the ways maps have been used in the centuries since.

Figure 45.1 illustrates the nature of this transformation. This map of Europe from a 1595 atlas contains obvious geographic inaccuracies, but it is unquestionably recognisable as a map: it is built on a grid of latitude and longitude and depicts the

Figure 45.1 Atlas map of Europe, Gerhard Mercator, *Atlas Cosmographicae,* 1595

Source: Courtesy of the Lessing J. Rosenwald Collection, Library of Congress. With permission.

continent as a set of territories defined by boundaries. In other words, this image speaks the visual language of modern mapping, and we are able to evaluate it in the same terms that the mapmaker or map user of the time would have done. It emphasises the spatial expanse of the earth's surface, does not accentuate any particular religiously or culturally important places, and purports to provide a complete picture of the geography of the region.

This transformation in the visual language of mapping – and its widespread adoption as a key tool of trade, learning and governance – made possible the shift from the complex, overlapping authority structures of the Middle Ages to the territorial exclusivity of the modern state. Of course, many other factors were involved in the transformation of politics in early modern Europe and the eventual consolidation of the territorial state (Spruyt 2002). Yet the visual medium of mapping provided the conditions of possibility for the ideas and practices of territorial rule. Without the means to depict space as a set of bounded territories – and thus the means to argue, fight or cooperate over those boundaries – it was simply not possible to conceive of territory as the exclusive foundation for political organisation. Rulers and other officials used maps to govern their realms and to rethink their external relations. Divisions between states came to take on the linear territorial character of modern boundaries, rather than the frontier zones or overlapping claims of the medieval period.

The technologies and techniques of mapmaking played a dual role in the emergence of the territorial state. On the one hand, more accurate and detailed mapping of frontier regions gave rulers the tools needed to claim a bounded territory – in this way, mapping *enabled* the assertion of territorial boundaries. On the other hand, the very nature of mapping as a dominant visual medium encouraged rulers to even begin to think in this way – in other words, mapping *constituted* the very interest in asserting those linear boundaries to begin with. One way to see the importance of the latter, constitutive effect of mapping is in the timing by which mapping was adopted as a tool of governing territory. Rulers and officials did eventually come to use maps extensively for tasks such as determining taxation, administering territories and planning military actions (Woodward 2007). This was preceded, however, by a century or more of mapping by commercial printers, during which the very *idea* of mapping the world, using visual images with particular characteristics, came to dominate among the governing elite. John Pickles (2004: 77) puts it best: "cartographic reason seems to have been so power-ful a force in the sixteenth and seventeenth centuries that it came to signify the most important forms of reason. *To map was to think*" (emphasis in original). It was in this context that rulers began to pursue policies that were enabled by increasingly accurate mapping.

This cartographic way of thinking and acting made possible and encouraged a new form of political authority, focused exclusively on linear divisions between homogeneous territories. In the Middle Ages, authorities were rarely depicted in maps, with written descriptions much more commonly used for political claims. Moreover, the maps that did show some form of political marking (such as flags occasionally placed on cities on portolan charts) further emphasised places rather than boundary-defined spaces. Early modern mapping, in contrast, quickly came to depict land surfaces as the modern jigsaw puzzle of mutually exclusive territories, often color-coded and labelled. By the middle of the seventeenth century, "large format world atlases typically had 90 percent or more of their maps showing boundaries" (Akerman 1995: 141). Yet this was not simply a reflection of a growing use of linear boundaries in practice, of territorial demarcation on the ground. Instead, until significantly later, political rule and interaction continued to be defined by a complex mix of place-focused territorial authorities and non-territorial claims over persons.

The gradual nature of the transformation of political authority – and thus the way in which mapping preceded and shaped that transformation – is demonstrated by the terms used in peace treaties and other documents. These terms reveal how actors thought about what it was they were negotiating over and ruling. Fifteenth- and sixteenth-century treaties often settled political claims over places without reference to linear boundaries or territorial demarcation. Settlements were presented as lists of towns, feudal rights and jurisdictions, and maps were rarely if ever a part of the discussions. Even in the seventeenth century, the treaties signed at the 1648 Peace of Westphalia continued to operationalise political control without extensive discussion of boundaries, demarcation, or exclusive sovereignty – contrary to the conventional interpretation of this as a founding moment of territorial statehood (Osiander 2001). It was only in the late eighteenth century and then in the post-Napoleonic settlements that we see the clear imposition of territorial divisions in practice. The treaty signed at the 1814–15 Congress of Vienna, for example, divides territories in terms of states possessing lands within geographically described lines "in full sovereignty and property" (Article II). Maps are also appended to the treaties, and feudal right and claims are directly renounced in favor of linear territorial divisions.

These changes in political practices came *after* the changes in mapping. Maps depicted a new way of seeing the world, ideas about how spatial political claims could and should be made changed next, and finally the practices of governance and interaction followed.

Mapping and territory today

Mapping has been transformed in the past several decades to a degree unseen since the sixteenth and seventeenth centuries. The intervening period saw continual improvements and new tools, to be sure, but the basic goals and practices of mapping remained consistent: the production of ever more accurate and detailed printed images of the earth's surface. With digitisation, however, not only is mapping improving by traditional measures (in terms of accuracy, for example) but transformations are also occurring in who is able to make maps, how maps are distributed and used, and even what it means to map something (Crampton 2010). These changes are altering the connections between mapping and territory, potentially creating the conditions for the emergence of new forms of political authority, spatial or otherwise.

The information technology revolution has both transformed the tools available to mapmaking experts (with, for example, Geographic Information Systems, or GIS) and created easily accessible online systems like Google Maps or Google Earth. All of these new tools share certain characteristics that dramatically depart from the centuries of paper-based cartography, characteristics that may affect the connections between mapping and the territorial structure of politics. For example, these new tools have implications for the emphasis placed on linear boundaries. Digital maps are not nearly as tied to the standard display of color-coded spatial units (such as states or other administrative territories); instead they can show spatial relationships and information of a much more complex nature, or remove political boundaries with a single mouse-click. Yet GIS and other digital tools remain wedded to the coordinate grid of latitude and longitude, and in many ways continue the long-standing pursuit of greater cartographic detail and accuracy. Even the addition of satellite imagery (easily available on many online tools) is a further step toward the goal of mapmakers for centuries: creating a perfect "mirror" to reality.

There may also be implications for how these tools are brought to bear on traditional territorial issues in world politics, such as negotiations over disputed boundaries. More complex forms of territorial division are able to be visualised and negotiated over with digital tools, making it theoretically possible to yield new types of settlements. Yet, even the most advanced systems have, thus far, been applied only toward the traditional goal of drawing clear linear boundaries between territorial jurisdictions. Nonetheless, possibilities remain for more dramatic effects, either by giving actors the tools to negotiate difficult divisions that have been impossible to sort out with a line or by destabilising existing divisions as more actors are able to get involved in measuring, challenging and demarcating (officially or unofficially) territorial boundaries.

Wider participation in mapmaking opens up the possibility for new depictions, new visual representations of political ideas and practices. The ideational power of the territorial state has been reinforced for centuries, not only through state actions like service provision and border enforcement, but also in everyday forms of socialisation through maps in schools or mass media. Mapping in the digital age may offer new visual depictions that could undermine the territorial structure of the state, or give new spatial formations evocative visual support. Mapping is not the only technology with an impact on spatial politics, or even necessarily the only visual technology with such a connection. The implications of related areas – such as cyberspace – could have as dramatic an impact on emerging political ideas. Yet so long as maps are used to measure, understand and influence the world around us, these evolving images will continue to shape the territorial state and its possible future transformation.

46 Time

Michael J. Shapiro

When it comes to making events intelligible, national cultures exhibit radically different communities of sense. A critical perspective on those differences emerges when we explore different media genres. For purposes of illustration, I invoke two of my media experiences decades ago: it is August 1966 and I'm exposed to two media events at roughly the same time.

First, several of us, leaving a dinner party shortly after midnight, decided to take in "the late show" at the Nippon, a Honolulu theatre showing Japanese films: a sentimental genre (e.g. stories about beloved elementary school teachers) in the early evening and a (soft) pornography genre around midnight. That evening, the late show was Hiroshima native Kaneto Shindo's *Lost Sex*, a film featuring as the protagonist, "the Master" (Hideo Kanze), a Noh theatre director who had been rendered impotent by the nuclear fallout of the Hiroshima bombing. The film's story foregrounds sex, focusing initially on the Master's potency regained as he is lying in a hospital bed while being subject to the hand manipulations of a young nurse (the scene is shown while being narrated to the Master's housekeeper in a flashback at the beginning of the film). Apart from its sex theme, what the story provides is a window into one aspect of the adversities that were an immediate legacy of the bombing, the physical and mental traumas that disrupted intimate relations. The story doesn't end well for the Master. After a failed marriage, when his potency has once again become fugitive, his 37-year-old housekeeper, a war widow, is able briefly to restore his sexual efficacy by staging erotic scenes in which she is involved. But because he misinterprets the staging (she solicits other seducers to stimulate him), he breaks off the relationship out of jealousy, only to learn after her death that the seduction scenes were staged for his benefit. The film ends with him as a lonely, unloved man, watching the snow fall at his mountain residence.

The second media event had a different kind of ending. It was a showing of military potency, a simulated bombing run staged on the 6 August anniversary of the Hiroshima atomic bombing and shown during a newscast on a local Hawaiian television station. The setting of the broadcast was an open field at a military base on the island of Oahu. While a group of military families were seated in temporary bleachers flanking the field, an air force bomber did a flyover and dropped a smoke bomb. As the smoke rose, a voice announced over the temporarily installed loudspeakers: "There's the bomb that ended the war." The people in the bleachers then applauded. For them, as for many participating in US collective memory, the bombing was "the end" of the Hiroshima event.

The different endings I've glossed testify to radically different experiences of the bombing and different practices of historico-cultural memory in Japan and the US.

Since the dropping of the atom bomb on Hiroshima and Nagasaki, it has been experienced in the US as a distant, abstract event. In contrast, as is evident for example in Kenzabouro Oe's *Hiroshima Notes* (prepared after several returns to Hiroshima, roughly two decades after the bombing), the event remains emotionally vivid and enduring for those who were on the scene. As Oe (1996: 35) puts it, while observing people visiting the Memorial Cenotaph for the Atomic Bomb Victims: "How often have I seen . . . people standing still and silently in Hiroshima. On that fateful day in 1945, they saw hell unleashed here. Their eyes are deep, darkened, fearful."

Out of touch with the Japanese experience after Hiroshima, much of the historical emphasis in diverse American media genres (and to a large extent in academic security studies) has been on futuristic visions of nuclear apocalypse. As for the past, the primary public exposure of the Hiroshima bombing in the US has been a relatively static story: a bombing run as the apex of the US war strategy, glossed in war history books and in a museum display in Washington DC's Aeronautical and Space Museum, which is part of the Smithsonian complex. There, as one of Oe's (1996: 67) interlocutors laments, "the atomic bomb is known better for its immense power [than] . . . for human misery it causes." Thanks to congressional lobbying that prevented material testifying to the bombing's victims, the Smithsonian's version of the episode eschews Japanese experiences and perspectives and is rendered as part of the history of military flight. The display, a celebration of a US war victory, effectively frames the bombing within a discourse that "attributes national security to air power" (Deutsche 2010: 16).

Remediating the event

However static its museum display may be, the Hiroshima bombing is a never-ending event; it endures as a variety of artistic and cultural texts pondering it, especially in the affective lives of those who have confronted its consequences directly – for example Oe (1996: 23), who wrote that "the Hiroshima within me does not come to an end with this publication."

I want to emphasise a particular grammar of temporality, the future anterior, to reflect how visual media continuously interpret and reinterpret Hiroshima. Recognising the radically different national communities of sense (in France and the US, as well as in Japan), I focus on a variety of media genres that intervene in the gap between the initial event and its various subsequent interpretations. The existence of disputes and negotiations effectively challenges the Kantian view of such sublime events. In his *Analytic of the Sublime*, Kant argues that overwhelmingly vast events, which initially stagger the imagination, ultimately end in a shared comprehension, in what he famously calls a "subjective finality." For Kant, the apprehension–comprehension gap is traversed rapidly and wholly cognitively as the subject, whose imagination is initially overwhelmed, quickly realises that its reasoning mind is greater than the event and experiences the negative pleasure of recognising that something fearsome is not to be feared (Kant 1952).

To enact that challenge to Kant's version of sublime experience, I draw on the Marguerite Duras/Alain Resnais film *Hiroshima Mon Amour* (1959) and a remediation of the film (and thus the event) in Silvia Kolbowski's video *After Hiroshima Mon Amour*, which "returns to Hiroshima to confront the legacy of the atomic bombing, linking it to the present invasion and occupation of Iraq" (Deutsche 2010: 10). Recasting the Duras–Resnais film and interspersing images from Iraq, Kolbowski creates a heterogeneous temporal association of the two wars, giving both the past and the present different significance.

The two temporalities

Addressing the significance of Kolbowski's temporal articulation of the Hiroshima bombing and the Iraq invasion and occupation, Deutsche writes, "The word *after* in Kolbowski's title raises the question of time and therefore of history, which is to say of the meaning of past events" (Deutsche 2010: 21). To situate Kolbowski's intervention and creative play with the temporality of *Hiroshima Mon Amour*, we have to revisit the temporal play in the Marguerite Duras/Alain Resnais screenplay (and in Resnais' cinematic realisation of the script). One way to construe the film narrative is to see it as "a documentary on Emmanuel Riva [the actress who plays an unnamed French woman having a post-bombing affair with an unnamed Japanese man]" (Domarchi *et al.* 1959: 63).

The film opens with the two lovers in bed. We see body parts whose morphology is indistinct because they are too close and the scene is too cropped to allow the viewers certainty of what they are seeing. Duras (in Mavor 2012: 115) describes the opening:

> As the film opens, two pairs of bare shoulders appear little by little. All we see are these shoulders – cut off from the body at the height of head and hips – in an embrace, and as if drenched with ashes, rain, dew, or sweat, whichever is preferred. The main thing is that we get the feeling that this dew, this perspiration, has been deposited by the atomic "mushroom" as it moves away and evaporates. It should produce a violent, conflicting feeling of freshness and desire.

In contrast with a strategic story in which the bodies of Japanese victims are rendered in an abstract war discourse as "casualties," the film renders those bodies in two experiential registers: the bombing's effects on relations of intimacy and the specifics of the bombing's inscription on bodies. Bringing the two registers together – the event time of the devastating bombing and the temporality of the rhythms of intimacy – the lovers "seem to be under a rain of ash," as the skin of the bodies simultaneously registers moments of "both pleasure and pain" (Mavor 2012).

In accord with Kaneto Shindo's *Lost Sex* on the bombing's disruption of processes and structures of desire and intimacy, the film links a love story with the material and social destruction of the city. The film's main narrative thread is a love affair between an unnamed French actress from the city of Nevers, referred to as Elle, and an unnamed Japanese architect from Hiroshima referred to as Lui. The film enacts a critical disjuncture at the outset as their bodies connect in mutual passion while their conversation is dissensual. The lovers begin their conversation this way: "Lui: You saw nothing in Hiroshima. Nothing." Elle: "I saw everything. Everything." At the same time that the conversation is dissensual, there is a dissensus between what Elle narrates and what the viewer sees. She notes for example that by the 15th day, a vast profusion of blooming flowers are poking up through the ashes, "unheard of in flowers before then." At that moment, however, what is shown is morbidity rather than vitality; damaged, grotesque bodies are on screen, being treated by medical staff. The musical score also underlines the dissensus. Early on, it has a rapid, frenetic pace, which adds to the tension between Elle's statements of what she sees and what is shown. In contrast, during Lui's rebuttals, his remarks are backed by a contrapuntal, single instrument (seeming to be a woodwind), which contrasts with the flute and string accompaniment to Elle's insistences.

With such disjunctive juxtapositions and other aspects of film form, *Hiroshima Mon Amour* establishes a temporal trajectory for what is described in Masuji Ibuse's (2012: 149) classic novelistic account of the Hiroshima bombing, *Black Rain,* as "moral damage." The film literally puts flesh on that expression, animating the process of bodily disintegration. At the same time, it tracks processes of witnessing while producing a disruption between witnessing and knowing. In response to Lui's frequent assertions that she saw nothing, Elle reports the evidence of her eyes: for example, "I saw the hospital, I'm sure of it . . . how could I not have seen it." However, when stating that she saw what was in the museum in Peace Square "four times," she introduces uncertainty into that witnessing by invoking the concept of lack; referring to how the museum reconstructs the Hiroshima event, she calls it a "reconstruction for lack of anything else."

As Elle's narrative voice proceeds, the film evokes a distrust of fixed images and iconic representations. An epistemology of the gaze must give way to an epistemology of becoming, an articulation of sense memory with a grammatical framing of history that reaches toward an uncertain future. That valuing of becoming operates in the interface between narrative and image. During her remarks about seeing and knowing what is in the museum, there is a tracking shot of a mother and children approaching the museum and further tracking shots that explore the outside and inside of the building. What can we make of those cinematic moments? Jean Luc Godard's provocative suggestion is that the aesthetic and moral aspects of the film coincide. In response to a query about whether the film is jarring aesthetically or morally, he says, "Tracking shots *are* a question of morality" (Godard in Domarchi *et al.* 1959: 62).

Affirming Godard's observation, the film incessantly juxtaposes the memory of the Hiroshima bombing to the movement of bodies involved in war tourism, especially by cutting from tracking shots of the memorial venues in Peace Square to hands caressing skin. What is therefore contrasted is a fixed institutionalised realisation of the bombing and a dynamic bodily sense memory, as the two lovers caress each other's skin while at the same time verbally questioning the different trajectories that have brought them together. That they represent two different temporal trajectories – the war experience of Elle, who is shamed in her city of Nevers because of an affair with a German soldier, and of Lui who has resided in Hiroshima but was not near ground zero during the bombing – is subtly represented by the crossing of their two wristwatches on the night stand of the bed where they are exploring each other's bodies.

To amplify Godard's observation about the morality of tracking shots, we can heed the way other aspects of the film's form articulate a morality. It is through *montage*, the cutting back and forth between the scenes of devastation and the lovers that the film makes its primary moral statements, which are about the disruption of the temporal rhythms of the life world. At the same time that the lovers are engaged in a slow caressing of each other's smooth, unblemished skin, Elle mentions that when the bomb dropped there resulted 200,000 dead and 80,000 wounded in nine seconds. And earlier, as the camera tracks the displays in the museum, there is a long take of glass containers with (what Elle's voiceover refers to as) "human flesh, suspended, as if still alive – its agony still fresh." Subsequently, we see the badly burned flesh of a man's back. The references to both instantaneous and rapid morbidity are followed by a scene of

Figure 46.1 Elle's and Lui's watches, from Alain Resnais' film *Hiroshima Mon Amour* (1959)
Source: *Hiroshima Mon Amour* (1959).

the lovers slowly caressing each other's smooth skin. The contrast between the slow indulgence with which healthy skin is appreciated and the suddenly damaged flesh resulting from the bombing is underscored with a display of scorched metal, which Elle describes as looking as vulnerable as flesh. In accord with Elle's indulgence in an erotic *jouissance*, the film suggests that enjoyment of the flesh – of the intimate rhythms of bodily exchange – is what the bombing specifically and the war as a whole have disrupted. In place of the slow, intimate rhythms of life, the war has produced an accelerated decrepitude.

Through both its cinematic form and discursive narration, the film suggests that Hiroshima (in contrast to the way it is rendered in abstract policy discourses and treatises on apocalypse) is an atrocity that took the forms of instantaneous destruction, sudden impairment, and then the accelerated decrepitude of bodies. At one point Elle provides a brief phenomenology of the war's attack on the body. After looking in a mirror, she wistfully exclaims that she was young once.

Along with the destruction and impairment of physical bodies, the film dwells on the ethics of memory, which through Elle's narration is articulated as a primary aspect of the film's morality. She dwells on the importance of not forgetting Hiroshima, which she says is as important as never forgetting either her former love for a German soldier in Nevers or the current one in Hiroshima.

The ethics of remembering/forgetting is doubtless an inspiration for Silvia Kolbowski's *After Hiroshima Mon Amour*, which simultaneously counters the forgetting of the bombing's devastation of Japanese life and suggests an equivalence with the Iraq war. Kolbowski is similarly inspired, especially by the "you will have seen me"

Figure 46.2 The two bodies, from Silvia Kolbowski's video *After Hiroshima Mon Amour* (2008)

Source: *After Hiroshima Mon Amour* (2008). Printed with permission from Sylvia Kolbowski.

grammar. As Rosalyn Deutsche (2010: 21) points out: "The word *after* in Kolbowski's title raises the question of time and therefore of history, which is to say of the meaning of past events." In accord with Duras' grammatical imposition through Elle's narration, Kolboswki's "after" is therefore also governed by the future anterior or will have been. That grammar is the analytic with which she reinserts Hiroshima in the present – that is, the invasion and occupation of Iraq – and thereby rethinks both events.

The vehicles for animating the "after" are bodies involved in intimacy and the exercise of sense memory – instead of the geo-strategic concerns and the technological preoccupations that have shaped US collective memory. Kolbowksi's video is a critical intervention into the way that cultural memory will be incessantly renegotiated, not only with respect to the Hiroshima bombing but also with respect to another catastrophe, the devastation of the African American neighbourhood by Hurricane Katrina. Deutsche (2010: 16) puts her temporal intervention with respect to the former in clear perspective: "Kolbowski's *After Hiroshima Mon Amour* has a kind of flash-forward structure, one that suggests what Hiroshima 'will have been' by substituting a movement forward from Resnais' film to the present for Resnais' movement backward from narrative present to the past." With respect to the latter, Kolbowski's remediation summons a reflection on the Katrina event by using different ethnic bodies – a black woman and Middle Eastern man – to create a bridge between the Iraq War and Katrina, a connection she affirms by interspersing video clips of the aftermath of Katrina.

Kolbowski's remake invites critical political reflection because it "fractures the mind of the viewer – causing her or him to enact an alternate, yet simultaneous, mode of thought."

47 Trauma

Emma Hutchison

Trauma imagery holds immense political power. By bringing hardship, pain and suffering into focus, trauma images shock and horrify. They present what witnesses perceive as an impossible spectacle: tragedy so difficult to comprehend that, in the words of Maurice Blanchot (1995: 7), it "escapes the very possibility of experience." Trauma turns our understanding of reality upside-down. Seeing human hardship, pain and death, it is as if our eyes are deceiving us. Yet, as we look, we know our eyes are not. And it is here, in this sheer impossibility of witnessing trauma, that trauma can also captivate. Trauma can hypnotise, fascinate, enthral, aggravate, anger and dismay. Trauma can motivate us.

A prominent recent example illustrates the compelling visual politics of trauma: the image of three-year-old Syrian refugee Alan Kurdi washed up on the shores of Turkey. So tragic and traumatic was this image it rallied countless movements in support of refugees worldwide (Feneley 2015; Withnall and Dathan 2015). Some nations, prominently Germany, made dramatic shifts in their humanitarian intake policies as a consequence.

What is it about images of trauma that they can so decisively frame – and seemingly almost shape – political debate and policy? All trauma imagery is shocking in its own right. So why do some images resonate and gain political traction while others fail to evoke an active response? How can images of trauma draw viewers together in solidarity and in pursuit of particular political ends?

I examine the politics and possibilities that can be both opened – and somewhat paradoxically, closed – by imaging trauma. I focus specifically on the role of affect and emotion, showing how the emotions communicated, interpreted and enacted through imagery are key to trauma's political potentials. This may, at first glance, seem a commonsensical proposition. Of course witnessing trauma is an act laden with intense emotions. But how exactly emotions work in times of crisis – that is, the emotions that are signified and elicited through images and the social significance and capacities they hold – is a culturally, contextually bound process. How and, indeed, whether images of trauma can resonate with and mobilise viewers is contingent upon historically embedded forms of feeling that shape how and for whom viewers should feel. But trauma can in this way, through its various visualisations and the ensuing affective dynamics and agency at play, be politically instrumental. Images of trauma can be part of a complex array of social processes through which existing forms of political power and order are reinstated. Or, on the contrary, trauma imagery can disrupt established political patterns and sow seeds of genuine political transformation.

The emotional politics of imaging trauma

Images have for long been considered central to communicating and "making sense" of trauma (see Kaplan 2005: 136–8). Imagine trying to comprehend, for instance, the horrors of the current global struggle against Islamic State, the spate of recent terrorist attacks around the world, or any of the various recent devastating natural disasters such as the 2015 Nepali and 2011 Fukushima earthquakes, without the arresting portrayals proliferating throughout the media. Traumatic imagery seems to illuminate the visceral nature of tragedy and human hardship far better than can any words.

For many scholars, the communicative power of trauma imagery lies in its unique ability to capture aspects of tragedy that are difficult to say: the deeply emotional dimensions (for instance Baer 2001: 1–21; Berger 1991). Images of trauma are intensely emotional. They lay bare the pain and distress of victims and survivors, capturing and communicating powerful emotions and affects. In so doing, images can create under-standings of tragedy that elicit equally distressing emotions. Seeing is in this sense about feeling. Images act as receptacles of emotion; they resonate affectively, procuring and enacting emotions that enable viewers to make sense and meaning of what is being seen, even when the trauma being visualised seems so utterly devoid of sense or meaning (Bronfen 2006: 33–4; Zelizer 2010: 7). Emotions are thus a critical element of how viewers perceive trauma through images. Emotions help to make trauma know-able and, significantly, in turn influence the conditions through which individual and collective responses to trauma are made possible. Whether it be political outcry or paralysis, action or inaction, emotions are embedded within, and help to produce, the social understandings that can mobilise (or fail to mobilise) political agency and community after pivotal traumatic events.

Recognising that emotions are grounded in cultural contexts therefore provides a crucial link: it allows for an understanding of how images and emotions "work" together after trauma. Simply put, emotions can be "pulled upon" in response to visualising trauma, and this process can take place in politically significant ways. Witnessing trauma through imagery can "steer" an audience's emotions, affectively resonating – "pulling" – in this or that way depending on what is seen and how feelings have been historically cultivated to prompt viewers to perceive the respective trauma. Trauma imagery can in this way solicit emotions – and wider social meanings – that pull people together and mobilise collectives around hardship and suffering (Fierke 2012: 79, 28). Boundaries of responsibility and care may consequently be expanded. Somewhat paradoxically, imaging trauma can also be practice whereby "us/them" and "inside/ outside" communal boundaries are collectively intensified.

Trauma imagery and political restoration

Even though traumatic events suggest the vulnerability and insecurity of established forms of power and order, images of trauma often confirm and entrench prevai-ling forms of political power and community (Brassett and Vaughan-Williams 2012; Edkins 2003). In other words, the very community that trauma undermines can – through visual representations and ensuing meanings – end up being restored. Trauma images become icons of the very communities they belie.

Political traumas, such as those of war, civil conflict or terrorism, are one occasion when we frequently see images playing this kind of restorative role. Let us examine one example more closely: a transnational terrorist attack that became a distinctly "national trauma" rallying a nation together: the Bali bombing of 2002. Late on the evening of 12 October, the Islamist group Jemaah Islamiyaah set off two bombs outside the popular expatriate-only Sari Bar in Kuta, on the island of Bali, Indonesia. The bombing resulted in the deaths of 202 people. 88 victims were Australian. Australia thus quickly became the country in which the impact of the attack was most sharply felt. Indeed, in the aftermath an incredible solidarity and strengthening of the national community was observed: it seemed that the nation was "at one" with the victims. Within the media, an ensuing sense of trauma – the shock and the gravity of loss – was invoked as damaging Australia's "collective soul" (Ragg 2002: 5).

Dominant visual portrayals of the bombing in the media demonstrate the combined emotional and political potentials of imaging trauma. They show how images "frame" trauma, guiding an audience to emotionally enact a sense of injury and loss and producing social understandings that prompt trauma to become a politically restorative collective experience (Alexander 2012: 3).

Consider images employed to depict the bombing and its aftermath in Australia's sole national print news source, *The Australian*. The visual narrative they created told of a uniquely Australian national tragedy. Initial images brought forth the sublime horror and shock of the violence and harm: they graphically presented the horror and pain of victims and survivors, encouraging distant Australian viewers to imagine and empathise with the trauma of experiencing the blasts first-hand.

The front page in Figure 47.1, on the first day of newspaper coverage, is particularly poignant.

Graphically presenting the pain and horror of unknown others, the image stops viewers short. The extent of the carnage is shocking. It seems to present things as they really "are," giving the viewer a sense of authenticity, of being there and experiencing the horror alongside direct victims. Viewing the image in conjunction with the headline – "Terror hits home" – moreover creates a powerful "image-text" (Mitchell, Chapter 34): it pushes the trauma into the lives of Australians, explicitly directing viewers to make sense of the bombing as an injustice and tragedy perpetrated upon all fellow nationals.

Ensuing media coverage furthered the "national trauma" narrative, yet it did so through imagery that provided the grounds for emotional understandings based not only on the collective harm but also on the shared loss and need for a collective response. These images shifted away from those depicting the initial destruction to those that visualised the more exact impact of the bombing: the young, seemingly resilient lives that were lost. Portraits of smiling faces – the young Australians who were either missing or pronounced dead – were posted on front pages. Victims were pictured as they were before: drinking beer with mates, cradling infant children, sitting on beaches soaking in the sun. Later on, families and schoolchildren were shown – heads bowed and weeping – at church and public memorial services. Images of mourning were also complemented with those portraying the compassion, outrage and expediency of the Australian political and security response. Then Prime Minister John Howard was shown surveying the bomb site and the media pronounced that Australians were the victims of a new "Season of Terror."

This type of commemorative and political imagery undoubtedly seems expected in the wake of a shocking terrorist attack. Countless other examples of political traumas imaged prominently in the media could be drawn upon: the terrorist attacks in Washington and New York on 11 September 2001, the London bombings of 7 July

Figure 47.1 "Terror hits home," front page of *The Australian*, 14 October 2002

Source: *The Australian*, 14 October 2002. With permission from *The Australian*/Newspix.

2005, or the recent November 2015 and March 2016 European bombings in Paris and Brussels. Following these attacks the abundance of visuals – of the bomb sites, ensuing trauma and stages of mourning – drew citizens together around shared understandings of loss and pain (Kaplan 2005; Miller 2003; Weber 2006a). Yet, there nevertheless remains a distinct visual politics at play: It is precisely in the supposed "normality" and obviousness of such imagery that it gains representational authority and political power (Tagg 1988: 21–2). As Judith Butler (2009) famously puts it, such imagery distinguishes the tragedy as "grievable." It provides an emotional object of identification, in this case (of the Bali bombing) for the Australian community, and as such brings the attack into focus as an injury and loss endured by all Australians and not simply by the individuals directly impacted. They suggest that the trauma is distinctly national trauma with which all Australians should identify and should feel.

As commonplace as this emotional, visual framing of political trauma may appear, it is politically significant in so far as it frequently functions to enable, reconstitute and restore an established community – the nation-state – as the preferred arrangement of political power, order and control. Even though the trauma (of terrorist attacks, civil conflict, war, etc.) in fact suggests the vulnerability, fragility and insecurity of the nation-state, images can appeal to affective sentiments that consolidate and recentralise agency and community at the national level. Such was the situation in this case: the nation-state as community was, paradoxically, strengthened. Power and order were "secured through a failure to secure" (Heath-Kelly 2015). Alternative or marginalised identities and forms of political community (either within or beyond the bounded community of the nation-state) were simultaneously silenced and closed off.

Trauma, images and political transformation

Although trauma often generates this kind of conservative – restorative – political effect, images can, paradoxically, enact an emotional politics that helps to disturb and transgress established political patterns. Trauma imagery can, simply put, be politically transformative. But, how is it that traumatic imagery can generate these seemingly dual, at-odds political ends? If images function to reinforce and restore the political status quo, how is it that they can also mobilise audiences to reflect upon existing orders and to actively participate to effect political change?

The capacity of images to disrupt and transform established political patterns lies likewise in part in emotions – in how traumatic images can affectively resonate with those who view them. So, just as the emotional dimensions of imaging trauma can limit or close off forms of political agency and community, they can also help produce feelings and meanings that reframe how individuals and communities perceive their attachments, identities, affiliations and responsibilities. Emotions and affects that may turn communities inwards, and be collectively mobilised to reinforce the existing political order after, say, the trauma of a terrorist attack, can in particular circumstances be engaged in ways that re-orientate individuals and communities. The emotional dimensions of trauma imagery may as such hold the seeds of political renewal or transformation.

Humanitarian crises are one situation when the transformative potentials of imaging trauma are particularly pronounced. Specifically, viewing the trauma of often distant disaster resonates with historically engrained, yet often marginalised or dissident, discourses of compassion and humanitarianism towards the unfortunate or less-privileged.

Shocking, abject images of suffering – of "the body in pain" and of especially emotive humanitarian symbols, such as "the mother and child" – are typically key (Dauphinee 2007; Manzo 2008). Such imagery appeals to historically cultivated emotional norms that suggest audiences should feel sympathy at the sight of bodies in pain and be motivated to reach out to alleviate others' suffering (Abruzzo 2011).

The incredible transnational response after the Southeast Asian tsunami catastrophe in December 2004 is, for instance, a telling case in point. When the giant wave struck the shores of more than fourteen countries on 26 December, Boxing Day, an unprecedented outpouring of international solidarity and aid was summoned. Key to this response was the inundation of intensely traumatic and emotional images (Brauman 2009: 108–17; Chouliaraki 2006: 4). Indeed, images of the tsunami created a context in which the catastrophe – the trauma of devastation and loss of life – was perceived as an exceptional humanitarian disaster for which viewers worldwide should feel and mobilise. Images – such as those in Figures 47.2 and 47.3 – achieved this by repeatedly visualising the vast scale of the destruction, human suffering and dependence, and death. They are the type of images that suggest audiences should not just feel in compassionate ways, but in so doing also reconsider their obligations towards those affected.

Figure 47.2 Amid trash and debris, the shrouded bodies of the deceased lay on a street in downtown Banda Aceh, Sumatra, Indonesia, following the massive tsunami that struck the area on 26 December 2004. Photograph 1 January 2005

Source: Photograph 1 January 2005. Wikimedia Commons, https://commons.wikimedia.org/wiki/File%3ABodies_in_Banda_Aceh_after_2004_tsunami_DD-SD-06-07373.JPEG (in the public domain).

Figure 47.3 Trash and debris line the streets in downtown Banda Aceh, Sumatra, Indonesia, following the massive tsunami that struck the area on 26 December 2004. Photograph 1 January 2005

Source: Photograph 1 January 2005. Wikimedia Commons, https://commons.wikimedia.org/wiki/File:Street_in_downtown_Banda_Aceh_after_2004_tsunami_DD-SD-06-07374.JPEG (in the public domain).

Traumatic, distressing images can also be influential in cultivating less obvious seeds of political debate and change. The haunting images of systematic prisoner abuse emerging from Abu Ghraib in 2003 sparked major public discussion in the US as well as worldwide on the politics and ethics of torture. Such was also certainly the case following the traumatic image of three-year-old Alan Kurdi. The stark visual of the small boy refugee washed up on the shores of Turkey tugged at heartstrings around the world, prompting a radical shift in public perceptions of the European refugee crisis and mobilising nations worldwide to reconsider their asylum-seeker policies.

Significant in all of these examples are the parallel politics of emotions and trauma. In these cases, images prompted audiences to emotionally enact and perceive trauma in ways that transgressed the status quo. Even if temporal, new forms of political agency ensued. Entrenched political orders, and in some cases, policies, were usurped.

The visual politics of trauma

Images of trauma possess a distinct visual politics. Trauma imagery can either fashion viewers' emotions to help buttress and strengthen established forms of political order, agency, and community or, indeed, often the very same types of emotions can be orientated in new or changed ways to abet the constitution of alternative, purposive political configurations. Yet, how trauma images function depends on the context in which they are seen. In this respect trauma images neatly highlight what is at stake in visual global politics. Like all representations, images are subjective. The meanings they attain are contingent. But often much more clearly than words, images are interpreted through the forms of feeling through which individuals and collectives have been socially, culturally and historically conditioned. Like the images that prompt them, these emotions can reveal and also conceal particular perceptions, choices and prerogatives. Understanding the power and politics of imaging trauma is thus a process of recognising and appreciating the sociality of emotions and in how emotions have been conditioned to make each of us feel and respond.

Note

This chapter draws on some of my previously published work, most notably Hutchison 2010, 2014 and 2016.

48 Travel

Debbie Lisle

The spread of photography from Europe to the rest of the world from the middle to the end of the nineteenth century is an extremely important origin point for a politically attuned understanding of visuality. The early globalisation of photography was systematically enabled by the existing structures and power relations of colonialism. It also reproduced, strengthened and extended those relations in ways that substantially reduced the freedom of colonised populations. Indeed, we cannot separate the birth of photography from its colonial context – from the fact that the early photographers who took their cameras around the world to visually document "exotic" scenes carried with them the assumptions and prejudices of a supposedly superior European culture.

In analysing the power relations that photography enabled and reproduced in the context of colonialism, many scholars have explained how a visual logic of coloniser/colonised was supported by attending hierarchies of race, gender and sexuality (Hight 2004; Osborne 2000; Ryan 1997). I am particularly interested in how this fundamental entwining of photography and colonialism was also shaped by the rise and spread of mass tourism. As companies like Thomas Cook & Sons began taking middle-class tourists around the world in the mid-nineteenth century, new tourist infrastructures – including photography studios and souvenir shops – developed in "exotic" destinations like Cairo, Istanbul and Jerusalem (Hazbun 2007). Along with posing for portraits themselves, many European tourists to the Middle East, Asia and Africa in the late nineteenth century purchased, collected and traded souvenir *cartes-de-visite* – the precursors of modern postcards – that depicted local "tribes" (e.g. a "Nubian" in traditional dress), famous landmarks (e.g. the Pyramids) and "typical street scenes" (e.g. an Egyptian market) (Gregory 2003, 2001).

I explore the visual politics that connect colonialism, photography and tourism. I examine how practices of tourist photography – of capturing the everyday encounters between different cultures – often reinforce dominant understandings of global politics that further entrench long-standing colonial asymmetries. Using two separate photographs – one from 1919 and the other from 2015 – as examples of colonialism–photography–tourism intersections, the chapter asks three important questions:

1 How do tourist photographs both reflect and produce prevailing colonial asymmetries?
2 How did the global spread of photography within a colonial context develop through the attending practices of tourism?
3 To what extent are practices of tourism and photography still shaped by a lingering colonial imaginary?

What particularly interests me is how prevailing global power relations at the structural level (e.g. between states, cultures, civilisations) circulate in unexpected and everyday spaces of leisure. In this case, I am interested in how a colonial global order resonates between those who take photographs (subjects), those who pose for them (objects), and those who look at them (viewers). Like any politically attuned account of visuality, this is a story of reflection *and* production. If it is the case that we document the world through visual representations like photographs, it stands to reason that our images will reflect existing asymmetries within that world. But the more we look at images in a visually saturated culture, the more we come to see them as constituting our world – as actually producing the world before us. For example, the more pictures depict Syria as violent, dangerous and chaotic, the more everyone's encounters with, and responses to, Syria will reflect that assumption. Pretty soon, the life-worlds, activities and relations of Syria will be determined by a prevailing understanding that Syrians are, indeed, violent, dangerous and chaotic. If this is all that is reflected back to someone living in Syria – if the global image bank only contains negative images of Syrians (i.e. destitute refugees or violent extremists) – it also stands to reason that some people living in Syria might *become* what the pictures tell them they are.

Pictures have enormous power in this way – even the most throwaway tourist image contains the capacity to produce the world as well as reflect it. These visual relations are complex, circuitous and entwined, but it is important to try to disentangle them so we can identify and understand how the power relations that constitute photography often align with the power relations that constitute global politics.

The dangers of photography

Drawing together colonialism, photography and tourism provides us with a *context* within which we can work out the dominant global power relations embedded in specific tourist photographs. So, for example, we could read any number of mid-to-late nineteenth-century *cartes-de-visite* depicting "natives" and explain how they reproduce familiar logics of Orientalism in which the West (Occident) constitutes itself as superior in relation to a subordinated East (Orient) (Said 1979). Here, the privileged viewer (e.g. an English tourist who collects souvenir *cartes-de-visite*) has all the power over an objectified Other (e.g. "A Native Lady") who is rendered silent, exotic and disempowered in the photograph (Behdad and Gartlan 2013). This context-driven reading is an important starting point because it shows us how a circulating imaginary – in this case a colonial imaginary – shapes how we encounter and represent the world in ways that privilege some and disempower Others.

However, that context-driven reading requires further elaboration to draw out how prevailing imaginaries shape the actual *content* of the photographs themselves. There are two primary sets of relationships that can help us in this task.

First, there are the relationships between the photographer who frames, produces and takes the photograph, and the object that is captured within the resulting image. The photographer controls the means of visual reproduction and therefore has the power to decide what is included within the image and what is excluded. As a consequence, the object – the Other – is mute, captured and made to signify through someone else's parameters. That central modality of framing (deciding what is in and what is out) is enabled through creative techniques of composition that dictate how the objects and Others that are included in the image are arranged to produce a preferred meaning.

Here, we need to pay attention to the relationships between light and dark, between foreground and background and between lines and shadows. What draws the eye in and what makes it focus? What disappears from view? Which aspects are privileged and which are neglected? What is left out of the frame?

Second, there are the relationships between the viewers of photographs and the objects and Others captured within the image. This set of relationships is important because it effaces the productive and creative efforts of the photographer who suddenly disappears from view. Here, the labour invested in the photograph – all the work that goes into framing, setting, arranging and directing the gaze – is forgotten as the viewer looks directly at the object or Other frozen in the image. Because that direct engagement between viewer and picture negates the act of mediation perpetrated by the photographer, the viewer is able to believe that the photograph actually represents an unmediated slice of reality: this really *is* a "Native Lady!" All "Native Ladies" must dress like this and look like this!

What is interesting in both sets of relationships is the extent to which the photographer encodes unacknowledged messages into the image (and thus inadvertently and/or unconsciously includes things that don't "fit"), and the extent to which the viewer brings unexpected prejudices to the photograph (and thus fails to "get" the preferred meaning by reading other things into it). These moments of slippage are extremely important in terms of disrupting the prevailing colonial imaginary underscoring tourist photographs because they open up the possibility of *reading the picture otherwise*. Taking hold of this possibility also helps us re-think the agency of those being photographed. For example, a reductive logic of Orientalism that silences Arab Others and robs them of their agency is too blunt to capture the complex meanings that circulate in and through tourist photographs. The hierarchical "looking"/"being looked at" relations of photography always contain within them a powerful return gaze through which the Other can re-order dominant viewing relations (Eileraas 2003; Gillespie 2006). For example, the direct stares that anchor colonial portraits of "Natives" can be read as confrontational rather than passive – as articulating a defiant resistance to Orientalist tropes rather than meekly accepting them. Foregrounding the possibilities of resistance inherent in the return gaze helps us re-imagine both the context of a photograph's interpretation (i.e. the alignment between colonialism, photography and tourism) as well as the compositional elements that encourage a preferred meaning to prevail.

Objectification and ambivalence

Given that colonial subjects fought valiantly for both sides during the First World War, and clashes between the Great Powers took place at the far reaches of empire, it was unsurprising that the structures of European colonial rule began to dissolve at the end of the war. At the same time, European populations emerging from the First World War were eager to re-establish a culture of tourism that had been thriving before the war. Deep in the Imperial War Museum Archives in London, there is a particularly arresting photograph that demonstrates these strange post-war intersections between decolonisation and tourism. In the summer of 1919, Mrs L.K. Briggs of North Yorkshire visited the First World War battlefields near Ypres with her two daughters. She initially made the trip to find the grave of her son Claude who was killed in battle, but subsequently the Briggs family returned to enjoy the growing phenomenon of battlefield tourism that characterised the inter-war years (Lisle 2016: 89–92; Lloyd 1998). One

A CHINAMAN BY A DERELICT TANK AT THE TOP OF OBSERVATORY RIDGE, HOOGE. 1919.

AUG: 30ᵗʰ

Figure 48.1 A "Chinaman" by a derelict tank at the top of Observatory Ridge, Hooge, 1919

Source: Cat. No. Documents 21795. Courtesy of the Imperial War Museum Archives, London.

of the daughters brought a Kodak personal camera to document their journeys, and Mrs Briggs arranged these tourist photographs into an annotated album that described the ruined landscapes and broken objects they encountered (Briggs n.d.). The Briggs themselves are seldom seen in these photographs, and the tone of both the images and accompanying text is overwhelmingly objective, documentary and dispassionate. There is one moment, however, that breaks through this distancing framework and destabilises Mrs Briggs' efforts to treat the war-torn battlefields of Europe as a commodified and exotic tourist destination. Near the Hooge battlefield in August 1919, the Briggs family came upon a "Chinaman" – a member of the Chinese Labour Corps that had been brought over by the British government to help with manual labour and support work during the war (O'Neill 2016).

In the annotated album, Mrs Briggs describes the "Chinaman" in racist terms as lazy, ungrateful and dangerous, but also indicates a fear of the "interloper" as his strange presence disrupts their reverent contemplation of rusting tanks, scattered shells and bomb craters. Indeed, the off-centre framing, blurred edges, and washed-out colour of the image suggest that it was perhaps taken quickly as the Briggs family hurried away from the stranger. When this photograph is read in conjunction with the rest of the annotated album, the "Chinaman" becomes a photographable object equivalent to the collapsed buildings, ruined landscapes and debris of battle that populate the rest of the photographs. Unlike the "Frenchmen" and "Belgians" that the Briggs regularly meet on their travels, the "Chinaman" is singled out: his racial inferiority equates him with the other objects deemed worthy of being photographed by Miss Briggs and methodically annotated by Mrs Briggs. In the photograph, the "Chinaman" is rendered equivalent to the derelict tank that he stands beside. Despite his efforts to help the Allied forces during the war, he cannot be lifted out of his position as an objectified Other: he is worth taking a picture of (like a tank or a crater or a grave), but his racial inferiority renders him unworthy of human engagement.

While this photograph can be understood as reinforcing prevailing colonial relations, I think the figure of the "Chinaman" is actually quite ambivalent. His "out of place" position on the European battlefield means he can be easily objectified and consumed within a prevailing tourist gaze; in other words, he is a "sight" – something worthy of being photographed. However, Mrs Briggs' description of him as threatening and violent suggests that the "Chinaman" might not be passive or mute; indeed, he might be active, full of agency and capable of movement and decision – a fully fledged *human.* This active agency is a form of return gaze that breaks out of the Briggs' efforts to objectify him and equate him with the ruined objects of Europe's post-war landscape. For me, the "Chinaman" is never fully captured by the prevailing colonial imaginary that underscores the Briggs' photographic project. His pose in the photograph reinforces this indeterminacy: he has stopped for the moment and is resting on his back foot (suggesting that he is happy to be photographed), but he also appears to be on the verge of pursuit – possibly towards the Briggs' tourist party, but possibly in a different direction altogether. The Briggs' album never refers to this strange and spectral encounter again, but the way this moment disrupts an otherwise straightforward documentary of a tourist experience is important because it unravels our assumptions about the superiority of both the tourists who take photographs and the viewers who look at them. No matter how powerful the visual and narrative efforts are to constrain the "Chinaman" and keep him in his place, he cannot help but make himself felt outside of these coordinates in ways that express independent will, agency and vitality.

Dehumanisation and narcissism

Over a hundred years after Mrs Briggs' son perished on the battlefields of Europe, we can see another strange entanglement between colonialism, photography and tourism – this time on the tourist beaches and resorts of southern Europe. During the summer of 2015, over 350,000 refugees made treacherous journeys across the Mediterranean Sea: many used all their savings to gain passage on crowded and unsafe boats and over 3000 drowned in the process (International Organization of Migration 2015). Many of these refugees were fleeing the war zones of Syria and Northern Iraq, but some were also travelling from places like Afghanistan, Eritrea and Yemen. At the same time as this mass migration of refugees and migrants pushed northwards, thousands of European tourists were making their annual summer journeys southward to the holiday resorts of Italy, Greece, Turkey and Cyprus. Unsurprisingly, these two populations ended up occupying the same territory: one group bringing all the possessions they could carry (and if they were lucky, a lifejacket to keep them alive), the other group bringing sunscreen, light summer clothing, and camera phones. One site where this clash of life-worlds was particularly stark was the small Greek tourist island of Kos, close to the beaches of Western Turkey. As the migration "crisis" reached its peak in August 2015, tourists and locals were confronted with over 7000 refugees landing on "their" beaches, and occupying "their" leisure space. As the numbers of migrant arrivals became overwhelming for the small island, the Greek government sent the cruise ship *Eleftherios Venizelos* to house, shelter and process 2,500 Syrian refugees (Mac Con Uladh 2015). The cross-overs here are dizzying: a cruise ship docked at a tourist resort but housing refugees; a beach front with sun-loungers placed between the discarded lifejackets of refugees; and tourists supposedly on holiday but distributing food, medicine and aid instead (McVeigh 2015).

Amid all this, of course, people were taking photographs – not just tourists, but also photojournalists and migrants themselves. German photographer Jörg Brüggemann's (2015) photo-essay *Tourists vs. Refugees*, reproduced in a number of European newspapers, visualised these strange juxtapositions. In one photograph, a young German tourist uses a selfie stick to take a picture of himself in front of a row of migrant tents assembled on the beach front (see Figure 48.2).

The looking-relations of this photograph are similar to the Briggs' "Chinaman" image in that both work as forms of documentary proof: they are meant to show viewers that the photographer was *actually there* (i.e. wandering through the smouldering battlefields of Ypres, or witnessing the arrival of thousands of Syrian migrants). But rather than evacuate the photographer from the scene and erase the labours of production (which

Figure 48.2 Brüggemann selfie

Source: with permission from Jörg Brüggemann.

is what the Briggs photograph does), this selfie increases the power of the producer who becomes both the author and the object of the photograph. This re-insertion of the photographer into the image increases his/her power to frame the scene and intensifies the practices of objectification. Becoming the author *and* object of the photograph means that all other elements of the scene are pushed further into the background and made to signify more completely around the central figure (the photographer). In this selfie, the tourist-photographer's privilege is secured to such an extent that the migrants in the background are not just objectified like the "Chinaman" (i.e. equated with an object), they are also dehumanised. Not only are the migrants rendered equivalent to the surrounding tents, trees and boats, but these "background" objects are then forced to signify only in ways that serve the narcissistic frame of the photographer (i.e. by lending "authenticity" and "exoticism" to his superior position). He is the central spectacle in his own exciting life and they are the "colourful background" serving his narrative. More to the point, that objectified background is totally replaceable: today some migrants, tomorrow some palm trees, the next day some ancient ruins.

Hope

The alignments between colonialism, photography and tourism certainly reproduce powerful hierarchies that secure the supposed superiority of colonising cultures. It is absolutely necessary that we attend to these alignments by revealing the complex ways that they privilege some subjects by rendering Others mute, immobile and often invisible. But just as important as exposing these asymmetries is unravelling them – showing how they are always resisted and re-ordered by both the objects/Others in the frame and viewers outside it. With the Briggs photograph, this means opening some interpretive space through which the "Chinaman's" agency can emerge on its own terms to puncture the dominant colonial framing in which his Otherness was commodified as an "intriguing" but threatening tourist object. With Brüggemann's photograph of the tourist selfie, this moment of instability is more difficult to locate. Perhaps the complete indifference of the migrants gives us a starting point: they are not interested in the tourist-selfie taker at all, but are instead getting on with their new lives in radically changed circumstances (e.g. bringing home food; staying out of the sun; re-grouping for the next stage of their journey). Not only does that indifference negate the narcissism of the tourist, it leads us to another hopeful scene currently being repeated across the Mediterranean. Migrants, of course, also carry camera phones. After calling home to assure friends and family that they are safe on the shores of Europe, they often take group selfies to document their relief at surviving. The spirit of those joyful group selfies is precisely what should direct our efforts to deconstruct the colonial relations of tourist photographs more generally. Even if they are initially obscured from view, the vibrant lives of photographed objects and Others are always present: the challenge is to make them more visible, intelligible and familiar.

Note

I would like to thank the University of Minnesota Press who have given permission to reproduce the spirit, if not the letter, of my arguments about the Briggs photograph. A more elaborate discussion of these issues can be found in chapter 2 of my book *Holidays in the Danger Zone: Entanglements of War and Tourism* (Lisle 2016).

49 Violence

Mark Reinhardt

Throughout its history, photography has had an intimate relationship with violence (Sontag 2003). For just as long, the relationship has fuelled anxiety. Critics worry when no photographs record a violent conflict *and* when photos abound. With good reasons: if the absence of pictures renders plights invisible or lives insignificant, a surfeit may make matters worse. Photographs not only document violence around the globe but also extend its repertoire and reach. Think, for example, of terrorism and the imperial violence carried out in the name of counter-terrorism: the very real business of killing is staged for the mass media in an attempt to create "images that traumatise their beholders" (Mitchell 2011: 12). If our image world is political, that's not only because powerful actors, movements and institutions affect what pictures we see. It is also because images and visual practices shape political subjects, verbs and objects – the categories (including, say, "terrorist") through which we perceive, experience, act within and demarcate the political arena. We should not be surprised, then, that the manner of picturing violence generates concern: the stakes are high.

That's only half the story, however. The visual shaping may be politically salutary, fuelling a social movement's confidence or putting pressure on existing hierarchies and prevailing perspectives. Taking, circulating and responding to photographs have long played an important role in civic life and democratic struggle (Sliwinski 2011; Azoulay 2012), an importance only likely to grow amid the proliferation of social media (Hariman and Lucaites 2016). Photographs can, for instance, prompt scrutiny of hitherto unrecognised or disavowed acts, forms, perpetrators or subjects of violence – they are part of how we imagine where violence happens, to whom and even what *counts* as violent. And if there are good reasons for concern about how those imaginings play out, there are dubious reasons, too. Although critics have warned against images' baleful effects at least since Plato and the Hebrew Bible (might iconophobia be as old as image-making?) photographs provoke controversies that do not attend other kinds of pictures. In some strands of criticism, not this or that photograph but the medium itself plays the culprit's role (Linfield 2012). Nowhere is this seen more clearly than when photography is indicted for "aestheticising" violence (or suffering, or the whole world). The indictment's terms deserve scrutiny. They would immediately appear untenable if applied to other media. They also deform and obscure much about photographs, so their enduring place in photo criticism offers an important clue: they reveal something about what we want from photography and even, in a distorted way, something about how photographs work. The debate over aestheticisation thus makes a good starting point for considering photography's role in the visual politics of violence. Working through the critique and its limits can put our analysis on a sounder footing, enabling us to discuss more clearly the problems peculiar to photographs engaging violence, the political uses of such photos and – despite the aestheticisation critique's distortions – the importance of aesthetics to those uses.

Aestheticisation and its discontents

Susan Sontag (1977: 109) put the critique in its broadest terms: "Photographs can and do distress. But the aestheticising tendency of photography is such that the medium which conveys distress ends by neutralising it." The nuances depend upon the critic and era, but critiques of aestheticisation from the early Frankfurt School through the twenty-first century all offer variations on that theme (e.g. Benjamin 1999 [1934]; Jansson 2001; Solomon-Godeau 2005; Chouliaraki 2006). Even when intended to confront injustice, the argument goes, images that aestheticise are artistically and politically reactionary. Mistreating their subjects, they invite passive consumption, narcissism, or even sadism on the part of viewers.

How? For that matter, what does "aestheticising" *mean*? Answers prove more elusive than one might expect, for the term tends not to be used clearly or consistently. We might begin, though, with what some philosophers call "the aesthetic attitude," in which "disinterested and sympathetic contemplation" of an "object of awareness . . . for its own sake alone" (Stolnitz 1988: 79) makes possible "delight in what resides intrinsically" in that object (Eaton 1998: 87). Perhaps aestheticisation, most narrowly construed, renders a scene in a way that invites such responses. The perils of aestheticising violence then become evident. Who would not be appalled when a photograph's composition invites viewers to do no more than take pleasure in how real acts of violence have been given visual form? As Arthur Danto (2003: 110) observes, only a "monster" would witness a bombardment and merely respond, "How beautiful those mourning women are beside the shattered pots of their burned and bombed houses" – and any photo soliciting that response would have a monstrous quality, too.

But which photos do this? For whom? Under what circumstances? Whatever their political shortcomings, not even the photos of James Nachtwey, perhaps the documentarian most often accused of aestheticising, ask for indifference to the violence or suffering they render with such formal power (Reinhardt 2007; Linfield 2012). The charges must fit some photos, somewhere, but how many? And are those pictures really the *only* targets? Recall Sontag's complaint, which invokes the aestheticising work of the medium itself and thus bears on a wide array of pictures, topics and styles. Her sweep and lack of specificity are representative: even a cursory review of the critical literature reveals how the meaning of "aestheticisation" shifts and slides, moving unreflectively between "inviting only formal pleasure" and something like "having any kind of formal properties." What might seem merely an objection to a kind of morally obtuse obscuring or exploitation of violence repeatedly becomes an anxiety – often inchoate and unstated, but perhaps thereby more powerful – about the formal choices, conventions and qualities inherent in the work of visual representation. Yet "to represent is to aestheticize," as David Levi Strauss (2003: 7) observes, "that is, to transform." It is not as though a photograph of a violent scene could have *no* aesthetic properties.

Few would contest the proposition outright (What could one say?) but many critiques do so implicitly and perhaps unawares. The potential inheres in the critical terms themselves. Consider how the *Oxford English Dictionary* (1971: 148) defines "aestheticize": "To render æsthetic, or agreeable to a refined taste, to refine." Do the latter clauses provide additional meanings or clarification of the first? Must rendering a scene "aesthetic" make it agreeable, and to the refined? One might seek answers in the meaning of the adjective, "aesthetic," but here, too, we find slippage: aesthetic means both "pertaining to sensuous perception, received by the senses" and "pertaining to the appreciation or criticism of the beautiful" (1971: 177–8). Of course, we need not feel bound by dictionaries, particularly when a term has so rich and contested a philosophical history. Aesthetic categories today extend beyond the beautiful and its traditional partner, the sublime to encompass, for example, the disgusting, the interesting and the cute (Danto 2003; Ngai 2012). Yet aestheticisation discourse follows the dictionary, beginning with something as narrow as beautification-in-the-service-of-pleasure and becoming as broad as sensory perception and the diverse ways in which photographic representation engages it.

That breadth should press us to ask why photography's inevitable form-giving and sensory engagement provoke anxiety. One key reason is the way pictures elude attempts to fix meaning through language. As Sontag (1977) herself observes, those most worried about photographs often hope captions will control viewer response – hopes that may end in disappointment. But *all* kinds of images are elusive in this way, so understanding the concerns about photographs that "aestheticise" violence requires additional work. Taken together, three further points may help us solve the puzzle. First, such photos, unlike some other varieties, engage human actions, structures and consequences (whether or not any person appears in them, as a picture featuring only, say, the debris left by a missile attack asks us to imagine the source). Second, even in an era that has made cheap editing software ubiquitous and computer-generated imagery a staple of the media environment – when, in short, we can assume everyone is aware of photography's intrinsic artifice and capacity to recombine, transfigure or deceive – our default response to most photographs is to take those human settings or actors as in a distinctive sense real. We often *want* photographs to serve as faithful records. Third, when photographers capture violence involving real people, then – to echo this chapter's opening – the pictures may become active participants in the events they depict. And the manner of depiction influences the part the photos play: though not in ways captured well by the critical indictments, photography's political uses and effects are intimately linked to photographic aesthetics. In elaborating, let us examine the violence of one infamous photograph.

Constitutive violence

To begin, consider its context. Spectacle lynching functioned as one of the main forms of racial terror enforcing white supremacy in the United States for over 50 years, particularly between the latter decades of the nineteenth century and the end of the 1930s. When targeting black men and (less frequently) other men and (occasionally) women of colour, lynch mobs aimed not only to kill the proximate victims while degrading them in the process but also to humiliate and intimidate the broader subordinated population. Far from random events, the killings were sometimes publicised in advance in mass media, and the crowds' actions were patterned, routinised, scripted. Often present throughout the proceedings, photographers contributed to the script

Figure 49.1 Thomas Shipp and Abram Smith, lynched in Marion, Indiana, on 7 August 1930

Source: https://en.wikipedia.org/wiki/File:ThomasShippAbramSmith.jpg/ With permission from the copyright holder, the Indiana Historical Society.

(Marriott 2000; Apel 2004; Goldsby 2006; Apel and Smith 2008; Wood 2011). Although taking pictures was of course neither the primary crime nor necessary to it, photography was nevertheless *integral* to this form of violence. The photographs were as a rule taken by those who actively joined the mob or by professionals known to be sympathetic to its aims. Both taking and viewing the pictures became important ways of elaborating lynching's conventions and meanings. For whites who advocated, engaged in or sympathised with lynching, the pictures "served to normalise" its brutality, making it "socially . . . even aesthetically acceptable" (Wood 2011: 75).

The photographers' complicity emerges most clearly from their practice of turning lynching photographs into souvenir postcards. The cards, "a huge industry by the early twentieth century," provided a key visual means through which white supremacists fashioned their ideology and even identity, while sustaining solidarity (Apel 2008: 44; Marriott 2000). But even as they served as tokens of exchange among advocates of racialised violence, the postcards had broader effects on more heterogeneous publics. They were, for instance, advertised in Southern newspapers and displayed for sale in stores, where anyone could see them. They were also sent – the threat as obvious as the insult – to black activists. We have every reason, then, to see the postcards as important to the practice of racial terror. Photography enacted humiliation and degradation; the circulation of the pictures sustained or even extended the dynamic. The postcards present the viewpoint of a crime's perpetrators, helping to spread the criminality.

Return, if you can bear it, to Figure 49.1. Lawrence Beitler's 1930 postcard presents the lynching of Thomas Shipp and Abram Smith, two black men accused of murdering a white man and raping a white woman in Marion, Indiana. The bloody bodies of Shipp (left) and Smith (right) testify to the ferocity of the violence unleashed upon them – the mob had, in fact, *already* beaten and killed both men – prior to their being hung from a tree in Marion's courthouse square. The cloth draped around Smith's waist and legs suggests both the sexualised fury that had led the crowd to remove his pants and the subsequent effort to cover the nudity – and disavow the sexual investment – in composing the scene for photographs. One needs evidence from outside the frame to establish that the cloth was a Klansman's robe and that Smith's pants were torn apart as members of the crowd sought souvenirs of their involvement (Madison 2001: 10–11), but the smiling, unembarrassed, even festive responses of the men and women inside the frame (a small fraction of the several thousand who gathered) provide more than enough visual evidence to confirm both the ritual character of this murder and the place of photography within the ritual.

The man pointing to the bodies while looking at the camera is obviously part of a wider, elaborately choreographed, exchange of gestures and glances. The visual interchange certainly includes the photographer as an active agent in this scene of violence and violation; by extension, the photograph invites viewers to incorporate themselves in a similar way. We might call that way "constitutive," insofar as the photo initiates a circuit of violence completed only when the picture finds a sympathetic audience.

Yet, even as a brief and simplified telling, the account of lynching photography given so far is misleadingly one-sided: it neglects the uses of photographs in the struggle against lynching, uses revealing the political complexity and contingencies of how constitutively violent images are viewed, and to what effect. Anti-lynching activists often reframed the photographs, shifting how they signified and what affects they produced, for instance by attaching militant captions or by using irony to turn the lynch mob's slogans against their authors – for instance, by giving Beitler's photograph captions such as "American Christianity" (Smith 2008: 21). They did so not in ignorance of the ways in which lynching photographers and photographs often worked to advance the cause of white violence but *because* this commitment was so visible in the pictures themselves: that the photographs put the perpetrators' perspective on display is what helped make them effective weapons for forging opposition to lynching. The viewpoint taken by the photographs – the solicitation offered the spectator, the attempt to enact and extend violence – was thus integral to constructing both pro- *and* anti-lynching publics. The pernicious power of the former public should not obscure the political importance of the latter: the photographs were key tools of mobilisation in the assertive protests that largely curtailed spectacle lynching by 1940.

Black activists waging the visual campaign against lynching earlier in the century were well aware that exhibiting constitutively violent images is fraught with peril. Knowing intimately that "race" has always been, at least in part, a matter of visual politics, its inequities tied to systems and habits of seeing human difference and organising the perceptual field, the activists worried that their use of the pictures might fortify white fantasies of black criminality. Yet, the campaigns proceeded, employing

Do not look at the Negro.

His earthly problems are ended.

Instead, look at the seven WHITE children who gaze at this gruesome spectacle.

Is it horror or gloating on the face of the neatly dressed seven-year-old girl on the right?

Is the tiny four-year-old on the left old enough, one wonders, to comprehend the barbarism her elders have perpetrated?

Rubin Stacy, the Negro, who was lynched at Fort Lauderdale, Florida, on July 19, 1935, for "threatening and frightening a white woman," suffered PHYSICAL torture for a few short hours. But what psychological havoc is being wrought in the minds of the white children? Into what kinds of citizens

Figure 49.2 Circular of the National Association for the Advancement of Colored People, 1935
Source: NAACP.

visual strategies designed to mitigate the dangers. During the peak years of the anti-lynching struggle, for example, the African American press rarely pictured lynched bodies in isolation and, even when doing so, nearly always focused commentary less on black pain than on the barbarism of the white crowd (Wood 2011: 199, 206).

Aesthetics and/as visual politics

Even this brief recounting of one particular case illustrates a few general conclusions about photography and the visual politics of violence. The first was asserted at the beginning of this chapter: taking and displaying photographs of violent scenes involves not only recording and conveying information but also producing effects and affects by fashioning a way of seeing. Second, we can now recognise the role of pragmatics in doing that work: visual politics is, crucially, a matter of how photographs are *used*, and by whom. Third, however, critical engagement with a *constitutively violent* photograph must not simply denounce the photographic gaze in question (although denunciation may prove helpful) but show its workings, undermining it by constructing, inviting or reinforcing another optics and, thereby, in Haraway's (1991: 193) words, another "politics of positioning." That leads to a final claim, one complementing but complicating the emphasis on pragmatics: whereas "aestheticising" is rarely the political problem when photographs engage violence, aesthetics *are* integral to photography's political work. In concluding, let us elaborate the point, one so fundamental yet so often overlooked or disputed.

Begin with Alexander Nehamas' (2007: 92) understanding of an object's "aesthetic features" as those it "shares only with other objects from which it can't be distinguished," features that can be established only by experiencing the object "or an identical copy of it." The political importance of a photograph's distinguishing, hence aesthetic, features – matters of what we call both "form" and "content" – is not at odds with the contingency and variability of meaning and effects seen in the history of lynching. Consider, again, how the use of lynching postcards in creating both white supremacist and anti-lynching publics relied on the perspective lodged inside the frame. In many political contexts, a description of an image, no matter how detailed, accurate and effective, cannot substitute for the image itself. For the same reasons, it matters – at least it can and often will – whether a protest deploys one image or another. To assume otherwise is to treat the signifying, affective and performative possibilities of any given picture in any given context as infinitely malleable, denying images' non-verbal qualities and ignoring *how* photography and photographs help fashion ways of seeing. It is, essentially, to deny the visual shaping of the political. Stressing the importance of visual shaping entails acknowledging the entanglement of politics and aesthetics.

But what follows from this acknowledgement? Even a brief answer requires pursuing the claim in a broader way than Nehamas's account allows. Jacques Rancière (2009: 72), however, can aid the pursuit. "Aesthetic experience," he argues, "has a political effect to the extent that . . . it . . . disrupts the way in which bodies fit their functions and destination," creating "a multiplicity of folds and gaps in the fabric of common experience," and thereby changes "the cartography of the perceptible, the thinkable and the feasible." Such "cartographic" changes, we might say, enable violence to be perceived differently – and picturing differently is one key way to make the cartography shift. Such shifts are often the stuff and the stakes of political life. Rancière (2003: 226) thus rightly takes his line of inquiry as not simply a commentary on images or artworks but an account of the political: "politics," he argues, "is aesthetic in that it makes visible what had been excluded from a perceptual field," thereby inscribing "one perceptual world within another." Making visible in this way is one of the most important tasks photography can perform. Aesthetics lies at the heart of visual politics.

50 War

James Der Derian

Every age has its own kind of war, its own limiting conditions, and its own peculiar
preconceptions.

Carl von Clausewitz, *On War* (1989: 593)

Were he to teleport from his age to ours, Clausewitz might understandably be pleased
to discover that *On War,* with considerable credit due to his wife, had taken on the
timeless category of a "classic." But what would Clausewitz make of our age's "own
kind of war?" Ever the dialectician, he might weigh the new against the persistence
of his own "peculiar preconceptions" of war, as a duel on a larger scale, a forceful
act to compel others to do our will as well as a continuation of politics by other means.
He could also accommodate the current decline in state-sponsored wars as merely a
matter of differing *appearances*, a thought that Clausewitz famously mooted (if never
fully pursued) when he wrote of war as "planned in a mere twilight, which in addition
not infrequently – like the effect of a fog or moonlight – gives to things exaggerated
dimensions and unnatural appearance."

A question, then, for Clausewitz in our over-mediated times: What if the essence
of war, diffused by ubiquitous media, now lies firmly in its *spectral* phenomenology?

We might then posit as the peculiar preconception of our age a new kind of war:
visual war, defined by acts of observing highly affective images that enable as well
as delimit new conditions of violence. Such wars take as little as two clicks to launch:
one to capture and one to send an image, most often by mobile phone. This is obviously
not just any image but one that entangles neural and external networks in a collective
paroxysm of pain and pleasure, that effectively (and perversely) locates pleasure in
the meting out of pain to others. After the big bang of a singular act of violence, visual
war is then amplified through the *e*-motive power of the image, in the dual sense of
emotional images observed and radially transmitted at high speeds.

From the image of war to the war of images

After a few thousand shares of such images, the captured moment scales up into a
free-floating incident; after a million hits the incident becomes a global event; and
then, between the blink of an eye and one bad decision, a crisis erupts. At light-speed,
an electromagnetic battlespace subsumes the kinetic battlefield; informational stratagems
displace military strategies; and non-, para- and anti-state actors vie with states for
full-spectrum dominance in a new global heteropolarity. As visual effect, the image

of war is displaced by a war of images. Recorded, transmitted and observed on multiple platforms, visual war becomes the continuation of politics by means of a networked global media.

Up to this point, not too much violence has been done to Clausewitz and the classical sense of war. However, when the new actors, new technologies and new configurations of power constantly reshaping the nature of visual war are entangled by ubiquity, simultaneity and interconnectivity of multiple media, classical war gives way to a much weirder version of visual war.

The historical evolution of visual war tracks – but is not wholly determined by – new technologies of representation. From the first use of cameras in the Crimean, US Civil and Franco-Prussian Wars, visual war has been part of official war-making. Tracking black budgets and gnomic bureaucratic acronyms in the US after the Second World War and the beginning of the Cold War, one finds an early proliferation of national security organisations in which imagery plays a critical role. At the apex of surveillance and secrecy would be the National Reconnaissance Office, set up in 1960 but only officially (and accidentally acknowledged) in 1973, to collect image as well as signals intelligence for the US Defence Department and other intelligence agencies, including the National Geospatial-Intelligence Agency, which was known as the National Imagery and Mapping Agency until 2003. Most recently, linking boots on the ground to eyes in the sky, Information, Surveillance, Target Acquisition and Reconnaissance (ISTAR) gives a technological edge and asymmetrical advantage to visual warriors. Operating across strategic levels and symbolic fields, visual war is tasked to oversee, foresee and if necessary pre-empt any potential threat; or in military parlance, to deter, disrupt and destroy the seen enemy.

The globalisation of the threat matrix through open and closed networks of information and imagery, many of them extra-terrestrial, augment regular, irregular, as well as hybrid warfare. No longer delimited by national borders, imminent threats and the ability to identify proximal foes from homogeneous friends, visual war takes on an amorphous, even spectral, quality.

The surveillant nature and targeting imperatives of visual war produce a convergence of warfare and software, or what we might call *warware*: a digitally enabled form of full-spectrum violence that phase-shifts from kinetic to electro-magnetic, visible to invisible in a blink, literally, of an eye. (Perhaps the Greeks, who thought sight came from fires in our head, were not too far off the mark.) A combination of hard and soft technologies of power, warware operates – or at least is designed to operate – as a system of systems for a world of random and unpredictable events with non-linear and emergent effects produced by multi-variant and multi-versal causes. However, like all new technologies of power, warware comes with its own particular accidents, commensurable forms of resistance, and, as every new form of power produces new forms of resistance (*viz* Foucault), the risk of *malware* that insinuates its way into a system by offering itself as cure, say, for a slow micro-processor or better drone-imaging, but, like all pharmacotic algorithms, has the capacity to do much more harm than the disease or original problem. Hidden in code, they take on the character if not the incredibility of conspiracy.

At the very moment when we most need to comprehend the changing nature of warfare, official secrecy and proprietary interests step in to cloud our understandings of visual war. There is as well a technological lag at work that can produce metaphysical effects: viewers once searched the new phenomenon of photography for spectral evidence of dead loved ones; audience members rushed from theatres when first shown cinematic images of an oncoming train. The *ancien régime* of perception is replaced by new modes of technological representation.

However, it is not merely a question of "catching up" to technological advances or uncovering some truth hidden by misperception. Any attempt to understand visual war must also consider, in a highly reflexive manner, how our modes of observation and comprehension have a direct impact if not constructive effect on phenomena under scrutiny; and, in turn, how networked modes of observation can actually "produce" new global conflicts.

A few media theorists, perhaps most consistently Paul Virilio (1989) and Friedrich Kittler (1997), have written perceptively on this coeval development of new modes of visual media and modern warfare. Looking back while projecting forward, Virilio (1988: 4–7) wrote:

> From now on everything passes through the image. The image has priority over the thing, the object, and sometimes even the physically-present being. Just as real time, instantaneousness, had priority over space. Therefore the image is invasive and ubiquitous. Its role is not to be in the domain of art, the military domain or the technical domain, it is to be everywhere, to be reality. . . . I believe that there is a war of images. . . . And I can tell you my feelings in another way: winning today, whether it's a market or a fight, is merely not losing sight of yourself.

Indeed, most of the largest and boldest headlines of the twenty-first century – technologically enabled, media-amplified terror against the US, a global financial crash, coming cyberwars, and the transformation of the internet into a "systematic snooping operation" – seem to have already been previewed by Virilio in the twentieth century (Virilio 1998).

Virilio's analysis of the shifting technological aspects of visual war offers the best update of Clausewitz. Emerging from the Second World War innovation of radar, television provided the medium and the motive for a videographic revolution. By the first Gulf War, video – cheaper to shoot, faster to edit and easier to broadcast than film – had become the medium of choice on, and even more critically, above the battlefield. As has been the case with almost every preceding format of media, video conveys as well as exercises a spectral (in both senses of the word) power that often exceeds conventional modes of perception and cognition. When electro-magnetic and kinetic spectra converge in visual wars, perceptual fields and rational analysis strain to keep up.

When social media is added to the visual mix, matters become even more complicated. Networked, proliferated and accelerated by multi-platform transmedia, images of war are instantaneously googled, wikied and twittered into branded identities and virtual realities. We have seen, from the first smart-bomb images of the Gulf War to the WikiLeaked gun-camera images of the Iraq War, how images of violence, no matter how degraded, night-scoped or pixelated, grab more eyeballs and engender more controversial interpretations than even the most well-crafted print story. We have seen how the shrink-sized video camera, made ubiquitous by the mobile phone, amplifies a local incident into a global crisis. And we have seen what happens when the same cameras shift focus to the next war; the crisis of the moment disappears into the blackest of news holes.

Visual war

As the modes of observation, representation and execution of war become complexly entangled on multiple screens and platforms, we must venture even further afield from the traditional social as well as physical sciences. This means recognising that while one particular kind of war might be in decline, global violence remains as a viable option in the face of intractable political differences, social injustices, cultural struggles for recognition. The emergence of the nation-state and the concomitant spread of reason, rights and prosperity might well have resulted in global decrease in the level of state-on-state violence. But these metrics, based on linear Enlightenment demarcations of space and time, fail to account for the displacement, acceleration and perception of violent effects emanating from pre-, post- and non-state actors that shift identities and addresses with every attempt to deter, disrupt and destroy them.

Visual war, peculiarly preconceived, as Clausewitz would have it, is on the rise. This kind of reiterative and emergent violence does not lend itself to the assumptions of rational action, methods of linear regression or hopes for a progressivist future that drive much of international relations thinking today. States, democratic or not, might be inclined less to use violence to achieve political goals. However, now individuals with access to networked technologies for the preparation, execution and *visualisation* of violence, can do more damage to a system, be it state or corporate, organic or inorganic, physical or psychological, than at any time in history. Following pathways worn by conditions of uneven development, visual war will continue to oscillate from classical to quantum and back again. But networked global media, as the trigger and transmitter, catalyst and conveyor of global events, has produced a multiverse of wars, a virtual realm but with all too real effects. If that sounds weird, so be it: to morph the gonzo journalist Hunter S. Thompson and theoretical physicist Freeman Dyson, "when the going gets weird, the weird need to go quantum."

51 Witnessing

Alex Danchev

For many of those who traffic in images, producers and consumers alike, witnessing is an essential part of the project. Witness testimony is evidence, and something more than evidence. The act of witness is not confined to the laws or the scriptures, though it smacks a little of both. Witnessing shapes history and memory. All over the world, the political culture is saturated in images and image-makers clamouring to bear witness.

It is often remarked that artists bear witness. They have done so since the beginning of time. It is less often remarked that works of art themselves bear witness (Danchev 2009, 2016). The most celebrated example in recent memory may be Picasso's *Guernica* (1937), reproductions of which were worn as a badge of honour by anti-war protestors on the eve of the Iraq War in 2003: warning and witnessing at the same time. Another example is Klee's *Angelus Novus* (1920) – Walter Benjamin's "angel of history" – a survivor who bears witness to the terrible twentieth century. Ironically, when it comes to witnessing, the testimony of the author of the act is not always to be trusted. Artists (and other makers of graven images) are rarely explicit or programmatic; often they obfuscate their purpose. Occasionally, someone makes a statement. The mottos of Goya's *Disasters of War* (1810–20) are legendary: "One cannot look at this." "I saw it." "This is the truth." In the Western canon, or the Western way of witness, Goya is the gold standard. He testifies from personal observation, according to the simplest definition of the witness: one present as spectator or auditor (hence eye-witness or ear-witness). His testimony is ineradicable; it is etched in the cultural memory of an entire continent.

War artists who came after him, war photographers in particular, have Goya on their shoulders. Don McCullin, one of the best of them, made those mottos his own. In his autobiography he recalls coming on a father and two sons lying in a pool of their own blood in a stone house in Cyprus during the conflict of the 1960s. He is riveted by the scene, as much for the tableau as the tragedy. It is as if he has been called upon to act; that is to say, to witness. McCullin is an ethical professional, with an active conscience. Still rooted to the spot when the rest of the family returns, he is suddenly conscious of trespassing with his camera. But the survivors are content for him to do what he has to do. "When I realised I had been given the go-ahead to photograph," he writes:

> I started composing my pictures in a very serious and dignified way. It was the first time that I had pictured something of this immense significance and I felt as if I had a canvas in front of me and I was, stroke by stroke, applying the composition

to a story I was telling myself. I was, I realised later, trying to photograph in a way that Goya painted or did his war sketches.

(McCullin 2002: 47)

McCullin's counterpart James Nachtwey is perhaps the most exacting ethical professional in the business. He is remorseless. At the beginning of his signature collection, *Inferno* (1999), he quotes Dante: "Through me is the way to join the lost people." Nachtwey has been to Hell on our behalf; he is intimately familiar with the place, all nine circles of it. He keeps going back to tell the tale – to bear witness – whether we like it or not. "Nachtwey's photographs are an odd, compelling combination of misery and serenity, of horrible content and stylised form," observes Susie Linfield. "But the perfection of their compositions – their so-called beauty – should not deflect us: Nachtwey's photographs are brutal, and they show us more than we can bear. But not more than we need to see" (Linfield 2010: 211).

Moral witness

There are many ways of witnessing, and a degree of fuzziness to much of the thinking about it. Despite a vast outpouring of historical studies, cultural studies, memory studies and even philosophical studies, it remains a rather elusive subject, as to the basics of who, and when, and how, and why, and larger questions of equal pertinence: to what end, and to what effect? Part of the problem may be its excess baggage – juridical, ethical and even spiritual – as the *Oxford English Dictionary* serves to reveal. "Applied to the individual testimony of conscience," it says, citing a verse from the Bible (2 Corinthians 1: 12): "For our rejoicing is this, the testimony of our conscience, that in simplicity and godly sincerity . . . we have had our conversation in the world." Witnessing may not change the world, but having that conversation marks it, tempers it, and sometimes rubs it red raw. The act of witnessing is not a neutral act. It does not leave things as the witness finds them. It does not spare feelings. The witness spares nothing and nobody, not even the witness. That is the idea – to prick the conscience, to lodge in the memory, or stick in the throat. In this sense, the witness is more akin to an agitator than a bystander, but also more purposive, more principled, more pure. If the bystander is a deeply compromised figure, the witness is a profoundly elevated one. Put differently, the witness is a historical agent with a moral purpose and a militant faith, in Avishai Margalit's (2002: 155) words, "that in another place or another time there exists, or will exist, a moral community that will listen to their testimony."

Margalit's exposition of the "moral witness" is a scrupulous and suggestive treatment, deservedly influential. His moral witness has a lot to live up to, however, being at once special case and ideal type. Margalit applies strict criteria for admission to this select company. The only ones who qualify are those who have direct, personal experience of radical evil and its consequences, those who have "knowledge-by-acquaintance of suffering," as he puts it. The paradigm case is probably a survivor of the camps, like Primo Levi or Elie Wiesel, or the Terror and the Gulag (Vasily Grossman, Aleksandr Solzhenitsyn), or torture (Henri Alleg, Jean Améry). Somewhat weaker cases might include those with knowledge-by-acquaintance of systemic persecution and incarceration in the Eastern Bloc in its Cold War heyday (Václav Havel, Adam Michnik), or the multiple degradations of military dictatorships (Ariel Dorfman, Wole Soyinka), or –

bringing it all back home – Guantánamo (Moazzam Begg, Mohamedou Ould Slahi). Astonishingly, Slahi wrote 122,000 words of his Guantánamo diary in a single-cell segregation hut in Camp Echo, in 2005. It was published ten years later, after a prolonged legal battle. The author remained in captivity, but his book was free at last (though heavily redacted). His account is untutored, and surprisingly measured. He is insistent on only one thing: he must make himself heard. He must testify. "Please," he tells his Administrative Review Board, "I want you guys to understand my story okay, because it really doesn't matter if they release me or not, I just want my story understood" (Slahi 2015: xix) As a witness, he has a conspicuous virtue: he is eminently capable of imagining a moral community that will listen to his testimony. He addresses them in his summing up:

> I don't even know how to treat this subject. I have only written what I experienced, what I saw, and what I learned first-hand. I have tried not to exaggerate, nor to understate. I have tried to be as fair as possible, to the US government, to my brothers, and to myself. I don't expect people who don't know me to believe me, but I expect them, at least, to give me the benefit of the doubt. And if Americans are willing to stand for what they believe in, I also expect public opinion to compel the US government to open a torture and war crimes investigation. I am more than confident that I can prove every single thing I have written in this book if I am ever given the opportunity to call witnesses in a proper judicial procedure, and if military personnel are not given the advantage of straightening their lies and destroying evidence against them.
>
> (Slahi 2015: 369)

For Margalit, moral witnesses of this ilk are insiders rather than outsiders; they are inside the story they have to tell, unlike photographers or filmmakers or reporters, concerned or unconcerned, embedded or unembedded. They are "special agents of collective memory," promoting "thick identity" based upon "thick relations," that is to say, a felt sense of shared ties, human and cosmopolitan. Their moral standing is assured, not only by their fortitude, but also by their resolve – the moral witness deliberately accepts the personal risk.

The notion of the moral witness is a compelling one. Undaunted by the excess baggage, it succeeds in capturing the ethical impulse that is fundamental to the very idea of witnessing. The act of witness is axiomatically linked to the exercise of conscience. The moral witness is a kind of conscientious objector. But is she alone in that? The Margalit model of moral witness is persuasive enough, as far as it goes, yet it appears to impose certain limitations on the subject – in particular, as to who, and when, and how.

The thrust of the argument about insider and outsider is surely right – witnessing is not a spectator sport, and witness tourism no more acceptable than war tourism – but the distinction is not so simple to maintain. During the Occupation, for example, the artist Jean Fautrier moved in Resistance circles in Paris; his studio was a *rendez-vous*. In 1943, he was arrested by the Gestapo and briefly imprisoned. After his release, he went into hiding in a sanatorium on the outskirts of the city, and began work on a series of abstract, head-like forms called *Hostages* (1943–5), a response to the sounds he could hear from his window: screams of torture and shots of executions. Fautrier was an ear-witness. Ostensibly, he had nothing to say, but *Fautrier l'enragé*, as Jean

Paulhan called him, was impelled to act. "One can't be painting apples while heads are rolling," he declared. His testimony, in his own idiom, was as searing as any. The *Hostages* were exhibited in 1945, immediately after the Liberation. They testified eloquently to man's inhumanity to man. At the same time they were an attestation to human dignity. Fautrier had found a way to imagine the unimaginable. Championed by the likes of André Malraux and Francis Ponge, his extraordinary act of witness echoed across post-war Europe. It continues to resonate.

Witnessing (moral or otherwise) may be done after the fact. Paradoxical as it may seem, the act of witness need not be instantaneous or contemporaneous. Robert Capa's celebrated dictum, "If your pictures aren't good enough, you're not close enough," does not apply, if the burden of that dictum is to prescribe a kind of action shot, a close-up in the moment. Unquestionably, "I was there" can deliver a visceral charge. Capa's D-Day landings are sufficient proof of that; and McCullin's shell-shocked soldier returns to haunt us at regular intervals. But powerful witnessing happens after the battle – after the war – sometimes long after. Simon Baker has noted "the capacity of photography to bear witness even (or especially) at removes of several decades" (Baker and Mavlian 2014: 200).

Post-witness

This form of witness we might call "post-witness," by analogy with "post-memory," the term proposed by Marianne Hirsch to comprehend the folk memory (or family memory) of successor generations, whose connection to the original event or source is not through recollection, as she says, but through "imaginative investment and creation" (Hirsch 1997: 21). Post-witness is exemplified in a recent project, which is also an anniversary project, by Chloe Dewe Mathews (born 1982), *Shot at Dawn* (2014). Arresting alike in its clarity and its humanity, *Shot at Dawn* is not immediately recognisable as an act of witness, or indeed as a morally cogent act at all. It is at first sight a suite of landscape photographs: bucolic scenes, for the most part, a path beaten through a field, a snow-covered wood, a stream. They are plainly titled, as if marked on the map: "Vanémont, Vosges, Lorraine," "Verbranden-Molen, West-Vlaanderen," "Klijtebeek stream, Dikkebus, Ieper" – Ypres or "Wipers" to the Tommies who had the misfortune to fetch up there. They are big – big enough for the viewer to lose himself, or his bearings, but not his moral compass. These are the sites at which British, French and Belgian soldiers were executed for cowardice and desertion during the Great War.

The complete series comprises 23 photographs, of which a sample may be inspected in various exhibitions. Inspection is invited, or incited, by a gnawing awareness of their back story – the slow realisation of their slow realisation – and by the deadpan data accompanying each one.

Here are two examples of Chloe Dewe Mathews' *Shot at Dawn,* commissioned by the Ruskin School of Art at the University of Oxford as part of 14–18 NOW, WW1 Centenary Art Commissions.

In an era of the "global War on Terror," the naming itself is an act of witness. *Shot at Dawn*, it transpires, is a resurrection – not a body-snatching but a revisiting, an investigation of the record, an invitation to think again.

The record was effectively concealed for a long period; the story remained untold until very recently. In 2006, the Ministry of Defence announced that 306 soldiers

Figure 51.1 Image of woodland in winter: Soldat Ahmed ben Mohammed el Yadjizy; Soldat Ali
        ben Ahmed ben Frej ben Khelil; Soldat Hassen ben Ali ben Guerra el Amolani;
        Soldat Mohammed Ould Mohammed ben Ahmed, 17:00/15.12.1914. Verbranden-
        Molen, West-Vlaanderen. Chloe Dewe Mathews

Source: Chloe Dewe Mathews, *Shot at Dawn*, commissioned by the Ruskin School of Art at the University of
Oxford as part of 14–18 NOW, WW1 Centenary Art Commissions.

convicted of desertion in the face of the enemy and executed during the Great War
were to be posthumously pardoned. Each of the countries immediately involved is
wrestling with its own painful history, though in each case the brutality of summary
justice was leavened with a certain residual compassion (or caution). In Britain, the
vast majority of those sentenced to death were pardoned at the time; of over 3,000
convictions for capital offences, 346 were carried out. In Belgium, the proportions
were somewhat similar: of 220 convictions, 18 were carried out. In France, of 412
convictions during a summer of mutinies in 1917, 55 were carried out. The names,
dates and times of these executions appear in court-martial proceedings. The locations,
however, are difficult to establish with precision. Dewe Mathews is the first person to
explore them systematically, camera at the ready.

Shot at Dawn is a documentary project, first and foremost, but there is more to it
than that. These photographs bear witness, one hundred years after the event. Like her
distinguished forebears, Dewe Mathews is not merely a shutter-operator but a thinker-
photographer. "These places have been altered by a traumatic event," she reflects. "By

photographing them, I am reinserting the individual into that space, stamping their presence back onto the land, so that their histories are not forgotten" (Baker and Mavlian 2014: 211). Every photograph is a certificate of presence, as Roland Barthes pointed out. Fundamentally, this is a moral position. Dewe Mathews is a moral witness. *Shot at Dawn* is excavatory, testamentary, perhaps even reparatory. In every sense, the plot is subject to scrutiny. Those bucolic scenes, soaked in meaning, are sites of memory, no doubt, but also sites of self-examination, for spectators of all sorts. In the final analysis, these photographs are little histories of conscience – a centenary of conscience – inventories of its excitation and reinterpretation over time.

They are also examples of exactitude: an ethical attribute. Witnessing imposes its own exacting requirements. In the case of *Shot at Dawn*, an approximate location or an approximate time of day would nullify the core concept. Similarly, for Simon Norfolk, a photographer who follows the wars and the massacres, inspecting the ground and the guilty secrets sown there, precise knowledge of the gravesites and the killing fields is of vital importance, for the credibility of the work and the veracity of the witness (Kennedy and Patrick 2014: 223–6). As Mr Cogito knew, in these matters accuracy is essential. From "Mr Cogito on the Need for Precision," in Zbigniew

Figure 51.2 Image of dyke: Private Henry Hughes, 05.50/10.4.1918. Klijtebeek stream, Dikkebus, Ieper, West-Vlaanderen. Chloe Dewe Mathews

Source: Chloe Dewe Mathews, *Shot at Dawn*, commissioned by the Ruskin School of Art at the University of Oxford as part of 14–18 NOW, WW1 Centenary Art Commissions.

Herbert's *Report from a Besieged City* (1983), a witnessing of Warsaw under martial law:

> a spectre is haunting
> the map of history
> the spectre of indeterminacy
>
> . . .
>
> we count the survivors
> and an unknown remainder
> neither known to be alive
> nor definitively deceased
> are given the bizarre name
> of the lost
>
> . . .
>
> but in these matters
> accuracy is necessary
> one can't get it wrong
> even in a single case
> in spite of everything
> we are our brothers' keepers

(Herbert 2008: 404–8)

The witness stands against indeterminacy. "Something that furnishes evidence or proof of the thing or fact mentioned," offers the *OED*; "an evidential mark or sign, a token." On the battlefields of the Great War, many of the lost are still missing. The Thiepval Memorial to the Missing of the Somme (1928–32) is one such sign, inscribed with the names of the 72,195 officers and men who died there between 1915 and 1918, who have no known grave. Memorials, too, bear witness. Lost and found, we have need of this token. Witnessing does not right wrongs; it makes possible their reappraisal.

Witnessing is intimately bound up with suffering. Death is the common currency. "And so they are ever returning to us, the dead," as W.G. Sebald reminds us. Bearing witness is good, it seems, but occasionally it is too much. After 9/11, public witness to the "jumpers" from the World Trade Center was disallowed, and the photograph of the famous "falling man" effectively suppressed; the deaths are recorded as homicide due to blunt trauma. Suicide (on our side) is indeed more than we can bear. "We cannot bear reality," muses David Levi Strauss (2003: 185). "But we bear images – like stigmata, like children, like fallen comrades. We suffer them. We idealise them. We believe them because we need what we are in them." Sometimes, we refuse them. Yet they have a way of getting under our skin. In the preamble to the remarkable work of witness to the lives of the poor sharecroppers of Alabama in the Great Depression, *Let Us Now Praise Famous Men* (1941), in collaboration with the photographer Walker Evans, the writer James Agee poses a series of unforgettable questions (Agee and Evans 2006: 7). Every act of witness asks the same. "Who are you who will read these words and study these photographs, and through what cause, by what chance, and for what purpose, and by what right do you qualify to, and what will you do about it?"

Acknowledgements

I

I would like to start by thanking everyone at Routledge: Nicola Parkin, Lucy Frederick, Craig Fowlie, Lydia De Cruz as well as the series editors, Jenny Edkins and Nick Vaughan-Williams. They have been exceptionally supportive and patient with me and I am grateful to them for this. Like most books, this one took far longer to complete than I would have liked. I had been working for most of my academic career on issues related to aesthetics and images. So I jumped at the opportunity when, half a dozen years ago, Jenny approached me with the idea of a volume on images and politics. I wrote a proposal and received exceptionally insightful comments from three referees. It is completely my fault that it took so long to translate all this into these pages.

A particularly big thanks goes to all the contributors. They have been great to work with. I know that book chapters don't count for much in the academic world, so I appreciate all the more their commitment, effort and expertise. Some of the contributors I have known for a long time, others I have "met" in the context of this project. Either way I hope this is the beginning of a continuous dialogue on visual politics.

I am grateful to Bill Callahan for our ongoing conversations about visual global politics over several years – and, in particular, for pushing me to embrace not just images but also visual artefacts and the myriad ways in which they "do" things. Thanks also for his invitation to present my introduction to the Visual International Politics workshop at the LSE in June 2016. Although the discussion and feedback were virtual, it was exceptionally useful: thanks, in particular, to Debbie Lisle, Iver Neumann and Cindy Weber. Feedback was also much appreciated when I presented aspects of this project at other venues. Thanks to Shine Choi and Erzsébet Strausz for the invitation to their September 2014 workshop on "What does Aesthetics Want from IR?" at the University of Warwick, and for comments from James Brassett, Nick Robinson, Rune Saugmann, Shirin Rai, Marysia Zalewski and, again, Debbie Lisle. Thanks also for invitations to two workshops at the University of Sydney, one by James Der Derian in February 2014 on "Peace and Security in a Quantum Age," and one by Megan MacKenzie in November 2015 on "Images in International Politics." I appreciated feedback from the organisers and all the participants, most notably Rebecca Adler-Nissen, Stefan Elbe, Jairus Grove, Charlotte Epstein, Caitlin Hamilton, Carolin Kaltofen, Katina Michael, Christopher Neff, Laura Shepherd, Johan Spanner, Colin Wight and, especially, Lene Hansen, who has provided feedback and exceptionally insightful comments on numerous other occasions too. Indeed, I am very grateful to Lene – as well as to David Campbell – for years of ongoing discussions on visual politics. May these conversations continue.

For concrete and exceptionally useful feedback on various drafts of the introduction I would like to thank Alex Bellamy, Sally Butler, Bill Callahan, David Campbell, Stephen Chan, Alex Danchev, Constance Duncombe, Simone Molin Friis, Lene Hansen, Frank Möller, Iver Neumann, Cindy O'Hagen, Eric Louw, Anca Pusca, David Shim, Gillian Whitlock.

My home institution, the University of Queensland, kindly gave me a sabbatical in semester I/2016, which allowed me to complete a big part of the editing job. Thanks to Tim Dunne, Richard Devetak and Kath Gelber. I am particularly grateful to UQ's Faculty of Humanities and Social Science for funding our Visual Politics Strategic Research Program. Thanks in particular to Joanne Tompkins, Rachel Smith and Justin Nicholls. This allowed us to establish a supportive interdisciplinary community of like-minded scholars. We are over fifty researchers so I can't name them all here, but let me just symbolically thank those who provided feedback on parts of the project: Dan Angus, Morgan Brigg, Sally Butler, Nicole George, Matthew Horsey, Sebastian Kaempf, Marguerite La Caze, Tom O'Regan, Heloise Weber, Martin Weber, Gillian Whitlock and everyone at the seminar I presented on the ominous day of 9 November 2016. Also big thanks to Shreya Singh, Eglantine Staunton, Federica Caso and Paul Crawford for their fantastic work on the text and on copyright issues.

Special thanks go to my partner Emma, my fellow thinker-writer and always my first and most acute and insightful reader. She is an inspiration in every sense of the word. This text – and my life – is so much better thanks to her. Work on this book coincided with numerous and far bigger challenges we had to face together. It is only thanks to our teamwork that we emerged victorious at the other end. Thanks also to my mother and sister, Lucia and Brigitte, who are half a world away for much of the year but at the same time always there.

II

This book is dedicated to Alex Danchev, who very unexpectedly died in August 2016 while we were in the process of completing this book. Alex was a good friend and one of the most generous, genuine and creative scholars I have ever met: a true role model in every sense of the word.

I consciously refrained from writing a conclusion to this book, as I had originally planned. I wanted to give Alex the last word. His chapter on "Witnessing" serves as a conclusion. I would like to finish here with a few short remarks in his honour because his work inspired much of the approach we took in this book.

III

Alex followed his passions, and his passions lay in creative research and writing and in exploring ever new ways of understanding the political. Alex got his hands dirty. He did it in archives, in libraries, in museums, and he did it wherever his research took him.

I remember, decades ago, how my supervisor at the University of British Columbia, Kal Holsti, told us how the formidable Susan Strange juxtaposed scholars who work like farmers and those who work like rangers. The former dutifully plough their well defined fields and do not dare to move beyond them. Rangers, Strange is said to have said, are those who branch out and venture beyond delineated fields into the dangerous but rewarding unknown.

Alex was neither farmer nor ranger: he was an astronaut. He went further than anyone else. He completely disregarded – and in doing so dismantled – disciplinary boundaries. He was traditional but had no time for narrow intellectual traditions. He defied all expectations of what an international relations scholar is meant to be and do.

Alex wrote extensively on the Anglo-American alliance. He wrote biographies of military figures and moral philosophers, such as Oliver Franks and Basil Liddell Hart. He wrote on a range of international relations topics, from war to terrorism and foreign policy. And then, at some point, he started to branch out into other realms, most notably by exploring links between art and politics. He wrote two fascinating books on that topic (Danchev 2009, 2016; see also Danchev and Lisle 2009). But he went much further than that. He started to write biographies of artists, first a short one on Picasso (2008b) and then two massive and very well received and widely discussed volumes on Braque (2005) and Cézanne (2012).

The very idea that an international relations professor would write artist biographies is heretic. But that he became very successful and highly respected in both of these fields is truly remarkable. Add to this that he regularly wrote commentaries on a wide range of topics for more popular outlets, most notably, but not only, for the *Times Higher Education Supplement*, where he had been a regular commentator for over two decades. In an obituary, Matthew Reisz (2016) called him a "polymath who was happy to stray well beyond the expected boundaries of his day job." And so he did. Alex wrote on an incredibly wide range of topics, from politics to art and society. In a piece about the jazz musician Charles Lloyd's innovative late period, Alex found the very model for his own compulsion to branch out and explore ever new worlds: "The elders mix freely, regardless of tribe. Lloyd plays tenor and alto saxophone, bass and alto flutes, and a modern ecstatic tarogato, a Hungarian folk instrument" (Danchev 2008a). And so did Alex.

IV

An issue that was very close to Alex's heart – and an issue I passionately share with him and we tried to apply in this book – is the one of writing style. Alex hated academic jargon. He did not write of norm entrepreneurs, of biopolitics, of ontologies, of empty signifiers or of dependent and independent variables. Alex wrote straight from the heart, in clear and compelling sentences. His language was music: it was infused with rhythm and sound and it encapsulated his passion for art and the political. The editor of the *Times Literary Supplement*, Ann Mroz, called him "the best writer I ever commissioned; I suspect he always will be" (cited in Reisz 2016).

The only way to appreciate Alex's appreciation for language and his ability to mould words and ideas is to read him. His biography of Cézanne is a good example. Go and read it. But, for now, just a short illustration, taken from a passage in which Alex discusses Georges Braque's *The Guitar Player,* painted in 1914:

> An entire tradition of visual representation was overthrown, as if a hand grenade had been tossed into the placid world of the reclining nude, the wedding feast and the woman reading a letter. Everything was shattered, discomposed, only to be remade anew, askew, back-to-front, inside-out, all around. Space itself was reconceived and reconstructed. Instead of receding tidily into the background, as prescribed by traditional perspective, the forms in Cubist paintings advance towards

the spectator. Landscapes become landslips. Still life pushed forward, begging to be touched, or sampled, or played. We see into things, round things, through things, without prejudice; we see the component part of things; we see things become things.

(Danchev 2009: 58)

V

Finally and most importantly is Alex's passion for and contribution to visuality and creativity in the study of global politics.

Alex was never one to play it safe. He took risks in his research by crossing taboo disciplinary boundaries. He ignored academic conventions and wrote about what mattered to him – and to many others – in real life.

Creativity was at the heart of what Alex did, and he combined it with visuality. He pioneered the study of art and politics. He did so because he had a deep conviction that, as he once put it, "contrary to popular belief, it is given to artists, not politicians, to create a new world order" (Danchev 2016: 91). He was convinced that works of art – as works of the imagination – can help us address some of the most pressing political themes of our times. And he convincingly showed us so, covering topics that ranged from terrorism and torture to memory and identity, and though aesthetic fields

Figure A.1 Village outside Champagne

Source: Roland Bleiker, September 2013.

Figure A.2 Village outside Champagne
Source: Roland Bleiker, September 2013

as diverse as photography, painting, film, novels and poetry. Alex forced us to see the world anew, to notice things that were not there before, to challenge assumptions that we had taken for granted. There were no limits to his curiosity. In his own words, he wanted to "put the imagination to work in the service of historical, political and ethical inquiry" (Danchev 2009: 2, see also Danchev 2014 and 2016: 1). Photography – just to pick one of many aesthetic and visual realms he engaged – was for Alex an "instrument of the imagination." War photography, which was traditionally shot in black-and-white, was for Alex the new war poetry: "Men-at-arms are shot and shot again, shot in black-and-white. . . . The dead and the wounded bleed black blood; the young bleed into the old" (Danchev 2009: 33).

In view of Alex's passion to combine words and images and the imagination, I offer two Magritte-like photographs here. I took them on the train home after a conference in Bordeaux in 2013. Alex and I were presenting together on panels about "Art and Politics." The photographs depict the very same view of the very same village, just outside of Champagne. There is only one difference: an alteration in shutter-speed and aperture. It is the kind of subversive and playful visual exploration Alex would have liked. Or so I hope, for they remind us that we always frame the world in particular ways and, in doing so, reveal as much about us and our choices than about the actual world out there.

VI

I can't say for sure, of course, but my sense is that all these issues were in Alex's mind when he died. I know he was working hard to complete his third artist biography, another massive volume, on Magritte. I know he was close to finishing a draft and his wife Dee says there is hope that the book will come out posthumously.

He was also preoccupied with exploring how artists serve as moral witnesses of our time – or of times past (Danchev 2016: 28). He did so at the last conference panel we were on together, in Glasgow in 2014. And he died just a few days before he was meant to speak on this topic at the Edinburgh Book Festival.

Alex will live on through his work. He will continue to pose difficult questions to us and he will give us the courage to take risks and be creative.

The book is dedicated to you, Alex. You wanted witnessing to be a process that makes us see the world anew, that "rubs it red raw" (Danchev, Chapter 51). You always tried to resist all forms of finalities and the sense of complacency that comes with them (Taylor 2016). You always wanted to pose new questions – questions that would help us re-think, re-view and re-feel the world around us. You were a moral witness of your time. May your writings live on and may they continue to rub us red raw.

Note

My remarks on Alex Danchev draw, with permission, on Bleiker 2016: 13–21.

Contributors

Linda Åhäll is Lecturer in International Relations at Keele University, UK. Her research covers the intersections of gender politics and security studies, often through popular/everyday culture. She is the author of *Sexing War/Policing Gender: Motherhood, Myth and Women's Political Violence* (2015), and co-editor of *Emotions, Politics and War* (with Tom Gregory, 2015) and *Gender, Agency and Political Violence* (with Laura J. Shepherd, 2012).

Ariella Azoulay is Professor of Modern Culture and Media and the Department of Comparative Literature, Brown University. Her books include *From Palestine to Israel: A Photographic Record of Destruction and State Formation, 1947–1950* (Pluto Press, 2011), *Civil Imagination: The Political Ontology of Photography* (Verso, 2012) and *The Civil Contract of Photography* (Zone Books, 2008).

Roland Bleiker is Professor of International Relations at the University of Queensland, where he coordinates an interdisciplinary research program on Visual Politics. His research has introduced aesthetics, visuality and emotions to the study of global politics. Recent publications include *Aesthetics and World Politics* (2009/2012) and, as co-editor with Emma Hutchison, a forum on "Emotions and World Politics" in *International Theory* (2014).

Jordan Branch is Assistant Professor in the Department of Political Science at Brown University. He received his PhD in political science from the University of California, Berkeley, and was the Hayward R. Alker Postdoctoral Fellow at the Center for International Studies, at the University of Southern California in 2011/12. His first book, *The Cartographic State: Maps, Territory, and the Origins of Sovereignty*, was published in 2014 by Cambridge University Press. His research has also been published in *International Organization*, the *European Journal of International Relations*, and *International Theory*.

James Brassett is Reader in International Political Economy at the University of Warwick. He works on the politics of global ethics with a focus on everyday discourses of global governance, crisis and resistance. His first book is entitled *Cosmopolitanism and Global Financial Reform* (Routledge, 2010/2013) and he is currently working on the portrayal of morality and tragedy in films about the global financial crisis.

Sally Butler is Associate Professor in Art History in the School of Communication and Arts, the University of Queensland. Her publications are in the area of contemporary and twentieth-century visual arts. She has curated numerous exhibitions about Australian Indigenous art and photography. Her most recent publication, co-authored with Roland Bleiker, is 'Radical Dreaming: Indigenous Art and Cultural Diplomacy,' *International Political Sociology*, 2016.

William A. Callahan is Professor of International Relations at the London School of Economics and Political Science. As part of his research on culture, politics and visual international relations, Callahan makes documentary films: *China Dreams* was broadcast on KCET (Los Angeles) in 2015, and *toilet adventures* (2015) was shortlisted for a major award by the UK's Arts and Humanities Research Council. For these and other films, see Callahan, 'Digging to China' on Vimeo.

David Campbell is a writer, professor and producer, with interests in visual journalism, the changing media economy and international politics. He is an Honorary Professor in the School of Political Science and International Studies at the University of Queensland, and Director of Communications and Engagement, World Press Photo Foundation, Amsterdam.

Stephen Chan OBE is Professor of World Politics at SOAS University of London, where he was also the Foundation Dean. He was 2015 Konrad Adenauer Chair of Academic Excellence at Bir Zeit University, and 2016 George Soros Chair of Public Policy at Central European University. Cambridge University Press will be publishing his study of the 2013 Zimbabwean elections and Polity Press his new book on non-Western international relations thought and practice.

Shine Choi is Lecturer in the School of People, Environment and Planning at Massey University. Her publications include *Reimagining North Korea in International Politics: Problems and Alternatives* (Routledge, 2015) and journal articles and book chapters on love, the colour grey, conflict and aesthetics.

Mark Chou is Associate Professor of Politics at the Australian Catholic University, Melbourne. His writings on democracy have been published in numerous scholarly outlets and include his latest book, *Democracy against Itself: Sustaining an Unsustainable Idea* (Edinburgh University Press, 2014). He is the co-editor of *Democratic Theory: An Interdisciplinary Journal* (Berghahn).

Lilie Chouliaraki is Professor at the Department of Media and Communications, LSE. She has published extensively on the nature of mediated public discourse, particularly on the relationship between spectatorship, distant suffering and cosmopolitan citizenship. Her books include *Discourse in Late Modernity* (Edinburgh University Press, 1999), *The Spectatorship of Suffering* (SAGE, 2006/2011) and *The Ironic Spectator: Solidarity in the Age of Post-humanitarianism* (Polity, 2012) which received the ICA Best Book Award in 2015.

Costas M. Constantinou is Professor of International Relations at the University of Cyprus. His research interests cover cross-cutting diplomacy, conflict, international political theory, and legal and normative aspects of international relations. He has published extensively in these areas, including, more recently, *The SAGE Handbook of Diplomacy* (2016; co-edited with P. Kerr and P. Sharp).

Alex Danchev was Professor of International Relations at the University of St Andrews at the time of his death in August 2016. He wrote extensively on art and violence, broadly conceived. Some of this work is collected in two volumes of essays, *On Art* *and War and Terror*, and *On Good and Evil and the Grey Zone*. He also wrote a number of internationally acclaimed biographies, most recently *Cézanne: A Life*.

Elizabeth Dauphinee is Professor in the Department of Political Science at York University in Toronto, where she researches and teaches in international relations, ethics and critical methodologies. She is the author of *The Politics of Exile* (Routledge, 2013), and the editor of the *Journal of Narrative Politics*.

James Der Derian is Michael Hintze Chair of International Security and Director of the Centre of International Security Studies at the University of Sydney. He writes books and produces documentaries on war, media and technology, including *After 9/11* (2003), *Virtuous War: Mapping the Military-Industrial-Media-Entertainment Network* (2009), *Human Terrain: War Becomes Academic* (2010) and *Project Z: The Final Global Event* (2015).

Klaus Dodds is Professor of Geopolitics at Royal Holloway, University of London. His latest book with Lisa Funnel is entitled *The Geographies, Genders and Geopolitics of James Bond* (Palgrave, 2017).

Nicole Doerr is Associate Professor of Sociology at the University of Copenhagen. Her work addresses questions of democracy, power and communication in culturally diverse societies. She also writes about social movements. Among her recent publications is a co-authored book with Alice Mattoni and Simon Teune on *Advances in the Visual Analysis of Social Movements*.

Jenny Edkins is Professor of International Politics at Aberystwyth University. Her research examines personhood, politics and aesthetics through studies of face politics, missing persons and trauma time. Her interests in creative practice in international politics span performance, contemporary art, image, story and memory. Her publications include *Face Politics* (2015); *Missing: Persons and Politics* (2011); and *Trauma and the Memory of Politics* (2003).

Lene Hansen is Professor of International Relations in the Department of Political Science, University of Copenhagen. She is the author of *Security as Practice: Discourse Analysis and the Bosnian War* (Routledge, 2006) and co-author (with Barry Buzan) of *The Evolution of International Security Studies* (Cambridge University Press, 2009). Since 2014 she has directed a large project on "Images and International Security" funded by the Danish Council for Independent Research.

Robert Hariman is a Professor of Rhetoric and Public Culture in the Department of Communication Studies at Northwestern University. He is the author of *Political Style: The Artistry of Power* and two volumes co-authored with John Louis Lucaites: *No Caption Needed: Iconic Photographs, Public Culture and Liberal Democracy* and *The Public Image: Photography and Civic Spectatorship*. His other publications include edited volumes on popular trials, prudence, post-realism and the texture of political action.

Emma Hutchison is an Australian Research Council DECRA Fellow in the School of Political Science and International Studies at the University of Queensland. Her work focuses on emotions and trauma in world politics, particularly in relation to security, humanitarianism and international aid. She has published widely on these topics in a range of scholarly journals and books. Her first book, *Affective Communities* *in World Politics: Collective Emotions after Trauma*, was published by Cambridge University Press in March 2016.

Heather Johnson is Senior Lecturer in International Studies at Queen's University Belfast. Her book, *Borders, Asylum and Global Non-Citizenship: The Other Side of the Fence*, was published in 2014 with Cambridge University Press and her work has appeared in journals such as *International Political Sociology*, *Security Dialogue* and *Third World Quarterly*. She is currently working on a project about irregular migration in the maritime space, funded through the ESRC Future Research Leaders scheme.

Sebastian Kaempf is Senior Lecturer in Peace and Conflict Studies at the University of Queensland. His research interests are in the ethics and laws of war, asymmetric conflicts, and the mediatisation of conflict in a transforming global media landscape. He co-convenes a website called www.thevisionmachine.com.

Katrina Lee-Koo is Associate Professor of International Relations at Monash University, Melbourne, Australia. Her research interests cover the United Nations' "Women, Peace and Security," and "Youth, Peace and Security" agendas, as well as the experiences of children and women in peace and conflict. She is the co-author of *Children and Global Conflict* (Cambridge University Press, 2015) and *Ethics and Global Security* (Routledge, 2014).

Susie Linfield is the author of *The Cruel Radiance: Photography and Political Violence* (University of Chicago Press, 2010), which was a finalist for the National Book Critics Circle Award in Criticism and has been translated into Italian, Turkish and Korean. She writes about culture and politics for a variety of publications, including the *New York Times*, the *New Republic*, *Dissent*, the *Nation*, *Guernica* and the *Boston Review*. Linfield was formerly editor in chief of *American Film*, deputy editor of the *Village Voice*, arts editor of the *Washington Post* and a book critic for the *Los Angeles Times*. She is currently an Associate Professor at New York University, where she teaches cultural journalism. She is completing a book that analyzes the writings on Zionism and the Arab–Israeli conflict of eight leftwing intellectuals in France, England and the United States.

Debbie Lisle is Professor of International Relations in the School of History, Anthropology, Philosophy and Politics at Queen's University Belfast. Her work explores the intersections of travel, power, war, mobility, security, technology, culture and visuality, and tries to uncover global politics in unexpected sites (e.g. museums, hotels, the Olympics, marathons). Her latest book is *Holidays in the Danger Zone: Entanglements of War and Tourism* (University of Minnesota Press, 2016).

John Louis Lucaites is Provost Professor of Rhetoric and Public Culture, Department of English, Indiana University. He is co-author with Celeste Condit of *Crafting Equality: America's Anglo-African World* (1993) and co-editor with Jon Simons of *In/visible War: The Culture of War in Twenty-First Century America* (2017). He and Robert Hariman are co-authors of *No Caption Needed: Photography, Public Culture, and Liberal Democracy* (2007) and *The Public Image: Photography and Civic Spectatorship* (2016).

Kate Manzo is Senior Lecturer in Human Geography in the School of Geography, Politics and Sociology at the University of Newcastle, England. Kate is a postcolonial development geographer, whose work explores the theories, policies and consequences of international development, especially as they affect the African continent. Her current research centres on images of climate change and climate policy, as well as images of Africa in Western media.

Noa Milman is a lecturer in the Sociology Department at Copenhagen University. She is working on a manuscript that explores the role of culture in shaping media response to social movements of minority women in Israel and in the United States. Her work focuses on movements of welfare mothers who resist austerity measures and welfare reforms imposed in the context of neoliberal economic globalisation.

W.J.T. Mitchell is Gaylord Donnelley Distinguished Service Professor of English and Art History at the University of Chicago. He edits the interdisciplinary journal *Critical Inquiry*. He is the author of a number of influential books on the history and theories of media, visual art and literature, including *What do Pictures Want? Essays on the Lives and Loves of Images* (Chicago, 2005), *Picture Theory* (Chicago, 1994) and *Iconology: Image, Text, Ideology* (Chicago, 1986).

Susan D. Moeller is Professor of Media and International Affairs and director of the International Center for Media and the Public Agenda at the University of Maryland. She is the author of a number of books, including *Packaging Terrorism: Co-opting the News for Politics and Profit*; *Compassion Fatigue: How the Media Sell Disease, Famine, War and Death*; and *Shooting War: Photography and the American Experience of Combat*.

Frank Möller is a Senior Research Fellow at the Tampere Peace Research Institute, Faculty of Social Sciences, University of Tampere, Finland, and co-convenor of the ECPR (European Consortium for Political Research) Standing Group on Politics and the Arts. He is the author of *Visual Peace: Images, Spectatorship and the Politics of Violence* (Palgrave, 2013) and the co-editor of *Art as a Political Witness* (Budrich, 2017). Among his most recent publications is "Politics and art," *Oxford Handbook of Political Science* (Oxford University Press, 2016).

Nayanika Mookherjee is Reader of Socio-Cultural Anthropology at Durham University. She has published extensively on the anthropology of violence, ethics and aesthetics. Recent publications include *The Spectral Wound: Sexual Violence, Public Memories and the Bangladesh War of 1971* (Duke University Press, 2015). She was guest editor of the special issue on *Aesthetics, Politics, Conflict* (*Journal of Material Culture*, 2015) and co-editor of the *Journal of the Royal Anthropological Institute* special issue *The Aesthetics of Nation*. She is currently finishing a manuscript on *Arts of Reconciliation and the Bangladesh Liberation War* for Stanford University Press.

Tanja R. Müller is Senior Lecturer in Development Studies at the Global Development Institute, and founding member and former Director of Research at the Humanitarian and Conflict Response Institute, University of Manchester. She is the author of *The Making of Elite Women: Revolution and Nation Building in Eritrea* (Brill, 2005) and *Legacies of Socialist Solidarity: East Germany in Mozambique* (Lexington, 2014). Her most recent work interrogates visual representations of development and activist citizenship as a politics of resistance among refugee populations.

Iver B. Neumann is Montague Burton Professor in International Relations at the London School of Economics and a lifelong associate of the Norwegian Institute of

International Affairs. His most recent books include *Diplomacy and the Making of World Politics* (Cambridge University Press, 2015) and, with Kevin C. Dunn, *Undertaking Discourse Analysis for Social Science Research* (University of Michigan Press, 2016).

Simon Philpott is Senior Lecturer in International Politics at Newcastle University (UK). He is the co-editor of the Routledge *Popular Culture and World Politics* book series and has long-standing interests in the intersections between politics and popular culture. Much of his research focuses on neglected areas of inquiry in international politics studies including documentary film and sports as well as the politics of electronic media.

Anca M. Pusca is an International Relations, Development and Area Studies editor at Palgrave Macmillan New York. She was previously Senior Lecturer in International Studies at Goldsmiths, University of London. Her work examines the relationship between aesthetics and politics in the post-communist, East European context. Her most recent book, *Post-Communist Aesthetics: Revolutions, Capitalism, Violence*, was published in 2015.

Shirin M. Rai is Professor in the Department of Politics and International Studies at the University of Warwick. Her current work has three strands: feminist international political economy, gender and political institutions, and politics and performance. Her latest books include *New Frontiers in Feminist Political Economy* (with Georgina Waylen), *Democracy in Practice: Ceremony and Ritual in Parliament* (editor, Palgrave, 2014) and *The Grammar of Politics and Performance* (editor, with Janelle Reinelt, Routledge, 2015).

Mark Reinhardt is Professor of Political Science and American Studies at Williams College. Among his visual projects are books he co-edited for shows he co-curated: *Kara Walker: Narratives of a Negress* (MIT, 2003, Rizzoli, 2007) and *Beautiful Suffering: Photography and the Traffic in Pain* (Chicago, 2007). He is currently working on a book titled *Visual Politics: Theories and Spectacles*.

Nick Robinson is Associate Professor in Politics and International Studies at the University of Leeds, UK. His research focuses on the militarisation of social media and the politics of videogames. He has published in journals such as *Perspectives on Politics*, *Political Studies* and *Millennium: Journal of International Studies*. He is presently working on a book about military videogames for Routledge and on a project about militarisation, gender and social media, funded by the Swedish Research Council.

Piers Robinson is Professor of Politics, Society and Political Journalism at the University of Sheffield. He researches communications, conflict and world politics with a current focus on organised persuasive communication and contemporary propaganda. He is co-author of *Pockets of Resistance: British News Media, War and Theory in the 2003 Invasion of Iraq* (Manchester University Press, 2010) and *The CNN Effect: The Myth of News, Foreign Policy and Intervention* (Routledge, 2002).

Rune Saugmann is a Post-doctoral Fellow at University of Tampere, where he conducts interdisciplinary research on the visual mediation of security. His work has appeared in outlets such as *Security Dialogue*, *European Journal of International Relations*, *Journalism Practice* and *European Journal of Communication*.

Michael J. Shapiro is Professor of Political Science at the University of Hawaii. He has published widely on such diverse topics as political theory and philosophy, critical social theory, global politics, politics of media, politics of aesthetics, politics of culture, and indigenous politics.

Laura J. Shepherd is Professor of International Relations at the University of Sydney. She has published widely on gender and security in scholarly journals such as *Journal of Narrative Politics*, *European Journal of International Relations*, and *International Feminist Journal of Politics*. She is the author/editor of eight books, including *Gender Matters in Global Politics* (Routledge, 2015) and *Gender, Violence and Popular Culture: Telling Stories* (Routledge, 2013).

David Shim is Assistant Professor at the Department of International Relations and International Organization at the University of Groningen. He is interested in the modes of representation that are central for the constitution of global politics. Among others, he has explored comics, film, photography and satellite imagery with regard to their specific politics of representation. His work appeared in *International Political Sociology, International Studies Review, Geoforum* and *Review of International Studies*. His book *Visual Politics and North Korea* is available at Routledge. David has translated some of his research activities into teaching practice and can be viewed on his blog "Visual Global Politics."

Sharon Sliwinski is Associate Professor of Information and Media Studies at the University of Western Ontario in Canada. She is author of *Human Rights in Camera* (2011), *Dreaming in Dark Times: Six Exercises in Political Thought* (2017), and co-editor, with Shawn Michelle Smith, of *Photography and the Optical Unconscious* (2017).

Brent Steele is the Francis D. Wormuth Presidential Chair and Professor of Political Science at the University of Utah. His research and teaching focus on US foreign policy, aesthetics, international security, international relations theory, collective memory, and international ethics. He is currently working on a project investigating restraint in global politics.

Elspeth Van Veeren is Lecturer in Political Science in the School of Sociology, Politics and International Studies at the University of Bristol and a resident at the Pervasive Media Studio at the Bristol Watershed. Specialising in the security cultures and foreign policy of the United States, she has published work on torture and popular culture, and on the visual and material power associated with detention and interrogation practices at Joint Task Force Guantanamo. Her latest project is a study of power, secrecy and security.

Cynthia Weber is Professor of International Relations at the University of Sussex, UK, and a documentary filmmaker. Her work critically engages various forms of hegemony, particularly those found in US foreign policy, gender and sexuality, and constructions of US Americanness. Her latest book is *Queer International Relations: Sovereignty, Sexuality and the Will to Knowledge* (Oxford University Press, 2016).

Lauren Wilcox is University Lecturer in Gender Studies and Deputy Director of the University of Cambridge Centre for Gender Studies. Her book *Bodies of Violence: Theorizing Embodied Subjects in International Relations* was published in 2015 with Oxford University Press and was awarded the Best Book prize from the ISA

Theory Section in 2016. Her current work addresses questions of global violence, posthumanism and feminist/queer theory.

Erin K. Wilson is the Director of the Centre for Religion, Conflict and the Public Domain, Faculty of Theology and Religious Studies, University of Groningen, the Netherlands. She works at the intersection of religious studies and international relations, deploying critical perspectives on religion and secularism to analyse contemporary global political issues. Her current research interests include global justice, forced migration, freedom of religion or belief, gender and development, climate change, and the politics of countering violent extremism.

Kalpana Wilson is a lecturer in Geography at Birkbeck, University of London. Her research explores questions of race/gender, labour, neoliberalism and visual representations in development. She is the author of *Race, Racism and Development: Interrogating History, Discourse and Practice*, Zed Books, 2012.

Marysia Zalewski is Professor of International Relations at Cardiff University. Her research focuses on feminist enquiry. She is currently working on critical projects on sexual violence and knowledge production in international relations. Key publications include her 2013 *Feminist International Relations: Exquisite Corpse* (Routledge) and the "man question" books (with Jane Parpart).

Illustrations

Figures

Table

Bibliography

Abe, Kobo (2003) *The Face of Another*, New York: Vintage Books.

Abruzzo, Margaret (2011) *Polemical Pain: Slavery, Cruelty, and the Rise of Humanitarianism*, Baltimore, MD: Johns Hopkins University Press.

Abu-Lughod, Lila (2002) 'Do Muslim women really need saving? Anthropological reflections on cultural relativism and its others,' *American Anthropologist* 104, 3: 783–90.

Abu-Lughod, Lila (2013) *Do Muslim Women Need Saving?*, Cambridge, MA: Harvard University Press.

Ad Council (2004a) *I am an American (2001–Present)*, www.adcouncil.org/default.aspx?id.141 (accessed March 2013).

Ad Council (2004b) *I am an American (2001–Present)*, available from: www.aef.com/exhibitions/social_responsibility/ad_council/2486 (accessed August 2007).

Adams, Parveen (1996) *The Emptiness of the Images: Psychoanalysis and Sexual Differences*, London: Routledge.

Adamson, Fiona (2006) 'Crossing borders: International migration and national security,' *International Security* 31, 1: 165–99.

Adib (1957) 'Life and letters: Art by the square yard,' *Times of India*, 14 June: 6.

'Aesthetic' (1971) in *The Compact Edition of the Oxford English Dictionary*, Oxford: Oxford University Press.

'Aestheticize' (1971) in *The Compact Edition of the Oxford English Dictionary*, Oxford: Oxford University Press.

Agamben, Giorgio (1998) *Homo Sacer: Sovereign Power and Bare Life*, Stanford, CA: Stanford University Press.

Agee, James and Walker Evans (2006) *Let Us Now Praise Famous Men*, London: Penguin.

Ahmed, Sara (2004) *The Cultural Politics of Emotion*, London: SAGE.

Ahmed, Sara (2014) *The Cultural Politics of Emotion*, 2nd ed. Edinburgh: Edinburgh University Press.

Akerman, James R. (1995) 'The structuring of political territory in early printed atlases,' *Imago Mundi* 47:138–54.

Akhtar, Shaheen, Suraiya Begum, Hameeda Hossein, Sultana Kamal and Meghna Guhathakurta, eds (2001) *Narir Ekattor O Juddhoporoborti Koththo Kahini* [Oral history accounts of women's experiences during 1971 and after the war], Dhaka: Ain-O-Shalish-Kendro.

Alexander, Jeffrey C. (2012) *Trauma: A Social Theory*, Cambridge: Polity.

Allan, Stuart (2011) 'Documenting war, visualizing peace: towards peace photography' in Ibrahim Seaga Shaw, Jake Lynch and Robert A. Hackett, eds, *Expanding Peace Journalism: Comparative and Critical Approaches*, Sydney: University of Sydney Press, 147–67.

Allan, Stuart and Kari Andén-Papadopoulos (2010) '"Come on, let us shoot!": WikiLeaks and the cultures of militarization,' *TOPIA: Canadian Journal of Cultural Studies* 23–4: 244–53.

Allemang, John (2001) 'Day of infamy communicating horror,' *Globe and Mail*, 12 September, available at: www.theglobeandmail.com/arts/day-of-infamy-communicating-horror/article4152803/ (accessed October 2017).

Alloula, Malek (1986) *The Colonial Harem*, Minneapolis: University of Minnesota Press.

Alsultany, Evelyn (2007) 'Selling American diversity and Muslim American identity through nonprofit advertising post-9/11,' *American Quarterly* 59, 3: 593–622.

Alsultany, Evelyn (2012) *Arabs and Muslims in the Media: Race and Representation after 9/11*, New York: New York University Press

Amer, Amena (2015) 'A white British Muslim,' LSE Research Festival Exhibition, available at: http://eprints.lse.ac.uk/63004/ (accessed October 2017).

Amoore, Louise (2007) 'Vigilant visualities: The watchful politics of the War on Terror,' *Security Dialogue* 38, 2: 215–32.

Amoore, Louise (2013) *The Politics of Possibility: Risk and Security beyond Probability*, Durham, NC: Duke University Press.

Amnesty International (2014) 'Ukraine: Mounting evidence of war crimes and Russian involvement,' available at: www.amnesty.org/en/latest/news/2014/09/ukraine-mounting-evidence-war-crimes-and-russian-involvement (accessed October 2017).

Anaïs, Seantel and Kevin Walby (2016) 'Secrecy, publicity, and the bomb: Nuclear publics and objects of the Nevada Test Site, 1951–1992,' *Cultural Studies*, 30, 6: 949–68.

Anderson, Barton L. and Jonathan Winawer (2005) 'Image segmentation and lightness perception,' *Nature* 434: 79–83.

Anderson, Benedict (1983) *Imagined Communities: Reflections on the Origin and Spread of Nationalism*, London: Verso.

Anderson, Carol (2016) *White Rage: The Unspoken Truth of Our Racial Divide*, London: Bloomsbury.

Ankersmit, Franklin R. (1996) *Aesthetic Politics: Political Philosophy beyond Fact and Value*, Stanford, CA: Stanford University Press.

Anonymous (2000) *A Woman in Berlin: Eight Weeks in the Conquered City – A Diary* (trans. Philip Boehm), New York: Picador.

Anonymous (2015) 'Awkward Apec fashion: What the world leaders wore in pictures,' *Guardian*, 17 November, available at: www.theguardian.com/world/gallery/2015/nov/17/awkward-apec-fashion-what-the-world-leaders-wore-in-pictures (accessed October 2017).

Antonowicz, Anton (2002) '20M face starvation in world's worst tragedy since Ethiopia,' *Daily Mirror*, 21 May, available at: www.thefreelibrary.com/20M+FACE+STARVATION+IN+WORLD'S+WORST+TRAGEDY+SINCE+ETHIOPIA%3B+Crops. . .-a086118731 (accessed October 2017).

Apel, Dora (2004) *Imagery of Lynching: Black Men, White Women, and the Mob*, New Brunswick, NJ: Rutgers University Press.

Apel, Dora (2008) 'Lynching photographs and the politics of public shaming,' in Dora Apel and Shawn Michelle Smith, eds, *Lynching Photographs*, Berkeley: University of California Press.

Apel, Dora (2012) *War Culture and the Contest of Images*, New Brunswick, NJ: Rutgers University Press.

Apel, Dora and Shawn Michelle Smith (2008) *Lynching Photographs*, Berkeley: University of California Press.

Arendt, Hannah (1949) 'The rights of man, what are they?' *Modern Review* 3, 1: 24–36.

Arendt, Hannah (1951) 'The decline of the nation state and the end of the rights of man,' in Hannah Arendt, *The Origins of Totalitarianism*, New York: Schocken Books.

Arendt, Hannah (1992) *Lectures on Kant's Political Philosophy*, ed. Ronald Beiner, Chicago: University of Chicago Press.

Arendt, Hannah (2000) *The Portable Hannah Arendt*, ed. Peter Baehr, New York: Penguin.

Arnon, Ben (2011) 'How Obama "hope" poster reached a tipping point and became a cultural phenomenon,' *Huffington Post*, 25 May, available at: www.huffingtonpost.com/ben-arnon/how-the-obama-hope-poster_b_133874.html (accessed January 2017).

Asad, Talal (2003) 'Redeeming the "human" through human rights,' In *Formations of the Secular: Christianity, Islam, Modernity,* Stanford, CA: Stanford University Press, pp. 127–58.

Ashworth, Lucian (2014) *The History of International Thought*, New York: Routledge.

Augé, Étienne (2002) 'Hollywood movies: Terrorism 101,' *Cercles,* 5: 147–63.

Austin, Naomi (2006) 'The world's first face transplant,' BBC *Horizon,* available at: www.youtube.com/watch?v=iMYzvBfqoq4 (accessed October 2017).

Azoulay, Ariella (2001) *Death's Showcase: The Power of Image in Contemporary Democracy*, Cambridge, MA: MIT Press.

Azoulay, Ariella (2008) *The Civil Contract of Photography*, New York: Zone Books.

Azoulay, Ariella (2012) *Civil Imagination: A Political Ontology of Photography*, New York: Verso.

Bach, Steven (2007) *Leni: The Life and Work of Leni Riefenstahl*, New York: Alfred A. Knopf.

Baer, Ulrich (2002) *Spectral Evidence: The Photography of Trauma*, Cambridge, MA: MIT Press.

Baines, Erin K. (2004) *Vulnerable Bodies: Gender, the UN and the Global Refugee Crisis*, Aldershot: Ashgate.

Baines, John (1989) 'Communication and display: The integration of early Egyptian art and writing,' *Antiquity* 63, 240: 471–82.

Bains, Inderdeep (2013) 'How we can't stop complaining about the weather: Average Briton whines about the elements for four MONTHS of their life,' *Daily Mail*, 13 April, available at: www.dailymail.co.uk/news/article-2316861/Average-Briton-whines-weather-months-life.html (accessed October 2017).

Baker, John C., Kevin M. O'Connell and Ray A. Williamson, eds (2001) *Commercial Observation Satellites: At the Leading Edge of Global Transparency*, Santa Monica, CA: RAND.

Baker, Simon and Shoair Mavlian, eds (2014) *Conflict, Time, Photography*, London: Tate.

Bakir, Vian (2013) *Torture, Intelligence and Sousveillance in the War on Terror: Agenda-Building Struggles*, London: Ashgate.

Bal, Mieke (2005) 'The commitment to look,' *Journal of Visual Culture* 4, 2: 145–62.

Barad, Karen (2007) *Meeting the Universe Halfway: Quantum Physics and the Entanglement of Matter and Meaning*, Durham, NC: Duke University Press.

Barber, Benjamin R. (2000) *A Passion for Democracy: American Essays*, Princeton, NJ: Princeton University Press.

Barber, Peter (1979) *Diplomacy: The World of the Honest Spy*, London: British Library.

Bartelson, Jens (2006) 'We could remember it for you wholesale: Myths, monuments and the construction of national memories,' in Duncan Bell, ed., *Memory, Trauma and World Politics: Reflections on the Relationship between Past and Present*, London: Palgrave, pp. 33–53.

Barth, Fredrik, ed. (1969) *Ethnic Groups and Boundaries*, Oslo: Norwegian University Press.

Barthes, Roland (2003 [1964]) 'Rhetoric of the image,' in Liz Wells, ed., *The Photography Reader*, London and New York: Routledge, pp. 114–25.

Barthes, Roland (1967) 'The death of the author,' *Aspen*, 5–6.

Barthes, Roland (1977) *Image, Music, Text* (trans. Stephen Heath), London: Fontana Press.

Bauman, Richard (1989) 'Performance' in *International Encyclopedia of Communications*, New York: Oxford University Press, vol. 3, pp. 262–6.

Beaman, Lori G. (2012) 'Battles over symbols: The "religion" of the minority versus the "culture" of the majority,' *Journal of Law and Religion* 28, 1: 101–38.

Beaman, Lori G. and Winnifred Fallers Sullivan (2013) 'Neighbo(u)rly misreadings and misconstrues: A cross-border conversation,' in Lori G. Beaman and Winnifred Fallers Sullivan, eds, *Varieties of Religious Establishment*, Abingdon and New York: Routledge, pp. 1–13.

Bearak, Barry (2003) 'Why famine persists,' *New York Times Magazine*, 13 July, available at: www.imaging-famine.org/images/pdfs/12.pdf (accessed October 2017).

Beck, Ulrich (2006) *The Cosmopolitan Vision*, Cambridge: Polity Press.

Becker, Jo and Scott Shane (2012) 'Secret "kill list" proves a test of Obama's principles and will,' *New York Times*, 29 May, available at: www.nytimes.com/2013/05/29/world/obamas-leadership-in-war-on-al-qaeda.html (accessed October 2017).

Behdad, Ali and Luke Gartlan (2013) *Photography's Orientalism: New Essays on Colonial Representation*, Los Angeles: Getty.

Beier, J. Marshall, ed. (2009) *Indigenous Diplomacies*, New York: Palgrave Macmillan.

Bellamy, Alex J. (2012) *Massacres and Morality: Mass Atrocities in the Age of Civilian Immunity*, Oxford: Oxford University Press.

Benjamin, Walter (1968) 'The work of art in the age of mechanical reproduction,' in Hannah Arendt, ed., *Illuminations*, New York: Schocken Books.

Benjamin, Walter (1999 [1934]) 'The author as producer,' in *Walter Benjamin: Selected Writings, Volume 2, part 2, 1931–1934*, ed. Michael W. Jennings et al., Cambridge, MA: Harvard University Press.

Benthall, Jonathan (1993) *Disasters, Relief, and the Media*, London: I.B.Tauris.

Berger, John (1972) *Ways of Seeing*, London: Penguin Books.

Berger, John (1991) *About Looking*, New York: Vintage Books.

Berlant, Lauren (1997) *The Queen of America Goes to Washington City: Essays on Sex and Citizenship*, Durham, NC: Duke University Press.

Berlin, Isaiah (1982) 'The originality of Machiavelli,' in *Against the Current: Essays in the History of Ideas*, ed. Henry Hardy, London: Penguin Books, pp. 33–100.

Bhabha, Homi K. ed. (1990) *Nation and Narration*, London: Routledge.

Bigo, Didier (2006) 'Security, exception, ban and surveillance' in David Lyon, ed., *Theorizing Surveillance: The Panopticon and Beyond*, Cullompton: Willan, pp. 46–68.

Bjola, Corneliu and Marcus Holmes, eds (2015) *Digital Diplomacy: Theory and Practice*, Abingdon: Routledge.

Black, Ian (2015) 'Middle East still rocking from First World War pacts made 100 years ago,' *Guardian*, 30 December, available at: www.theguardian.com/world/on-the-middle-east/2015/dec/30/middle-east-still-rocking-from-first-world-war-pacts-made-100-years-ago (accessed October 2017).

Blanchot, Maurice (1995) *The Writing of Disaster* (trans. Ann Smock), Lincoln: University of Nebraska Press.

Bleiker, Roland (2000) *Popular Dissent, Human Agency and Global Politics*, Cambridge: Cambridge University Press.

Bleiker, Roland (2001) 'The aesthetic turn in international political theory,' *Millennium: Journal of International Studies* 30, 3: 509–33.

Bleiker, Roland (2002) 'Activism after Seattle: Dilemmas of the anti-globalisation movement,' *Pacifica Review: Peace, Security and Global Change*, 14, 3: 191–207.

Bleiker, Roland (2009) *Aesthetics and World Politics*, Basingstoke: Palgrave Macmillan.

Bleiker, Roland (2014) 'Visual assemblages: From causality to conditions of possibility,' in Michele Acuto and Simon Curtis, eds, *Reassembling International Theory: Assemblage Thinking and International Relations*, New York: Palgrave Macmillan, pp. 75–80.

Bleiker, Roland (2015) 'Pluralist methods for visual global politics,' *Millennium* 43, 3: 872–90.

Bleiker, Roland (2016) 'Visuality and creativity: In memory of Alex Danchev,' *New Perspectives*, 24, 2: 13–21.

Bleiker, Roland and Sally Butler (2016) 'Radical dreaming: Indigenous art and cultural diplomacy,' *International Political Sociology* 10, 1: 56–74.

Bleiker, Roland, David Campbell and Emma Hutchison (2014) 'Visual cultures of inhospitality,' *Peace Review* 26, 2:192–200.

Bleiker, Roland, David Campbell, Emma Hutchison and Xzarina Nicholson (2013) 'The visual dehumanization of refugees,' *Australian Journal of Political Science* 48, 3: 398–416.

Bleiker, Roland and Emma Hutchison (2008) 'Fear no more: Emotions and world politics,' *Review of International Studies* 34, S1: 115–35.

Bleiker, Roland and Amy Kay (2007) 'Representing HIV/AIDS in Africa: Pluralist photography and local empowerment,' *International Studies Quarterly* 51, 1: 139–63.

Bogost, Ian (2007) *Persuasive Games: The Expressive Power of Videogames*, Cambridge, MA: MIT Press.

Boltanski, Luc (1999) *Distant Suffering: Morality, Media, and Politics* (trans. Graham Burchell), Cambridge: Cambridge University Press.

Bolter, Jay David (2005) 'Preface,' in Geoff King, ed., *The Spectacle of the Real: From Hollywood to Reality TV and Beyond*, Bristol: Intellect Books.

Bolter, Jay David and Richard Grusin (2000) *Remediation: Understanding New Media*, Cambridge, MA: MIT Press.

Bolton, Alec (1964) *Walkabout's Australia: An Anthology of Articles and Photographs from Walkabout Magazine*, Sydney: Ure Smith in association with Australian National Travel Association.

Boone, Pat (2008) 'Hate is hate, in India or America,' *World Net Daily*, 6 December, available at: www.worldnetdaily.com/index.php?fa=PAGE.view&pageId=82830 (accessed October 2017).

Booth, Charlotte (2005) *The Hyksos Period in Egypt*, Princes Risborough, Buckinghamshire: Shire.

Bourdieu, Pierre (1977) *Outline of a Theory of Practice*. New York: Cambridge University Press.

Bourdieu, Pierre (1984) *Distinction: A Social Critique of the Judgement of Taste* (trans. Richard Nice), London: Routledge.

Bourke, Joanna (2007) *Rape: Sex, Violence, History*, London: Virago Press.

Bourke, Joanna (2014) *The Story of Pain*, New York: Oxford University Press.

Brassett, James and Chris Clarke (2012) 'Performing the sub-prime crisis: Trauma and the financial event,' *International Political Sociology* 6: 4–20.

Brassett, James and Lena Rethel (2015) 'Sexy money: The hetero-normative politics of global finance,' *Review of International Studies* 41, 3: 429–49.

Brassett, James and Nick Vaughan-Williams (2012) 'Governing traumatic events,' *Alternatives: Local, Global, Political* 37, 3: 183–7.

Brauman, Rony (2009) 'Global media and the myths of humanitarian relief: The case of the 2004 tsunami,' in Richard Ashby Wilson and Richard D. Brown, eds, *Humanitarianism and Suffering: The Mobilization of Empathy*, Cambridge: Cambridge University Press, pp. 108–17.

Briggs, Mrs L.K. (n.d.) 'Index and notes of 500 lantern slides, Ypres and District, 1919–1939,' in *Private Papers of Mrs L.K. Briggs*, Catalogue number: Documents 21795. Imperial War Museum Archives.

Britton, Celia (1999) *Edouard Glissant and Postcolonial Theory: Strategies of Language and Resistance*, Charlottesville: University of Virginia Press.

Bronfen, Elizabeth (2006) 'Reality check: Image affects and cultural memory,' *differences: A Journal of Feminist Cultural Studies* 17, 1: 20–46.

Brown, Michelle and Nicole Rafter (2013) 'Genocide films, public criminology, collective memory,' *British Journal of Criminology* 53, 6: 1017–32.

Brown, Rebecca M. (2009a) *Art for Modern India 1947–1980*, Durham, NC: Duke University Press.

Brown, Rebecca M. (2009b) 'Reviving the past,' *Interventions* 11, 3: 293–315.

Brown, Wendy (2002) 'Suffering the paradoxes of rights,' in Wendy Brown and Janet Halley, eds, *Left Legalism/Left Critique*, Durham, NC: Duke University Press, pp. 420–34.

Brown, Wendy (2006) *Regulating Aversion: Tolerance in the Age of Identity and Empire*, Trenton, NJ: Princeton University Press.

Brüggemann, Jörg (2015) 'Distant shores: Tourists and refugees on Kos – in pictures,' *Guardian*, 4 September, available at: www.theguardian.com/world/gallery/2015/sep/04/distant-shores-tourists-and-refugees-on-kos-in-pictures (accessed October 2017).

Brunton, Finn and Helen Nissenbaum (2015) *Obfuscation: A User's Guide for Privacy and Protest*, Cambridge, MA: MIT Press.

BT TV (2009) 'Minister: Præsten lyver,' *BT TV*, available at: www.bt.dk/bttv/clip/229/4483 (accessed Octobber 2017).

Bull, Hedley (1977) *The Anarchical Society: A Study of Order in World Politics*, New York: Columbia University Press.

Burgert, Thomas (2013) 'Metaphors in American politics: Your guide to political metaphors used in American media,' available at: www.politicalmetaphors.com/2013/12/05/cold-weather-metaphors/ (accessed October 2017).

Burke, Edmund (1790) *Reflections on the Revolution in France*, ed. L. G. Mitchell (1991), Oxford University Press: Oxford.

Burman, Erica (1994) 'Innocents abroad: Western fantasies of childhood and the iconography of emergencies,' *Disasters* 18, 3: 238–53.

Burman, Erica (2008) *Developments: Child, Image, Nation*, New York: Routledge.

Burrington, Ingrid (2016) *Networks of New York: An Illustrated Field Guide to Urban Internet Infrastructure*, New York: Melville House.

Bush, George W. (2001) 'Address to a Joint Session of Congress and the American People,' *White House*, 20 September, available at: www.whitehouse.gov/news/releases/2001/09/20010920-8.html (accessed October 2017).

Bush, Laura (2001) 'Radio address by Mrs Bush,' *The American Presidency Project*, available at: www.presidency.ucsb.edu/ws/?pid=24992 (accessed October 2017).

Butler, Judith (1990, 2006) *Gender Trouble*, London: Routledge.

Butler, Judith (1993) 'Endangered/endangering: Schematic racism and white paranoia,' in Robert Gooding-Williams, ed., *Reading Rodney King, Reading Urban Uprising*, New York: Routledge, pp. 15–22.

Butler, Judith (2009) *Frames of War: When is Life Grievable?*, London: Verso.

Butler, Judith (2011 [1993]) *Bodies that Matter: On the Discursive Limits of "Sex"*, London: Routledge.

Buzan, Barry and Lene Hansen (2009) *The Evolution of International Security Studies*, Cambridge: Cambridge University Press.

Buzan, Barry, Ole Wæver and Jaap de Wilde (1998) *Security: A New Framework for Analysis*, Boulder: Lynne Rienner.

Cadwalladr, Carole (2012) 'Don McCullin: "Photojournalism has had it: It's all gone celebrity",' *Guardian*, 22 December, available at: www.theguardian.com/artanddesign/2012/dec/22/don-mccullin-photojournalism-celebrity-interview (accessed October 2017).

Callahan, William A. (2015) 'The visual turn in IR: Documentary filmmaking as a critical method,' *Millennium* 43, 3: 891–910.

Cameron, Hazel (2013) *Britain's Hidden Role in the Rwandan Genocide: The Cat's Paw*, London: Routledge.

Campbell, David (1992) *Writing Security: United States Foreign Policy and the Politics of Identity*, Manchester: Manchester University Press.

Campbell, David (2004) 'Horrific blindness: Images of death in contemporary media,' *Journal of Cultural Research* 8, 1: 55–74.

Campbell, David (2007) 'Geopolitics and visuality,' *Political Geography* 26: 357–82.

Campbell, David (2011) 'The iconography of famine,' in Geoffrey Batchen, Mick Gidley, Nancy K. Miller and Jay Prosser, eds, *Picturing Atrocity: Reading Photographs in Crisis*, London: Reaktion Books, pp. 79–92.

Campbell, David (2014a) 'Satellite images, security and the geopolitical imagination,' in Peter Adey, Mark Whitehead, Alison Williams, eds, *From Above: War, Violence, and Verticality*, Oxford: Oxford University Press, pp. 289–98.

Campbell, David (2014b) 'The myth of compassion fatigue,' in Liam Kennedy and Caitlin Patrick, eds, *The Violence of the Image: Photography and International Conflict*, London: I.B.Tauris, pp. 97–124.

Campbell, David and Marcus Power (2010) 'The scopic regime of Africa,' in Fraser MacDonald, Rachel Hughes and Klaus Dodds, eds, *Observant States: Geopolitics and Visual Culture*, London: I.B.Tauris, 167–98.

Capra, Frank (1971) *The Name above the Title: An Autobiography*, New York: Macmillan.

Carrier, Peter (2005) *Holocaust Monuments and National Memory: France and Germany since 1989*, Oxford: Berghahn.

Carroll, John (1993) *Humanism: The Wreck of Western Culture*, London: Fontana Press.

Cartwright, Lisa (1995) *Screening the Body: Tracing Medicine's Visual Culture*, Minneapolis: University of Minnesota Press.

Carusi, Annamaria, Aud Sissel Hoel, Timothy Webmoor and Steve Woolgar, eds (2014) *Visualization in the Age of Computerization*, London: Routledge.

Carver, Terrell, ed. (2003) 'The forum: Gender/feminism/IR,' *International Studies Review*, 5, 2: 287–302.

Caso, Federica and Caitlin Hamilton, eds (2015) *Popular Culture and World Politics*, London: E-IR.

Casper, Monica J. and Lisa Jean Moore (2009) *Missing Bodies: The Politics of Visibility*, New York: NYU Press.

Chaim, Gabriel (2014) 'The sons of war: Syria's refugees – in pictures,' *Guardian*, 16 October, available at: www.theguardian.com/media/gallery/2014/oct/16/the-sons-of-war-syrias-refugees-in-pictures (accessed October 2017).

Chamayou, Grégoire (2015) *A Theory of the Drone* (trans. Janet Lloyd), London: New Press.

Chant, Sylvia (2016) 'Women, girls and world poverty: Empowerment, equality or essentialism?' *International Development Planning Review* 38, 1: 1–24.

Chant, Sylvia and Caroline Sweetman (2012) 'Fixing women or fixing the world? "Smart Economics," efficiency approaches, and gender equality in development,' *Gender and Development* 20, 3: 517–29.

Châtelet, Noëlle (2007) *Le baiser d'Isabelle: L'aventure de la première greffe du visage*, Paris: Seuil.

Chatterjee, Partha (1989) 'The nationalist resolution of the women's question,' in Kumkum Sangari and Sudesh Vaid, eds, *Recasting Women: Essays in Indian Colonial History*, New Brunswick, NJ: Rutgers University Press, pp. 233–53.

Chauhan, Riddhi (2012) 'An analysis of the Almerisa series,' Rineke Dijkstra's series: *Almerisa*, available at: http://macaulay.cuny.edu/eportfolios/seriesblog/2012/09/22/almerisa (accessed October 2017).

Cheney, Lynne V. (1988) *Humanities in America: A Report to the President, the Congress, and the American People*, Washington, DC: National Endowment for the Humanities.

Chimni, B.S. (1998) 'The geopolitics of refugee studies: A view from the South,' *Journal of Refugee Studies* 11, 4: 350–74.

Chimni, B.S. (2009) 'The birth of a "Discipline": From refugee to forced migration studies' *Journal of Refugee Studies* 22, 1: 11–29.

Chong, Denise (1999) *The Girl in the Picture: The Story of Kim Phuc, the Photograph and the Vietnam War*, New York: Penguin Books.

Chou, Mark, Roland Bleiker and Nilanjana Premaratna (2016) 'Elections as theatre,' *PS: Political Science & Politics*, 49, 1: 43–7.

Choudhary, N.S. (1955) 'Murals: To the editor, "Times of India",' *Times of India*, 3 February.

Chouliaraki, Lilie (2006) *The Spectatorship of Suffering*, London: SAGE.

Chouliaraki, Lilie (2010) 'Post-humanitarianism: Humanitarian communication beyond a politics of pity," *International Journal of Cultural Studies*, 13, 2: 107–26.

Chouliaraki, Lilie (2013a) 'Re-mediation, inter-mediation, trans-mediation: The cosmopolitan trajectories of convergent journalism,' *Journalism Studies* 14, 2: 267–83.

Chouliaraki, Lillie (2013b) *The Ironic Spectator: Solidarity in the Age of Post-Humanitarianism*, Cambridge: Polity.

Christafis, Angelique (2010) 'Cornered: Princess Hijab, Paris's elusive graffiti artist,' *Guardian*, 11 November, available at: www.theguardian.com/artanddesign/2010/nov/11/princess-hijab-paris-graffiti-artist (accessed October 2017).

Chute, Hillary L. (2010) *Graphic Women: Life Narrative and Contemporary Comics*, New York: Columbia University Press.

Claridge, Amanda (2010) *Rome: An Oxford Archaeological Guide*, Oxford: Oxford University Press.

Clarkson, Thomas (1808) *The History of the Rise, Progress, and Accomplishment of the Abolition of the Slave-Trade by the British Parliament*, Vol. II, London: Taylor.

Clausewitz, Carl von (1989) *On War*, ed. and trans. Michael Howard and Peter Paret, Princeton, NJ: Princeton University Press.

Clay, Jason W. and Bonnie K. Holcomb (1985) *Politics and the Ethiopian Famine 1984–1985*, Cambridge, MA: Cultural Survival.

Clemmensen, Lillan (2009) 'Brorson-optagelser er politiets imagepleje,' *Information*, 5 September, available at: www.information.dk/202705 (accessed October 2017).

Clifford, Bob (2002) 'Merchants of morality,' *Foreign Policy* 129: 36–45.

Cloud, David S. (2011) 'Anatomy of an Afghan war tragedy,' *Los Angeles Times*, 10 April, available at: www.latimes.com/world/la-fg-afghanistan-drone-20110410-story.html (accessed October 2017).

Clowes, Daniel (2005) *Ice Haven*, New York: Pantheon Books.

Cohen, Raymond (1987) *Theatre of Power: The Art of Diplomatic Signalling*, London: Longman.

Cohen, Stanley (2001) *States of Denial: Knowing about Atrocities and Suffering*, Cambridge: Polity.

Cohen, Will (2012) 'The Roma are coming: Ed Kashi on the misuse of photography,' *Open Society Foundations*, 13 April, available at: www.opensocietyfoundations.org/voices/roma-are-coming-ed-kashi-misuse-photography (accessed October 2017).

Cohn, Carol (1987) 'Sex and death in the rational world of defense intellectuals,' *Signs* 12, 4: 687–718.

Collins, Jane (2003) *Threads: Gender, Labor, and Power in the Global Apparel Industry*, Chicago: University of Chicago Press.

Cold War Museum (n.d.) 'Fall of the Soviet Union,' Cold War Museum, available at: www.coldwar.org/articles/90s/fall_of_the_soviet_union.asp (accessed October 2017).

Connolly, William E. (1991) *Identity/Difference: Democratic Negotiations of the Political Paradox*, Ithaca, NY: Cornell University Press.

Connolly, William E. (2016) 'Donald Trump and the new fascism,' *The Contemporary Condition*, 14 August, available at: http://contemporarycondition.blogspot.com.au/2016/08/donald-trump-and-new-fascism.html (accessed January 2017).

Constantinou, Costas M. (1994) 'Diplomatic representations . . . or who framed the Ambassadors?' *Millennium-Journal of International Studies* 23, 1: 1–23.

Constantinou, Costas M. (1996) *On the Way to Diplomacy*, Minneapolis: University of Minnesota Press.

Constantinou, Costas M. (2006) 'On homo-diplomacy,' *Space and Culture* 9, 4: 351–64.

Constantinou, Costas M. (2013) 'Between statecraft and humanism: Diplomacy and its forms of knowledge,' *International Studies Review* 15, 2: 141–62.

Constantinou, Costas M. (2016) 'Everyday diplomacy: Mission, spectacle and the remaking of diplomatic culture,' in Jason Dittmer and Fiona McConnell, eds, *Diplomatic Cultures and International Politics: Translations, Spaces and Alternatives*, Abingdon: Routledge, pp. 23–40.

Constantinou, Costas M. and James Der Derian (2010) 'Sustaining global hope: Sovereignty, power and the transformation of diplomacy' in Costas M. Constantinou and James Der Derian, eds, *Sustainable Diplomacies*, New York: Palgrave Macmillan, pp. 1–22.

Conway, Eric D. (1997) *An Introduction to Satellite Image Interpretation*, Baltimore, MD: Johns Hopkins University Press.

Conway, Janet M. (2013) *Edges of Global Justice: The World Social Forum and its 'Others'*, New York: Routledge.

Cook, Michael (2010a) *Broken Dreams*, exhibition catalogue, Brisbane, Australia: Andrew Baker Art Dealer, available at: www.andrew-baker.com/mc.html

Cook, Michael (2010b) *Through My Eyes*, exhibition catalogue, Brisbane, Australia: Andrew Baker Art Dealer, available at: www.andrew-baker.com/mc.html

Cook, Michael (2010c) *Undiscovered*, exhibition catalogue, Brisbane, Australia: Andrew Baker Art Dealer, available at: www.andrew-baker.com/mc.html

Cook, Michael (2012) *Civilised*, exhibition catalogue, Brisbane, Australia: Andrew Baker Art Dealer, available at: www.andrew-baker.com/mc.html

Cook, Michael (2013) *Majority Rule*, exhibition catalogue, Brisbane, Australia: Andrew Baker Art Dealer, available at: www.andrew-baker.com/mc.html

Cooper, Andrew F. (2008) *Celebrity Diplomacy*. Boulder: Paradigm.

Copeland, Daryl (2009) *Guerrilla Diplomacy: Rethinking International Relations*, London: Lynne Rienner.

Copenhagen Police (2011) Research interview with Copenhagen Police operational planner, Mogens Jensen.

Cornago, Noé (2013) *Plural Diplomacies: Normative Predicaments and Functional Imperatives, Leiden*: Martinus Nijhoff.

Corner, John (2007) 'Mediated politics, promotional culture and the idea of propaganda,' *Media, Culture & Society* 29, 3: 669–77.

Costello, Diarmuid (2012) 'The Question concerning Photography,' *Journal of Aesthetics and Art Criticism*, 70, 1: 101–13.

Cottle, Simon and David Nolan (2007) 'Global humanitarianism and the changing aid-media field: "Everyone was dying for footage",' *Journalism Studies* 8, 6: 862–78.

Cox, Robert W. (1981) 'Social forces, states and world orders: Beyond international relations theory', *Millennium: Journal of International Studies*1 10, 2: 126-55.

Crampton, Jeremy W. (2010) *Mapping: A Critical Introduction to Cartography and GIS*, Malden, MA: Wiley Blackwell.

Crossette, Barbara (1995) 'US seeks to prove mass killings,' *New York Times*, 11 August, available at: www.nytimes.com/1995/08/11/world/us-seeks-to-prove-mass-killings.html (accessed October 2017).

Curthoys, Ann (2002) *Freedom Ride: A Freedom Rider Remembers*, Sydney: Allen & Unwin.

Czuperski, Maksymilian, John Herbst, Eliot Higgins, Alina Polyakova and Damon Wilson (2015) 'Hiding in plain sight: Putin's war in Ukraine,' Atlantic Council of the United States, available at: www.atlanticcouncil.org/publications/reports/hiding-in-plain-sight-putin-s-war-in-ukraine-and-boris-nemtsov-s-putin-war (accessed October 2017).

Daggett, Cara (2015) 'Drone disorientations: How "unmanned" weapons queer the experience of killing in war,' *International Feminist Journal of Politics* 17, 3: 361–79.

Damon, Arwa, Michael Pearson and Ed Payne (2014) 'Ukraine: Photos show undercover Russian troops,' *CNN*, 22 April, available at: http://edition.cnn.com/2014/04/21/world/europe/ukraine-crisis (accessed October 2017).

Danchev, Alex (2005) *Georges Braque: A Life*, London: Penguin Books.

Danchev, Alex (2008a) 'Off piste: Never out of the groove,' *Times Higher Education Supplement*, 5 June, available at: www.timeshighereducation.com/features/off-piste/off-piste-never-outof-the-groove/402226.article (accessed January 2017)

Danchev, Alex (2008b), *Picasso Furioso*, Paris: Editions Dilecta.

Danchev, Alex (2009) *On Art and War and Terror*, Edinburgh: Edinburgh University Press.

Danchev, Alex (2012), *Cézanne: A Life*, London: Profile Books.

Danchev, Alex (2014), 'Anselm Kiefer at the Royal Academy,' *Times Higher Education Supplement*, 2 October, available at: www.timeshighereducation.com/features/culture/anselm-kiefer-atthe-royal-academy-cataclysmic-transformational-stupendous/2016079.article (accessed January 2017).

Danchev, Alex (2016) *On Good and Evil and the Grey Zone*, Edinburgh: Edinburgh University Press.

Danchev, Alex and Debbie Lisle (2009) 'Introduction: Art, politics, purpose,' *Review of International Studies* 35, 4: 775–9.

Danto, Arthur (2003) *The Abuse of Beauty: Aesthetics and the Concept of Art*, Chicago: Open Court.

Daston, Lorraine (2015) 'Epistemic images,' in Alina Payne, ed., *Vision and its Instruments: Art, Science, and Technology in Early Modern Europe*, University Park, Pennsylvania: Penn State University Press.

Dauber, Cori (2001) 'Image as argument: The impact of Mogadishu on US military intervention,' *Armed Forces & Society* 27, 2: 205–29.

Dauphinee, Elizabeth (2007) 'The politics of the body in pain: Reading the ethics of imagery,' *Security Dialogue* 38, 2: 139–55.

Dauphinee, Elizabeth (2008) 'War crimes and the ruin of law,' *Millennium: Journal of International Studies* 37, 1: 49–67.

Dauvergne, Elizabeth (2007) 'Security and migration law in the less brave world,' *Social and Legal Studies* 16, 4: 533–49.

Davies, Matt and Simon Philpott (2012) 'Militarization and popular culture,' in Kostas Gouliamos and Christos Kassimeris, eds, *The Marketing of War in the Age of Neo-Militarism*, London: Routledge.

De Carvalho, Benjamin and Iver B. Neumann (2014) *Small State Status-Seeking*, London: Routledge.

De Certeau, Michael (1986) *Heterologies: Discourse on the Other* (trans. Brian Massumi), Minneapolis: University of Minnesota Press.

De Goede, Marieke (2000) 'Mastering lady credit,' *International Feminist Journal of Politics* 2, 1: 58–81.

De Waal, Alex (1997) *Famine Crimes: Politics and the Disaster Relief Industry in Africa*, Oxford: James Currey.

Dean, Jodi (2002) *Publicity's Secret: How Technoculture Capitalizes on Democracy*, Ithaca, NY: Cornell University Press.

Debord, Guy (1994) *The Society of the Spectacle*, New York: Zone Books.

Debrix, François and Cynthia Weber, eds (2003) *Rituals of Mediation: International Politics and Social Meaning*, Minneapolis: University of Minnesota Press.

DeChaine, D. Robert (2005) *Global Humanitarianism: NGOs and the Crafting of Community*, Lanham, MD: Lexington.

Deibert, Ronald J. (2013) *Black Code: Inside the Battle for Cyberspace*, New York: Signal.

Deleuze, Gilles and Félix Guattari (1980) *A Thousand Plateaus: Capitalism and Schizophrenia* (trans. B. Massumi), London: Athlone Press.

Dell, Simon (2010) 'Mediation and immediacy: The press, the Popular Front in France, and the Spanish Civil War,' in Cynthia Young, ed., *The Mexican Suitcase: The Rediscovered Spanish Civil War Negatives of Capa, Chim, and Taro*, Vol. 1: The History, New York: International Center of Photography/Göttingen: Steidl.

della Porta, Donatella and Mario Diani (1999) *Social Movements: An Introduction*, Oxford: Basil Blackwell.

Der Derian, James (1987) *On Diplomacy: A Genealogy of Western Estrangement*, Oxford: Basil Blackwell.

Der Derian, James (2001) 'Global events, national security, and virtual theory,' *Millennium* 30, 3: 669–90.

Der Derian, James (2009) *Virtuous War: Mapping the Military-Industrial-Media-Entertainment Network*, 2nd edn. London: Routledge.

Derrida, Jacques and Anne Dufourmantelle (2000) *Of Hospitality*, Stanford, CA: Stanford University Press.

Descartes, René (1998) 'Optics' in Nicholas Mirzoeff, ed., *The Visual Culture Reader*, London and New York: Routledge.

Deutsche, Rosalyn (2010) *Hiroshima after Iraq: Three Studies in Art and War*, New York: Columbia University Press.

Deuze, Mark (2011) 'Media life,' *Media, Culture & Society* 33, 1: 137–48.

Devereux, Linda (2010) 'From Congo: Newspaper photographs, public images and personal memories,' *Visual Studies* 25, 2: 124–34.

Devereux, Stephen (2000) *Famine in the Twentieth Century*, Brighton: Institute of Development Studies.

Devereux, Stephen (2002) *State of Disaster: Causes, Consequences and Policy Lessons from Malawi*, London: ActionAid International.

Devereux, Stephen (2006) 'Introduction: From "old families" to "new families",' in Stephen Devereux, ed., *The New Famines: Why Famines Persist in an Era of Globalisation*, Abingdon: Routledge, pp. 1–26.

Devetak, Richard (2005). 'The Gothic scene of international relations: Ghosts, monsters, terror and the sublime after September 11,' *Review of International Studies* 31, 4: 621–43.

Dewe Mathews, Chloe (2014) *Shot at Dawn*, Madrid: Ivory Press.

DeYoung, Karen (2014) 'US releases images it says show Russia has fired artillery over border into Ukraine,' *Washington Post*, 27 July, available at: www.washingtonpost.com/world/national-security/us-releases-images-it-says-show-russia-has-fired-artillery-over-border-into-ukraine/2014/07/27/f9190158-159d-11e4-9e3b-7f2f110c6265_story.html (accessed October 2017).

Dictionary.com (n.d.) 'Climate,' Dictionary.com, available at: http://dictionary.reference.com/browse/climate (accessed October 2017).

Dieter, Heribert and Rajiv Kumar (2008) 'The downside of celebrity diplomacy: The neglected complexity of development,' *Global Governance* 14: 259–64.

Dikovitskaya, Margaret (2005) *Visual Culture: The Study of the Visual after the Cultural Turn*, Cambridge, MA: MIT Press.

Dittmer, Jason (2005) 'Captain America's empire: Reflections on identity, popular culture, and post-9/11 geopolitics,' *Annals of the Association of American Geographers* 95: 626–43.

Dodds, Klaus (2014) 'Shaking and stirring James Bond: Age, gender and resilience,' *Journal of Popular Film and Television* 42: 116–30.

Dodds, Klaus, Merje Kuus and Joanne Sharp, eds (2013) *The Ashgate Companion to Critical Geopolitics*, Farnham: Ashgate.

Dodge, Martin and Chris Perkins (2009) 'The "view from nowhere"? Spatial politics and cultural significance of high-resolution satellite imagery,' *Geoforum* 40, 4: 497–501.

Doerr, Nicole (2010) 'Politicizing precarity, producing visual dialogues on migration: Transnational public spaces in social movement,' *Forum Qualitative Social Research* 11, 2: 30.

Doerr, Nicole and Alice Mattoni (2014) 'Public spaces and alternative media practices in Europe: The case of the EuroMayDay Parade against precarity,' in Kathrin Fahlenbrach, Erling Sivertsen and Rolf Werenskjold, eds, *Media and Revolt: Strategies and Performances from the 1960s to the Present*, New York: Berghahn, pp. 386–405.

Doerr, Nicole and Noa Milman (2014) 'Working with images' in Donatella della Porta, ed., *Methods of Social Movement Analysis*, Oxford: Oxford University Press, pp. 418–45.

Doerr, Nicole, Alice Mattoni and Simon Teune, eds (2013) *Advances in the Visual Analysis of Social Movements*, Bingley: Emerald.

Dollinger, André (2003) 'The instruction of Merikare,' Reshafim, available at: www.reshafim.org.il/ad/egypt/merikare_papyrus.htm (accessed October 2017).

Domarchi, Jean, Jacques Doniol-Valcroze, Jean-Luc Godard, Pierre Kast, Jacques Rivette and Eric Rohmer (1959) 'Hiroshima Notre Amour,' *Cahiers du Cinema*, 97, July.

Donini, Antonio (2010) 'The far side: The meta functions of humanitarianism in a globalised world,' *Disasters* 34, S2: S220–S237.

Donnelly, Laura (2011) 'The high price of face transplants,' *Telegraph*, 27 March, available at: www.telegraph.co.uk/health/8408844/The-high-price-of-face-transplants.html (accessed October 2017).

Doty, Roxanne Lynn (1996) *Imperial Encounters: The Politics of Representation in North–South Relations*, Minneapolis: University of Minnesota Press.

Douzinas, Costas (2000) *The End of Human Rights*, Portland, OR: Hart.

Douzinas, Costas (2007) 'The many faces of humanitarianism,' *Parrhesia* 2: 1–28.

Dowd, Maureen (2003) 'Powell without Picasso,' *New York Times*, 5 February.

Duffield, Mark (2007) 'The symphony of the damned: Racial discourse, complex political emergencies and humanitarian aid,' *Disasters* 20, 3: 173–93.

Dyer, Richard (1997) *White*, London and New York: Routledge.

Eaton, Marcia Muldar (1998) 'Locating the aesthetic,' in Carolyn Korsmeyer, ed., *Aesthetics: The Big Questions*, Oxford: Blackwell, pp. 84–90.

Edkins, Jenny (2000) *Whose Hunger? Concepts of Famine, Practices of Aid*, Minneapolis: University of Minnesota Press.

Edkins, Jenny (2003) *Trauma and the Memory of Politics*, Cambridge: Cambridge University Press.

Edkins, Jenny (2006) 'The criminalisation of mass starvations: From natural disaster to crime against humanity,' in Stephen Devereux, ed., *The New Famines: Why Famines Persist in an Era of Globalisation*, Abingdon: Routledge, pp. 50–65.

Edkins, Jenny (2015) *Face Politics*, London: Routledge.

Edwards, Steven (2006) *Photography: A Very Short Introduction,* Oxford: Oxford University Press.

Eileraas, Karina (2003) 'Reframing the colonial gaze: Photography, ownership, and feminist resistance,' *MLN*, 118, 4: 807–40.

Eisele, John C. (2002) 'The Wild East: Deconstructing the language of genre in the Hollywood eastern,' *Cinema Journal* 41, 3, 68–94.

Eisenstein, Elizabeth L. (1980) *The Printing Press as an Agent of Change*, Cambridge: Cambridge University Press.

Eisner, Will (2008 [1985]) *Comics and Sequential Art: Principles and Practices from the Legendary Cartoonist*, New York: W.W. Norton.

Elbe, Stefan (2006) 'Should HIV/AIDS be securitized? The ethical dilemmas of linking HIV/AIDS and security,' *International Studies Quarterly* 50, 1: 119–44.

Elden, Stuart (2013) *The Birth of Territory*, Chicago: University of Chicago Press.

Elias, Juanita (2004) *Fashioning Inequality: The Multinational Company and Gendered Employment in a Globalizing World*, Aldershot: Ashgate.

Elkins, James (2003) *Visual Studies: A Sceptical Introduction*, New York: Routledge.

Elkins, James (2013) 'An introduction to the visual as argument,' in James Elkins, Kristi McGuire, Maureen Burns, Alicia Chester and Joel Kuennen, eds, *Theorizing Visual Studies: Writing Through the Discipline*, New York: Routledge, pp. 25–61.

Elkins, James, Kristi McGuire, Maureen Burns, Alicia Chester and Joel Kuennen, eds (2013) *Theorizing Visual Studies: Writing Through the Discipline*, New York: Routledge.

Ellison, Ralph (1952) *The Invisible Man*, New York: Random House.

Elsaesser, Thomas and Malte Hagener (2010) *Film Theory: An Introduction through the Senses*, London and New York: Routledge.

Eltahawy, Mona (2015) *Headscarves and Hymens: Why the Middle East Needs a Sexual Revolution*, London: Weidenfeld & Nicolson.

Engle, Karen (1992) 'International human rights and feminism: When discourses meet,' *Michigan Journal of International Law* 13: 517–80.

Enloe, Cynthia (1996) 'Margins, silences and bottom rungs: How to overcome the underestimation of power in the study of international relations,' in Steve Smith, Ken Booth and Marysia Zalewski, eds, *International Theory: Positivism and Beyond*, Cambridge: Cambridge University Press.

Enloe, Cynthia (2007) *Globalization and Militarism: Feminists Make the Link*, Lanham, MD: Rowman & Littlefield.

Erickson, Hal (2012) *Military Comedy Films: A Critical Survey and Filmography of Hollywood Releases since 1918*, Jefferson, NC: McFarland.

Evans, Brendan and Andrew Taylor (1996) *From Salisbury to Major: Continuity and Change in Conservative Politics*, Manchester: Manchester University Press.

Evans, Martin (2010) 'Harold Macmillan's "Never had it so good" speech followed the 1950s boom,' *Telegraph*, 19 November, available at: www.telegraph.co.uk/news/politics/8145390/Harold-Macmillans-never-had-it-so-good-speech-followed-the-1950s-boom.html (accessed October 2017).

Eveleth, Rose (2015) 'How many photographs of you are out there in the world?' *The Atlantic*, 30 November, available at: www.theatlantic.com/technology/archive/2015/11/how-many-photographs-of-you-are-out-there-in-the-world/413389/ (accessed October 2017).

Ewald, Francois (1999) 'The return of the crafty genius: An outline of a philosophy of precaution,' *Connecticut Insurance Law Journal* 6: 47–79.

Fabian, Johannes (1983) *Time and the Other: How Anthropology Makes its Object*, New York: Columbia University Press.

Fanon, Frantz (1986) *Black Skin, White Masks* (trans. Charles Lam Markmann), New York: Pluto Press.

Farova, Anna (2002) *Josef Koudelka*, Prague: Foto Torst.

Fehrenbach, Heide and Davide Rodogno (2015) *Humanitarian Photography*, Cambridge: Cambridge University Press.

Feldman, Allen (2005) 'On the actuarial gaze: From 9/11 to Abu Ghraib,' *Cultural Studies* 19, 2: 203–26.

Feneley, Rick (2015) 'The picture that moved a world: Why it took little Aylan to make us notice,' *Sydney Morning Herald*, 4 September, available at: www.smh.com.au/national/the-picture-that-moved-a-world-why-it-took-little-aylan-to-make-us-notice-20150903-gjebs5.html (accessed October 2017).

Ferenbok, Joseph and Andrew Clement (2012) 'Hidden changes: from CCTV to 'smart' video surveillance,' in *Eyes Everywhere. The Global Growth of Camera Surveillance*, eds. Aaron Doyle, Randy Lippert and David Lyon, London & New York: Routledge.

Fierke, Karen M. (2012) *Political Self-Sacrifice: Agency, Body and Emotion in International Relations*, Cambridge: Cambridge University Press.

Flinders, Matthew (2012) *Defending Politics*, Oxford: Oxford University Press.

Flood, Alison and Alan Yuhas (2015) 'Salman Rushdie slams critics of PEN's Charlie Hebdo tribute' *Guardian*, 27 April. available at: www.theguardian.com/books/2015/apr/27/salman-rushdie-pen-charlie-hebdo-peter-carey (accessed October 2017).

Foister, Susan, Ashok Roy and Martin Wyld (1997) *Holbein's Ambassadors: Making and Meaning*, London: National Gallery.

Foley, Fiona (2006) *The Art of Politics, the Politics of Art: The Place of Indigenous Contemporary Art*, Southport, Queensland: Keeaira Press.

Foley, Gary, Andrew Schaap and Edwina Howell, eds (2013) *The Aboriginal Tent Embassy: Sovereignty, Black Power, Land Rights and the State*, London: Routledge.

Forbes Martin, Susan (1992) *Refugee Women*, London: Zed Books.

Ford, Peter (2001) 'Europe cringes at Bush "crusade" against terrorists,' *Christian Science Monitor*, 19 September, available at: www.csmonitor.com/2001/0919/p12s2-woeu.html (accessed October 2017).

Foreign Service Institute (2013), *Protocol for the Modern Diplomat*, US Department of State.

Fortier, Anne-Marie (2008) *Multicultural Horizons: Diversity and the Limits of the Civil Nation*, London: Routledge.

Foucault, Michael (1973) *The Order of Things: An Archaeology of the Human Sciences*, Random House: New York.

Foucault, Michel (1979) *Discipline and Punish: The Birth of the Prison* (trans. Alan Sheridan), New York: Vintage Books.

Franks, Suzanne (2010) 'The neglect of Africa and the power of aid,' *International Communication Gazette* 72, 1: 71–84.

Franks, Suzanne (2013) *Reporting Disasters: Famine, Aid, Politics and the Media*, London: Hurst.

Franks, Suzanne (2014) 'Ethiopian famine: How landmark BBC report influenced modern coverage,' *Guardian*, 23 October, available at: www.theguardian.com/global-development/poverty-matters/2014/oct/22/ethiopian-famine-report-influence-modern-coverage (accessed October 2017).

Friday, Jonathan (2000) 'Demonic curiosity and the aesthetics of documentary photography,' *British Journal of Aesthetics*, 40, 3: 356–75.

Friedberg, Anne (2009) *The Virtual Window: From Alberti to Microsoft*, Cambridge, MA: MIT Press.

Friis, Simone Molin (2015) ' "Beyond anything we have ever seen": Beheading videos and the visibility of violence in the war against ISIS,' *International Affairs* 91, 4: 725–46.

Friis, Simone Molin (2017) 'Behead, burn, crucify, crush: Theorizing the Islamic State's public display of violence,' *European Journal of International Relations*. Online first.

Frosh, Paul and Amit Pinchevski, eds (2009) *Media Witnessing: Testimony in the Age of Mass Communication*, New York: Palgrave.

Funnell, Lisa and Klaus Dodds (2017) *Geographies, Genders and Geopolitics of James Bond*, London: Palgrave.

Gadamer, Hans Georg (1986) *The Relevance of the Beautiful and Other Essays* (trans. N. Walker), Cambridge: Cambridge University Press.

Gadamer, Hans Georg (1999) *Truth and Method* (trans. J. Weinsheimer and D.G. Marshall), New York: Continuum.

Gallagher, Jake (2013) 'Dropping knowledge: The cargo pant,' *GQ*, 27 May, available at: www.gq.com/style/blogs/the-gq-eye/2013/05/dropping-knowledge-the-cargo-pant.html (accessed October 2017).

Gallagher, Jake (2015) 'Why men can't stop buying camouflage prints,' *Wall Street Journal*, January 2, available at: www.wsj.com/articles/why-men-cant-stop-buying-camouflage-prints-1420207782 (accessed October 2017).

Galtung, Johan (1996) *Peace by Peaceful Means: Peace and Conflict, Development and Civilization*, London, Thousand Oaks, New Delhi: SAGE.

Gambino, Lauren, Patrick Kingsley and Alberto Nardelli (2015) 'Syrian refugees in America: separating fact from fiction in the debate' *Guardian*, 19 November, available at: www.theguardian.com/us-news/2015/nov/19/syrian-refugees-in-america-fact-from-fiction-congress (accessed October 2017).

Garlan, Yvon (1975) *War in the Ancient World: A Social History,* London: Chatto & Windus.

Gelézeau, Valérie (2011) 'The inter-Korean border region: "Meta-border" of the Cold War and metamorphic frontier of the peninsula,' in Doris Wastl-Walter, ed., *The Ashgate Research Companion to Border Studies*, Farnham and Burlington: Ashgate, pp. 325–50.

Gelézeau, Valérie (2013) 'Life on the lines: People and places of the Korean border,' in Valérie Gelézeau, Koen De Ceuster and Alain Delissen, eds, *De-Bordering Korea: Tangible and Intangible Legacies of the Sunshine Policy*, Abingdon: Routledge, pp. 13–23.

Gillmor, Dan (2010) *Mediactive*, available at http://mediactive.com/wp-content/uploads/2010/12/mediactive_gillmor.pdf (accessed August 2015).

Gillespie, Alex (2006) 'Tourist photography and the reverse gaze,' *Ethos* 34, 3: 343–66.

Girleffect (2008) 'The Girl Effect,' YouTube, available at: www.youtube.com/watch?v=WIvmE4_KMNw (accessed October 2017).

Girleffect (2010) 'The Girl Effect: The clock is ticking,' YouTube, available at: www.youtube.com/watch?v=1e8xgF0JtVg (accessed October 2017).

Girleffect (2014) 'Smart Economics,' YouTube, available at: www.youtube.com/watch?v=7kGUynM-VP0 (accessed October 2017).

Giroux, Henry (2004) 'War on Terror: The Militarising of public space and culture in the United States,' *Third Text* 18, 4: 211–21.

Giroux, Henry A. (2008) 'Militarization, public pedagogy, and the biopolitics of popular culture,' in Diana Silberman-Keller, Zvi Bekerman, Henry A. Giroux and Nicholas Burbules, eds, *Mirror Images: Popular Culture and Education*, New York: Peter Lang, pp. 39–54.

Gjerding, Sebastian, Anton Geist and Lillan Clemmensen (2009) 'Også politiets fjerde forklaring var forkert,' *Information*, 3 September, available at: www.information.dk/202529 (accessed October 2017).

Goldsby, Jacqueline (2006) *A Spectacular Secret: Lynching in American Life and Literature*, Chicago: University of Chicago Press.

Goodman, J. David (2012) 'Cover of Swiss magazine draws accusations of racism,' *The Lede*, 12 April, available at: http://thelede.blogs.nytimes.com/2012/04/12/cover-of-swiss-magazine-draws-accusations-of-racism (accessed October 2017).

Goodwin-Gill, Guy S. (1996) *The Refugee in International Law*, 2nd edn, Oxford: Clarendon Press.

Gordon, Michael R. (2014) 'Syrian's photos spur outrage, but not action,' *New York Times*, 31 October, available at: www.nytimes.com/2014/11/01/world/middleeast/syrian-photographers-record-of-deaths-generates-outrage-but-little-action.html?_r=0 (accessed January 2017).

Graham-Harrison, Emma (2016) 'Yemen famine feared as starving children fight for lives in hospital,' *Guardian*, 5 October, available at: www.theguardian.com/world/2016/oct/04/yemen-famine-feared-as-starving-children-fight-for-lives-in-hospital (accessed October 2017).

Gregg, Robert W. (1998) *International Relations on Film*, London: Lynne Rienner.

Gregory, Derek (2001) 'Colonial nostalgia and cultures of travel: Spaces of constructed visibility in Egypt,' in Nezar Alsayyad, ed., *Consuming Tradition, Manufacturing Heritage: Global Norms and Urban Forms in the Age of Tourism*, London and New York: Routledge, pp. 111–51.

Gregory, Derek (2003) 'Emperors of the gaze: Photographic practices and productions of space in Egypt, 1839–1914,' in Joan M. Schwartz and James R. Ryan, eds, *Picturing Place: Photography and the Geographical Imagination*, London and New York: I.B.Tauris, pp. 195–225.

Gregory, Derek (2011) 'From a view to a kill: Drones and late modern war,' *Theory, Culture, Society* 28: 118–215.

Gregory, Thomas (2015) 'Drones, targeted killings, and the limitations of international law,' *International Political Sociology* 9: 197–212.

Griffin, Penny (2015) *Popular Culture, Politican Economy and the Death of Feminism*, New York: Routledge.

Grossman, David (1995) *On Killing: The Psychological Cost of Learning to Kill in War and Society*, New York: Back Bay Books.

Grossman, Lev and Hannah Beech (2006) 'Google under the gun,' *Time*, 5 February, available at: http://content.time.com/time/magazine/article/0,9171,1156598,00.html (accessed October 2017).

Guha-Thakurta, Tapati, (1992), *The Making of a New Indian Art: Artists, Aesthetics and Nationalism in Bengal, c. 1850–1920*, Cambridge: Cambridge University Press.

Gunn, Tim and Ada Calhoun (2012) *Tim Gunn's Fashion Bible*, New York: Gallery Books.

Gutierrez, Miren (2006) 'A world addicted to hunger: Part 1,' Global Policy Forum, available at: www.globalpolicy.org/component/content/article/217/46189.html (accessed October 2017).

Gutkowski, Stacey (2014) *Secular War: Myths of Religion, Politics and Violence*, London and New York: I.B.Tauris.

Halbwachs, Maurice (1925, 1980, 1992) *On Collective Memory* (trans. Lewis A. Coser), Chicago: University of Chicago Press.

Hall, Amy (2011) *UNWATCHABLE*, Red Pepper, available at: www.redpepper.org.uk/unwatchable (accessed October 2017).

Hall, Rodney Bruce (1999) *National Collective Identity*, New York: Columbia University Press.

Hall, Stuart (1985) 'Signification, representation, ideology: Althusser and the post-structuralist debates,' *Critical Studies in Mass Communication*, 2, 2: 91–114.

Hall, Stuart (1997) *Representation: Cultural Representations and Signifying Practices*. London: SAGE.

Hall, Stuart (2001 [1992]) 'The West and the rest' in Stuart Hall and Bram Gieben, eds, *Formations of Modernity*, Oxford: Blackwell, pp. 257–330.

Hansen, Lene (2006) *Security as Practice: Discourse Analysis and the Bosnian War*, New York: Routledge.

Hansen, Lene (2011) 'Theorizing the image for security studies: Visual securitization and the Muhammad cartoon crisis,' *European Journal of International Relations* 17, 1: 51–74.

Hansen, Lene (2014) 'Annual Michael Hintze Lecture in International Security,' lecture presented at the University of Sydney, February 20.

Hansen, Lene (2015) 'How images make world politics: International icons and the case of Abu Ghraib,' *Review of International Studies* 41, 2: 263–88.

Hansen, Lene (2017) 'Reading comics for the field of international relations: Theory, method and the Bosnian War,' *European Journal of International Relations*, 23, 3: 581–608.

Hanusch, Folker (2015) 'Disproportionate coverage of Paris attacks is not just the media's fault,' *New Statesman*, 16 November, www.newstatesman.com/politics/media/2015/11/disproportionate-coverage-paris-attacks-not-just-media-s-fault (accessed January 2016).

Haraway, Donna (1988) 'Situated knowledges: The science question in feminism and the privilege of partial perspective,' *Feminist Studies* 14, 3: 575–99.

Haraway, Donna J. (1991) *Simians, Cyborgs, and Women: The Reinvention of Nature*, New York: Routledge.

Hariman, Robert and John Louis Lucaites (2003) 'Public identity and collective memory in US iconic photography: The image of "accidental napalm",' *Critical Studies in Media Communication* 20: 35–66.

Hariman, Robert and John Louis Lucaites (2007) *No Caption Needed: Iconic Photographs, Public Culture, and Liberal Democracy*, Chicago: University of Chicago Press.

Hariman, Robert and John Louis Lucaites (2016) *The Public Image: Photography and Civic Spectatorship*, Chicago: University of Chicago Press.

Harley, J.B. (2001) *The New Nature of Maps: Essays in the History of Cartography*, Baltimore, MD: Johns Hopkins University Press.

Harley, J.B. and David Woodward, eds (1987) *The History of Cartography*, Vol. 1: *Cartography in Prehistoric, Ancient, and Medieval Europe and the Mediterranean*, Chicago: University of Chicago Press.

Harris, Beth and Steven Zucker (2011) 'Magritte, *The Treachery of Images (Ceci n'est pas une pipe)*,' Khan Academy, available at: www.khanacademy.org/humanities/art-1010/art-between-wars/ surrealism1/v/magritte-the-treachery-of-images-ceci-n-est-pas-une-pipe-1929 (accessed October 2017).

Harrison, Paul and Robin Palmer (1986) *News out of Africa: Biafra to Band Aid*, London: Hilary Shipman.

Hartsock, Nancy (2006) 'Globalization and primitive accumulation: The contributions of David Harvey's dialectical Marxism,' in Noel Castree and Derek Gregory, eds, *David Harvey: A Critical Reader*, Oxford: Blackwell, pp. 167–90.

Harvey, David (2004) 'The "new" imperialism: Accumulation by dispossession,' *Socialist Register* 40: 63–87.

Hattori, Tomohisa (2003a) 'The moral politics of foreign aid,' *Review of International Studies* 29, 2: 229–4.

Hattori, Tomohisa (2003b) 'Giving as a mechanism of consent: International aid organizations and the ethical hegemony of capitalism,' *International Relations* 17, 2: 153–73.

Haughney, Christine (2013) 'News media weigh use of photos of carnage,' *New York Times*, 17 April, available at: www.nytimes.com/2013/04/18/business/media/news-media-weigh-use-of-photos-of-carnage.html (accessed October 2017).

Hawkins, Virgil (2011) 'Media selectivity and the other side of the CNN effect: The consequences of not paying attention to conflict,' *Media, War and Conflict* 4, 1: 55–68.

Hazbun, Waleed (2007) 'The East as an exhibit: Thomas Cook & Son and the origins of the international tourism industry in Egypt,' in Philip Scranton and Janet F. Davidson, eds, *The Business of Tourism: Place, Faith, History*, Philadelphia: University of Pennsylvania Press, pp. 3–33.

Heath, Jennifer, ed. (2008) *The Veil: Women Writers on its History, Lore, and Politics*, Berkeley: University of California Press.

Heath-Kelly, Charlotte (2015) 'Security through a failure to secure? The ambiguity of resilience at the bombsite,' *Security Dialogue* 46, 1: 69–85.

Heidegger, Martin (1977) *The Question concerning Technology and Other Essays*, New York, London: Harper Perennial.

Helleiner, Eric (2014) *The Status Quo Crisis: Global Financial Governance after the Financial Meltdown*, Oxford: Oxford University Press.

Herbert, Zbigniew, (2008) *The Collected Poems* (trans. Alissa Valles), London: Atlantic.

Herman, Edward and David Peterson (2014) *Enduring Lies: The Rwandan Genocide in the Propaganda System, 20 Years Later*, Baltimore, MD: Real News Books.

Herring, Eric and Piers Robinson (2014) 'Report X marks the spot: The British government's deceptive dossier on Iraq and WMD,' *Political Science Quarterly* 129, 4: 551–84.

Hesford, Wendy (2011) *Spectacular Rhetorics: Human Rights Visions, Recognitions, Feminisms*, Durham, NC: Duke University Press.

Higgins, Elliot (2015) 'MH17: The open source evidence,' bellingcat, available at: www.bellingcat.com/ news/uk-and-europe/2015/10/08/mh17-the-open-source-evidence (accessed October 2017).

Hight, Eleanor M. (2004) *Colonialist Photography (Documenting the Image)*, London: Routledge.

Hirsch, Marianne (1997) *Family Frames: Photography, Narrative and Post-Memory*, Cambridge, MA: Harvard University Press.

Hobbes, Thomas (2008) *Leviathan*, Oxford: Oxford University Press.

Hobsbawm, Eric and Terence Ranger, eds (1999) *The Invention of Tradition*, Cambridge: Cambridge University Press.

Höijer, Brigitta (2004) 'The discourse of global compassion: The audience and media reporting of human suffering,' *Media, Culture & Society* 26, 4: 513–31.

Holloway, David (2008) *9/11 and the War on Terror*. Edinburgh: Edinburgh University Press.

Hollyer, James, Peter Rosendorff and James R. Vreeland (2011) 'Democracy and transparency,' *Journal of Politics* 73, 4: 1191–205.

hooks, bell (1992) *Black Looks: Race and Representation*, Boston: South End Press.

Huddart, Stephen (2005) *Do We Need Another Hero? Understanding Celebrities' Roles in Advancing Social Causes*, Montreal: McGill University.

Hughes, Rachel (2003) 'The abject artefacts of memory: Photographs from Cambodia's genocide,' *Media, Culture & Society*, 25: 23–44.

Hughes, Rachel (2013) 'Geopolitics and visual culture,' in Klaus Dodds, Merje Kuus and Joanne Sharp, eds, *The Ashgate Companion to Critical Geopolitics*, Farnham: Ashgate, pp. 69–88.

Human Rights Watch (2014) 'Ukraine: Widespread use of cluster munitions,' Human Rights Watch, available at: www.hrw.org/news/2014/10/20/ukraine-widespread-use-cluster-munitions (accessed October 2017).

Huntington, Samuel (1996) *The Clash of Civilizations and the Remaking of World Order*, New York: Simon & Schuster.

Hur, Youngman (1995) *O! Hangang* [*Oh! Hangang*], Vols 1–4, Seoul: Seju Munhwa Publishing Team Mania.

Hur, Youngman (1997) 'Naui jeulmeum, naui sarang manhwaga Hur Youngman 6' [My youth, my love manhwa artist Hur Youngman 6), *Kyunghang Shinmun*, March 21: 33.

Hurd, Elizabeth Shakman (2015) *Beyond Religious Freedom: The New Global Politics of Religion*, Princeton, NJ: Princeton University Press.

Hutchison, Emma (2010) 'Trauma and the politics of emotions: Constituting identity, security and community after the Bali bombing,' *International Relations* 24, 1: 65–86.

Hutchison, Emma (2014) 'A global politics of pity? Disaster imagery and the emotional construction of solidarity after the 2004 Asian tsunami,' *International Political Sociology* 8, 1: 1–19.

Hutchison, Emma (2016) *Affective Communities in World Politics: Collective Emotions after Trauma*, Cambridge: Cambridge University Press.

Hutchison, Emma and Roland Bleiker (2014a) 'Art, aesthetics and emotionality,' in Laura J. Shepherd, ed., *Gender Matters in Global Politics*, London: Routledge, pp. 349–60.

Hutchison, Emma and Roland Bleiker (2014b) 'Theorizing emotions in world politics,' *International Theory* 6, 3: 491–514.

Hutchison, Emma, Roland Bleiker and David Campbell (2014) 'Imaging catastrophe: The politics of representing humanitarian crises,' in Michele Acuto, ed., *Negotiating Relief: The Dialectics of Humanitarian Space*, London: Hurst.

Huynh, Kim (2015) 'Child soldiers,' in Kim Huynh, Bina D'Costa and Katrina Lee-Koo, eds, *Children and Global Conflict*, Cambrdige: Cambridge University Press.

Hyndman, Jennifer (2000) *Managing Displacement: Refugees and the Politics of Humanitarianism*, Minneapolis: University of Minnesota Press.

Ibuse, Masuji (1969, 2012) *Black Rain* (trans. John Bester), New York: Kodansha.

Imaging Famine (2002a) 'Africa's dying again,' Imaging Famine, available at: www.imaging-famine.org/images/pdfs/02.pdf (accessed October 2017).

Imaging Famine (2002b) 'Children in Malawi are starving,' Imaging Famine, available at: www.imaging-famine.org/images/pdfs/01.pdf (accessed October 2017).

Infante-Cossio, Pedro *et al.* (2013) 'Facial transplantation: A concise update,' *Medicina Oral Patologia Oral y Cirugia Bucal* 18, 2: e263–71.

Inside Job (2011), DVD, Culver City, CA: Sony Pictures Home Entertainment.

International Organization of Migration (2015) 'IOM monitors latest migrant arrivals, deaths in Mediterranean,' International Organization of Migration, available at: www.iom.int/news/iom-monitors-latest-migrant-arrivals-deaths-mediterranean (accessed October 2017).

Introna, Lucas D. and Helen Nissenbaum (2000) 'Shaping the web: Why the politics of search engines matters,' *The Information Society* 16, 3: 169–85.

Iyer, Pico (1998) 'The unknown rebel,' *Time*, 13 April, available at: http://content.time.com/time/magazine/article/0,9171,988169-2,00.html (accessed October 2017).

Jansson, Peder (2001) 'Photography's dissidents: Documentarism vs. visual art? The aesthetic transformation of the documentary photograph,' *Katalog*: 42–6.

Jarvis, Mark (2005) *Conservative Governments, Morality and Social Change in Affluent Britain, 1957–1964*, Manchester: Manchester University Press.

Jay, Martin, ed. (2005) *The State of Visual Culture Studies*, special issue of *Journal of Visual Culture* 4, 2.

Jenkins, Holman W. (2010) 'Google and the search for the future,' *Wall Street Journal*, 14 August, available at www.wsj.com/articles/SB10001424052748704901104575423294099527212 (accessed October 2017).

Jenni, Karen E. and George Loewenstein (1997) 'Explaining the identifiable victim effect,' *Journal of Risk and Uncertainty* 14: 235–57.

Jha, Dwijendra Narayan (2006) 'Looking for a Hindu identity,' Campaign to Stop Funding Hate, available at: www.stopfundinghate.org/resources/DNJhaHinduIdentity.pdf (accessed October 2017).

Johnson, Carol (2002) 'Heteronormative citizenship and the politics of passing,' *Sexualities* 5, 3: 317–36.

Johnson, James (2011) 'The arithmetic of compassion: Rethinking the politics of photography,' *British Journal of Political Science* 41, 3: 621–43.

Jolie, Angelina (2015) 'A new level of refugee suffering: Angelina Jolie on the Syrians and Iraqis who can't go home,' *New York Times*, January 27, available at: www.nytimes.com/2015/01/28/opinion/angelina-jolie-on-the-syrians-and-iraqis-who-cant-go-home.html?_r=1 (accessed October 2017).

Jolly, Jihi (2014) 'How algorithms decide the news you see,' *Columbia Journalism Review*, available at: www.cjr.org/news_literacy/algorithms_filter_bubble.php (accessed October 2017).

Jönsson, Christer and Martin Hall (2003) 'Communication: An essential aspect of diplomacy,' *International Studies Perspectives* 4, 2: 195–210.

Joppke, Christian (2009) *Veil: Mirror of Identity*, Cambridge: Polity.

Kaempf, Sebastian (2013) 'The mediatisation of war in a transforming global media landscape,' *Australian Journal of International Affairs* 67, 5: 586–604.

Kahn, Douglas and John Heartfield (1985) *Art and Mass Media*, New York: Tanam Press.

Kant, Immanuel (2001 [1798]) 'An old question raised again: Is the human race constantly progressing?' in *Kant on History* (trans. Robert E. Anchor), ed. Lewis White Beck, New York: Macmillan.

Kant, Immanuel (1952) *The Critique of Judgement* (trans. James Creed Meredith), Oxford, UK: Clarendon Press.

Kaplan, E. Ann (2005) *Trauma Culture: The Politics of Loss in Media and Literature*, New Brunswick, NJ: Rutgers University Press.

Kaplan, Robert D. (1994) 'The coming anarchy,' *The Atlantic*, February, available at: www.theatlantic.com/magazine/archive/1994/02/the-coming-anarchy/304670/ (accessed October 2017).

Kapoor, Ilan (2013) *Celebrity Humanitarianism: The Ideology of Global Charity*, London and New York: Routledge.

Kattago, Siobhan (2009) 'War memorials and the politics of memory: The Soviet war memorial in Tallinn,' *Constellations* 16, 1: 150–66.

Keane, John (2009) 'Monitory democracy and media-saturated societies,' *Griffith Review* 24: 47–69.

Keane, John (2013) *Democracy and Media Decadence*, Cambridge: Cambridge University Press.

Kellner, Douglas (2004) 'Media culture and the triumph of the spectacle,' University of California, Los Angeles, available at: https://pages.gseis.ucla.edu/faculty/kellner/essays/mediaculturetriumph spectacle.pdf (accessed October 2017).

Kennedy, Liam (2008) 'Securing vision: Photography and US foreign policy,' *Media, Culture & Society,* 30, 3: 279–94.

Kennedy, Liam (2014) ' "Follow the Americans": Philip Jones Griffith's Vietnam War Trilogy,' in Liam Kennedy and Caitlin Patrick, eds, *The Violence of the Image: Photography and International Conflict*, London and New York: I.B.Tauris, pp. 34–59.

Kennedy, Liam and Caitlin Patrick, eds (2014) *The Violence of the Image: Photography and International Conflict*, London and New York: I.B.Tauris.

Kerry, John (2014) 'Joint press conference by Secretary Hagel, Secretary Kerry, Foreign Minister Bishop, and Minister of Defence Johnston at AUSMIN in Sydney, Australia,' available at: www.defense.gov/News/Transcripts/Transcript-View/Article/606910/joint-press-conference-by-secretary-hagel-secretary-kerry-foreign-minister-bish (accessed January 2017).

Kirby, Paul (2016) 'auto/bio/graph' in Naeem Inayatullah and Elizabeth Dauphinee, eds, *Narrative Global Politics: Theory, History and the Personal in International Relations*, London: Routledge, pp. 153–8.

Kirkpatrick, David (2011) *The Facebook Story*, London: Random House.

Kirkpatrick, Marie (2016) *Photography, the State and War: Mapping the Contemporary War Photography Landscape*, PhD thesis, University of Ottawa.

Kittler, Friedrich (1997) *Literature, Media, Information Systems*. New York and Oxford: Routledge.

Klausen, Jytte (2009) *The Cartoons that Shook the World*, New Haven, CT: Yale University Press.

Klein, Grady and Yoram Bauman (2014) *The Cartoon Introduction to Climate Change*, Washington, DC: Island Press.

Klein, Naomi (2005) ' "Never before!" Our amnesiac torture debate,' *The Nation*, 8 December, available at: www.thenation.com/article/never-our-amnesiac-torture-debate (accessed October 2017).

Kleinman, Arthur and Joan Kleinman (1996) 'The appeal of experience, the dismay of images: The cultural appropriation of suffering in our time,' *Daedalus* 125, 1: 1–23.

Knorr Cetina, K. (2009) *Epistemic Cultures: How the Sciences Make Knowledge*, Boston: Harvard University Press.

Koffman, Ofra and Rosalind Gill (2013) ' "The revolution will be led by a 12-year-old girl": Girl power and global biopolitics,' *Feminist Review* 105: 83–102.

Kogut, Tehila and Ilana Ritov (2005) 'The "identified victim" effect: An identified group, or just a single individual?' *Journal of Behavioural Decision-Making* 18: 157–67.

Koudelka, Josef (2007) *Josef Koudelka (Photofile)*, London/New York: Thames & Hudson.

Kozol, Wendy (2004) 'Domesticating NATO's war in Kosovo/a: (In)visible bodies and the dilemma of photojournalism,' *Meridians: Feminism, Race, Transnationalism* 4, 2: 1–38.

Kozol, Wendy (2014) *Distant Wars Visible: The Ambivalence of Witnessing*, Minneapolis: University of Minnesota Press.

Kracauer, Siegfried (1995) *The Mass Ornament* (trans. Thomas Y. Levin), Cambridge, MA: Harvard University Press.

Kurgan, Laura (2013) *Close Up at a Distance: Mapping, Technology, and Politics*, Cambridge, MA: MIT Press.

Lafrance, Marc (2010) " 'She Exists within Me': Subjectivity, Embodiment and the World's First Facial Transplant," in *Abjectly Boundless: Boundaries, Bodies and Health Work*, ed. Trudy Rudge and Dave Holmes, Farnham, Surrey: Ashgate.

Lakoff, George and Mark Johnson (2003) *Metaphors We Live By*, London: University of Chicago Press.

Langley, Paul (2008) *The Everyday Life of Global Finance: Saving and Borrowing in Anglo America*, Oxford: Oxford University Press.

Laustsen, Carsten Bagge (2008) 'The camera as a weapon: On Abu Ghraib and related matters,' *Journal for Cultural Research* 12, 2: 123–42.

Leatherman, Janie L. (2011) *Sexual Violence and Armed Conflict*, Cambridge: Polity Press.

Lee-Koo, Katrina (2011) 'Horror and hope: (Re)presenting militarised children in global North/South relations,' *Third World Quarterly* 32, 4: 725–42.

Lee-Koo, Katrina (2013) 'Not suitable for children: The politicisation of conflict-affected children in post-2001 Afghanistan,' *Australian Journal of International Affairs* 67, 4: 475–90.

Lefort, Claude (1986) 'Politics and human rights,' in *The Political Forms of Modern Society Bureaucracy, Democracy, Totalitarianism*, Cambridge: MIT Press, pp. 239–72.

Leibold, James and Timothy Grose (2016) 'Veiling in Xinjiang: The battle to define Uyghur female adornment,' *China Journal* 76: 1–25.

Leonard, Andrew (2013) 'Why facial recognition failed,' *Salon*, 23 April, available at: www.salon.com/2013/04/22/why_facial_recognition_failed (accessed October 2017).

Leslie, Donna (2008) *Aboriginal Art: Creativity and Assimilation*, Melbourne: Macmillan Art Publishing.

Levi Strauss, David (2003) *Between the Eyes: Essays on Photography and Politics*, New York: Aperture.

Levinas, Emmanuel (1969) *Totality and Infinity*, Pittsburgh, PA: Duquesne University Press.

Lichfield, John (2006) 'Face transplant recipient Isabelle Dinoire faces the world,' *Independent*, 7 February, available at: www.independent.co.uk/news/world/europe/face-transplant-recipient-isabelle-dinoire-faces-the-world-343723.html (accessed October 2017).

Lidchi, Henrietta (1997) 'The poetics and the politics of exhibiting other cultures' in Stuart Hall, ed., *Representation: Cultural Representations and Signifying Practices*, London: SAGE, pp. 151–222.

Lillesand, Thomas, Ralph W. Kiefer and Jonathan Chipman (2008) *Remote Sensing and Image Interpretation*, 6th edn, Madison: University of Wisconsin.

Linfield, Susie (2010, 2012) *The Cruel Radiance: Photography and Political Violence*, Chicago: University of Chicago Press.

Limbaugh, Rush (2004). Statements aired on WNBC, 4 August.

Liptak, Adam (2009) 'Images, the law and war,' *New York Times*, 16 May, available at: www.nytimes.com/2009/05/17/weekinreview/17liptak.html?pagewanted=all (accessed October 2017).

Lisle, Debbie (2000) 'Consuming danger: Reimagining the war/tourism divide,' *Alternatives* 25, 1: 96–116.

Lisle, Debbie (2009) 'The "potential mobilities" of photography,' *M/C Journal* 12, 1: available at: http://journal.media-culture.org.au/index.php/mcjournal/article/viewArticle/125 (accessed October 2017).

Lisle, Debbie (2016) *Holidays in the Danger Zone: Entanglements of War and Tourism*, Minneapolis: University of Minnesota Press.

Lissner, Jørgen (1979) *The Politics of Altruism*, Geneva: Lutheran World Foundation.

Litfin, Karen T. (2002) 'Public eyes: Satellite imagery, the globalization of transparency, and new network of surveillance,' in James N. Rosenau and J.P. Singh, eds, *Information Technologies and Global Politics: The Changing Scope of Power and Governance*, New York: State University of New York Press, pp. 65–90.

Littler, Jo (2008) ' "I feel your pain": Cosmopolitan charity and the public fashioning of the celebrity soul,' *Social Semiotics* 18, 2: 237–51.

Lloyd, David William (1998) *Battlefield Tourism: Pilgrimage and the Commemoration of the Great War in Britain, Australia and Canada, 1919–1939*, London: Berg.

Los Angeles County Museum of Art (2015), 'Exhibition advisory: Delacroix's *Greece on the Ruins of Missolonghi*,' Los Angeles County Museum of Art, available at: www.lacma.org/sites/default/files/Delacroix-exhibition%20advisory%2010.28.14_0.pdf (accessed October 2017).

Louw, Eric (2010) *The Media and Political Process*, London: SAGE.

Louise, Martin-Chew (2014) 'Majority rule' in Michael Cook, *Majority Rule*, Brisbane: Andrew Baker Art Dealer. www.andrew-baker.com/Michael%20Cook_Majority_Rule.pdf (accessed October 2015).

Lovecraft, Howard Phillips (1927, 1945) *Supernatural Horror in Literature*, North Chelmsford, MA: Courier.

Luckerson, Victor 'Here's how Facebook's news feed actually works,' *Time Magazine*, 9 July, available at: http://time.com/3950525/facebook-news-feed-algorithm/ (accessed October 2017).

Luke, Timothy W. (1992) *Shows of Force: Power, Politics and Ideology in Art Exhibitions*, Durham, NC: Duke University Press.

Luke, Timothy W. (2002) *Museum Politics: Power Plays at the Exhibition*, Minneapolis: University of Minnesota Press.

Lutz, Catherine (2002) 'Making war at home in the United States: Militarization and the current crisis,' *American Anthropologist* 104, 3: 723–35.

Lyon, David (1994) *The Electronic Eye: The Rise of Surveillance Society*, Minneapolis: University of Minnesota Press.

Mac Con Uladh, Damian (2015) 'Greek cruise ship to provide shelter to Kos migrants,' *Irish Times*, 14 August, available at: www.irishtimes.com/news/world/europe/greek-cruise-ship-to-provide-shelter-to-kos-migrants-1.2316379 (accessed October 2017).

MacDonald, Fraser, Rachel Hughes and Klaus Dodds, eds (2010) *Observant States: Geopolitics and Visual Culture*, London: I.B.Tauris.

Madison, James H. (2001) *A Lynching in the Heartland: Race and Memory in America*, New York: Palgrave Macmillan.

Malkki, Liisa H. (1995) *Purity and Exile: Violence, Memory, and National Cosmology among Hutu Refugees in Tanzania*, Chicago: University of Chicago Press.

Mamdani, Mahmood (2002) 'Good Muslim, bad Muslim: A political perspective on culture and terrorism' *American Anthropologist* 104, 3: 766–75.

Mancini, Livio (2012) 'A completely different picture: Inciting hatred against Roma,' Open Society Foundations, 13 April, available at: www.opensocietyfoundations.org/voices/completely-different-picture-inciting-hatred-against-roma (accessed October 2017).

Manhwa Gwangjang (1987a), May.

Manhwa Gwangjang (1987b), June ('Je-3-Segye Jakga-deul-eui Hyangbyeon' [Manifesto of Third World Artists].

Manning, Stuart W. (2014) *A Test of Time and A Test of Time Revisited: The Volcano of Thera and the Chronology and History of the Aegean and East Mediterranean in the Mid-Second Millennium BC*, Oxford: Oxbow.

Manzo, Kate (2008) 'Imaging humanitarianism: NGO identity and the iconography of childhood,' *Antipode* 40, 4: 632–57.

Manzo, Kate (2010a) 'Beyond polar bears? Re-envisioning climate change,' *Meteorological Applications* 17: 196–208.

Manzo, Kate (2010b) 'Imaging vulnerability: The iconography of climate change,' *Area* 42, 1: 96–107.

Manzo, Kate (2012) 'Earthworks: The geopolitical visions of climate change cartoons,' *Political Geography* 31: 481–94.

Marciniak, Katarzyna (2006) *Alienhood: Citizenship, Exile, and the Logic of Difference*, Minneapolis: University of Minnesota Press.

Marcoci, Roxana (2010) 'What's in a portrait? Rineke Dijkstra's *Almerisa*,' INSIDE/OUT: A MoMA/MoMA PS1 Blog, available at: www.moma.org/explore/inside_out/2010/01/14/what-s-in-a-portrait-rineke-dijkstra-s-almerisa (accessed October 2017).

Marcuse, Herbert (1978) *The Aesthetic Dimension: Toward a Critique of Marxist Aesthetics*, Boston: Beacon Press.

Margalit, Avishai (2002) *The Ethics of Memory*, Cambridge, MA: Harvard University Press.

Marmor, Kathy (2008) 'Bird watching: An introduction to amateur satellite spotting,' *Leonardo* 41, 4: 317–23.

Marriott, David (2000) *On Black Men*, New York: Columbia University Press.

Marsh, Nicky (2011) 'Desire and disease in the speculative economy: A critique of the language of crisis,' *Journal of Cultural Economy* 4, 3: 301–15.

Martin, Randy (2014) *Routledge Companion to Art and Politics*, New York: Routledge.

Marx, Karl (1844, 1992) 'On the Jewish question,' in Karl Marx, *Early Writings* (trans. Rodney Livingstone and Gregor Benton, 2nd edn), London: Penguin Books.

Mattoni, Alice (2012) *Media Practices, Protests Politics and Precarious Workers*, London: Ashgate.

Mattoni, Alice and Simon Teune (2014) 'Visions of protest: A media-historic perspective on images in social movements,' *Sociology Compass* 8, 6: 876–87.

Mavor, Carol (2012) *Black and Blue*, Durham, NC: Duke University Press.

McAlister, Melani (2005) *Epic Encounters: Culture, Media, and US Interests in the Middle East*, rev. edn, Berkeley: University of California Press.

McChesney, Robert W. (2013) *Digital Disconnect*, New York: New Press.

McCloud, Scott (1994) *Understanding Comics: The Invisible Art*, New York: Harper Perennial.

McConnell, Fiona, Terri Moreau and Jason Dittmer (2012) 'Mimicking state diplomacy: The legitimizing strategies of unofficial diplomacies,' *Geoforum* 43, 4: 804–14.

McCullin, Don (1992, 2002, 2003) *Unreasonable Behaviour*, London: Vintage.

McLachlan, Shelley and Peter Golding (2000) 'Tabloidisation in the British press: A quantitative investigation into changes in British newspapers, 1952–1997,' in Colin Sparks and John Tulloch, eds, *Tabloid Tales: Global Debates over Media Standards*, London: Rowman & Littlefield, pp. 75–90.

McLean, Ian (1998) *White Aborigines: Identity Politics in Australian Art*, Melbourne: Cambridge University Press.

McLuhan, Marshall (1962) *The Gutenberg Galaxy: The Making of Typographic Man*, London: University of Toronto.

McRobbie, Angela (2008) *The Aftermath of Feminism: Gender, Culture and Social Change*, London: SAGE.

McSweeney, Bill (1999) *Security, Identity and Interests: A Sociology of International Relations*, Cambridge: Cambridge University Press.

McVeigh, Tracey (2015) 'Sympathy and solidarity for migrants on Kos beaches as two worlds collide,' *Observer*, 6 June, available at: www.theguardian.com/world/2015/jun/06/kos-migrants-tourists-greece-traffickers-sympathy-solidarity (accessed October 2017).

Megill, Allan (1998) 'History, memory, identity,' *History of the Human Sciences* 11, 3: 37–62.

Menon, Roshni (2008) 'Famine in Malawi: Causes and consequences,' United Nations Development Programme, available at: http://hdr.undp.org/en/content/famine-malawi-causes-and-consequences (accessed October 2017).

Merlan, Francesca (2009) 'Indigeneity global and local,' *Current Anthropology* 50, 3: 303–33.

Met Office (2013) 'What do we mean by climate?' Met Office, available at: www.metoffice.gov.uk/climate-guide/climate (accessed October 2017).

Michel, Franck (2015) 'How many pictures are uploaded to Flickr every day, month, year?' available at: www.flickr.com/photos/franckmichel/6855169886 (accessed November 2015).

Mill, John Stuart (1991) *Considerations on Representative Government*, Buffalo, NY: Prometheus.

Miller, Nancy K. (2003) ' "Portraits of grief": Telling details and the testimony of trauma,' *differences: A Journal of Feminist Cultural Studies* 14, 3: 112–35.

Milman, Noa (2013) *When do Mothers Matter? An Intersectional Analysis of Media Welfare Discourses in Israel and Massachusetts*, Dissertation. Boston College.

Milman, Noa (2014) 'Mothers, Mizrahi and poor: Contentious media framings of mothers' movements,' *Research in Social Movements, Conflicts, and Change* 37: 53–82.

Miodrag, Hannah (2013) *Comics and Language: Reimagining Critical Discourse on the Form*, Jackson: University of Mississippi Press.

Mirzoeff, Nicholas, ed. (1998) *The Visual Culture Reader*. London: Routledge.

Mirzoeff, Nicholas (1999) *An Introduction to Visual Culture*, London: Routledge.

Mirzoeff, Nicholas (2006) 'Disorientalism: minority and visuality in imperial London,' *TDR* 50, 2: 52–69.

Mirzoeff, Nicholas (2011) *The Right to Look: A Counterhistory of Visuality*, Durham, NC: Duke University Press.

Mitchell, Amy and Jesse Holcomb (2015) 'The State of the News Media 2015,' Pew Research Center, 29 April, available at: www.journalism.org/2015/04/29/state-of-the-news-media-2015/ (accessed October 2017).

Mitchell, W.J.T. (1986) *Iconology: Image, Text, Ideology*, Chicago: University of Chicago Press.

Mitchell, W.J.T. (1994) *Picture Theory: Essays on Verbal and Visual Representation*, Chicago: University of Chicago Press.

Mitchell, W.J.T. (2005a) 'The unspeakable and the unimaginable: Word and image in a time of terror,' *ELH*, 72, 2: 291–308.

Mitchell, W.J.T. (2005b) *What do Pictures Want? The Lives and Loves of Images*, Chicago: University of Chicago Press.

Mitchell, W.J.T. (2011) *Cloning Terror: The War of Images, 9/11 to the Present*, Chicago: University of Chicago Press.

Mitter, Partha (1995) 'Review: Western orientalism and the construction of nationalist art in India,' *Oxford Art Journal* 18, 1: 140–43.

Mitter, Partha (2007) *The Triumph of Modernism: India's Artists and the Avant-Garde, 1922–47*, London: Reaktion.

Moeller, Susan D. (1999) *Compassion Fatigue: How the Media Sell Disease, Famine, War and Death*, New York: Routledge.

Mohanty, Chandra Talpade (1986) 'Under Western eyes: Feminist scholarship and colonial discourses,' *Boundary 2* 12, 3: 333–58.

Mohite, V.A. (1955) 'Murals: Letter to the editor,' *Times of India*, 4 February: 6.

Möller, Frank (2013) *Visual Peace: Images, Spectatorship, and the Politics of Violence*, Basingstoke: Palgrave Macmillan.

Molyneux, Maxine (2008) 'The "neoliberal turn" and the new social policy in Latin America: How neoliberal, how new?' *Development and Change* 39, 5: 775–97.

Mookherjee, Nayanika (2006) ' "Remembering to forget": Public secrecy and memory of sexual violence in Bangladesh,' *Journal of the Royal Anthropological Institute* 12, 2: 433–50.

Mookherjee, Nayanika (2015) *The Spectral Wound: Sexual Violence, Public Memories and the Bangladesh War of 1971*, Durham, NC: Duke University Press.

Moore, Cerwyn and Laura J. Shepherd (2010) 'Aesthetics and international relations: Towards a global politics,' *Global Society* 24: 299–309.

Morozov, Evgeny (2011) *The Net Delusion: The Dark Side of Internet Freedom*, London: AllenLane.

Mortensen, Mette (2015) *Journalism and Eyewitness Images: Digital Media, Participation, and Conflict*, London: Routledge.

Moyn, Samuel (2010) *The Last Utopia: Human Rights in History*, Cambridge, MA: Harvard University Press.

Müller, Marion G. and Esra Özcan (2007) 'The political iconography of Muhammad cartoons: Understanding cultural conflict and political action,' *Politics and Society* 4: 287–91.

Müller, Tanja R. (2013a) ' "The Ethiopian famine" revisited: Band Aid and the antipolitics of celebrity humanitarian action,' *Disasters* 37, 1: 61–79.

Müller, Tanja R. (2013b) 'The long shadow of Band Aid humanitarianism: Revisiting the dynamics between famine and celebrity,' *Third World Quarterly* 34, 3: 470–84.

Murphy, M. (2012) 'The girl: Mergers of feminism and finance in neoliberal times,' *The Scholar and Feminist Online*, 11, 1–2, available at: http://sfonline.barnard.edu/gender-justice-and-neoliberal-transformations/the-girl-mergers-of-feminism-and-finance-in-neoliberal-times/#sthash.s4NK fpmI.dpuf (accessed October 2017).

Mutua, Makau (2008) *Human Rights: A Political and Cultural Critique*, Philadelphia: University of Pennsylvania Press.

Myers, Garth, Timothy Klak and Thomas Koehl (1996) 'The inscription of difference: News coverage of the conflicts in Rwanda and Bosnia,' *Political Geography* 15, 1: 21–46.

Nash, Kate (2008) 'Global citizenship as show business: The cultural politics of Make Poverty History,' *Media, Culture & Society* 30, 2: 167–81.

Nath, Anjali (2014) 'Beyond the public eye: On FOIA documents and the visual politics of redaction,' *Cultural Studies ↔ Critical Methodologies* 14, 1: 21–8.

NATO (2014a) 'Imagery reveals destabilizing Russian forces near Ukrainian border,' NATO Allied Command Operations, available at: www.aco.nato.int/imagery-reveals-destabilizing-russian-forces-near-ukraine-border-nato-plans-balanced-response-to-reassure-allies.aspx#prettyPhoto (accessed October 2014).

NATO (2014b) 'NATO defends accuracy of satellite images with additional proof,' NATO Allied Command Operations, available at: www.aco.nato.int/nato-defends-accuracy-of-satellite-images-with-additional-proof-2.aspx (accessed October 2014).

NATO (2014c) 'NATO releases satellite imagery showing Russian combat troops inside Ukraine,' North Atlantic Treaty Organization, available at: www.nato.int/cps/en/natohq/news_112193.htm (accessed October 2014).

Navarria, Giovanni (2014) 'Can democracy survive the rise of surveillance technology?' *Democratic Theory* 1, 2: 76–84.

Nehamas, Alexander (2007) *Only a Promise of Happiness: The Place of Beauty in a World of Art*, Princeton, NJ: Princeton University Press.

Neuman, Klaus (2004) *Refuge Australia: Australia's Humanitarian Record*, Sydney: University of New South Wales Press.

New York Times (2007) 'Ending famine in Malawi,' *New York Times*, 2 December, available at: www.nytimes.com/slideshow/2007/12/01/world/20071202MALAWI_index.html?_r=0 (accessed October 2017).

Newman, David (2003) 'On borders and power: A theoretical framework,' *Journal of Borderland Studies*, 18, 1: 13–24.

Newton, Paula and Thom Patterson (2015) 'The girl in the picture: Kim Phuc's journey from war to forgiveness,' *CNN*, 25 June, available at: http://edition.cnn.com/2015/06/22/world/kim-phuc-where-is-she-now/ (accessed October 2017).

Nexon, Daniel H. and Iver B. Neumann, eds (2006) *Harry Potter and International Relations*, Lanham, MD: Rowman & Littlefield.

Ngai, Sianne (2012) *Our Aesthetic Categories: Zany, Cute, Interesting*, Cambridge, MA: Harvard University Press.

Nguyen, Mimi Thi (2012) *The Gift of Freedom: War, Debt, and Other Refugee Passages*, Durham, NC: Duke University Press.

Nicolson, Harold (1963) *Diplomacy*, Oxford: Oxford University Press.

Nietzsche, Friedrich (1969) *On the Genealogy of Morals* (trans. W. Kaufmann), New York: Random House.

Nietzsche, Friedrich (1982) *Die fröhliche Wissenschaft*, Frankfurt: Insel.

Niezen, Ronald (2003) *The Origins of Indigenism, Human Rights and the Politics of Identity*, Berkeley and Los Angeles: University of California Press.

Nike Foundation (2006) 'I dare you' (re-uploaded in 2008 as 'The girl effect: I dare you to see I am the answer') YouTube, available at: www.youtube.com/watch?v=-Vq2mfF8puE (accessed October 2017).

NiqaBitch (2010) 'NiqaBitch shakes Paris,' vimeo, available at: http://vimeo.com/15747849 (accessed October 2017).

Nora, Pierre (1989) 'Between memory and history: Les lieux de mémoire' (trans. Marc Roudebush), *Representations* 26: 7–25.

Nordberg, Jenny (2014) *The Underground Girls of Kabul: In Search of a Hidden Resistance in Afghanistan*, New York: Penguin Random House.

Nordstrom, Carolyn (1999) 'Wars and invisible girls, shadow industries and the politics of not-knowing,' *International Feminist Journal of Politics* 1, 1: 14–33.

North, John (2004) *The Ambassadors' Secret: Holbein and the World of the Renaissance*, London: Hambledon Continuum.

North, Peter (2014) 'Ten square miles surrounded by reality? Materialising alternative economies using local currencies,' *Antipode* 46, 1: 246–65.

Nunez, Bryan (2012) 'Tips for activists using the YouTube face blur tool,' WITNESS, available at: http://blog.witness.org/2012/08/tips-for-activists-using-the-youtube-face-blur-tool (accessed October 2017).

O'Mahony, Jennifer (2012) 'Britain "worst in the world" for weather complaints on Twitter,' *Telegraph*, 12 December, available at: www.telegraph.co.uk/technology/twitter/9736843/Britain-worst-in-the-world-for-weather-complaints-on-Twitter.html (accessed October 2017).

O'Neill, Mark (2016) *The Chinese Labour Corps: The Forgotten Chinese Labourers of the First World War*, London: Penguin.

Obama, Barack (2012) 'Remarks by the President at the Sandy Hook Interfaith Prayer Vigil,' *The White House*, 16 December, available at: www.whitehouse.gov/the-press-office/2012/12/16/remarks-president-sandy-hook-interfaith-prayer-vigil (accessed October 2017).

Oe, Kenzaburo (1996) *Hiroshima Notes* (trans. David L. Swain and Toshi Yonezawa), New York: Grove Press.

Olesen, Thomas (2015) *Global Injustice Symbols and Social Movements*, New York: Palgrave.

ORLAN (1993) *Omnipresence*, Myriapodus Films and ORLAN, vimeo, available at: https://vimeo.com/66967753 (accessed October 2017).

Orwell, George (1941) 'Work: Essays: The Lion and the Unicorn,' George Orwell: 1903–1950, available at: www.k-1.com/Orwell/site/work/essays/lionunicorn.html (accessed October 2017).

Osborne, Peter (2000) *Travelling Light: Photography, Travel and Visual Culture*, Manchester: Manchester University Press.

Osiander, Andreas (2001) 'Sovereignty, international relations, and the Westphalian myth,' *International Organization* 55, 2: 251–87.

Otto, Kate (2015) *Everyday Ambassador: Make a Difference by Connecting in a Disconnected World*, New York: Atria.

Ó Tuathail, Gearóid (1996) *Critical Geopolitcs*, London: Routledge.

Owusu, Kwesi and Francis Ng'ambi (2002) 'Structural damage: The causes and consequences of Malawi's food crisis,' World Development Movement, available at: www.globaljustice.org.uk/sites/default/files/files/resources/malawi_exec_summary.pdf (accessed October 2017).

Paasi, Anssi (2011) 'A border theory: An unattainable dream or a realistic aim for border scholars?' in Doris Wastl-Walter, ed, *The Ashgate Research Companion to Border Studies*, Farnham and Burlington: Ashgate, pp. 11–32.

Padrón, Ricardo (2004) *The Spacious Word: Cartography, Literature, and Empire in Early Modern Spain*, Chicago: University of Chicago Press.

Paglen, Trevor and Rebecca Solnit (2010) *Invisible: Covert Operations and Classified Landscapes*, New York: Aperture.

Paine, Thomas (2000) *Political Writings*, Cambridge: Cambridge University Press.

Pallister, David (2009) 'Sri Lanka satellite images show Tamil refugees massing on beach,' 24 April, available at: www.theguardian.com/world/2009/apr/24/sri-lanka-tamil-tigers-satellite-images (accessed October 2017).

Pamment, James (2014). 'The mediatization of diplomacy,' *Hague Journal of Diplomacy* 9, 3: 253–80.

Paolo Favero (2014) 'Learning to look beyond the frame: Reflections on the changing meaning of images in the age of digital media practices,' *Visual Studies* 29, 2: 166–79.

Parks, Lisa (2005) *Cultures in Orbit: Satellites and the Televisual*, Durham, NC: Duke University Press.

Parliament Secretariat (1953) *Report of the Planning Sub-Committee on a Scheme of Decorating the Parliament House*, New Delhi.

Perlmutter, David D. (1998) *Photojournalism and Foreign Policy: Icons of Outrage in International Crisis*, Westport, CT: Praeger.

Perlmutter, David D. (1999) *Visions of War: Picturing Warfare from the Stone Age to the Cyber Age*, New York: St. Martin's Griffin.

Perrons, Diane (2012) ' "Global" financial crisis, earnings inequalities and gender: Towards a more sustainable model of development,' *Comparative Sociology* 11, 2: 202–26.

Peston, Robert (2009) 'Why men are to blame for the Crunch,' BBC, 29 July, available at: www.bbc.co.uk/blogs/thereporters/robertpeston/2009/07/why_men_are_to_blame_for_the_c.html (accessed October 2017).

Peterson, Peter G., Morris Goldstein and Carla A. Hills (1999) *Safeguarding Prosperity in a Global Financial System: The Future International Financial Architecture*, New York: Council on Foreign Relations.

Pfanner, Michael (1983) *Der Titusbogen*, Mainz am Rhein: Philipp von Zabern.

Physicians for Social Responsibility (2015) *Body Count: Casualty Figures after 10 Years of the War on Terror; Iraq, Afghanistan, Pakistan*, Washington, DC: PSR.

Pickles, John (2004) *A History of Spaces: Cartographic Reason, Mapping, and the Geo-Coded World*, New York: Routledge.

Pinney, Christopher (1997) *Camera Indica: The Social Life of Indian Photographs*, Chicago: University of Chicago Press and Reaktion Books.

Plantinga, Carl and Greg M. Smith, eds (1999) *Passionate Views: Film, Cognition, and Emotion*, Baltimore, MD: Johns Hopkins University Press.

Podolny, Shelley (2015) 'If an algorithm wrote this, how would you even know?' *New York Times*, 7 March, available at: www.nytimes.com/2015/03/08/opinion/sunday/if-an-algorithm-wrote-this-how-would-you-even-know.html?_r=0 (accessed October 2017).

Powell, Colin L. (2003) 'Remarks to the United Nations Security Council,' US Department of State Archive, 5 February, available at: https://2001-2009.state.gov/secretary/former/powell/remarks/2003/17300.htm (accessed January 2017).

Power, Matthew (2013) 'Confessions of a drone warrior,' *GQ*, 13 October, available at: www.gq.com/news-politics/big-issues/201311/drone-uav-pilot-assassination (accessed October 2017).

Pronk, Jan (2005) 'We need more stories and more pictures,' Jan Pronk, 8 October, available at: www.janpronk.nl/speeches/english/we-need-more-stories-and-more-pictures.html (accessed October 2017).

Puar, Jasbir (2007) *Terrorist Assemblages: Homonationalism in Queer Times*, Durham, NC: Duke University Press.

Pusca, Anca, ed. (2009) *Walter Benjamin and the Aesthetics of Change*, London: Palgrave Macmillan.

Queller, Donald E. (1967) *The Office of Ambassador in the Middle Ages*, Princeton, NJ: Princeton University Press.

Rabinowitz, Paula (1994) *They Must be Represented: The Politics of Documentary*, London: Verso.

Radwan, Hassan (2015) 'Muslims can reinterpret their faith: It's the best answer to ISIS,' *Guardian*, 16 December, available at: www.theguardian.com/commentisfree/2015/dec/16/muslims-faith-isis-religion-islam (accessed October 2017).

Ragg, Mark (2002) 'The numbers no-one wants to figure out,' *Sydney Morning Herald*, 17 October: 5.

Rai, Shirin M. (2014) 'Political aesthetics of the nation: Murals and statues in the Indian parliament,' *Interventions: International Journal of Postcolonial Studies*, 16, 6: 898–915.

Rajaram, Prem Kumar (2002) 'Humanitarianism and representations of the refugee,' *Journal of Refugee Studies* 15, 3: 247–64.

Rajaram, Prem Kumar and Carl Grundy-Warr (2007) *Borderscapes: Hidden Geographies and Politics at Territory's Edge*, Minneapolis and London: University of Minnesota Press.

Ramamurthy, Anandi (2003) *Imperial Persuaders: Images of Africa and Asia in British Advertising*, Manchester: Manchester University Press.

Rancière, Jacques (2003) *The Philosopher and his Poor* (trans. John Drury, Corinne Oster and Andrew Parker), Durham, NC: Duke University Press.

Rancière, Jacques (2004) *The Politics of Aesthetics: The Distribution of the Sensible* (trans. Gabriel Rockhill), London: Continuum.

Rancière, Jacques (2009) *The Emancipated Spectator* (trans. Gregory Elliot), New York: Verso.

Rancière, Jacques (2010) 'Who is the subject of the rights of man?' in *Dissensus: On Politics and Aesthetics*, London: Continuum, pp. 62–75.

Razumovskaya, Olga (2014) 'Russia presents its account of Malaysia Airlines Flight 17 crash,' 21 July, available at: www.wsj.com/articles/russia-presents-its-account-of-malaysia-airlines-flight-17-crash-1405952441 (accessed October 2017).

Rebergen, Gert and Janneke Rebergen (2015) 'Teardrops of a candlelight in Kliptown,' interview with Bolo Blom aka David Meyers, Zutphen, available at: www.izarte.nl/index.php?mm=0&pp=22 (accessed October 2017).

Reinhardt, Mark (2007) 'Picturing violence: Aesthetics and the anxiety of critique,' in Mark Reinhardt, Holly Edwards and Erina Duganne, eds, *Beautiful Suffering: Photography and the Traffic in Pain*, Chicago: University of Chicago Press.

Reinhardt, Mark, Holly Edwards and Erina Duganne, eds (2007) *Beautiful Suffering: Photography and the Traffic in Pain*, Chicago: University of Chicago Press.

Reisz, Matthew (2016) 'In praise of Alex Danchev (1955–2016),' *Times Higher Education*, 13 August, available at: www.timeshighereducation.com/blog/praise-alex-danchev-1955-2016 (accessed October 2017).

Rentschler, Carrie (2011) *Second Wounds: Victims' Rights and the Media in the US*, Durham, NC: Duke University Press.

Rethel, Lena and Timothy J. Sinclair (2012) *The Problem with Banks*, London: Zed Books.

Reynolds, M. (2014) 'Meet this war of mine: A war game where you play as civilians,' *Digital Spy*, 19 October, available at: www.digitalspy.com/gaming/previews/feature/a603503/meet-this-war-of-mine-a-war-game-where-you-play-as-civilians/ (accessed October 2017).

Rice, Bob (1941) 'July 1941: US freezes Japanese assets,' Aunt Ethel's War, available at: http://ww2cartoons.org/july-1941-u-s-freezes-japanese-assets/ (accessed October 2017).

Richey, Lisa Ann and Stefano Ponte (2011) *Brand Aid: Shopping Well to Save the World*, Minneapolis: University of Minnesota Press.

Rid, Thomas and Marc Hecker (2009) *War 2.0: Irregular Warfare in the Information Age*, Westport, CT: Praeger Security International.

Ritchin, Fred (2013) *Bending the Frame: Photojournalism, Documentary, and the Citizen*, New York: Aperture.

Ritzau and information.dk (2009) 'Politiet filmede også uden for kirken,' *Information*, 4 September, available from: www.information.dk/202626 (accessed October 2017).

Robinson, Nick (2015) 'Have you won the War on Terror? Military videogames and the state of American exceptionalism,' *Millennium: Journal of International Studies* 43, 2: 450–70.

Robinson, Piers (2002) *The CNN Effect: The Myth of News Foreign Policy and Intervention*, New York: Routledge.

Robinson, Piers (2014) 'Media empowerment vs. strategies of control: Theorizing news media and war in the 21st century,' *Zeitschrift für Politik* 4: 461–79.

Robinson, Piers, Peter Goddard, Katy Parry, Craig Murray and Philip M. Taylor (2010) *Pockets of Resistance: British News Media, War and Theory in the 2003 Invasion of Iraq*, Manchester and New York: Manchester University Press.

Rockhill, Gabriel (2009) 'The politics of aesthetics: Political history and the hermeneutics of art,' in Gabriel Rockhill, ed., *Jacques Rancière*, Durham, NC: Duke University Press, pp. 195–215.

Rodogno, Davide (2012) *Against Massacre: Humanitarian Interventions in the Ottoman Empire, 1815–1914*, Princeton, NJ: Princeton University Press.

Rømer, M. (2009) 'Politiet: Vi har flere optagelser,' *Ekstra Bladet*, 4 September, available at: www.ekstrabladet.dk/112/article1216835ece (accessed October 2017).

Rosenhaft, Eve (2008), 'Exchanging glances: Ambivalence in twentieth-century photographs of German Sinti,' *Third Text* 22, 3: 311–24.

Rotha, Paul and Richard Griffith (1967) *The Film till Now: A Survey of World Cinema*, London: Spring Books.

Ruggie, John G. (1993) 'Territoriality and beyond: Problematizing modernity in international relations,' *International Organization* 47, 1: 139–74.

Runciman, David (2013) *The Confidence Trap*, Princeton, NJ: Princeton University Press.

Russ, Andrew R. (2013) *The Illusion of History: Time and the Radical Political Imagination*, Washington, DC: Catholic University of America Press.

Ryan, James (1997) *Picturing Practices: Photography and the Visualization of the British Empire*, London: Reaktion Books.

Sachs, Albie, (1983) *Images of a Revolution*, Harare: Zimbabwe Publishing House.

Sack, Robert David (1986) *Human Territoriality: Its Theory and History*, Cambridge: Cambridge University Press.

Sahlins, Peter (1989) *Boundaries: The Making of France and Spain in the Pyrenees*, Berkeley: University of California Press.

Said, Edward W. (1979) *Orientalism*, New York: Vintage.

Said, Edward W. (2001) 'The clash of ignorance,' *The Nation*, 22 October: 1–5.

Salzinger, Leslie (2003) *Genders in Production: Making Workers in Mexico's Global Factories*, Berkeley, CA: University of California Press.

Sanchez, Maria Carla and Linda Schlossberg, eds (2001) *Passing: Identity and Interpretation in Sexuality, Race, and Religion*, New York: NYU Press.

Sartori, Leo (1983) 'Effects of nuclear weapons,' *Physics Today* 36, 3: 32–8, 40–1.

Saugmann Andersen, Rune (2015) *Remediating Security: A Semiotic Framework for Analyzing how Video Speaks Security*. PhD thesis, University of Copenhagen.

Saugmann Andersen, Rune and Frank Möller (2013) 'Engaging the limits of visibility,' *Security Dialogue*, 44, 3: 203–21.

Saward, Michael (2011) 'Slow theory: Taking time over transnational democratic representation,' *Ethics & Global Politics* 4, 1: 1–18.

SBS (2015) 'Healing Camp, guipuji an-neun-ga' [Healing Camp, happy, are we not?], television programme, SBS, 18 May.

Scales, Robert H. (2006) 'Clausewitz and World War IV,' *Armed Forces Journal*, 1 July, available at: http://armedforcesjournal.com/clausewitz-and-world-war-iv/ (accessed October 2017).

Scarry, Elaine (1985) *The Body in Pain: The Making and Unmaking of the World*, New York: Oxford University Press.

Scarry, Elaine (1994) *Against Representation*, Oxford: Oxford University Press.

Schlag, Gabi and Axel Heck (2012) 'Securitizing images: The female body and the war in Afghanistan,' *European Journal of International Relations* 19, 4: 891–913.

Scott, James C. (1998) *Seeing like a State: How Certain Schemes to Improve the Human Condition have Failed*, New Haven, CT: Yale University Press.

Scott, Joan Wallach (2007) *The Politics of the Veil*, Princeton, NJ: Princeton University Press.

Sebald, W.G. (2004) *On the Natural History of Destruction* (trans. Athena Bell), New York: Modern Library.

Sekula, Allan (1982) 'On the invention of photographic meaning,' in *Thinking Photography*, ed. Victor Burgin, London: Macmillan.

Sekula, Allan (1986) 'The body and the archive,' *October* 39: 3–64.

Shaheen, Jack G. (2001) *Reel Bad Arabs: How Hollywood Vilifies a People*, New York: Roundhouse.

Shaheen, Jack G. (2008) *Guilty: Hollywood's Verdict on Arabs after 9/11*, Ithaca: Olive Branch Press.

Shaheen, Jack G. (2015) *Reel Bad Arabs: How Hollywood Vilifies a People*, 4th edn. Victoria, BC: Interlink Books.

Shaheen, Kareem (2015) 'Syria War: "Unthinkable atrocities" documented in report on Aleppo,' *Guardian*, 5 May, available at: www.theguardian.com/world/2015/may/05/syria-forces-war-crime-barrel-bombs-aleppo-amnesty-report (accessed October 2017).

Shapiro, Michael J. (1988) *The Politics of Representation: Writing Practices in Biography, Photography and Policy Analysis*. Madison: University of Wisconsin Press.

Shapiro, Michael J. (1990) 'Strategic discourse/discursive strategy: The representation of "security policy" in the video age,' *International Studies Quarterly* 34, 3: 327–40.

Shapiro, Michael J. (1999) *Cinematic Political Thought: Narrating Race, Nation and Gender*, Edinburgh: Edinburgh University Press.

Shapiro, Michael J. (2004) *Methods and Nations: Cultural Governance and the Indigenous Subject*, New York: Routledge.

Shapiro, Michael J. (2008) *Cinematic Geopolitics*, London: Routledge.

Sharp, Joanne P. (2000) *Condensing the Cold War*, Minneapolis: University of Minnesota Press.

Sharp, Paul and Geoffrey Wiseman, eds (2007) *The Diplomatic Corps as an Institution of International Society*, London: Palgrave Macmillan.

Shaw, Kara (2009) *Political Theory and Indigeneity: Sovereignty and the Limits of the Political*, New York: Routledge.

Shell, Hanna Rose (2012) *Hide and Seek: Camouflage, Photography, and the Media of Reconnaissance*, Cambridge, MA: MIT Press.

Shepherd, Laura J. (2006) 'Veiled references: Constructions of gender in the Bush Administration discourse on the attacks on Afghanistan post 9/11,' *International Feminist Journal of Politics* 8, 1: 19–41.

Shepherd, Laura J. (2013) *Gender, Violence and Popular Culture*: Telling Stories, London: Routledge.

Shepherd, Laura J. (2015) 'Sex or gender? Bodies in global politics and why gender matters,' in Laura J. Shepherd, ed., *Gender Matters in Global Politics*, London and New York: Routledge, pp. 24–35.

Shildrick, Margrit (2002) *Embodying the Monster: Encounters with the Vulnerable Self*, London: SAGE.

Shildrick, Margrit (2008) 'Corporeal cuts: Surgery and the psycho-social,' *Body and Society* 14, 1: 31–46.

Shim, David (2014) *Visual Politics and North Korea: Seeing is Believing*, London: Routledge.

Shirazi, Faegheh (2001) *The Veil Unveiled: The Hijab in Modern Culture*, Miami: University Press of Florida.

Shirky, Clay (2008) *Here Comes Everybody*, London: Penguin Books.

Sieff, Kevin (2016) '"A famine unlike any we have ever seen",' *Washington Post*, 13 October, available at: www.washingtonpost.com/sf/world/2016/10/13/they-survived-boko-haram-now-millions-in-nigeria-face-a-new-threat-starvation (accessed October 2017).

Silverstone, Roger (2006) *Media and Morality: On the Rise of the Mediapolis*, Cambridge: Polity.

Simon, Taryn (2007) *An American Index of the Hidden and Unfamiliar*, Göttingen: Steidl.

Singer, Peter (1972/2008) 'Famine, affluence, and morality,' *Philosophy & Public Affairs* 1, 3: 229–43.

Sjoberg, Laura (2015) 'Seeing sex, gender, and sexuality in international security,' *International Journal* 70, 3: 434–53.

Slahi, Mohamedou Ould (2015) *Guantánamo Diary*, Edinburgh: Canongate.

slavick, elin o'Hara (2009) 'Hiroshima: A visual record,' *Asia-Pacific Journal* 7, 30: 3.

Sliwinski, Sharon (2004) 'A painful labour: Responsibility and photography,' *Visual Studies* 19, 2: 150–61.

Sliwinski, Sharon (2006) 'The childhood of human rights: The Kodak on the Congo,' *Journal of Visual Culture* 5, 3: 333–63.

Sliwinski, Sharon (2011) *Human Rights in Camera*, Chicago: University of Chicago Press.

Slovic, Paul (2006) '"If I look at the masses I will never act": Psychic numbing and genocide,' *Judgement and Decision Making* 2, 2: 79–95.

Small, David (1997) 'Development education revisited: The New Zealand experience', in Vandra Masemann and Anthony Welch, eds, *Tradition, Modernity, and Post-modernity in Comparative Education*, New York: Springer, pp. 581–94.

Smillie, Ian (1995) *The Alms Bazaar: Altruism under Fire*. London: Non-profit Organisations and International Development Intermediate Technology.

Smith, Shawn Michelle (2008) 'The evidence of lynching photographs,' in Dora Apel and Shawn Michelle Smith, eds, *Lynching Photographs*, Berkeley: University of California Press.

Smith, Shawn Michelle (2013) *At the Edge of Sight: Photography and the Unseen*, Durham, NC: Duke University Press.

Sobel, Lester A., ed. (1979) *Refugees: A World Report*, New York: Facts on File.

Soguk, Nevzat (1999) *States and Strangers: Refugees and Displacements of Statecraft*, Minneapolis: University of Minnesota Press.

Soguk, Nevzat, (2007) 'Border's capture: Insurrectional politics, border-crossing humans, and the new political,' in Prem Kumar Rajaram and Carl Grundy-Warr, eds, *Borderscapes: Hidden Geographies and Politics at Territory's Edge*, Minneapolis and London: University of Minnesota Press, pp. 283–308.

Sollors, Werner (1996) *Theories of Ethnicity: A Classical Reader*, New York: New York University Press.

Solnit, Rebecca (2010) 'The invisibility wars,' in Trevor Paglen and Rebecca Solnit, eds, *Invisible: Covert Operations and Classified Landscapes*, New York: Aperture Press.

Solomon-Godeau, Abigail (2005) 'Lament of the images: Alfredo Jaar and the ethics of representation,' *Aperture* 181: 36–47.

Sontag, Susan (1975) 'Fascinating fascism,' *New York Review of Books*, 6 February, available at: www.nybooks.com/articles/1975/02/06/fascinating-fascism (accessed October 2017).

Sontag, Susan (1977) *On Photography*, New York: Farrar, Straus and Giroux.

Sontag, Susan (2003) *Regarding the Pain of Others*, New York: Farrar, Straus and Giroux.

Sontag, Susan (2004a). 'Regarding the torture of others,' *New York Times Magazine*, 23 May.

Sontag, Susan (2004b) 'What have we done?' *Guardian*, 24 May: G2–G3.

Spivak, Gayatri C. (1988) 'Can the subaltern speak?' in Cary Nelson and Lawrence Grossberg, eds, *Marxism and the Interpretation of Culture*, Urbana, IL: University of Illinois Press, pp. 271–314.

Spivak, Gayatri C. (1994) 'Can the subaltern speak?' in Patrick Williams and Laura Chrisman, eds, *Colonial Discourses and Post-Colonial Theory: A Reader*, Hemel Hempstead: Harvester Wheatsheaf, pp. 66–111.

Spruyt, Hendrik (1994) *The Sovereign State and its Competitors*, Princeton, New Jersey: Princeton University Press.

Spruyt, Hendrik (2002) 'The origins, development, and possible decline of the modern state,' *Annual Review of Political Science* 5: 127–49.

Stahl, Roger (2010) *Militainment, Inc.: War, Media, and Popular Culture*, New York: Routledge.

Steele, Brent J. (2010) *Defacing Power: The Aesthetics of Insecurity in Global Politics*, Ann Arbor, MI: University of Michigan Press.

Steele, Valerie (2006 [1997]) *Fifty Years of Fashion: New Look to Now*, New Haven, CT: Yale University Press.

Stiglitz, Joseph (2002) 'Transparency in government,' in Roumeen Islam, Simeon Djankov and Caralee McLeish, eds, *The Right to Tell*, Washington, DC: World Bank.

Stolnitz, Jerome (1998) 'The aesthetic attitude,' in Carolyn Korsmeyer, ed., *Aesthetics: The Big Questions*, Malden, MA: Blackwell, pp. 78–83.

Stone, Oliver (1987) *Wall Street*, DVD, Los Angeles: Twentieth Century Fox Film Corporation.

Strong, Roy (1984) *Art and Power: Renaissance Festivals, 1450–1650*, Berkeley: University of California Press.

Struck, Doug (2014) 'How the "global cooling" story came to be,' *Scientific American*, January 10, available at: www.scientificamerican.com/article/how-the-global-cooling-story-came-to-be/ (accessed October 2017).

Sturken, Marita (1997) *Tangled Memories: The Vietnam War, The AIDS Epidemic and the Politics of Remembering*, Berkeley: University of California Press.

Sullivan, Winnifred Fallers (2005) *The Impossibility of Religious Freedom*, Princeton, NJ: Princeton University Press.

Sullivan, Winnifred Fallers (2013) 'Religion, land, rights,' in Winnifred Fallers Sullivan and Lori G. Beaman, eds, *Varieties of Religious Establishment*, London: Ashgate, pp. 93–106.

Switzer, Heather (2013) '(Post)feminist development fables: The Girl Effect and the production of sexual subjects,' *Feminist Theory* 14, 3: 345–60.

Tagg, John (1988) *The Burden of Representation: Essays in Photographies and Histories*, Basingstoke: Macmillan.

Taylor, Diana (2003) *The Archive and the Repertoire: Performing Cultural Memory in the Americas*, Durham, NC: Duke University Press.

Taylor, Garry (2016) 'Sudden death of a cultural polymath,' University of St Andrews, 11 August, available at: http://slippedisc.com/2016/08/sudden-death-of-a-cultural-polymath-60/ (accessed January 2017).

Taylor, Victor E. (2000) 'Recalling modernity: Aesthetics before the abyss,' *International Journal of Politics, Culture and Society* 14, 2: 411–20.

Taylor-Alexander, Samuel (2013) 'On face transplantation: Ethical slippage and quiet death in experimental biomedicine,' *Anthropology Today* 29, 1: 13–16.

Teshigahara (1966) *The Face of Another*, DVD, Japan: Eureka.

Tester, Keith (2010) *Humanitarianism and Modern Culture*, University Park, PA: Pennsylvania State University Press.

The Australian (2015) 'Sharrouf, Elomar, and the mess they left in Islamic State's Raqqa,' *The Australian*, 26 June, available at: www.theaustralian.com.au/in-depth/community-under-siege/sharrouf-elomar-and-the-mess-they-left-in-islamic-states-raqqa/news-story/841b124decc47a91274d53c1589ad1d6 (accessed October 2017).

The Nation (2004) 'The horror of Abu Ghraib,' *The Nation*, 6 May, available at: www.thenation.com/article/horror-abu-ghraib (accessed October 2017).

Thesiger, Wilfred (1980) *The Life of My Choice*, London: Norton.

Thompson, Jerry L. (2013) *Why Photography Matters*, Cambridge, MA: MIT Press.

Thornton, Pip (2015) 'The meaning of light: Seeing and being on the battlefield,' *Cultural Geographies* 22, 4: 567–83.

Tillim, Guy (2009) http://verbal.co.za/2009/07/guy-tillim/ (accessed 2010, no longer available today).

Tilly, Charles (1975) 'Reflections on the history of European state-making,' in Charles Tilly, ed., *The Formation of National States in Western Europe*, Princeton, NJ: Princeton University Press.

Tilton, Jennifer (2010) *Dangerous or Endangered? Race and the Politics of Youth in Urban America*, New York: New York University Press.

Tocqueville, Alexis de (2000) *Democracy in America*, Chicago: University of Chicago Press.

Tynan, Jane (2013) 'Military chic: Fashioning civilian bodies for war,' in Kevin McSorley, ed., *War and the Body: Militarisation, Practice and Experience*, London: Routledge, pp. 78–90.

UN News Centre (2014) 'UN sounds alarm to end "global pandemic" of violence against women,' UN News Centre, available at: www.un.org/apps/news/story.asp?NewsID=49443#.VpJ8cFJzKqU (accessed October 2017).

UNHCR (United Nations High Commissioner on Refugees) (1951) '1951 Convention on the Status of Refugees,' available at: www.unhcr.org/en-au/1951-refugee-convention.html (accessed October 2017).

UNHCR (United Nations High Commissioner on Refugees) (1991) *Images of Exile 1951–1991*, Switzerland: UNHCR.

UNHCR (United Nations High Commissioner on Refugees) (2000) 'The State of the World's Refugees 2000: Fifty Years of Humanitarian Action,' available at: www.unhcr.org/en-au/publications/sowr/4a4c754a9/state-worlds-refugees-2000-fifty-years-humanitarian-action.html (accessed October 2017).

United Nations Permanent Forum on Indigenous Issues (2015) *Who are Indigenous Peoples?*, Indigenous Voices Fact Sheet 1, www.un.org/esa/socdev/unpfii/documents/5session_factsheet1.pdf (accessed October 2015).

UNWATCHABLE (2011) vimeo, available at: https://vimeo.com/25341404 (accessed October 2017).

Unwatchablethefilm (2011) 'Masika tells her story,' YouTube, available at: www.youtube.com/watch?v=fYUsMD3BbZg (accessed October 2017).

US Air Force (2011) "Transcripts of a US drone attack" *Los Angeles Times*, available at http://documents.latimes.com/transcript-of-drone-attack/ (accessed September 2016).

US Department of Defense (2010) 'News transcript: ABC News interview with Secretary Gates and Secretary Clinton,' *ABC News*, 11 April, available at: http://archive.defense.gov/transcripts/transcript.aspx?transcriptid=4718 (accessed October 2017).

van der Gaag, Nikki and Cathy Nash (1987) *Images of Africa: The UK Report*, Oxford: Oxfam.

Van Veeren, Elspeth (2011) 'Captured by the camera's eye: Guantanamo and the shifting frame of the global War on Terror,' *Review of International Studies* 37, 4: 1721–49.

Van Veeren, Elspeth (2013) 'Clean war, invisible war, liberal war: The clean and dirty politics of Guantánamo,' in Andrew Knapp and Hilary Footitt, eds, *Liberal Democracies at War: Conflict and Representation*, London: Bloomsbury.

Van Veeren, Elspeth (2014) 'Materializing US security: Guantanamo's object lessons and concrete messages,' *International Political Sociology* 8, 1: 20–42.

Vaux, Tony (2001) *The Selfish Altruist: Relief Work in Famine and War*, London: Earthscan.

Virilio, Paul (1986) *Speed and Politics*, New York: Semiotext(e).

Virilio, Paul (1988) *Block 14*, autumn: 4–7.

Virilio, Paul (1989) *War and Cinema: The Logistics of Perception*, New York: Verso.

Virilio, Paul (1998) *The Paul Virilio Reader*, ed. James Der Derian, Oxford: Blackwell.

Vis, Farida and Olga Goriunova (2015) *The Iconic Image on Social Media: A Rapid Research Response to the Death of Aylan Kurdi*, Sheffield: University of Sheffield, available at: http://visualsocialmedialab.org (accessed January 2017).

Voluntary Service Overseas (2002) 'The Live Aid legacy: The developing world through British eyes. A research report,' VSO, available at: www.eldis.org/vfile/upload/1/document/0708/DOC1830.pdf (accessed October 2017).

Wæver, Ole (1995) 'Securitization and desecuritization,' in Ronnie D. Lipschutz, ed., *On Security*, New York: Columbia University Press, pp. 46–86.

Walker, R.B.J. (1990) 'International relations/world politics,' unpublished paper.

Walker, R.B.J. (1993) *Inside/Outside: International Relations as Political Theory*, Cambridge: Cambridge University Press.

Walzer, Michael (1967) 'On the role of symbolism in political thought,' *Political Science Quarterly* 82, 2: 191–204.

Watson, Adam (1982) *Diplomacy: The Dialogue between States*, London: Methuen.

Watts, Michael (1991) 'Entitlements or empowerment? Famine and starvation in Africa,' *Review of African Political Economy* 51: 9–26.

Weber, Cynthia (2003) 'Epilogue: Romantic mediations of September 11,' in François Debrix and Cynthia Weber, eds, *Rituals of Mediation*, Minneapolis: University of Minnesota, pp. 173–88.

Weber, Cynthia (2005) *International Relations Theory: A Critical Introduction*, London: Routledge.

Weber, Cynthia (2006a) 'An aesthetics of fear: The 7/7 London bombings, the sublime and werenotafraid.com,' *Millennium* 34, 3: 683–711.

Weber, Cynthia (2006b) *Imagining America at War: Morality, Politics, and Film*, London: Routledge.

Weber, Cynthia (2007) '"I am an American": Video portraits of post-9/11 US citizens,' I am an American, available at: www.iamanamericanproject.com.

Weber, Cynthia (2008a) 'Popular visual language as global communication: The remediation of United Airline Flight 93,' *Review of International Studies* 34, 1: 137–53.

Weber, Cynthia (2008b) 'Designing safe citizens,' *Citizenship Studies* 12, 2: 125–42.

Weber, Cynthia (2010) 'Citizenship, security, humanity,' *International Political Sociology* 4, 1: 80–85.

Weber, Cynthia (2011) *'I am an American': Filming the Fear of Difference*, Chicago: University of Chicago Press.

Weber, Cynthia (2013) '"I am an American": Protesting advertised "Americanness",' *Citizenship Studies* 17, 2: 278–92.

Weber, Cynthia (2016) *Queer International Relations: Sovereignty, Sexuality and the Will to Knowledge*, Oxford: Oxford University Press.

Wei, Jin (2015) 'Burqas, hijabs and beards in the governance of Xinjiang,' University of Nottingham: China Policy Institute Blog, available at: http://blogs.nottingham.ac.uk/chinapolicyinstitute/2015/04/29/regulating-burqas-hijabs-and-beards-to-push-or-pull/ (accessed October 2017).

Weldes, Jutta, ed. (2003) *To Seek Out New Worlds: Science Fiction and World Politics*, New York: Palgrave Macmillan.

Weldes, Jutta, Mark Laffey, Hugh Gusterson and Raymond Duvall, eds (1999) *Cultures of Insecurity: States, Communities, and the Production of Danger*, Minneapolis: University of Minnesota Press.

Wells, Karen (2009) *Childhood in a Global Perspective*, Cambridge: Polity.

Wessells, Michael G. (1998) 'Children, armed conflict, and peace,' *Journal of Peace Research* 35, 5: 635–46.

Westwell, Guy (2011) 'Accidental napalm attack and hegemonic visions of America's war in Vietnam,' *Critical Studies in Media Communication* 8, 5: 407–23.

Whelan, Richard (2007) *This is War! Robert Capa at Work*, New York: International Center of Photography/Göttingen: Steidl.

White, Sarah (2002) 'Thinking race, thinking development,' *Third World Quarterly* 23, 3: 407–19.

Whitebrook, Maureen (1992) 'Introduction,' in Maureen Whitebrook, ed, *Reading Political Stories: Representations of Politics in Novels and Pictures*, Lanham, MD: Rowman & Littlefield, pp. 1–22.

Wigham, Nick (2015) 'Children of Australian terrorist at centre of heated national debate,' news.com.au, 30 June, available at: www.news.com.au/national/crime/children-of-australian-terrorist-at-centre-of-heated-national-debate/story-fns0kb1g-1227420635724 (accessed October 2017).

Wikipedia (n.d.) 'Manga iconography,' Wikipedia, available at: https://en.wikipedia.org/wiki/Manga_iconography (accessed October 2017).

Wilcox, Lauren (2009) 'Gendering the cult of the offensive,' *Security Studies* 18, 2: 24–40.

Wilcox, Lauren (2015a) *Bodies of Violence: Theorizing Embodied Subjects in International Relations*, New York: Oxford University Press.

Wilcox, Lauren (2015b) 'Drone warfare and the making of bodies out of place,' *Critical Studies of Security* 3, 1: 127–31.

Wilcox, Lauren (2017) 'Embodying algorithmic war: Gender, race, and the posthuman in drone warfare,' *Security Dialogue* 48, 1: 11–28.

Wilkes Tucker, Anne and Will Michels with Natalie Zelt (2012) *War/Photography: Images of Armed Conflict and its Aftermath*, Houston: Museum of Fine Arts/New Haven, CT: Yale University Press.

Williams, Michael C. (2003) 'Words, images, enemies: Securitization and international politics,' *International Studies Quarterly* 47, 4: 511–31.

Williams, Raymond (1974) *Television: Technology and Cultural Form*, Fontana: London.

Wilson, Erin K. (2012) *After Secularism: Rethinking Religion in Global Politics*, Basingstoke, UK: Palgrave Macmillan.

Wilson, Erin K. (2017) ' "Power differences" and "the power of difference": The dominance of secularism as ontological injustice,' *Globalizations* 14, 7: 1076–1093.

Wilson, Erin K. and Luca Mavelli (2016) 'The refugee crisis and religion: Beyond conceptual and physical boundaries' in Luca Mavelli and Erin K. Wilson, eds, *The Refugee Crisis and Religion: Secularism, Security and Hospitality in Question*, London: Rowman & Littlefield International, pp. 1–22.

Wilson, Kalpana (2008) 'Reclaiming "agency", reasserting resistance,' *IDS Bulletin* 39, 6: 83–91.

Wilson, Kalpana (2011) ' "Race," gender and neoliberalism: Changing visual representations in development,' *Third World Quarterly* 32, 2: 315–31.

Wilson, Kalpana (2012) *'Race,' Racism and Development: Interrogating History, Discourse and Practice*, London: Zed Books.

Wilson, Kalpana (2015) 'Towards a radical re-appropriation: Gender, development and neoliberal feminism,' *Development and Change* 46, 4: 803–32.

Winn, Steven (2004) 'Photos that will haunt us more than words ever could,' *SFGATE*, 19 May, available at: www.sfgate.com/entertainment/article/Photos-that-will-haunt-us-more-than-words-ever-2757827.php (accessed October 2017).

Withnall, Adam and Matt Dathan (2015) 'The public's extraordinary response to the Syrian refugee crisis,' *Independent*, 24 September, available at: www.independent.co.uk/news/uk/home-news/refugee-crisis-the-true-extent-of-the-british-publics-extraordinary-response-revealed-10514341.html (accessed October 2017).

Wood, Amy Louise (2011) *Lynching and Spectacle: Witnessing Racial Violence in America, 1890–1940*, Chapel Hill, NC: University of North Carolina Press.

Wood, Denis (2010) *Rethinking the Power of Maps*, New York: Guilford Press.

Wood, Marcus (2000) *Blind Memory: Visual Representations of Slavery in England and America 1780–1865*, London: Routledge.

Woods, Chris (2015) *Sudden Justice: America's Secret Drone Wars*, London: Hurst.

Woods, Ngaire (2009) 'Analysis: Financial tsunami,' BBC Radio Documentary, 19 March, available at: http://news.bbc.co.uk/nol/shared/spl/hi/programmes/analysis/transcripts/19_03_09.txt (accessed October 2017).

Woodward, David, ed. (2007) *The History of Cartography*, Vol. 3: *Cartography in the European Renaissance*, Chicago: University of Chicago Press.

Woollaston, Victoria (2013) 'Revealed: What happens in just ONE minute on the internet,' *Daily Mail*, 30 July, available at: www.dailymail.co.uk/sciencetech/article-2381188/Revealed-happens-just-ONE-minute-internet-216-000-photos-posted-278-000-Tweets-1-8m-Facebook-likes.html (accessed October 2017).

World Bank (2006) 'Gender Equality as Smart Economics: A World Bank Group gender action plan (fiscal years 2007–10),' World Bank, available at: http://siteresources.worldbank.org/INTGENDER/Resources/GAPNov2.pdf (accessed October 2017).

World Bank (2011) *The World Development Report 2012: Gender Equality and Development*, Washington, DC: World Bank.

World Food Programme (2005) 'Niger: A chronology of starvation,' WFP, available at: www.wfp.org/stories/niger-chronology-starvation (accessed October 2017).

World Health Organization (2016) 'Violence against women: Intimate partner and sexual violence against women,' WHO, available at: www.who.int/mediacentre/factsheets/fs239/en/ (accessed October 2017).

World Meteorological Organization (n.d.) 'What is climate?' WMO, available at: www.wmo.int/pages/prog/wcp/ccl/faqs.php (accessed October 2017).

Wright, Melissa W. (2006) *Disposable Women and Other Myths of Global Capitalism*, London and New York: Routledge.

Wyatt, Chad Evans (2014) *RomaRising*, available at: www.romarising.com.

Youde, Jeremy (2009) 'Selling the state: State branding as a political resource in South Africa,' *Place Branding and Public Diplomacy*, 5, 2: 126–40.

Zalewski, Marysia (2015) 'Feminist international relations: Making sense . . .,' in Laura J. Shepherd, ed., *Gender Matters in Global Politics*, London and New York: Routledge, pp. 3–13.

Zalewski, Marysia and Anne Sisson Runyan (2015) 'Unthinking sexual violence in a neoliberal age of spectacular terror,' *Critical Studies on Terrorism*, 8, 3: 1–17.

Zelizer, Barbie (2002) 'Finding aids to the past: Bearing personal witness to traumatic public events,' *Media, Culture & Society*, 24, 5: 697–714.

Zelizer, Barbie (2005) 'Death in wartime: Photographs and the "other war" in Afghanistan,' *Harvard International Journal of Press/Politics*, 10, 3: 26–55.

Zelizer, Barbie (2010) *About to Die: How News Images Move the Public*, New York: Oxford University Press.

Žižek, Slavoj (1989) *The Sublime Object of Ideology*, London: Verso.

Žižek, Slavoj (2005) 'Against human rights,' *New Left Review* 34: 115–31.

Žižek, Slavoj (2010) 'The neighbor in burka,' *The Symptom* 11, available at: www.lacan.com/symptom11/?p=69 (accessed October 2017).

Index

Entries in *italics* refer to figures

Abu Ghraib *see* images, of torture
aesthetic *see* visual
Afghanistan: *bacha posh* 150–155; and
    conflict 20, 50, 52, 248; and drones 17,
    112, 114; and films 147, 158; press in 32;
    refugees 318; Taliban 66, 109, 226; *see*
    also refugees
Africa 102, 314; African 96–97, 280; African
    Union 109; child-soldier 49–54, *50*;
    colonies 246; conflict 20, 65, 281; famine
    127–128, *129*; maps *see* cartographic
    techniques; refugees 247;
    stereotypes/representations 9, 26, 42–47,
    131–132, 282, 285; *see also* refugees
Âhäll, Linda 25, 150–156
Al-Qaeda 8, 159, 226, 286
Al-Shabaab *see* Islamic, militia
America *see* US
Amnesty International 18, 32, 165, 227
Anderson, Barton 14
Arab: "Arab" 82, 134–137; Arab/Muslim 27,
    46; Arab Spring 6, 102, 173, 229; women
    82–83
architecture 11, 108, 213, 216, 219, 251
Arendt, Hannah 33, 174–175
art 258–259, 330, 332; and aesthetics 173;
    indigenous 28, 189–195; performance
    84–85; power/role of 23, 28–29, 215–219;
    socialist realist 26
atomic bomb 31–21, 300–302
Australia: artist *see* Rankin, David; and
    Bali bombing 308, *309*, 310; indigenous
    28, 108, 189–19; and jihad 48, 52;
    Leader of Opposition 52; and refugees
    65
Australian, The 49, 308, *309*

Band Aid 42–47
Barthes, Roland 12, 16, 189, 233, 291, 337
BBC 42–43, 46–47, 63, 124, 133
Benjamin, Walter 193, 224–225, 229,
    258–259, 264, 268, 332
Berger, John 10, 16, 29
Berlin 58, 225, 238, *240*, 241–242, 286
Bin Laden, Osama 23, 146
body, the 30–34, 180, 241, 283; black 113;
    face 121–126; in pain 30, 311; war 304
borders 182, 210, 244–245, 272, 284; buffer-
    zone *22*, 36; inter-Korean 35–41
Boston Marathon 9, 289
Bourdieu, Pierre 167, 215
Bourke, Joanna 33, 34
Brassett, James 21, 139–143
Britain *see* UK
British Cartoon Archive 55, *58*, 60
Bush, George W. 31, 138, 146, 276; *see also*
    US, President
Bush, Laura 50, 52
Butler, Judith 113, 150, 152, 310
Butler, Sally 16, 28, 189–195

Callahan, William A. 25, 81–87
Capa, Robert 220, 223, 227, 229, 335
caricatures 35–36, 38–39, 55, 115, 252, 254,
    256; *see also* comics
cartographic techniques 3, 22, 157,294–299,
    327, 329
cartoon 24, 78, 84, 141, 178, 180; cartoonist
    35, 55, 171; *Charlie Hebdo* 24, 55, 81, 84,
    226, 252, 254, 256–257, 275–276; climate
    see climate, iconography; Cold War
    56–58; Danish controversy 252, 254,
    256–257, 275–276; *see also* comics